# A
# DEFIANT
# LIFE

Other books by Howard Ball

*Changing Perspectives in Contemporary Political Analysis*

*The Warren Court's Perceptions of Democracy*

*The Vision and the Dream of Justice Hugo L. Black*

*No Pledge of Privacy: The Watergate Tapes Litigation*

*Judicial Craftsmanship or Fiat:*
*Direct Overturn by the U.S. Supreme Court*

*Constitutional Powers*

*Courts and Politics: The Federal Judicial System*

*Compromised Compliance: Implementation of*
*the 1965 Voting Rights Act*

*Controlling Regulatory Sprawl*

*Federal Administrative Agencies*

*Justice Downwind: America's Atomic Testing Program in the 1950s*

*Of Power and Right: Justices Black and Douglas and*
*America's Constitutional Revolution*

*"We Have a Duty": Watergate in the U.S. Supreme Court*

*"Cancer Factories": The Tragedy of America's Uranium Miners*

*The U.S. Supreme Court: From the Inside Out*

*Hugo Black: Cold Steel Warrior*

*Multicultural Education in Colleges and Universities*

# A DEFIANT LIFE

## THURGOOD MARSHALL AND THE PERSISTENCE OF RACISM IN AMERICA

# HOWARD BALL

*The University of Vermont*

CROWN PUBLISHERS, INC. • NEW YORK

FRONTISPIECE: Thurgood Marshall waiting to argue a case in Supreme Court, ca. 1961. *(Library of Congress)*

Published by Crown Publishers, Inc., 201 East 50th Street, New York, New York 10022. Member of the Crown Publishing Group.

Random House, Inc. New York, Toronto, London, Sydney, Auckland

www.randomhouse.com

CROWN and colophon are trademarks of Crown Publishers, Inc.

Printed in the United States of America

Design by Leonard Henderson

Library of Congress Cataloging-in-Publication Data

Ball, Howard, 1937–

A defiant life : Thurgood Marshall and the persistence of racism in America / Howard Ball. — 1st ed.

p.  cm.

1. Marshall, Thurgood, 1908–1993. 2. United States. Supreme Court—Biography. 3. Judges—United States—Biography. 4. Afro-Americans—Civil rights—History.  I. Title.
KF8745.M34B35  1999

347.73'2634

[B]—DC21                                                               98-23031

CIP

ISBN 0-517-59931-7

10  9  8  7  6  5  4  3  2  1

First Edition

*For Thurgood Marshall:*

*"I can remember my mother talking about the 'Moses.' It wasn't until I became older that I realized the invisible angel Marshall was."*

—SHELLY HARVARD, AFRICAN AMERICAN HOUSEWIFE

# CONTENTS

# CHRONOLOGY OF
# "A LIFE WELL LIVED"

| | |
|---|---|
| July 2, 1908 | Thurgood Marshall born, Baltimore, Maryland |
| | 1909: NAACP formed |
| 1929 | Marries Vivian "Buster" Burey |
| 1930 | Graduates from Lincoln University |
| 1933 | Graduates from Howard Law School |
| 1934–36 | Counsel, Baltimore Branch of the NAACP |
| 1936–38 | Assistant Special Counsel to the NAACP |
| 1938–40 | Special Counsel to the NAACP |
| 1940–50 | Special Counsel, NAACP Legal and Educational Fund, Inc. |
| | 1944: *Smith v. Allwright* |
| 1946 | Recipient of Spingarn Medal, NAACP |
| 1950–61 | Director-Counsel, NAACP Inc Fund |
| 1951 | Special Investigator, NAACP: Racism in Army, Korea and Japan |
| 1954 | *Brown v. Board of Education* |
| February 1955 | Vivian Marshall dies |
| December 1955 | Marries Cecilia "Cissy" Suyat |
| 1961–65 | Judge, U.S. Second Circuit Court of Appeals |
| 1965–67 | U.S. Solicitor General |
| 1967–91 | Associate Justice, U.S. Supreme Court |
| October 1, 1991 | Retires from U.S. Supreme Court |
| January 24, 1993 | Thurgood Marshall dies |

# ACKNOWLEDGMENTS

A great many people helped me in the researching and writing of this book. The librarians and staff of the following libraries and archival collections were generous with their advice and assistance: the Library of Congress Manuscript Division; the Harry S Truman Presidential Library; the Dwight David Eisenhower Presidential Library; the John F. Kennedy Presidential Library; and the Lyndon Baines Johnson Presidential Library. University library staffs also helped me in my discovery of Thurgood Marshall's life and professional career. These include the Moorland-Spingarn Archives at Howard University; the University of Kentucky archives; the Columbia University Oral History archives; and the University of Texas Law School library archives.

In support of my research on Thurgood Marshall and his times, the following organizations supported my research, and I am very grateful for their help: the University of Vermont (the Department of Political Science and its M.P.A. program, the College of Arts and Sciences, the Graduate School, and the Provost's Office); the Jacobson Fund at UVM; the John F. Kennedy Foundation (for selecting me as the 1996–97 Theodore Sorensen Fellow); the Harry S Truman Foundation; and the Dwight D. Eisenhower Foundation.

Once again I must thank two close friends—Phillip Cooper, the Gund Chair of Liberal Arts at the University of Vermont, and Thomas P. Lauth, Professor and Chair of Political Science at the University of Georgia—for their invaluable assistance, counsel, and friendship over the years. Three others must also be acknowledged for their help and advice to me as I worked on this book: Laryn Ivy was a student of mine at the University of Vermont who did some extraordinary work for me, including some very fine interviews with former Thurgood Marshall law clerks, while she was attending the Washington, D.C., Semester program at American University. She is a brilliant law student at the University of Virginia, and will be an outstanding legal advocate upon graduation. John Burke, a colleague of mine here at the University of Vermont, was another person who helped me a great deal, finding books for me to look at and helping me with my planning for the work at the presidential libraries. My friend and editor, Jim O'Shea Wade, has been enormously helpful in the final preparation of the manuscript.

The recently deceased U.S. Supreme Court justice William J. Brennan Jr., who wrote the foreword to this book, graciously allowed me to examine all his papers at the Library of Congress. Brennan shared over two dozen years with his friend Thurgood Marshall, and the two of them have secured places in the pantheon of legal greats in America. I gratefully acknowledge Justice Brennan's help and encouragement.

Finally, I want to acknowledge, with love, the support I have always received from my family. My wife, Carol, and my three daughters, Sue, Sheryl, and Melissa, have been a continuing font of love and friendship for a long time, and I appreciate it more than they will ever know.

# FOREWORD

Thurgood Marshall was one of our century's legal giants. Before he joined the judiciary, he was probably the most important legal advocate in America and the central figure in this nation's struggle to eliminate institutional racism.

On the Supreme Court, he played a crucial role in enforcing the constitutional protections that are the hallmarks of our democracy. Perhaps what made him such a towering figure, and one to whom the entire nation owes a debt of gratitude, is that he brought to his work not only the authority of experience but also a unique combination of courage, humanity, and mastery of legal reasoning.

I hope that, just as Thurgood during his lifetime profoundly enriched our nation, this story of his life will embolden others to carry on the work left undone.

William J. Brennan Jr.
Associate Justice, U.S. Supreme Court (Retired)
March 1997

# 1

# Born into Racism
## and Segregation in America

Thurgood Marshall was born in 1908. That year an African American named Jack Johnson knocked out Tommy Burns, the then world heavyweight champion. This was the first time a black man had taken the title away from a white man. As soon as Johnson won, the search was on for the "great white hope" who would take the crown away from him. For African Americans, Johnson's victory may have been the only joy they had that year.

On July 2, Thurgood Marshall's birthday, there were stories in the newspapers about race riots, accompanied by crude racial jokes, reminders of the inferiority of the African American in a world dominated by whites. The sociology of the day, as exemplified by the work of Herbert Spencer, U.S. Supreme Court decisions of that era, and Admiral Alfred Thayer Mahan's treatise on world power, all argued scientifically and legally for the racial inferiority of Thurgood's people.

Although vastly outnumbered by the colored peoples of the world, whites used their power and technology ruthlessly to dominate the lives of nonwhites, particularly in America, where African Americans were worse off than impoverished serfs of some feudal kingdom. Since the end of the Civil War, they had been seen as a societal problem that called for a final resolution. By the turn of the century, that solution was state-ordered Jim Crow segregation of white and black, America's version of white South Africa's policy of apartheid. This was the America into which Thurgood Marshall was born.

## SLAVERY, RACE, AND RACISM:
## THE HISTORIC CONTEXT

In August 1619, the first shipment of Negro slaves, comprising about twenty persons, arrived at Point Comfort, near Jamestown, Virginia. In 1640, a Virginia judge set the tone for America's history of racial discrimination when he sentenced three indentured servants who had run away and had been captured by local authorities. He punished the two white indentured servants by adding one year apiece to their indenture. The third indentured servant, an African American, was punished for his failed escape "by [being] sentenced...to a lifetime of service."[1]

During the early seventeenth century and continuing up to 1865, slavery was legally recognized in law and politics. African Americans were seen as chattel property, much like oxen and wagons, to be bought and sold at the whim of the slave owner. From the earliest days of British colonialization of North America, African American slaves had no legal or civil rights. By the time the U.S. Constitution was adopted in 1787—almost two centuries after slavery had come to America—every Southern state constitution contained clauses that perpetuated slavery by forbidding state legislators from emancipating slaves.

The U.S. Constitution referred to the slaves only in property and electoral enumeration terms. Despite the new nation's commitment to equality, pronounced in the Declaration of Independence, slavery was sanctioned. Slaves were not citizens, but merely properties valued, for purposes of determining each state's electoral representation, as three-fifths of a human being. The 1793 Fugitive Slave Act further extended the property rights of slave owners to all the states. When the nation's capital was established in 1801, only "free white inhabitants" could elect members of the Washington, D.C., city council.

In 1842, in the case of *Prigg v. Pennsylvania,* the U.S. Supreme Court held that a slave owner's property rights took precedence over a state's right to protect African Americans. The 1850 amendment to the Fugitive Slave Act reaffirmed that slaves were chattel property. It appointed and authorized U.S. marshals to hold hearings and return slaves to their masters.[2]

The ultimate sanction was the U.S. Supreme Court's *Dred Scott v. Sandford* decision of 1857, confirming that slavery was the law of the land. Dred Scott, a slave, sued for his freedom in federal court in a non-slave state. By a seven-to-two vote (five of the seven justices were born and raised in the South), the Supreme Court said, in part, that Scott was property and had "no rights a white man has to respect." Scott, because he was black, did not have legal "standing" to bring a suit in any federal court, even if he were a free black. Chief Justice Roger Taney wrote in blunt terms: "It is difficult at this day to realize the state of public opinion in relation to that unfortunate race.... They had for more than a century before been regarded as beings of an inferior order, and altogether unfit to associate with the white race, either in social or political relations; and so far inferior, that they had no rights which the white man was bound to respect."[3]

## HOODED TERROR AND THE
## CIVIL WAR AMENDMENTS

After the Civil War's end and Lincoln's assassination, the radical Republican Reconstruction Congress succeeded in introducing and getting ratified, between 1865 and 1870, the Thirteenth through Fifteenth Amendments to the Constitution, the so-called Civil War Amendments. The Thirteenth Amendment, ratified in 1865, ended slavery.

The Fourteenth Amendment, ratified in 1868, was a direct response to Black Codes enacted in localities across the South after 1865 to control and limit the legal and political status—and conduct—of their recently freed slaves. In some cases, these codes "amounted to a virtual re-enslavement of blacks."[4] They deprived African Americans of their basic individual rights. Louisiana's code, for example, starkly stated that "the people of African descent cannot be considered as citizens of the United States." The congressional response was swift: The Fourteenth Amendment proclaimed citizenship for all persons born or naturalized in the United States, and restricted states from abridging the privileges or immunities of citizens of the United States, or depriving any person of life, liberty, or property without due process of law, or denying any person the equal protection of the laws. Both amendments provided that "Congress shall have power to enforce this article by appropriate legislation."

Accompanying the passage of the Black Codes was the reemergence of paramilitary groups in local communities across the South, similar to the South's pre–Civil War "night patrols," most notably the Ku Klux Klan. The Klan was founded in December 1865, in Pulaski, Tennessee, by six ex-Confederate soldiers, and led by former Confederate general Nathan Bedford Forrest, who became its first Imperial Wizard. Within months of Appomattox, these grassroots hate groups had unleashed "a campaign of terror designed to deter blacks from voting, to destroy the Republican party, and to reestablish white dominance."[5]

Hundreds of white Republican party leaders in the occupied South were killed by these nighttime marauders, and many more thousands were intimidated by the actions of the Klan and other groups. The freed slaves were terrorized as well, in order to make sure they did not participate in local and state elections. The national rejoinder was the drafting and ratification, in 1870, of the Fifteenth Amendment. In it, Congress ensured that the right of citizens to vote would not be abridged or denied "by the United States or by any state on account of race, color, or previous condition of servitude." Its second section gave the Congress power "to enforce this article by appropriate legislation."

Additionally, using the enforcement powers in these amendments, Congress passed a series of civil rights acts in the 1860s and 1870s to protect blacks from violent lawlessness and racial discrimination. U.S. attorneys general aggressively attacked, in federal courts, the racist vigilantism; the first incarnation of the Klan ended its reign of terror in the 1880s because of more than six hundred indictments brought against the Klan's membership by the national government.

The civil rights statutes punished those who acted to deprive African Americans of their new political and legal freedoms, and prohibited any discrimination against African Americans in places of "public accommodations," such as theaters, restaurants, hotels, and other businesses open to the general public. The Congress, through the mid-1870s, was committed to a national public policy that would, in the end, remove all the "badges of slavery" that African Americans, after the Civil War, still wore.

However, the "great sin of the North after 1865 was to destroy slavery and yet not destroy the culture that slavery had generated."[6] By the time of the presidential election of 1876, the pendulum had swung against the Radical Reconstruction Congress's civil rights policies, and in the early 1880s, because of changes and compromises in national politics and the conservatism of the U.S. Supreme Court, its civil rights legislation was eviscerated.

This era of Southern history, called the "Redemption" period, began in 1877 with the "withdrawal of federal troops from the South, the abandonment of the Negro as a ward of the Nation, the giving up of the attempt to guarantee the freedman his civil and political equality, and the acquiescence of the rest of the country in the South's demand that the whole [Negro] problem be left to the disposition of the dominant Southern white people."[7] There soon followed racially discriminatory legislation passed by the Redeemers, the white politicians who negotiated the Redemption, or Compromise, of 1877. A set of lawful policies and practices, especially segregation, or Jim Crow statutes, maintained the physical and psychological "badges of slavery" and led to a reaffirmation of second- and third-class citizenship for the recently freed African Americans.

The plight of the African American became extremely dire just about the time America was celebrating the centennial of the U.S. Constitution. Eerily similar to the hateful rhetoric spewed out by the Nazis in the 1930s and 1940s, these new Southern state-ordered race segregation statutes were, according to C. Van Woodward, "regarded as the 'final settlement,' the 'return to sanity,' the 'permanent system'" for dealing with the Negro problem.

## REDIRECTING CIVIL RIGHTS: THE U.S. SUPREME COURT STRIKES DOWN CIVIL RIGHTS LEGISLATION, 1883-1896

This redirection of civil rights values and policy toward the African American community was seen most clearly in U.S. Supreme Court opinions that invalidated most of the legislation passed by the Radical Reconstruction Congress. (The Court also began to validate state segregation policies challenged by African Americans.) Using its power of judicial review, the Court concluded that the Congress had acted unconstitutionally in trying to protect the newly freed slaves from racial segregation and discrimination: Congress did not have the power to tell private individuals how to behave toward African Americans. The Civil War Amendments prohibited only *state* action, not private actions, and therefore the Congress had overstepped its authoritative use of power when it attempted to redress purely private behavior, however intolerant and discriminatory, against African Americans. Conservative Supreme Court decisions such as the *Civil Rights Cases* (1883), declaring the 1875 Civil Rights Act unconstitutional, drained the energy from the Civil War Amendments.

By 1885, an observer could note that "there is scarcely one public relation in the South where the Negro is not arbitrarily and unlawfully compelled to hold toward the white man the attitude of an alien, a menial, and a probable reprobate, by reason of race and color." The badges of slavery, those remnants of the "Times of Sorrows," were still present, and for most in the African American community, these were the days of "secret tears."[8]

In 1887, the centennial of the Constitution, the more than 7 million African Americans were still effectively an enslaved people. For Frederick Douglass, "so far as the colored people are concerned, the Constitution is but a stupendous sham...keeping the promise to the eye and breaking it to the heart." An observer noted that "race and the badges of slavery entered into every type of legal matter during the centennial era and thereafter."[9] Roy Wilkins, one of Thurgood Marshall's NAACP associates, best summed up the plight of the African American when he wrote about his grandfather: "If the Civil War liberated [him], the Supreme Court circumscribed his possibilities. Like millions of other Negroes, he responded by becoming a stoic; he endured."[10]

### PLESSY V. FERGUSON: LEGITIMIZING JIM CROW

The tragic 1896 case of *Plessy v. Ferguson* was the watershed litigation in which the U.S. Supreme Court, with but one dissenting vote, gave its official stamp of approval to the constitutional validity of racial segregation. Homer Plessy, an African American living in Louisiana, challenged the constitutionality of the state's 1890 Railroad Bill, which segregated African Americans and whites by requiring separate railway cars for the two races. In a 7–1 ruling, the court majority affirmed the 1890 act, stating that "racial instincts" were real, that the white race was superior to the African American race, and that a legislature could establish "separate but equal" facilities to ensure the separation of the races in social settings. The majority held that the equal-protection clause of the Fourteenth Amendment did not prohibit Louisiana from enacting and enforcing racial separation.

With the decision in *Plessy*, the Supreme Court legitimized the era of formal racial segregation, known as Jim Crowism. (The term Jim Crow evidently originated in 1831 as the name of a blackface song-and-dance routine, and became an adjective for segregation of races by 1838.)[11] This formal state-ordered policy of segregation existed for almost sixty years, until, in 1954, another Supreme Court, in *Brown v. Board of Education*, determined that *Plessy*'s "separate but equal" doctrine lacked constitutional validity. As a consequence of *Plessy*, the legal and political status of the African American plummeted to pre–Civil War levels.

By 1900, the racial mores that were at the heart of the *Plessy* decision, racial segregation and Jim Crowism, had permeated the South. As Edward Ayers wrote, "Once [state-ordered] segregation began, there was no logical place for it to stop." And it did not stop until *all* conceivable social actions (from birth to death and burial) were segregated and separated based on race and color.[12] Jim Crowism was the "single most prominent characteristic that set the South apart from the rest of the country." Separation of the races provided a basic form of "psychic security" for most white southerners; integration of the races was categorically opposed by the overwhelming majority.[13]

The nineteenth century, for African Americans, was a time in which their civil rights were continually compromised. It was also a time for reconciliation between the central and state governments, between the North and the South, between those who fought for the Union and those who fought for the Lost Cause.

It was also a century that saw the development of a small number of middle-class African American families. Toward the end of the nineteenth century, industrialization came to the South, and with it the dramatic growth of the railroads and the small cities. Many young men and women began leaving the rural farm towns and villages to make a new life for themselves in those cities. Small towns like Birmingham, Alabama, changed significantly in a few decades. Their steel mills and other industries attracted both African American and white workers.

Paralleling this demographic change in the South was the development of African American businesses. In spite of racial segregation, or perhaps because of it, some enterprising African Americans began accumulating property and wealth by catering to the needs of their own race. By 1900, a self-contained African American world—doctors, athletes, businessmen, dentists, lawyers, authors, editors, and druggists—had emerged out of the shrillness and cruelty of *Plessy's* "separate but equal" doctrine.

In 1901 the National Negro Business League was organized in an effort to enhance the successes of black middle-class businessmen across the South and the nation. It was one of many dozens of racially segregated business, civic, literary, church, and fraternal organizations created by African Americans to reflect the reality of race segregation and the economic responses by the African American community.

As the young black activist W. E. B. Du Bois observed in 1900, an African American

> may arise in the morning in a house which a black man built and which he himself owns, it has been painted and papered by black men;...He starts to work walking to the car with a colored neighbor and sitting in a car surrounded by colored people;...Once a week he reads a colored paper; he is insured in a colored insurance company; he patronizes a colored school with colored teachers; and a colored church with a colored preacher; he gets his amusements at places frequented and usually run by colored people; he is buried by a colored undertaker in a colored graveyard.[14]

Despite this nascent development of a black middle and professional class, the overarching restrictions imposed by *Plessy* dramatically restricted employment possibilities for the community. The result was that the overwhelming number of those African Americans living in the cities worked as unskilled and semi-skilled laborers, low-paid factory workers, haulers, and, like Thurgood Marshall's father, railroad porters. One African American writer, Sutton E. Griggs, observed in an 1899 novel:

> It is true that there were positions around by the thousands which he could fill, but his color debarred him. He would have made an excellent drummer, salesman, clerk, cashier, government official (county, city, state or national), telegraph operator, conductor, or anything of such nature. But the color of his skin shut the doors so tight that he could not even peep in.[15]

By the turn of the century there was total capitulation to Jim Crowism in the South. If there was any lingering animus on the part of white liberals, by this time such assaults, feeble though they might have been in face of the South's political realities, were no longer heard. Editorial writers and abolitionist-minded essayists for *The Nation, Harper's,* or *The Atlantic Monthly,* instead of writing about the true equality of African Americans and the larger white American community, were "mouthing the shibboleths of white supremacy regarding the Negro's innate inferiority, shiftlessness, and hopeless unfitness for full participation in the white man's civilization."[16]

At the same time, young white children growing up in the South had their Southern racist values developed by their parents, grandparents, relatives, and family friends. White children were taught to address African American males as "nigger" or "boy," but never by their right name, and to call African American women "auntie." When a young white boy "referred to a respected black man as 'Mr. Jones,' [the boy's] aunt quickly corrected him. 'No, son. Robert Jones is a nigger. You don't say "Mister" when you speak of a nigger. You don't say "Mr. Jones," you say "nigger Jones."' Children soon learned the lesson."[17]

By 1900, there emerged, as a consequence of state political actions through-out the South, a rigid racially segregated system affecting hospitals, hotels, cemeteries, churches, schools, playgrounds, and all other social activities. The racist ideal of a completely circumscribed world of white and black was estab-lished. While there were a handful of exceptions, an inferior, third-class citizen-ship for African Americans was accepted by whites in the South, as well as by federal and state courts, by presidents, Congresses, even by churches and orga-nized labor.

African American resistance to these realities was at an ebb. Booker T. Washington, the leading accommodationist African American, preached a pro-gram of "submission" to white power, one that called for blacks to set aside demands for integration, civic equality, and full political participation. "In all things purely social," he said to a white audience in Atlanta in 1895, "we can be as separate as the five fingers, and yet one as the hand is in all things essential to mutual progress." These words were "an invitation to further [Southern white] aggression," and did much, to the anger of younger African American leaders like W. E. B. Du Bois, to smooth the path to proscription.[18]

As Du Bois wrote, Washington's program, popular with whites, called for "industrial education, conciliation with the South, and [African American] sub-mission and silence as to civil and political rights....Mr. Washington distinctly asks that black people give up, at least for the present, three things,—First, polit-ical power, Second, insistence on civil rights, Third, higher education of Negro youth,—and concentrate all their energies on industrial education, and accumu-lation of wealth, and the conciliation of the South."[19] In his 1895 Atlanta speech, Washington urged his fellow African Americans to "cast down your bucket where you are" and come to terms with the cultural and political realities of the South.

In 1900 the South, for the tens of millions of people living in the eleven states of the old Confederacy, was a "feudal land, an Americanized version of a European society in the Middle Ages." It had its ruling nobles, its lords of plantation estates, its poor peasants, and its black vassals. Its "values were rooted in the land, in stability and permanence, in hierarchy and status, in caste and class, and race. The highest virtues were honor and duty, loyalty and obedience." In such an organic hierarchical society, "placeness" was all-important. Everyone, male and female, black and white, adult and child, knew his or her place.[20]

## RACE, SEX, AND LYNCHING

Edward Ayers notes, correctly, that "the history of segregation shows a clear connection to gender: the more closely linked to sexuality, the more likely was a place to be segregated." Race and sex are the dominant themes in understanding white southerners' intense, irrational commitment to racial segregation: Their fear of African American sexuality led to some of the worst cruelties associated with racial segregation. "One of the oldest and most complex dimensions of the racial dilemma was sexuality. It hung like an albatross about the neck of the South."[21]

By 1900, three distinct mentalities had emerged in the South, all clinging to the sexual fear of African Americans held by the white community:

The first, held by most southerners, was that the African American was, in a way, a zoolike curiosity: "a child's brain implanted in an adult's body"; the African American was perceived as a perpetual child with a limited capacity and capability for learning.[22]

A second view, held by a very small group of white southerners, was that the African American had some potential, but what that potential might be remained undefined. This conservative mentality accepted the notion of African American inferiority and believed that the only way African Americans could live happily was to have the white community strictly define, in law and in custom, their place in society. Blacks were seen as docile and manageable.

The third, or radical, mentality emphasized savagery and bestiality as the African Americans' natural state.[23] For the radicals, the Civil War and emancipation had led to a retrogression of African Americans to their natural state of bestiality, a condition evident in attempts by black males to rape white women. These assaults on an "idealized" white womanhood by the "nigger beast" had to end, and lynching, including social lynching, where the killing of an African American was watched by the entire community of whites, was the answer.

Sexual contact of any sort between African Americans and other races, defined as "miscegenation," was legally forbidden throughout the South (and elsewhere in the nation) in order not to defile the superior white race. Of course, the reality of relationships in the South was quite different. Ada Sipuel Fisher, the plaintiff in an important 1948 NAACP-initiated higher education lawsuit (Marshall was one of Fisher's lawyers), recalled that her grandmother was one of two wives of a Captain Anderson. Her grandmother was black and the captain was a white southerner who also had a white wife. The captain fathered seven white children who lived in the large house and seven black children who lived in a small cabin about a mile from the big house. All fourteen were "brothers" and "sisters" to each other.[24] But real social equality between African Americans and whites was, for the white South, an abomination. The white majority feared that the principle of equality found in the Civil War Amendments, if implemented, would destroy the white Anglo Saxon race.

"The New South was a notoriously violent place," wrote Ayers. The mythic beliefs whites held about the African American male's insatiable sexual drives, his primitive bestiality, and his lust for white women led to a dramatic surge of lynchings in the South. Between 1882 and 1968, almost five thousand persons were lynched in the South, 3,446 of whom were African American men. As Stephen J. Whitfield writes, "death [by lynching] was a penalty that fell disproportionately on black males who were accused—and sometimes convicted—of sexual assault."[25]

For the African American community, the message in the myth was a clear one: Black boys and men should stay out of the line of sight of white women in the South, even if it meant looking down at one's feet or crossing a street to avoid too close an encounter. An African American who "stepped too far out of line risked the real possibility of facing a lynch mob."[26]

Lynching was an "object lesson [that] touched the entire black community and not merely the victims and their families….In the wake of one [lynching], the local black community was terrorized: 'None of 'em would come out on the streets.'" As Charles S. Johnson, a noted African American educator, said in 1941: The effect of "such terrorism on black children in the rural South [at the turn of the twentieth century] was profound and permanent….Lynching or the possibility of lynching [was and remained] a part of the cultural pattern."[27]

## 1903: W. E. B. DU BOIS'S
### SOULS OF BLACK FOLK

It was a brilliant African American who put the pieces of the American racial puzzle together in an epochal book written in 1903. "The problem of the Twentieth Century is the problem of the color line," wrote William Edward Burghardt Du Bois in his classic *The Souls of Black Folk*. The African American experience was and remained quite different from that of whites, according to Du Bois. They were a spiritual people cruelly treated by whites in both the North and South in an industrial, materialistic America. He wrote, with racial pride, of the distinct qualities of the African American community.

> Your country? How came it yours? Before the Pilgrims landed we were here. Here we have brought our three gifts and mingled them with yours: a gift of story and song;...the gift of sweat and brawn to beat back the wilderness, conquer the soil, and lay the foundations of this vast economic empire two hundred years earlier than your weak hands could have done it; the third, a gift of the Spirit....Would America have been America without her Negro people?[28]

Du Bois was an African American sociologist with a Ph.D. from Harvard University and advanced graduate study in Berlin. He had written a powerful book—indeed a revolutionary and dialectical one—that gave voice to the pain of stigmatic, psychological injuries suffered by African Americans in what he called

> this American world—a world which yields him no true self-consciousness, but only lets him see himself through the revelation of the other world. It is a peculiar sensation, this double-consciousness, this sense of always looking at one's self through the eyes of others, of measuring one's soul by the tape of a world that looks on in amused contempt and pity. One ever feels his twoness,—an American, a Negro; two souls, two thoughts, two unreconciled strivings; two warring ideals in one dark body, whose dogged strength alone keeps it from being torn asunder. The history of the American Negro is the history of this strife,—this longing to attain self-conscious manhood, to merge his double self into a better and truer self....He simply wishes to make it possible for a man to be both a Negro and an American, without being cursed and spit upon by his fellows, without having the doors of Opportunity closed roughly in his face.

For Du Bois, African Americans, because of state-created and -enforced racial segregation, "descended rapidly into the caste status of subhumans in the South."[29] They were treated scarcely better in the North, where they were ghettoized and marginalized. Indeed, Jim Crowism had first appeared in Boston, New York, and Philadelphia, prior to the Civil War.

By the beginning of the twentieth century, African Americans had been constitutionally disenfranchised by such techniques as the poll tax, property and literacy tests, and—the most potent weapon—the whites-only state primary election, as well as economic pressures, terror, and violence. The dramatic effectiveness of these techniques is seen in voting statistics of African American registered voters in Louisiana. In 1896 there were over 130,000 voters. Eight years later there were only 1,342 African American voters registered in that state.[30]

In 1906, at Harper's Ferry, West Virginia, the site of the John Brown rebellion a half-century earlier, Du Bois announced the formation of the Niagara Movement, which would fight for all the rights he felt African Americans deserved and needed to take their rightful place in American society. In its public "Address to the Country," the movement issued a clarion call, expressed in Du Bois's powerful language:

> Against this [violence and discrimination] the Niagara movement eternally protests. We will not be satisfied to take one jot or tittle less than our full manhood rights. We claim for ourselves every single right that belongs to a freeborn American, political, civil, and social; and until we get these rights we will never cease to protest and assail the ears of America....How shall we get them? By voting where we may vote, by persistent unceasing agitation; by hammering at the truth, by sacrifice and work....Justice and humanity must prevail.

The activist program advocated by Du Bois attracted few of his fellow African Americans. In 1910, Du Bois and most of the Niagara Movement's followers joined the newly formed National Association for the Advancement of Colored People.

In the first two decades of the century, more than a million African Americans fled the South to Northern cities in hopes of finding safer and better living conditions and economic opportunity. But for most of the 10 million African Americans in the United States, emigration, whether to the North or to the promised land of Marcus Garvey's Back to Africa Movement, was not an option. They either had to accept the way things were or find a way to struggle against segregation and discrimination. To the frustration of the founding generation of the NAACP, the great majority of their brothers and sisters chose to live quietly, meekly, with Jim Crow and its white-hooded terror rather than attempt to overcome it. However, this passivity is understandable given the history of violent riots by whites directed at black communities across America: African Americans feared for their lives.

There were few choices available to them. Most turned to the ministers in their black churches for guidance and solace, consoled by the promise of a better afterlife. Many turned to the accommodationist vision of Washington. Few followed Du Bois's call to action. The NAACP had to set its own, different course.

## 1908: GROWING UP IN BALTIMORE

The second of two sons of Norma Arica and William Canfield Marshall, Thoroughgood Marshall was born in the racist and totally segregated city of Baltimore, Maryland. Marshall soon got tired of writing his unusually long first name, the name of his paternal grandfather, and in the second grade, he simply shortened it to Thurgood. His birth came just twelve years after the U.S. Supreme Court's *Plessy* opinion was handed down and two years after two events became indelibly engraved on the national psyche and that of the African American community.

In Texas in 1906, 167 African American soldiers, including a few who had been awarded the Congressional Medal of Honor for their heroism under fire in the Spanish-American War of 1898, were dishonorably discharged from the service. They had allegedly incited a riot in Brownsville, Texas, that led to the death of a white bartender and the wounding of a white policeman. This mass action against the African American soldiers was approved by President Theodore Roosevelt, who, ironically, had been their leader in the Cuban campaign.[31] The President had brushed aside pleas from prominent African Americans to show leniency. (Some sixty years later, the army cleared the records of the 167 dishonorably discharged soldiers.)

The second mind- and body-searing event in 1906 was the Atlanta, Georgia, race riot, a pogrom led by thousands of angry whites against African Americans. Liberal, advanced, and gentle Atlanta, Georgia, the home of Coca-Cola, and of then-modernistic seven-story skyscrapers, was "the symbolic heart of the New South." Yet Atlanta newspapers wrote about "bad niggers" moving into the city from the surrounding rural areas, frightening its white citizens. White Atlantans, stirred to a wild frenzy by eight-column-wide headlines in the Atlanta news dailies, developed an irrational fear of potential African American sexual attacks on the pure white women of Atlanta. In late September 1906, "more than 10,000 white men, many of them carrying guns, marched through the city searching out blacks." In less than a day, twenty-five African Americans were murdered and hundreds injured—and no one in authority intervened or apologized or took action against the leaders of the white mobs.

Walter White, the future NAACP leader and colleague of Thurgood Marshall, was living in Atlanta at the time and vividly recalled how the marauding white mob moved down his street like a tidal wave, shooting and stabbing and beating African Americans who were in their path. His recollection of that event, a pure nightmarish hell for a thirteen-year-old boy, is nothing less than a Gothic horror tale of a young African American who found out who he was on that terror-filled, dark, torch-flickering night in racist and segregationist Atlanta.

Walter was one of nine "light-skinned Negroes" in his family, and "on a day in September 1906," he found out "that there is no isolation from life." After the first day of race rioting, the family was warned that the mob was going to "clean out the niggers" that evening. While his mother and sisters hid in a safe part of their brick home, he and his father armed themselves with rifles, turned out all the lights, and, "full of apprehension," waited at the windows for the mob to appear. The father told the young son not to fire until "the first man puts his foot on the lawn and then—don't you miss!"

> In the flickering light the mob swayed...and began to flow toward us. In that instant there opened in me a great awareness; I knew then who I was. I was a Negro, a human being with an invisible pigmentation which marked me a person to be hunted, hanged, abused, discriminated against, kept in poverty and ignorance, in order that those [whose] skin was white would have readily at hand a proof of their superiority....It made no difference how intelligent or talented my millions of brothers and I were, or how virtuously we lived. A curse like that of Judas was upon us, a mark of degradation fashioned with heavenly authority....In the quiet that followed [the mob dispersed without White having to fire his gun], I was gripped by the knowledge of my identity....It was all just a feeling then, inarticulate and melancholy, yet reassuring in the way that death and sleep are reassuring, and I have clung to it now for nearly half a century.[32]

Maryland, a Northern state, had all the characteristics of a state of the Old Confederacy. It was a city whose white citizens were proud of the fact that Baltimore, latitudinally and ideologically, was south of the Mason-Dixon Line or, as Marshall often referred to it, "the Smith and Wesson Line." For a mature Thurgood Marshall, Maryland was a "mean state," a "way up South" state.[33]

Baltimore's residential segregation pattern, created at about the time of Thurgood's birth, was one that "designated all-white and all-Negro blocks in areas occupied by both races." It was a housing segregation plan that was to be copied throughout the Deep South by other municipal authorities.

Thurgood's home in the Druid Hill Avenue section in northwest Baltimore was a part of that plan. It was a middle-class neighborhood area where white and African American families lived in separated groups of blocks. Druid Hill was the African American area; four blocks away was the all-white area, called Bolton Hill. Druid Hill was the best of the three black residential areas in the city. "If you were a black person and owned a house on Druid Hill Avenue in those days, you had arrived," observed a woman whose family published Baltimore's *Afro-American* newspaper.[34]

An Urban League study in 1930 concluded that "segregation in Baltimore was more rigid than [in] any other city in the country, including Jackson, Mississippi." In 1908, Baltimore had separate, segregated schools, parks, and stores. No department stores opened their doors to black customers, and "if you went in the store, you were told to get the hell out," recollected Thurgood Marshall decades later.

There were no rest rooms for African Americans in all of downtown Baltimore, and Marshall recalled one urgent moment when "the only thing I could do was get on a trolley car and try to get home. And I did get almost in the house, when I ruined the front doorsteps." Marshall attended Division Street public school, the small home for eight full elementary grades of African American students. There was a white Catholic school two blocks from Division Street. Because frequent fights broke out between the students at the respective schools, the parochial school let its students out fifteen minutes before Division Street.

Thurgood's maternal great-grandfather, whose name has been forever lost, was brought to America by slavers in the 1840s. In a *Time* interview in 1962, Marshall said his forebear was "one mean man, the baddest nigger" in Maryland. Freed by his owner, he married a white woman and settled in Maryland. His paternal grandfather was a freedman who, during the Civil War, fought for the Union with almost 200,000 other African American soldiers. During the war, he took the name Thoroughgood. When the war ended, he joined the U.S. Merchant Marine, sailed around the world a few times, and then settled in Baltimore, marrying a Virginia mulatto named Annie, who was the offspring of a white Virginia slaveholder and an African American slave.

Thurgood's maternal grandfather, Isiah Olive Branch Williams, was also a Union soldier and then a sailor in the merchant marine, who, after his seafaring days, married and settled down in Baltimore. He was an activist battler for civil rights in the last decades of the nineteenth century, leading the first public African American demonstration ever seen in Baltimore to protest the beatings of African Americans by the Baltimore police. Both grandfathers opened up competing grocery stores, and by the turn of the twentieth century, they had the two largest African American grocery stores in Baltimore.

Marshall's mother was named Norma Arica because her father had sailed into the port of Arica, Chile, where he went to a performance by a local opera company and fell in love with Bellini's opera *Norma*. She attended a black college and became a public-school teacher in Baltimore. When she was seventeen she married a longtime school chum, twenty-one-year-old, straight-haired, blue-eyed William Canfield Marshall. Both of them were very light-skinned, and Thurgood, who, years later, was to be called a "tall, yeller nigger" by a redneck sheriff in Tennessee, inherited their genes.

Marshall recalled that while his father was "the noisiest and loudest, my mother was by far the strongest." He loved her dearly, often recalling with joy his getting "her drunk every Mother's Day because she was a sucker for sweet drinks, and I'd just put a lot of Cointreau and stuff in her glass, real thick."

At the time of Thurgood's birth, William Marshall, who had little education, was a Pullman dining car waiter on the Baltimore & Ohio Railroad's Washington-to-New York run. Later on, when Thurgood was attending Lincoln University, his father took a job as a waiter at the posh Gibson Island Club. He eventually became chief steward at the yacht club and occasionally had Thurgood work at the club when the young man was on school vacation.

William Marshall, like all blacks, felt racism. "He felt it doubly because he was blond and blue-eyed," said Marshall. "He could have passed for white, and a lot of times, he would get in a big fight because someone would think he was white." Marshall's father was also an inveterate gambler and a drinker. When he drank too much, which was regularly, "my mother was afraid of him," recalled Marshall. He was a man who always stood up for his rights, even though it meant he lost many jobs. Marshall recalled one occasion when his father quit a posh butler's job. His father "was working for a widow woman, very wealthy. One night, she decided to show off her little poodle, Nanky. 'Nanky,' she said, 'show the people which you would rather be, a nigger or dead.' The dog lay on its back with four feet up as if to say it would rather be dead. Pop walked right out the door and never went back."

Thurgood's older brother by four years, William Aubrey Marshall, after contracting and then overcoming tuberculosis, became a surgeon and researcher specializing in the disease. Like Thurgood, he battled racism all his life and, Thurgood felt, was ultimately one of its tragic victims. Marshall bitterly described his brother's life—and death: "He started out as an assistant (in a TB sanitarium) and ended up as the assistant, and might have had twenty people promoted over him."

> I used to tell him to fight about it, but he was not a fighter.... The last thing they did was to put a [white] guy over him who was not a doctor...who knew nothing about medicine. The officials insisted he clear everything with this guy. He told 'em he wasn't gonna do it. They said, "do it or go."...He called me, and I told him to tell them to go to hell. I said, "Why not go into private practice and make yourself some money, boy?" He said that he would be giving up on all the poor people in the sanitarium who needed him. He hung up and just sat grieving about it. His wife went to the market, and when she came back he was dead. From his heart. His heart just gave out.[35]

Thurgood's parents provided a comfortable, protected environment in which the family ate dinner together most nights and, afterwards, engaged in heated debates about the events of the day. Thurgood first learned the art of debate at his dinner table. William Marshall loved to debate, and young Thurgood was forced by his father to offer evidence to support his youthful assertions. As Marshall recalled, his father never told him to become a lawyer, "but he turned me into one. He did it by teaching me to argue, by challenging my logic on every point, by making me prove every statement I made."

He was, from a fairly young age, a pretty tough kid. Behind his highly respectable, middle-class Druid Hill Avenue house, "there were back alleys where roughnecks and the tough kids hung out. When it was time for dinner, my mother used to go to the front door and call my older brother. Then she'd go to the back door and call me." His principal often punished Thurgood for his poor behavior by sending him to the school basement with a copy of the U.S. Constitution. To be let out from the cellar, Thurgood had to show that he had memorized a passage from the Constitution. As Marshall later recounted, "Before I left that school I knew the whole thing by heart."

A black scholar observed correctly that "probably the single most important event in the life of any African American child is his recognition of his own coloredness, with all the implications of that fact." Whether the initial realization is a neutral experience or a rude shock, the result is a "new understanding of the self [that] influences the child's every thought and emotion from that day forth."[36] Marshall, like Walter White and all other African Americans, came to that recognition early in life. His initiation, at age seven, into a form of self-realization was not as traumatic as White's, but it was a powerful one.

Until the event occurred, Thurgood was not conscious of either the potency or the portent of his "coloredness." He recounted the incident to a reporter decades later:

> I heard a kid call a Jewish boy I knew a "kike" to his face. I was about seven. I asked him why he didn't fight the kid. He asked me what I would do if somebody called me "nigger"—would I fight? That was a new one on me. I knew "kike" was a dirty word, but I hadn't known about "nigger." I went home and wanted to know right that minute what all this meant. That's not easy for a parent to explain so it makes sense to a kid, you know.

After a brief definition of the term, along with a quick lecture on the history of slavery, racism, and segregation, his father told him something he took to heart: "Anyone calls you nigger, you not only got my permission to fight him— you got my orders to fight him."[37] From that time on, Thurgood fought, in a variety of ways, the racist name-callers.

In 1977 he recalled one such racial incident in Baltimore. While attending high school he worked for a hat company owned by Mr. Schoen, a local Jewish merchant. His job was delivering the store's merchandise to clients living in the city. Thurgood had a "whole lot of hats in boxes to be delivered" and was getting on a trolley with them. A man grabbed the young Thurgood, pulled him back, and shouted at him, "Nigger, don't you push in front of white people!" Marshall proceeded to "tear into him" for calling him "nigger," and was promptly arrested. Mr. Schoen came down to the police station to bail out his young employee, who was truly contrite, for he had ruined the shipment of hats during the brawl. Thurgood apologized to him, "because the five hats were wrecks and it was a complete loss to him, and he said, 'Forget about them, what about you?' I told him. And he asked the man, how much was the bail money, or what have you, and the man said, 'Well, Mr. Schoen, it's up to you.' Mr. Schoen got his lawyer, and that was the end of that."[38]

But Marshall soon learned the costs of being black in a white-dominated world. His father found a waiter's job for Thurgood on the B&O Railroad. When Thurgood arrived at work the first day, the white dining car chef gave the tall youth a waiter's outfit. Thurgood found the pants too short, and asked for a different pair. The angry chef retorted, "Boy, we can get a man to fit the pants a lot easier than we can get pants to fit the man. Why don't you scroonch down a little more?" As Marshall recalled, "I scroonched."[39]

There were to be, in his lifetime, more insidious and dangerous incidents than those recounted above. Thurgood, like all African Americans, was always made aware of his color and his status as an outsider in racist America. He was "marked by segregation, mistaken [years later, he recalled] for an electrician when anyone should know that no African American could be an electrician in New York City—much less...a federal judge."[40]

# 2

---

# THE RISE OF THE NAACP
# AND CHARLIE HOUSTON'S
# "SOCIAL ENGINEERS"

One month after Marshall's birth, another race riot occurred, this time in Springfield, Illinois. It lasted two days, during which two black men were lynched—one a barber and the other an eighty-four-year-old man whose only crime was being long married to a white woman. Six more African Americans were killed by racist mobs. Two thousand black people had to flee for their lives. It took 4,200 state militia to restore order in Abraham Lincoln's birthplace.

The August 14, 1908, race riot showed Americans that the "color line" was not just a Southern problem, but a national one. Such riots and lynchings would increase dramatically in the next two decades, leading historian Nancy MacLean to note that many Southern whites found "killing a Negro less reprehensible than eating with him."[1] The terrible events in Springfield did trigger a response on the part of a handful of concerned whites, one from the South and three others from the distant city of New York.

## THE BIRTH OF THE NAACP

Three white people were so horrified by the events in Springfield that they resolved to do something about racism in America. A social worker in New York City, Mary White Ovington, wrote to William E. Walling, a southerner who had covered the riot for *The Independent,* a radical populist magazine, and suggested that they issue an appeal to America's conscience. Joined by another social worker, Dr. Henry Moskowitz, Ovington and Walling decided to publish a broadside attacking racism and urging the creation of an organization that would address its evils. "The Call: A Lincoln Emancipation Conference to Discuss

Means for Securing Political and Civil Equality for the Negro" was largely written by Oswald Garrison Villard, the grandson of one of the nineteenth century's great abolitionist leaders, William Lloyd Garrison, and published in his paper, the *New York Evening Post,* on February 12, 1909, the centennial of Lincoln's birth.

"The Call" pointed out the broken promises and denial of justice by whites to blacks since 1865—disenfranchisement, the establishment and judicial legitimization of Jim Crow laws and the perpetuation of the customs and "badges of slavery"—and cited the denial of educational opportunities for African Americans:

> Added to this [is] the spread of lawless attacks upon the negro, North, South, and West—even in the Springfield made famous by Lincoln—often accompanied by revolting brutalities, sparing neither sex, nor age nor youth, could not but shock the author of the sentiment that "government of the people, by the people, for the people, shall not perish from the earth."

The broadside concluded by noting that "silence under these conditions means tacit approval.... Discrimination once permitted cannot be bridled.... This government cannot exist half free and half slave any better today than it could in 1861. Hence we call upon all believers in democracy to join in a national conference for the discussion of present evils, the voicing of protests, and the renewal of the struggle for civil and political liberty."

The document was signed by fifty-three prominent social workers, educators, lawyers, and clergy, mostly white, including Jane Addams, John Dewey, the Reverend Walter Laidlaw, Rabbi Stephen S. Wise, Rabbi Emil Hirsch, Lincoln Steffens, Lillian D. Wald, Susan P. Wharton, J. G. Phelps-Stokes, and Oswald Garrison Villard, with a very small number of African American signers, including Ida Wells-Barnett and Du Bois, then teaching in Atlanta.

In May 1909, the National Negro Committee was formed. In February 1910, after meeting in a tiny office on Vesey Street in New York City, the NNC reorganized itself as the National Association for the Advancement of Colored People. (That same year also saw the emergence of another African American civil rights organization, the National Urban League, which sought support for black equality from those in America's cities. In 1911, Marcus Garvey created another, controversial organization, in Jamaica, the Universal Negro Improvement Association. It soon spread to and grew rapidly in America.)

Although many members felt the NAACP's name was a bit too long and cumbersome, it was retained because the Executive Committee felt it was "comprehensive, and inclusive, and can offend no one who is interested in the advancement of colored people." Among the early supporters of the Association were Jewish Americans, especially those recently arrived from Russia and eastern Europe. They knew all too well the cost of discrimination and prejudice, and could identify with the plight of African Americans.

W. E. B. Du Bois, as part of an effort to bring more African Americans into the leadership structure, was given the post of director of publications and research. This led to his appointment as editor of the Association's monthly publication, *The Crisis*. Du Bois brought a small contingent from the Niagara Movement with him.

Although there were more than 11 million African Americans living in America in 1909, they were so beaten down that such an initiative had to be taken by whites. In 1914, one could find in the "land of opportunity" only one African American judge, two African American legislators, and two thousand African American college students.[2]

The goals and objectives of the NAACP have remained fairly constant since its initial meeting as the NNC in May 1909. From its inception, the Association was an organization that welcomed whites as well as blacks and challenged the "mainstream [white] public to accept ever-greater civil and social rights for the nation's historic minority."[3] It hoped to accomplish this general end through litigation, legislative and political action, and public education, "all unified, coordinated, and centrally directed."

The NAACP's goals, as published in the January 1996 issue of *The Crisis*, sadly mirrored the message in the 1909 broadside:

1. To eliminate racial discrimination and segregation from all aspects of public life in America.
2. To secure a free ballot for every qualified American citizen.
3. To seek justice in the courts.
4. To secure legislation banning discrimination and segregation.
5. To secure equal job opportunities based on individual merit without regard to race, religion, or national origin.
6. To end mob violence and police brutality.

The organizational structure of the NAACP was simple and efficient, with a committee of one hundred members serving as its National Council. An executive board of thirty functioned as the policy-approving body. The field secretary would act as liaison with the local NAACP chapters that the organizers hoped would (and, very quickly, did) sprout up across the nation. In addition, there were bureaus that handled publicity; legal, educational, political, and civil rights; and press and industrial relations.[4]

Initially, apart from Du Bois, the leaders of the organization were white. In 1918, Moorfield Storey, a prominent Boston attorney and former president of the American Bar Association, was its president. The chairman of the executive board was Mary White Ovington; John R. Shillady was the secretary; J. E. Spingarn was the treasurer; and Arthur Spingarn was the chairman of the Legal Committee. The predominance of whites in the leadership structure created tensions inside the organization and in the African American community. The problem was eventually addressed by putting African Americans into the positions of secretary and chairman of the Legal Committee. Also, two young African Americans had been appointed to important secondary positions. James Weldon Johnson was the field secretary, and a young man named Walter White came up from the Atlanta chapter to take the post of assistant secretary.

The NAACP's executive secretary ran the national office and made sure, with the assistance of the field secretary, that all the bureaus were working properly, that the national association's policies were followed in the chapters, and that public relations reached the press, the President, and the Congress. But the most essential role of the secretary was to raise funds to pay for NAACP operations.

The post of secretary was held by a white person until 1919. John Shillady was the last of these. In that year, while in Austin, Texas, to fight the state's demand for a list of Texas members, Shillady was severely beaten by a local judge, the sheriff, and other county officials. The organization was unable to find an attorney willing to bring suits against these officials in the state courts. After a long and painful recuperation, Shillady resigned as executive secretary. The position was filled by James Weldon Johnson. Since then the post has been held by African Americans.

When Johnson took over, the NAACP had little money and plenty of creditors. But the growth of the organization was phenomenal—it was meeting the needs of oppressed African Americans. Local chapters quickly began to form: by 1930 there were 378 branches in forty-four of the then forty-eight states. Recruiting thousands of new members every year, these new chapters provided information to the national office, helping it to carry out the Association's litigation and lobbying work. Yet many black people were afraid to support the organization openly, and others were opposed to the NAACP's very visible activism. This lack of a binding consensus among African Americans would be a problem for decades.

African American church leaders were essential to the development of the NAACP chapters. Thurgood Marshall recalled that "eighty percent of the branches of the NAACP when I went there [in 1936] were run by ministers, in churches. Ninety-eight percent of the meetings were held in Negro churches. The Negro church support was beautiful, from one end of the country to the other." He told the story of one of these branch leaders, a Reverend Lucas, the pastor of one of the largest African American Baptist churches in Houston, Texas. "One of the finest gentlemen you'd run across. In the glove compartment of his car, he had two items—a Bible and a .45. And his answer [when queried about them] was very simple: 'I'll try the Bible first.'"[5]

## THE NAACP'S FIRST TWO DECADES, 1910-1930

The NAACP initially sought to put an end to lynchings in the South. By 1911 the organization had "published its first pamphlet against lynching and held its first large meeting of protest."[6] In the July 1916 issue of *The Crisis,* the NAACP ran a special supplement on a lynching in Waco, Texas. Replete with gruesome photographs and statistics, it was titled "The Waco Horror." Race riots, accompanied by lynchings, had become, tragically, too "uncomfortably common" and would continue for another generation.

Lynching was defined, by the Association and its allies in Congress, as death at the hands of a mob, whether by hanging, beating, gunshot, stabbing, drowning, burning, or mutilation. All too often it was a combination of these ways of killing. In a 1930 letter to Republican President Herbert Hoover, Walter White cited that year's twenty-five lynchings. The particulars were horrific: "Beaten to death," "shot," "hanged and shot," "burned (in jail)," "shot (body burned)," and "Hanged."[7]

Arthur Spingarn, other legal officers of the NAACP, and members of the NAACP's Anti-lynching Committee, worked with public relations firms to raise money for full-page ads in major newspapers in Atlanta, Chicago, New York City, and Boston. Spingarn and others in the NAACP appealed to the American Fund for Public Service and other agencies and individuals, using the argument that publicizing the ugly facts about lynching was necessary because "the American public at large is either ignorant or apathetic about the facts. We believe," Spingarn wrote to Roger Baldwin, the secretary of the fund, "that when the facts are put before their eyes we shall be able to arouse them."

The NAACP's legal officers believed that the "justification for a federal anti-lynching law is to be found in the peculiar nature of the crime itself, and the consequences flowing from it."

> When a prisoner is violently taken from the custody of the law by mob and lynched, the orderly processes of government are successfully assaulted and set at naught. Let the state agencies complacently submit or negligently fail or refuse to apprehend or prosecute the known participants in the lynching, then in effect the state abdicates her sovereignty in favor of the mob and acquiesces in her own over-throw.... The constitutional guarantee of the equal protection of the laws becomes reduced to a mere platitude.[8]

Unfortunately, the NAACP did not get anti-lynching legislation passed during these early years; it would continue the fight into the 1960s. By 1937, with Assistant Special Counsel Thurgood Marshall involved in the NAACP's lobbying efforts for passage of an anti-lynching bill, more than sixty such bills had been introduced in the House of Representatives. They were supported by other civil rights groups, including the ACLU, the National Urban League, the American Federation of Teachers, and even the League for Industrial Democracy (during the 1930s and 1940s a Communist-infiltrated organization in conflict with the NAACP). Each bill languished in Congress, crushed by Senate filibuster if it passed in the House.

In these early years, poignant letters from African American members poured into the national office begging the NAACP to investigate egregious criminal procedural violations that had sent their daughters or sons or husbands to prison for years—if they had not been preemptively lynched. In such cases, the letters pleaded for investigation of the tragic incidents and punishment of those responsible, who were often the local sheriff and his deputies.

In the early fall of 1914, the NAACP tried something new: it sent a questionnaire to all candidates for Congress, asking them to express their views on segregation and lynching. Arthur Spingarn told the candidates that the results would be published in *The Crisis*, "which reaches 150,000 readers, [as well as] the white and colored press of the country, and in handbills for distribution by our branches." Those running for Congress but not replying would have their names printed in *The Crisis*, "and colored voters and their friends [would be] advised to vote against them."[9] In addition to publicizing the evils of racial segregation and discrimination, the NAACP soon found itself responding to a flood of requests for information about civil rights.

In those early years, the national headquarters would occasionally send two officers, one white and the other black, into a particular state, equipping them "with a small camera" to try to capture the reality of Jim Crow segregation on film. This evidence would be published in *The Crisis* and provide copy for newspapers, which could publicize Jim Crow life in the South. J. E. Spingarn went into Oklahoma on one such trip in 1914. W. E. B. Du Bois was sent to the South and Southwest to investigate racial incidents. In July 1917 he went to East St. Louis, Missouri, after a race riot, a particularly dangerous fact-finding trip. When Walter White joined the NAACP in 1918 as its national assistant secretary, he found himself taking similar trips to the South to investigate race riots and lynchings. Because of his fair skin—he could easily "pass" as a white man—he was able to travel without the "trustworthy colored man" accompanying him.

The emergence of the second Ku Klux Klan began in 1915 in Atlanta, Georgia, fueled by the screening of the film *Birth of a Nation*, which glorified the original post-1865 Klan. It reached the apex of its political power in the 1920s. Between 1918 and 1929 the Klan experienced a dramatic growth in membership. It was one that, not coincidentally, paralleled the NAACP's own growth in membership. This growth of both organizations reflected the impact of the African American military veterans returning from service in World War I, who greatly worried the Klansmen. Given their military training and experience in combat (40,000 of the 200,000 African Americans in uniform saw action in the trenches), they were seen as a new threat to white supremacy. These black soldiers had fought a war "to make the world safe for democracy," only to return to Jim Crow—and their anger would lead them to the NAACP.

In 1919, the year of the "Red Summer," more than one hundred African Americans were murdered (eighty were lynched) and some one thousand were wounded in twenty-five race riots.[10] Even the nation's capital was the scene of a terrible race riot, one observed firsthand by another future NAACP leader, Charles Houston. In the postwar decade, lynchings and race riots had increased in number and intensity, in cities in the South and the Southwest, as well as Chicago and other cities in the Midwest. One of the worst took place in Tulsa, Oklahoma, on June 1, 1921, after a nineteen-year-old black man allegedly assaulted a teenaged white female elevator operator. A lynch mob gathered at the jail but, thanks to the local sheriff, was deterred from seizing the young man. (He was later freed when it was determined that he had stumbled getting off the elevator and accidentally brushed against the operator.)

Later that day, forty blocks of Greenwood, the fairly prosperous African American section of Tulsa, then labeled the "Negro Wall Street of America," were looted and leveled by torch-bearing white mobs. According to conservative estimates, more than one hundred residents were killed. In the end, in addition to the deaths—on both sides, because black Americans fought back—twenty-three neighborhood churches were razed and more than one thousand homes and businesses destroyed.[11] The Klan was deeply involved in stirring up the fears of whites and leading mobs against African Americans. In this same period, too, the Klan played a decisive role in the elections of mayors, councilmen, governors, and U.S. senators in Alabama (Hugo Black), Georgia (Tom Watson, Walter George, William J. Harris), and other Southern and Southwestern states.

By the end of the 1920s, the KKK's power had diminished dramatically because of changes in the political climate and the growing revulsion of many moderate Southern whites who were appalled by lynchings and race riots. Unlike the first Klansmen, the revived Klan's typical member was a middle-aged, middle-class parent. Civic leaders such as mayors, bankers, salesmen, businessmen, college professors, councilmen, justices of the peace, sheriffs, notary publics, and even ministers and Sunday school teachers made up its nucleus.

Whether in Georgia, Utah, Alabama, Colorado, New Jersey, Connecticut, or Indiana, they were "mainstream" men—nativistic, evangelical Protestants who were alarmed about what they saw as a crisis in American values caused by the influx of alien Catholics, Jews, socialists, Bolsheviks, anarchists, and other "deviants."[12] Race, however, was at the center of the Klan's politics. Its members were fundamentally committed to protecting Anglo-Saxon "purity" from potential racial pollution by 12 million African Americans. They believed these inferior but dangerous people were encouraged to fight for civil and political equality by "outside agitators" like the NAACP.[13]

In 1915, David Wark Griffith's blatantly racist film *The Birth of a Nation* opened to rave reviews across the country, particularly in the South and the Southwest, where it played right into the 1920s. It depicted the first Klan as heroes during Reconstruction and portrayed African Americans as subhuman. The NAACP did everything it could to ban its showing. For them, it was an "obnoxious and dangerous film," one that had incited acts of terrorism against African Americans. For almost two decades, Walter White and others vigorously complained about this motion picture, writing letters and articles pressuring local film censorship boards to block its exhibition.

This led to conflicts not only with the Klan but also with the American Civil Liberties Union. In 1931 the ACLU's national director, Roger Baldwin, while accepting the NAACP argument that the film was obnoxious propaganda, stated, "we hold that the right of propaganda—even bad propaganda—must be protected against interference by the civil authority.... [The] NAACP, by invoking the civil authority to prevent the showing of 'The Birth of a Nation,' is placing itself in exactly the position of...any other group of self-appointed censors when they attempt to restrict forms of expression objected to on special grounds." Walter White continued to encourage local chapters to protest screenings of the film. This forced Baldwin to complain to White again in 1936 about NAACP efforts to ban the film in Milwaukee and Denver. The NAACP actually gave serious consideration to the idea of producing a major Hollywood film to present a true history of the period. Ultimately, however, there was not enough money available and the project died quietly.

From its inception and certainly in its first two decades, the NAACP had few friends in Congress or in the White House. It wasn't until the administration of Harry S Truman (1945–1953) that the NAACP was able to work closely with the presidency in dealing with the dilemmas facing African Americans, politically, economically, and socially. Until then, their only recourse was the federal courts.

President Woodrow Wilson was probably the most openly racist of the Chief Executives in the eyes of the NAACP leadership. A Virginian, Wilson had grown up in the post-Reconstruction era, and his racist attitudes formed then were, in the opinion of some, reinforced while he was president of Princeton University, the only major Northern university to exclude African Americans and an institution "spiritually located in Dixie."[14] Although Wilson knew a number of the white leaders of the NAACP (Spingarn and Storey), he refused to work with them on the elimination of racism in America. Indeed, he fostered it by allowing the "'Jim Crowing' of the colored clerks in the Departments at Washington,"[15] thereby infecting the federal bureaucracy with racial segregation and discrimination. And after expressing some faint support to the NAACP's leadership for creating a commission to examine racial discrimination, Wilson declined to take action on the pretext that opposition from the Senate would make it impossible. And when challenged in 1913 by the Association to take a firm stand against racial discrimination, Wilson refused even to invite them to a meeting.

In 1930 the NAACP faced a watershed political challenge: defeating a U.S. Supreme Court nominee of Herbert Hoover's, federal appeals court judge Frank J. Parker, who had been identified as a segregationist Southern politician by African Americans. In 1920, running for governor of North Carolina on the Republican ticket, Parker had given a speech in which he said he believed in the disenfranchisement of Negroes, that the Republican Party did not want the Negro to vote, and that participation of the Negro in politics was a source of evil and danger to the society.[16]

President Hoover nominated the Republican judge for a seat on the U.S. Supreme Court on March 21, 1930. Parker's claim that his 1920 speech was misinterpreted by the press and that he had "no prejudice whatever against the colored people" was not accompanied by a denial that he had actually said that African Americans were a source of evil and danger in politics. The NAACP board, led by Spingarn and Walter White, immediately marshaled the chapters and obtained the support of the American Federation of Labor to lobby for the defeat of Parker's nomination in the U.S. Senate. On May 7, 1930, the vote was taken in the Senate. Parker was not confirmed by a vote of 39–41. The rejection of Hoover's nominee was a signal victory for the NAACP. The fight to block Parker,* led by Walter White, "transformed the NAACP into a leading civil

---

*Interestingly, Judge Parker was still serving on the Fourth Circuit U.S. Court of Appeals when, in 1951, Thurgood Marshall appealed a South Carolina district court decision involving school segregation. The *Briggs* lawsuit was one of a quartet of cases, under the name of the seminal *Brown v. Board of Education of Topeka, Kansas,* that came to the U.S. Supreme Court in 1953 challenging *Plessy's* continued validity as constitutional doctrine. He would continue to sit and hear appeals from the NAACP during Marshall's tenure with the NAACP, much to the unhappiness of the Association lawyers litigating in Parker's Fourth Circuit Court of Appeals.

rights organization [and] brought about the recognition that the black vote in the North and in border states was a force to be reckoned with."[17]

By 1930, the end of the Association's second decade, it could justifiably claim to be "the first line of defense" for African Americans. That year the NAACP published a pamphlet, summarizing its legal and civil rights work over the preceding twenty years in the "civil rights struggle for American Negroes." In its fight against lynching, which it called the "Shame of America," it spent close to $65,000 for ads and publicity. From 1910 to 1930, it spent $95,000 in legal costs (not including additional costs covered by chapter treasuries). This had funded "six decisive victories before the U.S. Supreme Court....This legal work of the Association is directed to the affirmation of fundamental civil rights affecting not alone Negroes but every citizen of the country. The Negro represents the shock troops in this long struggle for democracy."[18] The Association's initial ventures in the legal arena were remarkably successful, especially when one considers that there was no full-time lawyer in the National office in those years.

## EARLY LITIGATION EFFORTS, 1915–1936

The NAACP was the very first organization to try to secure the civil and political rights of its constituents through litigation in state and, critically important, federal courts. The NAACP's initial venture into the federal courts came in 1915 when its national president, Moorfield Storey, filed a successful *amicus* brief in an Oklahoma voting case. From 1915 through 1936, the year Thurgood Marshall joined the NAACP as assistant special counsel, the civil rights organization participated in ten cases before the U.S. Supreme Court, either as a major party to a lawsuit or, once, as an *amicus curiae*, a "friend of the Court." It was victorious in nine of these cases. The lawsuits involved state primary elections, *Nixon v. Herndon,* 1927, and *Nixon v. Condon,* 1932; voting procedures, *Guinn v. United States,* 1915 *(amicus);* state-enforced racial segregation, *Buchanan v. Warley,* 1917, and *Harmon v. Tyler,* 1927; *City of Richmond v. Deans,* 1930; private restrictive covenants, *Corrigan v. Buckley,* 1926 (the NAACP's argument was rejected by the Court: the Civil War Amendments did not prohibit private discrimination); and procedural rights in criminal cases, *Moore v. Dempsey,* 1923, *Hollins v. Oklahoma,* 1935, and *Brown v. Mississippi,* 1935. There was no litigation involving segregated education's unfair consequences, either secondary, college, or postgraduate and professional school, prior to 1935.

By 1934 it was clear that the NAACP needed a full-time lawyer just to deal with the litigation. (Spingarn, in addition to his role as chairman of the legal committee, had his own business and was also involved in other NAACP activities, as chairman of the National Board and a member of the Joint Committee.)

In that year the NAACP turned to Charles H. "Charlie" Houston. Walter White had been working hard on Houston to work for the Association full-time as its legal counsel. (He had been doing legal work for the NAACP part-time in addition to his full-time work as vice-dean and professor of law at Howard University.) In late 1934, White finally convinced Houston to leave Howard to become the Association's first full-time legal advocate.

## CHARLIE HOUSTON'S "SOCIAL ENGINEERS"

Houston was a brilliant lawyer and educator who, during his tenure from 1929 to 1935, turned Howard Law School into the "West Point of the civil rights movement in America."[19] In a 1977 program at Amherst College honoring Houston, Thurgood Marshall said of his friend and teacher: "We wouldn't have been any place if Charlie hadn't laid the groundwork for it." Even U.S. Supreme Court Justice William O. Douglas, though no friend and admirer of Marshall when the two served on the U.S. Supreme Court, had a positive view of Houston: "I sincerely believe that he was one of the top ten advocates to appear before this Court in my thirty-five years." In his autobiography, Douglas called Houston "a veritable dynamo of energy guided by a mind that has as sharp a cutting edge as any I have known."[20]

Born in the District of Columbia in 1895, one year before *Plessy* came down, Houston graduated from Amherst College, magna cum laude and Phi Beta Kappa, in 1915. He was a tall, handsome, imposing man with a massive head and lively, engaging eyes, not someone to be taken lightly by anyone. Through his father's influence, Charlie secured a position teaching English in Howard University's Commercial Department. That department offered a program of study for nonmatriculating African American students interested in business careers. In 1917 he left the teaching position to serve in the segregated military as an officer in the world war. Houston returned from Europe full of bitterness. He had experienced a great many racist incidents, including a near-lynching in France, discrimination "more virulent than he had ever known before."[21] He also contracted tuberculosis while in the army, the effects of which overshadowed the rest of his life.

In 1919, Houston received an honorable discharge and was admitted to Harvard Law School, where he was the first African American to be elected editor of the *Harvard Law Review*. After graduating in 1921, Houston continued his legal education at Harvard, receiving a Doctor of Juridical Science degree the following year. He subsequently traveled in Europe and, in 1924, worked as a junior partner at Houston and Houston, his father's law firm in the District of Columbia. Then Houston was recruited by the dynamic president of Howard

University, Mordecai Johnson, to revise the law school's curriculum and thereby attract the best African American professors. However, he was appointed vice-dean. The politically astute Johnson, knowing that Howard's funds came from congressional appropriations, also appointed a white man, retired judge Fenton Booth, as dean. "He was barely doing anything," Marshall recalled years later. "He was just 'retired.' But he had one qualification [Houston didn't have]—he was white."[22]

When Houston arrived at Howard in 1929, he was thirty-four years old and facing the enormous challenge of replacing Howard's unaccredited evening law program with one that was accredited by the American Bar Association before he left. For more than five years, until he left to work full-time for the NAACP, Houston "taught, litigated, and ran the law school."[23] His impact on the law, and on African Americans practicing it, was phenomenal. Houston was primarily responsible for developing a cadre of African American lawyers, including Thurgood Marshall, who would fight segregation in the only forum available to African Americans, the federal courts.

As the vice-dean, he turned the law school around overnight with his strict discipline, his dedication to excellence, and his vision of the role of the African American legal advocate. At the time, Houston confronted some daunting realities: there were about one thousand African Americans out of 160,000 attorneys practicing law in 1929. A great majority of those lawyers had received their degree from Howard's unaccredited law school. Perhaps one dozen of them, according to Houston and others, were well qualified, competent lawyers.[24] Houston saw his task as turning out extremely competent—"superior" was the word he often used to describe his graduates—attorneys to serve as his "social engineers" in the battles against racism in America. The role Houston envisioned for these "capable and socially alert Negro lawyers" was a complex one:

> The Negro lawyer must be trained as a social engineer and group interpreter. Due to the Negro's social and political condition...the Negro lawyer must be prepared to anticipate, guide, and interpret his group advancement. [He must also be a] business advisor...for the protection of the scattered resources possessed or controlled by the group....He must provide more ways and means for holding within the group the income now flowing through it.[25]

Houston's practical jurisprudence, in class and in practice, came down to a few basic principles: "(1) face the facts, (2) relate to the past, (3) convince the public, and (4) seek and agitate for truth."[26] He conceived a "grand strategic framework" and proceeded quickly, during his tenure at Howard, to lay the groundwork and build the educational structure that would prepare for its implementation.[27]

Thurgood Marshall, his best student, said that Charlie Houston "insisted that we get out into the field and become 'social engineers' and not just lawyers. You had to be as good [as] if not better than the white lawyer in order to win and he wanted the Negro lawyers to a make a contribution to the overall picture of the country.... He touched all of us, but I think me more than anybody else because he worried with me. Including breaking up my crap games, things like that."[28]

A younger (by nine years) distant cousin of Houston's, and mentor and friend to Marshall, was William "Bill" Hastie. Following his cousin Charlie, Hastie attended Amherst College and Harvard Law School (making Law Review as well). Hastie, only four years older than Marshall, was one of the new instructors Houston brought to Howard. He would become a major force in Marshall's evolution as a lawyer and judge. Both Houston and Hastie took Howard's number one student under their wings. Houston was a decisive influence on Marshall and many other African American law students, several of whom worked with Marshall in the Association's legal section. (Included in this cohort were Spottswood Robinson III, Leon Ransom, Robert Carter, Constance "Connie" Baker Motley, Arthur Shores, Sidney Redmond, and George Crockett.) Houston and his faculty taught their students that they would have to function, in both state and federal courts, under a major constraint—the *Plessy* separate-but-equal legal precedent. It was a precedent firmly woven into the nation's legal, social, economic, and political fabric. The 1896 doctrine seriously limited the possibility of victory in court.

*Plessy* was, in 1930, an essential thread in the fabric of the Rule of Law. Houston never let his students forget that the black-letter law (court opinions and statutes) constituted the rules of the legal game: "We have to figure out how we can use them to our advantage, or else show, in case after case, the weakness and the error of the rules until an appellate court decides to change the rules."

From the time Marshall joined the NAACP until the late 1940s, he had to argue for African American equality within the framework of the bitterly hated *Plessy* doctrine. He never deviated from his belief—hammered into his head by Charlie Houston—that "Rules is Rules" and a good lawyer or a good judge litigated and adjudicated within their framework, however constraining, until the Rules were changed. As an advocate for the NAACP, Marshall "just took the Rules as they were.... We just learned to use them." It was only after World War II that Marshall concluded that *Plessy* had been weakened enough for him to challenge the Rule itself before the Supreme Court.

Houston's "First Commandment" of legal behavior guided Marshall throughout his years as lawyer and judge. During the 1987 term of the Supreme Court, one of Marshall's law clerks recommended that the judge grant certiorari review even though the petitioner's petition, *Greene v. Polk County, Iowa,* was not properly filed with the Court because it was typed space-and-a-half rather than double-spaced. The clerk wrote Marshall: "The Legal office recommends that we enforce our double-spacing rule and make [petitioner] retype the petition, [petitioner] claims he can't afford to have it retyped, even though he is not proceeding [*in forma pauperis*]. The cert. [petition] is completely readable and I don't think it needs to be retyped. I recommend *GRANT*-md-10/26/87." Marshall's terse reply to his clerk: "Deny—'Rules is Rules!'"[29]

Marshall saw this principle work even in federal courts in the deep South. Some—not all—Southern federal district court judges reluctantly followed the Rules, especially after they had been changed by a federal appeals court. He vividly recalled one such federal judge's commitment to the theory. The man, a white supremacist, sat in Richmond, Virginia, and was presiding over a teacher's salary inequity case. The judge ruled against the NAACP, and the judgment was appealed to the Fourth Circuit U.S. Court of Appeals. The appeals court overturned the federal trial judge's ruling, and the case was remanded to that judge for further action.

When the case was returned, the school superintendent refused to follow the new order requiring equal pay for African American and white schoolteachers, saying in the trial court that "I will not be a party to paying a nigger the same money I pay a white person. And I refuse to do it." Marshall immediately filed contempt proceedings before the same judge. The judge told Marshall, "Do you know that that's my best friend?" Then he said, "Despite that, I'm going to go with you" (on the civil contempt charge). Years later, Marshall noted: "That's the same man. He was getting ready to put his friend in jail. Because, you see, in his mind, the law had changed. He thought the law was one way. When the Court of Appeals tells him the law is the other way, that's the way he went. Yes, I can find plenty [of judges] like that, too. I'm for federal judges."[30]

There was yet another concern of Dean Houston, the importance of detailed, careful preparation of the legal briefs and oral arguments by African American lawyers. He did not overestimate the enormous value of presenting a written brief that was well written, correct regarding the black-letter law, free of errors or poor grammar that would detract from the presentation. In the eyes and minds of white readers, anything less would be dismissed as a "nigger brief."

Marshall remembered being told by a federal court clerk that even he "could look at a pleading filed by a lawyer and tell from looking at it whether it was done by a white or a Negro lawyer." Marshall said that that message stuck in his mind. "From that day until I stopped practicing law, I never filed a paper in any court with an erasure on it. If I changed a word, it had to be typed all over, because I didn't want that on it."[31]

Marshall's views on this matter were always clearly and forcefully expressed to the men and women who worked with him in the Association's legal section, the LDF, or "Inc Fund." Jack Greenberg was one of the handful of the Association's bright young lawyers brought into the New York office by Marshall in the late 1940s. He recalled that Thurgood insisted "we would never file 'nigger briefs.'"[32] Not "practice, practice, practice," but "preparation, preparation, preparation" was, for Marshall, the only way to perform successfully in *his* Carnegie Hall, the U.S. Supreme Court.

Charlie Houston, Marshall recalled, "was a perfectionist, and he insisted that we each be, and if we did a slipshod job, boy, he would lay it on you....He insisted on perfection." A mediocre African American lawyer was a disaster not only for his client but for his entire community. Houston was a tough teacher and administrator because of his "unwillingness to accept the mediocre."[33]

Marshall and others remembered how Houston worked them without letup. "No tea for the feeble, no crepe for the dead" was a common refrain of the dean to his students. Where once, as an undergraduate student at Lincoln University, Marshall had been able to breeze by his studies and play a great deal of pinochle, once he came under Charlie's tutelage, he had to change his behavior quickly: "I never worked hard until I got to the Howard Law School and met Charlie Houston....I saw this man's dedication, his vision, his willingness to sacrifice, and I told myself, 'You either shape up or ship out.' When you are being challenged by a great human being, you know that you can't ship out."[34]

Marshall, when attending Howard Law School between 1930 and 1933, was fully aware that Houston's potential "social engineer" students had to be outstanding for them to receive their law degree—as long as Houston was running things. Only six of the thirty students who entered with him graduated because of Charles Houston's heavy demands on their time and on their intellect. Those who dropped out, Marshall noted, were "the casualties of Houston's war on racial stereotypes."[35]

## THE SCOTTSBORO INCIDENT, 1931

Houston said of the Scottsboro Incident that it marked another "historic departure" for African Americans. In northern Alabama in late March 1931, nine black male teenagers, ranging in age from thirteen to nineteen, were accused of raping two white women while riding a freight train from Chattanooga to Memphis. It was quickly revealed that the women were prostitutes who catered to unemployed men riding the freight trains across Alabama.

Taken off the train at Paint Rock, Alabama, by local sheriffs, the nine youths were locked up in the Scottsboro, Alabama, county jail. In less than two weeks they were on trial for rape. In under four days, hardly sufficient time for their lawyers to mount a defense, four juries found eight of them guilty and sentenced them to death. (The youngest, Roy Wright, saw his trial end in a mistrial, but was convicted of rape after a second trial.) The trials and the environment in which they took place were mockeries of justice. Mobs estimated at over ten thousand persons came in from the countryside each day and "thronged this town of 1,500 inhabitants, yelled for a lynching and greeted the death verdict for the first two boys with cheers and music from a brass band. The uproar was plainly audible to the jury."[36]

Thus began the tragic odyssey of the Scottsboro Nine, as they were referred to in the Northern press. For one, the tragedy lasted two decades. Despite many appeals, all grew into manhood in prison while imprisoned for crimes they did not commit. A number sat on death row in the Alabama prison for many years. They endured seven retrials and secured two separate Supreme Court judgments in their favor. Four spent six years and one nineteen years in state prison.[37]

The NAACP was appalled by this judicial travesty and provided a defense attorney through its Chattanooga, Tennessee, chapter. The court appointed a local lawyer to assist in the defense. After the convictions, the attorneys prepared appeal briefs and submitted them to the Alabama Supreme Court. They were joined by additional lawyers hired by the Alabama NAACP and by Clarence Darrow, the noted trial lawyer, who was a member of the NAACP's National Legal Committee and its National Board.

A clash between defense organizations developed immediately, for the American Communist Party saw in the Scottsboro travesty an opportunity to recruit blacks, and their lawyers became involved in the defense. Both the NAACP and the Communist Party wanted to control the appeals process of the Scottsboro boys. After being visited by NAACP lawyers, Walter White, and field secretary William Pickens, as well as by lawyers from the American Communist Party's legal front organization, the International Labor Defense (ILD), the families decided to let the Communists defend their sons. The ILD, much to the anger of the NAACP, exploited this opportunity to make recruitment inroads in black communities throughout the South. The young men soon became martyrs in the Soviet Communist Party's worldwide campaign against capitalism in the 1930s.

Marshall and the rest of the NAACP leadership despised American Communists and would fight them right up into the 1960s. Houston warned White in 1934 to stay away from them: "My advice is to keep out....Keep the Association free and clear...." This advice created a dilemma for White because African Americans, many of them members of the NAACP, wanted the Association to do something for the young men facing death for crimes they did not commit. In December 1935, after four years of arguments and recriminations, with the nine Scottsboro boys still in prison awaiting death, the contending organizations reached a compromise. A Scottsboro Defense Committee, consisting of members of the NAACP, the ILD, the League for Industrial Democracy, and the ACLU, was formed to carry on the defense.

In July 1937, Alabama dropped charges against four of the defendants, who then began making vaudeville appearances across America! In a memo to the chapters in August 1937, Marshall advised them that under no circumstances was a chapter to work with the former defendants' booking agent. They all took Marshall's advice and stayed out of it. In June 1950, the last of the Scottsboro defendants, Andy Wright, was paroled and left Alabama for New York.

## THE MARGOLD REPORT

In 1977, Justice Thurgood Marshall recalled that there was "never any strategy in this [civil rights litigation] business;...we took them case by case. The only thing was Margold's Report, that's all, and that's way back in '32 or '33."[38]

The Margold Report evolved from a grant to the NAACP from the American Fund for Public Service, Inc., also known as the Garland Fund. In May 1930, the fund allocated $100,000 to the Association "to be used in financing a nation-wide legal and educational campaign to secure for Negroes a fuller and more practical enjoyment of the rights, privileges and immunities theoretically guaranteed them by the Constitution of the United States."[39] (Because of the Depression and the "decline of the security market," the fund actually gave the Association only about $27,000 of the promised $100,000.)

The first step was hiring a "competent lawyer,...and [having him recommend] the bringing of cases at the most vital, strategic and advantageous points. ...[There was a need for a full-time lawyer] to work in conjunction with the NAACP's Executive Secretary and under the joint supervision of the five-person Joint Committee [made up of three members selected by the fund, Morris Ernst, Roger Baldwin, and Lewis Gannett, and two men appointed by the NAACP, Arthur Spingarn and James W. Johnson] in preparing for the successive steps that are to be taken."

In October 1930, at the urging of Charles Houston, William Hastie, and one of the members of the NAACP's National Legal Committee, Harvard Law School professor Felix Frankfurter, Nathan Margold, then an assistant U.S. attorney in New York, left his federal post to work for the NAACP. Margold, who had been a student of Frankfurter's, worked with the NAACP until he was appointed Solicitor of the Department of the Interior in the spring of 1933. As soon as he took up his new job, he reviewed the large body of legal precedents and other legal material. Margold submitted detailed reports, in 1932 and 1933, on how to attack the four "primary evils in this country": segregation and the unequal apportionment of school funds; residential segregation; segregation on common carriers; and disenfranchisement. His final report outlined a number of possible NAACP legal strategies in these areas, as well as jury discrimination against qualified African Americans and racial segregation and discrimination. His observations and recommendations formed the basis for most of the NAACP's legal section's actions for the next thirty years.

Margold found great disparities in Southern state funding for white and African American schools, from two to ten times greater for white schools in the ten Southern states he examined. His recommendation was the bringing of tax-payer suits to force "equal if separate accommodation." The hoped-for results: the "cost of the dual system [would] be demonstrated as prohibitive," would "focus the public's attention on vicious discrimination," and would ultimately lead to the financial breakdown of the dual public school systems.

Given the *Plessy* precedent, Margold concluded that "segregation is not contrary to the Fourteenth Amendment unless accompanied by other discriminations." Therefore, he proposed litigation that would challenge "the constitutional validity of segregation if and when accompanied irremediably by discrimination" and make a *prima facie* case that the coupling of segregation with discrimination was a denial of the Fourteenth Amendment's equal-protection clause. The threat of destroying segregation would potentially "exert a real force in compelling enormous improvement in Negro schools from voluntary official actions."

Residential segregation was accomplished either by state or city/municipal ordinance or by a private property owner's restrictive covenants. The Supreme Court had already decided that the former violated the Fourteenth Amendment. Margold suggested a line of attack on private residential segregation that involved "serious but I hope not insurmountable difficulties," and required funding "to prepare a case in which the U.S. Supreme Court cannot avoid a definite decision [regarding restrictive covenants]." The NAACP had to find "an appropriate litigant...willing to cooperate with us, [in litigation] in the Supreme Court which will really test the propriety under the Fourteenth Amendment of enforcing a property owner's covenant discriminating against Negroes solely on the basis of color."

Segregation on common carriers, like segregated schools, had to be tackled in the face of the reality of the *Plessy* doctrine. For Margold, the most effective tactic for the NAACP was to bring suits to compel railroad and bus companies doing business in the South to provide "equal accommodation." Margold advocated filing at least ten separate actions, simultaneously, against all the Southern states.

Margold concluded that there was no clear line of attack on the disenfranchisement of African Americans, since no Southern state had a "statutory provision which is itself subject to constitutional objections." Whites used terror, combined with economic and social pressures, to deny black people the right to vote. Voting registrars employed arbitrary standards and tests to determine who was qualified to vote. The "white primary" and the poll tax enforced the exclusion of nonwhites. But none of these abuses of power were of the sort prohibited by the Fourteenth Amendment.

Margold was unable to attribute the bar against jury service by blacks "to [any] invalid statutory requirements nor to open disobedience of valid ones, nor to any discriminatory practices which are susceptible of actual proofs." A test case, based on sufficient data showing numbers of registered African American voters and the actual makeup of trial and grand juries over a significant period of time, could, he argued, demonstrate that this denial of participation was deliberate and systemic. The case could be bolstered if it could be shown that the same officer had been in charge of drawing up the jury list over that period. "It will not be easy to find such a case," he warned the Joint Committee and the NAACP.

Margold left to join the Roosevelt administration in 1933. Acting on his recommendations, the NAACP began to "map out a broad frontal attack on the basic causes of discrimination instead of waiting to handle the manifestations" in the case-by-case fashion the Association had previously followed.[40]

By 1934, Arthur Spingarn had served as the chair of the NAACP's National Legal Committee for twenty-seven years. Assisted by a few other white attorneys such as Darrow and Storey, all working *pro bono*, Spingarn had handled the litigation brought by the organization in the state and federal courts, despite the heavy demands of each man's law practice. There was an obvious need to find a full-time legal advocate for the NAACP. After Margold's departure, nothing was done to implement his legal strategy until Charles Houston joined the NAACP as its Special Counsel in 1935. (William Hastie had been expected to take over and to become the Association's full-time attorney. But Margold recruited Hastie to serve as his assistant solicitor in the Department of the Interior.) His reports provided the foundation for hundreds of NAACP lawsuits in state and federal courts challenging racial segregation.

In October 1934, Houston responded to the final Margold recommendations. He targeted all segregated educational facilities, including secondary as well as university, postgraduate, and professional schools. Houston also recommended that the Association attack segregation and discrimination in transportation and teacher salary inequalities. The legal assault of the NAACP on higher education was quickly launched.

## THE DU BOIS CRISIS, 1934

Houston, starting with Margold's reports, quickly developed his own legal agenda for the NAACP. The Du Bois battles with Walter White, Roy Wilkins, and the National Board came to a traumatic conclusion in this period. James W. Johnson, the NAACP's first African American executive secretary, had resigned. Walter White took over in 1930 and immediately brought Roy Wilkins, from Missouri, into the national office as assistant secretary. Du Bois did not like White, and the feeling was mutual. He was utterly contemptuous of White's intellectual limitations, regarding him as nothing more than an office manager and a public-relations shill for the Association.

Ironically, the NAACP's litigation led to the final controversy between Du Bois and White. In 1928, *The Crisis* was undergoing financial scrutiny by the National Board because of the growing deficits of the in-house journal. For thirteen years the NAACP had not spent a cent on *The Crisis*. By 1934 the growing deficits angered many in the NAACP. Du Bois, in *The Crisis*, began to editorially criticize Walter White as well as Charles Houston. The final blow-up came at the 1934 Annual Spring Meeting of the NAACP, in Philadelphia. Du Bois resigned his position on July 1, 1934, and returned to Atlanta University. In a series of controversial essays early in 1934 in *The Crisis*, Du Bois insisted that the struggle for legal and political equality for African Americans had failed. It would be much better, he said, to seek economic independence before demanding equality.

Du Bois, much like Booker T. Washington, argued that African Americans had to unite as a race, and held that this could only occur through voluntary segregation. He believed it was better for black people to "stand erect in a mud puddle and tell the white world to go to hell, rather than lick boots in a parlour."[41] His views were totally contrary to the NAACP's strategies to end Jim Crow and create an integrated environment. They were in fundamental conflict with Margold's proposals and with Houston's coming on board as Special Counsel.

According to Wilkins, Du Bois appeared to call for African Americans to "embrace Jim Crow." Bill Hastie, at that moment involved in litigation challenging segregation, blasted Du Bois, saying that "any Negro who uses [Du Bois's arguments] as a justification for segregation is either dumb, mentally dishonest, or else he has, like Esau, chosen a mess of pottage."[42] By May 1934, Du Bois knew that White had won the battle. He returned to Atlanta and moved in a different direction from that time on. Although he briefly returned to the NAACP in 1944, by that time he had committed himself to socialism. He left the Association for good a few years later, and joined the Communist Party. He was self-exiled; toward the end of his long life, he moved to Africa, where he died.

The battle between Du Bois and the others was an example of the "classic and perpetual schism within Black America"; a clash between those who believed in legal remedies and Du Bois, joined by Ralph Bunche and other "economic instrumentalists."[43] In 1940, Bunche, who was to become America's ambassador to the United Nations after World War II, continued his criticism of the organization: "In an era in which the Negro finds himself hanging ever more precariously from the bottom rung of an economic ladder that is itself in a condition of not too animated suspension, the Association clings to its traditional faith, hope, and politics."

This fierce internecine battle continued to plague the Association. In the late 1940s, Thurgood Marshall concluded that it was time to challenge the notorious *Plessy* doctrine directly in the U.S. Supreme Court. His decision to initiate the complex, multi-state litigation process would be greeted by criticism from within the NAACP and from many of its chapters across the nation. When that moment of decision arrived, the opposition lacked the fire and brimstone, the intellectual genius, of W. E. B. Du Bois.

By 1936, the year twenty-eight-year-old Thurgood Marshall joined the NAACP as assistant special counsel, Jim Crowism was firmly implanted in America. His joining the NAACP was, he later recalled, a most exciting time for a young, bright African American lawyer eager to confront the reality of racial segregation.

# 3

---

# MARSHALL JOINS THE NAACP

While working on a civil rights case in Little Rock, Arkansas, during the mid-1950s, Marshall received one of the many death threats sent to him throughout his life—including those he received while serving as an Associate Justice of the U.S. Supreme Court. William T. Coleman, a friend of Marshall's and a politically active African American public figure himself, recalled what happened next. "He was sharing a room with another attorney and their names were written on the beds. But Marshall changed the names, saying if someone cased the joint and decided to shoot, they'd hit the wrong guy. Thurgood could joke about things that were very important."[1]

Humor was his lifelong tonic. "Buffoonery relaxes his tense spiritual muscles. Buffoonery and work," wrote a *Time* reporter in 1955. Of these twin characteristics, a great capacity for sheer hard work and an irrepressible zany sense of humor, the latter led classmates from Lincoln and Howard, and even his mentor, Houston, to saddle him with some colorful nicknames. A college classmate, years later, recalled that Thurgood had a "dual personality—on the one hand studious, on the other crazy."

Beneath his unflagging sense of humor, there was a "tense personality," one that reflected "the tensions of his job and his time and his nation."[2] He lived at a time of great change and, consequently, a time of great danger to himself and the handful of other African Americans working in the field of civil rights. It was arduous, dangerous work, done without any relief from the prejudices, threats, and injustices Marshall confronted wherever he traveled. He worked long and hard, often into the early hours of the morning, to prepare his cases. He did all this in the backseats of cars, in railroad stations, in cold flats in the African American sections of small Southern towns. Marshall was occasionally protected by armed African American men.

By the time he moved to New York City's Harlem, Thurgood Marshall was known by a wide variety of people, from the poor African Americans in Baltimore who were his "freebie" clients, to the white merchants who felt his wrath as the leader of the Baltimore chapter of the Association. After taking on the position of assistant special counsel in October of 1936, the beginning of a lifetime of legal advocacy and adjudication, he would become a friend of presidents, attorneys general, senators and congressmen, generals, labor and religious leaders, the leaders of newly independent nations in Africa, and other world-famous personalities. But what really mattered to him, as he said in 1947, was "meeting the plain people on the street to find out how they think and feel. As soon as I reach any town, I talk to the shoe-shine boys or the barbers or the people in the restaurants, because it's Mr. Joe Doakes who is very close to reality."[3]

Throughout his life, Marshall was always aware of the millions of "Joe Doakeses" living at the margins of society. He knew them, their wives, their children, their grandparents—and he knew about their problems. His life was dedicated to making their lives less tough, less brutal, more humane, and more free.

## "NO GOOD TURKEY"

Growing up in Baltimore, young Thurgood was called a "bum" by his uncle because "he was such a hellion as a kid." He had a "penchant for exploiting every seeming advantage he had."[4] He was still a bit of a handful when, in 1925, he graduated from high school and went off to attend predominantly African American Lincoln University, in Oxford, Pennsylvania.

By then he had become a tall (six feet two inches), lanky, handsome young man who loved women—in general and enthusiastically. Ada Sipuel, one of the Association's higher education plaintiffs in the 1940s, recalled her first memory of Thurgood. She was a seventh-grader in Oklahoma when he came to town to argue a criminal case in court. "He was," she thought, "the most handsome, articulate, brilliant, and charismatic man I had ever seen."[5] Jack Greenberg described the young Marshall as "over six feet tall, slender, handsome, with a Levantine nose, narrow, triangular mustache, and thick wavy black hair combed straight back [and with] an accent and a manner that he could shift from refined Southern diction to Southern country style."[6] Another longtime friend and Association colleague, Roy Wilkins, remembered Thurgood as "lean, hard, and Hollywood-handsome, a black Ronald Colman"; a good dresser, always wearing "natty, double-breasted suits with immaculate white handkerchiefs sticking out of the breast pocket."[7]

Colleagues, news reporters, and friends often noted Marshall's common sense and his ability to express himself so well and so forcefully, characteristics he had acquired at his family dinner table during arguments with his father and brother.

Thurgood was seen by them, and others, long after he played out his college hijinks, as a "formidable opponent" because he was an objective assessor of reality—a trait developed through the discipline imposed by Charles Houston. He had a "clarity of reasoning" that was never "befogged by his emotions."[8]

Others observed that Marshall was a very self-assertive young man—and remained so for the rest of his life. Walter White, the executive secretary of the NAACP and a lifelong friend and colleague, recalled his first sighting of Marshall:

> It was a lanky, brash young senior law student who was always present [when White met with Charlie Houston to discuss legal strategy at Howard's law library]. I used to wonder at his presence and sometimes was amazed at his assertiveness in challenging positions by Charlie and other lawyers. But I soon learned of his great value to the case and doing everything he was asked, from research on obscure legal opinions to foraging for coffee and sandwiches.[9]

While attending Lincoln University, he was a popular fraternity ladies' man who was "pinned" to and actually dated no less than seven young coeds—all at the same time. Thurgood occasionally attended church services in Philadelphia because, he later admitted, "we learned that's where all the cute chicks went." He wound up marrying a very "cute chick," a Lincoln coed, Vivian "Buster" Burey, while he was still an undergraduate and she quickly got him under some kind of control for as long as they were together. (She died of cancer in February 1955.)

Although Marshall claimed that they first met either at a football game or in a drugstore in 1927, and that it was love at first sight that led to marriage in September 1929, she maintained that she met him "in Harrison's restaurant in Washington but [he] was so busy arguing and debating with everybody at the table that [he] didn't even give me a second glance." Thurgood finally relented and agreed with Buster's version of their first meeting. "You have a better chance of winning a decision in court [than winning against Buster!]," he told a reporter, Ted Poston, in 1949.[10]

While he discussed politics, led the Lincoln University debate team, became enthralled with the new African American literature that sprang out of the Harlem Renaissance, and actually led a successful protest march against the local movie house in Oxford, Pennsylvania, Thurgood, until he came under the spell of Buster and Houston, was a fairly wild goof-off, according to most who knew him. He was "something of a playboy," a classmate recalled, an irresponsible student who mostly wanted to have a great time. Friends of the young couple "charged that Thurgood 'is as foolish as a man can be with his money,'" and he countered by saying, "'If I had more money, I could be more foolish.'" Marshall got into the habit, early on, of turning all his paychecks over to his wives. "'I'm supposed to have my allowance but I always manage to borrow a little extra and I never, never pay it back.'"[11]

Marshall was "an enthusiastic eater," one reporter noted, easily downing two steaks, potatoes, and a lot of salad in one sitting. He also enjoyed wine and spirits, especially good bourbon, and most especially a brand called Wild Turkey. He was known to have "booted up a few" drinks on many occasions, recollected his law-school friend Oliver Hill. And, early on, he developed a lifelong taste "for a martini before lunch, and a couple before dinner."[12] Playing long and often late-night card games, especially poker and pinochle, was another "bad" Marshall avocation. He also smoked two and sometimes three packs of cigarettes a day and proudly boasted that the smoking and the drinking and the carousing wouldn't kill him: "I expect to die at 110, shot by a jealous husband."[13]

He had a glorious "gift of gab" that always stood him in good stead throughout his life. Roy Wilkins, who worked with Marshall for over two decades when both were with the NAACP, once said that the gift came about because "he came from Baltimore, and his tactics combined a shrewd Southern way of leaving white foes enough rope to hang themselves with a Northern spare-me-the-sorghum style."[14]

He never forgot the rules of the game when he spoke in a small Southern courtroom in an affected Southern dialect. Robert Carter, the Association's assistant special counsel under Marshall, recalled that

> having grown up in Maryland, Marshall had a slight Southern accent. But when our opponents were Southern lawyers, which was virtually all the time, his accent would become much more pronounced. Before and after the case was called, Marshall would joke with the opposing counsel or exchange some pleasantry, all in a Southern accent so broad that it sounded as if he lived all his life in the deep rural South. The practice irritated me at first. The very lawyers Marshall's Southern drawl would put at ease were defending a system we detested. [I gradually came to understand that Marshall] was attempting to communicate to these men that, although we were on opposite sides of an emotionally charged lawsuit, we were lawyers representing our clients and had no personal quarrel with each other.[15]

Marshall always seemed relaxed and self-confident, even though he might be inwardly boiling with rage or terrified. Elmer Carter, a black member of the New York State Commission Against Discrimination in the 1940s, worked with Marshall in New York and said of his speaking style, "It's very important that we have a man who is at home in the Supreme Court and equally at home with the man on the street. Thurgood can talk on terms of equality with a social scientist like Sweden's Gunnar Myrdal, but he talks the argot of Harlem with the man on the street corner. He creates confidence on all levels of life."[16]

His college and law school friendships were lifelong ones, and well into Marshall's later years he got letters that addressed him variously as "Nogood," "Dum Dum," "Turkey," or "Monkey," and were signed "Andy," "Little Bits," "Blackie," or "Smitty." Even Charlie Houston, who rarely drank hard liquor and never cursed, got to calling his favorite student "Hey, Turkey." Invariably, after getting rid of the serious business in their letters, his friends kidded him about his being too busy to write, occasionally sending him postage stamps so that he could write to the "little fellows" back home.

All of these early friends adored Buster and typically ended their notes with love and regards to her. They knew of his constant travels, which meant that Buster was home alone. One of them, writing in June 1941 while Marshall was in Washington, D.C., felt compelled to remind "Dum Dum" that "you still have a wife and she still lives at 409 Edgecombe Avenue, New York."

Marshall enjoyed sports, especially baseball and football, but only as an observer. After his team, the Yankees, defeated the Brooklyn Dodgers in the 1941 World Series, Thurgood took great pleasure in passing around the composite box-score to his NAACP colleagues, especially to Roy Wilkins, the office's main Dodger fan. Wilkins responded, briefly, that even though the Bums had lost, "I still believe"; another staffer wrote to Marshall: "Them Bums can still play. Wait till next year." When, in 1947, Jackie Robinson broke the baseball color barrier to become the first African American player in the major leagues, with the Brooklyn Dodgers, Marshall immediately switched his loyalty from the Yankees to the Dodgers. This, of course, gratified Wilkins.

Never much of an athlete, he once told a reporter: "I gave up baseball when two sandlot teams down in Baltimore threatened a sitdown strike if either side had to accept me. I couldn't hit the side of a barn with a paddle or catch cold in a rainstorm." Nor did he believe in any physical exercise, other than driving his car "very fast."

When Marshall moved to Harlem in late 1936 to begin work for the NAACP, he and Buster arrived at the height of the Harlem Renaissance, a cultural blossoming of art, literature, and great jazz. They loved jazz, and when Marshall was in the city, they went out regularly to hear Duke Ellington, Cab Calloway (an old Lincoln University classmate), Alberta Hunter, and Dinah Washington, among other greats. When he was not on the road, as the Association's "backroads ambassador" to the isolated African Americans living in small, rural towns in the South, he and Buster regularly joined their NAACP friends, Roy Wilkins and Walter White, at a major Harlem "nite spot," "Happy" Rhone's club on Lenox Avenue and 143rd Street.[17]

While Marshall "always ma[de] a great show of despising work or physical exertion, and contend[ed], 'There's no call for a man to ever lift anything much heavier than a poker chip'…he…work[ed] steadily since he took his first job as an errand boy at Hale's grocery store, in Baltimore, at the age of seven." He took many different jobs—delivery boy, bellhop, waiter on a railroad dining car, porter, and others—in order to earn and save enough money to pay for college and law school. Invariably, he, like all other African Americans, soon learned that he did not have to look in a mirror to see that he was "colored"; he just had to get used to being called "boy" by his white customers.[18] Aware of the frequently brutal reality of racial segregation in America, Marshall challenged Jim Crow only in the courtroom. "I wrapped my civil rights in cellophane," he told Greenberg, "and put them in my pocket" when he traveled in the South.

After graduating from Lincoln University and deciding, because he did not do well in science courses, not to become a dentist, Marshall chose to enter law school. Rejected by the University of Maryland solely because of his color, he entered Howard University. By the end of his first academic semester he was captured by Charlie Houston's visions. Thurgood knew what he wanted to be: a civil rights lawyer, a "social engineer." Though he also knew he would not be making a great deal of money, and that civil rights litigation work entailed a great deal of traveling in a pretty scary part of the country, he was committed.

Later, Marshall noted that he succeeded not only because he was willing to forgo a comfortable middle-class life, but because both his wives, Buster and Cissy, never complained about his being away three-fourths of the time and in town one-fourth: "Well, some wives will say they won't take that. Or, 'Why can't I have more money?' Neither one of my wives ever asked for more money. They could have used it." Marshall was fortunate. Both wives, as he said, "fit into" his lifelong commitment to securing justice for African Americans. They "wanted it done as much as I did." He "never heard [them] grumble once.…I was lucky."[19]

## THURGOOD MARSHALL, ESQ.: JOINING THE NAACP'S NATIONAL OFFICE, 1936

Charles Houston was appointed Special Counsel for the NAACP in October of 1934 but did not begin full-time work in the New York office until July 11, 1935. He wanted to finish the academic year at the law school and take an official leave of absence before moving up to New York "to devote his entire time to the work of the special legal campaign." Bringing Houston in meant that the NAACP leadership, especially Walter White, was committed to a lengthy struggle in the courts to eliminate segregation and to achieve social and political equality.

It was, for Houston, a difficult decision to leave Howard for the hard work of the NAACP's special counsel. Charlie spent as much time as he could, the final half year, with his beloved students and his law faculty. In this final six-month period, Houston spoke and wrote to the Howard community about the critical importance of creating a trained cadre of African American lawyers to fight the battles against segregation and racial discrimination. Such a lawyer's social justification, he said, was "in the social service he can render the race as an interpreter and proponent of its rights and aspirations, [a role, experience has shown,] that the average white lawyer, especially in the South, cannot [perform]."[20]

However, it was a timely move for him and for the NAACP. At this very time, Charlie's first marriage was ending sadly, but not bitterly. His move to New York led to divorce a short time later. He was brought into the civil rights organization as a full-time legal counsel with a strategic plan for using the federal courts to achieve some of the major goals of that Association, an important first for the NAACP.

His friend, cousin, and legal colleague, William Hastie, said that Houston was "truly the Moses of [the African Americans'] journey through the legal wilderness of second-class citizenship."[21] Like Moses, who did not live to see the Hebrews enter the Promised Land, Charlie Houston did not live to see the formal overturn of *Plessy* by the Supreme Court's historic *Brown* decision in 1954. He died of a massive heart attack in 1950. Marshall paid tribute to him, saying that "the school case was really Charlie's victory. He just never got a chance to see it."

The Marshall who had returned to Baltimore to practice law in 1933 was a very bright, very brash, and very hungry lawyer with great ambitions. In the early days, while attempting to build a practice, he lived with his wife in his parents' house in the Druid Hill section. At this point, Marshall had an excellent if inexperienced mind. Charlie Houston, working with Bill Hastie, took on the task of continuing to train him by giving him work to hone his advocacy skills. Marshall respected Hastie almost as much as he did Houston. Later on, Marshall would say that Hastie, and not Thurgood Marshall, should have been the first black American to sit on the U.S. Supreme Court. "He's a great man. Much better than I am. Much better than I ever will be. Honest. His opinions [Hastie was the first black appointed to a federal appeals court] are among the best I've ever read. Hastie [was] just great."[22]

In law school and after graduation, he was being taught the practice, not the theory, of law: "how to get it done," Marshall told an Amherst College audience decades later. In 1932, while still a second-year law student, he was doing legal clinic work in the field. He helped Hastie prepare the briefs in a civil rights case involving higher education discrimination. This was Marshall's very first civil rights litigation, the *Hocutt v. University of North Carolina* case. The suit brought by Hastie for the NAACP involved an African American who had sought entry into the segregated School of Pharmacy of the University of North Carolina. It was initiated by two local lawyers who, after the briefs had been filed, asked the NAACP for legal assistance. Hastie was sent to work with them, and Marshall was assigned by Houston to do the legal research for Hastie.

Hastie was brilliant in the courtroom, so much so that "young white students" from nearby Duke University as well as the University of North Carolina began attending the trial daily. At the conclusion of each day's trial activity, they "surrounded Hastie and his fellow counsel for Hocutt to congratulate them, much to the annoyance of the Attorney General." [23] (*Hocutt* was lost on a technicality; the student's undergraduate college transcript had not been sent to the school. Since Hocutt had not "fully complied with the admission requirements," the case failed. Houston chose not to appeal the decision because it wasn't a solid suit for appeal to the U.S. Supreme Court.)

*Hocutt* did lead, however, to a successful 1935 effort, *Pearson v. Murray*, to desegregate the University of Maryland's School of Law. The case was argued in the Maryland courts by Houston, with the legal research assistance of the recently graduated Thurgood Marshall, who was especially pleased with this 1935 victory: the University of Maryland had declined to admit him to its law school in 1930. "I filed it the first year after I left [law school] to get even with the bastards....To get even with the whole segregated system," Marshall said years later. (The litigation was successful at the state level. No appeal was taken by the university to the U.S. Supreme Court, so no national precedent was announced until the Supreme Court handed down, in 1938, its *Gaines* opinion, which desegregated Missouri's law school.)

Marshall's continuing education included heated arguments with Houston and Hastie over the litigation strategy they were implementing—and such disputes invariably involved criticisms of Thurgood's writing style. He recalled one incident involving the preparations for the 1944 Texas white primary case, *Smith v. Allwright*. Marshall, Houston, and Hastie were working on the brief for the Supreme Court. Marshall, over a number of days, had pared down a segment of the brief from fourteen pages to four, "and figured that was it. You couldn't cut it anymore....I showed it to Bill Hastie and Bill said it's still too long. I said, 'God damn it, you do it.' He took it over the weekend, one paragraph. And I said 'oh, man,' and he said, 'read it and tell me what's not in it.'...Hastie could do that. Of the writers Charlie and Hastie were the best." [24]

In 1934 he took an automobile trip with Charlie Houston to the Deep South to see firsthand its "raw racism." It was a shattering experience for Marshall, who had never traveled south beyond the Washington, D.C., area. He never forgot that first of hundreds of trips deep into the enemy camp. He also recalled

Charlie's dedication to the "social engineering" task. On the trip to the South, Marshall recalled that the two of them would "sit in the back of the car with typewriters in our laps and type out pleadings and everything. He could type as well as any secretary."

Until 1935, Marshall did legal work, without remuneration, for the NAACP's Baltimore chapter, including the *Murray* case, but he also led a boycott of the stores of white merchants who refused to hire African Americans, and he had begun to prepare an NAACP lawsuit seeking equal pay for African American schoolteachers in Maryland (including his mother and some of his relatives). Marshall had also picked up a few clients who could pay him. He was, as he wrote in a letter applying for a job at Howard Law School, counsel for the largest "colored laundry" in town, as well as for the only "Negro building and loan association in the city, counsel for the colored Funeral Directors' Association, and counsel for several prominent individuals in the city." He had won some important criminal cases, and he "took part in a civil action taken against a white policeman charged with killing a Negro while under arrest, which case resulted in a verdict and judgment of $12,000 in favor of the widow."

But he was spending an inordinate amount of time, with no compensation, on NAACP business. This greatly concerned Houston. In September 1935, during Marshall's work on *Murray*, Charlie wrote to him, "I do not advise that you drop everything for NAACP work. Keep a finger on your office practice whatever you do. You can get all the publicity from the NAACP work but you have to keep your eye out for cashing in." [25]

On April 22, 1936, the struggling twenty-seven-year-old lawyer received a letter from a former law school friend, informing him that the School of Law at Howard University had two faculty vacancies for the 1936–1937 school year. "Dear No-Good," it began, "I suggest you get in touch with George Crawford, Chairman of the Law School Committee, and ask him about the possibility of an opening....If you do make application, let Charlie know and suggest to him that he write [Crawford] about you. Give my love to all the folks, especially Buster. Tell her that I want you over here teaching next year, so that I can see her oftener."

The very next day, Marshall typed a two-page letter to Crawford, a letter that made application "for a position on the faculty." It was a very strong letter, talking about his "diversified" criminal and civil legal experiences in Maryland, urging consideration of a graduate of Howard for the position, and closing with the following: "If there is a possibility of an appointment on the faculty of the law school, I do hope that this application will be considered, and I stand ready for a personal interview at your convenience." On April 25 he received a reply from Crawford, informing him that his name would be brought before the committee and instructing him to write to the dean of the law school. In May, Marshall formally applied to the law school for the position and his letter was acknowledged, on May 15, 1936, by the president of Howard University, Dr. Mordecai W. Johnson (who was the first African American to hold that position since the founding of the school after the Civil War).

Houston was deeply concerned about the possibility of losing Marshall to the Howard teaching job. He recognized Marshall's potential greatness as an advocate and knew about his practical struggles to get ahead in private practice in Baltimore. Houston understood how attractive to Marshall a regular salary and a teaching job at Howard Law School would be. So, in the late summer of 1936, he began to lobby within the NAACP to create a position for him with the national organization. On September 17 of that year, Charlie wrote a confidential memo to Walter White about Marshall's financial dilemma and the improbability that things would get better as long as he devoted so much time to NAACP litigation. He urged White to give Marshall a salaried position with the Association:

> You would not be able to find a more faithful person than Thurgood or a more dependable office man. But I am afraid he is just not the type to make a success in private practice. He needs to be in a school or on a salary where he could work to his heart's content in the exhausting way he likes to work, without financial worry. He is perhaps too conscientious and painstaking to be a commercial scuffling lawyer.[26]

Houston added that he would need office help while he was on the road, traveling as the Association's "evangelist and stump speaker…stirring up the colleges to fever heat." Hiring Marshall was well "worth the gamble," for it would enable the NAACP to continue to work on litigation while Houston was raising hell—and money to cover litigation costs.

White, who knew Marshall from earlier meetings with Charlie Houston at Howard University, accepted Houston's suggestion. After the board, meeting in mid-October, approved the recommendation, the job offer was formally extended to Marshall. Marshall immediately accepted it, even though it was a temporary six-month appointment. Even before the formal appointment was announced by the board, Marshall was hard at work on the Missouri higher education litigation that would, in a few years, come to the U.S. Supreme Court. The November 1936 issue of *The Crisis* contained a brief personnel announcement: "October 15, 1936. Thurgood Marshall joins the legal staff—work with Charles Hamilton Houston on the campaign for educational equality. Appointment: 6 months." Instead of joining the faculty of Howard's law school in the fall of 1936, Marshall became the NAACP's assistant special counsel. Less than two years later, Houston left the NAACP, and Marshall, then only thirty years old, became its new special counsel. By the end of his tenure with the NAACP in 1961, his "temporary" appointment had lasted twenty-four years, based on annual contracts from the Association. The fact that he would initially be working with Houston made the move to the New York headquarters of the NAACP very easy for him.

But, just as Houston had found it hard to leave his students behind in Washington when he moved to New York, Marshall found it impossible to sever all contacts with his clients, many of whom desperately needed the advice of their "freebie" lawyer. And so, for a period after his appointment, he commuted between New York and Baltimore to assist his clients "until they adjusted over to new lawyers."[27] He rapidly had his "private practice, whatever little there is of it," he wrote White, "transferred to Mr. Warner McGuinn who is going to take it over."

Once officially on board, Marshall got right to work. He took an automobile trip to Virginia, North and South Carolina, Georgia, Alabama, and Mississippi to speak to Howard Law School graduates, trying to convince them "that they had an obligation to help by taking NAACP cases in their towns."[28] Back in New York, he was able to relieve Charlie Houston of office chores and began to plan tactics for the legal office to follow in filing its legal briefs, with "major emphasis on educational discrimination."

The very month Thurgood Marshall joined the national office, Charlie Houston had the NAACP announce the start of the first orchestrated legal action, the NAACP's Public Education Initiative.

## THE NAACP'S 1936 PUBLIC EDUCATION INITIATIVE: BEGINNING THE ATTACK ON *PLESSY V. FERGUSON*

"In the Southern states the Negro goes to separate schools by force of law. These schools are invariably inferior to the white schools in the same community. The school term is shorter, equipment poorer and the teachers less well paid." These were the opening words in Walter White's October 1936 publicity release informing the public of the NAACP's new endeavor in civil rights litigation.

This was the first step: implementing a strategic plan that focused on discrimination in public education. It was one that promised to "reach all levels of public education, from the nursery school through the university....EDUCATIONAL INEQUALITIES MUST GO!!!!" When White wrote these words, nineteen of the forty-eight states had statutes that required educational segregation. In 1930 there were 230 counties in the South, with over a million African American students, that did not provide any high school education whatsoever.[29]

The initiative was planned and written by Charlie Houston; it was the first organized legal effort planned by the Association's first full-time special counsel. Underscoring the strategy and tactics in the Margold Report, Houston crafted an educational plan that laid out six specific objectives. It was an educational litigation strategy premised on Houston's noble vision, one he spoke of in 1939: "Can't you conceive of the inspiring effect [of our successful litigation effort] when the little Negro boy in the South sees he no longer has to go to an unpainted, one room wooden school room for a term of no more than four months of the year, to teachers who do not make enough for even subsistence....Can't you envision the difference?"

Given Houston's natural caution, however, and his correct understanding of the reality of precedent and the rules of the game, it was a plan that allowed for *Plessy*'s continuing precedential validity. As he wrote in a January 1937 letter to a Michigan law professor:

> All we can insist upon is equality of treatment. *The state can separate the races provided it keeps the educational opportunities equal.* This means that where there is a Negro state college and a white state college in the same state, offering substantially the same courses under the same conditions, the state may constitutionally bar whites from the Negro college and Negroes from the white college [my emphasis].[30]

Houston proposed "to use every legitimate means at [the NAACP's] disposal to accomplish actual equality of educational opportunity for Negroes" in an enumerated list of specific areas:

1. Equality of school terms
2. Equality of pay for Negro teachers having the same qualifications and doing the same work as white teachers
3. Equality of transportation for Negro school children at public expense
4. Equality of buildings and equipment
5. Equality of per capita expenditure for education of Negroes
6. Equality in graduate and professional training

The Maryland case, *Pearson v. Murray,* had been won but not at the national level. At the moment of the announcement of the legal initiative in education, they were already hard at work on *Gaines,* hoping that it would go to the U.S.

Supreme Court. (The Court did hear *Gaines* in its 1938 term, and ruled in favor of the NAACP position. It ruled that Missouri must either have a separate law school for African Americans, substantively equal to the white law school, or else allow African Americans to enroll in the formerly all-white University of Missouri law school. Subsequently, Missouri admitted blacks to its state law school.)

The NAACP's legal section—which consisted entirely of Marshall and Houston—was also preparing litigation involving disparities in teacher salaries in Maryland and other Southern states, and moving full steam ahead with lawsuits challenging separate but unequal educational facilities. (The Association's second generation of social engineer lawyers were still hard at work in the educational opportunity field a half-century later.)

Even before they both came to New York, Houston and Marshall had developed an amazingly symbiotic relationship in their litigation work. They seemed to naturally complement each other, and worked harmoniously from the early 1930s until Charlie's death in 1950. The older advocate "was low-key, well organized, formal in his demeanor, and a stickler for the most minute detail." The younger man "was the gregarious extrovert, a backslapper who quickly won friends. Houston was smart. Marshall was shrewd. Houston was the better writer, Marshall the better speaker, lacing his conversations with humor, logic, salty and streetwise language, and black dialect that appealed to less educated black people."[31]

While Houston was the NAACP's special counsel, and even after he left in 1938, he was "Mr. Outside," and Thurgood was "Mr. Inside." As he noted when he offered Marshall the job as assistant special counsel, and also said in a letter to his father in 1938, "I am much more of an outside man than an inside man.…I will grow much faster and be of much more service if I keep free to hit and fight wherever the circumstances call for action."[32] When Charlie found an appropriate case for litigation, there was Marshall in New York, running the office and doing the legal research, preparing and filing the briefs, and providing him with whatever else was needed to bring the suit into court.

Houston and Marshall worked with the handful of cooperating African American attorneys in the Southern towns and cities where the lawsuits commenced. In 1936 there were about one dozen competent African American lawyers practicing in the South; Marshall and Houston knew and worked with every one of them over the years.

Until Charlie's untimely death in 1950, these two men were the "lonely warriors" in the NAACP's litigation battles for civil rights. They were the "shock troops" of the NAACP, and, as Jack Greenberg recounted, "shock troops don't occupy towns."[33] Even after Houston formally left the NAACP in 1938, the two continued to strategize until Houston's death, at the age of fifty-five. Although he took over all his colleague's work when Charlie left, Thurgood Marshall was formally appointed special counsel only a year later, in the spring of 1939.

Charlie Houston returned to Washington, D.C., and his father's law firm, explaining to Marshall, "I think I better go back to Washington and rebuild [the business], so that you and Hastie and the others will have a place to come, when the [NAACP] money runs out." He also believed that civil rights litigation wouldn't last forever. According to Marshall, though, Houston had another reason for leaving: his father's poor health. Charlie's health, too, was not good; he suffered from TB and developed a serious heart condition. Ironically, sadly, the father outlived the son.[34]

Unfortunately, Houston's belief about the temporary nature of civil rights litigation work proved wrong. For almost two dozen years, Thurgood Marshall was an inordinately busy civil rights advocate, generally involved with hundreds of cases and, like Houston, traveling 50,000 to around 75,000 miles annually. He traveled continuously and "was in charge of as many as 450 cases at a time. 'I was on the verge of a nervous breakdown for a long time, but I never made the grade,' he once said."[35] When Marshall left the NAACP in 1961 to begin his public service as a federal court of appeals judge, the Association's civil rights docket was more crowded than it had been in 1936.

## MARSHALL'S COLLEAGUES IN THE NAACP

Charles Houston and William Hastie continued to work closely with Marshall even though both had no formal connections with the Association after 1938. With Marshall working as special counsel and the other two helping out from Washington, D.C., Charlotte Amalie (the capital of the U.S. Virgin Islands), and other locales, the trio prepared and argued some very significant civil rights cases before the U.S. Supreme Court for another decade.

Between 1939 and 1949, under Marshall's leadership, the NAACP brought nineteen cases to the U.S. Supreme Court. Hastie was co-counsel with Marshall in twelve of these and, as Marshall said later, he was "important in [the preparations for] all of them."[36] Hastie, for example, with assistance from Houston and Marshall, successfully argued the Texas white primary case, *Smith v. Allwright*, for the Association in 1944 and the important interstate transportation case of *Morgan v. Virginia* in 1946. Because Houston and Hastie were more experienced and available for litigation despite involvement in private civil law practice (Houston) or part-time government service (Hastie) outside the Association, Marshall did not engage in oral arguments before the U.S. Supreme Court until its 1943 term.

When Marshall began work as the new assistant special counsel in 1936, the Association office was quite small. For him, as he recounted many years later, "those were the best days, the early days, because we didn't have anything to fight about except the enemy. We didn't have to fight among ourselves. And when I went there in 1936, the whole budget [for the national office] was seventy or eighty thousand dollars. My whole legal department's budget was $7,000. That included Houston, Marshall, and a secretary plus calls and everything else."[37]

After Houston left in 1938, the national office consisted of just three full-time men and the secretarial staff. The full-timers were Marshall; Walter White, the executive secretary; and Roy Wilkins, the Association's assistant secretary and, since 1934, editor of *The Crisis*. Walter White, recalled Marshall, "was the front man. He went out. He met with the Presidents. He did this, he made that public statement and all. We went along." Roy Wilkins, the assistant secretary, "was the one that actually ran the organization, the day by day nuts and bolts— Roy ran that." And, naturally, Marshall's responsibility "was the legal side."

The three of them got along fairly well, in great part because White was out of the office a great deal, as was Marshall. Their on-the-road travels for the Association consumed anywhere from six to nine months annually. Both worked to raise funds for the NAACP and recruit new members; both also held rallies, seminars, and meetings in the many chapters to bring the national office and its policies to the masses of African American victims of segregation and racial discrimination and terror.

For Marshall, travel also meant working with local attorneys across the South and Southwest, in and out of court, preparing briefs, arguing in trial courts, and appealing verdicts in appellate tribunals. He was always careful while traveling in the South. Commenting in 1947 on the dangers he faced from the Ku Klux Klan and other racists, Marshall said softly, "'These are the chances I just have to take.'"[38]

White and Marshall were close personal friends. They and their wives socialized, frequently with Roy Wilkins and his wife. They all loved jazz and the night life of Harlem. Walter White and Thurgood Marshall got along fine, so long as White kept out of Marshall's legal business. Given White's personality, it was impossible for White not to "get into it." And when he did, "we didn't get along," Marshall recalled. White's poking around in legal matters was a perennial problem for Marshall "because Walter White always thought he was a lawyer, and he would interfere with my legal business and he'd get his head chopped off." These persistent clashes between the two men continued unabated until White's death in 1955. Although annoyed, Marshall never let White's behavior interfere with his work and their friendship. "He had an idea of telling a lawyer how to handle a lawsuit. You don't do that," Marshall explained—but he always forgave White's behavior.

Roy Wilkins was, in Marshall's mind, "the salt of the earth, there's no more dedicated person."[39] White and Wilkins worked well together—when White was out of town. In the office, the older man created problems for Wilkins, ones that were similar to the problems Marshall had with the diminutive executive secretary. In 1926, Roy Wilkins had met Walter White while Wilkins was the secretary of the NAACP's Kansas City, Missouri, branch and White was visiting the city on Association business. They struck up a friendship that lasted almost thirty years, until White's death.

In 1931, after he became the executive secretary of the Association, White wrote to the younger Wilkins, who was a highly regarded reporter for a Kansas City African American newspaper, the *Kansas City Call*. White asked Wilkins to become the Association's, and White's, assistant secretary. Wilkins spoke with his wife, Minnie, and then quickly wired White accepting the position. For Wilkins, like Marshall a few years later, civil rights work was a lifelong calling.

What impressed Wilkins about White was that the new executive secretary had brought fresh fighting blood to the NAACP, marshaling a variety of civil rights and labor organizations to block the confirmation of Judge Parker as a member of the Supreme Court. As Wilkins wrote much later, "Here at last was a fighting organization, not a tame band of status quo Negroes."[40]

These three, then, were the hub and the core of the NAACP's leadership from 1931 through 1955, when White died, and up to 1961, when Marshall left for the Second Circuit U.S. Court of Appeals. The trio, with the vital assistance of Houston and Hastie (who worked primarily with Marshall) and, after 1941, a small number of additional assistant special counsel, were responsible for carrying on the mission of the Association in the courts, in Congress, in the executive branch, and before the public.

When Marshall became the special counsel in 1938, he brought his brashness, bravery, shrewdness, and gregarious sense of humor with him. He was now the HNIC, "Head Nigger in Charge," as he referred to himself, and he did not shirk any of the responsibilities that came with the job. From eight in the morning to midnight every day, alone and with colleagues in the crowded office, consulting constantly with Houston and Hastie, Marshall worked to implement the education strategy developed primarily by Houston. In addition, as a few more social engineers were added to the national legal staff, the Association took on other legal challenges in the areas of voting, restrictive covenants, transportation, and criminal justice.

Their education litigation strategy was based on their conviction that the Association, with the timely help of favorable U.S. Supreme Court rulings, had to force white southerners to equalize expenditures in no less than the six areas enumerated by Houston. Educational equity, if achieved, was only a stepping-stone to the NAACP's eventual frontal assault on *Plessy*.

Voting equality was the other part of their strategy; by securing improved educational facilities and the right to vote, essential to democracy, the African American community could begin to share in the American dream. In 1977, Marshall said that *Smith v. Allwright*, the 1944 white primary case, and *Brown v. Board of Education of Topeka, Kansas*, were the two most important victories won by the NAACP during his tenure as the leader of the legal section.

Marshall was barely thirty years old when he replaced his idol, Charlie Houston, in 1938. The civil rights battles in the state and federal courts would be led by young, gregarious Thurgood "No Good" Marshall.

# 4

# "THURGOOD'S COMING":
# MR. CIVIL RIGHTS

In 1938, Thurgood Marshall had been married less than ten years; it was a
childless marriage, but never a loveless one, and was to remain so until
Buster's death from cancer in 1955. (Buster experienced the joy of three
pregnancies followed in rapid course by the trauma of three miscarriages.
Marshall's second wife, Cecilia, called Cissy, gave birth to two sons, Thurgood
junior and John William. Thus Marshall, at the age of fifty, finally experienced
the pleasures and responsibilities of fatherhood.)

Marshall was building on the work of a handful of men who had preceded
him. These lawyers included Arthur Spingarn and his small band of affluent,
white, successful NAACP volunteer lawyers, as well as Houston and Hastie. As
Marshall would note in 1959, "so far as the legal work [of the Association] is
concerned, I dare say that the NAACP will forever be more indebted to Arthur
Spingarn and Charles H. Houston than any of the other individual lawyers."[1]

Bill Hastie, as a biographer observed, was a man who "sparkled like a diamond, [like] a black diamond, for he is rare, precious, special."[2] During the
course of his career, he was a teacher at Howard Law School with his cousin
Charlie Houston; an assistant solicitor in the Department of the Interior; a federal district court judge in the U.S. Virgin Islands; the dean of Howard Law
School; a civilian aide (while remaining dean) to the Secretary of War (until he
resigned in 1943, in protest against racial segregation in the army). Hastie was
also the first African American to be appointed governor of the Virgin Islands,
and the first African American appointed to a federal court of appeals (the Third
Circuit), on which he served from 1949 until his death in 1976.

By the time Marshall took over the leadership of the NAACP's legal section
in 1938, there had developed a very small but close-knit network of civil rights
groups and individuals. It was an alliance that included some liberal religious

groups (the Society of Friends, or Quakers, and some Catholic archdioceses in the Deep South); labor organizations such as the American Federation of Labor; and the ACLU and a small number of brave, individual attorneys who either defended black Americans charged with crimes or brought civil suits on behalf of plaintiffs who claimed a lack of equality in such areas as teacher salaries or their children's educational facilities. Marshall knew all these people well; there were not too many organizations and individuals doing civil rights work in the 1930s and 1940s.

As important as these organized groups and the civil rights core made up by the NAACP and Howard Law School were, Marshall believed that the future depended on a few ordinary African Americans living in segregated, terror-filled towns of the South who agreed to become plaintiffs in the civil suits. "The real protagonist in the struggle in the courts," he always reminded people, "is the rank and file Negro determined to get his rights." While Marshall was "appalled" by the apathy and "docility" of the great mass of African Americans toward the legal revolution he and Houston were leading,[3] he had nothing but the highest admiration for that handful of African American parents, schoolteachers, and workers who took their lives in their hands when they made the decision to become plaintiffs for the NAACP. Marshall knew that while he could leave town before sunset, his clients had to remain to endure the angry, vengeful responses of their white neighbors.

## CREATING THE "INC FUND," OCTOBER 1939

Marshall assumed his position at just the time when the Treasury Department refused to recognize the NAACP as an "educational" organization, making it impossible for contributors to deduct their gifts to the organization as charitable for income tax purposes. Because the NAACP was denied tax-exempt status by the Internal Revenue Service, owing to its intensive lobbying efforts, the Association set up the NAACP Legal Defense and Educational Fund, Inc. (thereafter known to all connected with the Association as the "Inc Fund" or the LDF). As Marshall explained later, "When they wouldn't let us have a tax exemption, Arthur Spingarn...and I got this idea of getting a tax exemption for the new one, and all of a sudden we realized that there wasn't any real problem, because Arthur Spingarn was the closest friend of a man by the name of Henry Morgenthau, who was then Secretary of the Treasury."[4]

After negotiating the problem with the IRS in 1939, Marshall drafted the charter for the new, "nonpartisan" wing of the Association. In a memo to the board, Marshall urged the creation of the Inc Fund and specified that cases would be carefully selected by a small committee of lawyers and laymen.

Acceptance of the cases brought to the Inc Fund would be based on three factors: the innocence of the individual, the presence of injustice because of race or color, and the "possibility of establishing in the courts a precedent for the benefit of Negroes in General."[5]

The new entity, as Marshall observed, was a "legal aid society for the advocacy of Negro rights in the courts as contrasted to the legislative halls and areas of general protection handled...by the NAACP." (The Inc Fund was to become, very quickly, the legal model for other civil rights groups in America, organizations representing Native Americans, Japanese Americans, and other oppressed minority groups.) There were a number of reasons enumerated by Marshall in his memo for creating and incorporating the Inc Fund. They became the basis for the granting of the Inc Fund Charter. In addition to the "legal aid" function, the Fund was established to "conduct research, collect, collate, acquire, compile, and publish facts, information, and statistics concerning educational opportunities for Negroes and the inequality in the educational opportunities provided for Negroes out of public funds;...[and] to receive and administer funds, contributed solely for legal aid to worthy Negroes suffering from injustice because of race or color and for educational purposes in the promotion of equality in the distribution of public funds for education." The charter also specified that the LDF would not "engage in any activities for the purpose of carrying on propaganda, or otherwise attempting to influence legislation, and [would] operate without pecuniary profit to its members."

The charter of incorporation was granted by New York State in March 1940. The two main components of the Inc Fund's mission made it necessary to secure the approval of New York State's education department and the state's highest court, the New York Court of Appeals. Given Spingarn's highly placed legal and education connections in the state, as well as the presence on the Inc Fund board of New York governor Herbert H. Lehman, the approvals were received and the Inc Fund became a corporate entity in 1940.

After formally separating, although still operating out of the same crowded offices at 69 Fifth Avenue, the two groups had somewhat more clearly defined responsibilities. But until Marshall's power asserted itself, the Inc Fund was a subsidiary, "a controlled instrumentality," of the NAACP. White and Wilkins were the executive secretary and assistant secretary, respectively, of both the NAACP and the newly created Inc Fund. Marshall ran the fund and retained his position as special counsel to the Association.

The Inc Fund had an initial budget of $13,900 in 1941. Marshall was its director-counsel until he stepped down in 1961. In helping to create it, Marshall was also creating "a bailiwick of his own." As Wilkins later wrote, he left the "lobbying and politicking to Walter and me."[6] The fund's tax-exempt status provided the means whereby desperately needed money was made available to the Association to hire additional civil rights lawyers and also support Marshall's litigation efforts.

By 1940 the fund met its initial goal of hiring not more than four lawyers to work out of the New York office under Marshall's supervision and control. Their primary task was to work with local cooperating civil rights attorneys across the nation in tactically implementing the civil rights legal strategies developed by Houston, with Marshall's help, a few years earlier.[7]

White's continual intrusions into the legal arena were a major problem for Marshall, leading to friction not just with Marshall but with other Inc Fund lawyers. Once, when Marshall was on the road, Bob Carter, the Inc Fund's assistant counsel, assumed interim leadership of the fund. In a confidential memo— one of the many complaints he would have to make to Marshall, White, Wilkins, and the board—Carter wrote that he was "exceedingly astounded...to find that legal decisions are being made without my knowledge or consultation." White, in Marshall's absence, was giving advice to chapter directors about restrictive covenant litigation and legal opinions on important matters (such as whether a person should consent to be interviewed by FBI agents) on his own, without consulting the Association's lawyers.[8]

Marshall's struggles with White spilled over even into the sacred precincts of the Supreme Court, where, to his astonishment and annoyance, he found White sitting in the section of the Court reserved for lawyers who had been admitted to the Court's bar. After unsuccessfully reproving White for doing something that might well affect his standing in the Court, Marshall had to threaten to get a guard to expel White from the section. Undaunted, White had his old friend Justice Hugo Black arrange for him to sit in the section reserved for justices' guests! In contrast, Marshall's leadership of the Inc Fund had no effect on his long-standing friendships with Association leaders like Spingarn and Wilkins. When the latter became the executive secretary after White's death, the relationship between the Inc Fund and the parent organization improved dramatically.

At the time of White's death, the Eisenhower Administration was bowing to demands from Southern legislators in Congress that something be done about the tax-exempt status of the Inc Fund. Marshall believed that the Secretary of the Treasury had been receiving letters "from the southern Senators and Congressmen, [asking] 'How come they're [the NAACP's Inc Fund] tax exempt?'...As soon as the Eisenhower Administration took over, they came after us," Marshall recalled in 1969. He was very concerned because, if the Treasury Department took away the Inc Fund's tax-exempt status, "it would be two years before we could litigate it—complete the litigation. With a reserve fund of about twenty or thirty thousand dollars, we couldn't take that chance."[9]

The IRS began to discuss the situation with Marshall while they continued their intensive audit of both the Inc Fund and the Association for almost a year. After examining the practices and the policies of the two organizations, the agents told Marshall that (1) the Inc Fund and the NAACP were interlocking units, with both using the NAACP name; (2) the Inc Fund was using its funds to assist NAACP chapters that were involved in civil rights litigation; and (3) the Inc Fund was really not operating as a legal aid society because it had plaintiffs who could pay some costs. Something had to be done, or else the tax-exempt status would be lost.

In a successful effort to maintain the group's tax-exempt status, in 1956 Marshall resigned as the NAACP's special counsel. The NAACP created a new position, that of general counsel, and it was formally though not functionally separated from the Inc Fund. Bob Carter, the Inc Fund's assistant special counsel, moved over from the Inc Fund to serve as the first general counsel of the NAACP. He remained in that position until he was appointed to the U.S. District Court. As Marshall noted years later, the formal separation between Fund and Association did not impair the working relationship between the two operations. "In most of the trials we tried them together," he recalled. "I don't know of any case of mine [for the Inc Fund] that Bob [Carter] didn't have a piece of it."[10]

## ADDING STAFF TO THE NAACP'S LEGAL OFFICE

Through the early 1950s, there were never more than five full-time Inc Fund staff lawyers, including Marshall. The additions to the Inc Fund's legal staff were bright, young, and dedicated civil rights lawyers who were carefully chosen by Marshall. In 1949, at the beginning of the final Inc Fund push to overturn *Plessy,* the five were Marshall, Bob Carter, Connie Motley, Jack Greenberg, and Frank Williams. Two others had part-time work—his old friend Spottswood W. "Spotts" Robinson III and Annette Peyser, a sociologist who, as the Inc Fund's socioeconomic analyst, did data collection for the group on extralegal matters related to the Association's civil rights litigation. Over the years, others on the full-time staff included Clarence Mitchell and Derrick Bell.

Marshall never had to persuade any of them to take jobs that promised minimal pay, huge workloads, and a great deal of hard travel. "Didn't have to," he said. "They all wanted to. They knew enough about it." But he never allowed people to work without pay. When Connie Motley volunteered to work without pay while going to Howard's law school, Marshall refused. "I just had a theory that I didn't allow people to work for nothing. Pay them something—if it was peanuts it didn't matter. That's about what we paid."[11]

He assigned responsibilities to his staff in job descriptions he wrote at the time. His own job description involved overall supervision of the legal department, "argument of appeals, trial of cases, setting of policy and strategy pursuant to the Board, Executive Committee, and Secretary of the Association."

Bob Carter's tasks, as the Inc Fund's senior assistant special counsel, paralleled that of his boss. He was in charge of "all the administrative details of the legal department," including the entire professional and clerical staff. In Marshall's absence, Carter had the authority to act as special counsel. He also participated in the argument of appeals and in the trial of cases.

The assigned duties of the other professional lawyers in the office, the assistant special counsel, were clearly delineated by Marshall. They were the "associates" in the office, and were assigned duties such as "legal research, preparation of memoranda of law, preparation of briefs, answering of routine correspondence, advice to branches, interviews with branch people...[a] reasonable number of speaking engagements as assigned, [and] other work which [they] do at their own request with the approval of Special Counsel."

Marshall was "not only the boss, he was the commanding presence."[12] "Tall, burly, gregarious, light skinned and light hearted," as one newspaper account described him,[13] he filled every room he entered, with his relaxed, casual, down-to-earth, "enormous" presence. His management style reflected his personal characteristics. His personality made the office work well, despite the crowded space and the heavy workload. Marshall did not have his own private office for over a decade. By the late 1940s, however, an increasing workload and the growth of the Inc Fund staff forced the legal department "to do the most careful research in the preparation of the trial and appeal of cases in quarters that are so cramped as to make it impossible to do either."[14] It wasn't until Marshall wrote a four-page letter in October 1947, threatening to halt the work of the legal department if the space problem was not addressed, that the Association's "bureaucrats" dealt with the matter. While it was an angry and forceful message, it did not include any threat by Marshall to resign, because he and everyone else knew that he would never quit the Association. The new space was found, and that office crisis ended quickly.

In the world outside the office, Marshall *always* worked very closely with his cooperating attorneys. He knew how difficult and dangerous it was for an African American lawyer to work with the NAACP—and how even more perilous it was for a white southerner to defend African Americans in a small Southern courtroom. There was a good chance that the local attorney would, at the very least, "lose his paying practice" if he worked with Marshall, and possibly much more than that. Of these lonely, brave civil rights attorneys, Thurgood said that "there isn't a threat known to men that they do not receive. They've never been out from under pressure. I don't think I could take it for a week. The possibility of violent death for them and their families is something they've learned to live with like a man learns to sleep with a sore arm."[15]

After every legal victory, Greenberg recalled, Marshall would call local cooperating attorneys and the chapter leaders to inform them of the decision. These were people he knew and cared about. Because segregation denied him access to restaurants and accommodations, he would stay in their homes. As a dividend, he got the good home cooking he appreciated so much—and often armed protection as well. As late as the mid-1960s, there were only a small number of such courageous local legal advocates working with the NAACP. One was Arthur Shores, a lonely, brave civil rights lawyer in Alabama, the only black attorney in the state until the early 1950s. His home had been bombed at least twice, but he refused to knuckle under to the threats and violent actions of the racists. (He died in December 1996, at the age of ninety-two.)

A. P. Tureaud was "Thurgood's man in New Orleans" and other areas of Louisiana. He was one of fewer than five African American lawyers working in that state until the 1950s. James Nabrit, who lived in the District of Columbia and was the dean of the Howard Law School, was another lawyer who worked with Marshall for many years on important litigation in courtrooms all over the country and served as one of his major helpers during the dynamic years leading up to the 1954 education decisions.

## THE INC FUND'S LEGAL STRATEGIES, RULES, AND POLICIES

The NAACP's legal strategies had to serve at least two purposes. Cases were taken and argued in order to chip away at the evils of racial segregation and discrimination. And, as Marshall said in 1952,

> A lawsuit is an educational process in itself. It educates not only the defendant and his lawyers, it also enlightens the general public in the area. When we were fighting to get Herman Sweatt into the University of Texas, more than 200 white students set up an NAACP branch on the campus. They even built and manned a booth on campus, to collect funds to help defray our legal expenses. They were a little worried the first day when they saw a policeman, on the opposite side of the street, eyeing the booth for a long time...until he walked over to the booth, said, 'If you kids want that cullud [sic] man in your school so bad, you sure got a right to have him,' and handed them five dollars.[16]

And while the Margold and Houston strategic plans took the long-range, strategic view, Marshall always prescribed the "one case at a time" tactic, even though at times this guideline, in practice, turned into hundreds of cases at a time for Marshall and the Inc Fund staff lawyers. Carefully selecting cases to argue that, if won, would bring the Association and the African American community closer to victory over race segregation and discrimination enforced and maintained by state laws, he developed an Inc Fund policy that categorically rejected litigation that did not involve discrimination. Thus a situation in which a young, local African American man planned to marry an underage white Jewish girl from New Jersey, wrote Bob Carter to a branch head, was "emphatically not a problem for the Association."

Other letters from the Inc Fund office informed branch leaders requesting legal assistance that the NAACP "never filed briefs *amicus curiae* on behalf of the NAACP in any cases involving conviction under the Smith Act," national legislation directed against the Communist Party and other subversive organizations.[17] Bob Carter, on yet another occasion, wrote to the head of the Buffalo, New York, NAACP branch, stating that since the person involved "is not being charged with any criminal act because he is a Negro, [it] is not a case involving racial discrimination. It can well be an issue of due process of law, but the NAACP assists only those persons who have been victims of discrimination because of their race or color."[18]

With regard to criminal cases, Marshall's ruling, as expressed in a note to his staff, was that the Fund stuck by the policy set at its creation in 1939: "In order to secure our active support, all criminal cases must have the following factors present: (1) That there is injustice because of race or color, (2) The man is innocent, (3) There is a possibility of establishing a precedent for the benefit of due process and equal protection in general and the protection of Negroes' rights in particular."

During World War II and the decade that followed, with the key exception of the Communists and their front organizations, Marshall and White were in regular communication with other civil rights groups and unions, essentially in response to requests from them for information, and support, and alliance formation to address crucial civil rights matters. For example, Marshall assisted the National Congress of American Indians in a number of ways, from training its key administrators to issuing statements about the abrogation of Indian rights. The NAACP even responded to a request for assistance in the hiring of a tribal policeman for the Northern Cheyenne Indians of Montana.

The Society of Friends had always supported the NAACP's quest for racial equality. Its Committee on Race Relations made clear, in the Association's early years, their opposition to segregation. The more militant young African Americans who sat in restaurants and took to the streets to protest segregation in the early 1960s were supported by the Quakers. The Japanese American

Citizens League sought advice from the NAACP, especially during the painful, humiliating World War II years when more than 120,000 Japanese, including more than 70,000 American citizens of Japanese descent, were incarcerated without due process of law. Though the Association expressed opposition to the treatment of the Japanese (cautiously, given America's wartime hysteria), when the Japanese exclusion cases, *Hirabayashi, Korematsu* and *In Re Endo,* did come to the U.S. Supreme Court, during its 1943 and 1944 terms, the NAACP did not file briefs *amicus curiae.*

The ACLU and the Communist Party had long-standing, but fundamentally different, associations with the NAACP. The only clashes with the ACLU, as noted earlier, took place when Roger Baldwin objected to NAACP attempts to restrict the First Amendment freedoms of the KKK. As seen in the clashes accompanying the defense of the Scottsboro Nine, the Communists were another matter entirely.

## MARSHALL, THE COMMUNIST PARTY, AND THE FBI

William T. Coleman Jr., an African American lawyer and political administrator, one of Marshall's longtime friends in the NAACP, said of him that "he was someone who spent his whole life trying to use the Constitution as a real force in his civil rights efforts, and I think his reaction against communists is one you would expect it to be against people who wanted to undermine the Constitution."[19]

For Marshall, African American Communists and the Communist Party were serious competitors for the hearts and minds of the masses of African Americans.[20] He knew that the Communists were not friends of African Americans but were committed to overthrowing the government by organizing blacks and others "as a fifth column in the international struggle to undermine capitalism."[21]

Early in his career with the NAACP, deeply concerned by Communist attempts to infiltrate the NAACP and compromise it as a legitimate civil rights organization, Marshall became part of the anticommunist establishment in America. The Communists and their sympathizers had no place in the NAACP, he and other leaders believed, and they fought hard to force all Communists out of the organization. It was a tough fight, because the Communist message was an attractive one to the millions of black Americans who still had to bear the stigma and consequences of slavery. Right through the early 1950s, Marshall, White, and Wilkins fought to keep the Communists from taking over the NAACP.

Communists made inroads into some NAACP affiliates in the Midwest and on the West Coast. At the annual 1950 NAACP convention, almost 20 percent of those in attendance voted against Marshall's successful effort to "eradicate" Communists from the Association. For a long time, Marshall supported the efforts of the FBI and other federal agencies to clamp down on these Communist activists. Indeed, for over two decades, Marshall provided the FBI with information about the Communists that affected the NAACP. He also provided similar information to the Truman White House.

Recently released FBI files, totaling almost 1,300 pages, indicate that Marshall cooperated with the FBI from the 1930s through the late 1950s. But he did not allow himself to be exploited by this agency. Marshall had two strategic goals in mind when he passed information to the FBI: to rid the NAACP of Communists who were threatening its existence, and to "inoculate" the Association from charges that it somehow was sympathetic to, or being influenced by, the Communist Party.

He was clearly an "uneasy ally" of the FBI.[22] He certainly had no love for J. Edgar Hoover. The FBI director was viewed by Marshall and others in the NAACP as an extremely powerful racist. Again and again, in the FBI files, as well as those of Attorney General Tom Clark, the NAACP, and Stephen Spingarn covering the period of the Truman administration, one sees harsh criticism by Marshall of the "one-sided" efforts of the FBI to deal with the brutality of white racists in the South.

In December 1946, for example, he wrote a blistering letter to Clark, complaining about the apparent inability of the FBI "to identify any members of the lynch mob in the Monroe, Georgia, lynchings." He wrote that "the FBI has been unable to identify or bring to trial persons charged with violations of federal statutes where Negroes are the victims. Such a record demonstrates the uneven administration of federal criminal statutes [by the FBI], which should not be tolerated."[23] This led to an exchange of letters between Clark, Hoover, Marshall, and Walter White. Hoover wrote to White to complain about Marshall's criticism of the FBI. Marshall was, he wrote, both "untruthful" and "unfairly critical of the work of the Bureau in investigating cases involving the civil rights of Negroes." Hoover claimed that Marshall and others in the "legal branch of the NAACP have not rendered full and complete cooperation to the FBI."[24]

Clark also fired back at Marshall in mid-January 1947, with a lengthy letter refuting Marshall's four charges that the FBI was acting in a one-sided manner. "I know that Director Hoover of the FBI," wrote Clark, "has made vigorous efforts to conduct thorough, complete, and impartial investigations in every case in which there has been an allegation of a violation of civil rights." He ended the letter by asking Marshall to try to be more cooperative with the FBI. A meeting was held in early 1947 between Clark and Marshall, and then another one between Marshall and Hoover to address the concerns Marshall had about the FBI, but the matter was never resolved. As Marshall said to White, on January 23, 1947, "I have no faith in either Mr. Hoover or his investigators and there is no use in my saying I do."[25]

Members of the Truman administration were aware of Marshall's attitude toward Communists and Communist front organizations. He was especially critical of Communist-front legal operations like the Civil Rights Congress of 1950. Communists were continually trying "very hard to horn into cases that the NAACP is handling," observed a White House staff member. Marshall, in a letter to William Patterson, the secretary of the Congress, condemned that organization for labeling the Supreme Court a "Pontius Pilate" and for trying to take cases away from the Inc Fund. Arguing that the Civil Rights Congress had no right to interfere with the activities of the NAACP in civil rights matters, Marshall closed his letter with a lecture: "These cases...and any other cases under the jurisdiction of this Association will be carried forward in a law-like manner within the lawful machinery of our Government. We have never been convinced that the Civil Rights Congress is primarily interested in the protection of the rights of Negroes."

## BE COOL, STAY COOL

Another policy of Marshall's was extremely important for the Association, given the grim realities faced by Inc Fund lawyers. Marshall warned his staff, in New York and in the hinterlands, "Lose your head, lose your case."[26] There were many occasions on which state segregationist judges or local prosecutors would speak and act in totally unprofessional ways. Many local judges and a few U.S. district court judges addressed African American plaintiffs and witnesses as "boy" or "nigger." But Marshall and his Inc Fund lawyers never responded to those insults in other than legal and professional fashion, even though they would have been justified. Jim Nabrit, Marshall's courtroom betting partner in the *Sipuel* trial, was with him in another courtroom, this time in Texas (it was the *Sweatt* trial, involving the University of Texas's law school segregation policy):

> Marshall had the rare ability to know where to draw the line in his fervor. He was fuming over a judge in Austin, and he said to me before court began one morning, "I'm gonna tell that judge what I think of him today." I told him to take it easy. He said nothing in court, but after the case was over and we were all heading for the cars, there was Thurgood over in the corner apparently muttering to himself. When he came back to join us, I asked him what that was all

about, and he said, "I told you I was gonna tell that judge what I thought of him—and I just did." He could do that.[27]

The Inc Fund staff had its work cut out for it. From Marshall's perspective, there were three distinct legal periods in the NAACP's history through the early 1950s. Two of these were not very productive, and the Association had a lot of work to do in a short period because of this spotty history.

The first era dated from *Plessy* through 1930, and was the "separate but equal" period of legal history. *Plessy*'s precedent "became ingrained in our case law through a lack of carefully planned legal action."[28] No effort was made, by the NAACP or any other group, to present data that challenged the validity of segregation statutes in the Southern states. Since there was no critical analysis of *Plessy* in this era, it "thus became a rule of law sacred and apparently beyond legal attack."

The second period of litigation was from 1930 to 1945. Starting in 1930, the NAACP began its planned assault on racial segregation, with its glaring inequities, in public education. The attack got off to a slow start. Marshall pointed out that the lack of "full support from the Negro community in general" meant there was great difficulty finding appropriate plaintiffs. As always, there was a "lack of sufficient money to finance the cases."

During the third period, which extended from 1945 through the early 1950s, when *Plessy* was overturned by a unanimous U.S. Supreme Court, there was a greater responsiveness to the actions of the NAACP by the African American community. Veterans of World War II, men and women who had faced humiliating racial segregation in the American military while fighting a war against the fascists, were much more vocal about Jim Crowism when they returned from the war. The final stage was the one in which Marshall, Houston, and Hastie committed the Association to the "only solution to the problem…an all out attack against segregation in public education." By 1945, plans were ready "for a direct attack on the validity of segregation statutes insofar as they applied to public education on the graduate and professional school level."[29]

Why start at the postgraduate and professional school levels? According to Marshall, "those racial supremacy boys somehow think that little kids of six or seven are going to get funny ideas about sex and marriage first from going to school together, but for some equally funny reason youngsters in law school aren't supposed to feel that way. We didn't get it [the reasoning of whites], but we decided if that was what the South believed, then the best thing for the movement was to go along."[30]

When Marshall was a bit more serious, he gave another reason for attacking segregation in higher education. "At the university level," he commented in 1959, "no provision for Negro education was the rule rather than the exception."

Moreover, the cost of providing separate but truly equivalent graduate schools would be fundamentally ruinous for the states under attack, so they might well capitulate and not engage in extended litigation.

In addition to the education litigation, some of which led to substantial success in forcing the equalization of public school teachers' salaries across the South, Marshall had the Inc Fund focus on voting inequities. The white primary became the major target of the Association in the early 1940s.

## MR. CIVIL RIGHTS: "THURGOOD'S COMING"

Marshall traveled out of New York City every month of the year. In 1942, for example, his average monthly mileage was over 5,000 miles, from almost 7,000 miles in February to a low of 2,680 miles in June of that year.[31] From the first months on the road to his departure from the Inc Fund in 1961, travel took its toll on his health. But Marshall shrugged off the constant dangers, the broken-down cars he was forced to use, the Jim Crow railroad cars he rode, occasionally standing, eating at irregular intervals and sleeping in four-hour stretches. Because of the NAACP's perennial lack of funds, Marshall frequently traveled alone, increasing the danger to his life. But he felt that the local African Americans he was working with in these small towns throughout the South were in even greater danger. As he recalled, "although I lay awake nights wondering when the lynch mob might come…I don't deserve the credit. The people who dared to stand up, to file lawsuits, were beaten and sometimes murdered after I spoke my piece and took the fastest goddamn train I could find out of the area [were the real heroes]."

He was never out of harm's way. In the early evening of November 28, 1946, near Columbia, Tennessee, a lynch mob, consisting of a few carloads of local police and state troopers, stopped his car, seized him, and led him to a tree near the Duck River. Since the early spring, Marshall had been working closely with Maurice Weaver and Alexander Looby, attorneys for more than two dozen fellow African Americans, many veterans of the war, indicted for attempted murder in a race riot in Columbia.

In February 1946, marauding bands of whites drove into the black section of town, Mink Slide, and shot indiscriminately at the residents, who returned the fire. Police surrounded the area and invaded the area at dawn. They arrested almost seventy African Americans, holding all of them without bail. Later that month, two of the prisoners were shot to death in the county jail by sheriffs, killed for allegedly reaching for guns in the interrogation room while being questioned by police—without the presence of their attorneys.

Weaver and Looby were the Tennessee attorneys employed by the NAACP to represent the twenty-five men ultimately charged and brought to trial. In a major victory, twenty-three of them were found not guilty. In November 1946, Marshall, who had appeared in the earlier trials with Weaver and Looby, returned to defend the last two prisoners. One of them was acquitted and the other was given a five-year sentence, a judgment that infuriated the local and state police.

At the trial's conclusion, Marshall, Weaver, and Looby left Columbia for Nashville, where Marshall could get a train to New York. They were accompanied by Harry Raymond, a reporter for the *New York Daily Worker* (the Communist Party daily newspaper). Their car was followed by an angry horde of Tennessee law enforcement officers who stopped the auto, pulled Marshall, "the tall yaller nigger," out of it, and told the others to drive away.

The others, refusing to abandon Marshall, got out of the car and followed the mob "down to the river." Outwardly calm but filled with fear, the lawyers and the reporter insisted on staying with Marshall. Perplexed, perhaps unwilling to lynch four men, the police drove Marshall back to Columbia.

Taking Marshall out of the car, the police asked him to cross the street to the office of the local justice of the peace. Marshall refused, saying, "I'm not going to go over there so you can shoot me in the back and claim that I was escaping." The police reluctantly crossed the street with Marshall, brought him into the local justice of the peace, and charged Marshall with drunk driving, hoping to get him locked up in the city jail. The magistrate smelled Marshall's breath, declared that the man had not had any drinks, and dismissed the charge.

After leaving that office, Marshall went over to a group that included Looby, Weaver, and, by now, other African Americans who had heard about the incident. They changed cars, and Looby, under cover of darkness, quickly drove Marshall to Nashville, where, with great relief, he caught the train to New York the following morning. On his arrival in New York, he had more than one bourbon to try to erase the horrors of his past few days in rural, brutal Tennessee.

All across the nation, NAACP chapters sent angry telegrams to Attorney General Clark and to President Truman about the "near lynching of attorney Thurgood Marshall near Columbia, Tennessee." They demanded that "criminal charges be pressed against the officers participating in the incident in which Mr. Thurgood Marshall was intimidated on a trumped up charge of being drunk."[32]

Walter White, on November 26, 1946, wrote to Truman personally, urging "prosecution under Section 20 of the United States Criminal Code of the peace officers who viciously attacked Thurgood Marshall.... This is the latest outrage... encouraging mobs to take the law into their own hands not only against individual citizens but now upon the lawyers engaged in defending victims of mob attack."

(In 1968, twenty-two years later, memories of the incident came flooding back to Marshall because of a case being argued in the Supreme Court. Mr.

Justice Marshall wrote to Chief Justice Earl Warren to disqualify himself from *Anderson v. Johnson, Warden.* "Upon examination of the record...I now recall that petitioner was one of a group of defendants I represented in several actions arising out of a 1946 racial disturbance in Tennessee, and therefore I find it necessary to disqualify myself from all further participation in this case."[33]

Marshall, undaunted by his close call, continued to travel across the South to represent African American plaintiffs in civil suits involving education, teacher salaries, and restrictive covenants, as well as others who faced serious criminal penalties. While it was rewarding for him to win these suits, and to have the U.S. Supreme Court adjust, modify, and even discard precedent in the general area of civil rights, his inner life was shaped by sacrifice, anxiety, and terror. By 1950, the lawyer once known as "the black Ronald Colman" had added about thirty pounds to his large frame. The classic, neatly pressed double-breasted suits with the silk handkerchiefs were now rumpled, some spotted with cigarette burns and ashes. Where once newspaper stories had written of his style and grace, his slimness and his good looks, in 1950 *Newsweek* described Marshall as "a disheveled bear of a man."

This change in his appearance was largely due to the demanding pressure of litigation. Marshall would have worked twenty-three hours a day if he had possessed the strength. As it was, his average day when preparing for litigation ran close to sixteen hours. When working in New York, Marshall would arrive in the office before 8:00 A.M. and would work until past midnight daily for months at a time until the case had been tried and the appeals had been argued. Given the raggedness of this time schedule, Marshall lived on far too much fast food, cigarettes (at least two packs a day), liquor, and coffee.

Stress and an erratic lifestyle did not compromise his meticulous preparation and attention to detail. Getting ready for trial or appeal work in any court, whether a county court in Arkansas or the U.S. Supreme Court, Marshall would carefully prepare a tabbed notebook containing the summaries of pertinent cases for quick reference by him while on his feet in court. And when in Washington, D.C., for argument before the U.S. Supreme Court, he would convene his legal staff and some Howard law faculty members in a Howard Law School mock courtroom for a dry run before he faced the nine justices the following day. And before a major appearance in a courtroom he would limit his consumption of wine or bourbon. For an entire week before his court appearance, Marshall limited himself to a single glass of wine with his dinner.[34]

A compulsive perfectionist and worrier, he would regularly "moan and groan" about the tremendous burden and jurisprudential weaknesses of the NAACP briefs. As one reporter observed, after seeing Marshall prior to a number of court appearances, "for all his flair, he was a nervous Nellie who was almost semi-paralyzed by fear that he was about to lose a case."[35] Once inside the courtroom, he was a tiger, whether in a trial court or in an appellate tribunal. At trial, he was, by everyone's judgment, the master at examination and particularly cross-examination. He was a vicious, slashing advocate, when it came time to cross-examine the state's "prize witnesses," recalled one of his plaintiffs who sat and watched in awe.[36] To maintain his cool self-control when confronted with par-ticularly bad segregationist judges, Marshall would even quietly engage in some betting with his co-counsel on which way a judge would go with bench rulings. It helped pass the time.

By the early 1940s, Marshall became widely known in black communities as "their" litigator. African American newspapers across the nation, lauding his courage, good looks, bravery, and legal victories, helped him become known as "Mr. Civil Rights." The magical words to communities that were struggling against racial segregation were simply, "Thurgood's coming."

Yet he retained his self-deprecating humor in the face of this adulation. His letters to the Inc Fund staff from the road in 1941 reflect his attitude toward fame. For example, Marshall would preface each one by writing, "attached hereto is the _____ installment in that stirring saga of unselfish devo-tion to a great cause, 'SAVING THE RACE,' by Thurgood Marshall." After talking about problems he had with a group of Texas NAACP leaders, he told his New York colleagues how one of the white segregationists said that "'the powers that be here cannot afford to let a "northern nigger" win against them so they want to settle.' Will you please respect the fact that I am now a *northern nigger*."

In one memo back to the office, written in New Orleans on January 18, 1943, Marshall's humor stood out. After describing no less than seven meetings with blacks in the city, including addressing a mass meeting of the local chapter with "the usual baloney," he ended the memo with the following observation: "Very important meeting at one of the bars in town for the purpose of forgetting about the other meetings—*this* meeting was a great success."

Often he would complain of the transportation he had to use to get to the various branches in the South. In March 1943, in a memo to the office from New Orleans, he wrote: "The available autos are getting worse. Started out for Baton Rouge yesterday in a car with 'lace' tires. Then changed to a car which could only go backward....Ended up by driving a car that could not be driven over 30 miles an hour because of bad bushings in the front wheels."[37]

## THE INC FUND'S EDUCATIONAL EQUITY LAWSUITS

The onset of World War II in 1941 sidetracked education litigation for a few years. By 1945, however, Marshall and his staff were preparing litigation in this area to follow up the precedents established in the earlier higher education cases. When the troops came home from the war, there was an increasing demand on the Inc Fund to force open the doors of higher education for African Americans.

In the seventeen states of the South, there was no African American institution offering a Ph.D. in any field, while all seventeen state universities had such programs for white students. There were no African American engineering schools, although thirty-seven existed for white students. There were only two schools of medicine and law for African Americans, while there were, respectively, twenty-nine and twenty schools for white professional students across the South. The South had one doctor for every 843 whites; there was one doctor for every 4,409 blacks. Similar statistics showed disproportionate disparities between black and white lawyers and dentists.[38]

If there was no lawyer, doctor, or dentist in the African American community, Marshall argued in speeches and briefs, then blacks were deprived of their services. In 1947, Marshall and Jim Nabrit brought suit in Oklahoma to force the University of Oklahoma's law school to admit qualified African Americans. (Oklahoma did not have a separate law school for African Americans.) Ada Lois Sipuel was the plaintiff; she had been denied admission solely because of her race and color.

Marshall and Nabrit lost in the state courts, although there was a good story that came out of that defeat, one that was added to Marshall's store of anecdotes about Southern justice. The state court judge hearing the case in the first instance was an Oklahoma redneck. He was, however, greatly impressed with the NAACP witnesses who testified in his courtroom, learned professors from Harvard, Yale, and the University of Chicago. "'Just before he made his ruling,' Marshall recalled, 'he took me aside and said, "These men have opened my eyes. They are the smartest men I've come across. They've done something to me right here," he said, pointing to his chest and heart. And having delivered himself of that informal opinion, he climbed back up on the bench and promptly ruled against us. Our arguments may have affected his heart, but he certainly didn't let them affect his decision.'"[39]

Marshall appealed to the U.S. Supreme Court. In his certiorari brief, he not only challenged the lack of educational facilities for African Americans at the University of Oklahoma, he also raised the question of the continued validity of *Plessy:* "Beyond that [the immediate issue of the lack of legal education for African Americans in Oklahoma], the petitioner contends that the separate but equal doctrine is basically unsound and unrealistic and in the light of the history of its application, it should now be repudiated." (Marshall brought *Sipuel* and a restrictive covenant case, *Shelley,* to the Supreme Court and had to argue both cases in the span of a single week. It was the equivalent, said one of his assistants, of an "iron man feat of pitching a doubleheader.")[40]

The U.S. Supreme Court was not prepared to overturn *Plessy*. In an unsigned, short *per curiam* opinion, *Sipuel v. University of Oklahoma*, it held that the state was required to provide African Americans with equal educational opportunities as soon as such facilities were available to white students.

In June 1949, Ada Sipuel Fisher (she had been married in the interim) was finally admitted to the law school. The only African American attending the law school, she was segregated after her admission. She had to sit "in back of the last row of seats, [where] there was a single large wooden chair behind a wooden rail. Attached to a pole on the back of the chair," she recalled, was a large printed sign that said "COLORED."[41] This cruel treatment continued until June 1950, when the *McLaurin* case was decided by the Supreme Court. After that important higher education decision, Ada recalled that she finally "moved down to the front row."

In 1948, Marshall, again joined by Jim Nabrit, was arguing other higher education cases in Texas, such as *Sweatt v. Painter*, and, in Oklahoma, *McLaurin v. Oklahoma State Regents for Higher Education*. After losing their cases, begun in 1946 in the courts in both states, Marshall took them to the U.S. Supreme Court. During the 1950 term of the Court, the justices handed down opinions favorable to the NAACP's position. Unlike *Sipuel* and *Shelley*, which Marshall had to argue in the same week, in *Sweatt* and in *McLaurin*, Marshall had to prepare for oral argument before the Supreme Court *on the very same day* when both cases came before the Court in early April of 1950.

In the Texas law school case, Herman Sweatt, a qualified African American, was initially refused admission to the all-white University of Texas law school because of his race and color. After *Gaines* and the new litigation initiated by the Inc Fund, the Texas legislature funded a law school for African Americans. Maceo Smith, Marshall's administrative man in Texas, tried to push him to move quickly in Texas, before the state created a bona fide law school at the African American college in Prairie View, Texas. The consensus among blacks in Texas was that "we do not wish to have a professional school at Prairie View."[42]

Sweatt refused to attend the new "colored" law school, and sued for admission to the University of Texas. Promising to move forward and to attend the University of Texas's law school—a promise "I mean to keep even at the cost of my life if necessary"—he wrote to the president of the NAACP's chapter in Houston, Texas. "I can think of no greater cause for which to give myself without count of cost." He lost in the state courts because they maintained that there were substantially equal facilities offered by the law school open only for African Americans (with no library, no accreditation, three rooms, and three part-time law instructors in a basement in Austin). Although Marshall was willing to raise the question of *Plessy*'s continuing viability, as he did in the *Sipuel* brief, he was talked out of that approach by his co-counsel and his witnesses.

Erwin Griswold, then the dean of Harvard's law school, was one of the many expert witnesses who testified in these higher education law school cases and who cautioned Marshall about raising the *Plessy* issue. They were excellent cases to argue on the "inequality issue," but poor ones to argue for the overturn of *Plessy*. He then wrote, "I know it must be difficult to be content to proceed inch by inch. Except for rare occasions, though, I feel that you will go further in the long run that way than you will if you try to do everything at once."[43] In a unanimous opinion, the U.S. Supreme Court ruled that Sweatt had to be admitted to the University of Texas law school because the clearly inferior African American school did not afford Sweatt equal educational facilities.

While *Sweatt* moved through the appellate process, Marshall took on another Oklahoma higher education case, involving a sixty-eight-year-old African American educator, George W. McLaurin, and the University of Oklahoma's graduate school of education. McLaurin had a master's degree in education and wanted to pursue studies that would lead to his receiving an Ed.D. from the university. He was admitted under a federal court order. Once admitted, he found himself, like Ada Sipuel Fisher, thoroughly segregated within the graduate school. McLaurin was required to use a special table in the cafeteria, a designated bench in the library, and a specified chair in his classes. All had "Reserved for Colored" signs attached to them. Marshall went back to local federal court, lost there, and appealed directly to the U.S. Supreme Court. Marshall was also informed, in February 1950, by acting U.S. Solicitor General Philip Elman, that the Truman administration was filing briefs *amicus curiae* in both cases in support of the NAACP's arguments. The Court heard oral arguments in both cases on April 1, 1950. In early June 1950, in another unanimous decision, handed down the same day as *Sweatt,* the Court held that McLaurin had to receive the same treatment as any other student; he could not be segregated within the university!

The Court once again refused to overturn *Plessy:* the justices feared violence if "separate but equal" was invalidated. While all of them, with the exception of Stanley Reed, from Kentucky, were in "substantial agreement with the views that there can be no equality in a segregated school system and that segregation was a violation of the equal protection clause,"[44] there was not a majority to overturn *Plessy*. As Chief Justice Fred Vinson, who wrote the opinions in *Sweatt* and *McLaurin,* said to Justice Felix Frankfurter, "I certainly would not want to have anything in the opinion which would stir up feelings of anger and resentment in any portion of the country."[45]

Tom Clark, a Texan recently appointed to the Court after serving as Truman's attorney general, sent around a memo to the brethren after oral arguments were heard. He firmly believed that segregated education was unequal education, and sought to provide his colleagues with some pertinent information about the general issue. "Since these cases arise in 'my' part of the country it is proper and I hope helpful for me to express some views concerning...the 'horribles' following reversal of the cases."

Clark, who was opposed to the maintenance of the *Plessy* doctrine, thought the potential "horrible" were greatly exaggerated. He noted that for over a decade there had been fairly good relations between white and African American college and professional school students, and that colleges in the South had already allowed African Americans to enter formerly all-white state institutions. The cases, he said, did not involve "desegregation of swimming pools" or "grammar schools," two very different segregation issues. He recommended, and the Court accepted the advice, that it declare that segregated graduate education denied equal protection of the laws. Concluding his memo to his colleagues, he wrote, prophetically, "if some say this undermines *Plessy* then let it fall, as have many nineteenth century oracles."[46]

Teacher salary equalization litigation initiated by Marshall and the Inc Fund across the South was, simultaneously, very attractive and difficult to litigate. Statistics clearly indicated the gross disparities in the salaries of white and African American public school teachers. A 1941 report prepared by the U.S. Office of Education regarding the salaries of "Negro Teachers" concluded that it would take over $26 million in additional funds to bring "the salaries of Negro teachers in the 17 Southern states into parity with those of white teachers. In addition," the report continued,

> our specialist estimates that a minimum of $3 million would be needed for supplies in order to bring Negro schools into even approximate equality with white. Actually, $7 or $8 million would be needed to do the job properly. Further, $9 million additional would be needed to add Negro teachers if the proportion of pupils per Negro teacher is to be maintained in the same ratio as pupils per white teacher. (This ratio as it stands now is 29 pupils per white teacher and 39 pupils per Negro teacher.)[47]

For African American teachers, including Marshall's mother, who was an elementary school teacher, "the economic injustice of discriminatory salaries affecting colored school teachers" had to be remedied. Beginning in 1936, the NAACP initiated dozens of suits to equalize salaries. By 1939, more than one-third of Maryland's counties had equalized teacher salaries (increasing black teacher salaries in the state by over $100,000 annually). Suits were begun in South Carolina, North Carolina, Alabama, Virginia, Georgia, Florida, Louisiana, and Mississippi. By 1944, there were suits in every one of the Southern states. A great deal of Marshall's road travels during this period of time was occasioned by equalization of teacher salary cases in local and state courts across the nation.

The cases proceeded at a snail's pace, in great part owing to the initial difficulty in obtaining plaintiffs and then trying to keep them in the litigation. Many plaintiffs' teaching contracts were not renewed by the school board, and the local chapter had to find another plaintiff. The slow pace was also due to the enormous amount of funding that local school boards would have to find to equalize the salaries of their black schoolteachers. For example, the Alabama teacher salary lawsuit begun in 1936 was not finally resolved until a federal judge issued a final consent decree in April 1945, ordering the equalization of salaries.

These were mostly local legal battles, with occasional federal district court activity. The U.S. Supreme Court did not hear a teacher salary equalization case during this time. In 1940, in the case of *Alston v. School Board of Norfolk, Virginia* (112 F2d 999, 4CA), the U.S. Supreme Court denied certiorari (311 U.S. 693), and, by not acting, it let the judgment of the court of appeals stand (which was a remand of the case to the district court for a decision on the merits).

## VOTING AND VOTER REGISTRATION LITIGATION

Houston and Marshall saw voting equality for African Americans as the other side of the educational equality coin. "The voting [primary decisions]," said Marshall in 1977, "were probably the most important [victories for African Americans]."[48] As early as 1915, in *Guinn v. United States,* the very first case the NAACP participated in, the Supreme Court invalidated a voting registration device, the "Grandfather Clause" that had discriminated against African Americans. (That device, a part of the Oklahoma Constitution since 1910, allowed illiterates to vote who had, prior to January 1866, lived in a foreign land, or had been eligible to register to vote prior to that date, or if a lineal ancestor—a "grandfather"—had been eligible to register prior to 1866.)

Immediately after *Guinn* was decided, Oklahoma passed a statute that allowed all those not registered to do so within twelve days (April 30, 1916, through May 11, 1916) or be forever barred from registering and voting. In 1939, in the case of *Lane v. Wilson,* the Supreme Court invalidated the legislation on Fifteenth Amendment grounds. Justice Frankfurter, for the majority, wrote that that amendment "nullifies sophisticated as well as simple-minded modes of discrimination," and that the Oklahoma statute retained an "unfair discrimination...by automatically granting voting privileges for life to the white citizens...while subjecting colored citizens to a new burden."

The "white primary" was a most effective mechanism for disenfranchising

African Americans in the South. The NAACP had challenged their constitutionality in the Texas cases *Nixon v. Herndon,* 1927, and *Nixon v. Condon,* 1932. The Court had agreed with the NAACP that Texas had limited African Americans' rights to participate in the Democratic Party primary, but state legislators had continued to restrict African American voting in the primary.

In *Grovey v. Townsend,* 1935, however, a *unanimous* Court upheld the discriminatory action of leaders of the Texas Democratic Party. They had limited participation in the primary to whites only. The Court concluded that the constitutional prohibitions on racial discrimination in voting did not cover purely private acts of groups.

By 1940, given the existence of this racially exclusionary process, only 3 percent of African Americans were registered to vote in the South. By 1947, after the 1944 *Smith* decision, the figure had increased to 12 percent, and, by 1950, 20 percent of black people in the South were registered to vote. African American veterans were in the forefront in the drive to register, and they were dramatically helped by the Supreme Court decision in the later Texas white primary litigation, *Smith v. Allwright,* decided in 1944. For Marshall, *Smith* was the "first real big one I had." Even the federal judge who ruled against him in the case encouraged him to file his certiorari petition because "you know you're going to win [in the Supreme Court]."[49]

Hastie, with Marshall's courtroom help, succeeded in showing that the primary was an essential part of the electoral process in the South, and therefore covered by the proscriptions of the Fourteenth and Fifteenth Amendments. The Court, in an opinion written by Stanley Reed, overturned the unanimous *Grovey* opinion. In part, the Court said that the Constitution granted all citizens the right to vote "without restriction by any state because of race. This grant to the people of the opportunity for choice is not to be nullified by a state through casting its electoral process in a form which permits a private organization to practice racial discrimination in the election." The private party primary was an integral part of the electoral process in Texas and was therefore subject to the commands and constraints of the Constitution's "state action" language in the Fifteenth Amendment.

Interestingly, behind the scenes and unknown to Marshall and Hastie, the Court had a mini-crisis of sorts. It was a not a problem regarding the substantive judgments on the merits, but rather a disagreement over who should write the opinion for the nearly unanimous Court (there was a single dissenter, Owen Roberts). The Chief Justice, Harlan F. Stone, assigned the *Smith* opinion to Felix Frankfurter. Another justice, Robert Jackson, voiced a great deal of anxiety over the assignment to a former member of the NAACP's legal committee. Jackson's concern, stated in a communication to Stone, was blunt: Frankfurter, in addition to his connection with the NAACP, was a foreign-born (Austrian) Jew, raised in New England, and a former professor at the very elitist Harvard Law School. It would be difficult enough to make whites comply with the decision without adding to the fires of Southern discord by having someone like Frankfurter write the opinion. Stone and Frankfurter agreed with Jackson: Reed, a Southern WASP, was given the assignment.

The opinion, when published, was a forthright statement. Reed, for the Court, said that *Grovey* was "erroneous" and that "we are applying, contrary to the recent decision in *Grovey,* the well established principle of the Fifteenth Amendment, forbidding the abridgment by a state of a citizen's right to vote. *Grovey v. Townsend* is overruled."

After the victory, Marshall went out with Buster, Roy Wilkins, and a few others to celebrate this signal victory for the Association and for every African American. He missed a call from Associate Justice Frank Murphy, one of the liberal members of the U.S. Supreme Court who had sided with Marshall. The next day, Marshall called to apologize, but Murphy told him "that a guy has a right to get drunk at a time like that."[50] And Marshall was forever grateful to that fine, white Texas politician, Tom C. Clark. Unlike his predecessor at Justice, Francis Biddle, who Marshall believed was unresponsive to NAACP requests for the U.S. Department of Justice to enforce Supreme Court opinions, Clark was fully supportive of the goals of the NAACP. Less than a month after *Smith* was announced, Clark, then assistant attorney general, sent a letter to the U.S. attorneys in all the states informing them that, in his judgment, *Smith* "applies to all primaries which are an integral part of the election process, whether federal, state, county, or municipal." After presenting his analysis of the broad sweep of *Smith,* Clark closed by stating publicly "that the Department feels that it is its duty to institute an investigation of the cases reported to it which involve such an alleged violation. In order that there may be consistent enforcement of this law, all such cases should be referred to the Department for approval of investigation or prosecution."[51]

Indeed, during his subsequent tenure as attorney general, Clark saw to it that the Department of Justice, for the very first time, filed briefs *amicus curiae* in support of the NAACP position in the restrictive covenant cases. As Marshall recalled, Clark, after taking over, "told the other states that they'd better fall in line or he'd whack them one. And they all fell in line except Georgia and South Carolina, and we had to file two more cases [which were won by the NAACP]."

Fittingly, poignantly, Thurgood Marshall was appointed to the U.S. Supreme Court in 1967 to fill Tom C. Clark's seat. Clark retired from the Court because his son, Ramsey Clark, had been appointed U.S. attorney general by another Texas friend of Marshall's, President Lyndon B. Johnson.

## THE CRIMINAL JUSTICE CASES

In his extensive travels across the South, beginning with the 1934 trip he took with Charlie Houston, Marshall was personally made aware of the host of violations of due process of law perpetrated against African Americans by whites, ranging from the common use of brutal, cruel, and terrifying police methods for eliciting confessions from black defendants to the exclusion of black citizens from service on juries. The 1923 case of *Moore v. Dempsey* was one of the initial due-process victories for the NAACP. The Court overturned the convictions and death sentences of twelve African Americans. Justice Oliver W. Holmes, for the majority, condemned the lynch-mob environment, the "wave of public passion" that all were caught up in, including the judge and the jury, which led to conviction and sentencing of the innocent African American defendants in less than an hour.

In 1936, in another one of the "horrible" criminal justice cases, *Brown v. Mississippi,* heard in this era of police cruelty, the Supreme Court overturned the conviction and death sentences of three African Americans who had been accused of murdering a white farmer. However, as the NAACP argued on appeal, physical and psychological torture had been used to elicit confessions from the men, including the near hanging of one of them, as well as beatings and other cruel treatment. The Supreme Court of Mississippi affirmed the convictions, but the U.S. Supreme Court reversed, arguing that the Constitution's due-process clause prohibited the "rack and the torture chamber" to obtain coerced confessions.

Hastie was NAACP counsel when *Brown* was argued orally, and wrote White to describe the strange scene in the courtroom.

> For once the Supreme Court was literally shocked out of its judicial detachment....Although Brandeis remained silent, with an occasional sardonic smile, and Cardozo listened impassively, the other five—McReynolds and Butler were absent—were at no pains to conceal their indignation....Roberts was continually interrupting...to inquire whether there was any substantial evidence of guilt other than the confession....Van Devanter became positively sarcastic about the testimony of the sheriff....Even Sutherland seemed to be aroused.

"I think that a scorching opinion is to be anticipated."

*Chambers v. Florida,* another coerced confession case decided during the Court's 1940 term, was the occasion of Marshall's first written brief filed in the Court. The case was another example of police brutality and fundamental denial of due process of law. The Supreme Court overturned the convictions because the convictions were based on coerced confessions. In the opinion, symbolically announced on Lincoln's Birthday in 1940, Hugo Black wrote that "to permit human lives to be forfeited upon confessions thus obtained would make of the constitutional requirement of due process of law a meaningless symbol."

The *Chambers* opinion was, for its author, Hugo Black, always his favorite opinion. Late at night, he would have his wife, Elizabeth, read it to him many times over the decades. Listening to it usually brought tears to his eyes. Unfortunately, as Black found out in a letter from one of the Florida judges who heard the case, the toll on Chambers was grim. Within months after his conviction was overturned, Chambers "lost his mind" and spent the rest of his life in a hospital for the insane.

The following year brought on a difficult loss in the Supreme Court for Thurgood Marshall and the Association. W. D. Lyons, a local black handyman in the tiny town of Hugo, Oklahoma, had been convicted of murdering a white family of four and setting their house on fire to conceal the crime. The NAACP was convinced by the local African Americans that Lyons was innocent and that the dead family had been murdered as part of a vendetta by rival bootleggers. Marshall went to the town to serve as Lyons's defense counsel. Because of the great fear of violence in Hugo, he had a hard time finding lodgings for the night, even though he had an "unofficial" armed guard protecting him. Finally, an elderly woman agreed to put him up, saying proudly, "I ain't scared!"

Marshall was never so frightened in his life as he was that first night in Hugo, Oklahoma. He stayed up all night and, years later, admitted that he was scared to death: "I never wanted anyone, I mean nobody, to know that during that first night in Hugo I lay on the bed sweating in fear. I think I remembered every lynching story that I read about after World War One. I could see my dead body lying in some place where they let white kids out of Sunday School to come and look at me, and rejoice."

Marshall's presence in the small Hugo, Oklahoma, courtroom was unprecedented; Hugo and other small Oklahoma towns in the area "dismissed their high schools in order for the students to attend what the authorities may have regarded as a circus."[52] What was thought to be the spectacle of a black lawyer from the North defending a black defendant turned into an amazing event. The white Southerners saw a riveting trial performance by Marshall. "On the very first day, the whites were so astonished at Marshall's presentation of his case that their hostility turned to curiosity. He'd hardly finished his opening statement before he had half of them pulling for him," said one local observer.[53]

Prior to Marshall's arrival, Lyons had been questioned continuously, beaten by the local police, and psychologically tortured by having a pan of bones, allegedly those of the victims, thrust onto his lap while he was being questioned by the police. He confessed after these horrific methods were employed. He was then taken from the local jail to the state penitentiary, where he confessed a second time. At the trial, the prosecution used only the second confession.

Marshall argued, and lost, at the trial. He maintained that the terror Lyons felt was so strong that it carried over to the second confession, given that same evening. As he noted afterwards, "the jurors were shocked" by the brutal methods of the local police, "but they couldn't break altogether with their backgrounds. They found Lyons guilty and then salved their consciences by giving him life imprisonment. Had they really thought a Negro guilty of such a crime, they would surely have given him the chair."

After losing in the Oklahoma supreme court, Marshall sought review by the U.S. Supreme Court. However, in a surprising 1944 opinion, the Court, in a six-to-three opinion, affirmed Lyons's conviction. The majority concluded that the second confession was not "brought about by the earlier mistreatments." Three justices dissented: Marshall's friend Hugo L. Black, Frank Murphy, and Wiley Rutledge. Marshall had one bitter consolation: "The father of the slain white woman took up the fight for Lyons' freedom and eventually became president of the Hugo branch of the NAACP."[54]

Throughout this period, with the exception of the *Lyons* case, Marshall and the Association successfully challenged coerced confessions in the federal courts. In cases such as *Lee v. Mississippi*, 1948, and *Watts v. Indiana*, 1949, the Court invalidated the convictions because they were coerced in violation of the due-process clause of the Fourteenth Amendment.

## SEGREGATED TRANSPORTATION AND TRAVEL CASES

In 1946, Marshall's Inc Fund won a major victory in *Morgan v. Commonwealth of Virginia:* Irene Morgan, an African American citizen, had been convicted in the Virginia courts for violating a state statute requiring segregation of the races on all public vehicles. Traveling from Richmond to Baltimore, Maryland, on a Greyhound bus, she had refused orders to move to the back of the bus. After conviction and a fine of fifteen dollars, she appealed, with the help of the NAACP. Once again, Hastie and Marshall prepared the briefs and participated in the oral argument before the Supreme Court. They contended that the Virginia statute, as applied in Irene Morgan's case, was an "undue burden" on interstate commerce and was therefore unconstitutional.

In June of 1946, the Supreme Court accepted their argument and ruled that passengers on interstate carriers were not under the jurisdiction of Jim Crow state statutes like Virginia's. Such statutes, it said, burdened interstate commerce and were therefore unconstitutional. Justice Stanley Reed, from Kentucky, wrote the opinion for a seven-to-one Court majority.

Less than two years later, Marshall, working with Hastie and "Spotts" Robinson, quickly put together and filed a brief *amicus curiae* in another transportation discrimination case that had come to the Supreme Court. The case, *Bob-Lo Excursion Company v. Michigan,* involved the question of foreign commerce. The facts were significantly different from those in the *Morgan* litigation.

The company ran two excursion boats between Detroit, Michigan, and Bob-Lo Island, in Canada. The company owned both the boats and the island, and sold only round-trip tickets, so that the excursions began and ended in Michigan. An African American had been sold a ticket, allowed to board, and then forced off "solely because of race or color." Michigan had a civil rights statute that prohibited such racial discrimination, but the company argued that since it was engaged in "foreign commerce," the Michigan statute was inapplicable.

The Michigan supreme court held that the statute was valid and covered the actions of the excursion company. The company, arguing that it was a private commercial operation and not an interstate public common carrier, took its appeal to the U.S. Supreme Court. In part, the company argued that the *Morgan* decision established a precedent that prevented a state statute from interfering with interstate or foreign commerce.

The NAACP's friend-of-the-court brief, joined by the ACLU and the National Lawyers Guild, argued that there was a difference between the statutes in Virginia and Michigan. One (Virginia's) *required* segregation, while the other (Michigan's) *prohibited* segregation. The brief urged the Court to distinguish between the two statutes and to rule, clearly, in favor of the nondiscriminatory statute. For the NAACP and the other joiners, the Michigan statute "was in keeping with the principles established in the Thirteenth, Fourteenth, and Fifteenth Amendments; that the rule of decision should be that statutes [such as Michigan's] in keeping with the principles of the amendments should be upheld and the others knocked down."[55]

The Court, in a seven-to-two opinion written by Wiley Rutledge, upheld the judgment of the Michigan Supreme Court. While Chief Justice Vinson, joined in dissent by Justice Jackson, argued that the Michigan statute "cannot interfere with commerce," the majority judged that there was no burden placed on foreign commerce by the Michigan statute. Although Marshall succeeded in getting the Court to void Jim Crow practices on interstate carriers, it would be many years before black Americans could freely travel on interstate and intrastate common carriers.

## RESIDENTIAL DISCRIMINATION AND RESTRICTIVE COVENANTS LITIGATION

From its inception, the NAACP had wrestled with laws that allowed residential segregation. Beginning around 1910, as Arthur Spingarn wrote, "a wave of residential segregation laws swept the country, city after city in the southern and border states passed ordinances....No one for a moment believed that they were anything but the initial step in an attempt to create Negro ghettos throughout the United States."[56]

More than a dozen large cities, including Baltimore, Dallas, St. Louis, and Louisville, had ordinances that banned the sale, lease, or rental of property to African Americans, as well as to persons of Japanese or Chinese ancestry, Filipinos, Koreans, Indians, Catholics, and Jews. Moorfield Storey took Louisville to court to challenge discriminatory ordinance. In a 1918 case, *Buchanan v. Warley,* the Supreme Court unanimously concluded that such local residential housing ordinances that prohibited whites from living in black areas of Louisville, Kentucky, and vice versa, violated the due-process clause of the Fourteenth Amendment.

In 1927, in the case of *Harmon v. Tyler,* the Court used the *Buchanan* precedent to strike down a New Orleans ordinance that, like Louisville's, discriminated against African Americans. In 1930, in *City of Richmond v. Deans,* a Richmond, Virginia, restrictive residential housing ordinance was declared unconstitutional by a federal court and the Supreme Court affirmed the judgment.

The NAACP was not as successful initially in challenging private covenants that restricted the sale or rental of housing to African Americans and other minorities. In 1926, in *Corrigan v. Buckley,* a state court issued a judgment prohibiting Corrigan from selling her home to an African American woman. On appeal to the Supreme Court, the high court said that since "nothing in the Constitution prohibits private individuals from entering into contracts respecting...their own property," there was no case or controversy. Therefore, the state court order remained in force.

Things did not change in this area of *private* housing discrimination until 1947, when the Supreme Court granted certiorari in a number of restrictive covenant cases coming from Missouri, Michigan, and the District of Columbia. In the spring of 1944, Thurgood Marshall asked Spottswood Robinson to prepare a plan for attacking the restrictive covenant. After Spotts made suggestions for challenging the restrictive covenant, Marshall began to prepare for arguments before the Supreme Court.

By 1947, because of postwar demands for better housing, Marshall and his staff had brought to the Court petitions for certiorari challenging the restrictive covenant in a number of states and the District of Columbia. Once again, Marshall recruited a number of lawyers to prepare the briefs and the oral arguments in these cases: *Shelley v. Kramer,* from St. Louis, Missouri; *McGhee v. Sipes,* from Detroit, Michigan; and *Hurd v. Hodge,* from the District of Columbia. It was to be the last occasion when Houston, Hastie, and Marshall stood together before the U.S. Supreme Court.

In September 1947, after discussions with Marshall, White wrote Attorney General Clark requesting that the Justice Department file briefs in the restrictive covenant cases. After months of review, on October 30, 1947, the Solicitor General, Philip Perlman, informed White and Marshall that the attorney general would file a brief *amicus curiae* and that Perlman would participate in oral argument in the cases.[57] This was a historic first for the national government; never before had the Justice Department filed a brief supporting the NAACP.

When the cases were argued, three of the justices—Stanley Reed, Wiley Rutledge, and Robert Jackson—did not participate because they had purchased homes with restrictive covenants attached. In a unanimous six-member decision, the Court held that while the restrictive covenant was a valid private contract, it could not be enforced by state courts or any other state agency. Such enforcement was deemed a form of "state action" prohibited by the Fourteenth Amendment.[58]

After a celebratory evening with Buster, Roy, and the Inc Fund staff, a tired but happy Marshall confessed, in a letter to one of his college chums, "The favorable decision is therefore most gratifying because, frankly, *we were all scared to death!*" Under Marshall's leadership, the Inc Fund was participating in hundreds of legal suits across the South. If he was frightened, he rarely showed it; instead, his demeanor convinced black Americans that their champion possessed "the broadest shoulders of all."[59]

## THE POLITICS OF RACE DURING THE ROOSEVELT AND TRUMAN ADMINISTRATIONS

While Marshall was plotting the attack on *Plessy*, Walter White and Roy Wilkins focused on the politics of race in Washington and sought to influence successive presidents.[60] Occasionally, White, Wilkins, and Marshall worked together on a particular task that they all felt would help the Association.

In January 1941, for example, there was a remarkable effort to try to have the Association "enlist the support of the steadily growing number of intelligent, courageous, and educated young white Southerners." They sponsored a meeting of an unusual small group of interested parties to discuss how to accomplish this. The meeting took place at the Willard Hotel in Washington, D.C. In attendance, besides Houston, Hastie, Marshall, White, and Wilkins, were U.S. Supreme Court Associate Justices Hugo Black and Felix Frankfurter and a small number of educators, including the president of the University of North Carolina, Dr. Frank Graham, Dean George Payne of New York University, and Archibald MacLeish, to "discuss how this could be done."[61]

Black and Frankfurter should not have been there, for they would continue to hear cases from the NAACP and their presence was ethically improper. But to Felix Frankfurter, the Jewish "outsider" who had to deal with that status throughout his life, and who empathized with the "colored" community's similar problem, it was imperative that ways be found to connect good, decent white people in the South with their black neighbors. He had been a member of the NAACP's legal committee until he went on the Court in 1939, and felt that he should participate in such conversations.

Justice Hugo Black, the Alabaman on the Court, who had joined the Ku Klux Klan in 1923 and had been elected to the U.S. Senate in 1926 with Klan support, had changed dramatically by the time he was appointed to the Court in 1937. He spoke about and longed for the emergence of a "New South" of freedom and equality. Black believed that, working with White and Marshall, two men he had known and highly respected for a number of years, a bridge could be built between blacks and young white men and women in the Southern states.

From that meeting and others like it, a small network of black and white southerners began to emerge. The whites were liberals, like Alabama's Clifford and Virginia "Jinksie" Durr, who deeply believed in the justice and necessity of the NAACP's struggle to achieve these goals.[62]

### THE "NEW DEAL" AND AFRICAN AMERICANS

Unfortunately for the African Americans who had voted heavily for the Democratic candidate in the 1936 election (the first time a majority of African Americans cast votes for a Democrat in almost a century), it was not really a "New Deal" for them. Franklin Delano Roosevelt frequently went down to Warm Springs, Georgia, to enjoy the therapeutic effect of the warm spring water on his polio-crippled legs. Many of his friends in that state, including its U.S. senators, were Klansmen or politicians who had been elected with Klan support. While his wife, Eleanor, spoke out openly in support of anti-lynching legislation, the President did not. He claimed that he could not risk alienating the Southern Democrats who chaired all the key Senate committees. He needed them to pass his New Deal legislation and to help him move an isolationist America to military preparedness before a second world war engulfed the nation.

As a consequence, Marshall quickly lost whatever admiration he had for Roosevelt because of the President's "refusal to antagonize [the Southern chairmen] by bold, open displays for America's non-whites." As he told a reporter in 1987, "the biggest trouble of all was [the President]. He was [not] worth a damn so far as Negroes were concerned....When it came to just the Negro, Roosevelt was not a friend....I don't know of any place in government in Roosevelt's time where the Negro really got what he was entitled to."[63]

In a January 30, 1939, memo to White, Marshall cataloged all the discriminatory actions by federal agencies taken against African Americans. The list included charges against the TVA, the WPA, the Resettlement Administration, the federal civil service generally, the army and the navy, the Federal Housing Administration, and the National Maritime Commission.

Probably the most searing event in the relationship between Marshall and the President occurred when he was in Attorney General Biddle's office discussing a particularly bad racial incident in Virginia. Biddle telephoned the President to discuss the matter with him, and asked Marshall to pick up an extension phone. Unaware that Marshall was listening in, Roosevelt told Biddle: "I warned you not to call me again about any of Eleanor's niggers. Call me one more time and *you* are fired." The President, Marshall said later, "only said 'nigger' once, but once was enough for me."[64]

In October 1940, Walter White prepared a report card on Roosevelt's debits and credits "in relation to the Negro." He cited the administration's failure to support anti-lynching legislation, integrate the federal bureaucracy, or end discrimination against African Americans in the armed forces. The administration had not banned discrimination in hiring for work done under federal contract or funding, nor had it moved on "violations of civil rights of Negroes as provided for in federal laws." It had ignored the sequestering, by whites, of farm benefits and "other payments [due] to Negroes" and remained silent in the face of "vicious denunciation of the Negro by Southern senators."

While the President was, to say the least, diffident about civil rights and the NAACP's goals, his wife, Eleanor, was most definitely not timid about speaking out on behalf of black Americans. Time and again, her presence at NAACP annual meetings and award banquets, as well as the interviews she gave, showed her to be a friend of the NAACP and of all oppressed peoples. In 1939, when the Daughters of the American Revolution refused to allow famed African American opera singer Marian Anderson to perform in their auditorium, Eleanor promptly resigned from that organization in protest, and then helped arrange the use of the Lincoln Memorial as the site for Anderson's concert.

Roosevelt's reluctant incrementalism in moving toward equality and equity for African Americans is illustrated by the creation of the Fair Employment Practices Commission (FEPC), by Executive Order 8842, in 1941. The FEPC was created in response to threats by A. Philip Randolph, the president of the Brotherhood of Sleeping Car Porters, and Walter White to stage a major march down Pennsylvania Avenue, in Washington, D.C., by 100,000 African Americans to show their anger at continuing employment discrimination in the expanding defense industries and demanding abolition of this by executive order.

The White House responded to the threat with "fear and anxiety." Roosevelt refused to discuss the employment discrimination problem with Randolph and White. But the President was so alarmed by the specter of thousands of black Americans coming to the national capital to protest that in early June, in a critical meeting with the two leaders, he asked what it would take to call off the march. An executive order restricting discrimination based on race, they responded.

The President had a young lawyer, Joseph Rauh (who would, a decade later, work with Marshall on civil rights litigation), draft the proposed order. On June 25, Roosevelt signed it. The order called for employers and labor unions "to provide for the full and equitable participation of all workers in defense industries, without discrimination because of race, creed, color, or national origin." A five-person Fair Employment Practices Commission was established. The FEPC was to have a stormy history as the target of attacks by congressional leaders, the media, and labor unions, which had for decades discriminated against racial and religious minorities. In spite of the hostility directed toward it, the FEPC achieved some early successes. By the beginning of 1942, the commission had pressured industry and labor so effectively that black people began to get jobs in the defense industry, positions not confined to janitorial and maintenance functions.

### THE WORLD WAR II RACE RIOTS

While the FEPC was an adequate remedy in the eyes of African Americans who still experienced harsh discrimination, it was repugnant to white labor unionists and others who wanted to restrict blacks to menial positions. By 1943, the tensions between blacks and whites exploded in race riots at home while America was fighting the Axis in Europe and Asia. Marshall and the NAACP leadership, in New York and in the chapters across the nation, faced new outbreaks of racial violence during and after the war.

This "mob terror," as White termed it, was the white response to growing demands by blacks for equal rights in employment, education, the military, and the voting booth. White and others pleaded, in vain, for legislative and executive leadership "to destroy the cancer of racism in American life."[65] Instead, such demands triggered riots in several major cities, including Detroit and New York, all during two summer months in 1943.

The Detroit riot occurred in late June, sparked by an incident a few weeks earlier, in which a wildcat strike of 25,000 workers took place in a defense factory because the company had promoted three African American workers. One of the strikers, thinking that Walter White was indeed white, told him, "I'd rather see Hitler and Hirohito win the war than work beside a nigger on the assembly line."[66] The strike was ended quickly, but the anger remained and festered.

A few weeks later, on June 20–21, rioting broke out. Some minor scuffles on a bridge near a segregated amusement park escalated overnight into full-scale civil disturbance in downtown Detroit. More than 100,000 people were involved, and the hatred and rage on both sides were palpable. Three thousand Detroit police could not contain the violence, so the governor declared a state of martial law, called in state police, and asked the army commander in the area to order soldiers into the city. After President Roosevelt gave permission to use the troops, the army quickly occupied parts of Detroit. Within a day, the riot was over. The casualties included 34 dead (25 were African Americans, 17 of them killed by white policemen) and another 340 injured.[67]

The race riot in Harlem, in August, was equally violent and ignited by anger in the African American community. For weeks before both riots, African American newspapers had published story after story about black military personnel being assaulted, viciously beaten up, and, in more than a few instances, brutally murdered by whites, primarily near military bases located in the South. In the spring of 1943, Marshall and Hastie visited a number of these bases to investigate some of the complaints, after which they wrote a report of their findings and sent it to the War and Justice Departments. Their analysis "grimly stated," as White reported in a *New Republic* article published on August 16, 1943 (after the Harlem rioting), that

> civilian violence against the Negro in uniform is a recurrent phenomenon....It may well be the greatest factor now operating to make *13,000,000 Negroes bitter and resentful* and to undermine the fighting spirit of three-quarters of a million Negroes in arms. Yet, no effective steps are being taken and no vigorous, continuing and comprehensive program of action has been inaugurated by state or federal authorities to stamp out this "evil."...To address a Negro soldier as "nigger" is such a commonplace in the average Southern community that little is said about it. But *the mounting rage* of the soldier himself is far from commonplace....In such a climate resentments grow until they burst forth in violent and unreasoning reprisal. (My emphasis.)

On August 1, 1943, a white policeman shot a black military policeman, setting off the rioting in Harlem. Although the soldier was not fatally wounded, the rumor quickly spread that he had been killed right in front of his mother. As White recounted, "blind, unreasoning fury swept the community with the speed of lightning."[68] During the height of the riot, Wilkins, Marshall, and White rode together in a police radio car and used its loudspeaker to tell people milling about in the hot Harlem streets to "cool it, cool it."[69] When the Harlem riot was over, there were five dead, more than three hundred injured, and over $5 million in damages.

## THE VITAL CHANGE: HARRY S TRUMAN

These acts of race violence continued throughout the Roosevelt administration and into the Truman administration. Roosevelt was absolutely unwilling to do anything publicly to address these horrors. His attorney general, Francis Biddle, following Roosevelt's lead, did little to use the powers of the Justice Department to deal with the discrimination that fueled black anger.

Truman and his attorney general, Tom Clark, however, publicly condemned racial violence, lynchings, and inequality in general. For example, after the 1946 murders of two African American couples in Monroe, Georgia, Clark moved quickly to collect evidence and convene a grand jury to try to indict the men who murdered the four African Americans. Even though the federal grand jury failed to return any indictments, the message to the public was clear. The Truman Justice Department, led by Clark, would protect black Americans.[70]

Whether the violence took place in a state prison in Georgia (where a crazed warden machine-gunned to death eight African American prisoners), in Columbia, Tennessee, or in a tiny Delta town in Mississippi, Clark's vigorous legal efforts were appreciated by Marshall and the rest of the African American community. Marshall had known Clark from the time the Texan first came to Washington to work in the Justice Department. He also knew Clark's mother and his brother. Marshall knew that Clark was a decent and principled man. As he recalled in 1977, Clark "has always been great."

The Roosevelt administration did little to defuse the rage and prevent the violence spreading across the country during the war. Racial riots and lynching incidents increased in volume and violence when people came home from the war in 1945 and 1946, particularly racial violence against returning black servicemen in the South.

Harry S Truman, a feisty, plain-talking senator from Missouri, had been picked as Roosevelt's vice-presidential running mate in the 1944 presidential election. When Truman took over the presidency after Roosevelt's death in April 1945, most African Americans were concerned because, as Roy Wilkins said, "he was an untested haberdasher from Klan country."[71] But Wilkins knew Truman from their days in Kansas City, and felt that Truman's heart was very different from Roosevelt's when it came to equality of opportunity and just plain fair treatment of people, regardless of color.

Truman grew up in segregationist Independence, Missouri, where its black community lived in a segregated area of the town called "Nigger Neck" and the children attended a separate "colored" school. African Americans could not shop in the white-owned downtown stores or use the local library. Words such as "nigger" and "coon" were "used as a matter of course in so-called 'polite society.' And below the surface always lay a threat of violence, should any blacks forget their 'place.'"[72]

Even though Truman used the ugly racist words of his childhood throughout his life, he did not accept support from the Klan, and lost local elections in the 1920s. From the time he arrived in Washington, D.C., in 1934, he was one of a handful of Southern and border-state senators who supported federal anti-lynching legislation and who called for the abolition of the poll tax as well. In 1948 he introduced a major omnibus civil rights program that included a strong anti-lynching measure.

Marshall, like most black Americans, felt that Truman was "somebody to rely on. Who would go the whole hog...you know he's there when you need him."[73] After the gruesome murders of four African Americans in Monroe, Georgia, in 1946, Truman met with six black leaders to discuss the crimes. He promised to appoint a strong civil rights committee to recommend steps that the federal and state governments could take to improve and strengthen the civil rights of all Americans. By Executive Order 9808, signed in December 1946, he created the President's Committee on Civil Rights.

Ten months later, the Committee's report, *To Secure These Rights*, called upon the federal government to take immediate and aggressive action—as both a "sword" and a "shield"—on behalf of citizens whose rights had been denied for too many decades. It said a "moral dry rot" had set into the fabric of American democracy, and something had to be done quickly to repair the damage to America's fundamental values.

It recommended no less than thirty-five legislative initiatives that, when enacted, would guarantee four essential rights for all citizens: the right to safety and security of the person; the right to citizenship and its privileges; the right to freedom of conscience and expression; and the right to equality of opportunity. In response to the recommendations, Truman presented to the Congress, on February 2, 1948, a Ten Point civil rights message containing significant and highly controversial legislative proposals, including another federal anti-lynching statute. Truman had the guts to introduce this legislation before the next election, knowing that it would adversely affect his chances of winning the South. (He paid a real price for his stand; Southern Democrats walked out of the Democratic National Convention and formed a Dixiecrat Party, which took electoral votes away from Truman in the November general election.)

Truman called on the Congress to enact legislation for

- establishing a permanent Commission on Civil Rights, a Joint Congressional Committee on Civil Rights, and a Civil Rights Division in the Department of Justice
- strengthening existing civil rights statutes
- preventing lynching
- protecting "more adequately" the right to vote

- establishing a permanent FEPC "to prevent unfair discrimination in employment"
- prohibiting discrimination in interstate transportation facilities
- providing home rule and suffrage in presidential elections for the District of Columbia
- providing statehood for Alaska and Hawaii
- equalizing the opportunities for residents of the United States to become naturalized citizens
- settling the evacuation claims of Japanese Americans.[74]

This omnibus proposal covered a great part of what the NAACP had fought for from its inception. The African American press hailed Truman as the first presidential champion of civil rights in almost a century.

Shortly after Truman's 1948 upset electoral victory, Marshall had an opportunity to be nominated by Truman for a U.S. district court judgeship. In the spring of 1949, the Congress passed legislation, HR 1826, which, in part, created four new federal trial court judgeships in the Southern District of New York, with the understanding that one of the four would be filled by an African American.

Arthur Spingarn, the NAACP president, wrote to his cousin Steve, a staff member in the Truman White House, and suggested that Marshall, an outspoken supporter of the President and someone untainted by any left-wing affiliations, would be an ideal candidate. At Steve Spingarn's request, Marshall submitted biographical information for presentation to key people in the White House. As late as September 1949, Marshall was still being considered by Truman for the appointment. Ultimately, although he appreciated the lifetime tenure and relative peace, safety, and security of the federal judgeship, Marshall withdrew his name from consideration. He was playing leading roles in education litigation in Texas and Oklahoma and in the NAACP's preparations for the frontal attack on segregated public school education in state courts in South Carolina, Kansas, Virginia, and Delaware. Marshall could hardly leave the battlefield at such a crucial period in the struggle.

## THE ASSAULT ON PUBLIC SCHOOL SEGREGATION AND THE *PLESSY* DOCTRINE

By 1948, the NAACP had more than half a million members in some 1,600 branches across the nation. Some members, especially the young African American veterans of World War II, were demanding more aggressive action against racial discrimination. But a great many other members, and black people in general, feared the consequences of such aggressiveness. This was to create some serious practical problems for the Inc Fund director-counsel.

Marshall knew that those pressing for a more vigorous confrontation were the plaintiffs so desperately needed by the Association in the years to come. Even before 1948, he was plotting the strategy that would, in the education field, frontally challenge *Plessy's* continued constitutional validity. The NAACP would go beyond pressing for equalization of educational opportunity and argue that separate could not be equal. The dual school system had to be dismantled. While neither Marshall nor the rest of the NAACP leadership knew what would happen when and if the Supreme Court ordered an end to *Plessy* and desegregated school systems, they believed this was the only road to equality for African Americans.

In September 1947, Marshall persuaded the NAACP board to issue a statement to all the branches about the Association's policy in education cases. Coming just at the time the *Sipuel* appeal was moving to the Supreme Court, the new policy signaled a change in litigation strategy for cases involving elementary and high schools. The NAACP would no longer ask the courts for separate but truly equal, and would no longer "recognize the validity of separate school statutes":

> This is necessary if we are to keep our position clear which is that we do not consider segregation statutes legal, do not recognize them as being legal and will continue to challenge them in legal proceedings. Finally, it must be pointed out that…the NAACP cannot take part in any legal proceeding which seeks to enforce segregation statutes, which condones segregation in public schools, or which admits the validity of these statutes.[75]

Marshall, while he believed *Plessy* had to be attacked and overturned, nevertheless feared the immediate costs of such a judicial overturn of separate but equal. The jobs of African American schoolteachers would be in jeopardy (because of white parents' refusal to allow them to teach their children). It would provoke increased violence, especially in Georgia, Florida, Alabama, Mississippi, and Louisiana. Marshall also acknowledged the discouraging possibility that African American communities might not really want integration but would prefer good "deluxe" Jim Crow schools for their children.[76]

The unwillingness of many African Americans to move toward desegregation frustrated Marshall. Sometimes he would exclaim to his staff that "the easy part of the job is fighting the white folks!"[77] In the months just before initial public school segregation trials in four states and the District of Columbia that would eventually lead to the overturn of *Plessy,* he was writing letter after letter to local chapters to underline the change in policy. Marshall wrote Roy Wilkins a letter expressing his frustration at the evident lack of support by the branches for the policy change:

I *had* assumed that the NAACP really meant business about an all-out attack against segregation, especially in the public school system. I *had* assumed that we not only realized that segregation was an evil but had come to the conclusion that *nothing* can be gained under the doctrine of "separate but equal." I *had* assumed that the Board of Directors...were in agreement on this. I *had* assumed that the resolutions...meant exactly what they said.[78]

Marshall's explosion led Wilkins to convene a "thrashing out" meeting of the national board. All reaffirmed the new policy announcement and agreed that the message had to get to the branches clearly and firmly.

Tragically, during this exciting but stressful period, Charlie Houston died on April 22, 1950. Even though the fifty-five-year-old Houston had been in poor health, Marshall was stunned. At Houston's funeral in Washington, D.C. (which was attended by Justices Hugo Black and Tom C. Clark), a friend noted that Marshall "grieved for Charlie as if he were a brother, and I think his grief was compounded by the fact that sitting there in Rankin Chapel, staring at Charlie's casket, Thurgood suddenly realized he had lost a man who had been as important in his life as his father had been."[79]

# 5

## SEGREGATION IN THE MILITARY: A SPECIAL HUMILIATION

While serving in the army in Europe during World War I, Charlie Houston learned the bitter lesson that American racial prejudice and Jim Crowism were just as pervasive "over there" as in his native land. The moral authority of the United States, fundamentally compromised first by slavery and then by its legacies, was particularly impaired as long as the nation allowed black men to die for it but would not accord them the dignity and equality enjoyed by the white majority. America's enemies would seek to exploit this contradiction.

The January 28, 1938, issue of the *Volkischer Beobachter*, Nazi Germany's major newspaper, lashed out at America's disapproval of Nazi Germany's race theory and persecution of the Jews, saying that such criticisms will not "make any impression on us."

> We very humbly just pointed out the *lynchjustice* on Negroes and answered that these actions did not very well fit in with the beautiful gleaming soap bubble of democracy....We German barbarians, as far as we know, do not lynch Jewish race polluters in this inhuman way, we don't even kill them....Our means of punishment for race pollution is much more refined...than America's democratic *lynchjustice.*[1]

In 1937, while rejecting democratic "lynchjustice" for the Jews, the Schwarze Korps, a military wing of the secret police and the Hitler Elite Guard, demanded that Germany promulgate "an anti-Jewish 'Jim Crow' decree. It would segregate (in special 'Jew compartments' or separate cars) all Jews, including those of foreign citizenship, traveling on German railways." Such a decree would, after all, be comparable to "a documented democratic example. For the world's freest country...does not permit its State citizens, with equal rights but a darker hue, to sit, much less sleep, next to a white person, even if the white is only a sewage worker and the black a world-class boxing champion or other national hero."[2]

America's Jim Crowism was the perfect Nazi propaganda tool, useful to "cultivate attitudes in the Negro which will render him disloyal to American institutions," and to stir up "the resentment of the anti-Negro white population in America."[3] Some German radio broadcasts focused on racial discrimination in America, race violence (lynchings, rioting), and discrimination by government agencies, with particular emphasis on discrimination against "the Negro in the Army and in the war effort in general." To inflame the resentment of white racists, the Nazis predicted the full emancipation of African Americans after the war.

Though crude and not very effective, this propaganda did exploit essential frustrations of both African Americans and Southern whites, who feared what might happen when black frustrations were combined with military training and combat experience. There was certainly enough truth behind the Nazi propaganda. While "no black Americans supported Nazism or condoned the Japanese attack on Americans at Pearl Harbor, [it] was difficult, however, for blacks to fight in defense of the 'four freedoms' with which they had little to no acquaintance."[4]

Black Americans had experienced the humiliation of segregation when they fought the Germans in World War I. The humiliation continued in World War II, fought ostensibly to preserve democracy. The military high command willfully maintained rigid segregation in all the armed forces. Roy Wilkins summed up the terrible anger smoldering in the hearts and minds of African Americans at this time in the nation's history:

> A country that denied democracy to millions of its citizens in the South was suddenly rousing itself to defend democracy thousands of miles away across the Atlantic; a country that placidly countenanced lynch ropes...was suddenly expressing horror over the persecution of minorities in Europe; a country that abominated Nazis still winced at the Ku Klux Klan and the white master race ideology of Southern Democrats. Obviously Hitler had to be dealt with...but anyone with eyes, ears, and a sense of justice knew that segregation at home was also an evil that had to be wiped out. Yet the country seemed oblivious to this obvious truth.[5]

Despite this anger, young African American men would serve when called. However, Wilkins, White, and Marshall felt that the NAACP had to somehow address, politically and legally (where possible), racial segregation in the military, a practice followed by America's leaders for nearly two centuries, throughout all its wars.

## MILITARY SEGREGATION IN WORLD WAR I

In World War I, more than 400,000 African Americans served in the army; some 140,000 of them were sent to France to fight the Germans. Of that number, only 40,000 were combat troops, and the rest served in labor battalions.[6] It was a thoroughly segregated war for these men.

Charlie Houston's experiences in World War I were all too representative. He was twenty-two when America entered the war in 1917. He volunteered, unwillingly, for a segregated army officer training program, obtained his commission, and went overseas in 1918. He felt that the segregation would be easier to deal with if he were an officer volunteer than if he waited to be drafted into the army. Houston's unit was transferred from one region in France to another and finally relieved from duty, seeing little action but a great deal of discrimination. Wherever they went, these black American officers experienced horrible treatment, from fellow officers and white troops and even from Red Cross workers in America and Europe. When a bitter, angry Houston finally came home from France, in February 1919, he recalled thinking, "I felt damned glad I had not lost my life fighting for this country."[7]

A 1925 Army War College report on Negro manpower placed this kind of observation in an official document shared by general officers at the highest levels. In part, the report observed:

> In the process of evolution, the American negro has not progressed as far as other *subspecies* of the human family.... The cranial cavity of the negro is smaller than whites.... The psychology of the negro, based on heredity derived from mediocre African ancestors, cultivated by generations of slavery, is one from which we cannot expect to draw leadership material.... He cannot control himself in fear of danger.... He is a rank coward in the dark.[8]

On August 6, 1934, after military budget cuts reduced the number of African American active duty regiments from four to one, Houston wrote a letter of complaint to the Chief of Staff of the U.S. Army, Douglas MacArthur. As "a Negro veteran and former reserve officer," he offered sober "friendly advice" to MacArthur about how African Americans resented the continuation of Jim Crow segregation in the army. He urged MacArthur to "lift the ban on discrimination against Negroes in the Army, and to see that Negroes are accorded full representation in all arms of the service with equal opportunity for advancement according to their ability."[9]

MacArthur wrote back a few weeks later, categorically rejecting all of Houston's observations and ignoring his recommendations for integrating the army and giving equal opportunity to all in the service to advance on the basis of merit. MacArthur closed with the incredible assertion that "there has been and will be no discrimination against the colored race in the training of the national forces."

Not surprisingly, the situation was unchanged at the time of America's entry into World War II. In 1940, the year before the Japanese attack on Pearl Harbor, there were exactly *two* African American officers and only 4,700 African American soldiers in the army (out of nearly 500,000 men). The navy had 4,000 black sailors in 1940, but the only ranking they had was mess attendant. These men were serving their nation—by serving their white naval officers coffee and meals, and doing their laundry.

Only four African Americans had ever graduated from the U.S. Military Academy and none from the Naval Academy. Furthermore, there "was not a single Negro in the Marine Corps, the Tank Corps, the Signal Corps, or the Army Air Corps."[10] As an official army report noted, "certain branches (Air Corps, Signal Corps, Light Artillery, etc.) were considered *too technical* for mastery by Negroes [my emphasis]."[11]

Any African American who complained to higher-ups in the military about the discrimination he experienced was punished quickly, generally by a bad-conduct discharge from the service. But as the war went on, complaints multiplied and were often reported in the African American press. The NAACP had to do something about the segregation in the military. Lines were drawn for a battle on the home front, where many African Americans were in perhaps greater danger than they would be in combat.

## SEGREGATION IN THE ARMED SERVICES IN WORLD WAR II

On September 27, 1940, Roosevelt had a meeting with Walter White, A. Philip Randolph, and T. Arnold Hill, the acting secretary of the National Urban League, to listen to their concerns about segregation throughout the military services. Secretary of the Navy Frank Knox and Assistant Secretary of War Robert Patterson were also present. White soon understood that none of the administration officials, including the President, "had even thought of non-segregated units in the Army."[12] On October 4, 1940, a modest White House press release was issued. African American military units would be created in all the armed services, including the army air corps. But segregation in all the services would be maintained. The black American community's "disappointment turned to fury when, in announcing it to the press, White House press secretary Steve Early gave the false impression that the three Negro leaders had agreed with the wording and countenanced the policy of segregation."[13]

A firestorm erupted, for the "statement fell like a bomb on public opinion," White recalled afterwards. Within a week, on October 11, 1940, the three black leaders issued a statement to the press denying that they had ever approved the President's military segregation policy and flatly stating that "official approval by the Commander-in-Chief of the Army and Navy of such discrimination and segregation is a stab in the back of democracy...[and] a blow at the patriotism of twelve million Negro citizens." During the final weeks of the presidential campaign, the NAACP organized protest meetings of thousands of African Americans in Northern cities, which served to underline evidence of their increasing support for FDR's opponent, Wendell Wilkie.

In a second, late-October meeting with White, Randolph, and Hill, Roosevelt promised to try to do something to end the restrictions in the army and the navy. He also appointed, evidently at the urging of Supreme Court Justice Felix Frankfurter,[14] William Hastie as civilian aide to the very unsympathetic secretary of war, Henry Stimson, and promoted Colonel Benjamin O. Davis, the only African American army officer of that rank, to brigadier general. Another African American, Campbell Johnson, was appointed civilian aide to the director of the Selective Service.

Stimson was livid at the President's cave-in to these demands. He told the President that the Hastie and Davis appointments were mistakes. By the end of January 1943, Bill Hastie had quit his job as civilian aide to Stimson because he was absolutely cut out of all informational and decisional loops in the department.

Segregation in the military continued during the war, with African Americans gaining only very modest incremental improvements through constant political pressures on the President and his key advisers, and through threats of lawsuits by Marshall. For example, the army set up a Jim Crow training program at Tuskegee College for thirty-three pilots to staff a brand-new but still very segregated 99th Pursuit Squadron. At the time, the army was training thirty thousand white Army Air Corps pilots annually: the thirty-three African American flyers were to become one thousandth of America's air force![15]

The American Red Cross's racial policies paralleled the military's in both world wars. All its activities, from collecting blood for wounded soldiers to serving black soldiers doughnuts and coffee in segregated facilities, followed Jim Crow principles. After January 1942, the Red Cross separated the blood of white and African American donors and, as a matter of policy, practiced blood segregation.

While the Red Cross received protestations from White, Hastie, and others in the Association, its policies remained basically unchanged throughout the war. The Red Cross established "white and colored" Red Cross detachments sent to overseas fighting areas in Europe and the Pacific to give aid and comfort separately to white and African American personnel.

When White and others protested blood segregation and demanded that the Red Cross do the right thing and act "in consonance with the ethical standards upon which the Red Cross was founded," the organization told White that the racist policy was a "matter of tradition and sentiment rather than of science, as there is no known difference in the physical properties of white and Negro blood."[16] However, the discrimination remained during the war.

During World War II, there was a severe shortage of volunteers for the Army Nurse Corps. However, the army refused to use black nurses; at war's end, only 479 served out of a total of 60,000. It was "unthinkable that black nurses could care for white American soldiers. (In June 1944 one unit of sixty-three African American nurses went to a hospital in England, to care for German POWs.)"[17]

## WORLD WAR II "SOLDIER TROUBLES"

Despite a statement by General Benjamin Davis in early October 1942, after a visit to England, that African American soldiers were being well treated and made no complaints to him, African American soldiers *were* complaining about the brutal treatment they were receiving in the military, both at home and in Europe. Just a few weeks after Davis's comments, *Time* magazine, in its October 19, 1942, issue, ran a story titled "Black and White." The article focused on British complaints about the importation into their nation of Jim Crow customs and white soldiers' violence against African American soldiers. The article concluded with this observation: "Much of the trouble that had occurred pointed to the failure of the U.S. Army command to take a strong line against discrimination among its own troops."

By 1942 the NAACP offices in New York and in many branches across the nation were regularly receiving dozens of letters from soldiers and their families about the terrible mistreatment the soldiers experienced in America, England, and Australia. Filed in the NAACP offices under "Soldier Troubles," they told one horror story after another about black soldiers being beaten, shot, and killed by white soldiers and white civilians living in areas around the military bases in the South. The letters and telegrams had a common theme: a plaintive plea for help from their parents and from the NAACP.

The publication of the "Soldier Troubles" stories in the African American press infuriated government agencies, particularly the War and Justice Departments, and led President Roosevelt, in December 1942, to warn White that consideration was being given to issuing indictments of some African American editors and publishers for "sedition" and "interference with the war effort" because of their shrill criticism of the Roosevelt administration and their coverage of "soldier troubles."[18] John Sengstacke, publisher of one of the leading black newspapers, the *Chicago Daily Defender,* outraged at the President's threat, "led a delegation [of black publishers] to Washington, essentially to call the Administration's bluff." He confronted Attorney General Biddle, "telling him 'if you want to close us, go ahead and attempt it.'"[19] The administration took no action against the black press.

The stories continued to appear in both the white and the African American press. One told of "murder, flogging, lynching, desertion and possible treason," and of how white military policemen had flogged and murdered two African American soldiers at Fort Benning, Georgia. The Columbus, Ohio, branch of the NAACP wrote to White asking that the Association "launch the investigation" because, "with thousands of Negroes being inducted into the Army monthly, this matter concerns every Negro home in these United States and also answers the question as to what the National Association does for local causes."[20]

If these accusations of racial brutality were valid, the letters were a damning indictment of the military command's lack of concern about the consequences of allowing racism to continue in the armed forces. Marshall and the Association made plans to investigate all credible, verifiable incidents, using a variety of examiners and help from NAACP branches.

The stories received by the NAACP covered all the services, though the great majority of alleged incidents took place on and off army bases in the South. These "troubles" included allegations involving white soldiers shooting and killing black soldiers, beatings and shootings by white police officers, brutal treatment in military hospitals, and sadistic handling of black soldiers in the field by their white noncommissioned officers (who were mostly from the South).

Other complaints focused on discriminatory treatment of African American soldiers by their officers, including refusal to allow religious services, and failure to provide promised or required technical training as well as base facilities such as recreation halls, movie theaters, chapels, libraries, and post exchanges. African American in-hospital patients were even forced to clean their own hospital wards.

Still other cases involved vicious assaults on African American servicemen by local civilians; in some cases black soldiers were forcibly removed from public buses and beaten. A few letters to the NAACP demanded some kind of justice for families of African American *civilians;* one letter to White came from a grieving widow of a redcap who was killed by a drunken white soldier—and nothing was done to the murderer.[21]

By late 1941, the NAACP's national office began giving these reports case file numbers, and referring ones believed to be credible or verifiable. Arthur Shores and a few other African American attorneys working with Marshall on litigation in the South were asked by White to investigate some of these allegations of racial brutality in Alabama, Mississippi, and Texas. By this time, Marshall had moved to New York City with his wife, and had taken up permanent residence in Manhattan. He did not get to see much of the city because he was crisscrossing America, especially the South and Southwest, arguing dozens of cases, many criminal, involving African Americans accused of major crimes.

But there was a world war on, and millions of men, including more than a million African Americans, were being drafted. There were no exemptions for civil rights attorneys. By 1943, the Inc Fund legal staff consisted only of Marshall and a small number of unpaid cooperating lawyers. On May 4, 1943, Walter White received a letter from William Hastie, at the time still the part-time civilian assistant to Secretary of War Henry L. Stimson: "I want to call to your attention the seriousness of the situation which would confront the NAACP and the general community if Mr. Thurgood Marshall, our Special Counsel, should be taken away from his legal duties" to serve in the military. Referring to the white primary Negro voting rights case then in preparation, as well as teacher salary equalization negotiations then taking place in Florida, Georgia, Alabama, Louisiana, Texas, and Arkansas, all involving Marshall, Hastie noted that the "community value of Mr. Marshall's efforts is incalculable." Furthermore, Hastie pointed out that Marshall was "engaged in activities involving the protection of Negro soldiers in the civilian community."

The executive secretary, who was keenly aware of Marshall's prominent legal role in the NAACP, got the clear message and relayed their concerns to Marshall's draft board, located in Harlem. While Marshall never sought a deferment, and always kept his local draft board in Harlem informed of his activities and his travels, he was never called for military service. He continued his travels in the South, defending African Americans in local trial courts and in the U.S. Supreme Court, winning significant cases, helping African American soldiers who found themselves in great trouble in wartime America.

Marshall was so inundated with nonmilitary litigation that a large number of these "soldier trouble" allegations were passed on to Hastie's office in the War Department for his review and possible investigation of the complaint. Because Hastie was not involved in significant War Department policy matters, he could spend time investigating these complaints. From January through August 1942, over sixty case files were created by the NAACP, in at least twenty of which Hastie intervened and conducted investigations of the complaints.

In some of these cases, where the Department of Justice refused to take action against white persons accused of killing African American soldiers, Marshall got directly involved. In one case from Alexandria, Louisiana, involving an African American military police soldier, Raymond Carr, who was killed by a white civilian police officer, Marshall was committed to the litigation for an entire year.

On November 1, 1942, Carr was shot dead by the policeman, who had ordered Carr to leave his military guard post. Carr refused to disobey orders not to leave his post and was shot in what White described as a "coldblooded murder." After strong protests from the NAACP and a War Department investigation, in March 1943 a state grand jury refused to indict the policeman, forcing Marshall to write to Attorney General Francis Biddle, asking that the Justice Department prosecute the officer under Sections 52 and 54 of Title 18 of the United States Code. "Negro soldiers now present in camps in the South," Marshall wrote, "are there solely by reason of the fact that they are under the jurisdiction of the War Department. Failure of the United States government to protect these soldiers destroys the morale of Negro soldiers and civilians....We once again urge the Department to prosecute in this case."[22]

But, as it had done in earlier cases in Louisiana, Texas, and Arkansas, the Justice Department refused to prosecute, thereby sending what must have seemed a clear signal to white racists that it was okay to shoot down African American soldiers in cold blood. Marshall continued to press for federal prosecution, but no indictment or information was ever presented in federal district court against the white policeman, who continued to patrol the streets of Alexandria, Louisiana. As Marshall noted, in a short, sad letter to a friend, "We have been given the usual run around."

In August 1944, Marshall was involved in a major case involving 50 navy stevedores who had been charged with mutiny and were facing general courts-martial. On July 17, 1942, over 600 African Americans were loading ammunition and incendiary bombs on a ship at the Naval Ammunition Depot at Port Chicago, California, when an explosion tore the ship apart. Over 200 men were killed in the blast, and 240 others were wounded. Fifteen percent of *all* African American naval personnel casualties occurred that night in California. Port Chicago "was the worst homefront disaster of World War II."[23]

Although all personnel were moved out of the area after the disaster, by early August, repairs had been made and work crews were assigned to load ammunition on another navy ship. According to the official navy report, on August 10, 1942, all three divisions of African American navy stevedores, 328 men, refused to perform their duties. After the orders were repeated, 258 still continued to refuse to obey.

The next day the commandant of the Twelfth Naval District visited the men, explained the serious trouble they were in, and asked them to comment about their reasons for refusal. Basically, the reason they gave was the "mass fear arising out of the Port Chicago explosion." Marshall saw it differently, and said that if there had been a few white sailors killed in the Port Chicago explosion, "I don't think it [the mutiny] would have happened. No, that was a racial point with them. No ...white guys were there."[24]

After this meeting with the commandant, all but 50 returned to work. The 208 men who at first refused to perform but then changed their minds and went back to work were tried "by Summary Courts Martial on charges of refusing to obey orders." The fifty who refused to load ammunition were brought "to trial by General Courts Martial on charges of mutiny." Mutiny was a capital crime. If convicted, the men faced the possibility of a death sentence for their actions.[25]

President Roosevelt interceded quickly on behalf of the 208 who, after initially refusing to obey the order, had gone back to work. In a memo to James Forrestal, the new secretary of the navy, he wrote, "It seems to me we should remember in the summary court martials of these 208 men that they were activated by mass fear and that this was understandable. Their punishment should be nominal. FDR."

The NAACP was contacted immediately by families of some of the fifty men facing the much more serious general court-martial charges. Marshall flew out to San Francisco to lead the defense. He had the assistance of one junior naval legal officer. The men were found guilty and sentenced to between eight and fifteen years at hard labor. Marshall contended that "these men are being tried for mutiny solely because of their race and color." As Marshall recalled, "After all the appeals were over, it was in Forrestal's lap." In January 1946, all of them had their sentences commuted and were set free by order of the secretary of the navy.

Marshall traveled to base after base, defending men facing general courts-martial. Things got so hectic that Marshall had Bob Carter, his Inc Fund assistant special counsel, work with him in some of those trials and on the appeals that followed conviction. As Marshall observed ruefully in later years, the navy and army brass "were treating Negroes something awful. And I gave them someplace they could come to. If it got real rough, I'd be there."[26] One positive consequence of the Port Chicago disaster was that it confirmed Forrestal's belief that the discriminatory treatment of African Americans in the navy was wrong. Immediately after the explosion, Forrestal ordered white navy personnel assigned to do ammo depot work at Port Chicago and all other ammunition-loading naval facilities, allowed African Americans to serve on fighting ships, insisted on admission of qualified African Americans to the Naval Academy, and ordered an end to separate facilities for all navy personnel taking advanced training.

Marshall thought the world of Forrestal and considered him "very sympathetic to blacks." As he put it, "Forrestal really got screwed good" because of his policy of fairness. The senior line officers in the navy, who refused to implement Forrestal's policies, "just clobbered him every time they got a chance."[27] The war took its toll on both Jim Forrestal and Bill Hastie. Truman made Forrestal the first secretary of defense (after the reorganization of the services), but lost confidence in him and asked for his resignation. Shortly afterwards, owing to his poor health—both mental and physical—Forrestal was a patient in the navy's hospital at Bethesda, Maryland. On May 22, 1949, evidently in great despair, he committed suicide. Before taking his life, he left a note with some lines from Sophocles' *Ajax:* "Worn by the waste of time / Comfortless, nameless, hopeless save / In the dark prospect of a yawning grave." [28]

Bill Hastie, too, was spiritually "worn by the waste of [his] time" in the War Department. The establishment of the Jim Crow Army Air Corps training facility at Tuskegee, opposed by Hastie, the NAACP, and other civil rights groups, had produced over one hundred young, commissioned African American fighter pilots. But a year later these flyers still had not been given any overseas combat assignments by the War Department. "On the other hand," wrote Roy Wilkins in a letter to Stimson in July 1943, "white cadets who have been graduated [over the past year] are already flying, fighting, and winning medals on the battlefronts in Europe, North Africa, and the Southwest Pacific." [29]

The Tuskegee beating, along with the unwillingness of both the War and Justice Departments to act positively with regard to segregation, discrimination, and racial violence directed toward African American servicemen, was the last straw for Bill Hastie (who had continued his work as dean of Howard's law school while serving in the War Department). As soon as Hastie began presenting his recommendations for integrating the military and all ancillary services, including the nursing corps and the Red Cross, he discovered that he was, as his biographer wrote, an "unwanted appendage," someone forced on the lily-white War Department by a President pressed by the NAACP. [30] His January 31, 1943, resignation was another embarrassment to Roosevelt's administration. He explained that he was resigning because of "reactionary policies and discriminatory practices of the Army Air Force in matters affecting Negroes." Such "racial barriers and humiliating practices" continued to confront the African American soldier and sailor. On the positive side, after leaving his dispiriting War Department assignment, Hastie was able to spend more time working with Marshall and Houston on NAACP litigation, which included preparation and argument of Association cases before the Supreme Court.

Newspaper stories about the naked, ugly reality of Jim Crow in uniform were read and discussed by the African American community. The brutal, violent race riots that took place in 1943 were one consequence of ongoing "soldier troubles" and segregation in the military. Such stories fed the anger and resentment felt by African Americans during the war. Inevitably, the riots were preceded by clashes involving whites and black military personnel.

All it took were minor incidents, a fender bender on a bridge in Detroit, a wild rumor about the death of a black soldier in Harlem, killed by a white police-man while the soldier's mother watched in horror, and the hatred and pent-up wrath from generations of Jim Crow discrimination boiled over into furious, and violent, rioting and killing in the streets of America's cities and towns. These were the unforgettably painful legacies of racial discrimination in World War II. With the war's end, there was no great rejoicing in the African American com-munity. Jim Crow segregation still existed in the military, in the Red Cross, and in every small town and village in the South. While well-meaning military administrators like Forrestal tried to change the racist customs of the military, without the visible imprimatur of the Commander in Chief, not a great deal happened. Things began to change only when Truman became President.

## FROM WAR'S END TO THE KOREAN WAR

After the war, the War Department continued to report to the White House on clashes between African American servicemen and local whites across the nation. The NAACP sent letters to Truman, the secretary of war, and other offi-cials, protesting the continuation of discriminatory treatment of African American servicemen assigned to bases in the South. When White complained about discrimination at Fort Benning, Georgia, and requested a "thorough investigation," his letter was ignored.

The stereotype of the African American had not changed at all. The War Department, in 1945, had issued a brief document titled "Certain Character-istics of the Negro Which Affect Command of Negro Troops." It listed dozens of "characteristics" of the African American soldier for commanders to bear in mind when they led their "colored" troops. Nothing had changed, really, since the 1925 army report. The African American soldier was still stereotyped by the army. He was, the document said,

- Gregarious, extroverted…
- Loud in speech—argumentative…
- Very sensitive: Resentful of correction. Takes same as highly personal. Easily hurt by criticism, especially in public. Appreciative of praise, even the slightest…
- Hot-tempered, to the point of physical reaction…
- Mentally lazy, not retentive, forgetful.
- Ruled by instinct and emotion rather than by reason…
- Stubborn no end. Hard-headed as a Swede.
- Has keen sense of rhythm…
- Difficult to make assume responsibility…[31]

As the veterans came home, many African American servicemen were greeted with violence and brutal beatings, and some were killed on American soil after having survived years of war abroad. The NAACP was informed of lynchings of veterans; the murders took place in Mississippi, Georgia, Louisiana and other Deep South states. That time was referred to by White as the "terrible summer of 1946."[32]

One incident of violence shocked the entire nation. Sergeant Isaac Woodard had spent three years in the army, fighting the Japanese in the South Pacific. He was discharged that summer of 1946 from an army base in Georgia and took a bus for his home in North Carolina. While on the bus, he asked the driver if he could go to a rest room. As White recalled:

> When he returned, Woodard was cursed and threatened by the driver because he had been gone longer than suited the driver's wishes....The driver asked the chief of police to arrest the veteran for being "drunk and disorderly," although Woodard did not drink. When Woodard protested, the chief beat him unmercifully with a blackjack and struck him in both eyes with the end of his nightstick, blinding him forever. The soldier was then thrust into a cell and kept there overnight without food or medical treatment.

Unable to see, Woodard was dragged before a local judge, found guilty and fined fifty dollars. The judge, seeing the defendant's terrible medical state, finally had someone call a veterans' hospital for assistance. It was later determined that, because of the beating, the "corneas of both eyes had been injured beyond repair."

The national outrage at this unspeakable cruelty led Truman to order Clark to investigate and to help in the federal government's prosecution of the police chief. The FBI, with the assistance of local NAACP workers, identified the man and a federal grand jury indicted him. However, as was so typical of Southern justice, "upon being brought to trial he was acquitted to the cheers of a crowded courtroom."[33]

The brutal murder and torture of African American servicemen—and, in the Monroe, Georgia, lynching, of their wives as well—led President Truman, outraged by these attacks, to sign the executive order that created the President's Committee on Civil Rights.

In Memo 615-500-4, dated November 21, 1946, the War Department ordered all African American personnel to Fort Jackson, South Carolina, for their basic training. After the spate of lynchings of black servicemen, the War Department rescinded that order in February 1947 and had all African American soldiers receive their training at Fort Dix, New Jersey (two-thirds of personnel) and Fort Knox, Kentucky (one-third of personnel). Additional training sites were located in California, Washington, and North Carolina. Of course, White and others in the Association complained about the continuation of a segregated military training system, although these segregated camps would be in localities that were less dangerous for black soldiers than those in Georgia, Louisiana, Mississippi, and South Carolina.

The prime question for the War Department, after hostilities ended, was what could be done to improve the military environment for African Americans, from recruitment and training to advancement. In October 1945, General Alvin Gillem, at the request of the secretary of war, was asked to head a Board of Officers on Utilization of Negro Manpower in the Post-War Army to make policy recommendations, after a careful review of the African American soldier's role in America's wars, "his capabilities and his weaknesses, his successes and failures." [34]

The 1946 Gillem Board Report called for an African American soldier quota of 10 percent, which was the proportion of the African American population in the larger society. It also recommended that, "initially, Negro units...be stationed in localities where community attitudes are most favorable." [35] The report caused an immediate controversy within the African American community. The new policy would force African American soldiers out of the army: 16 percent of the army was black, and at least 6 percent would have to be discharged to keep within the Gillem quota. Further, there had to be a "suspension" of African American recruitment until the 10-percent target was reached by attrition.

Moreover, the new policy set a requirement for the entry of African Americans to the service—high school graduation, or else a score of 99 on the army general classification test. There was no graduation requirement for white applicants, and a minimum score of 70 on the same test enabled whites to enter the army. This "special treatment" of the African American triggered instant criticism from the NAACP and the African American press. White charged the War Department with "conscienceless discrimination." However, the Gillem Report became, as the *Daily World*, an Atlanta, Georgia, African American newspaper, noted, the "War Department's Bible." [36]

The report's policies remained in force until the years immediately after Truman's executive order, issued in 1948, that ended discrimination by race or color in the military. In the spring of that year, Congress began debates on the new selective service process, embodied in the proposed Universal Military Training (UMT) Selective Service bill.

In March of that year the Senate Armed Services Committee heard testimony from the Committee Against Jimcrow in Military Service and Training, organized in October 1947 by "non-Communist liberals" and African American leaders.[37] Speaking for the committee were its two African American leaders, Grant Reynolds and A. Philip Randolph. Both urged Congress to pass a substantive conscription bill that would end, once and for all, injustices against African Americans in the military. Randolph warned that if there was "passage now of a Jimcrow draft [bill], it may only result in a mass civil disobedience movement along the lines of the magnificent struggles of the people of India against British imperialism":

> In refusing to accept compulsory military segregation, Negro youth will be serving their fellow men throughout the world....This time Negroes will not take a jimcrow draft lying down. The conscience of the world will be shaken as by nothing else when thousands and thousands of us second-class Americans choose imprisonment in preference to permanent military slavery...."Never again."[38]

On July 26, 1948, President Truman responded to the anger of Randolph, White, and other African Americans. Where President Roosevelt had been overly cautious, President Truman moved aggressively to try to end segregation in the armed services. That day he issued Executive Order 9981, in which he declared that "there shall be equality of treatment and opportunity for all persons in the armed services without regard to race, color, religion, or national origin," and that it "shall be put into effect as rapidly as possible." The EO also created the President's Committee on Equality of Treatment and Opportunity, chaired by former solicitor general Charles Fahey, to work with the Department of Defense and the three major services "in order to determine in what respect [the military's] rules, procedures, and practices may be altered or improved with a view to carrying out the policy of this order." The committee was charged with making appropriate recommendations to the President.

In 1949 the committee, in a memorandum to Truman, applauded recent efforts of the army to end segregation practices, but expressed concern about the Gillem quota: "There remains the problem of the over-all racial quota. The Army presently restricts Negro strength to 10% of total army strength. The Committee has contended that the quota system should be eliminated because its racial limitation is directed solely at Negroes."[39] The committee and the army agreed to address the quota problem together over the following months. The army command indicated that it would not reject the committee's recommendation to do away with the racial quota.

On February 7, 1950, Fahey sent Truman a memo describing the policy change. An "achievement quota" would replace the existing racial quota. Under the policy, all recruits, regardless of race or color, would be required to score at least 90 on the army's classification test. Fahey could not predict, with any great accuracy, what percentage of African American servicemen would be in uniform under the new policy. He did, however, tell Truman that it might be as high as 17 percent and, given the achievement quota, they would be better suited for military life than in the past. On March 27, 1950, the new army policy was formally put into practice. It was not fully implemented for some time.

On May 22, 1950, the Fahey Committee could inform the President that the air force and the navy had started to move forward: navy personnel were integrated on all ships, and "Negroes are presently serving in every navy general rating throughout the fleet." The report also noted that the air force "has opened up all Air Force jobs and schools to Negro airmen." Within the first eight months of the new policy, "75 percent of the 25,000 Negroes in the Air Force had been transferred to integrated units."

Commenting on these significant changes, on June 5, 1950, *Time* magazine, in a story appropriately titled "Armed Forces: Ahead of the Country," applauded the "quiet progress" taking place in the military. In just twenty-two months, *Time* reported, the President's new integration policy had led to what "amounted to the greatest change in service custom since the abandonment of the cat-o'-nine-tails." One African American soldier summed up the change when he was quoted as saying, "It's better in the Army than outside."

## THE KOREAN WAR

Less than a month after the *Time* story appeared, the North Korean Communist forces invaded U.S.-occupied South Korea, and America was at war again. Racism in the military persisted, the most glaring example of which was afforded by America's commander in the Far East, General of the Army Douglas MacArthur, in his treatment of black troops under his command. There was still a segregated army fighting in Korea during the first year of the Korean War because of the general's belief that African American troops were inferior in battle.

An African American newsman, Jimmy Hicks, just back from Korea, informed Thurgood Marshall about "drumhead" courts-martial of more than fifty African American army men. At the same time, Marshall and the NAACP office had begun receiving letters from African American soldiers fighting in Korea about the continued discriminatory treatment they were receiving from their white officers. The letter-writers spoke, as they had in World War II, of the disproportionate number of courts-martial of African American soldiers and the harsh sentences meted out when they were convicted. As Marshall wrote, in his 1951 "Report on Korea," "[What] has happened in Korea is an old, old story—as old as Jim Crow in the armed services. It is a story of the sacrifice of Negro troops upon the altar of segregation."[40]

One particular court-martial conviction—of an African American officer, Leon A. Gilbert, charged, convicted, and sentenced to death for "misbehavior in the face of the enemy"—finally led the NAACP to send Marshall to Korea to investigate that and other courts-martial. In September 1950, Marshall heard about the Gilbert sentence while at the same time the Association received letters requesting NAACP help from the three dozen other African Americans, all from Gilbert's 24th Infantry Battalion (colored) of the 25th Army Division and all "tried and convicted of cowardice, of misbehavior in the presence of the enemy, of failure to perform their assigned duties."

"Something had to be wrong," Marshall wrote, and the Association decided "that we must get to the root of this trouble." This would be, observed Marshall in his report, "the most important mission thus far of my career." Initially, both the State Department and MacArthur tried to stop Marshall from going over to Korea, but the President overruled them.[41] (Years later, Marshall recalled wryly that the NAACP, concerned about his safety in the war zone, had taken out a $100,000 life insurance policy for him. "When I got on the plane and looked at the policy, it was not valid in Korea and Japan—which was where I was going.")[42]

Marshall arrived in Japan on January 14, 1951. He spent the next five weeks examining the trial records of the thirty-six men who had asked for NAACP assistance, interviewing all but two of them in the stockade where they were confined, and reviewing the records of twelve other African Americans who had been convicted of less serious offenses. Accompanied by one of MacArthur's staff officers, Marshall visited the front lines to interview close to one hundred witnesses to the alleged acts of cowardice and misbehavior. He visited Lieutenant Gilbert on six different occasions to get the full story of his behavior at the front.

Marshall wrote in his diary, on January 21, that "things are beginning to shape up. These men are guilty of 'speedy justice,' if nothing more."[43] During the interviews with the convicted men and the many witnesses, "one unbelievable story after another came to my attention." In addition to the common complaint of the convicted soldiers that their white officers despised their "niggers" and treated them poorly, Marshall heard about suppressed evidence and factual data that would have acquitted many of them.

Men "with air-tight defenses had not presented evidence clearly demonstrating their innocence of the charges," observed Marshall, explaining that "the men were seized with despair...and hopelessness." As one said, "It wasn't worth it. We knew when we went to trial that we would be convicted—and we were hoping and praying that we would only get life....We know the score."[44]

Some black soldiers, convicted of cowardice, were in army hospitals at the time of their alleged offenses. (When the NAACP appealed, the life imprisonment convictions were overturned and the soldiers returned to active duty.) Even men on mess duty well behind the lines were accused of cowardice, arrested, charged, convicted, and sentenced to ten years of hard labor. The NAACP again appealed, and the convictions were reversed by the army's Judge Advocate's Office in Washington, D.C. All told, Marshall's report indicated that sixty African American and eight white soldiers were accused of violating Article 75 of the Articles of War ("misbehavior in the face of the enemy"), although there were four times as many whites as blacks in the 25th Division. Thirty-two blacks were sentenced, against two whites. The white soldiers received modest sentences (five years and three years, with both sentences later reduced), while the African Americans received sentences ranging from death (one), life imprisonment (fifteen), fifty years (one), twenty-five years (two), twenty years (three), fifteen years (one), ten years (seven), and five years (two).[45]

What he found in Korea, he said time and again, was contemptible: "There were records of trials, so-called trials, in the middle of the night where men were sentenced to life imprisonment, in hearings that lasted less than ten minutes."[46] As Marshall noted in his 1951 report, "justice in Korea may have been blind, but [it was] not color blind." MacArthur had tried to hide the records of these drum-head courts-martial. "I think he was going to deep-six them," Marshall wrote, and he would have but for Marshall's insistence on reviewing them.[47]

Marshall presented MacArthur with a preliminary report of his findings before returning to New York. It was a grim meeting. He told the general that the men were tried "in an atmosphere making justice impossible," that the trials were "rooted in the Jim Crow policies still persisting in the Army," that, after his five weeks of intense research, "the NAACP has evidence to clear most of these hapless men of the unfounded charge of cowardice," and that "so long as we have racial segregation in the Army we will have the type of injustice of which these courts-martial are typical." As he noted years later, "we were able to bust every one of the convictions. Although we didn't get them all out scot free, we got most of them out scot free, and the others a very short term."

Finally, Marshall bluntly informed MacArthur that, while he "had no direct hand in the courts martial," he was responsible for the injustices perpetrated on the African American soldiers because he had "failed to implement the President's order for the elimination of segregation from the armed services.... While there are a few mixed units in the Army in Korea, the general practice is one of rigid segregation."

Upon his return to New York, Marshall gave his report to White and then presented it to the Association's National Board. He sent copies of the final report to both the President and General MacArthur. After the appeals were taken by Marshall to the army's Judge Advocate General's office in Washington,

D.C., twenty of the thirty-two men who were convicted for violating Article 75 had their sentences reduced. "But we have just begun," Marshall wrote in May 1951. "The NAACP is working to secure the appropriate exoneration or abbreviation of sentence for every man treated unjustly because of his race or color."

By the end of the Korean War (an armistice was signed that ended formal hostilities in June 1953), over 90 percent of the army units in Korea had been integrated. MacArthur, fired by Truman for insubordination some months after his meetings with Marshall, was replaced by General Matthew Ridgway, who immediately implemented Truman's 1948 executive order. While vestiges of discriminatory policies remained, by the end of the Korean War there were indeed significant changes in the armed forces.

After his defense of the convicted soldiers ended in 1951, Marshall returned, full-time, to the battles for an end to formal segregation and racial discrimination in America's civil society. Black veterans of World War II and Korea would become the core plaintiffs in the lawsuits leading to victory against Jim Crow in the 1950s.

# 6

## THE PUBLIC EDUCATION BATTLES BEGIN: *BROWN V. BOARD*

Thurgood,' said a psychologist friend, 'is a delicate balance of turmoils.'"[1] When he returned from his Korean investigation, he was worn out, physically and spiritually, not only by travel but by the weight of responsibility he bore. He had to bring appeals to the military's Judge Advocate General's office, make the reports to the board, write the formal report for the NAACP, and contact the families of the imprisoned African American soldiers.

Despite this fatigue in body and spirit, Marshall was soon fighting once more on the Southern battleground of segregated public school education. In 1951, twenty-one states and the nation's capital had some form of segregated public school education, as specified in the states' constitutions or through state statutes that either required or permitted public school segregation. Marshall and his legal colleagues were about to challenge the validity of all those statutes and constitutional requirements—against almost overwhelming odds.

By April of that year, lawsuits challenging public school segregation had been initiated in a number of states. The NAACP lawyers worked with brave African American parents and their children to attack segregation in public school education. In 1949, sixty-seven parents and their children in Clarendon County, South Carolina, led by navy war veteran Harry Briggs Jr., had demanded that the county school board provide them with equal school facilities. (As soon as Briggs became involved, he was fired from his job as an auto mechanic, and his wife lost her job as a maid for a local white family.) The almost three hundred white students in the county were taught in two well-built schools that boasted a student-teacher ratio of twenty-eight to one. In contrast, the county's eight hundred African American students were housed in three old, ramshackle buildings; there the ratio was one teacher to forty-eight students. While the white children were bused to school, black children had to walk as much as five miles one way. By the time the case entered the federal district court, initially in May 1950, the parents were asking the court to issue an injunction to prevent the school board, all white, from making any educational distinctions based on race or color.

In the District of Columbia, on September 11, 1950, African American parents, with help from James Nabrit, attempted, without success, to integrate Sousa Junior High School. This failed action led to a lawsuit brought by Nabrit in federal district court in the District of Columbia. In June 1951, Topeka, Kansas, African American parents asked a federal district court to invalidate a Kansas statute that allowed local school boards to segregate on the basis of color. In October 1951, black parents in Wilmington, Delaware, challenged the constitutionality, in state court, of separate public school systems. And, finally, in Virginia, in February 1952, a three-judge federal district court was asked by African American parents to invalidate the separate educational facilities in Prince Edward County. Thus began the frontal assault on *Plessy*—and Thurgood Marshall was scared to death about the outcome.

He wasn't too sure how the Court would go on the question of overturning the *Plessy* precedent, and he was concerned because so many people had invested so much—jobs, money, security, and safety—in the litigation effort. To keep faith with them, Marshall had to fight within the Association to press ahead and attack segregation itself. For them, as Marshall said in the Supreme Court during oral argument in December 1952, "slavery is perpetuated in these [school segregation] statutes."[2] For many in the NAACP, however, a good "colored" school was all that was desired. Gaining equalization of facilities meant better equipment, new books, a new building, new buses to take their children to school, and, most important, the continuation of jobs for African American teachers and educational administrators.

Marshall also knew that "separation provided its own psychic security [and that] integration was far riskier,"[3] but he continued to believe that educational equality for black Americans was the key to resolving the many problems they faced. Equal education provided "the basic tools and opportunities that might enable people to rise." A former law clerk of Marshall's, Cass Sunstein, commented that his decades-long battle against *Plessy* "was undertaken, first and foremost, with an eye toward the achievement of equal educational opportunity...the social service most indispensable for an equal chance in life. Segregated education stamped notions of racial inferiority into children at an early, even decisive stage."[4]

Marshall was all too aware that there were four kinds of federal trial judges working in the South, some of whom were "completely hostile," while others, though not openly hostile, were "completely evasive...[they] can find all types of legal gymnastics to either prevent a ruling, delay a ruling, or try to tie a ruling up so that it cannot be appealed." There were also judges who "rule correctly, rule as they believe the law to be." And there was the "new type of judge...who is willing not only to rule as he believes the law to be, but to rule with courage and sufficient firmness that everybody will not only respect the ruling as is but respect the ruling in all of its ramifications."[5]

Marshall also knew that there were very few of the "new type of judge," jurists "with heart," sitting and deciding cases brought by the NAACP. Among this minority were federal judges like Frank Johnson of Alabama and J. Waties Waring of South Carolina. The probability that Marshall would lose in the lower federal courts was high. Only the Supreme Court could overturn *Plessy v. Ferguson*—and only by appealing adverse rulings in the lower federal courts could Marshall and the NAACP question legally "whether the states and the District of Columbia have constitutional power to segregate white and Negro students in separate schools at the elementary and secondary levels." The strategy was straightforward: "NAACP attorneys, acting in behalf of the parents and Negro children, in each case maintain that segregation *per se* is discrimination and, accordingly, a violation of the equal protection clause of the Fourteenth Amendment to the Constitution of the United States. The D.C. case is based on the due process clause of the Fifth Amendment."[6]

## MARSHALL'S NAACP STRATEGY IMPLEMENTED: THE PUBLIC SCHOOL SEGREGATION CASES

In 1950, Juanita Hall received a Tony for her acting as Bloody Mary in South Pacific, the hit musical. Althea Gibson was the first African American tennis player to compete in the U.S. Tennis Open, and Chuck Cooper became the first African American player to be drafted by a professional basketball team, the Boston Celtics. Ralph Bunche, an ally of W. E. B. Du Bois, became the first African American to win the Nobel Peace Prize for his mediation work in Palestine.

It was also the year when a handful of suits went forward in the states and, first in South Carolina, launched the tactical attacks on *Plessy*. The lawsuits maintained that segregation per se could never be constitutional or ethical because it caused psychic injury to the young African American students attending segregated schools. For the first time, in *Briggs* (and in the other cases), Marshall presented a large body of evidence "of a sociological nature testifying to the debilitating effects of segregation on the mind and the emotions." He elicited testimony from thirty-two social scientists who all agreed that "regardless of facilities which are provided, enforced segregation is psychologically detrimental to members of the segregated group."[7]

Psychological and emotional injury, called "stigmatic injury" by the lawyers, was a new legal classification. It entered into these public school segregation cases because the NAACP had to show injury to the plaintiffs in order to sue in the federal courts for declaratory or injunctive relief. In 1950, in *Sweatt* and in *McLaurin*, Marshall had hinted at this type of injury, but the higher education cases rested on a total lack of educational facilities for black Americans. However, when Chief Justice Vinson, speaking for the unanimous Court, indicated that a graduate or a law student was adversely affected by the "intangibles" associated with enrollment at a hastily created African American graduate program or law school, he was talking in part about psychological injury suffered by such students because of the pattern and practice of segregation.

Psychological injury was central to the research of Kenneth Clark, an African American social psychologist and a member of the faculty at the City University of New York. He and his wife, Mamie K. Clark, had done extensive research on the general problem of "early levels in the development of consciousness of self in Negro preschool children with special reference to emergent race consciousness."[8] They had devised two tests to measure the attitudes of African American children toward race and racism. In the first test, children were shown four dolls, identical except for their color: two were brown, two were white. The kids were asked which they thought was the "nicest" or "prettiest." Clark found that the children showed "an unmistakable preference for the white doll and a rejection of the brown doll." In the second test, African American children were asked to represent themselves by using crayons to color in outline drawings of boys and girls. A surprising number chose white or pink crayons. Clark concluded that the children felt inferior to white children and unaccepting of themselves.

In a major piece, titled "Racial Prejudice Among American Minorities,"[9] Clark held that racial self-hatred was common and came about as a result of the African American's poor self-image, one developed in a racially discriminatory and segregated cultural environment. Not allowed to assimilate into the American melting pot, the black person remained an outsider, an "Invisible Man" in the larger, white, community and, as early as four to five years of age, exhibited "self-rejection."

Although Marshall read Clark's research and used him as an expert witness in the *Briggs* suit, he had already learned about stigmatic injury from his travels across the South. As he recalled years later:

> It [stigmatic injury] was so clear...and I realized that, talking to people. In the South, I knew a man in a poolroom in Little Rock, Arkansas, about 1941...and he said, "Lawyer, you got anything to do with this business of when you come back after you die?" I said, "You talkin' about reincarnation?" He said, "I don't know, is that what it is?" I said, "Yes." He said, "Well, if you got anything to do

with it, when I come back, I don't care whether it's a man, woman, dog, or cat, let it be *white*."[10]

In the South Carolina case, *Harry Briggs, Jr., et al. v. R. W. Elliott,* and in the other four cases winding their way through the court system, Marshall introduced findings about the psychological pain of stigmatic injury. He was challenging the constitutionality of South Carolina's provision, in Article II, Section 7, of its constitution, which stated that "separate schools shall be provided for children of the white and colored races, and no child of either race shall ever be permitted to attend a school provided for children of the other race."

The parents had originally challenged only the inequality of educational facilities and opportunities for their children, but now asked the federal district court in Charleston to issue an injunction "restraining and enjoining the school board from making a distinction on account of race or color in maintaining public schools." In November 1950, the NAACP argued that its goal was the abolition of the segregated school system and the case was then heard by a three-judge panel in federal district court in late May 1951. During the trial, the attorney for the county school board told the court that plans were under way to "equalize" the physical facilities and that it would be accomplished in a reasonable amount of time. Marshall was again reminded of the violent reality of African American life in South Carolina. As he was leaving the court, a local white attorney approached him while the trial was in progress and said, "If you show your black ass in Clarendon County again, you're a dead man."[11]

The judges ruled, two to one, that as long as black and white schoolchildren in a segregated school system were provided with equal accommodations, segregation was a constitutionally permitted public policy. U.S. District Court judge J. Waties Waring issued a forceful dissent, saying that, to him, "it was clearly apparent, as it should be to any thoughtful person, irrespective of having such expert testimony, that segregation in education can never produce equality and that it is an evil that must be eradicated."[12]

Waring, who practiced law in Charleston, was a white upper-class southerner born and reared in that city. He had been a federal district court judge since 1941. After over thirty years of marriage to an aristocratic Charlestonian, he had divorced her in 1945 to marry a Yankee from Detroit. His new wife, Elizabeth Avery, was openly critical of the racial norms of the South and had convinced her jurist husband of the evils of racial segregation. His change of heart was accelerated when, as a federal judge, Waring presided over cases involving peonage (in which blacks were forced to work for whites because of debts owed), black teacher salaries, and, in 1948, *Elmore v. South Carolina,* that state's own white primary case. In these three sets of cases, Waring saw the brutal ugliness of racism. In those cases and others, he ruled against the state and for the NAACP. Waring thus became a pariah, an outcast, in his hometown.

By 1945, Judge Waring had become acquainted with Marshall, Roy Wilkins, and Walter White. The association with White deepened after Waring presided over the 1946 federal trial of the South Carolina sheriff accused of blinding war veteran Isaac Woodard. When the white jury quickly acquitted the sheriff, Waring was truly "heartsick over the outcome." He later confided to a friend, "I was shocked by the hypocrisy of my government...in submitting that dreadful case."[13]

After 1946, Waring and his wife often met with the Whites and the Marshalls when they visited New York City. He was in constant written communication with White and, after 1946, with Marshall. After his dissent in *Briggs,* Waring sought to provide legal advice and counsel to the NAACP lawyers. For example, in June 25, 1951, he wrote to Marshall, suggesting a number of South Carolina cases that could be used to the NAACP's advantage in preparing Supreme Court briefs. In one of his warmly supportive letters, he predicted that the Supreme Court would rule the right way, for he had an "abiding faith that the right must and shall here prevail." Then he wrote, "Congratulations on your magnificent work for our people."[14] Shortly after his dissent in *Briggs,* in 1952, Waring retired from the court and moved to New York City, where he died in 1968. His body was returned to Charleston for burial. About a dozen whites attended the funeral—and more than three hundred African Americans.

## THE U.S. SUPREME COURT
## HEARS THE SCHOOL SEGREGATION CASES

After the split judgment against the NAACP's plaintiffs in *Briggs,* Marshall asked the Supreme Court, in June 1952, to note probable jurisdiction and hear arguments in *Briggs* regarding the question of "whether racial separation in public elementary and high schools is a constitutionally possible pattern."[15] The Court agreed, and oral argument for the *Briggs* case was scheduled for December 9–12, 1952. By that time, all the other cases had proceeded through the lower court systems and were ready or nearly ready for appeals to the Supreme Court. The Court therefore granted certiorari in the other four public school segregation cases (from Kansas, Delaware, Virginia, and the District of Columbia) shortly after announcing that the justices would hear the arguments in *Briggs.*

Opposing Marshall in the Court was John W. Davis, then seventy-eight years old, a well-known West Virginian, a Democrat who had been the party's nominee for President in the 1924 election. For thirty years, Davis "had been the most prestigious U.S. constitutional lawyer," observed *Time* magazine at the time. Davis was also a good friend and political ally of South Carolina's governor in 1952, James Byrnes. The two men had known each other since 1911, when both were Democratic congressmen. In 1952, Davis was living in retirement on Long Island. He had argued more than 250 cases before the Supreme Court, mostly in corporate litigation representing his Wall Street clients. Byrnes visited Davis in New York and persuaded the lawyer to lead the defense of school segregation in the litigation about to go to the Court.[16] It was to be the elderly lawyer's last appearance before the justices. In March 1955, less than a year after the Court announced its initial opinion in *Brown*, Davis, who always wintered in the South, died in Charleston, South Carolina.

Briefs from the contesting parties in all five school segregation cases had been presented to the Supreme Court during the summer and early fall of 1952. In late September, Marshall filed an appendix to appellants' briefs titled "The Effects of Segregation and the Consequences of Desegregation: A Social Science Statement." It was a masterful presentation of the stigmatic-injury argument, and it was presented by a distinguished group of thirty-two of the world's most renowned academics. The list included Floyd and Gordon Allport, Jerome Bruner, Hadley Cantril, Isidor Chein, Kenneth Clark, Else Frenkel-Brunswik, R. M. McIver, Robert K. Merton, Robert Redfield, Arnold Rose, and Samuel Stouffer, among others.

When the cases came to the Court for argument in December 1952, a majority of white Americans still held the hateful stereotypical views of African Americans. Letters to the justices of the Court overwhelmingly reflected this ugly prejudice. Justice Hugo Black's mailbox was inundated by letters from Southern whites, including some of his relatives and his former Sunday school students who pleaded with the Alabaman to "save our way of life."[17] And one Aurora Chestnut, in a letter to Chief Justice Fred M. Vinson, told him that "in a grocery you see peas with peas, beans with beans, corn with corn, beef with beef. Once in a while you will see everything jumbled up in vegetable soup. But each vegetable soup is with other vegetable soups. Like to like. Negro to negro. White to white."[18]

There were a few whites like Charles Hamilton, who wrote Vinson from his home in Corinth, Mississippi, to assure him that "if the implementation of any decision against segregation could be allowed five years or so to be worked out by grades…half the parents would take the elimination of segregation without hostility, unless urged on by…demagogs [*sic*] and press." But the overwhelming message received by the U.S. Supreme Court justices was a negative one.

Some of the brethren were not happy having the Court thrust into the center of the segregation controversy. According to Philip Elman, a former law clerk of

Frankfurter's who was in the U.S. Solicitor General's Office at this time, "the Court was nowhere near ready to take on the issue. The Justices (except for Black and Douglas) were deliberately pursuing a strategy of procrastination. The Court's strategy, and this was the Frankfurter-Jackson strategy, was to delay, delay, delay—putting off the issue as long as possible."[19]

Jackson's law clerk during the 1952 term was William H. Rehnquist, much later (after Rehnquist joined the Court in 1972) Marshall's nemesis. Rehnquist prepared a draft for his boss, Robert Jackson, titled "A Few Expressed Prejudices on the Segregation Cases," which urged retention of *Plessy*. "As I see it, either you accept *Plessy* or overrule it." Rehnquist's advice:

> To the argument made by Thurgood, not John, Marshall that a majority may not deprive a minority of its constitutional right, the answer must be that while this is sound in theory, in the long run it is the majority who will determine what the constitutional rights of the minority are....I realize that [this] is an unpopular and unhumanitarian position, for which I have been excoriated by "liberal" colleagues, but I think *Plessy v. Ferguson* was right and should be reaffirmed. If the Fourteenth Amendment did not enact Spencer's *Social Statics*, it just as surely did not enact Myrdal's *American Dilemma*.[20]

For Jackson, the "cryptic words of the Fourteenth Amendment solved nothing" in the area of public school education. But the cases were coming to the Court, and he needed help. While not agreeing with Rehnquist's views about *Plessy*, Jackson was "perplexed" by some of the questions these race relations cases raised: "What is the function of the Court in the matter?" Would the Court's intervention stir up virulent anticommunism in the country? "There is no doubt," he wrote to Charles Fairman, "that the present rather hysterical state of fear of communists, etc., is due in some large part to the identification of left-wingers with this movement to end segregation....Nothing promotes fascism as surely as a real and widespread popular fear of communism and 'radicalism.'"[21]

If Jackson was perplexed, the Chief Justice was not. Vinson was unwilling to accept the argument that *Plessy* was no longer viable precedent for the nation. For him, the "body of law [in] back of us [was very clear] on separate but equal. It was hard [for the Court to] get away from the long continued acceptance [of segregation] in the District of Columbia." Separate but equal "had been the law of the land for over a half-century, and he was not ready to change it....[Vinson] was not going to overrule *Plessy*."[22]

Felix Frankfurter was deeply concerned about the Court's growing involvement in the race segregation matter. "Issues legal in form but embroiled in explosive psychological and political attitudes [now] require disposition by this

Court," he wrote in September 1952, a few months before the Court heard arguments in the public education cases. He reminded his brethren that

> it is not our duty to give a Constitutional stamp to our merely personal attitudes toward these issues, however deep individual convictions may be. The opposite is true. It is our duty not to act on our merely personal views. However passionately any of us may feel, however fiercely any one of us may believe that such a policy of segregation undoubtedly expresses the tenacious conviction of Southern States is both unjust and shortsighted, he travels outside his judicial authority if on the basis of his private feelings he declares unconstitutional the policy of segregation.

For the cautious, conservative jurist, there was the danger that such "a decision...would be disobeyed, [and] would be the beginning rather than the end of a controversy."[23]

Justice Hugo Black was categorical about the issue of race segregation and *Plessy*. He was in fundamental disagreement with his fellow southerners on the Court. "Let's overrule *Plessy,*" Black urged his brethren. Justice Douglas joined Black on this issue.

Black's son, Hugo junior, recalled a conversation he had with his father in 1952 before the oral arguments in the school segregation cases. Living in Alabama, Hugo junior had been approached by local Democratic Party leaders. Would he be interested in running for Congress? He spoke to the judge about the possibility and "was surprised and a little alarmed by his answer." Black had asked his son to fly up to Washington to discuss the matter, and when the young attorney arrived, Black told him about the public education segregation cases on the docket that term, cases that were challenging *Plessy*. Said the father, "I agree with old Justice Harlan's dissent in *Plessy v. Ferguson*. I don't believe segregation is constitutional."[24]

The oral arguments took place on December 9–12, 1952. The Supreme Court building was extremely crowded; African Americans stood in line for hours in the cold mornings to get into the small Court chambers and hear Marshall and the others argue the cases. The justices were told by Virginia's attorney general, J. Lindsay Almond Jr., that if desegregation was ordered, the order "would destroy the public school system in Virginia." When the Chief Justice asked how that would happen, Almond replied that the taxpayers would not vote funds to maintain desegregated public schools. It was "hard, sound reality that the 5,243 Negro teachers in Virginia would not be employed to teach white children in a tax-supported system in Virginia."

Marshall argued that "the rank and file people in the South will support any decision this court hands down." Jackson, from the bench, suggested to Marshall that it was up to Congress, and not the Court, to establish a policy on segregation. And Frankfurter remarked that "we can argue for hours whether [public school segregation] is a violation of the Constitution." Justice Harold Burton asked Marshall whether or not "changing times" should lead to a changing interpretation of the Constitution's Fourteenth Amendment by the Court. Marshall responded that it was his "contention that if segregation was necessary in 1865, it is not necessary now."

During one point in the oral argument, Marshall was able to string a few sentences together before being interrupted by one of the brethren. There was absolute silence as Marshall spoke:

> I got the feeling on hearing the discussion yesterday that when you put a white child in a school with a whole lot of colored children, the child would fall apart or something. Everybody knows that is not true. Those same kids in Virginia and South Carolina—and I have seen them do it—they play in the streets together, they play on their farms together, they go down the road together, they separate to go to school, they come out of school and play ball together. They have to be separated in school. Why, of all the multitudinous groups of people in this country, [do] you have to single out the Negroes and give them this separate treatment?... The only thing it can be is an inherent determination that the people who were formerly in slavery, regardless of anything else, shall be kept as near that stage as is possible. And now is the time, we submit, that this court should make it clear that it is not what the Constitution stands for.

Marshall had made a direct attack on the constitutionality of the use of the *Plessy* precedent in public school education. The three days of oral arguments left him somewhat depressed. Davis was at his smooth, Southern best. A great deal of respect, Marshall felt, had been shown the octogenarian lawyer by the Court. Chief Justice Vinson and Justices Jackson, Frankfurter, and Reed had asked Marshall tough, troubling questions and made comments from the bench that could only be considered negative ones. He returned to New York very worried about the outcome of the cases.

On December 13, 1952, one day after the oral arguments had concluded, the Supreme Court held the first of a number of conference sessions to discuss the school segregation cases. As Marshall had seen in open Court, the justices were deeply divided about what the Court should, or could, do. Marshall and the NAACP, from the start of arguments in these cases, refused to "concede equality without integration," [25] according to another lawyer working with Marshall, William T. Coleman Jr. (who had been the first black law clerk at the Supreme Court—for Felix Frankfurter in 1948).

The December 13, 1952, conferees were sharply divided on the merits of retaining or overturning *Plessy*. According to the conference notes taken by Justices Burton, Clark, and Jackson, there were possibly five justices who leaned in favor of overturning *Plessy:* Black, Douglas, Burton, Minton, and Frankfurter. Four others, including Chief Justice Vinson and Associate Justices Jackson, Reed, and Clark, were unwilling to rule that, as a matter of law (as opposed to social or political policy), *Plessy* was unconstitutional.

Vinson was unwilling to act in an area in which Congress should legislate— if it desired to do so. If the Court acted, he said, its action would lead to the "complete abolition of public school systems in the South." In a remark aimed at Black, Vinson went on to say that while "boldness was essential, wisdom was indispensable" in this area of law. Black, however, undeterred by Vinson, said that while there "would be some violence," he was "compelled for [him]self to say that segregation is [an] idea of inferiority...segregation *per se* violates [the Fourteenth] Amendment....[He] votes to end segregation." As Justice Clark noted, in his record of the conversation, Black said that he knew that segregation came about because "Southerners saw the Negro as inferior." Because he believed that the Fourteenth Amendment had, "as its basic purpose, the abolition of castes," Black strongly urged *Plessy*'s immediatre overturn.

Reed defended *Plessy* because there had been "great progress in the South." He refused to acknowledge the NAACP's argument that "17 states are denying equal protection or due process....Ten [more] years," he suggested, "would make [the blacks] really equal." The Court should "uphold segregation as constitutional."

Frankfurter, concerned about the catastrophic effect of a Court opinion at that time, began to discuss the possibility of reargument in this conference session. He was the "grand strategist" of the Court in the working out of the process the Court was to follow in its effort to decide the segregation cases. He was, "to use the Yiddish word that Frankfurter used all the time, the *Kochleffel.* It means cooking spoon, stirring things up; the man stirring everything up inside the Court was Frankfurter." The Court "can't finish on [the] merits [and therefore Frankfurter] would reargue all [of the cases]."[26]

It was "very simple for me," said Douglas. The Court "can't avoid [the] conclusion reached that [a state] cannot classify on [the basis of] color. It is not in [the] realm of argument." Douglas's notes recorded that Burton would go "full length to upset segregation," whereas Clark was concerned about the fact that the Court had "led the states on to believe [that] separate but equal [was] OK." Minton believed that there should be "no classification on [the] basis of race." Justice Jackson, as Clark recorded in his notes, was "not conscious of the problem [of school segregation] until I came here [to Washington, D.C.]." He said that "nothing in the Marshall briefs tells me that this [*Plessy*] is unconstitutional,

Marshall's brief starts and ends with sociology." According to Burton's notes, Jackson suggested that a reading of the legislative and judicial history did not, until this point (1952), indicate that segregation was unconstitutional, and though the Court could abolish *Plessy* for policy reasons, he could not see a legal basis for overturning the 1896 opinion.[27]

No formal vote was taken in December 1952. The Court moved on to other cases on its docket, returning to the school segregation cases throughout the spring of 1953. In the meantime, in January 1953, an impatient, restless Marshall wrote to Bill Hastie (Charlie Houston had died two years earlier, and Hastie had since become Marshall's closest ally and counselor) to let him know that he was going to call a planning meeting of the NAACP legal staff and its cooperating attorneys to look at the education cases and also to continue the planning for additional litigation in other areas of racial discrimination, including housing.

At its May 29, 1953, conference, against the wishes of Black and Douglas, a divided and floundering Court agreed to set reargument in the cases for the following fall term, and developed five basic questions for the attorneys to address at reargument:

1. What evidence is there that the Congress which ratified the Fourteenth Amendment contemplated or did not contemplate, understood or did not understand, that it would abolish segregation in public schools?
2. What was the understanding of the framers about "abolishing such segregation"?
3. Is it within the Court's power, in construing the Amendment, to abolish segregation in the public schools?
4–5. What kinds of remedies could the Court devise should it conclude that the Fourteenth Amendment abolished segregation in the public schools?

Its reargument order contained another surprise, especially for the lawyers defending *Plessy*. The Court said that the "Attorney General of the United States is invited to take part in the oral argument and to file an additional brief if he so desires." Justice Black had urged the brethren not to invite the attorney general. "I do not think that this Court should permit itself to become involved in current political controversies." His was a solitary voice, and Eisenhower's new attorney general was invited to participate in the discussions.[28]

Black was correct about the invitation causing political repercussions. James Byrnes, then Democratic governor of South Carolina and a friend and supporter of Eisenhower in the 1952 presidential election, quickly put pressure on the

President to have the federal government refuse to file a brief in the Court. As Eisenhower's attorney general, Herbert Brownell, said, confirming Justice Black's apprehensions, "the president was bombarded during this period by southern friends who sought to have the federal government refuse to participate in *Brown*." [29]

Within weeks of the order, other Southern governors were writing President Eisenhower, urging him to have his attorney general support them in their fight in the Supreme Court. Allan Shivers, the governor of Texas, in a letter of July 16, 1953, pointed out that "this unusual Supreme Court invitation [is] an attempt to embarrass you and your Attorney General: I trust that he [Brownell] will see the implications involved and advise the Court that this local problem should be decided on the local and state level." [30] Louisiana's governor, Robert Kennon, wrote Eisenhower that any federal "edict contrary to the established order and customs could well disrupt many local school systems, particularly in the rural areas. Such a disruption would interrupt the present orderly improvement and do great damage to the fine racial relationships that have existed—and improved—over the years." Resolution of the "school problem," he wrote, is for the states and local communities to address.

The Eisenhower administration's position in the brief filed by the Justice Department confounded these and other Southern governors who wrote to the President to argue for states' rights, state sovereignty, and a passive federal executive position on this very local matter of public school education. Attorney General Brownell, assisted by holdover staff in the Solicitor General's Office, had the government's brief conclude that the "Fourteenth Amendment created a broad constitutional principle of full and complete equality of all persons under the law, and...forbade all legal distinctions based on color." [31]

When asked in oral argument to outline the government's position on segregation, the administration responded that school segregation was unconstitutional and that *Plessy* "had been wrongly decided." Brownell's recollection of the Vinson request is interesting. Vinson had verbally suggested to the attorney general, in January 1953, months before the formal order was issued, that the Court would be interested in the new administration's views on *Brown*. For the new attorney general,

> it appeared that the Court was not so uniformly in favor of school desegregation....It [struck] me as plausible that Vinson was soliciting the new administration's legal views to tip the balance, either by encouraging the waverers on the Court to overturn *Plessy* if the Eisenhower administration was on that side of the issue or to dodge the question until public and political support were greater and the Court would not have to risk its prestige in such a controversial area.

Attorney General Brownell "wanted the Justice Department to support desegregation," but after the June 8, 1953, order was received, he knew he "had his work cut out for him" because he had to persuade the President, who was a strong believer in states' rights, to go along with such a government brief. As Brownell suspected, Eisenhower felt that the government should not file a brief because the issue, equal educational opportunity, was a local one best left to state and local political forces to work out without federal intervention and federal "edicts."

After discussing with the President the professional and constitutional duty of the attorney general, as an officer of the Court, to respond positively to an invitation by the Court, Brownell persuaded Eisenhower, after several attempts, to allow him to file the brief—in support of desegregation.[32]

## GOING BACK TO THE COURT

As soon as the June 8, 1953, order was received, Marshall set the machinery going within the NAACP Inc Fund and reached out to his allies. Like his friend Hugo Black, he was enraged that the Court had invited the attorney general to participate in the cases. Brownell recalls that Marshall told him that "he considered the government an interloper in the case even if the Supreme Court had asked us to participate. He feared that if the Court was presented with several— potentially confusing—lines of argument, we might well undermine his legal strategy in making his case."[33]

By the end of the month, Marshall, with the invaluable help of William Coleman, had organized a set of task forces to answer each of the five questions posed by the Court. The network of academics and lawyers that made up these task forces, over 130 scholars in all, had taken Marshall two years to pull together. When they were needed by the Association, these men and women quickly responded to Marshall's requests for help. The NAACP Inc Fund had to prepare its brief and get ready for the oral argument scheduled for October 12, 1953. Like the other parties to the dispute, the NAACP had to answer some significant historical questions about legislative intent and the power and authority of the federal courts.

Another person was also busy during these summer months. James Byrnes, the governor of South Carolina, who had, very briefly, been a member of the U.S. Supreme Court in 1941, continued lobbying on behalf of retention of the status quo. In addition to appealing to Eisenhower, he paid a visit to the Supreme Court itself and spoke with two of the justices about the segregation cases: Chief Justice Fred Vinson and Associate Justice Felix Frankfurter. The message Byrnes brought to them was that good white men in the South were moving toward the equalization of separate facilities and that the Court should defer to these moderates working to better conditions for the African American within the framework of separate-but-equal. He warned them that if the Court issued a ruling that attempted to negate the separate-but-equal doctrine, demagogues would take over politics in the South, thus ushering in an era of terror and violence.[34]

At the direction of Herbert Brownell, government lawyers asked Chief Justice Vinson for what turned out to be a critical time extension during the summer of 1953, and Vinson granted it. The rearguments were postponed from October 12, 1953, until December 7, 1953.

Marshall took advantage of the extra time to convene a conference in New York City, on September 25–28, 1953. It was called, he wrote, "so that the research undertaken in connection with the preparation of the briefs and oral argument in the school segregation cases could be carefully evaluated from the point of view of the historian, educator, sociologist, political scientist and lawyer. The meshing of these disciplines should enable us to make the soundest and most persuasive argument possible against the validity of segregation."[35] The problem that Marshall and his researchers encountered was that there was little hard evidence to indicate what the men who had drafted and passed the Fourteenth Amendment thought of segregated education. As Louis Pollak, one of the new Inc Fund lawyers doing research on this historical question, had written:

> we've got a tough job proving that the equal protection clause was supposed to require integrated education. *I'm afraid it can't be done.* If we win, it'll be on the basis that the clause requires an increasingly high standard of achievement as times and mores change....The idea of educating Negroes at all was itself a largely novel one in the 1860s, etc. This is sort of another way of phrasing the changing standard argument. (My emphasis.)[36]

This strategy was seized upon by Marshall and became a significant part of his argument, in the written brief for the appellants and in his oral presentation before the Supreme Court in the fall of 1953. He incorporated Pollak's suggestions into the final written brief.

As presented to the justices, the NAACP's written brief's concluding words were sharp. Viewing the history of the Fourteenth Amendment,

> compels the conclusion that it was the intent, understanding, and contemplation that the Amendment proscribed all state imposed racial restrictions. The

Negro children in these cases are arbitrarily excluded from state public schools set apart for the dominant white groups. Such a practice can only be continued on a theory that Negroes, *qua* Negroes, are inferior to all other Americans. The constitutional and statutory provisions herein challenged cannot be upheld without a clear determination that Negroes are inferior and, therefore, must be segregated from other human beings. Certainly, such a ruling would destroy the intent and purpose of the Fourteenth Amendment and the very equalitarian basis of our Government.[37]

This would force the Court to go beyond the legal, political, and historical questions and focus, intensely, on the human and ethical dimension of the dilemma. If African Americans were not inferior to other humans, then how could a segregated public school system be constitutional?

On September 8, 1953, Chief Justice Fred Vinson suffered a major heart attack and died. Remarked Frankfurter to two of his former law clerks, upon hearing of Vinson's passing: "This is the first indication that I have ever had that there is a God."[38] For all the participants in the litigation, the death of Vinson meant that the Court had lost a defender of *Plessy* as well as the Court's chief manager of that litigation. Philip Elman voiced the views of many when he said, of Vinson's death: "Without God, we never would have had *Brown*, a unanimous decision.... Without God, the Court would have remained bitterly divided, fragmented, unable to decide the issue forthrightly. God won *Brown*, not Thurgood Marshall or any other lawyer or mortal.... He took care of the American people and the little children and *Brown* by taking Fred Vinson when he did."[39]

There is no doubt that Earl Warren's recess appointment to the Court, on October 2, 1953, to replace Vinson led to the dramatic shift to unanimity of the brethren on the question of *Plessy's* continued viability. An immensely popular and successful Republican politician, he was California's attorney general from 1939 to 1943 and Governor Thomas Dewey's vice-presidential running mate on the Republican Party ticket in 1948. He served as California's governor from 1943 to 1953.

At the 1952 Republican National Convention, he brought his state's delegation around to support Eisenhower for President. After the election, the President-elect promised Warren a seat on the Supreme Court as political payoff. Eisenhower kept his promise—and soon regretted doing so.

With Warren in as Chief Justice, in less than one year the Court went from 5–4 to 9–0 for overturn of *Plessy*. The dramatic turnaround was attributed to Warren's tact and social leadership of the fragmented Court. He also found Marshall's argument extremely persuasive; it was one Warren used in his discussions with his brethren. Outside of the conference room, Warren moved skillfully among them, discussing the legal, ethical, and moral issues with each of them privately.

After the December 7, 1953, oral arguments before the justices, the new Chief Justice, recalling Marshall's words in the Association's massive brief and Marshall's voice during oral argument, told his colleagues that, in his view, segregation was wrong: "I don't see how in this day and age we can set any group apart from the rest and say that they are not entitled to exactly the same treatment as all others. [The Civil War Amendments] were intended to make the slaves equal with all others. Personally, I can't see how today we can justify segregation based solely on race."[40]

The Warren strategy, after the oral argument ended, was to argue that *Plessy* was the repository of the "concept of the inherent inferiority of the colored race....If we are to sustain segregation, we...must do it upon that basis." If any of Warren's brethren defended *Plessy*, he also had to accept the concept of the inherent racial inferiority of the African American people. After he finished, the others spoke informally, and there was no "polarization" of the brethren at that time. Warren believed that there were six in support of a *Plessy* overturn; two (Jackson and Clark) were now wavering. Clark indicated to his colleagues that he would go along with an overturn if it were written properly and "provided relief is carefully worked out...in such a way that will permit different handling in different places." Jackson spoke much the same way. Only one of the brethren, Kentuckian Stanley Reed, still maintained that *Plessy* was viable law.

While this slow dance proceeded within the Court, Marshall was busy preparing his staff and the local leadership of the NAACP for decision day and afterwards. Planning ahead, he scheduled a meeting of all the NAACP state conference presidents, to be held in Atlanta, Georgia, on the Saturday or Sunday after the Court announced its decision in *Brown*. With the help of the president of the NAACP branch in Atlanta, preparations were made for the meeting in the early summer of 1954.

In March 1954, Marshall sent a letter to the branch presidents, telling them that, as soon as the *Brown* decision was announced, the Inc Fund staff would get detailed information about the meaning of the opinion to each of them, effectively setting the NAACP's response to the Court's judgment—whatever form it took. We want "accurate statements" about the decision, he told them, so just "delay speaking to the press until you receive the material from the Inc Fund."

Messages and memos circulated among the nine justices of the Court, and Warren had private conversations with all of them. In January 1954, Frankfurter sent his "typical" professorial memo to the brethren, sharing with them his concerns about the school segregation litigation. Although he had been a friend of the NAACP for many decades, he was concerned about the impact of a Court decree ordering an end to segregation at once. This was the NAACP's position, a view also held by his arch rival, Hugo Black. But it was not Frankfurter's view and he said so in his memo.

The "time for obedience to an order" was an important factor if there was to be a major transformation in public school education in the almost two dozen states that had segregated schools. It would be a transformation involving physical, educational, ethical, cultural, and social changes of the first magnitude. The transformation had to be done carefully, or else equality would lead to lowered educational standards in the public schools. In "enforcing the Fourteenth Amendment," he wrote,

> the Court is promoting a process of social betterment and not contributing to social deterioration. Not even a court can in a day change a deplorable situation into the ideal. It does its duty if it gets effectively under way the righting of a wrong. When the wrong is a deeply rooted state policy the Court does its duty if it decrees measures that reverse the direction of the unconstitutional policy so as to uproot it "with all deliberate speed."

In addition to implementing the transformation, "spreading the adjustment over time" through the use of the "all deliberate speed" standard (the phrase—and the strategy—adopted by the Court the following year), Frankfurter urged his brethren to consider issuing a decree that gave the task of implementing desegregation plans to disinterested, nonjudicial "masters." Such a person, "properly equipped would become immersed in the problem, undistracted by other judicial duties or the thought of them." He ended the memo by noting that while appointing a master would be a good way to handle the practical matters associated with desegregating public schools, "on the other hand, there are important things to be said for charging the District Courts with responsibility."[41] These ideas were to become essential parts of the Court's implementation decree announced a year later.

During the first months of 1954, Warren continued to have informal conversations with the others. By March, the Court had agreed, by an eight-to-one vote, to overturn *Plessy,* and Warren assigned himself the task of writing the opinion for the Court. In the end, the Chief Justice was able to persuade Reed to join with the others so that the Court could speak with one voice in the important issue of race segregation. Evidently, Jackson was planning on issuing a concurring opinion. But a heart attack incapacitated him, and in the end, after some hospital conversations with Warren, Jackson joined the rest of the brethren in standing behind Warren's opinion for the Court. Reed, after the unanimous opinion was announced, wrote to Frankfurter telling him that "while there were many considerations that pointed to a dissent…they did not add up to a balance against the Court's opinion.…The factors looking toward a fair treatment for Negroes are more important than the weight of history." [42]

## THE SUPREME COURT OVERTURNS *PLESSY*

In May 1954, the Chief Justice was hard at work putting finishing touches on the *Brown* draft, and circulating it to the others for review and reaction. In a May 7, 1954, memo to the brethren, Warren outlined the kind of opinion he was writing. (Actually, two were circulated, the *Bolling* opinion, involving the District of Columbia segregation suit, and the *Brown* opinion, the consolidation of the four state segregation lawsuits.) By this time, Warren had concluded, with Frankfurter, that there had to be two decisions. "No single decree," he wrote, "could meet the problems of all [the varying conditions in the states that authorize segregation]." Furthermore, the Court had been spending a great deal of time on the substantive question (the constitutionality of segregation per se) and "had little enlightenment on the subject of [what a decree should state]."

That question, Warren said, had to be put over to the following term of the Court "for further argument on Questions IV and V, consideration of which was blanketed this Term by the attention given to the substantive question in the briefs and on argument." On the constitutionality of segregation, the *Brown* opinion he was drafting "should be the end of the line case."

Finally, he told his colleagues that the opinion would hold that *Plessy* could not apply to public education, and that the opinion would be "short, readable by the lay public, non-rhetorical, unemotional and, above all, not accusatory. No section of the country and no segment of our population can justly place full responsibility for segregation on others. They must assume a measure of that responsibility themselves." [43]

On Monday, May 17, 1954, with an ailing Jackson out of the hospital and sitting with his brethren on the historic occasion, and Thurgood Marshall in the audience, Warren announced the unanimous opinion of the Court in *Brown v. Board of Education.*

The opinion was a short one, resting on a contemporary interpretation for the equal-protection clause:

> In approaching this problem, we cannot turn the clock back to 1868 when the Amendment was adopted, or even to 1896 when *Plessy v. Ferguson* was written. We must consider public education in the light of its full development and its present place in American life throughout the Nation. Only in this way can it be determined if segregation in public schools deprives these plaintiffs of the equal protection of the laws.

The opinion also addressed, very clearly, the harmful effects on black children of a segregated education:

> To separate them from others of similar age and qualifications solely because of their race generates a feeling of inferiority as to their status in the community that may affect hearts and minds in a way unlikely ever to be undone.... Whatever may have been the state of psychological knowledge at the time of *Plessy v. Ferguson,* this finding [that a sense of inferiority is developed in young black children who are educated in a segregated environment] is amply supported by modern authority.

And the opinion also underscored the contemporary importance of education in American life; it reflected the significantly changed role of education in society. "Today, education is perhaps the most important function of state and local governments....It is the very foundation of good citizenship....In these days, it is doubtful that any child may reasonably be expected to succeed in life if he is denied the opportunity of an education. Such an opportunity, where the state has undertaken to provide it, is a right which must be made available to all on equal terms."

Therefore, Warren wrote, "we conclude [when he reached this part of the opinion in open Court on that fateful Monday, Warren paused, looked toward Reed, and added the word "unanimously"] that in the field of public education the doctrine of 'separate but equal' has no place. Separate educational facilities are inherently unequal."[44]

Marshall was flabbergasted! A unanimous decision from a Court that was, as recently as a year ago, very divided on this constitutional issue. There was one moment during the reading that Marshall always remembered. It involved Justice Reed. Marshall and others believed that Reed, and a few other justices, would dissent from any Court overturn of *Plessy.* He had even heard that Reed had brought in an extra law clerk to help the jurist prepare his dissent in *Brown.* As Warren read the unanimous decision in *Brown,* Reed looked at Marshall and nodded almost imperceptibly. Marshall nodded back.[45]

George Mickum, Justice Reed's law clerk that year, was in the courtroom for the momentous event. He recalled that "when the opinion was read from the bench, [Reed] cried. He was really troubled by it." And the rumor Marshall heard about Reed bringing on an extra law clerk was correct. Jack Fassett, according to Mickum, helped Reed prepare "lots of drafts of dissents" that Reed was considering using in the *Brown* case. "It was the Earl Warren influence... that brought him around....It was a sense on Reed's part that it was in the best interests of the country that the opinion be unanimous."[46]

With that short opinion for a unanimous Court, the era of *Plessy* had formally come to an end. "I was so happy, I was numb" was Marshall's immediate reaction to the decision in *Brown*. The NAACP legal staff's response to *Brown* was joyous and euphoric. Roy Wilkins recalled that "after other victories we had broken out a quart of Scotch and celebrated," but this time "the decision was so overwhelming that for a while we forgot the toasts. We all just sat there looking at one another. The only emotion we felt at the moment was awe—every one of us felt it. Later in the day, Thurgood came back from Washington—laughing and cheering—[my] door flew open and Thurgood walked in with a grin as wide as Fifth Avenue. He walked right over and kissed me."[47]

The exultation lasted for all of a few days. After all, the Court had left open the question of implementing the constitutional principle it had just announced in the *Brown* decision. While Marshall was naturally overjoyed to see *Plessy* overturned by a *unanimous* Court, he knew that there was still a great deal to be done to dismantle the still-breathing monster called Jim Crow. However, for most blacks, the May 17, 1954, opinion of the Court was an important watershed: "[It]...was the day we won; the day we took the white man's law and won our case before an all-white Supreme Court with a Negro lawyer....And we were proud."[48]

The other side, the defendant states in the South, was not happy with *Brown*. Many demagogues, especially in the Deep South, were enraged with the Court's opinion, calling *Brown* decision day "Black Monday." As Roy Wilkins soon found out, the "sense of euphoria...was a bit naive. Swept away, elevated, exalted, I failed to anticipate the ferocity of the resistance that quickly grew up in the Deep South."

Marshall had another reason for his fall from joy to extreme sadness and depression just days after the *Brown* decision. Buster, his wife of twenty-five years, revealed a secret she had kept from him for the past six months: she was dying of cancer. During the following fall and winter of 1954–55, Marshall canceled all travel, except to Atlanta and Washington, to be with her as much as possible. She died in February 1955. Looking back, Marshall said, "I thought the end of the world had come."

There was also a very ebullient reaction in the Court after the opinion came down on May 17, 1954. Law clerks recalled that they "felt good—and clean. It [*Brown*] was so good."[49] Some of the brethren, in their euphoric state, wrote notes to Warren on his outstanding success in bringing the Court together. Frankfurter noted, in a handwritten letter, "*This* is a day that will live in glory. It is also a great day in the history of the Court and not in the least for the course of deliberation which brought about the result. I congratulate you." In a "Dear Chief" note, Justice Harold Burton wrote, "Today I believe has been a great day for America and the Court....To you goes the credit for the character of the opinions which produced the all important unanimity. Congratulations."[50]

## THE *BROWN* IMPLEMENTATION DECREE

The May 1954 opinion, however, did not address the remedial issue: When and how soon must segregated public schools cease functioning? The Supreme Court itself quickly got to work on the question of implementation of the *Brown* decision. A day after the decision was handed down, Frankfurter sent a detailed memo to the others. One of his former law clerks, Alexander Bickel, had prepared a detailed history of the Fourteenth Amendment, and Frankfurter wanted to share it with them, even though "my brethren may care to put the result of all of this labor in their files."[51]

On July 5, 1954, Frankfurter wrote Warren that "the most important problem is to fashion appropriate provisions against evasion." Frankfurter was concerned about the Court issuing a decree that "set forth with detailed particularity" how a segregated school system had to desegregate its facilities. In the letter, he presented two themes that he had already raised earlier in the year and that would ultimately see the light of day in the *Brown II* remedial decree written by Warren for a unanimous Court the following spring: (1) the need for flexibility in a realistic time frame for desegregating the public schools and (2) the need for lower federal court involvement with school authorities in fashioning a desegregation remedy rather than have the Supreme Court get bogged down in the minutiae of desegregation planning. One of Stanley Reed's law clerks left a memo for Reed before his departure in early July 1954. In it, the young man indicated that he had a conversation with Warren and that the Chief's "inclination...was to send the cases back to the trial courts for the entry of appropriate decrees."[52]

Warren put six law clerks to work during the summer and early fall of 1954 to prepare a "Segregation Research Project" for the Court. It was distributed in the fall and provided the Court with a statistical portrait of desegregation programs across the country. The clerks presented a set of recommendations for the desegregation decree that would be issued by the Court in the spring of 1955. Included in it were calls for federal district courts to handle the "supervision of the execution of the decrees," issuance of some general guidelines for the parties and the lower court judges (who should be given "considerable discretion"), and for sufficient time, some sort of "gradualism," for the South to comply with the general desegregation decree. "Whatever may be said for immediate desegregation at all levels of the Southern school systems, such a requirement is impractical."[53]

And so, while the Court did not formally agree on the general pattern of the decree until its April 16, 1955, conference session, almost a year before, most of

the justices had reached the conclusion that the Court should order desegregation of public schools "with all deliberate speed." While Marshall and his staff
spent hundreds of hours and months of work putting together their brief and
preparing for oral argument, the Court had very soon after the May 17, 1954,
announcement come to the conclusion that the NAACP's call for immediate
desegregation of the public schools was untenable.

As Marshall promised, there was a special meeting of all the state NAACP
presidents, held in Atlanta, Georgia, on May 22–23, 1954. It was limited, however, to the representatives of the NAACP branches in the seventeen southern
and border states and the District of Columbia. There were eighty-four delegates to the conference. Marshall presided over the meeting, joined by Wilkins
and White. After canvassing all the delegates and hearing their status reports,
Marshall quickly pieced together a document called the "Atlanta Declaration."
In it he laid out the strategy of the NAACP Inc Fund. The Association was
ready to get into the trenches for the struggle to implement *Brown*. The
Association, he wrote, stood "ready to work with law abiding citizens who are
anxious to translate this decision into a program of action to eradicate racial segregation in public education...speedily."[54] Unaware that the Court had already
reached a "with all deliberate speed" consensus on the question of implementation, Marshall worked feverishly to get all the data from the field into the brief.

Briefs were filed in *Brown II* in November 1954, and the oral arguments were
held in April 1955. Marshall again insisted that the Court issue a decree that
called for full desegregation in *all* the affected jurisdictions no later than
September 1955. Brownell's brief for the federal government called for gradual
desegregation, taking into account the varying commitment to the cultural norm
of segregation across the South. The Southern position was put to the Court by
the attorney general of Texas: "It is our problem. Let us solve it [in our own
time]."[55] Southern anger about *Brown I* came through during the oral arguments. Calling for an open-ended decree from the Court, to allow the Southern
states a great deal of time "to work something out," the South's advocates were
quite frank in oral argument.

When asked by Chief Justice Warren whether the South "would conform to
the decree" issued by the Court, whether there "would be an honest attempt to
conform to this decree," attorney Rogers responded, "Let us get the word 'honest' out of there." Warren: "No, leave it in." Rogers: "No, because I would have
to tell you that right now we would not conform—we would not send our white
children to the Negro schools....We do not want to say that we would violate
the decree. We are trying to work within it. We hope the Court will give us a
decree that we can work within....We are asking the opportunity to work the
matter out at the local level."[56]

At the April 16, 1955, conference, Warren said that he felt that the remedy should contain clear instructions to the federal district courts, but that there had to be flexibility in order to take into account different problems facing school districts in different parts of the South. Most of the Court supported Warren's remediation proposals. Stanley Reed, still somewhat sour about the May 1954 opinion, took a radical position in conference. He told the group that he was concerned about the increase in "social disease and promiscuity" that would come about as a consequence of rapid desegregation in his beloved South. Then he said, "it took this Court sixty years from *Plessy* to May 17th to change its mind. Prince Edward County [and the others] *ought to have a comparable term.*" (My emphasis.)

Black, however, suggested something else. As usual, he was supported by Douglas. He recommended that the Court issue "a decree and quit. The less we say the better off we are....Nothing could injure the Court more than to issue orders that cannot be enforced."[57] The Alabaman warned that it was "futile to think that in these cases we can settle segregation in the South." In the end, much to his later regret, he went along with the Chief's plans for a very gradual resolution of the segregation issue. Frankfurter urged Warren to consider using an expression Justice Oliver W. Holmes had used in earlier opinions. "I have only one further and minor remark to make. I still think that 'with all deliberate speed' is preferable to 'at the earliest practicable date.'" By May 1955, Warren had drafted a short opinion that was discussed at the May 27, 1955, conference. At that conference the Court unanimously agreed to go with the Warren opinion—including the words "with all deliberate speed."

The opinion came down on May 31, 1955, and it was unsettling to Marshall. Chief Justice Warren had written that "all provisions of federal, state or local law requiring or permitting" public school segregation "must yield to" the principle of integration announced in *Brown I.* However, given the existence of a variety of political, demographic, and social environments in the twenty-one states and the District of Columbia, the Court, after giving responsibility for implementing the decrees to local federal district courts, said that segregation must yield to desegregation according to the "all deliberate speed" prescription.

Marshall had hoped for the kind of decree Black had suggested, but the Court went in the direction of gradualism. After the initial disappointment, Marshall then got to work. As had been the case the preceding year, there was an Emergency Regional Conference of the NAACP, held in Atlanta a week after the second *Brown* decision came down.

By June 4, 1955, Marshall and the NAACP leadership had presented the Association's formal "interpretation" of the Court's ruling in *Brown II.* Marshall and Wilkins (Walter White had died a few months earlier, and Roy Wilkins had been appointed executive secretary of the NAACP) wrote the membership's leaders a very somber note. The Court had not set a "deadline date for either the beginning or the completion of desegregation in the public schools." Nor did the Court "outline a definite plan by which desegregation must proceed and by which the lower courts might judge the efforts of local school boards toward compliance with the May 17 (1954) and May 31 (1955) rulings."

What did the Supreme Court actually say in *Brown*? Marshall noted ruefully that while the justices nullified all laws that required or permitted segregation in public schools, they also gave the local school boards "the primary responsibility" for solving the desegregation riddle. The task of local NAACP branches, accordingly, was to "begin the campaign for desegregation with the local school authorities." The school board had to act in "good faith," and if there was no such showing, that board was to be brought before a federal district court judge for determination and action to remedy the lack of good faith. The Court stated that African Americans, Marshall wrote, have the right to admission to a public school on a nondiscriminatory basis "as soon as practical." The school boards had to start "promptly" to develop a plan to desegregate the public schools, after "eliminating" a "variety of obstacles" to desegregation in their communities. Even though the local officials might not like the May 17, 1954 decision, Marshall reminded the Association's branch leaders that the whites *"may not ignore, evade, or defy it."* [58] If there was not a prompt start, the burden was on the defendants (white local officials) to show clearly that there was a need for additional time to carry out a desegregation plan.

Thurgood Marshall closed with a wish: "In the overwhelming majority of instances it can be expected that compliance without legal action will be the rule, perhaps grudgingly and reluctantly in some areas, but compliance, nevertheless." Looking "confidently toward the future," the NAACP was ready to work "with qualified experts in public education and community organization to cooperate with any and all school boards willing to work toward desegregation."

Marshall was not sanguine, however, about the impact of a Court order that did not have beginning and ending dates for completing public school desegregation and did not formulate any guidelines for use by the federal district court judges, soon labeled the "58 Lonely Men," [59] as they struggled to implement the 1955 *Brown* opinion's general decree. He knew that the Inc Fund was going to be very busy "in the trenches," in another protracted legal civil war over the pace and quality of public school desegregation. It was a legal war that would be fought case by case, state by state, "county by county, school district by school district," all over the South and Southwest. [60]

A year later, in a *Time* magazine "report card" of the legal behavior of the seventeen Southern states, Marshall's grade for each state's progress toward ending segregation indicated where the critical war zones were located. One state, Missouri, received an A grade for its immediate desegregation of its public schools. Another, West Virginia, was graded A-minus by Marshall because more than half of its school districts had desegregated in time for the start of school in September 1955. Three other states, Kentucky, Maryland, and Oklahoma, received B-plus and B-minus grades for their desegregation activities. Five states—Arkansas, Delaware, North Carolina, Tennessee, and Texas—were graded in the C range by Marshall. Two other states, Florida and Virginia, received D's, and five—Alabama, Georgia, Louisiana, Mississippi, and South Carolina—received F's because there was absolutely no movement toward desegregation. Clearly, for Marshall, the trench warfare battles would be fought primarily in the Deep South states, where the African American population was much greater than in the other states.

Segregation seemed to be ending in those county and city school districts where the African American population was less than 10 percent; between 10 percent and 25 percent, "the fight may not be too hard. Where it approaches or exceeds 50 percent, the end can hardly be imagined," reported *Time* magazine in September 1955.

In 1955, however, Marshall and the others did not want to acknowledge the intensity and ingenuity of their opposition. They were to find out quickly how committed many in the South were to "ignoring, evading, and defying" the Supreme Court's mandate. By 1959, Marshall had seen the brutal reality of the South's ignoring, evading, and defying the Court's orders. As he told attendees at a Freedom Fund dinner:

> It was hoped, but not expected, that the decisions in these cases would have set-tled the "problem." This, of course, as subsequent events proved, was hoping for too much....Opposition in areas of the South has ranged from violence, killings, and lynchings to economic boycotts and threats of violence....While our struggle has been one within the law, with honor and supported by both the constitutional law and the moral law of our civilization, the opposition from these state officials and others has been a disgrace to our democratic ideals, our country, our religious and every other principle of ethics or simple democracy.[61]

Marshall, Wilkins, and the rest of the NAACP leadership in New York were simply not fully prepared for the open expressions of hatred that erupted in the Deep South after the first *Brown* decision on that "Black Monday" in May 1954. Medgar Evers and other local NAACP branch leaders knew what was coming because they had seen it daily, growing up in rural Mississippi. But, for all of them, the loathing was ugly and primeval. As Roy Wilkins wrote in 1982, "I still remember picking up a newspaper and reading an interview with a fourteen-year-old Dixie Belle who said, 'I'd rather grow up to be an idiot than go to school with a nigger in it.'"[62]

## MASSIVE RESISTANCE: THE WHITE DEEP SOUTH'S RESPONSE TO *BROWN*

Shortly after the May 17, 1954, victory, Marshall received an angry letter from J. E. Stockstill, a lawyer who practiced in Picayune, Mississippi. It was a response to Marshall's "braggadocio bigotry" statement after *Brown* came down. "The South," Stockstill wrote, "has heard such blah-blah statements for the last 80 years, and we want you to know that any law that is applied to the South is enforced by the citizenry of the South....When you, or the Supreme Court... think you are bigger than the solid South, you will find out different in the long run."[63] Southern politicians were planning their response to the Court's decision. On March 16, 1951, South Carolina's governor, James F. Byrnes, told a convention of the South Carolina Education Association:

> South Carolina will not, now nor for some years to come, mix white and colored children in our schools. If the Court changes what is now the law of the land, we will, if it is possible, live within the law, preserve the public school system, and at the same time maintain segregation. If that is not possible, we will abandon the public school system. To do that would be choosing the lesser of two great evils.[64]

Byrnes was joined in this threat by the governors of Georgia and Mississippi, who both threatened to "abandon the public school system" rather than desegregate it.

On May 18, 1954, Lyndon B. Johnson, then a moderate Democratic U.S. senator from Texas, spoke on the floor of the Senate about the *Brown* decision announced the preceding day. His speech was not that of a Southern agitator. He said that the decision was "an accomplished fact....It cannot be overruled now, and it is probable that it can never be overruled. Second, the Supreme Court in its ruling recognized the complexity of the problem. Personally, I think it would have been sounder judgment to allow that progress to continue through the processes of natural evolution. However, there is no point in crying over spilt milk."[65]

One week later, however, he wrote an acrimonious letter to a friend of his, Judge H. R. Wilson of Alpine, Texas. In it, Johnson condemned the action of the Supreme Court in *Brown:*

Like you, the Supreme Court decision left me shocked and dismayed....It is obvious that criteria other than law and equity were the governing factors in the ruling. Somehow, of course, we will find a method by which no one will be forced into distasteful or unpleasant associations....It is unfortunate that such things [as *Brown*] should arise and that institutions which have worked well for so many years be disrupted by an arbitrary decision.

Johnson, however, was the voice of moderation compared to his Senate and House colleagues from the South. After *Brown II*, 101 U.S. senators and congressmen, from every one of the eleven former Confederate states, signed what they called the Southern Manifesto. The Court's decision in *Brown* was labeled by these legislators as a "clear abuse of judicial power...creating chaos and confusion in the States...[and] destroying the amicable relations between the white and Negro races that have been created through 90 years of patient effort by the good people of both races."

The congressional delegation "pledged [themselves] to use all lawful means to bring about a reversal of this decision which is contrary to the Constitution." Lyndon Johnson and his political mentor, House Speaker Sam Rayburn, also from Texas, were not asked to sign the Manifesto. The only Southern legislators who did not sign were Albert Gore and Estes Kefauver, the two U.S. senators from Tennessee, and a handful of congressmen from urban centers in the South.

At the state level, immediately after *Brown,* a number of Southern governors (Alabama, Georgia, Mississippi, and Virginia) stridently denounced the ruling. They vehemently shouted to their constituents that everything would be done to continue segregated schools in their states—U.S. Supreme Court or not. As Justice Black warned his colleagues, the demagogues had taken over in his beloved Alabama and other Southern states. It would be, he correctly predicted, a long, terrible time for liberty and freedom in that part of the country. While Marshall optimistically reported to the NAACP branches that Kentucky, Oklahoma, Maryland, Missouri, Delaware, and West Virginia "have promised full compliance," that was not the message from the hard-core South. And that translated into the filing in federal district courts in the Deep South of hundreds of lawsuits, brought by the Inc Fund staff working with local cooperating attorneys, to try to force local officials to begin to act in good faith to end public school segregation.

The transition process was a complex and lengthy one. Petitions first had to be filed with a local school board that was not moving to desegregate its public schools. The petition would request the board to act in accordance with the May 31, 1955, order of the Court. There had to be periodic follow-ups by members of the local NAACP branch. If there was no action, then some of the members of the local community, acting as plaintiffs, had to file a lawsuit in the federal district court indicating that the local board was not acting in accordance with the Supreme Court order and seeking to have the federal judge issue an order to the school board to begin to develop a desegregation plan.

In those situations, and there were to be hundreds of incidents of ignoring, evading, and defying by local communities, "Court action is essential," said Marshall, in order for there to be "full compliance" with the Supreme Court's decision. At that point, he said, knowing the huge burden he was placing on himself and the Inc Fund, "the matter will be turned over to the NAACP's legal department and it will proceed with the matter in court."[66]

"Massive resistance" took the legal form of passage of school education laws in the South that attempted to evade the Court's mandate to end segregated schools. Statutes were passed that repealed compulsory attendance laws, allocated state funds to pay for private school education, withdrew education funds from any school district that developed and tried to implement a desegregation plan, as well as passage of "state laws threatening the direct closing of public schools if integration became inevitable."[67] South Carolina governor Byrnes led the Deep South's effort. He believed that constant challenging of Brown "at every opportunity in local courts and setting up church-sponsored schools to encourage the withdrawal of white students from the public school systems" would legitimately defy and evade the Court's ruling in Brown.[68]

All these statutory efforts to ignore and defy the Brown mandate were challenged in federal court by the Inc Fund lawyers, and became a basic part of the prolonged trench warfare taking place in federal district courts across the South. (So tiresome were these lawsuits that, after 1956, Inc Fund staff literally leaped at the opportunity to switch from these lawsuits to the defense of protesting African Americans who were arrested for mass demonstrations or sit-ins in restaurants that refused to serve them because of their color or race.)

Nullification and interposition was another, ultimately futile, effort by Southern legislators in Congress to evade the Court's mandate in Brown. The argument for interposition went back to the pre–Civil War ideas of a great Southern patriot and defender of states' rights, John C. Calhoun. Interposition suggested that a state could formally stand between its citizens and the national government if, in the eyes of state leaders, the national government had acted unconstitutionally. Nullification carried the idea of interposition to its logical conclusion. A state would declare an action of the Supreme Court or the Congress unconstitutional owing to its infringement on the reserved powers of the states, given to them and to the people in the Tenth Amendment.

State legislatures passed joint resolutions, signed with a flourish and a great deal of publicity by the governors, "condemning the... usurpation and encroachment on the reserved powers of the States by the United States Supreme Court." Typically, as in the South Carolina Resolution of February 14, 1956, the nullification and interposition resolution called upon the Congress and the states to prevent such encroachment by the Supreme Court.[69] While almost all lawyers in the South knew that this notion of interposition and nullification was a relic of an earlier century, and that the Civil War had "nullified" the viability of this strategy, die-hard segregationists were using everything they could to defy and evade the Court's orders in *Brown*. Economic threats and violent repression, unfortunately and tragically, became another all-too-common strategy in the Deep South after the school desegregation decisions.

Within days of the first *Brown* decision, white Southerners began the protracted campaign, often fierce and vicious, to block the implementation of the Court's decision. By October 1954, in Mississippi, the White Citizens' Council (WCC), an upscale Ku Klux Klan, was formed. Roy Wilkins noted that while WCC members "were too shrewd for bedsheets and burning crosses, the councils still breathed the spirit of the KKK. One of the council organizers said very early on: 'We intend to see that no Negro who believes in equality has a job, gets credit, or is able to exist in our communities.'"

Its members were "some of the leading citizens in the South," noted a 1956 FBI report to the President and his attorney general. The WCC recruited local businessmen, bankers, state legislators, industrialists, professionals, farmers, and other hard-line segregationists committed to maintaining their old way of life. They were encouraged to action by legislators such as Senators James O. Eastland of Mississippi and Strom Thurmond of South Carolina; Congressman Mendel Rivers of South Carolina; and Georgia's governor, Marvin Griffin. Eastland told twelve thousand cheering people at a WCC rally in Jackson, Mississippi, that "the Anglo-Saxon people have held steadfast to the belief that resistance to tyranny is obedience to God." In a rally held in Birmingham, Alabama, Georgia's attorney general, Eugene Cook, said that "the time has now come to use defiance, nullification and refuse to obey. We will not permit suicide in Georgia at any price. We want to persuade first but are determined to use force if necessary."[70]

By 1956 the WCC had 127 branches throughout the Deep South, with a total membership of over 116,000.[71] Their primary tactic was to use economic pressures and economic reprisals against local African Americans who worked with the NAACP and, after 1956, other African Americans who worked with more direct-action-oriented civil rights groups such as Martin Luther King Jr.'s Southern Christian Leadership Conference (SCLC).

If economic threats and reprisals did not convince the local African American not to file the petition with the local school board, they were usually followed by violence and terror, actions that led to lynchings or the local NAACP activists fleeing for their lives. For example, the FBI informed the attorney general that "one Negro was told that economic pressure would be applied if he didn't resign as president of the NAACP in Belzoni, Mississippi. *He didn't resign but we cannot say if this was the sole reason for his being shot and wounded on November 25, 1955.*" (My emphasis.)[72]

Aaron Henry, at the time involved in NAACP work in Mississippi with Medgar Evers, remembered that the first major WCC harassment came in 1955, one year after *Brown*.

> Some 455 or 460 heads of families signed the petition asking the school board here (Clarksdale, Mississippi) to abide by *Brown*. These parents were intimidated in many ways. Many were fired, many were abused, many were denied credit. This gave birth to the local credit union that we have here in town today, because so many farmers who signed this petition could no longer borrow money from the banks to carry out their farming enterprises. And of course this is the time of Reverend George Lee's murder, the time that Gus Coates was shot; this was the time of Dippy Smith being killed on the courthouse lawn at Brookhaven.[73]

E. J. Stringer, the president of the Mississippi branch of the NAACP in 1955, was one of the first to feel the rage of the WCC. His car insurance liability was canceled; his wife was fired from her job teaching high school; he received, nightly, threatening telephone calls, and was audited by the Jackson, Mississippi, office of the U.S. Internal Revenue Service (some of whose auditors were members of the WCC).[74]

In Yazoo City, Mississippi, members of the local NAACP branch signed a petition addressed to the local school board requesting compliance with the Supreme Court's school desegregation decision. In 1950 the per capita pupil expenditures in that small Mississippi Delta town reflected the education problem: $245 for each white schoolchild versus $3 spent for educating each black student. Fifty-three signed the petition. Immediately, the local WCC took out an advertisement in the town paper "setting forth the names of 53 Negroes who petitioned for integrated schools. As a result, many lost their jobs, those who were self-employed received no work, and grocery stores refused to sell the petitioners merchandise."[75] Within days of these economic pressures, fifty-one of the signers removed their names from the petition; the remaining two fled Yazoo City and went North. This campaign of terror and intimidation was very successful. As Ellis Wright, the head of the Jackson, Mississippi, WCC declared boastfully, "We now tell the NAACP people that they have started something they will never finish."[76] At the time of the second *Brown* decision, almost five thousand African American Mississippians were members of the Association. By 1959 the number had dropped to under 1,700 and was continuing to fall.[77]

Violence, committed by both the WCC and the KKK, was on the rise, especially in Mississippi. Medgar Evers, a World War II veteran, had been a member of the Mound Bayou, Mississippi, branch of the NAACP, and became Mississippi's first NAACP field secretary in 1954. He served as liaison between the New York office and the local branches in the state. Marshall knew him well because Evers, in January 1954, had applied for admission to the University of Mississippi's law school and Marshall had been his lawyer in the action.

While Evers's effort was unsuccessful, in October 1954 he was named the NAACP's Mississippi field secretary. The job was a sort of "suicide mission," for it entailed his monitoring compliance with *Brown* and gathering affidavits for use in court suits against Mississippi school boards.[78] But Evers did an excellent job in a treacherous culture, and was known across the state for his audacity and his bravery. And he never went anywhere without his gun. Evers and Marshall remained close friends until Evers was coldbloodedly murdered in his driveway when he returned home from an NAACP meeting in June 1963. Before his death, he had mourned the deaths of other African Americans who worked for the NAACP in the state. In four years, eight fellow civil rights leaders were murdered in Mississippi, and no one was ever charged with any of the crimes. Myrlie Evers (in 1996, the president of the national NAACP), Medgar's widow, recalled that her husband sat "and just pounded the desk or the chair or whatever in utter despair and grief and anger that these people's lives had been snuffed out like this."[79]

Protecting the NAACP's branch field secretaries became a primary and ultimately unresolvable problem for the NAACP. In December 1955, Roy Wilkins, the new executive secretary of the NAACP, and Marshall received a grim letter from Walter Lowe about the violence directed by the WCC and the KKK toward "some of the sturdy patriots who dare to become NAACP officials." After commenting on the killing of young leaders in Mississippi and Texas, he wrote, "these outrageous attempts to blunt the effectiveness of the NAACP must be met if you are to have a supply of leaders to carry out your programs on the state and local level.... Greater security should be provided for the officials of the NAACP.... Their families need protection too. I want to propose...a plan whereby protection will be provided for these men and their families." Sadly, almost pathetically, his suggestion was to have the NAACP place "$5,000 to $10,000 life insurance upon every president and secretary."[80] Mr. Lowe's suggestion illustrated the NAACP's dilemma. As Thurgood Marshall always said, the Association must play by the rules, even though the opposition does not. Other than providing life insurance policies for Medgar Evers and other brave men and women like him, there was little the NAACP could do. Law enforcement officers in the South were very often the enemy, centrally involved in acts of violence against African Americans for decades. Federal agency personnel in the South, born and raised there, were often members of the WCC or the Klan. There were few meaningful answers to the tragic dilemma, other than strapping on a gun or resting it on the gun rack of the truck one drove from branch to branch on the dusty, dark roads of Mississippi.

Attacking the NAACP in state courts was another very successful strategy for reducing the impact of the civil rights organization throughout the Deep South. In Alabama, Texas, Mississippi, Florida, and Georgia, suits were introduced by the state attorneys general, using their corporate filing laws, to acquire the organizational data and the Association's membership lists in each state. In the Alabama litigation, although the NAACP reluctantly turned over some documentation, it refused to surrender the membership rosters, arguing that to do so would subject its members to economic and employment harassment, violence, and terror.

The NAACP was held in contempt and fined $100,000. It appealed the judgment and, in 1958, in the case of *NAACP v. Alabama, ex rel Patterson,* the Supreme Court unanimously set aside the contempt citation. It stated that the Association had, under the First Amendment, freedom of association, and any forced surrender of the membership roster would deprive the NAACP members of their First Amendment right of freedom of association. Ultimately, owing to Alabama's defiance of federal court orders, the litigation went to the Supreme Court four times and the court battle turned into an eight-year marathon. In October 1964, the Association was finally allowed to do business in Alabama. By that time, given the threats implicit in the legal challenges, membership in the Alabama NAACP affiliates had dropped precipitously.

In other states, including Virginia, suits for barratry (the illegal solicitation of legal business) were introduced against the NAACP. According to Virginia's attorney general, given the barratry codes in the civil law, "attorneys who represented organizations having no 'pecuniary interest' in such litigation were subject to disbarment." In 1963, in the case from Virginia, *NAACP v. Button,* the Supreme Court, in a six-to-three opinion written by Justice William J. Brennan Jr., said that actions of Marshall and others from the Inc Fund on behalf of African Americans were protected by the First and Fourteenth Amendments.

In 1956, Mississippi created the State Sovereignty Commission. Its task was, through the use of illegal wiretaps and other covert investigations, to do anything necessary to protect the government of Mississippi from encroachment by the national government or any of its local branches, departments, and bureaus.

For decades it was the state's spy agency, investigating the NAACP and other civil rights groups and all persons thought to be sympathetic to these civil rights and "communist front" organizations. Files of those investigations were secreted in agency files in Jackson, Mississippi.[81]

In January 1955, government officials and private individuals from eleven states of the Old Confederacy met in Jackson, Mississippi, to organize a regional anti-desegregation group called the Federation of Constitutional Government. The governing board of the new organization included U.S. Senators Eastland and Thurmond, as well as six members of the U.S. House of Representatives and four former Southern governors. Its goal was to "fight racial integration and other efforts to destroy the Constitution" through coordinated actions of the various pro-segregation organizations that had been created or reborn since the Court's May 17, 1954, desegregation decision.[82] Despite the fanatical resistance to it, Marshall saw an immense value to *Brown,* one that went beyond the school segregation issue. The Supreme Court, in the years immediately after the decision, extended the case's constitutional reach beyond public school desegregation cases. The principle announced in *Brown* was quickly used to desegregate other public facilities and publicly operated recreational facilities in the South that had been operated on a segregated basis.

In very short, unsigned *per curiam* opinions, the Court ordered an end to segregation in a variety of public, state-connected places. Municipally owned parking-lot restaurants *(Burton v. Wilmington, Delaware, Parking Authority),* courthouses *(Johnson v. Virginia),* cemeteries *(Rice v. Sioux City Memorial Park Association),* hospitals *(Simkins v. Cone Memorial Hospital),* public parks and playgrounds *(Watson v. City of Memphis),* golf courses *(Holmes v. City of Atlanta),* and public buses *(Gayle v. Browder)* were ordered to desegregate. In addition, the Court used the same *per curiam* process to order desegregation of public beaches *(Dawson v. City of Baltimore)* and city-owned amphitheaters *(Muir v. Louisville, Kentucky, Park Theatrical Association).*

In another very fundamental way, *Brown* accounted for the birth and rapid growth of a new and massive civil rights movement, one that began in Montgomery, Alabama, in December 1955. *Brown,* said Marshall, "probably did more than anything else to awaken the Negro from his apathy to demanding his right to equality."[83] Demanding and fighting for civil rights for blacks, after 1955, was a responsibility that the NAACP was to begin to share, reluctantly, with other civil rights groups whose members were impatient with the slowness of the NAACP's litigation strategy in providing equal justice for African Americans.

# 7

## THE SEGREGATION BATTLES CONTINUE AND THE CIVIL RIGHTS MOVEMENT EMERGES

Accompanying Thurgood Marshall on a plane ride to Atlanta, Georgia, in 1956, Bernard Taper, who was doing a piece on him for *The New Yorker*, asked, "'What would the NAACP do if it found in the future that it won lawsuit after lawsuit and court decision after court decision but couldn't get the decisions put into effect?'" Marshall's worried response was, "'I don't know what we'd do. That's something I can't even contemplate. It would be anarchy. It would be the end of the country. I can't imagine it coming to that.'"[1]

In the years immediately following *Brown II*, Marshall saw the nation come perilously close to a sort of anarchy, encouraged by the absence of presidential leadership, a near insurrection he had once believed could never happen in a nation founded on the concept of the Rule of Law. Decent people, especially in the Deep South, white as well as African American, were effectively deprived of fundamental rights and freedom of expression because of the intimidation and outright terror they experienced at the hands of die-hard segregationists, particularly those in government who were sworn to uphold the law. Marshall observed that "the average person is afraid to even speak out in favor of what he knows is morally right—to follow the law as interpreted by the Supreme Court."[2]

When Kenneth Clark heard from an acquaintance, Max Spiegal, that Southern Jews were joining the White Citizens Councils across the South, he responded: "The plight of these Jews is a tragic one but no more tragic than a large and undetermined number of moderate potentially decent southern whites who have been terrorized into abject conformity and dare not express publicly an opinion which differs from the prevailing racial fanatic. These people are living under a terrible form of totalitarianism. They, even more than the Negro, need our help and our prayers."[3]

Decades later, Marshall admitted that the *Brown* victory in 1954 was the high point of his quarter-century struggle. Marshall's remaining years with the NAACP, from 1955 through 1961, were difficult and very painful, given the often violent resistance to desegregation of education. In 1955, Marshall was forty-seven years of age. He suffered through profound sadness over the death of his first wife but was gradually able to come to terms with his tragic loss. In December 1955, he married an NAACP staff secretary, Cecilia "Cissy" Suyat. Within a few years he experienced the joy of becoming the proud father of a son, Thurgood junior, followed two years later by another, John William.

Both sons attended the private Georgetown Day School. After school, Marshall often played cards with them. As he told a writer for *Jet* magazine, "I haven't pushed a [poker] chip in ten years. You know what cards I'm down to now! I play 'War' with my two boys. Now that's hot action for you, isn't it?" Looking back many years later, he recalled how much he enjoyed playing touch football (probably not very adroitly) with his boys and being able to have, at last, a happy family life that was not punctuated by constant travel. He said of his parenting role:

> I [didn't] give advice to either one...I had a deal with them. I would answer any question, but I wouldn't volunteer advice. And it ends up that one of them gave up a job paying $100,000 with the biggest law firm here to go to work for Ted Kennedy, and I said, "With all that money I spent on your education, why did you take that?" You know what he said? "I know somebody else who didn't give a damn about money, too." And my other son [John] is a [Virginia] state trooper...and he had the same kind of education, he graduated from Georgetown. And you know what he said? "I want to work for the people." So that's their way, not based on money.

John, while working as a Virginia State Police sergeant, secretly went back to Georgetown part-time and took a degree in government and sociology in 1986. John knew that his father was "disappointed" when he left college to become a policeman: "I told myself I was going to go back to school." John did not tell his father of his return to college until he sent him an invitation to his graduation. Marshall, his son recalled, "let out such a yell it scared me."

After graduation came law school. John needled his father a bit, telling him, "Of course, I'd want to be a prosecutor. I'd want to be on the prosecuting side. My dad, he'd shake his head again, I guess."[4] The other advocate in the family, Thurgood Marshall Jr., received his undergraduate and law degrees from the University of Virginia. In 1998, he was a part of Bill Clinton's administration, serving as secretary to the cabinet and as an adviser to the President. Both boys and their mother—and Marshall's wonderful, loving memories of Buster—did much to make up for the strain and sadness that was an ineluctable part of fighting for his fellow African Americans and all people, regardless of class or color, who suffered injustice and inequality.

However, the joy he experienced in family life was offset by his engagements in still more battles, in a war he thought had been won but would instead follow him into the very halls of the Supreme Court. As he said years later, while he was ready to "take a breather" from the civil rights wars after 1954, "we found out you can't take a breather. If you do, the other guy will run you ragged."[5] *Brown II* forced the Inc Fund into a legal war over school desegregation that went on for decades in the federal courts. Years later, Marshall said that the NAACP lawyers naively "put some trust in the decency of men....I'm afraid we assumed that after a short period of time of one to five years, the states would give in."[6] But the terrorism and economic repression directed against black Americans in those nightmarish years was as severe as in any other decade in the nation's history. Marshall knew that successful desegregation required a "mobilized African American community." Yet the men and women and their school-age children who had to be mobilized were confronted by the undisguised hatred and rage of die-hards, especially the members of White Citizens' Councils across the Deep South.

And the NAACP, especially its local field secretaries and other uncowed African Americans who dared to challenge local school policy with petitions and lawsuits in federal court, faced this vicious opposition *alone*. Much to the anger of Justice Hugo Black and the frustration of Marshall and the Inc Fund staff, the U.S. Supreme Court, during the years up through 1968, largely "abandoned the field of public school desegregation" to the local federal district court judges, who were "much too exposed" to the local politics of racism, in the hands of the "hometown [white] boys," in many parts of the South.[7] "The Supreme Court was not going to move, and we were caught in a bind," said Marshall as he reflected on the post-*Brown* era.

Until passage of the 1964 Civil Rights Act (which, in part, empowered the Civil Rights Division in the Justice Department to initiate litigation in federal courts challenging segregated school districts), the NAACP Inc Fund, *alone*, shouldered the burden of bringing litigation into the federal courts to challenge continued delay in the desegregation of schools in many parts of the South. As Marshall said in later years, the "leadership of President Johnson was most important, [because he] laid the groundwork" for the significant changes in the area of civil rights after 1964.

## THE "NEW WAVE" IN CIVIL RIGHTS

The key events that led to the emergence of an alternative civil rights movement unfolded in 1955. In late August of that year, fourteen-year-old Emmett Till, visiting relatives living in Money, Mississippi, from his home in Chicago, was killed for allegedly whistling at the white female owner of the local general store, and his body was dumped into the Tallahatchie River. Two men, the husband of the woman and his brother-in-law, were charged with the crime. At the trial they were identified in open court by the dead boy's relatives as the men who had abducted Emmett from his grandparents' home.

The two were acquitted by the all-white jury "in the time it takes to drink a bottle of soda pop."[8] Afterwards, for a modest fee, they had an interview with a *Life* magazine reporter and told him that they had indeed murdered Till in cold blood and thrown his body in the river. As Wilkins commented, ever so wearily, "massive resistance" was no longer just legal guerrilla warfare against the NAACP and the federal courts, nor was it simply evasion of desegregation orders, or the publishing of Southern Manifestos; instead, "it had become a blood issue."[9]

The terrible, brutal murder shocked the nation and radically changed black American responses to white segregationists' cruelties and injustices. As Anne Moody recalled in her 1968 book, *Coming of Age in Mississippi,* the Till murder was a tragic watershed event in her young life, one that screamed out for some kind of visible response to the evil that roamed the Mississippi Delta.

> Before Emmett Till's murder, I had known the fear of hunger, hell and the Devil. But now there was a new fear known to me—the fear of being killed just because I was black. This was the worst of my fears...[for] I didn't know what one had to do as a Negro not to be killed. Probably just being a Negro was enough, I thought.[10]

The Till lynching followed other coldblooded murders of African American civil rights workers living in Mississippi and working for the NAACP in the days after *Brown*. The leader of the Belzoni, Mississippi, NAACP branch, the Reverend George W. Lee, after getting four hundred black Americans to register to vote, was shot dead on a street in Belzoni on May 7, 1955. No one was ever charged with the crime. A co-worker, Gus Courts, was shot in November of that year but survived.

That summer, Lamar Smith, an NAACP field-worker from Brookhaven, Mississippi, and a World War II veteran, was shot and killed at midday in front of the courthouse. He was leading a voting rights drive in his county, and the local die-hards did not like what he was doing, so they gunned him down. Marshall, who knew Lamar, saw another one of his brave "Joe Doakeses" murdered by the segregationists. A local grand jury did not return an indictment.

The NAACP was powerless to stop these violent acts of murder and mayhem, or, at the very least, to act proactively to prevent future crimes. Most of the time there were no arrests, or if there was an arrest, there was no indictment. In the very few cases that went to trial, there was quick acquittal. Jury nullification effectively protected local white segregationists in these Deep South enclaves of race hatred if any of them somehow managed to be brought to trial.

At about the same time as the spate of lynchings were occurring in Mississippi, on December 1, 1955, "a revolution started in the aisle of a Cleveland Avenue bus, in Montgomery, Alabama."[11] Forty-three-year-old Rosa Parks, a local seamstress and NAACP worker, was arrested for refusing to give up her seat on a segregated public bus. Her arrest led to a 382-day boycott of the local buses by almost fifty thousand African Americans in the city. It also impelled E. D. Nixon, the local NAACP branch president, to establish the Montgomery Improvement Association, because the national office was slow to respond to the arrest. It was headed by a twenty-six-year-old Baptist minister, Martin Luther King Jr. A year later the MIA was replaced by King's Southern Christian Leadership Conference. A month into the boycott, things began to turn ugly. Bombs were thrown at the homes of Nixon and King. One hundred of the local African Americans were arrested by the police, and Fred Grey, the NAACP lawyer in Alabama working with the MIA, was harassed and "his draft board classified him as 1-A, taking away his deferment as a part-time minister."[12]

After a year of litigation, Marshall, aided by Alabama attorneys Fred Grey and Clifford Durr (a courageous white Alabama attorney related by marriage to Supreme Court Justice Hugo Black) and by his assistant, Robert Carter, won another case when the Supreme Court, in *Browder v. Gayle,* issued a *per curiam* opinion on November 13, 1956. It upheld the district court and federal court of appeals judgments that segregating public buses was unconstitutional and that the issuance by the federal district court judge of an injunction prohibiting Montgomery officials from enforcing these segregation statutes was valid.

## THE ALTERNATIVES TO THE NAACP: SCLC AND SNCC

The African American response to the segregationists' terror and intimidation was to move in a radically different direction, away from support of litigation undertaken by the NAACP—legal battles that often ended with Inc Fund victories in court but no implementation in the community—to more activist, nonviolent, direct-action *mass* protest. The new direct-action movements began "scooping up a whole generation of students by offering them something the NAACP could not: action."[13]

The human dynamics of these new mass movements were not fully grasped by Marshall, Wilkins, and other NAACP leaders but were, however, understood by social scientists and by charismatic ministers such as SCLC's King and one of his lieutenants, Andrew Young. As Young said, "Most people didn't realize that we were not in control [of the movement] in the sense that a movement is like an ocean tide. You don't really stop it; you might direct it constructively. That's all we were able to do…try to provide a constructive direction of the movement of people."[14]

Anne Moody gave expression to the feelings of rage this new generation of African American students felt about the continuing violence. Her hatred of people, white and black American alike for a time, began at age fifteen when Emmett Till was murdered in the Mississippi Delta. She hated the white segregationist murderers and all the other whites who did nothing to prevent these wanton killings. But she also hated "Negroes. I hated them for not standing up and doing something about the murders." Writing about the shotgun death of Samuel O'Quinn, a local NAACP field-worker, on a street in her town of Centreville, Mississippi, she said, "The blast left a hole through his chest large enough to stick a fist through."

> I lay in bed for two days after his death recalling [other murders of African Americans]. I hated myself and every other Negro in Centreville for not putting a stop to the killings or at least putting up a fight to stop them. I thought of waging a war in protest against the killings all by myself, if no one else would help. I wanted to take my savings, buy a machine gun, and walk down the main street in Centreville cutting down every white person I saw. Then, realizing that I didn't have it in me to kill, I slowly began to escape within myself again.[15]

For Anne Moody and for many others her age, the new civil rights groups were the answer. They gave her a constructive outlet for her rage and despair. It was much more meaningful and satisfying to take this path than to continue to help the NAACP's lawyers win a lawsuit in a Mississippi state court.

While Marshall and the Inc Fund lawyers continued to work with local citizens (in those states where it hadn't been forced to close up shop because of litigation against the Association itself) through litigation on school integration, voting rights, and criminal justice, many thousands of African Americans were fascinated with and accepted the new, nonviolent, mass direct-action philosophy of King and his SCLC. Local black communities in cities in the Deep South were being asked by SCLC leaders "to go into the streets and get battered and we were asking them to do this without ever raising a hand in their own defense," wrote Ralph Abernathy, King's chief aide.[16]

Marshall knew King's father, Martin Luther King Sr., and didn't like him very much; for the same reasons he didn't approve of the son. The elder King was a prominent Atlanta, Georgia, conservative Republican minister. In the mid-1940s he had headed the African Americans Citizens' Committee and was a constant critic of Marshall's efforts to challenge the Georgia white primary in federal court and of the Inc Fund's legal efforts to equalize the salaries of the city's black schoolteachers. King senior went so far as to visit the judge hearing the teacher salaries case, "and discussed the case with him," wrote Marshall to White in 1947.

> When Reverend King admitted this, I told him that he had placed the lawyers in such a position that it was necessary for us to withdraw from the case. The other members severely criticized Reverend King and urged us to remain in the case. I told them that I would hold the matter in abeyance. In the meantime, it looks as though Reverend King will be more cooperative in the future. If not, we will just have to get out of the case.[17]

A decade later, Martin Luther King Jr. was to cause Marshall quite different legal headaches arising from King's and his followers' mass demonstrations in the streets.

Marshall's first image of the younger King was of "this preacher jumping out of there [in Montgomery, in 1955]." Although he believed that King "came at the right time," Marshall had "lots of fights with Martin about his theory about disobeying the law":

"I didn't believe in that. I thought you did have a right to disobey a law, and you also had a right to go to jail for it. He kept talking about Thoreau, and I told him, 'If I understand it, Thoreau wrote his book in jail. If you want to write a book, you go to jail and write it.'"[18]

Marshall, the "Rules is Rules" advocate, never could accept King's mass demonstration tactics, especially his use of many hundreds of children in most of the SCLC demonstrations. Marshall had to admit, however, that King "was great, as leader. As an organizer," though, according to Marshall, Martin "wasn't worth diddley squat." In the end, Marshall was angry with King because he felt that he had "lost his touch" with the civil rights movement when he entered the heated national debate over the Vietnam War. King was, as Marshall concluded, "diluting the race issue…and I told him so—and it didn't change him.…And he said if his Lord told him to do something, he was going to do it. 'Well,' I said, 'no use arguing about that.'"[19]

The occasions on which King would rebuke the "gradualism" of the NAACP grew more frequent. Roy Wilkins was hurt by such criticism. For the leader of SCLC, wrote Wilkins, "to equate our faith in law with gradualism, the South's main device for resisting change, was a very low blow."[20] A few years later, in 1960, an offshoot of SCLC, consisting of young, mostly African American students, but including some whites, was created. The Student Nonviolent Coordinating Committee was also committed, in the early 1960s, to the religious, ethical values inherent in SCLC. When it was first organized, it saw itself as a community within a social struggle, one that followed the traditional teachings of Gandhi and other nonviolent protesters. SNCC's rhetoric was that of "nonviolent direct action and [it had a] moralistic orientation...[that] pervaded SNCC through the early 1960s," wrote one of their early leaders.[21]

SNCC began its nonviolent direct-action work with the reintroduction of the "sit-in" demonstration (a tactic used very briefly in the 1940s by CORE to protest racial segregation). On February 1, 1960, four black college freshmen from North Carolina A&T College sat down at a Woolworth's whites-only lunch counter in Greensboro, North Carolina, and requested service. They left after an hour; no arrests were made. Within days, their action spread like wildfire across the South. Black Americans used this tactic in all the states of the Old Confederacy that still had segregated public accommodations. Young college students also conducted "sympathy" protest marches in the North in front of national chains, such as Woolworth's and Kresge's, whose Southern stores were practicing segregation.

Marshall's initial move, after the February 1, 1960, sit-in, was to convene an Inc Fund strategy meeting to figure out how the NAACP should respond. According to Derrick Bell, then a young Inc Fund staff attorney, Marshall opened the three-day session by raging against "those crazy colored students [who] violated the sacred property rights of white folks by going into their stores or lunch counters and refusing to leave when ordered."[22] By the end of the marathon session, after figuring out how the NAACP could defend these SNCC protesters, Marshall announced that the Inc Fund would provide legal representation "for all Negroes unlawfully arrested while exercising their constitutional right to protest peacefully the refusal of stores open to the public to serve them on the same basis as white students."

Marshall honestly believed that King's mass demonstrators and the SNCC sit-in activists were implementing a very dangerous civil rights strategy that would cause more black Americans "to be arrested, thrown into medieval local jails in these crazed Deep South states, where they would be hurt, injured, or killed by the infuriated die-hard segregationists." Given this view of what could and would happen, Marshall reluctantly but immediately, came to their legal defense. "Even though Thurgood disagreed with our techniques," wrote John Lewis, one of the young SNCC leaders (and, in 1998, a member of Congress from Georgia), "he would make available the legal expertise and the legal resources of the Inc Fund, Jim Nabrit, Constance Baker Motley, Robert Carter, and a battery of just very bright and very smart people."[23]

SNCC leaders, influenced by an older generation of civil rights workers, especially two Southern African American women, Ella Baker and Septima Clark,
were committed to providing training for militant civil rights activists who, for
the first time in civil rights movement activity, were Thurgood's indigenous "Joe
Doakeses" of rural Alabama, Mississippi, and Georgia. Beyond training the new
leaders, SNCC had two primary goals: direct action to overturn segregation, primarily in Arkansas, Tennessee, Maryland, and Alabama; voter registration
drives in the Deep South, especially Mississippi, Georgia, South Carolina, and
Alabama.[24] They went into regions that neither the NAACP nor SCLC dared
go, particularly southwestern Georgia and Mississippi.

They were very courageous young men and women whose strategy was sum-
marized in their battle cry, "Jail, no bail." This strategy was a key difference
between SNCC and SCLC, and it created all sorts of additional problems for
Marshall and the Inc Fund, who were trying to get civil rights workers *out* of the
local jails! Through their actions, they "resolutely tested the limits of the nonviolent protest strategy." They willfully provoked "perilous confrontations with
Southern segregationists" in order to publicize the continuing evils of racism in
America.[25]

By the time of the 1964 Civil Rights Act, which, in part, provided for open
access to all public accommodations regardless of race, sex, color, religion, or
national origin (making sit-ins unnecessary), more than 70,000 students had
participated in these demonstrations across the South. Over 3,600 were arrested
and charged with a variety of crimes ranging from breach of the peace, trespass,
loitering, and vagrancy, to failing to obey an order to disperse. Like SCLC's mass
street marchers and protesters, these SNCC sit-in demonstrators regularly faced
violence from white segregationist onlookers as well as from the police who
arrested them.

The leaders of SNCC and SCLC were critical of the "old folks guard" of
fighters and organizations like Marshall and the NAACP. John Lewis, one of
these young militants, said, responding to Marshall's criticism of their strategy
and tactics, "I don't think some of the NAACP leaders and Thurgood Marshall
understood at that time the importance of creating mass movement. In a mass
movement you can involve more than just the plaintiffs, more than the lawyers,
the sort of just professional civil rights workers, but you can involve the masses
to help increase the tempo of change."[26]

In a letter to an African American White House staffer, Fred Morrow, written at the very start of the 1955 Montgomery bus boycott, Wilkins expressed his
frustration at the NAACP's evident inability to counter violence and intimidation of the segregationists. He spoke of the growing opposition to the NAACP's
legalistic response to white terror. The Association, he wrote Morrow, was

"being criticized for being 'too legal.' We are being told that the other side is stopping at nothing, while we proceed according to legal technicalities. Believe me, there is considerable support from hitherto fairly conservative areas of opinion for what may be termed a 'strike back' action, whether it is legal or not, or whether it is productive of anything except blind retaliation."[27] Marshall and others in the Association never accepted the notion of an irrational "strike back" strategy led by the NAACP—or even a mass demonstration against the continuation of violence. But many in the Inc Fund enjoyed defending demonstrators because it took them away, however briefly, from the NAACP's grinding, reactive litigation against educational inequality.

For Marshall and his small staff, their legal assistance for the protesters, including finding the money to cover all the fines and expenses incurred in defending the large numbers of those arrested, was "far more difficult to plan and control than the litigation culminating in *Brown.*" In the face of such discouraging odds in school segregation battles, Marshall persevered stoically. While he "realized that there was a change from the legal movement in the courts, to the protest movements in the streets,"[28] Marshall provided the essential courtroom leadership that enabled these new groups to succeed in ways that were, when they began, unimaginable to the leadership of the NAACP. While these new direct-action civil rights movements were directing the attention of the nation to segregation in the South, Marshall and his staff had to struggle on in the less dramatic forums of courtrooms to wear down Southern resistance in the face of the Supreme Court's desegregation order in the 1955 *Brown* opinion.

## THE LITTLE ROCK CRISIS

The first major firestorm of reaction occurred in Little Rock, Arkansas. It was one that involved the federal district court, the U.S. Supreme Court, and the President of the United States on one side and Arkansas's governor, Orval Faubus, along with state and local judges and other state political leaders, on the other.

It is ironic that the major clash between the national government and state segregationists in the long, bitter post-*Brown* struggle took place not in Mississippi or Alabama (which certainly had their share of traumatic incidents at the time) but in the relatively less racially polarized state of Arkansas. The school board in Little Rock had acted promptly to desegregate its public schools, showing the "good faith" requested by the Court in *Brown II.* On May 20, 1954, three days after the first *Brown* decision, the board adopted and, on May 23, 1954, made public its commitment to desegregate. After studying the administrative problems associated with desegregation, the board adopted the Blossom

Plan, named after a local high school superintendent, Virgil Blossom, on May 24, 1955.

The plan provided for desegregation of the high schools first, followed by junior high schools and, finally, elementary schools. The plan was to begin in September 1957, and by September 1963, desegregation would be completed. After public discussion of the plan, it was adopted by the board. African American parents challenged it, arguing for speedier desegregation. The federal district court upheld the plan, and the federal court of appeals, in April 1957, affirmed the lower court judgment. The parents chose not to appeal to the U.S. Supreme Court.

While the local leaders in the city were moving toward school desegregation, however, the state legislature and the state's governor were moving in the opposite direction and "actively pursuing a program designed to perpetuate in Arkansas the system of racial segregation which [the U.S. Supreme] Court had held violated the Fourteenth Amendment." Indeed, on August 29, 1957, Governor Orval E. Faubus went into the Arkansas state court system and received a restraining order from a chancery court judge that prevented the federal judiciary–approved desegregation plan from taking effect. The next day, upon petition of the school board, the federal district court judge issued an order enjoining enforcement of the state order. He "acted to prevent obstruction of a court order issued by a [federal district court judge] a year prior thereto," noted Attorney General Brownell, in a memo sent to President Eisenhower during the crisis.

Even in the face of repressive state laws passed in the fall and winter of 1956–57, and attempts by the governor to get state court action to "invalidate" the federal court action, the Little Rock school administrators continued to move toward public school desegregation. Nine African American high school students were scheduled for September 1957 admission into Central High School. On September 2, 1957, the day before school was to open, Governor Faubus, claiming to be fearful that "blood will run in the streets" if he did not act, ordered almost three hundred Arkansas National Guardsmen to surround Central High School, and placed the school "off limits" to African American students (as well as placing the African American high school, Horace Mann, "off limits" to white students). In part, Faubus's order stated that the military was there to restore the "peace and good order" of the community. "It is my conviction," the order read, "that it will not be possible to restore or maintain order and protect the lives and property of the citizens if forcible integration is carried out tomorrow in the schools of this community. The inevitable conclusion therefore must be that the schools in Pulaski County, for the time being, must be operated on the same basis as they have operated in the past."

Even as the troops arrived the day before school was to begin, "peace and good order" prevailed in Little Rock. There was no need for a military presence; there were no angry crowds surrounding the high school, nor had there been any hostile acts or even threats of violence. The governor did not discuss the deployment of the troops with any local officials. Faubus's action was not requested by the mayor of the city or by the local school authorities; it was, said the Supreme Court, "entirely unheralded."[29]

The governor's actions might well have been encouraged by something President Eisenhower said after the Deep South's massive resistance activities had begun in deadly earnest. In a July 17, 1957, press conference, he remarked, "I can't imagine any set of circumstances that would ever induce me to send federal troops...into any area to enforce the orders of a federal court....I believe [the] common sense of America will never require it...[but] I would never believe that [sending in the federal troops] would be a wise thing to do in this country."[30]

This hands-off position of the President was a none-too-subtle message to all Southern racists that the executive branch would not support the NAACP and other civil rights groups. Mrs. L. C. "Daisy" Bates, the President of Arkansas's NAACP branch who was leading the attempt to desegregate Little Rock, was shocked and outraged. "His words," she wrote afterwards, "electrified Little Rock....[We] were confused, and [we] were frightened."[31] She telegraphed Wilkins, telling him, "there is a real campaign of terror going on down here. A cross was burned in front of my house on Sunday. They broke my picture window on Tuesday night. We have set up floodlights in front of my home, and it is being guarded around the clock."

Roy Wilkins blasted Faubus's actions in a telegram to the President. "Negro Americans," he wrote, "are greatly concerned over the prevalent idea that states and regions are free to decide whether to abide by the Constitution and federal rulings or not as they see fit....This doctrine threatens the entire concept of a federal union and endangers a wide category of rights and privileges of the citizens of the United States wherever they may live."

The immediate consequence of the use of troops, as noted by the Supreme Court in its description of the events, "was to harden the core of opposition to the Plan and cause many persons who theretofore had reluctantly accepted the Plan to believe that there was some power in the state of Arkansas which, when exerted, could nullify the federal law and permit disobedience of the decree of the Court, and from that date hostility to the Plan was increased and criticism of the officials of the school district has become more bitter and unrestrained."[32]

Eisenhower equivocated. At a September 3, 1957, press conference, when asked about the governor's action, he expressed his personal view that "time and again, a number of people—*I, among them*—have argued that you cannot change people's hearts merely by laws." (My emphasis.) That same day the school board asked the African American students not to attend school until the legal problems were resolved. Within a day, federal district court judge Davies said that Faubus's action was not a sufficient reason for departing from the desegregation plan, and ordered the school board and its administrators to proceed with the plan's implementation. His order was disregarded by Faubus. On September 4, 1957, the National Guard refused to let the black students enter the high school. This prohibition continued for about three weeks.

On September 14, in an unprecedented meeting between Eisenhower and Faubus held at the naval station at Newport, Rhode Island, the President tried to persuade the governor that the state had to obey the orders of the federal district court. As the President wrote in his diary, "I suggested to him that he go home and not necessarily withdraw his national guard troops, *but just change their orders to say... that the Guard continue to preserve order but to allow the Negro children to attend Central High School....I did not want to see any Governor humiliated.*"[33] (My emphasis.) Faubus nodded in apparent agreement, stating that he would obey "a valid court order." But when he returned to Arkansas he remained defiant and his troops continued to prevent the African American children from attending Central High School.

At the same time, Attorney General Brownell asked the federal district court to issue an injunction prohibiting Faubus and the military from acting to prevent obedience to the court order calling for the plan to proceed. If Faubus did not obey the federal court order, he was "clearly in danger of a contempt citation from the judge, perhaps even arrest," wrote Brownell years later.[34] That would have triggered an even greater crisis. It was clear, however, that Faubus, running for reelection in November 1957, was unwilling to back down and accept an order from a bitterly despised federal judge. On September 20, 1957, Judge Davies issued a final order calling on Faubus to comply with the previous ruling.

On Saturday, September 21, the ever "cunning" Faubus,[35] knowing that there were over one thousand angry, irrational, die-hard segregationists from Arkansas and other Southern states in the streets surrounding Central High School, appeared on statewide television to announce that he was removing the National Guard from their posts at the high school. He knew all too well that the local Little Rock police would not be able to control the mob camped outside the school and that he was not going to send state troopers or the guard to prevent the violence that was virtually guaranteed to break out.

On Monday, September 23, the children were admitted to Central High School, under the protection of local police officers. When the nine youngsters entered the school, the crowd went wild. "After three hours of riot and tumult, the Negro children were removed from the school by orders of the Mayor and local officials," reported Brownell to the President. "Only one effective method remained to enforce the law: presidential use of federal troops." On the advice of Brownell, Eisenhower issued a proclamation on September 23, calling on the enraged mob of segregationists to disperse. That did not happen and so, the next day, he signed an executive order that sent regular army troops, a battalion of the crack 101st Airborne, to "aid in the execution of Federal law at Little Rock, Arkansas." (Ironically, the general in charge of the troops in Little Rock, Edwin Walker, would in 1962 be the racist civilian leading a segregationist mob of thousands at the University of Mississippi in an extended, pitched battle against federal marshals to prevent the integration of "Ole Miss." President John F. Kennedy, like his predecessor in 1957, reluctantly had to call in the regular army to restore order in a violent riot in which a number of people were killed.)

Eisenhower's action was necessary, Brownell believed, "to suppress the domestic violence, obstruction and resistance…then and there existing." The President, wrote his attorney general, has the constitutional power "to compel obedience to law and order."[36] That night, the President spoke to the nation about his actions:

> Under the leadership of demagogic extremists, disorderly mobs have deliberately prevented the carrying out of proper orders from a Federal Court.… Unless [I acted], anarchy would result.…Mob rule cannot be allowed to override the decisions of our courts. With deep confidence, I call upon the citizens of the State of Arkansas to assist in bringing about an immediate end to all interference with the law and its processes. If resistance to the Federal Court orders ceases at once, the further presence of Federal troops will be unnecessary and the City of Little Rock will return to its normal habits of peace and order and a blot upon the fair name and high honor of our nation in the world will be removed.

The President received letters of thanks from Little Rock school board members for his actions. The secretary of the school board, Wayne Upton, told Eisenhower, "While I am not in favor of integration, and in making this statement I believe I reflect the feelings of our individual board members, nevertheless, as a lawyer, I have respect for the lawful orders of all our courts and shall continue to do whatever I can to be in compliance with, and not in defiance of, the law."[37]

Other letter-writers were not so gracious. Among the dozen letters Eisenhower received from members of the Congress, a particularly damning one came from Senator Richard Russell of Georgia, the chairman of the Senate

Armed Services Committee. The powerful legislator claimed that the federal troops were "applying tactics which have been copied from the manual issued the officers of Hitler's Storm Troopers." That same day, September 27, 1957, Eisenhower responded to his good friend from Georgia. "Few times in my life have I felt as saddened as when the obligations of my office required me to order the use of force within a state to carry out the decisions of a Federal Court," he wrote.

After explaining why he had acted, the President closed with a comment about Russell's mention of Nazi storm troopers. "I must say that I completely fail to comprehend your comparison of our troops to Hitler's storm troopers. In one case military power was used to further the ambitions and purposes of a ruthless dictator; in the other to preserve the institutions of free government."

The regular army troops were soon replaced with state guardsmen "federalized" by President Eisenhower in November 1957. They remained on guard at Central High School for the remainder of the school year. The nine students were constantly harassed by about fifty white students (a small minority of a high school population of about two thousand students). Life for them, wrote Wilkins, "became a daily misery." They were jeered, kicked, hit with rocks, smeared with ink, had food spilled on them, were "hit with bowls of soup, bombarded with racist epithets." Nothing was done to stop such intimidation. Finally, in February 1958, one of the African American girls, Minnie Jean Brown, after being called "nigger bitch" by a white female student, was expelled from school for the remainder of the semester. The reason: she had turned to the white girl and exclaimed, "White trash!"[38]

Marshall and other NAACP people in Little Rock tried to protect the nine families whose children were involved. As he recalled, these were absolutely the best people in the world, all strong and seemingly undaunted by the violence around them, especially the children. Marshall recalled meeting with them all one night to let the families know that money had been found for bodyguards. One father said, "No way." He had been in World War II: "When I left the Army, I said I wouldn't touch a gun again, and I'm not going to." Marshall tried to persuade him to accept protection, but the man ended the conversation when he said, "I am just not afraid." In the end, without informing the family, Marshall stationed a guard across the street to safeguard them.[39]

The Little Rock crisis continued the following year. The school board, concerned about the continuing safety of the African American students, but not prepared to punish the small band of whites who were persecuting them, went to the federal district court to request a thirty-month delay in the implementation of the desegregation plan. The federal district judge, citing the "unfavorable community attitude...violence, chaos, bedlam, and turmoil," and the generally "intolerable" situation, granted the delay on June 20, 1958.

## THE U.S. SUPREME COURT REAFFIRMS
## BROWN: THE COOPER V. AARON DECISION

The parents, with Marshall and the NAACP Inc Fund appearing on their behalf in federal court, appealed to the Eighth Circuit U.S. Court of Appeals. In August 1958, the appeals court overturned the federal district court order. However, the court stayed its mandate to allow both parties to appeal to the Supreme Court. Both parties did appeal. Because of the importance of the issues raised in the litigation, the Court convened a Special Term on August 28 to determine whether Central High School would open on a desegregated basis that September. By September the justices found themselves listening to Marshall argue the Little Rock school segregation case before them. Just prior to the convening of this special session to hear oral arguments in *Cooper v. Aaron*\* on September 11, 1958, Attorney General William P. Rogers sent a letter to the Little Rock city manager and the school board members, telling them that "because of the possibility that the Supreme Court may affirm the decision of the Eighth Circuit Court of Appeals, it seems desirable that careful plans should be made now by responsible officials to prevent disorder or violence in the event of such affirmance." (Herbert Brownell resigned in late October 1957, after the initial Little Rock crisis had abated significantly, and his deputy, Rogers, took over.)

Rogers pledged his full cooperation with these local officials. Arrangements were made for the temporary expansion of the U.S. Marshal's office in order that it might "perform their proper functions to assist in the execution of the orders of the United States courts and do it cooperatively in a way that will be helpful to you." He hoped that through such advance preparation, "mob violence and disorder may be prevented." [40]

In the special session, the justices heard oral argument in the case on September 11, 1958. The following day, the Court met to examine what, for Justice Harold Burton, was the "first real test of the power of the federal courts to implement the *Brown* decision." [41] The justices were enraged by the behavior of the state officials, who were plainly disregarding the law of the land. Warren, at oral argument, pressed the attorney for the defendants to address the issue of violence and evasion of legal orders of the federal judiciary by the state. At the conference that immediately followed the oral arguments, the brethren took only a few minutes to uphold the court of appeals decision and to issue, dated

---

\*Both parties appealed to the Court and the cases *Aaron v. Cooper* and *Cooper v. Aaron* were joined. John Aaron was one of a number of blacks who asked the Court to vacate the federal appellate court's stay suspending the implementation of the Little Rock "plan to do away with segregated schools." William Cooper and other members of the board of directors of the Little Rock Independent School District asked the justices to allow the district court order to remain in effect.

September 12, 1958, a *per curiam* opinion that would, as Warren told the brethren, "reaffirm the duty of state officials to obey the law as laid down by the Supreme Court."[42] The full opinion was to follow shortly; it was announced on September 29, 1958.

After the September 12 conference, the Court met two more times, on September 24 and 26, to discuss the opinion then being hurriedly drafted by William J. Brennan, one of the three justices who had joined the Court after *Brown.* The Court's unanimity was threatened by a Clark dissent, but, after writing a longhand draft that indicated his concern that the "all deliberate speed" concept was being rejected, he joined the Brennan opinion. Brennan, a state supreme court judge from New Jersey who had recently (1956) been appointed to the Supreme Court by Eisenhower, "worked long and hard on writing a full opinion for the Court."[43] He had some difficulty with the initial draft opinion's style and "verbal differences." These were called to his attention by another recently appointed justice, John M. Harlan II (the grandson of John Marshall Harlan, the "great dissenter" in *Plessy*), when Brennan circulated the draft in mid-September.

He was, however, helped by a number of his colleagues, especially Hugo Black, who assisted him in the development of the critical opening paragraph in the case. In longhand, Black wrote this language for Brennan to use:

> As this case reaches us it involves questions of the highest importance to the maintenance of our federal system of government. It squarely presents a claim that there is no duty on state officials to obey federal court orders resting on this Court's deliberate and considered interpretation of the United States Constitution. Specifically, it involves actions by the Governor, Legislature and other agencies of Arkansas...that they are not bound by our holding in *Brown*...that the Fourteenth Amendment forbids states to use their governmental powers to bar children from attending schools which are helped to run by public management funds or other public property. We are urged to permit continued suspension of the Little Rock School Board's plan to do away with segregated public schools until state laws and efforts to upset [*Brown*] have been further challenged and tested in the courts. We have concluded that these contentions call for clear answers here and now.[44]

This was a very powerful and direct message telling all state officials that they were bound to obey the law of the land, including the orders of the Supreme Court.

Black's second modification of the Brennan opinion underlined the supremacy of the Constitution; the Fourteenth Amendment was "therefore the

supreme law throughout this nation, binding on state no less than federal officials." A few justices suggested another change that was quickly adopted by the
group. It was a significant one. "To show that we were all [especially the three
justices who joined the Court after *Brown*] in favor of [*Brown*], we should also
say so...by an opinion signed by the entire Court," said Chief Justice Warren.[45]
After Black's modifications were incorporated, the unanimous opinion was ready
for announcement on September 29, 1958.

Frankfurter, however, dropped a "bombshell," as Douglas put it, when he
announced, at the last conference, that he was publishing a concurring opinion,
because he thought it might influence many of his students now practicing law
in the South. Warren, Black, Douglas, and Brennan expressed their outrage so
strongly that Frankfurter reluctantly agreed to announce his concurrence separately, a week later.

That was not the end of the Little Rock crisis, however. The school board,
concerned for the continued safety of the students and threatened by the state
legislature with a cutoff of state education funds (the statute, quickly passed after
*Cooper* came down, denied funding to any integrated school district), closed the
schools for the balance of the 1958–59 academic year. Marshall succeeded in
getting the federal district court to quickly strike down the board order.
However, the board appealed and the justices found themselves, once again,
reading and listening to Marshall argue the Little Rock, Arkansas, school segregation case before them. They, too, once again agreed with Marshall. In a *per
curiam* order, the justices upheld the federal district court order and required the
Little Rock schools to reopen immediately. They did, but very briefly, remaining
closed for the rest of the 1958–59 school year.

When the Little Rock schools opened in September 1959, they did so "using
a pupil assignment desegregation plan," in which attendance zone lines were
redrawn to enhance desegregation. This arrangement was kept until 1964, when
the district instituted a "freedom of choice" plan allowing students in all grades
to attend the school of their choice if space was available.[46] This type of "desegregation" plan was a notorious one that was widely used to evade the *Brown*
mandate. It was challenged across the South by the Inc Fund because it really
was a way around the "good faith" requirement to desegregate schools. In Little
Rock, in *Clark v. Board of Education,* the federal district court invalidated the
plan because it did not achieve adequate racial balance. A court-ordered "pairing
plan" was agreed to by the board and by the NAACP Inc Fund. It took effect in
1973–74.

By the 1970s, however, Little Rock residents had *resegregated* themselves. As
*The New York Times* reported, "Whites have fled to the suburbs by the thousands
to escape school desegregation and the city is building itself racial islands, black

ones in the central city and white ones further out."[47] The London *Economist*'s reporter covering the events that led to the crisis noted, in 1958, that Faubus had lost, but he had fought a losing battle "in such a way as to cause the greatest loss to all concerned."

Forty years after the admission of the nine African American students into Little Rock's Central High School, President Bill Clinton visited Central High School. His remarks spoke to the continuing dilemma of racial segregation and discrimination in America. "Segregation is no longer the law, but too often separation is still the rule.... Today, children of every race walk through the same door, but then they often walk down different halls... they sit in different classrooms, they eat at different tables.... We retreat into the comfortable enclaves of ethnic isolation." In 1957 the Little Rock public school system had 74 percent white students and 26 percent African American. In 1997 there were 67 percent African American schoolchildren in the system and only 33 percent white. Most African American students attending Central High School in 1997 are in regular classes, while many more of the white students are enrolled in the advanced classes. Private all-white academies, created in 1957 in Little Rock, in 1997 enroll almost 50 percent of Little Rock's white student population. The Arkansas NAACP and its Little Rock affiliate did not participate in the fortieth anniversary commemoration; they "boycotted [the events] because they maintain that little progress has been made over the past 40 years."[48]

## EISENHOWER'S CIVIL RIGHTS VIEW: "MAKE HASTE SLOWLY"

Dwight David Eisenhower was six years old when *Plessy*'s "separate but equal" doctrine was formulated by the Court in 1896. "He had lived all his life with it. There were no Negroes in his hometown, none at West Point. As Ike's biographer, Stephen Ambrose, has written,

> Eisenhower had spent virtually all his prewar career at army posts in the South....During the war, he had commanded a Jim Crow Army....[He] had many southern friends and he shared most of their prejudices against Negroes. When he went down to Augusta [Georgia], he listened to the plantation owners tell their jokes about the "darkies"; when he returned to Washington, in the privacy of his family, he would repeat some of those jokes.[49]

Marshall had few good things to say about the President. He had formed an opinion about Eisenhower's racial views when the general, testifying before a congressional committee in 1947, opposed the elimination of racial segregation in the armed services.[50] Ike believed that separating military men based on race and color was appropriate. His association with African Americans was almost nil. After entering the White House, he maintained his friendships with some powerful Southern political leaders, Democrats who had worked for his election in 1952. Clearly, Eisenhower was comfortable in the South and with his Southern friends. Jimmy Byrnes was governor of South Carolina during most of the Eisenhower administration. When Eisenhower visited Columbia, South Carolina, during the last days of the 1952 presidential campaign, he "was seated after greeting Byrnes when a band struck up the martial strains of 'Dixie.' Eisenhower immediately rose from his chair and delighted the local crowd by saying, 'I always stand up when they play that song.'"[51]

Roy Wilkins was even less generous in his comments about Eisenhower. As executive secretary of the NAACP, he worked closely with legislators and other politicians in Washington, D.C., and his view was that "Eisenhower was doing as little as he could to help us."

> If the President had put his personal prestige and the influence of the White House solidly behind the Supreme Court right after the school-cases decision, it might have been possible to blunt massive resistance more quickly. As it was, the President's early actions were at best equivocations and at worst derelictions. They gave a false sense of legitimacy to obstructionists and nullifiers.[52]

Indeed, a few months after the 1954 *Brown* decision was announced by the Court, the President told a group of Southern governors, "I think *personally* the decision was wrong." The President "personally wished that the Court had upheld *Plessy v. Ferguson,* and said so on a number of occasions (but only in private)."[53] One of his White House aides characterized the President as someone who had a "'basic insensitivity' to the whole issue. Although revolted by individual acts of bigotry and fond of those few blacks he knew personally, Ike cared little about the problems of Negroes in general."[54]

Earl Warren recalled that just before *Brown* came down, Eisenhower invited him to a stag party at the White House. Present at the small gathering was John W. Davis, the lead counsel for the segregationists in *Brown* and the four other cases then before the Court. As Ambrose notes, "[Warren said, Eisenhower] went to great lengths to tell me what a great man Mr. Davis was. And, when the guests were filing out of the dining room, Eisenhower took Warren by the arm and said of the southerners, 'These are not bad people. All they are concerned about is to see that their sweet little girls are not required to sit in school alongside some big overgrown Negroes.'"[55]

At a May 19, 1954, press conference, just two days after *Brown,* the President was asked if he had "any advice to give the South as to just how to react to the recent Supreme Court decision banning segregation." His answer was instantaneous—and deeply troubling to Marshall and Wilkins. *"Not in the slightest,"* he said. "The Supreme Court has spoken, and I am sworn to uphold the constitutional process in this country. *And I am trying—I will obey it."* (My emphasis.) Again, on November 23, 1954, Ike was just as equivocal at another press conference, this one shortly after briefs had been filed with the Court for *Brown II.* When asked if he had any personal views on how *Brown* should be implemented, he answered, "Well, not particularly." Clearly, as Marshall and Wilkins had said, these were missed chances for the President to lead the nation. Instead, he did not offer any personal insight into his feelings about the equality issue— in public, that is.

On the one hand, he allowed his Department of Justice, under the fairly liberal leadership of Nebraska-born Herbert Brownell, to file strong briefs *amicus curiae* in the *Brown* litigation and allowed Justice to try to initiate aggressive civil rights legislation in Congress, while on the other hand the President refused, until it was far too late, to display any leadership in response to the massive resistance, including lynchings, in the Deep South to the *Brown* decision.

An example of this narrowness of view is afforded by Eisenhower's response to the 1955–56 black boycott of segregated public buses in Montgomery. When Martin Luther King pleaded with the President for federal help in the face of bombings and terror, his request was turned down. The response, in a letter from Warren Olney, the assistant attorney general in charge of the Criminal Division, said that "notwithstanding our deep aversion to violent acts of the sort you describe, the primary responsibility for the maintenance of law and order is lodged in state and local authorities. The federal government has no general police power." [56]

Another event illustrates Eisenhower's views about school desegregation. In August 1958, Eisenhower bluntly chastised his new attorney general after reading a draft of a speech Rogers was proposing to deliver. Eisenhower "recommended" that Rogers *"avoid predictions that the [Supreme Court's school desegregation] law will necessarily be permanent,"* and that he *"not give the impression that the Federal government is looking for opportunities to intervene on its own initiative; the key for success must be local."* Finally, the President noted that integration would be accomplished only at a very gradual rate: *"Indeed, I personally think that some of the plan, even in such places as Tennessee, may be 30 or 40 years in reaching the ideal."* [57] (My emphasis.)

Eisenhower never used the "bully pulpit" of his office to speak out in support of the values inherent in *Brown.* As one biographer of the President asserted, "What hurt was not Eisenhower's private disapproval of *Brown,* but his refusal to give it a public endorsement."[58] As Justice William O. Douglas noted in his autobiography, voicing an opinion shared by many,

> There was tragedy in Eisenhower's attitude....If he had gone to the nation on television and radio telling the people to obey the law and fall into line, the cause of desegregation would have accelerated. Ike was a hero, and he was worshipped. Some of his political capital spent on the racial cause would have brought the nation closer to the constitutional standards. Ike's ominous silence on our 1954 decision gave courage to the racists who decided to resist the decision ward by ward, precinct by precinct, and county by county.

Jackie Robinson, the black baseball player who broke the major leagues' color barrier when he joined the Brooklyn Dodgers in 1947, was the membership chair of the NAACP at this time. He, too, although a Republican Party activist, condemned the President: "If there had been vigorous and uncompromising leadership from the White House, America would never have had the shame of Little Rock."[59]

Marshall certainly shared these views of the President. He said many times that

> if President Eisenhower had used his good offices to say that "this is the law and it should be obeyed," that would have accomplished much. We hoped for it. And we found out too late that indeed, Eisenhower was opposed to it [Brown's rulings that called for school desegregation], and was working against it, and even went so far as to try to convince Chief Justice Warren to vote the other way. *That to my mind is the most despicable job that any president has done in my life.* (My emphasis.)[60]

Marshall was referring to an incident that took place between Eisenhower and Chief Justice Earl Warren while the Court was in the process of deciding *Brown I.* It was a story told to him by his colleague Ralph Bunche. At a luncheon the President pulled Warren aside and, with Bunche standing close by, proceeded to talk to him about the value of segregated schools. Bunche "distinctly heard Chief Justice Warren say to President Eisenhower, 'I thought I would never have to say this to you, but I now find it necessary to say to you specifically, you mind your business and I'll mind mine.'"[61]

It is ironic that Eisenhower appointed two men to the U.S. Supreme Court, Chief Justice Earl Warren in 1953 and Associate Justice William J. Brennan Jr. in 1956, both of whom were absolutely committed to the idea of racial equality of opportunity. In May 1961, Walter Cronkite and Fred Friendly, the CBS newsman and the producer, visited the former President at his home in Gettysburg, Pennsylvania, for a series of televised conversations. During a break, Friendly noted that Eisenhower's administration would be remembered for placing Earl Warren on the Supreme Court. "'I'm surprised to hear you say that, Fred,' [Eisenhower replied]. 'That was the worst mistake I ever made.' Friendly said he then asked, 'Are you saying that's one of the mistakes you made as President?' Eisenhower, Friendly said, put two fingers up: 'two, and they're both sitting on the Supreme Court—Earl Warren and William Brennan.' He said, 'Brennan's just as bad. Those are two very important jobs, and I didn't do a very good job with them.'"[62]

Herbert Brownell, Ike's first attorney general, grew up in the Midwest like his boss, but lived his adult life in New York and was a part of the Republican Party's "Eastern liberal establishment." Marshall and Wilkins believed that Brownell was "one of the more enlightened men in the Eisenhower Administration."[63] He continually tried to convince Eisenhower that the federal government must do more to deal with the violence and terror taking place in the Deep South, actions that were left unchecked and unpunished by local and state law enforcement agencies.

During the Eisenhower administration, the NAACP continued to push for an eight-point civil rights bill. A number of its suggestions were welcomed by Brownell, although not by the President. The NAACP leadership proposed an omnibus bill calling for equal employment opportunity, a permanent FEPC (still not in existence fifteen years after Roosevelt, under pressure from White and Randolph, created the first temporary FEPC), abolition of the poll tax, protection of the right to vote, establishment of a Civil Rights Division in the Department of Justice, creation of a Civil Rights Commission, integrated interstate travel, and an end to the rigid cloture rule in the Congress that enabled the small Southern delegation of senators to filibuster and kill civil rights proposals.

Roy Wilkins and a few other African American leaders, including Congressman Adam Clayton Powell, Martin Luther King Jr., A. Philip Randolph, and baseball great Jackie Robinson, did finally meet with the President toward the end of June 1958, in an effort to persuade Eisenhower that more needed to be done by the federal government to end the terror and violence taking place in the Deep South. The meeting was attended by Attorney General Rogers as well.

After telling the President that African Americans "have exhibited unparalleled patience in the face of decades of proscription and persecution," but that, in 1958, "they are frustrated and angry," and many of them "are questioning whether their forbearance and respect for orderly procedure are rewarding," the group presented Eisenhower with a prepared statement, one that contained the recommendations for a proposed civil rights bill.

Eisenhower's response to their comments was one of "extreme dismay," according to Rocco Siciliano, a White House staffer who kept a record of the meeting. According to Roy Wilkins, the President's response to the suggestions was stony silence.[64] Eisenhower then became defensive. He said he was shocked to hear that "after five and one half years of effort and action in this field these gentlemen were saying that bitterness on the part of the Negro people was at its height. He wondered if further constructive action in this field would not only result in more bitterness." When Randolph suggested that Eisenhower's imprimatur on these recommendations may "give it a high moral tone," the President replied that "there was only so much any President could do."[65]

The President did not again meet with a delegation of black American leaders. None of the recommendations were acted on by his administration. Republicans in the House and Senate, without any leadership from Eisenhower and in the face of opposition by senior Southern members who chaired key committees, did nothing.

## IKE'S AMBIVALENT SUPPORT OF THE 1957 CIVIL RIGHTS ACT

After Eisenhower's reelection in 1956, a modest civil rights bill was presented to Congress in 1957, as a result of heavy pressure from Brownell. He wrote, years later, that after *Brown* was decided in 1954, "I became convinced that the time was ripe for new civil rights legislation," a belief confirmed by Emmett Till's murder. His problem was his boss; Eisenhower would have little to do with a civil rights proposal that sought to assert the authority and use the powers of the national government more vigorously.

Eisenhower was finally persuaded that the Department of Justice needed civil rights legislation to do its job of ensuring that federal laws were implemented. He introduced its general parameters in his State of the Union message before a joint session of Congress on January 10, 1957. Almost immediately after he delivered the message to the nation, Eisenhower was pressured by Southern legislators to go easy on civil rights and warned that the proposed legislation would be, as Senator Richard Russell of Georgia told him, "vigorously resisted by a resolute group of Senators."[66]

Threatened with another Southern filibuster two days after he spoke about the proposal, Eisenhower immediately backed off from the controversial Title III, which would have given the attorney general direct power to sue in federal courts whenever there was a civil rights violation. For the Southern senators, as Russell said on behalf of the group, Title III, if allowed to stand, would put "the whole might of the federal government...to force the commingling of white and Negro children in the State-supported schools of the South."[67]

After discussions with the Cabinet about the proposed civil rights act, the President told Brownell that he could not support Title III but that Brownell could "send the bill to Congress as a Department of Justice proposal," and so he did.[68] This démarche by Eisenhower did not surprise Marshall or Wilkins; they were saddened by the unwillingness of the President to strike out proactively on behalf of African American citizens denied fundamental civil rights and liberties. Senate Majority Leader Lyndon B. Johnson told Roy Wilkins and other civil rights lobbyists that it was, fundamentally, a political decision; Title III had to go or there would be no civil rights act.[69]

A few weeks later, at his July 17, 1957, press conference, in response to a question about whether Title III was "a wise extension of federal power," the President said, *"I personally believe if you try to go too far too fast in laws in this delicate field, that has involved the emotions of so many millions of Americans, you are making a mistake."* The final version of Title III, worked out by Johnson and Brownell, gave federal judges the power to decide whether a defendant would receive a jury trial. This satisfied the Southern senators, for they knew the likelihood of jury nullification in civil rights trials. With these changes, the bill was passed by the Senate on August 7, 1957. The vote was 72 to 18. The only Southern senators voting for it were Johnson and his Texas senatorial colleague, Ralph Yarborough, along with Tennessee's Estes Kefauver and Albert Gore, and George Smathers of Florida. Southern congressional power was employed to weaken it—but for all that, the first national civil rights legislation passed since 1875 had finally been enacted.

At this time, Roy Wilkins, though not Marshall, became extremely critical of Senator John F. Kennedy's actions in the debate over the 1957 Civil Rights Act. By then, Washington pundits were viewing Kennedy as a possible candidate for the Democratic Party's presidential nomination in 1960. In a number of speeches in 1957 and 1958, Wilkins claimed that the Massachusetts senator, in his efforts to get the 1960 nomination, had buddied up to the very Southern senators who were the major opponents of the NAACP. (Kennedy had voted to keep Title III in the civil rights bill, but had voted for the jury trial amendment, much to the anger of Wilkins and others.)

In Massachusetts and elsewhere on speaking engagements, Wilkins repeatedly said that Kennedy was "fraternizing with such personages as Governor Griffin of Georgia and Senators Russell and Talmadge of that state. He has also been to South Carolina where Governor Timmerman is the chief executive. He has also been to Mississippi....We must be pardoned for exhibiting some alarm at the apparent wooing of Southern support three years before the nominating convention."[70]

Wilkins's criticisms grew so loud that Kennedy, who had been a supporter of civil rights legislation for the twelve years he had been in Congress, wrote to Wilkins a number of times to clear up the problem. In one letter, dated June 6, 1958, Kennedy said, "quite frankly, I am unable to understand [your criticisms]." In another letter, dated July 18, 1958, the senator wrote, "I think the time has come for you and me to have a personal conversation about our future rela-tions....It would be most unfortunate if an 'iron curtain' of misunderstanding were to be erected between our two offices." Wilkins's bad feelings about Kennedy never really dissipated, even after Kennedy became President in 1961.

Marshall thought that the bill was "barely progress." The loss of Title III was a bitter blow for him and the NAACP, "yet," he said later, "it was great progress, it seems to me, to get them [the Senate] to move at all" on civil rights legisla-tion. Although Marshall disagreed with Wilkins about Kennedy's commitment to civil rights, he conceded, "Roy ran the show. Being in Legal Defense I had to stay out of anything that looked like politics."[71]

It was good to get something called a civil rights bill out of a Congress dom-inated and controlled by men like Strom Thurmond, James Eastland, and Richard Russell. On the other hand, the weak bill sent a message to the South that the federal government was not yet fully committed to the effort to end the evils of racism and the violence associated with racism.

While Eisenhower had many opportunities to clarify the issue, "to speak out on racial injustice and to promote racial harmony...he would not seize them."[72] On the fifth anniversary of *Brown*, he once more passed up opportunities to lend the moral authority of the presidency to the supporters of racial justice. At his May 13, 1959, press conference (Eisenhower had more meetings with the press than any other previous president), he was asked to comment about the school desegregation cases. He did so, saying that *"Law is not going to do it.* We have never stopped sin by passing laws; and in the same way, we are not going to take a great moral ideal and achieve it merely by law."[73]

It was not surprising that, during the Eisenhower administration, another type of civil rights group arose, taking to the streets and directly confronting the segregationists. The advent of SCLC and SNCC brought home to Marshall the message that it was time for him to hand over the reins of Inc Fund leadership to the younger generation of African American lawyers.

## MARSHALL LEAVES THE NAACP

The events in Montgomery, Alabama, and other southern cities that experienced the new civil rights direct-action protests hastened Marshall's departure. Fundamentally, Marshall was a "test case" civil rights advocate. Going into court to challenge the evils of race discrimination and segregation was the only way he

knew to fight injustice, inequity, and inequality. His not-so-subtle disdain for
SCLC and SNCC actions, and, later on, his bitter disavowal of "Black Power"
advocates such as Stokely Carmichael and Malcolm X, demonstrated that
Marshall could not "embrace anyone or any group whose actions seemed to
undermine the chances for successful civil rights litigation."[74] But he knew that
"it was time for younger people to take over [the Inc Fund]."[75]

*Garner v. Louisiana,* 1961, one of many SNCC sit-in protest cases argued by
the Inc Fund in the federal courts, was the last case Marshall worked on at the
Inc Fund. *Garner* was one of more than a dozen major "sit-in" protest cases that
came to the Supreme Court between 1961 and 1964. It involved sixteen young
black college students, members of the local SNCC chapter, who sat in and tried
to get food service at a local Baton Rouge, Louisiana, Kresge's department store
that had a whites-only restaurant. They were arrested and charged with disturbing the peace, found guilty, fined fifty dollars, and sentenced to thirty days in the
city jail. In December 1961, Marshall defended the students, arguing that,
because there was discriminatory state action involved, the arrests were in violation of the Fourteenth Amendment. In a unanimous opinion, the Supreme
Court overturned the convictions of all sixteen students.

*Garner* was Marshall's thirty-sixth victory before the Supreme Court.[76] In a
way it was appropriate that his last case was one in which Marshall, in the briefs
he wrote, defended the right to due process for these nonviolent direct-action
protesters. As their lawyer, Marshall was a legal advocate wrestling with his
deepest beliefs. "Rules is Rules" was central to Marshall's advocacy for civil
rights, and these well-meaning young people challenged the Rules, not in the
law courts as the NAACP had been doing for decades, but by intentionally, and
very actively, violating them. When Marshall left the Inc Fund, he was somewhat
embittered by the younger African Americans' rejection of the decades-old and
successful strategy of using the federal courts to end racial segregation and discrimination. He was unwilling to embrace the new tactics of "direct action," and
said so unequivocally. Asked why he didn't participate in the SCLC and SNCC
marches for civil rights, Marshall replied acidly, "Why should I? I was on that
road before any of those [SCLC and SNCC] kids were born, and when their
parents wouldn't be caught within a mile of it."[77]

By 1961, after twenty-five years of battling on the lonely roads and in the
courts, Marshall "was ready to go...for two reasons: I thought I'd kind of outlived my usefulness, in original ideas, in the NAACP hierarchy. And I had been
shopping around, thinking of going in some law firm, making myself a good
hunk of money, and then this judgeship came through."[78] As he quickly found
out, it was not to be an easy or uncomplicated transition to the public life on the
other side of the bench.

# 8

# A NEW LIFE:
# THURGOOD MARSHALL, GOVERNMENT SERVANT

In September 1961, Thurgood Marshall was nominated by President John F. Kennedy to be a federal appeals judge on the Second Circuit U.S. Court of Appeals, serving New York, Connecticut, and Vermont. When confirmed, almost a year later, he was only the second African American to sit on a federal court of appeals. (His friend and mentor, Bill Hastie, nominated by President Truman in 1949, was the first. He was still sitting in 1961.)

Marshall believed that Kennedy was a closet moderate on civil rights during the 1950s, but he had not had an opportunity to sit down and talk with the senator until the spring of 1960. During the lengthy lunch meeting, they had "quite a frank discussion as to the possibility of his running for President," recalled Marshall a few years later.[1] Marshall was not optimistic about Kennedy's chances of electoral success, and said so. "While I was in favor of his running," Marshall remarked, "I was not sure he could be elected. As a matter of fact, I seriously doubted it." Marshall was "convinced that the South would not support a Northern Catholic and a person outspoken on civil rights." He told Kennedy "he shouldn't run, because I remembered what happened to Alfred E. Smith, and I wouldn't want that to happen to any friend of mine. He listened, as he always did. Didn't say anything. Didn't commit himself. But then he ran."[2] When Kennedy defeated Richard M. Nixon, Marshall was pleased because he believed that Kennedy's heart was in the right place on civil rights.

## THE "NEW FRONTIER" AND CIVIL RIGHTS

As a presidential candidate, JFK was supportive of the young SNCC protesters. He remarked that "it is in the American tradition to stand up for one's rights—even if the new way is to sit down."[3] Kennedy was very critical of Eisenhower's equivocation on civil rights, and promised the electorate a different kind of leadership if he was elected. The next president, Kennedy said, "must exert the great moral and educational force of his office to help bring about equal access to public facilities—from churches to lunch counters....If the President does not himself wage the struggle for equal rights—if he stands above the battle—then the battle will inevitably be lost."[4]

A dramatic incident in the weeks before the election gave hope to millions of black Americans that Kennedy was on their side in the battle against racial discrimination and inequality. In mid-October 1960, Martin Luther King and seventy other protesters participated in a sit-in in Atlanta, Georgia, and were arrested and charged with trespass. In a few days, all were released except King. He remained imprisoned because a state judge ruled that the trespass had violated King's parole (for driving without a valid driver's license) and reinstated the earlier conviction—four months' hard labor in a Georgia chain gang at the state prison in Reidsville, a rural area of the state, two hundred miles from Atlanta.

King's terrified wife called one of Kennedy's advisers, telling him that "they are going to kill my husband." On October 26, days before the election, Kennedy called and consoled her. In addition, the candidate's brother, Robert Kennedy, called up the state judge who had reinstated the King conviction to request that King be released. On October 28, the SCLC leader was released after paying a $2,000 fine. These actions by the Democratic candidate and his brother were decisive signals to Americans, both black and white. Blacks who had always voted for the party of Lincoln voted for Kennedy. Martin Luther King Sr. and Jackie Robinson, Republican Party loyalists, publicly switched their support and encouraged blacks across America to vote Democratic in 1960.[5]

Kennedy received more than 75 percent of the black vote, a significant statistic in light of the fact that Richard Nixon received 51 percent of the white vote. Kennedy won the election by the narrowest of popular vote margins, 118,500 votes. In addition, the Democrats lost two seats in the Senate and twenty-one in the House of Representatives. That political equation meant that Kennedy's New Frontier program would have difficulty enough getting through the Congress without the added burden of filibusters in the Senate "by the bitter enders" (as his civil rights adviser, Harris Wofford, called the Southerners in control of the Senate), if the President introduced his promised civil rights bill. Wofford told Kennedy, quite firmly, that there was no chance of passing such legislation. Even introducing a civil rights proposal would "endanger all the rest of the administration's program, including measures of great importance to most blacks....It would demonstrate the President's weakness at a time when he needed to build strength."[6] In a long report dated December 30, 1960, Wofford outlined a civil rights agenda for Kennedy: "Negro voting rights; token school desegregation…established in each Deep Southern state; employment and upgrading of Negroes in the Federal Service, Federal Government contracts and federal grant-in-aid programs [for minority businesses]; job opportunity and integrated housing." All of these issues should be dealt with by "strong Federal executive action," but, although "it is heresy in the civil rights camp to say this," there should be no civil rights legislation proposed in the upcoming term of Congress. Quite accurately predicting that the lack of a civil rights proposal would not please African Americans, Wofford "stressed the importance of keeping in touch with the top Negro leaders. Roy Wilkins, Martin Luther King, [they] are the keys [and so]…you need to see [them] and call [them] occasionally, and give [them] some recognition. Both are flexible and understanding."[7]

Kennedy faced a Congress whose leaders were hostile to any substantive civil rights legislation. His administration, therefore, in 1961 and 1962, began implementing Wofford's suggestions. The decision reflected "morality against math. It was yearning to lead against yearning to win. Winning won."[8] Marshall understood better than Wilkins that while JFK could not introduce a broad civil rights bill, he could and would take other effective steps. Marshall remarked that "the President was appalled by the fact that in 1960 there were Negroes in this country denied the right to register, denied the right to vote. That struck him as something entirely wrong and he decided to work on it first through the executive and then through the legislature." Marshall understood the political vise the President's head was in. "He had certain key domestic proposals he would have preferred to get through before the inevitable filibuster on the civil rights bill."[9]

Others were less patient with Kennedy's reluctance to introduce and defend a civil rights bill. Roy Wilkins and the NAACP led the attacks on Kennedy, joined by the leaders of SCLC and SNCC. As Wilkins said later, "my illusions [about Kennedy] faded very quickly.…We wanted Congress and the White House to come out of hiding and line up alongside the Supreme Court [against] segregation. We thought we had a clear promise from the Democrats and from Kennedy himself to do just that, but now he was backing down."[10]

Kennedy did take some important steps, in 1961 and 1962, through the use of the executive order and through aggressive actions by the Department of Justice. The Committee on Equal Employment Opportunity was created on March 6, 1961, by Executive Order 10925, to ensure that, for 20 million workers, no federal funds were used in ways that encouraged employment discrimination. Years later, commenting on the singular importance of that executive order, Marshall said that Kennedy "will go down in history as the President who *actually* put into effect the definite promise that Negroes were entitled to employment in the federal government on every single level without regard to race."[11] Kennedy also issued the very first presidential endorsement of public school desegregation. Publicly applauding the administrators, teachers, parents, and students who were "on the front lines of the problem," he concluded by saying their commitment to the law and the Constitution was "contributing to the education of all Americans."

Robert F. Kennedy, the thirty-five-year-old attorney general and the President's brother, quickly acted to "beef up" the Department of Justice, especially its new Civil Rights Division, in order to take more proactive actions in federal courts to end racial discrimination and segregation. The Civil Rights Division received more funds, saw a committed civil rights litigator, Burke Marshall, appointed as the new assistant attorney general for civil rights, and employed more legal staff in order to get into the field and attack the problems of racism there. As John Doar, one of the new lawyers in the Civil Rights Division of the Justice Department, said of Bobby Kennedy, "He was always wanting to move, get something done, accomplish something, and when I went up to see him—probably April 1961—he was for filing seventy-five cases by Thanksgiving."[12] For the first time, Marshall saw the federal government "inaugurating a new campaign of enforcing court decisions in the school [desegregation] cases, and doing it on the initiative of the Attorney General rather than on the initiative of private organizations such as NAACP."[13]

Kennedy's Justice Department filed a great many voting rights suits in Alabama, Mississippi, and Louisiana, but those actions did not significantly change the vote-denial situation in the South. Protecting African American voting rights did not begin to get resolved until after the Congress passed the Voting Rights Act in 1965. By that time, Marshall was solicitor general and took great pleasure, as America's advocate, in defending, successfully, the constitutionality of the act in the 1966 case of *South Carolina v. Katzenbach.*

The much-criticized President took immediate measures to address his black detractors. He appointed dozens of African Americans for significant positions in his administration and in the federal courts. But even that personnel recruitment, one that brought many African Americans into governmental service, did not placate the African American community. Black leaders wanted Kennedy to lead the movement for a new civil rights bill, and appointing a few African Americans would not do.

Both Kennedys were forced by congressional political reality to develop their own "Southern strategy" in the federal judicial appointment process. They had to deal with the arch-segregationist U.S. senator James O. Eastland, from Sunflower County, Mississippi, who was the powerful chairman of the Senate's Judiciary Committee. If John Kennedy nominated an African American, he occasionally followed with an announcement that a white segregationist, frequently a political crony of a Southern Democratic senator, had been appointed to a federal court position. Andrew Young recalled that "the Kennedy strategy in those days was to try to please everybody, so he would appoint a Thurgood Marshall in New York but also appoint a [William Harold] Cox in Mississippi. . . . Cox was part of a trade for Marshall."[14] Just before Cox's nomination for a seat on the federal district court in Mississippi, Senator Eastland reportedly told Bobby Kennedy, "Tell your brother that if he will give me Harold Cox, I will give him the nigger."[15]

SCLC and SNCC, along with the NAACP and other civil rights groups, responded to the Kennedy policy by increasing pressure on the administration through a variety of action-oriented civil rights tactics. These included Freedom Rides in 1961 to focus national attention on the continuing segregation, often violently maintained, of interstate travel facilities in the South. In 1961–63, mass demonstrations were held by SCLC in Albany, Georgia, and Birmingham, Alabama, that led to the arrests of thousands of young African Americans. In Birmingham, there were brutal attacks by the police and their dogs, led by Chief "Bull" Connor, on the peacefully protesting demonstrators. And, after the President finally introduced his civil rights legislation, there was the successful March on Washington in August 1963 to support the legislation and to pressure Congress to act on it.

The NAACP continued to press for integration of public schools and colleges in the South. One such effort took place in Mississippi in late September 1962, and evolved into a clash of wills between Mississippi's governor, Ross Barnett, and the President of the United States. It began when James Meredith, a black military veteran, sought admission to the all-white University of Mississippi. It ended with his admission under the protection of more than five hundred U.S. marshals, after a segregationist riot on the university campus forced Kennedy to use five thousand army troops to quell the rioters. Two onlookers were killed during the violent melee, and 160 U.S. marshals were wounded, twenty-eight by gunshots. Marshall saw a significant difference between Kennedy's actions and those taken by Eisenhower in Little Rock four years earlier. "In the Little Rock crisis," he said, "Eisenhower waited until the last moment. And in the Meredith case the President did not wait until the last moment."

By June 1963, Kennedy had seen enough of Southern intransigence, hatred, and continued cruelty toward African Americans. The last straw for the President was Governor George Wallace's defiant stand, in front of the doors of the University of Alabama, barring two black students from entering the all-white public university in Tuscaloosa. Wallace's actions, coming shortly after Governor Barnett's racist bravado in Mississippi, convinced the President that he had to introduce a major piece of civil rights legislation—regardless of the political fallout. He announced the plan on national television.

That night, June 11, 1963, was an epiphany for Kennedy. Caution was set aside as he spoke to the nation about the moral imperative of equal rights for African Americans. He said the nation could no longer tell black Americans to "be content with the counsels of patience and delay," nor could its citizens claim that America "had no class or caste system, no ghettos, no master race except with respect to Negroes." That night he promised America that he was going to submit to Congress legislation in order "to make a commitment it has not fully made in this century to the proposition that race has no place in American life or law."

Tragically illustrating the urgency of Kennedy's message was the brutal murder of Medgar Evers just hours after the speech was broadcast. Evers, Marshall's friend and the NAACP's activist Mississippi field secretary, was gunned down in his own driveway, shot in the back. He died in his wife's arms, in plain sight of his three young children. Within days, on June 19, 1963, Kennedy sent to Congress a proposal for a major civil rights act. By then, "there could be no turning back. The President had fully committed the authority of his office—and his political future—to continued civil rights progress."[16] Andrew Young observed that while the NAACP, SCLC, and SNCC tried to educate the President about the reality of racial discrimination, "I think George Wallace educated them [the Kennedy brothers]; and I think probably the most credit ought to go to Ross Barnett at the University of Mississippi. I think that's where [they] really began to understand the treachery that was present."

## MARSHALL'S APPOINTMENT TO THE U.S. COURT OF APPEALS, 1961

By 1963, the year Kennedy introduced the civil rights legislation—and the centennial of President Abraham Lincoln's issuance of the Emancipation Proclamation—Marshall had been on a federal appeals court for almost two years. His discussions about the judicial appointment were solely with Robert Kennedy. These were not easy conversations, to say the least. The attorney general had sought advice from Burke Marshall, because some critics maintained that Marshall was a "one-client lawyer, and he doesn't have the experience and breadth of practice, 'So he's basically second-rate,' is what they [the Wall Street lawyers] said." But Burke Marshall strongly supported Thurgood Marshall's nomination because he was "well qualified," the highest recommendation the American Bar Association can give a nominee for judicial office.[17]

Initially, partly because of some of the criticism he had heard, the attorney general wanted Marshall to take a federal district court judgeship. Marshall, however, told Bobby Kennedy that he was not district court material, because, as he said, his fuse was too short:

[Marshall continued:] "My boiling point is too low for the trial court. I'd blow my stack and then get reversed....And that wasn't good. But I would like to be on the Court of Appeals."

He said, "Well, you can't."

I said, "There's an opening."

He said, "No, but that one's been filled."

So he said, "Well, that's it. You don't seem to understand. It's that or nothing."

I said, "Well, I *do* understand. The trouble is that you are different from me. You don't know what it means, but all I've had in my life is nothing. It's not new to me, so good-bye." And I walked out.[18]

Three days after Marshall stormed out, Louis Martin, a highly respected African American newspaper publisher friend of Marshall's and one of JFK's black advisers (he was also the deputy chair for minorities for the Democratic National Committee) called his friend up and asked, "Are you still thinking about that Court of Appeals job?" Marshall said, "Sure, I would take it." (It was a lifetime appointment and came, in 1961, with an annual salary of $25,000.) The following day, President Kennedy made the public announcement. Evidently, after the blowup between Marshall and Bobby, the President spoke with Martin, indicating that he wanted to nominate Marshall for an appellate federal court judgeship. Marshall knew that his friend Louis was speaking for the President, and that his answer was all that was needed to seal the decision.

On September 21, 1961, Bobby Kennedy sent to the President the names of eight men nominated for positions on the federal judiciary. All the nominees, including Marshall, were to fill newly created judgeships. The attorney general's letter noted that Marshall had received the Bar Association's "well qualified" recommendation for appointment to the federal appeals court, and that he "bears an excellent reputation as to character and integrity, has judicial temperament, and is, I believe, worthy of appointment as a United States Circuit Judge."

Two days later, from Kennedy's summer home at Hyannisport, Massachusetts, Marshall's name was sent to the Senate, along with the seven others. The Congress ended its session a few days later, without any action on the judicial nominees. On October 3, 1961, all were given a recess commission by the President. By the end of that month, Marshall was fully engaged in the business of federal appellate adjudication. *Time* magazine predicted that "Southern senators who disagree with Marshall but respect his abilities, are expected to make only a token fight against his confirmation."[19]

*Time*'s projection was way off base. A vote on his nomination was delayed for over eight months by the Southern Democratic senators opposed to Marshall because of his leadership of the NAACP's Inc Fund. As Kenneth Keating, the

New York Republican serving as the point man in the Senate for Marshall's nomination, said: "opponents of civil rights were maneuvering to delay the confirmation, [and their] opposition centered not on the man but on the results he has achieved."[20]

There were six days of hearings, but they were held over a three-month period. The hearings took place before a three-man Senate subcommittee of the Judiciary Committee: Olin Johnston (D-S.C.) was the chairman, joined by Roman Hruska (R-Iowa) and John McClellan (D-Ark.) on May 1, July 12, and August 8, 17, 20, and 24, 1962. During August, Wilkins sent letters to every senator, formally complaining about the inordinate delay in confirming Judge Marshall. In the letters, he pointed out that two Deep South federal district court nominees had been nominated and confirmed in a matter of weeks, while Marshall was left twisting in the wind for almost one year. Finally, after some vicious questioning by a small number of "bitter ender" Southern senators, Marshall was confirmed, 56 to 14, by the Senate on September 11, 1962.

The confirmation marathon was a manifestation of the "massive resistance" sentiments of the white segregationist South toward the man they considered a virtual Antichrist. The hearings transcripts show that the handful of issues raised by Marshall's opponents—marginal issues at best—were brought up to harass the nominee, who was forthrightly defended by Keating, New York Republican senator Jacob Javits, and other moderate Republicans and liberal Democrats.

One issue that took two days of testimony was Marshall's connection with the Texas barratry suit brought against the NAACP. His defenders protested this, essentially asking the opponents to show how Marshall was involved and how, in any case, this could have any bearing on his capacity to serve as an appellate judge. As Keating said at one point, "We are not here concerned with investigating the NAACP. We are here concerned with the investigation of the qualifications of this nominee, as to his character, ability, and integrity, to be a U.S. circuit judge."

Another issue raised by staff counsel was the fact that Marshall was a member of only the bar of the state of Maryland, even though his work for the NAACP was done in New York. When Marshall told L. P. B. Lipscomb, the antagonistic staff counsel, that he did not practice in New York, counsel was taken aback. Marshall pointed out that he was admitted to the federal circuit bar, where he did most of his appeal work when working with the NAACP. On other occasions he worked in other states to assist a member of that state's bar in bringing a lawsuit into the courts. Marshall was also asked about his membership in the American Civil Liberties Union, the National Lawyers' Guild, and the National Committee of the International Juridical Association (the latter two organizations were identified as "Communist front" organizations). He replied that he was a member of the ACLU and had left the other two groups as soon as he found out about their Communist connections.

The final criticism of Marshall focused on his behavior as director-counsel of the NAACP's Inc Fund. It revolved around one article written by one of the historians who worked with Marshall over the summer of 1953 in preparing the second *Brown* brief. In the course of the essay, Al Kelly (a historian from Wayne State University) indicated that Marshall had yelled at his secretary, fabricated the history of the congressional debates surrounding the passage of the Fourteenth Amendment, and, finally and most ominously, had said that "when us colored folks take over, every time a white man draws a breath, he'll have to pay a fine."

Although the charges were ludicrous and totally out of line, Marshall's defenders had to bring Professor Kelly from Detroit to explain his remarks, especially the last one. Kelly, angry at the "die-harders'" use of his article, said that the "draw a breath" story was one of many humorous remarks made by Marshall. "The remark," Kelly testified, "was mordant humor, given exclamation by a man possessed of a powerful sense of humor, and who expresses something of the excitement of verbal exchange in humorous hyperbole of this kind.... To lift this remark out of context and treat it as a threat or even a philosophical observation is absurd, even grotesque, in its bizarre distortion of reality." The subcommittee ignominiously ended its hearing on that issue; the full Judiciary Committee pulled the nomination back without the subcommittee report and quickly voted, 11 to 4, to recommend confirmation.

It was quickly sent to the full Senate for final action. After five hours of debate, with the "bitter ender" opposition led by Senators Eastland and Johnston, and twelve days short of a year since nomination by Kennedy, the Senate confirmed Thurgood Marshall on September 11, 1962.

Marshall served on the federal appeals court from October 24, 1961, to August 23, 1965. In July 1965, he was asked by President Lyndon Baines Johnson to serve as the U.S. Solicitor General, the nation's advocate before the U.S. Supreme Court. Marshall stepped down from the appeals court at the end of August 1965, after confirmation by the Senate.

The Second Circuit was then and remains the premier, and most highly respected, of the thirteen federal appellate courts. Over its history, many judicial luminaries, such as Jerome Frank and Augustus and Learned Hand, had sat on it. Many significant constitutional cases and controversies were decided by this court, with its judgments then affirmed, on appeal, by the U.S. Supreme Court. The Second Circuit's case load, when Marshall joined the court, reflected changes in the larger society. The court's staples—"nautical 'fender benders' and copyright actions"—had decreased in number and importance, and the judges heard more and more appeals that raised questions about a person's constitutional and statutory rights.[21]

When Marshall joined the court in 1961, "an extraordinary array of litigants" appeared before it. "Defendants included black revolutionaries, Irish terrorists, Croatian nationalists, and Nazi collaborators...as well [as] the American Communist Party...the chairman of the board of governors of the New York Stock Exchange, a former dean of Harvard Law School, and a rabbi who owned substandard nursing homes."[22]

During his four years of service, Marshall wrote 118 opinions, including 98 majority opinions, 8 concurring opinions, and 12 dissenting opinions. The bulk of his opinions "dealt with litigation involving federal tort claims, admiralty and maritime law, suits brought under the Securities and Exchange Act, personal injury suits, labor relations, patents and trademarks, and deportation of aliens."[23] None of his opinions written for the appeals court majority were ever reversed by the U.S. Supreme Court. Marshall did participate in a number of civil liberties cases, dissenting in a civil disobedience case, *New York v. Galamison* (1965), and writing the majority opinion in a First Amendment case involving the use of loyalty oaths, *Keyishian v. Board of Regents of the University of the State of New York* (1965).

In a Fourth Amendment criminal appeal, *United States ex rel Angelet v. Fay* (1964), Marshall dissented from the court majority's view that the 1961 Supreme Court opinion *Mapp v. Ohio* was not to be applied retroactively by the federal judges. (In *Mapp*, the Warren Court ruled that the Fourth Amendment "search and seizure" constraints were applicable in state police actions. In addition, the majority concluded that a 1914 "exclusionary" rule, created by the Court in *Weeks v. U.S.*—prohibiting evidence seized in violation of the Fourth Amendment from being used in any criminal proceeding—was also applicable.)

In *Fay*, Marshall maintained that the federal court was "not free to circumscribe the application of a declared constitutional right." (Marshall's *Fay* dissent would be cited by his Senate opponents in 1967 when he was being considered for a seat on the U.S. Supreme Court.) And, in 1965, Marshall's forty-two-page opinion in *United States ex rel George Hetenyi v. Wilkins* spoke for the majority (also discussed by his die-hard senatorial opponents in his 1967 Senate confirmation hearings), which found that a defendant who was tried three times in New York State was deprived of due process of law. "Abhorrence to successive prosecutions is deeply rooted in our common law traditions," he wrote, "and the Bill of Rights' curb on the power of the federal government to reprosecute is ample recognition of how central this abhorrence is to our constitutional concept of justice."

Judge Irving R. Kaufman, one of Marshall's colleagues on the federal appeals court, observed that

> my most abiding memory of Thurgood on this court…was his ability to infuse his judicial product with the elements of the advocate's craft. As an attorney Thurgood stressed the "human side" of the case. *As a judge, he wrote for the people.*…He possessed an instinct for the critical fact, the gut issue, born of his exquisite sense of the practical.…Behind his jovial veneer is a precise and brilliant legal tactician who…was able to view the law…*as an effective instrument of social policy.* (My emphasis.)[24]

In court, Marshall, as his longtime secretary, Alice Stovall, recalled, was "so informal. When he became judge we kept saying: 'We've got to make you in the image of a judge,' but with him you just couldn't do it. He would never allow his chamber doors to be closed unless he was with another judge. He would ask us, 'What have I got to be locked up about?'"[25]

Throughout his service on the Second Circuit Federal Appeals Court, Marshall's "position on the bench was that of a liberal in social and economic thought. He was always willing to render a generous interpretation to the Bill of Rights and the Fourteenth Amendment and he consistently upheld government activity in areas not affecting civil rights." Marshall also was committed to the potency of precedent. For him, as always, "Rules is Rules," and given his "desire to maintain conformity in law," he always adhered closely to Supreme Court precedent.[26]

## LYNDON JOHNSON AND CIVIL RIGHTS

Marshall truly admired a small number of Texans, including Attorney General and then Supreme Court Justice Tom C. Clark and especially the President he considered to have done the most for African Americans, Lyndon Baines Johnson. This President, said Marshall, "intended to wipe as much of [discrimination] out as he could."

> He intended to be in this century what Abraham Lincoln was to the last century, and he was going to do it. I frankly believe that if he had four more years (Johnson did not seek re-election in 1968), he just about would have done it.… He rebelled at the discrimination against women.…He always did. He said he wanted to leave the presidency in a position that there was no government job with a race tag on it—none!…He was pushing [these ideas] like mad.[27]

At the time Johnson assumed the presidency, on November 22, 1963, upon the assassination of John F. Kennedy, the government's civil rights policy was generally reactive and cautious. Burke Marshall said that "we must realize the constitutional rights of Negroes in states where they are denied *but we must do so with the smallest possible federal intrusion into the conduct of state affairs.*" (My emphasis.) The deputy U.S. attorney general, Nicholas deB. Katzenbach, said that the Kennedy administration's civil rights strategy was to *"avoid at all costs an occupation of the South'* by federal troops, lawyers, registrars, and marshals."[28]

This was not Johnson's thinking. Within days of assuming the presidency, he told a joint session of Congress, "We have talked long enough in this century about equal rights. We have talked for a hundred years or more. It is time now to write the next chapter—and to write it in the books of law." President Johnson's views on civil rights were strikingly different from the ones held by *Senator* Johnson. LBJ the legislator was critical of both the Supreme Court's overturn of *Plessy* and of the continual pressures, in litigation, of the NAACP's Inc Fund.

For decades, Johnson had followed the advice of his mentor, Congressman Sam Rayburn (D-Texas), the venerated—and extremely powerful—Speaker of the House of Representatives. But as Vice President and then as President, Johnson moved light-years away from Rayburn's traditional views of racism and segregation. By the time of Marshall's 1967 nomination to the Supreme Court, Johnson had pushed through the Congress two of the most substantive pieces of civil rights legislation ever created in the United States. The first was the omnibus 1964 Civil Rights Act. This legislation, introduced in Congress a year earlier by President Kennedy, went through the Congress after the bloody summer riots in Birmingham, Alabama, and the deaths of the three civil rights workers in Mississippi. Senator Paul Douglas observed grimly that it was "a sorrowful mockery of our principles that it required the Birmingham, Alabama, [church] bombings [that killed four young African American girls] and the Philadelphia, Mississippi, murders to pass the Civil Rights Act of 1964."[29]

One year later, after viewing SCLC's bloody Selma-to-Montgomery, Alabama, massive march for voting rights, President Johnson engineered development and passage, in a remarkably short period of time (about three months), of the 1965 Voting Rights Act, one of the most radical pieces of legislation in this area. If it took the deaths of children and civil rights workers in Alabama and Mississippi to bring about swift passage of the 1964 Civil Rights Act, sadly it took the brutality and violence by implacable segregationists against peaceful marchers in Alabama to bring about the introduction and the passage of the 1965 Voting Rights Act.

It was a radical bill because it did not rely on litigation to ensure justice for

African Americans. Johnson told his attorney general, Nicholas deB. Katzen-bach, after winning the 1964 presidential election, to "write the god-damnedest, toughest voting rights act that you can devise." This was a crucial change in national civil rights policy, for Johnson quickly moved away from the incremen-tal, case-by-case litigative method to a strategy that was premised on "direct, aggressive national executive action on behalf of blacks."[30] The plan was formu-lated and given to the President on March 5, 1965. Johnson prepared to intro-duce the bill in 1966. But the murder of a white Unitarian minister, James Reeb, while marching from Selma to Montgomery to demand voting rights for African Americans moved up LBJ's timetable.

Johnson's March 15, 1965, speech to the joint houses of Congress, just ten days after receiving a draft of the voting rights legislation from Katzenbach, was one of the strongest, most moving speeches ever given by an American presi-dent. Broadcast to the nation over radio and television, Johnson's bully-pulpit speech was part Christian evangelical and part roof-raising political rhetoric: "At times history and fate meet at a single time in a single place to shape a turning point in man's unending search for freedom. So it was at Lexington and Concord....So it was last week in Selma, Alabama, where...one good man, a man of God [Reeb], was killed....Our mission...is to right wrong, to do justice, to serve man." Johnson announced that he was sending Congress a voting rights bill, one "designed to eliminate illegal barriers to the right to vote." Even when the bill passes, he said, "the battle will not be over." It "is not just Negroes, but really it is all of us, who must overcome the crippling legacy of bigotry and injus-tice. *And, we shall overcome.*" He concluded with stirring words about African Americans, public utterances that the NAACP and SCLC leaders had never before heard from any American President.

> The real hero of this struggle is the American Negro. His actions and protests, his courage to risk safety and even to risk his life, have awakened the conscience of this nation. His demonstrations have been designed to call our attention to injustice, designed to provoke change, designed to stir reform. He has called upon us to make good the promise of America. And who among us can say that we would have made the same progress if not for his persistent bravery, and his faith in democracy.

The voting rights bill was signed into law on August 6, 1965. It enraged Southern legislators because it created a legal environment that put Southern counties, and towns, and cities, on the defensive with respect to voting rights. The bill suspended all tests and devices, including a wide variety of literacy tests, that had been used to deny African Americans their right to register and to vote in the South. It sent federal monitors into the Deep South jurisdictions to help ensure the speedy registration of black Americans. And, in the most controversial title (Title V) of the voting rights bill, it forced the covered jurisdictions (the six Deep South states and parts of North Carolina) to submit all voting changes—*before they were put into practice*—for pre-clearance by the national government, either by the federal district court in Washington, D.C., or by the Voting Section of the Department of Justice's Civil Rights Division.

The first president from Texas did more to change the civil rights environment than any chief executive since Abraham Lincoln. By 1967, Johnson had appointed more African Americans to high governmental positions than all other presidents combined, including a number of "firsts" such as Marshall's appointment to the Supreme Court and Warren C. Weaver's Cabinet appointment as secretary of housing and urban development. Marshall's close NAACP associate Jim Nabrit was named America's ambassador to the United Nations and Constance Baker Motley, one of Marshall's bright young Inc Fund legal staffers, was sitting on one of New York's federal district courts. She joined Spotts Robinson (sitting on the federal district court in the District of Columbia) and other African Americans appointed to federal judicial positions by Johnson.[31]

Marshall and others would comment, sadly, that if Johnson had continued as president for another four years, he would have addressed many of the ongoing civil rights dilemmas, in the urban areas, in employment, housing, and economic discrimination. The tragedy in Vietnam closed that window of hope. In March 1968, Johnson sadly announced that he would not seek reelection that year. A brief era in aggressive national government enforcement of civil rights came to an end with the election of Richard Nixon the following November.[32]

## MARSHALL'S APPOINTMENT AS U.S. SOLICITOR GENERAL, 1965

On July 8, 1965, Attorney General Katzenbach wrote Johnson informing him that Solicitor General Archibald Cox was resigning. The attorney general recommended Marshall for the position. Katzenbach needn't have bothered to do so, for Johnson wanted to be the President who appointed the first African American to the U.S. Supreme Court. When Archibald Cox, an austere Harvard law professor, stepped down from his job as U.S. solicitor general, after four years of service, the Texan immediately asked Marshall, as an intermediate step, to serve as the advocate for the United States before the U.S. Supreme Court.

Johnson's wife, Lady Bird, in her diary entry dated July 2, 1965, recorded her husband's strategy: "Lyndon admires Thurgood Marshall and spoke today of the possibility of asking him to be solicitor general, and if he proved himself outstanding, perhaps when a vacancy on the Supreme Court opened up he might nominate him as a justice—the first of his race." Jack Valenti, one of the President's closest White House advisers, recalled that Johnson told him, "By God, I'm going to take Thurgood, and I'm going to make him solicitor general, and then when somebody says, 'He doesn't have a lot of experience for the Supreme Court,' by God, that son of a bitch will have prosecuted more cases before the Supreme Court than any lawyer in America. So how's anybody gonna turn him down?"[33] In less than two years, the unpublished, somewhat secret LBJ "plan" was successfully implemented by the President.

Marshall recalled the day in 1965 when he and Johnson spoke. He was having lunch with other judges when a bailiff approached and told him that the President was on the telephone for him. After a moment or two on the phone, Johnson told Marshall, "I want you to be my Solicitor General." Marshall thanked him and said he had to speak with the boss, Cissy Marshall. He did and she immediately said okay, even though there were personal costs involved for the family. The following day, Marshall traveled to Washington, D.C., to speak with the President about the job.

> He said, "You don't have to tell me. I can tell you everything including what you've got in your bank account. I'm still asking you to make the sacrifice." We talked for quite a while, and I said, "Okay with me." He wanted me, "number one, in his administration." Number two, he wanted me in that spot for two reasons. One, I could handle it. Second, he wanted people—young people—of both races to come into the Supreme Court Room…and somebody to say, "He's the Solicitor General of the United States." Somebody will say, "But he's a Negro!" He wanted that image.[34]

To take the political appointment meant giving up the lifetime tenured job of a federal appellate judge for a much less secure position in the Johnson administration. It also meant a loss of salary, from $33,000 to $28,500, and a move from New York City to Washington, D.C., where the cost of living was much higher. But these factors hardly diminished Marshall's desire to accept.

Although he said at the Senate confirmation hearing, "I am an advocate… and once you become an advocate, that is it," the fifty-seven-year-old Marshall suspected what Johnson's long-term strategy was. Although the President repeatedly insisted that "this has nothing to do with any Supreme Court appointment…there's no quid pro quo here," Marshall heard that statement too many times to believe it. Marshall was nominated on July 13, 1965. Before he was confirmed for the position, New York congressman Adam Clayton Powell, who represented Harlem, was on the phone to Marvin Watson, one of Johnson's senior advisers, telling him that Powell's "people very much want Marshall considered for the Supreme Court at the proper time."[35]

In marked contrast to his confirmation ordeal in 1961–62, the Judiciary Committee subcommittee spent less than a half-hour on July 29, 1965, on public hearings. The five person subcommittee, with no Southern senators sitting on it, met at 10:07 A.M. and, after saying good morning to Marshall, taking prepared statements from him and his senatorial supporters, adjourned at 10:22 A.M.! In less than one month, on August 11, 1965, he was confirmed by the U.S. Senate. He was the nation's thirty-third solicitor general, and the first African American to hold the office.

## THURGOOD MARSHALL, "GENERAL"

Marshall said that his job as solicitor general "was the best job I ever had."[36] As the third-highest-ranking lawyer for the government (behind only the attorney general and the deputy attorney general), he was the advocate not for the NAACP and its clients but for the United States of America and its clients, the people of the United States. He liked that idea very much. He *was* the United States in pinstripes, arguing in front of the Supreme Court for all the people.

As solicitor general, Marshall had the responsibility for determining which of the thousands of cases heard in the lower federal courts—three-judge district courts and courts of appeals—would be appealed to the U.S. Supreme Court. More than half the annual case load of the Supreme Court comes from the solicitor general's petitions to the justices. The justices rely on him to select only those cases that are worthy of Supreme Court review. (Typically, the solicitor general appeals only about 15 percent of the federal government's cases to the Supreme Court.) Marshall's discretionary judgment on which cases would be argued before the Court was the final one in the Department of Justice. It was an important, powerful position for an advocate, and Marshall seemed to relish the job. However, it was a political appointment, one good for as long as the President who did the appointing was in the White House—and liked the job "his" solicitor general was doing.

LBJ, however, simply wanted Marshall in that spot for the "exposure" it would give him, and because it would prepare him for appointment to the Supreme Court. According to Louis Martin, Johnson had a poor view of Marshall's capacity to manage the Solicitor General's Office. "He's not doing a job over there," the President told Martin on a number of occasions, "he ain't worth a damn as an administrator! He doesn't pay any attention to half the cases; he just gets those he likes!"[37]

The view of Marshall from inside the office was quite different. Louis Claiborne, who was one of the senior career legal staff in the Solicitor General's Office, thought that Marshall was an outstanding administrator and advocate. "Generosity and forbearance, with an acute sense of justice," were some of the characteristics Marshall exhibited as solicitor general, wrote Claiborne. "Although he was good at delegation, there was to be no abdication. Marshall read all the papers, with extraordinary speed and retention. Nor was he reluctant to take the really important decisions himself. And he backed his lawyers to the hilt, assuming full responsibility for what was done, even when the controversial act was initiated by us."[38]

As solicitor general, Marshall's work habits were "deceptive," as one reporter wrote in 1967. Though he often left early for home, Marshall always took work home with him. "Unlike his brilliant predecessor, Archibald Cox, he has not so much sparked off ideas of his own as chosen among those offered to him." And, much like the Inc Fund of earlier decades, Marshall's Solicitor General's Office lacked the "formal austerity" of his Harvard predecessor, Cox. "In the Cox days and before…annual staff pictures looked like photos of high school graduating classes, one stiff row sitting and another standing. Marshall's first year [photo] shows almost everyone in shirtsleeves, clustered around his desk, arguing."[39]

While he was seen as "lacking the erudition of Cox and other noted Solicitors General," Marshall "frequently earned high marks as a give-and-take courtroom advocate."[40] As solicitor general, he personally argued nineteen cases before the U.S. Supreme Court, winning fourteen of them. And he was solicitor general at a felicitous time in civil rights litigation. Both the 1964 Civil Rights Act and the 1965 Voting Rights Act became law before his tenure, and Marshall "would have an opportunity to give the new anti-discriminatory laws their most effective interpretation"[41] before the U.S. Supreme Court.

Furthermore, Marshall had the unique experience, as NAACP advocate, of arguing successfully for the overturn of *Plessy* and then, a decade later, as the nation's advocate, being able to broaden the *Brown* mandate. Included in the group of cases he argued for the United States before the Court were some important civil rights and civil liberties cases, including *United States v. Price* (the case involved the prosecution of the murderers of three young CORE workers, Andrew Goodman, Michael Schwerner, and James Chaney, in Philadelphia, Mississippi, in 1964); and *United States v. Guest*, a 1966 criminal conspiracy case in which the federal government successfully prosecuted the white segregationists who murdered an African American military officer near Athens, Georgia.

In two cases involving the constitutionality of sections of the 1965 Voting Rights Act, *South Carolina v. Katzenbach* (1966) and *Katzenbach v. Morgan* (1966), Marshall won again in the Court, successfully arguing the constitutionality of the critically important 1965 Voting Rights Act. And, in another voting rights case, *Harper v. Virginia Board of Education*, an important 1966 civil rights case that involved the constitutionality of a state poll tax, Marshall, filing a brief *amicus curiae*, maintained that the poll tax denied poor persons the equal protection of the law as guaranteed by the Fourteenth Amendment.

He successfully participated on behalf of the national government in other civil rights cases, filing an *amicus* brief in *Evans v. Newton* (1966; involving the desegregation of a public park in Macon, Georgia), and, again as *amicus curiae*, in the case of *Reitman v. Mulkey* (1967), in which Marshall challenged, successfully, the constitutionality of a California constitutional amendment that attempted to prohibit the state from enacting fair housing regulations.[42]

As the government's representative in the Supreme Court, however, Marshall also argued that the government could imprison Muhammad Ali for refusing induction into the army (he lost on appeal to the Supreme Court), and defended the constitutionality of the war in Vietnam.

As solicitor general, his view was that all discretionary treatment by government, whether state or national, against identifiable groups, as well as all governmental actions that had a disproportionate impact on disadvantaged groups in society—owing to their social, racial, economic, religious, or other neutral characteristics—had to be invalidated by the Supreme Court when brought to the high bench by the solicitor general.

## MARSHALL'S APPOINTMENT TO THE U.S. SUPREME COURT, 1967

The fifty-eight-year-old Thurgood Marshall's nomination to the Supreme Court was, in a way, poetic justice. The former NAACP advocate who, in the words of his arch-critic Senator Richard Russell, exercised "an almost occult power" over the Supreme Court would join the very "brethren" he had allegedly "mesmerized."

There was also sadness mixed in with the celebration of Marshall's appointment to the Court. As he revealed many years later, Marshall and other leaders in the African American community believed that William Hastie should have been the first from their ranks to sit on the Court, and had been deeply disappointed that Hastie was not nominated by Kennedy when a seat became available in 1962: "We had agreed on it....We had agreed that whenever any of us were asked about it, we would immediately all converge on Hastie. So that it wouldn't be split, all around....Hastie should have been on this court way back. He's a great man. Much better than I am. Much better than I will ever be. Honest."[43]

According to Burke Marshall, Hastie was discussed inside the Department of

Justice and mentioned to Chief Justice Earl Warren, but the word came back to President Kennedy that Hastie was "too pedestrian" (Nicholas deB. Katzenbach's assessment) as well as too conservative for service on the Court (Earl Warren's evaluation). Despite Burke Marshall's support for the nomination, Kennedy "didn't appoint Judge Hastie." [44] The man nominated by Kennedy and confirmed by the Senate, Byron White, a Colorado supporter of the President (who was, at the time, working in the Justice Department), ironically proved to be both pedestrian and conservative. It was probably for the best that Marshall was not aware of the discussion and evaluation of Hastie inside the administration, because he would have been outraged by this negative view of Hastie's qualifications.

On June 13, 1967, Marshall was sitting in his office at the Justice Department when the new attorney general, Ramsey Clark, dropped by the office. The night before, Marshall and his wife, Cissy, and others had attended a retirement party for Clark's father, Justice Tom C. Clark. The justice's son, who knew what was about to happen (as did his father), told Marshall to go over to the White House because "the boss wants to see you." When Marshall entered the White House, he found that two of his friends, Louis Martin and Cliff Alexander, the latter an African American White House staffer, had also been invited to the small meeting. As soon as Martin saw Marshall, he knew why they were there. "Thurgood walks in…and we all knew the story then. I think the President just had a ball."

The three of them sat down with Johnson, who turned to Marshall and said, "'You know something, Thurgood, I'm going to put you on the Supreme Court.' I said, 'Well, thank you, sir.' We talked a little while." Martin recalled the President calling up a number of people to let them know of the impending announcement. Johnson spoke with Vice President Hubert Humphrey, the Senate's minority leader, Everett Dirksen, and long-distance with Chief Justice Earl Warren, who was in California that day. [45]

After the phone calls, Marshall recalled, "we went out to the press and he announced it." At the press conference, the President said of his nominee, "I believe he earned that appointment. He deserves the appointment. He is the best qualified by training and by…service to the country. I believe it is the right thing to do, the right time to do it, the right man and the right place." Afterwards, Marshall called up Cissy. Before he could speak to his wife, Johnson took the phone and said, "'Cissy—Lyndon Johnson. I've just put your husband on the Supreme Court.'" [46]

Another version of what took place suggests that Thurgood and Cissy were not surprised by the nomination to fill the seat of the retiring Justice Clark. But Marshall told Johnson that Cissy would be "shocked" by the nomination. Johnson then put a call through to Cissy and put her on the speakerphone. After Marshall said, "It's me, honey," Cissy allegedly replied, "'Yeah, honey. Did we get the Supreme Court appointment?' Even Johnson, who had almost no sense of humor, guffawed."[47] In any event, Thurgood and Cissy were immensely gratified with the opportunity to serve on the Supreme Court. It was, Marshall said, every lawyer's dream to serve on the Court, and he was happy to have that opportunity to continue to serve his country.

Johnson, always the master political strategist, had to create a vacancy on the Court in order to get Marshall on it. He had therefore named Ramsey Clark to be his attorney general on February 28, 1967. Ramsey's father would have faced "conflict of interest" criticism had he remained on the Court while his son was the nation's chief law enforcement officer. As Johnson expected, Clark then submitted his retirement letter to the President on March 15, 1967. The way was then clear for Marshall's appointment. A day after the announcement, June 14, 1967, Cissy Marshall sent a short letter to Ramsey Clark in which she wrote, "Just a note to let you know how deeply grateful I am for the role you played (needless to say not a small one) with regard to Thurgood's nomination."[48]

Marshall's nomination elicited negative and covertly racist reactions from "a number of Eastern, Ivy League lawyers and their newspaper friends," who, "either on grounds of his liberalism or because they feel Marshall is not a sufficiently brilliant legal analyst, contend the Court needs a superior mind now more than a generous heart, and that Marshall supplies only the latter."[49]

Press reporting of the nomination reflected this genteel bias against Marshall. Most major dailies had the story on page one, with accompanying editorials that reflected some concern about Marshall's intellect. It was not the first time he had experienced such disparagement, and unfortunately, it would not be the last. The liberal *New Republic* commented, in a June 24, 1967, editorial, that "Mr. Marshall's performance [in the federal court and as solicitor general] was often less than brilliant."[50] And *The New York Times* editorialized:

> There are judges in the state and federal courts whose judicial work had been far more outstanding than Mr. Marshall's record during his brief service on the Second Circuit. Nor as Solicitor General did he demonstrate the intellectual mastery of Archibald Cox, his predecessor. But, apart from the symbolism, Mr. Marshall brings to the Court a wealth of practical experience as a brilliant, forceful advocate.[51]

While Marshall was enduring such criticism, Johnson was receiving congratulations on the nomination. "This is great news! *Also it is very clever politics.* But you couldn't have made a better choice for [Tom Clark's] successor. Again, congratulations," wrote Cornelius Vanderbilt Jr. to the President on June 13. On June 19, Chief Justice Warren wrote a letter to the President, in which he said,

I was pleased to hear the news. It was an excellent appointment. Few men come to the Court with better experience or a sounder preparation for our work. Also, it is in keeping with your policy of opening governmental opportunities to all without regard to race, religion, or economic status....All of us [on the Court] know Thurgood and will welcome him to the Court in the belief that he will make a real contribution to its jurisprudence during the many years we hope he will be able to serve.[52]

The Senate, in contrast to its treatment of Marshall in 1965, held five days of hearings on July 13–19 and July 24, 1967. Not only the Southern die-hards but, ironically, SNCC opposed the nomination. It was a very different SNCC in 1967, however. Gone were the young men and women who had a commitment to fundamental Christian values. John Lewis, Dianne Nash, Mary King, and Bob Moses had been replaced by secularist and exclusivist African American militants. By 1967, Stokely Carmichael, the Black Power advocate, was the fiery new leader of the civil rights organization.

There was little love between Marshall and the Black Power advocates. Carmichael didn't like Marshall "because he is too moderate, is middle class and has white friends," wrote Ralph McGill, the liberal editor of the *Atlanta Constitution*. The "Rules is Rules" advocate saw these new leaders as law-violating anarchists. Besides, Marshall "just didn't believe that everything that's black is right, and everything that's white is wrong."[53] His nomination, as one paper reported, came "at a time when Marshall must appear to be a conservative figure in the minds of many disaffected Negroes. The President chose Marshall precisely because he had become a symbol of orderly social change through the legal process, and the nominee has given no encouragement to the latter-day militants."[54]

In the Senate, predictable enemies were attacking Marshall during the hearings. The cast included Sam Ervin Jr. of North Carolina; John McClellan of Arkansas; the committee chair, James O. Eastland of Mississippi; and South Carolina senator Strom Thurmond. All objected to Marshall's liberal philosophy, especially in the areas of due process of law (Fourth through Eighth Amendments), which led to the growth of crime in the nation, and what the die-hards believed was the unconstitutionally expansive role of the judiciary in "interpreting" what Marshall always referred to as the "living Constitution."[55]

Sam Ervin was repeatedly frustrated by Marshall's refusal to answer questions about key liberal Warren Court decisions in these areas. In declining to reply, Marshall claimed that "it has been considered and recognized as improper for a nominee to a judgeship to comment on cases that he will have to pass on." Again and again, after being asked his views of *Mapp, Miranda,* and *Escobedo,* and other

Warren Court decisions that held that segments of the Bill of Rights created procedural protections for persons accused of crime, Marshall refused to answer, saying, "I can't comment, because it [the due process issue] is coming back up [to the Court]." Marshall did suggest that the senators read his appellate court opinions if they wanted an understanding of his jurisprudence in these controversial areas. A visibly angry Senator Ervin, however, demurred, acidly commenting, "I do not have time to read all of your opinions."

Marshall, however, was direct with his Senate critics on his view of the character of the Constitution. Senator Ervin, who was the major constitutional interrogator, asked Marshall, "Is not the role of the Supreme Court simply to ascertain and give effect to the intent of the framers of the Constitution and the people who ratified the Constitution?" Marshall answered, "Yes, Senator, with the understanding that the Constitution was meant to be a living document... [that] needs somebody to interpret it."

Then, on the next-to-last day of questioning, Strom Thurmond took over. Thurmond had a lawyer prepare a list of more than sixty questions about the minutiae, the "esoteric details" (as the committee majority labeled these questions) surrounding the drafting and the passage of the Fourteenth Amendment in the late 1860s. Thurmond hoped to show Marshall up as someone ignorant of the history of the key clauses in the Constitution that had been at the very heart of all the NAACP victories in the courts. Thurmond closely questioned Marshall about constitutional clauses in Marshall's "area of expertise," especially the Fourteenth Amendment.

"Do you know who drafted the Thirteenth Amendment to the U.S. Constitution?" began the South Carolinian. Marshall's reply was repeated many times that day: "No, sir; I don't remember." Thurmond: "Do you know from what provision of the prior law the language of this amendment was copied?" Marshall: "I do not." Thurmond: "What objections were made to the original draft of the first section of the Fourteenth Amendment in February 1866, which caused the framer to redraft it into its present form?" Marshall: "I don't know." And so it went for about an hour, "with both men unyielding, and unsmiling."[56]

Marshall, however, was not bothered by the questions. As he said afterwards, "When I saw the lawyer advising [Thurmond], I said, 'Well, I don't have much to worry about.' The questions he asked I expected. I wasn't going to answer them in the first place."[57] *Time* magazine compared Thurmond's questioning of Marshall "to a white registrar administering a literacy test designed to confound even the best-educated Negro." It labeled Thurmond's futile efforts a "Yahoo-type hazing" which "made it more unlikely that any serious Senator would want to question [Marshall] seriously."[58]

The hearings ended on July 24, 1967, as they began, with Senators Ervin and

McClellan attacking Marshall's liberal jurisprudence and condemning him for not answering questions about issues then before or on their way to the Supreme Court. On August 21, 1967, the committee issued its report, along with the minority views of Sam Ervin. By a vote of eleven to five, the Judiciary Committee recommended Marshall's confirmation. The five in opposition were Eastland, Ervin, McClellan, Thurmond, and George Smathers (Florida's Senator Smathers had supported some civil rights legislation, so he may have acted more from principle than prejudice.)

On August 30, 1967, "after six hours of mostly listless debate" in the Senate, by a 69-to-11 vote, Marshall was confirmed by the U.S. Senate.[59] His nomination had sat for seventy-eight days before final confirmation by the Senate—much longer than other Supreme Court confirmation hearings during this period: Kennedy's appointees Byron White (eight days) and Arthur Goldberg (twenty-six days), and Johnson's other appointee, Abe Fortas (fourteen days), were nominations acted on much more expeditiously than Marshall's.[60] Although it did not take the eleven months it took for Senate approval of Marshall's federal appeals court nomination, it was a much longer process than usual because the Southern senators, again, were still out to embarrass the nominee, knowing that they did not have the votes to defeat him.

As Stephen Carter, a constitutional scholar, observed harshly:

> when a black nominee is controversial, the battles seem far more bitter than when the controversial candidate happens to be white. No one has ever faced quite so vicious an onslaught as Thurgood Marshall, [who was] forced to sit through a demeaning constitutional law and history trivia quiz in order to demonstrate his intellectual acumen and gain Senate approval.[61]

On September 1, 1967, Marshall took his constitutional oath of office in the chambers of his old friend Justice Hugo L. Black. On September 2, 1967, Johnson received a short note from Marshall: "It has been rewarding to serve under a president who has led the nation to historic gains in the pursuit of equal justice under law. What can I say today but that I shall seek, in such measure as I can, to justify the further trust which you have placed in my hands."[62] Earl Warren, one of the men on the Court whom Marshall grew to admire and respect, asked Marshall to visit him at the Court. As Marshall recalled the conversation, Warren "said he just wanted to give me some advice, and his advice was very simple: that the same books are on both sides of the bench. You use the same books as lawyers or judges, and it's not any different. He said, 'Your real trouble is going to be lack of talking to people. You'll wander around the hall and say, 'Will somebody please talk to me?'"[63]

The first Monday in October 1967 found, for the first time in America's history, an African American sitting on the high bench. Unfortunately, even on the Supreme Court Marshall did not have to hold his hand in front of his face to determine his color. As he had in every other place he worked, Marshall was to find himself treated as a wandering outsider during his twenty-four years of service on the Supreme Court. Warren's prediction was even more accurate than he knew.

Marshall brought to the Supreme Court "a sense of how the world worked, and how it worked against those at the bottom."[64] But, as a justice, Marshall saw his new role as quite different from his previous ones as an advocate and an apellate judge. Karen Hastie Williams, the daughter of Bill Hastie and then one of Marshall's Supreme Court law clerks, recalled that he

> never lost sight of his previous experiences which he brought with him to the Court, but I think that he saw his focus, once he became a Justice, as being a bridge builder between advocates and the decision makers on the Court. He was not a mouthpiece for woman's rights, civil rights, or First Amendment rights advocates....Rather he saw himself as an interpreter of their positions; a filter through whom the issues could be presented to the Court. He went into each conference well prepared to discuss or argue positions he felt strongly about in terms that the justices would understand.[65]

Over the years he served as an associate justice, Marshall tried to persuade his colleagues on these issues, but the eloquence of his arguments did not yield commensurate success. By the mid-1970s, Marshall had a clear, disturbing sense of how the Court as a small group worked, and how, as an outsider, he was at the margins of Supreme Court decision making.

But this cold realization would come later on in Marshall's life on the Court. On Monday, October 2, 1967, he was escorted into the courtroom by the chief deputy clerk of the Court to a seat adjacent to the clerk's desk at the side of the high bench. The clerk read his commission to serve on the Supreme Court. Then, standing next to the clerk's desk, with his left hand on a Bible and his right hand raised, Marshall took the judicial oath administered by the Clerk of the Court. After that, the Marshal of the Court escorted Thurgood Marshall to his seat at the other end of the bench. "The audience and the Justices, who have been standing while you were taking the oath, will remain standing until you are seated," concluded the preparatory memorandum on the ceremony sent to Marshall by John F. Davis, the Supreme Court Clerk.[66]

A few years later, in 1973, in the months before he died, Lyndon Johnson spoke on the telephone with Marshall. He insisted that it was his nomination of

Marshall to a seat on the Supreme Court, not Vietnam, that cost him the presidency. "He thought," recalled Marshall, "that moving me here was what killed him off. He felt they used the Vietnam War as the excuse. He told me that as late as about a week before he died."

Thurgood Marshall was about to fill the last major professional role in his sixty-year career as an advocate. He must have chuckled at the thought that he was only the second person from Maryland to sit on the U.S. Supreme Court, and that the first was none other than Roger Taney, the Chief Justice who authored the infamous 1857 opinion *Dred Scott v. Sandford*.

# 9

## MR. JUSTICE MARSHALL

**M**arshall arrived at the start of the Supreme Court's October 1967 term, after the racial riots that raged in Newark, Detroit, and Chicago that summer, and just in time to join a liberal Warren Court that was on the downward slope of its exciting revolution in constitutional adjudication.[1] *Newsweek* characterized the new justice as "one of the special ones—a great, rumpled bear of a man with...the immutable dignity only those with a true calling ever achieve....America may romanticize its radicals but it more often rewards its reformers. And Marshall is a reformer in the best tradition of the rule of law."[2] In fact, Marshall was both reformer and radical, more radical than all but one of his fellow justices could accept. He joined a liberal, activist cohort that included the Chief Justice, Earl Warren, Associate Justices Brennan, Douglas, and Fortas, and, on certain issues, Associate Justice Black.

Two years later this era came to an end. Chief Justice Earl Warren retired and was replaced by Warren Earl Burger, a conservative federal appeals court judge who had been a member of Eisenhower's Justice Department and who was nominated by the newly elected Richard M. Nixon. By 1970, another member of the liberal Warren Court, Abe Fortas, had resigned in disgrace,[3] to be replaced by Burger's close friend and then-conservative federal appeals court jurist, Harry Blackmun.

By the spring of 1972, Nixon had selected two more men to serve on the Supreme Court, Associate Justices Lewis Powell of Virginia and William Rehnquist of Arizona. Powell replaced Hugo Black, who had retired in September 1971 (and died three weeks later), while Rehnquist replaced Black's distant cousin on the Court, John M. Harlan II, who also retired in September 1971 (and died a few months later).

Marshall, then, was a part of a liberal Court majority for only two years, 1967–69, of the twenty-four he served. "Within two years of Marshall's appointment to the Supreme Court, the tide of judicial liberalism had begun to ebb. From 1972 until his retirement in 1991, Marshall saw support for the values he held dear steadily eroding, and he could not suppress his indignation."[4]

Justice Byron White remembered that "Thurgood brought to the conference table years of experience in an area that was of vital importance to our work, experience that none of us could claim to match. He characteristically would tell us things that we knew but would rather forget; and he told us much that we did not know due to the limitations of our own experience."[5]

Marshall was also, uniquely, very much an outsider on the Court; owing to "changes in the Court's composition, Marshall relatively quickly found himself placed on the margins of the Court's work by many of his colleagues."[6] More troubling, however, was the fact that Marshall was an outsider on the Court because of his race and his class and caste.

It was also painful for Marshall to hear or to read scholars and jurists repeatedly claim, falsely, that he had no judicial ability to sit on any appellate court, much less the U.S. Supreme Court. Indeed, one of Marshall's appellate court colleagues, Judge Fred J. Friendly, wrote his friend, Justice Felix Frankfurter, in 1962 that, when confronted with differences of opinion in cases argued before the federal court, or, worse, on issues he did not understand, Judge Marshall would toss a coin to decide how to vote on the litigation! And Bernard Schwartz, a noted Court scholar, wrote of Marshall that "next to Charles Whittaker, he was arguably the least able Justice to sit on the Warren Court."[7]

Marshall did not expect to experience racism on the Court. When he encountered it, he was disappointed and, on occasion, fiercely angry, bitter, and disillusioned to find, after his fifty-nine years of experiencing discrimination, some of his colleagues reminding him of his race and his place.

## THE OUTSIDER ON THE COURT

In April 1991, just months before he retired from the Court, Marshall wrote a Memo to the Conference dissenting from a proposed amendment to the Court's own rules (Rule 39). His brief note of dissent encapsulated his views of the role of the justices of the Supreme Court and how the Constitution had to be addressed by them—and it underlined the outsider's role that Marshall played throughout his Court tenure.

This amendment to the rules "embraced an invidious distinction," charged Marshall. An indigent defendant, but not a "paying litigant," could be denied a "disposition on the merits of a petition...following a determination that the filing was 'frivolous or malicious.'

"This Court once had a great tradition," he wrote. "'All men and women are entitled to their day in Court.' That guarantee has now been conditioned on monetary worth. It now will read: 'All men and women are entitled to their day in Court only if they have the *means* and the *money*.' I dissent."[8]

His brethren had to be reminded of the "bitter past" of the impoverished, and of racial, gender, ethnic, and other minorities. Most members of the Court often seemed, in Marshall's view, to want to forget or simply could not imagine such realities because they were beyond their own experiences. Marshall spent most of his life being, as Ralph Ellison put it, "invisible and without substance, a disembodied voice,"[9] rather than "sharing hours with an intellectual elite."[10]

Like Louis Brandeis, who, as a Jewish justice, saw himself as an outsider, Marshall "saw himself standing alone at the margin of his society."[11] However, unlike Felix Frankfurter, another Jewish justice who wanted desperately to become a social and political insider and who worked, unsuccessfully, all his life to attain that goal, he always remained at the margins. One of his law clerks speculated that Marshall remained an outsider partly because he, unlike his friend Bill Brennan, did not have the will, temperament, or patience to work to pull a majority together on a constitutional issue. Marshall was at odds, philosophically and ideologically, with Court majorities on most of the controversial constitutional conflicts within the Court. While he was not particularly content with his outsider status, he never felt compelled, like Frankfurter, to overcome it. Another of his clerks said of Marshall, "Part of his greatness is reflected in his lifelong struggle to maintain his outsider status even as he 'made it' in a white world. Marshall never lost sight of the fact that the Court was, at the core, a white man's institution and that his fundamental commitments were elsewhere....He had no use for the pretense and mystification that surrounded the Court's processes."[12]

The same was true when he was on the federal court of appeals, when his staff tried (and failed) to get him to dress and act the role. Marshall's style on the Supreme Court was rather different from that of any present or past justice. As a reporter observed: "His un-Holmesian way of life included regular trips to the race tracks and Atlantic City casinos, copious consumption of Winston's and Wild Turkey and conversation filled with profanity and a 1940s *boulevardier*'s slang. He sometimes addressed his brethren as 'baby.'"[13]

Given his lifelong poor health habits, presidents from Nixon to Bush constantly expected Marshall to retire or be invalided from the Court because of ill health, and they hoped that he would leave quickly so that they could fill his seat with a very different kind of jurist. While on the Court, Marshall was admitted to Bethesda Naval Hospital for a variety of illnesses and procedures, including an appendectomy, a broken ankle, pneumonia, failing eyesight caused by glaucoma, hearing problems, and a minor heart attack. These incidents only encouraged his opponents in the White House. Once, in 1970, when Marshall was in Bethesda, President Nixon asked the doctors to give him the medical file on Marshall. When he heard of Nixon's request, Marshall took the file from the medical attendant and, on its cover, wrote in large, bold strokes, "Not Yet!"[14]

Rumors about his health circulated virtually until the day he retired. He had to deny such reports in the African American press as well as articles like the one in a 1973 issue of *Justice* magazine that reported Marshall was "frequently" off the bench because he had a bad back and, generally, "was not in good health." The word "'frequently,'" he wrote, "is about as accurate as the entire statement. The facts are that I have been off the bench two times in five years—once with pneumonia and the other time with appendicitis.... Your conclusion [about the poor state of my health] can only be attributed to wishful thinking or hoping."[15] He reacted to another such report on ABC News in 1980 by stating, "I intend to serve out my term which is for life!"[16]

He wanted to stay on the Court *literally* until he died, in order to continue to monitor and criticize the errors of the white majority. Marshall certainly didn't want to leave while a Republican administration was in the White House. He once said to his clerks, during the early years of Ronald Reagan's presidency, "If I die while that man's President, just prop me up and keep on voting."[17]

Another set of rumors greatly offended Marshall, but he could do nothing to put them to rest. It was alleged by many that Marshall did not do any work in chambers, and that he spent his days watching soap operas on television. For example, a recent biography of Marshall asserted that he "spent hours each day telling stories and watching daytime television." Marshall had the free time, claimed the author, because the work of the Court was done by others. Since "opinion writing did not interest him," Marshall "told his clerks precisely and emphatically what to do, then let them do it."[18]

In 1979, because of the general perception that Marshall was a "soaps" watcher, NBC's *Today* show actually requested that Marshall do a 30-second spot on soap operas! The request was rejected by the Court's public information officer, Barrett McGurn, who wrote Marshall a memo letting the justice see his response to the network. Marshall angrily returned the note to McGurn with a handwritten comment: "And I do not look at soap operas."[19]

Incidents like this reflected the disdain many people had for a black American sitting as a justice on the Supreme Court. Marshall saw such comments, including allegations that he was not interested in the business of the Court other than the area of African American civil rights, as racially motivated attacks on his competence. Of course, the truth was quite different. For one thing, *all* the justices who sat with Marshall used their law clerks to assist them substantively in reviewing petitions for certiorari as well as in preparing drafts of written opinions. Naturally, all the justices provided input for their clerks to incorporate in the drafts they were crafting. Just as he had done in his previous legal and judicial roles, Marshall as an associate justice "arrived at a judgment after examining the legal materials his highly competent subordinates presented to him, and then delegated to them the job of working out the details necessary to support that judgment."[20]

Derogatory comments about his work and competence angered him (particularly because critics had no way of determining the truth), but Marshall was for the most part disciplined in his responses to them. He never lost sight of his lifelong mission to serve as an African American "social engineer" in predominantly white America, and would do nothing to impair his efforts to ensure that African Americans would, in Martin Luther King's words, "one day live in a nation where they will not be judged by the color of their skin but by the content of their character." But Marshall was never less than candid in his conversations with his colleagues. Candor is the stating of what everybody should know, but doesn't, for any number of reasons. His self-imposed task was to educate his colleagues about a life beyond the Court's confines that they simply were unaware of, and to try to have them "acknowledge the realities of the world on which constitutional decisions act."[21] Marshall sugar-coated his candor in anecdotes employed to educate his judicial brothers and sisters on particular points of law and soften somewhat the raw brutality of his experience. As one of his law clerks observed, Marshall "had a brilliant ability to create and deploy narrative" to inform his colleagues.[22]

In his memos and in his dissents, Marshall chastised the majority for "imagining ideal circumstances in a non-ideal world" and for "either choosing to ignore or [failing to recognize] another world 'out there.'"[23] Especially in race cases, his candor was unmasked and he attacked the majority's "unfounded assumptions" about life that led the majority, in his view, to create terrible, cruel opinions.[24]

Yet even through the more gentle, anecdotal form of persuasion, he could not change many attitudes. Indeed, some ridiculed his storytelling, seeing in his stories only *"tall tales…*with which he *delighted* us [my emphasis]," as Chief Justice Rehnquist described them at a memorial service after Marshall died. A few, such as Justices Sandra Day O'Connor and Anthony Kennedy, respected Marshall and did appreciate his efforts; both admitted that Marshall affected them through his stories. O'Connor recalled that he "imparted not only his legal acumen but also his life experiences, constantly pushing and prodding us to respond not only to the persuasiveness of legal argument but also the power of moral truth" illustrated by his telling anecdotes. "Behind most of the anecdotes," she said, "was a relevant legal point."[25] As someone who had experienced gender dis-

ABOVE: Thurgood's mother,
Norma Arica Marshall.
*(Cecilia Marshall)*

RIGHT: A one-year-old
Thurgood Marshall.
*(Collection of the Supreme Court
of the United States)*

Thurgood's father, William C. Marshall.
*(Cecilia Marshall)*

Thurgood Marshall in high school.
*(Collection of the Supreme Court of the United States)*

Thurgood Marshall at Lincoln University *(middle row, second from right).*
*(Collection of the Supreme Court of the United States)*

Charles Hamilton Houston, cadet.
*(Moorland-Spingarn Research Center, Howard University)*

Charles Hamilton Houston, dean, Howard Law School/NAACP, ca. 1935.
*(Moorland-Spingarn Research Center, Howard University)*

William Hastie, Howard Law School/NAACP.
*(Moorland-Spingarn Research Center, Howard University)*

W. E. B. Du Bois, NAACP.
*(Moorland-Spingarn Research Center, Howard University)*

Arthur Spingarn, NAACP.
*(Moorland-Spingarn Research Center, Howard University)*

Thurgood Marshall with Franklin Williams, NAACP, ca. 1945.
*(Moorland-Spingarn Research Center, Howard University)*

Thurgood Marshall,
NAACP, ca. 1938.
*(Collection of the
Supreme Court of the
United States)*

Marshall with Donald
Gaines Murray, who
was denied entry into
University of Maryland
Law School, and
Charles Hamilton
Houston, court pro-
ceedings, Maryland,
ca. 1935–1936.
*(Library of Congress)*

Roy Wilkins, Walter White, and Thurgood Marshall, ca. 1940.
*(Library of Congress)*

W. D. Lyons, one of Marshall's clients, standing with six arresting officers,
Hugo, Oklahoma, ca. 1939–1940. *(Library of Congress)*

**NATIONAL ASSOCIATION FOR THE ADVANCEMENT OF COLORED PEOPLE**

**69 FIFTH AVENUE, NEW YORK**

TELEPHONE: ALgonquin 4-3551

*Official Organ: The Crisis*

New Orleans, La.
January 18, 1943.

Memorandum to office:

        Yesterday was quite a day had a total of six meetings starting at 10:30 and ending at 8:30 last night.

1. Meeting with a group of teachers from New Orleans who are interested in getting the teachers to put up some money for the NAACP and to give Donald Jones something for his services.

2. Meeting with officials of the state teachers' association for plans to continue the fight on a state basis (this is confidential for time being.

3. Meeting with group of citizens from state who are interested in same fight and who will organize into a citizens' committee--I hope.

4. Meetings with representatives from several branches in Louisiana interested in organizing a state conference of branches. I told them it could not be done unless all branches of the state were notified and approval obtained from N.O. We, however, made a temporary organization subject to approval of all branches and N.O. They are to send the full minute to the N.O. for approval They should be sent to all Louisiana branches explaining that it is temporary and must have their approval before a permanent organization can be set up. As soon as approval is obtained they are ready to meet in Baton Rouge and form a permanent organization. We need one to raise money for these cases and all at the meeting yesterday were more than enthusiastic and ready to go.

5. Addressed a mass meeting by the branch starting at 4:00 PM--usual baloney.

6. Met with teachers of Jefferson Parish about their case which is ready to be filed next week.

7. Met with larger group of New Orleans teachers about the same matters discussed in the first meeting.

8. Very important meeting at one of the bars in town for the purpose of forgetting about the other meetings--this meeting was a great success.

        HOT AS THE DEVIL DOWN HERE     Thurgood.

"On the road": Letter from Marshall to NAACP office staff, 1943.
*(Library of Congress)*

Marshall on steps of
Supreme Court, with
fellow NAACP counsel
George Hayes and James
M. Nabrit, in 1954 after
*Brown* was announced.
*(AP/Wide World Photo)*

Marshall with Ada Lois Sipuel Fisher *(seated)*, seeking enrollment at the University of Oklahoma School of Law. Others are Amos Hall, NAACP, and Dr. J. E. Fellows, 1948.
*(Library of Congress)*

Vivian "Buster" Marshall, first wife, ca. 1936.
*(Moorland-Spingarn Research Center, Howard University)*

Marshall, wife Cissy, and sons Thurgood Jr. and John, ca. 1969.
*(Library of Congress)*

Thurgood Marshall at work in NAACP office, ca. 1960.
*(Library of Congress)*

Earl Warren, the "Super Chief," during his 1948 campaign for vice president.
*(Collection of the Supreme Court of the United States)*

Marshall's brethren, 1967 term. First row: Harlan, Black, Warren, Douglas, Brennan; second row: Fortas, Stewart, White, Marshall. *(Hessler Studio/Collection of the Supreme Court of the United States)*

Justice Hugo L. Black, ca. 1970
*(Collection of the Supreme Court of the United States)*

Marshall, robing for first time as
associate justice, 1967, with his
family.
*(Library of Congress)*

A beaming Marshall at the
robing, 1967.
*(Library of Congress)*

William J. Brennan, Jr.
*(Collection of the Supreme Court of the United States)*

Chief Justice Warren E. Burger, ca. 1980.
*(Collection of the Supreme Court of the United States)*

Chief Justice William Rehnquist, ca. 1987.
*(Collection of the Supreme Court of the United States)*

Associate Justice Sandra Day O'Connor.
*(Collection of the Supreme Court of the United States)*

Justice William O. Douglas.
*(Peter Erenheft/Collection of the Supreme Court of the United States)*

Marshall, with Associate Justice Lewis Powell, ca. 1988.
*(Josh Mathes/Collection of the Supreme Court of the United States)*

Marshall in chambers, 1978.
*(Deborah L. Rhode/Collection
of the Supreme Court of the
United States)*

ABOVE LEFT: Marshall with William J. Brennan, Jr., 1985.
(Ray Lustig, Washington Post/Collection of the Supreme Court of the United States)
ABOVE RIGHT: Marshall, at retirement press conference, 1991.
(Lois Long/Collection of the Supreme Court of the United States)
BELOW: Marshall and Brennan: lonely liberals walking down a corridor in the Court,
1978.
(Deborah L. Rhode/Collection of the Supreme Court of the United States)

crimination, O'Connor "understood the stories so well. She also, upon hearing these stories, realized that her own experiences with discrimination were very mild in comparison."[26]

Kennedy was a young conservative jurist from California, appointed in 1987 by President Reagan after conservative Robert Bork's nomination was defeated in the Senate. Kennedy was a colleague of Marshall's for his last five terms, 1987–91, and was influenced by Marshall's storytelling as much as O'Connor was. Those stories, he said, "prove that his compassion and his philosophy flow from a life and legend of struggle. His gift of storytelling is not some incidental facet or adornment of Thurgood's character and personality. It is an essential part of his professional greatness."[27]

Marshall was sensitive to racism on the Court, and reacted accordingly when it reared its head. There were times, he confessed to a reporter, when "I did take a little [racial slurs]—in Court." As a consequence, to many of his colleagues he "seemed withdrawn and vaguely hostile....In race cases particularly, Marshall grew increasingly bitter. He stopped short of calling his colleagues racist—but just barely."[28] Even his law clerks noted that Marshall's disposition was always "tinged with a mockery and bitterness that never left him."[29] At the very least, Marshall thought that his brethren, including, during the *Bakke* controversy (over affirmative action), his best friend, William J. Brennan Jr., were insensitive and sometimes even callous about the impact of racism on human beings.

> "What do they know about Negroes?" he asked in 1990. "You can't name one member of this Court who knew anything about Negroes before he came to this Court." Most of all he resented the unwillingness of some of his colleagues to embrace minority preferences as a way of redressing past injustice. "There's not a white man in this country who can say, 'I never benefited by being white,'" insisted Marshall.[30]

Marshall felt the stings of Court slights, and always believed they were because of his race. On April 7, 1972, for example, Marshall wrote the Chief, Warren E. Burger, that his cherished aunt had died and that he was going to attend the funeral. "Please make an announcement from the bench that I may participate in the argued cases on the briefs," he requested of the Chief.[31] A new date for the conference was set by the Chief, and Marshall left for the funeral. On his return, he found that the conference had been held in his absence, despite his request to hold off. Evidently, Burger found out that the rescheduled conference was to be held on the date set for Jimmy Byrnes's funeral services. The segregationist governor of South Carolina while Marshall was trying to overturn *Plessy* was also, for a year, a member of the Court. Burger, thinking that some of the brethren would want to attend the funeral, canceled the rescheduled conference and held the conference on the original date, which meant that Marshall missed the important meeting. An angry Marshall wrote a stern letter to the conference:

> I am deeply disturbed as a result of the conference on argued cases being held in my absence. I know that this has not occurred during my few years here except where the Justice involved was ill and unable to be present and, even then, it was with the consent of the Justice involved. I had assumed that it was the usual practice here....I prefer that I just be listed as not participating in any opinions coming out of yesterday's conference. I will leave it to the press to speculate as to why I am not earning my salary.[32]

In the original draft of the letter, however, Marshall expressed his anger much more directly in a final paragraph not included in the letter actually sent: "One final and perhaps more personal note is that I think I am justified in considering the burial of my ninety-three-year-old aunt, who is the last member of that generation of my family, more important than the burial of Jimmy Byrnes. This, of course, is only insofar as I am concerned."

For Marshall, this slight was another example of the different, disrespectful treatment he received as a member of the Court. It just reaffirmed his belief that even on the Court there was an insidious form of racism. What bothered him as much as Burger's insensitivity was the response of the other seven justices. None of them, not even his friend Brennan, had complained to Burger when he rescheduled the conference in Marshall's absence. One account noted that, after the fact, they were "mortified" because they had not objected on Marshall's behalf. In the end, Burger rescheduled the conference session, with Marshall present, and every vote was retaken.[33]

Justice Antonin Scalia, appointed to the Court in 1986 by President Reagan, was an acid-tongued jurist who never pulled punches with brethren he disagreed with. His anger at Marshall came through clearly in a 1990 case before the Court, *Holland v. Illinois*. Daniel Holland, a white defendant, had been charged with a number of felonies, including rape, armed robbery, and aggravated kidnapping. The state's prosecutor had removed the two black jurors from the pool of possible jurors, and Holland's lawyers argued that such action violated their client's Sixth Amendment rights to be tried before a jury that was representative of the community. The majority, in a five-to-four decision written by Scalia, concluded that this was a frivolous constitutional argument, and upheld Holland's conviction.

Marshall's dissent, joined in by Justices Brennan and Blackmun (Justice John

Paul Stevens wrote a separate dissent), claimed that Scalia's opinion for the Court "decides today that a prosecutor's racially motivated exclusion of Afro-Americans from the petit jury does not violate the fair cross section requirement of the Sixth Amendment: To reach this startling result, the majority misrepresents the values underlying the fair cross section requirement...[and] insulates an especially invidious form of racial discrimination in the selection of petit jurors from Sixth Amendment scrutiny."

Scalia, writing for the majority in *Holland*, insisted that "race has nothing to do with the legal issue in this case," and that "it is not remotely true that our opinion today 'lightly sets aside' the constitutional goal of 'eliminating racial discrimination in our system of criminal justice,'" (quoting Marshall's criticisms). Scalia was so thoroughly disgusted with Marshall's intense focus on race that he wrote, "Justice Marshall's dissent rolls out the ultimate weapon, the accusation of insensitivity to racial discrimination—which will lose its intimidating effect if it continues to be fired so randomly."

Scalia's repeated assaults on Marshall, in open court, included "one of the most pointed personal attacks to appear in recent Supreme Court opinions," wrote two Scalia biographers.[34] Marshall, however, was not the only justice to feel Scalia's wrath. "Scalia," wrote one Court observer, "is rash, impulsive, and imprudent, a Justice who in case after case would rather insult his colleagues' intelligence than appeal to them."[35] But Marshall never backed away from Warren Burger's insensitivity and Scalia's bombast, even in the face of scathing personal attacks on him. He had heard and experienced far worse from Deep South die-hard sheriffs and other crude racists.

Justice William O. Douglas, another Supreme Court jurist who often clashed with Marshall, also recalled Marshall's cutting remarks in conference about racial matters. He, too, like Scalia and other jurists after him, believed that Marshall was only a one-issue jurist and that the Court really didn't need his insights on civil rights for African Americans. During its 1971 term, the Court quickly denied certiorari in a case from Arizona in which a white applicant for admission to the state's bar was rejected because of failing grades while African Americans with similar grades were admitted. The petitioner claimed he was the victim of reverse discrimination. Douglas wrote, "I was the only one to vote to grant [certiorari, and a vote of four is needed to hear the case], saying to the conference that racial discrimination against a white was as unconstitutional as racial discrimination against a black. The only one who replied was Thurgood Marshall, who said, 'You guys have been practicing discrimination for years. Now it is our turn.'"[36]

There were instances in which the social differences between Marshall and his colleagues were all too clearly evident. When a power failure left his Virginia home without electricity, Marshall's clerks suggested he call up Lewis Powell to see if the influential Virginian could help out. Marshall took their advice, and within minutes Powell had spoken to the chairman of the power company and "'the next thing I knew,' said Marshall, 'there were three trucks in front of the house.' Not only did Marshall get his electricity restored, but he had additional confirmation of the power of Lewis Powell and all the other rich white men who ran the South to get whatever they wanted by private contacts."[37]

Clearly, Marshall was a "first" for the Court. As a former law clerk noted recently, "unlike Marshall, none of his colleagues was the grandson of slaves. None had defended people on death row. None had been denied access to hotels or the law school of their choice because of the color of their skin. None knew what it was like to be in downtown Baltimore with no access to a bathroom or to be run out of town by the threat of violence."[38]

## FRIENDS, COLLEAGUES, AND ANTAGONISTS

It is deeply ironic that one of Marshall's friends and admirers was Hugo L. Black, a card-carrying member of the Alabama Ku Klux Klan in the 1920s, a very successful trial lawyer and then a county prosecutor, and a U.S. senator from Alabama elected in 1926 only because he had the electoral support of the state's Klansmen. Black had known Marshall since the mid-1930s, when he was a U.S. senator and Marshall, then the NAACP's assistant special counsel, frequently visited him along with Walter White and Charles Houston to talk about race and lynchings, desegregation, and aid to education.

In the early 1940s, Justice Black, along with Justice Felix Frankfurter, met secretly with Marshall and others to try to figure out a way to bring African Americans and liberal white Southerners together to address the race issue that was tearing up the region. By 1952, the beginning of the end of the *Plessy* doctrine, Black was regarded as a champion of African Americans' legal demands for equality. Black had written some major opinions, and had spoken out forcefully on the importance of equal rights for black people.

Marshall and Black occasionally communicated with each other. After Marshall's lengthy Senate hearings ended and he was confirmed as a member of the federal court of appeals, Black wrote him a short letter of congratulation. "Now that the protests against your appointment have been laid to rest and you are actively serving your country as a Judge of the Court of Appeals for the Second Circuit, I want to tell you how happy I am that you are there and to congratulate the nation on having a man of such ability, integrity, and patriotism."[39]

Black believed that Marshall had been a fine judge and an excellent advocate for both the NAACP and the government. He warmly welcomed Marshall to the Supreme Court. Black, who had sworn Marshall in when he became the solicitor general, was asked by Marshall to officiate at his swearing-in as a justice of the U.S. Supreme Court on September 1, 1967. He took the "constitutional" oath of office in Black's private chambers. Elizabeth Black, the justice's wife, was present for the ceremony, and wrote,

> Hugo called Bill Brennan, the only other Justice in the building at the time. Hugo asked Thurgood if he had a favorite chapter in the Bible, and Thurgood said he couldn't think of one, so Hugo said, "What about Corinthians 13: 'And now abideth faith, hope, charity, these three; but the greatest of these is charity.'" Thurgood loved it, and Hugo swore him in on his white Gideon Bible.... Thurgood wished his daddy could have been there, but he said he knew he was on some street corner in heaven shaking his finger and saying, "I knew my boy would do it." [40]

Although Black disagreed with Marshall's expansive view of the role of federal judges and his notion that the Constitution was to be read as an evolving, changing document, the Alabaman shared with the Marylander some very basic values about law and orderliness. For one thing, both believed in the primacy of the Rule of Law as well as in the value of Rules. For both men, "Rules is Rules," and violators of the Rules had to take the punishment associated with such acts of disobedience to law.

Both Black and Marshall disagreed with SCLC and SNCC taking to the streets to force changes in the law. For the two men, the forces for good marching and singing in the streets one day could easily be overwhelmed by the forces of evil walking the streets the following day. Black would have agreed categorically with Marshall's assertion that "I am a man of the law, and in my book, anarchy is anarchy." [41] Marshall was deeply saddened when Black retired in September 1971 and died shortly afterwards.

Thurgood Marshall, recounted one of his law clerks, "had a trial lawyer's personality." By instinct and training, Marshall "went for the jugular" in his courtroom battles with segregationists. And he was very successful in his job. So, too, was Hugo Black before coming to the Court in 1937. Black had become the most successful trial lawyer and prosecutor in Alabama by the time he decided to run for the Senate in 1925. [42] He became that body's most highly respected and, for some, most feared, investigator. He, too, always went for the jugular in trial courts and when chairing Senate investigating committees. So he saw in Marshall a kindred spirit: there were very few justices on the Court who had toiled in such a trial advocacy role prior to elevation to the Court. Black, listening to Marshall in Court while he was the NAACP's legal counsel, conversing with Marshall when the two men met outside the Court and in Black's Senate chambers, and reading Marshall's briefs, saw in him a colleague who had shared, in a way, Black's experiences in the courtroom.

Marshall's trial-lawyer personality also struck a positive chord with two other members of the Court. Both Chief Justice Warren and Associate Justice Brennan had similar experiences and traits. Both were outgoing and very friendly, and both worked with their clerks in a similar manner. As a law clerk at the time noted,

> all three were gregarious men who established working relationships by recounting interesting anecdotes and telling jokes. They all wanted to interpret the Constitution to promote justice, and were willing to leave to others the details of the arguments linking just results to the words of the Constitution and precedents. Warren expressed this perspective in his celebrated question to advocates who presented the Court with legalistic arguments: "Yes, but is it fair?"[43]

Warren was, in Marshall's words, "just one of the greatest people who ever lived, and I think history will record when both of us are long since dead that he is probably the greatest Chief Justice who ever lived. He had the opportunity [to change society]. He grasped it. He didn't duck it, and I think he did extremely well with it. But, in addition, he had a warmth....And he digs. He takes that briefcase. You should see that briefcase he takes home at night!...He must stay up all night."[44]

Brennan was Marshall's closest friend and ally on the Court. Cissy Marshall recently commented that the two were so close that they "behaved like brothers."[45] So highly regarded was Brennan in the Marshall household that one of Marshall's grandsons was named Thurgood William Marshall in his honor. Brennan was, in the opinion of many informed observers, the most energetic, personable, friendly, and persuasive jurist ever to sit on the U.S. Supreme Court. Even his arch jurisprudential opponents on the Court, Scalia and Rehnquist, called him friend. Brennan, a New Jersey Democrat who sat on that state's supreme court at the time of his nomination, was picked by President Eisenhower in 1956, and served on the U.S. Supreme Court for a near-record thirty-four years, until his retirement in 1990.

Bill Brennan, Marshall admitted many times, was "the coalition builder" throughout his tenure on the Court.[46] He was, clearly, the absolute master of implementing what he called the most important rule in Supreme Court adjudication: the Rule of Five. "Like all good political leaders, Brennan structured the process of decision and gave his colleagues reason for doing what he understood to be the right thing." From the moment he joined the Court in 1956 until his retirement in 1990, the elfin Irishman assiduously "sought to get five votes for the doctrine that he believed most compatible with his vision of fundamental rights."[47] Since Marshall was literally his partner in these doctrinal fights, he let Brennan, who was the acknowledged master, do the negotiating and the dealing. Brennan could almost always count on Marshall's vote. Clearly, in civil liberties, criminal justice, and civil rights cases, the two men voted as one. Their clerks also worked together very closely. As Susan Low Bloch, one of Marshall's bright young clerks, recalled, "we spent a great deal of time working with Brennan's clerks. Brennan's office was next to Marshall's and the flow of traffic between the two chambers was constant—we almost wore out the marble [floor] between them."[48] This working alliance was significant in the last decade of their service on the Court when they were usually in the minority on a great many civil rights and liberties issues.

There is a touching story told of Brennan's behavior after Thurgood Marshall's funeral, which took place on January 28, 1993. Brennan, then eighty-seven years old, had been retired a bit less than three years, but still maintained his chambers in the Supreme Court building. Because of a temporary estrangement, Brennan had not visited Marshall in the hospital in the month before he died. At the funeral, "Brennan regretted not having visited him." In terrible agony over his behavior toward his longtime friend, Brennan returned to the Court after the service and walked into Marshall's chambers, passing surprised staffers. He silently entered Marshall's office and locked the door behind him. "And there Bill Brennan sat, engrossed in thoughts of his departed friend, and his own future, until late into the evening....He checked the desk drawers to see if Thurgood had a bottle hidden somewhere. One never knew with Thurgood....But he found nothing he could imbibe to toast a fond farewell."[49]

There were three justices who stood out in Marshall's mind because of the continuous tension generated by their interactions with him. Justices Douglas, Powell, and Rehnquist were very different Supreme Court justices in their philosophies and judgments, and were Marshall's major adversaries on the Court—especially Rehnquist, who sat on the Court with Marshall for nineteen of his twenty-four years and who was by far the most conservative of his opponents.

William O. Douglas was, during his three and a half decades of service on the Court (1939–75), the "darling" of the liberals, a man who staunchly, vigorously defended the rights and liberties of individuals against the intrusive power of the state. Justice Powell was a moderately conservative jurist from Virginia nominated by President Nixon in 1971 to fill the seat vacated by Hugo Black. Justice, later Chief Justice (1986), William Rehnquist was a very conservative judicial ideologue nominated in 1971 by Nixon to fill the seat vacated by Justice Harlan. While they differed personally and jurisprudentially, the trio shared a less-than-positive view of the intellectual ability of Thurgood Marshall.

Douglas deeply disliked Thurgood Marshall and "thought little of him as a judge." [50] On the Court, Douglas "treated Marshall with an abruptness approaching contempt." [51] Marshall's response, according to Brennan, was to conclude that Douglas was a racist. Given his life experiences with such people, Marshall, said Brennan, "could never really believe it wasn't race." [52] According to Douglas, Marshall was named to the Court by Johnson "simply because he was black, and in the 1960s that was reason enough."

As early as 1968, less than a year after Marshall joined the Court, Douglas was writing disparaging comments, in private memos placed in his files, about his black colleague. In one such memo that he wrote after a contentious conference in April 1968, he said, "Marshall is a fine individual, but extremely opinionated and not very well trained in the law. His report [in the conference] was rather on the side of wasting a lot of time and in a lot of idle talk and irrelevant conversation." [53] At about the same time, in the late 1960s and early 1970s, Marshall invariably refused (as did most of the brethren) to join Douglas's votes to grant certiorari in cases that challenged the constitutionality of the war in Vietnam. Marshall strongly disagreed with Douglas about the war on at least two counts: its "rightness" and whether Lyndon Johnson had acted constitutionally as Commander in Chief in the Vietnam War.

Douglas recalled a particularly ugly clash he had with Marshall during the summer of 1973, when the Supreme Court was not sitting. New York congresswoman Elizabeth Holtzman, along with a small number of military officers, asked the federal courts to stop the U.S. bombing of Cambodia. In July 1973, a federal district court issued an order staying the secretary of defense from bombing Cambodia. The federal court of appeals, however—Marshall's own former Second Circuit—lifted the stay in the case *(Holtzman v. Schlesinger)*. The ACLU then made application to Marshall, who served as circuit judge of the Second Circuit, asking him to reinstate the stay of the bombing ordered by the federal district court judge. Because he knew the feelings of most of the members of the Court, Marshall issued an order upholding the court of appeals decision.

The ACLU, on behalf of Holtzman, then asked another justice, Douglas, for an order reinstating the federal district court order. After Douglas held a hearing in Yakima, Washington, he issued an opinion "granting the stay on the basis that only Congress had the power to declare war...and that no war had been declared." He called in his order and opinion from Washington State to his secretary; it was filed at the Court on August 4, 1973. The government then went to Marshall and asked him to intercede to prevent the district court from issu-

ing the order halting the bombing. Believing that "it was up to the full conference to decide whether to reverse [Douglas's order,] Marshall called Brennan,
who suggested a solution that would avert an embarrassing confrontation
between the Court and the Executive Branch, and at the same time avoid overruling Douglas....Marshall called each of the other seven Justices to secure their
agreement [on the order he was preparing]."[54]

Marshall's order in effect upheld the federal appeals court decision. The
bombing of Cambodia continued. Douglas was livid at Marshall's method of
overturning—the use of the telephone pool, which, for Douglas, did not "conform with our ground rules." To his law clerks, Douglas called Marshall
"spaghetti spine." As Douglas recounted the incident in his autobiography:

> Marshall had seen the order I signed....Yet Marshall falsely stated that the
> "only order extant in this case is the order of the District Court." He thereupon
> talked on the phone with all members of the Court except me and stayed the
> order of the District Court. That was *lawless* action, for only the Court [con-
> vened in Washington, D.C., with all members present] could vacate my order
> reinstating the order of the District Court.[55]

In addition to calling Marshall's actions cowardly and lawless, Justice Douglas
publicly speculated, without any proof whatsoever, that "I believe that some
Nixon men put the pressure on Marshall to cut corners. Sad to say, he did so and
thus emulated the 'law and order' men during the Watergate period."[56]

There was a special edge to Marshall's relationship to Justice Lewis Powell,
the jurist from Virginia who joined the Court in 1972 (filling Hugo Black's seat).
Only once in sixteen years did Marshall actually visit Powell in the latter's chambers. "Marshall held Lewis at a distance," said one of their colleagues, perhaps
because of Powell's attachment to the South. (Powell had filed a brief *amicus
curiae* in a school busing case, arguing against busing to achieve desegregation.
It came to the Court shortly after Marshall joined it and when Powell was deeply
involved in Richmond, Virginia, school board matters.)

> Powell's courtly ways and soft Virginia accent reminded Marshall of the edu-
> cated and impeccably well mannered southerners who for so long had main-
> tained the subjugation of blacks. Powell once made the mistake of saying in
> Conference that only he and Marshall would understand a certain point because
> they were the only southerners. Marshall's head snapped up in dismay. He came
> from the border state of Maryland, but in a more fundamental way than geog-
> raphy, he and Powell came from different worlds.[57]

The two men, coming from different worlds and different life experiences,
held widely divergent views of the value of education in overcoming the ravages

of segregation. Those differences stood out in a number of race discrimination cases that came to the Court during the 1970s. Marshall was deeply angered by Powell's position in these equal-protection and affirmative-action cases. His attitudes, expressed in the school property tax equalization case of *San Antonio School District v. Rodriguez* (1973), the Detroit, Michigan, interdistrict school busing case of *Milliken v. Bradley* (1974), and the medical school affirmative-action case of *Board of Regents v. Bakke* (1978), left little doubt in Marshall's mind that Powell was, indeed, a racist.

The only really positive comments Powell could make, and the only small praise he offered, about his colleague focused on Marshall's use of advocacy rather than the mass protest and noisy marching in the streets to achieve racial justice and equality. "I admire Thurgood Marshall," he said recently, "as much for *how* he advanced racial equality as for *what* he accomplished. Thurgood Marshall steadfastly chose the courts as the avenue by which he sought to change society. He promoted civil rights on account of, not in spite of, the rule of law."[58]

Associate Justice, and, after 1986, Chief Justice, William Rehnquist was another of the brethren who had little regard, personally and professionally, for Marshall's views, and for his self-appointed role of critical outsider. Rehnquist was Marshall's prime antagonist for nineteen years. Karen Hastie Williams recalled that Rehnquist "never took Marshall seriously. He disagreed at the core with Marshall's view on almost every subject which came before the Court."[59]

Rehnquist, a conservative jurist from Arizona, had a history of personal and professional actions that suggested to observers that he was less than admiring of the quest of African Americans for an end to racial segregation and for the realization of political and social equality under the law. When he clerked for Justice Robert Jackson during the Court's 1952–53 term, he wrote the memo cited earlier to Jackson arguing that *Plessy* should not be overturned. During both his 1971 and 1986 confirmation hearings before the Senate Judiciary Committee, Rehnquist had to defend himself against accusations that he harassed African American voters while he served as a poll-watcher in Arizona and that he purchased a home in Vermont that had a restrictive covenant attached to it. Rehnquist and Marshall clashed on these and other issues while both were on the Court. Marshall saw overt racial bias in Rehnquist's civil rights views. Whether the issue was affirmative action or the use of busing to desegregate public schools, the two were continuously at loggerheads. Marshall saw in these actions of the Chief a concerted effort to minimize the substantive impact of the 1954 *Brown* decision—one that Rehnquist had not liked when it was announced.

In another area, that of capital punishment, the categorical disagreement between the two men exploded in open court during oral argument. In 1981 the justices were hearing arguments in a death-penalty case. Rehnquist, then an associate justice, "suggested that the inmate's repeated appeals had cost the taxpayers too much money. Justice Marshall interrupted, saying, 'It would have been cheaper to shoot him right after he was arrested, wouldn't it?'" [60]

When Marshall retired at the end of the Court's 1990–91 term, he requested the occasional use of the Court's chauffeured automobile to take him from his home in Virginia to the Court. Rehnquist rejected the request from Marshall, saying that "while I am sympathetic to the request you make…I do not believe I can accede to it." The projected home-to-office use of the car for retired justices was, claimed Rehnquist, not official business, and he refused to provide transportation to Marshall. [61]

Nat Hentoff, after Marshall's death, wrote of Chief Justice Rehnquist's reaching "a new level of abominable *chutzpah*." After decades of continually working to undermine Marshall's efforts to achieve equal justice for all men and women, at a memorial service for Marshall, the Chief had intoned somberly, "Inscribed above the front entrance to the Supreme Court building are the words 'Equal Justice Under Law.' Surely no one individual did more to make these words a reality than Thurgood Marshall." For the enraged Hentoff (as well as many others who heard or read the homage offered by Rehnquist), the Chief's eulogy "went beyond friendship to hypocrisy." [62]

## "MY KNUCKLEHEADS": JUSTICE MARSHALL AND HIS LAW CLERKS

The Supreme Court is really nine small, independent law firms. Marshall brought with him into the Court his experiences as manager of a similar "small law firm," his old NAACP Inc Fund office. Each operation is headed up by a senior partner (a justice) and each has a small number of associates (two law clerks when Marshall joined the Court in 1967; four young men and women by the time of his retirement in 1991). In addition, there is the necessary secretarial and other administrative assistance to keep the small firm in business. [63]

Marshall's management styles at the Inc Fund and in the Court were quite similar: he delegated a great deal of work to his law clerks, including the drafting of opinions he was delegated to write. His view was that the clerks should spend their time working on the details needed for an opinion. He could quickly reach, usually, a sound judgment about the disposition of a case; his clerks took care of the minutiae. He would determine the appropriate remedy for a case that came to the Court. His sound judgment was a principal reason he was appointed to the Court by Johnson, he told his clerks.

One clerk recalled an incident she experienced that illuminated Marshall's view of his role, as the boss, and that of his clerks, as staff to the senior partner:

"Once when I suggested a change in the draft of an opinion we were working on, he commented: 'A pretty good idea, but you're missing two things.' Panicked, I wondered what I had left out. I had cite-checked, shepardized, proof-read...and could find no error. The judge filled me in: 'Nomination by the President and confirmation by the Senate!'"[64]

The clerks, much like the young lawyers who had worked for Marshall at the Inc Fund, were bright, highly motivated young men and women who had recently graduated at the top of their classes at law school. Some of Marshall's clerks came into his office with prior clerking experience in the lower federal courts. All were eager to work, and they did work hard for Marshall. After the heyday of the Warren Court, much of their work was devoted to preparing dissents with Marshall. By the mid-1970s, as one recalled, "the first question he asked potential clerks was invariably, 'How do you feel about writing dissents? If you don't like it, you are probably in the wrong office.'"[65]

He treated them as an extended family, with warmth and compassion. They were his "knuckleheads," a term of endearment he used when he was confident about their skills and their capacity to do the work expected of them. Marshall would get together with his clerks several times a week to discuss the pending cases and the status of each clerk's opinion drafting. According to one, their "survival" strategy in these sessions "was to treat these discussions like oral argument: Come prepared, know what you want to say, be able to summarize your main points quickly, and be ready to respond to a peppering of questions [from the judge]. If you acted like a well-prepared lawyer, the Judge was ready to listen and to reason with you—though when he disagreed, you could look forward to a grilling."[66]

Marshall's role as a judge, said another of his law clerks, was defined as clearly as his role as an NAACP advocate. His task in both professions was clear: Do the work, do the work, do the work. No deviation from that command was permitted. He did not participate in politics, on or off the Court, unlike many of his brethren, while serving on the Court. For most of his tenure, Marshall did not give very many speeches to bar associations, nor did he meet with other groups to discuss the Court and its work. His sole task, as he saw it, was to reflect and concentrate on cases as well as, when appropriate, to explain life's realities to his colleagues. As one clerk described it, Marshall's task was to "look hard at the subject matter, to review the briefs that were submitted and to work with his clerks in the development of opinions where he felt it was important to write."[67]

## THURGOOD MARSHALL'S JURISPRUDENCE

Thurgood Marshall's jurisprudence required a judge to use practical judgment in deciding cases and controversies, taking into consideration the *context* of the litigation. It was a view of "judging that is grounded in a reading and rendering—an ethnography—of the life, culture, and material existence of real poor people."[68] He rejected, totally, the use by judges of an abstract, rigid "legal formalism" to decide real cases presented to them for review and decision.[69]

For example, in a case heard during the Court's 1970 term, *Wyman, Commissioner, New York State Department of Social Services v. James,* Marshall dissented from the majority's view that welfare benefits could be terminated if a recipient refused to allow a caseworker to enter her home on an official visit. Justice Blackmun, one of the new justices appointed by President Nixon, joined by all the other Nixon appointees (and by Potter Stewart and Byron White), overturned the lower federal court by ruling that such a visit was not a "search" bound by the constraints of the Fourth Amendment's "search and seizure" requirements. The Warren Court holdovers, Douglas, Brennan, and Marshall, dissented.

In the past, Marshall wrote in his dissent, the Court had "pushed beyond established constitutional contours to protect the vulnerable and to further basic human values. I find no little irony in the fact that the burden of today's departure from principled adjudication is placed on the lowly poor. Perhaps the majority has explained why a commercial warehouse deserves more protection than this poor woman's home. I am not convinced; and, therefore, I must respectfully dissent."

Marshall believed that it was the responsibility of judges to ensure that all persons had the possibility of living in a "just and humane society."[70] He believed, as a study of his opinions on the Court indicates, that all persons had the right to be free of all forms of capricious discrimination; that all persons had to have access to decent education, decent housing, and decent jobs; and that all persons had a significant liberty interest in the Fourteenth Amendment's due-process clause to be free from governmental interference in their personal lives. And he was always critical of a Court majority that ignored the peculiar circumstances of the impoverished.

This meant that federal judges, including the justices on the Supreme Court, had an important, active—rather than passive—role to play in order to guarantee liberty for all persons. The Supreme Court justices' role in a constitutional republic was to give meaning to the evolving words of the Constitution in such a manner as to provide justice to the weak and the underclasses who needed its protections. For the justices of the Supreme Court to ignore their legal and constitutional oaths to provide justice for both the rich and the poor was an unforgivable lack of fundamental fairness. Unfortunately, decisions by the Court majority that failed this test of fairness were not uncommon during Marshall's tenure, and he protested in conference and in his dissents.

*United States v. Kras* (1972) was one of many cases where this "context" issue arose. It involved a poor man, Robert Kras, who was unable to file for bankruptcy because he did not have the fifty-dollar filing fee necessary for such an action under the Federal Bankruptcy Act. (The fee was a condition of discharge in a voluntary bankruptcy petition by a person who claimed not to have assets sufficient to pay the regular fee. The federal law also allowed a claimant to pay the fee over an extended period of time.) Kras lived on welfare with his extended family; he could not get a job and therefore had no money to pay the fee for an action that would have enabled him to start over. The Court majority, in an opinion written by Justice Harry Blackmun, ruled against Kras's argument that the filing fee was unconstitutional. At one point in the majority opinion, Blackmun had written that if Kras had really wanted to start over, he could have paid the fee in installments, which came to "less than the price of a movie and little more than the cost of a pack or two of cigarettes."

Marshall was livid at Blackmun's "unfounded assertions," his incorrect views, that entered the majority opinion. To Marshall, the majority did not understand "how close to the margin of survival" Kras and other poor persons lived. This arrogant attitude was one that, for Marshall, totally ignored the realities of living for the hopelessly poor in America. "The desperately poor," he wrote in dissent, "almost never go to see a movie, which the majority seems to believe is an almost weekly activity."

In the conference session after oral arguments were heard, he emphatically stated his belief that "no federal judicial proceeding can be denied anyone because he does not have the money."[71] He was joined, in conference, by only three other justices: Brennan, Douglas, and Potter Stewart. There were five who disagreed with him, however, and Marshall found himself again on the dissenting side of the case.

Blackmun, joined by Chief Justice Burger and Justices Byron White, Powell, and Rehnquist, concluded that the "case was a phony one," that it raised a "frivolous constitutional question," and that the federal law should be upheld. The majority opinion that followed the conference votes dismissed Kras's alleged inability to find even small amounts of money to be able to pay for the civil action he desperately sought. Blackmun was severely taken to task in Marshall's biting dissent, which stated that while it was "perfectly proper for judges to disagree about what the Constitution requires," it was "disgraceful for an interpretation of the Constitution to be premised upon unfounded assumptions about how people live."

He knew that his remarks about the Constitution, which he expressed publicly during the document's bicentennial celebrations in 1987, were highly controversial. In early April of that year, he sent a draft of his speech to a friend, African American historian John Hope Franklin, then an emeritus professor at

Duke University. In the covering letter, Marshall wrote, "I would appreciate it if you would go over…a draft of the guts of my speech concerning the 200th Anniversary of the Constitution.…Make any suggestions, etc." Franklin responded a few weeks later, saying that the speech was "excellent," offering some suggestions, and closing by telling Thurgood to, "as Harry Truman would say, somewhat more bluntly, 'Lay it on 'em.'"[72]

The speech was delivered in Hawaii in May 1987, and subsequently published in a number of law reviews, including those of Harvard and Vanderbilt law schools later that year. Marshall refused to celebrate the birth of the Constitution. "The focus of this celebration invites a complacent belief that the vision of those who debated and compromised in Philadelphia yielded the 'more perfect union' it is said we now enjoy." The Constitution, in Marshall's opinion, was not forever "fixed" in 1787; nor did he "find the wisdom, foresight, and sense of justice exhibited by the framers particularly profound." He then said that the government the Constitution created in 1787 was "defective from the start, requiring several amendments, a civil war, and momentous transformation to attain the system of constitutional government, and its respect for the individual freedoms and human rights, that we hold as fundamental today."

The Constitution "was a product of its times, and embodied a compromise which, under other circumstances, would not have been made." It reflected the racial and gender biases of the eighteenth century; though slavery was not mentioned, the document condoned the treatment of African Americans as property. The fundamental contradiction in the Constitution was that between "guaranteeing liberty and justice for all, and denying both to Negroes."

The adoption of the Fourteenth Amendment was a watershed event in the reconstruction of the Constitution, he maintained. "And yet," he said, "almost another century would pass before any significant recognition was obtained of the rights of black Americans to share equally even in such basic opportunities as education, housing, and employment, and to have their votes counted, and counted equally." During those two hundred years, black Americans "were enslaved by law, emancipated by law, disenfranchised and segregated by law; and finally, they have begun to win equality by law. Along the way, new constitutional principles have emerged to meet the challenges of a changing society. The progress has been dramatic, and it will continue."

The credit for these changes and new constitutional principles did not, Marshall said, belong to the men who wrote the document in 1787, but "to those who refused to acquiesce in outdated notions of 'liberty,' 'justice,' and 'equality,' and who strived to better them." Let us not lose our perspective on American history, he concluded. *"We will see that the true miracle was not the birth of the Constitution, but its life,* a life nurtured through two turbulent centuries of our own making....I plan to celebrate the bicentennial of the Constitution *as a living document,* including the Bill of Rights and the other amendments protecting individual freedoms and human rights." (My emphasis.)[73]

The last paragraph contained the core of Marshall's understanding of the Constitution and of the judiciary's responsibility for interpreting it. He was, as were Warren and Brennan, an exponent of a constitutional interpretation that was premised on viewing the 1787 document as an evolving instrument, one that had to be continuously reexamined and reinterpreted by judges to address the problems faced by their contemporaries, especially the problems of Americans "who continue to live in desperate conditions."[74]

That was the primary role of the Supreme Court's justices: to identify the cruel realities in the republic and, using the flexible terms of the fundamental law, to change them. "More than anyone else," wrote one of Marshall's former law clerks, Marshall was "responsible for the idea that social reform, through the Courts in the name of the Constitution, was both possible and desirable." He was to devote the rest of his life to defending that view of the role of the Court and his concept of constitutional interpretation.

# 10

## THE MEANING OF EQUALITY IN THE FOURTEENTH AMENDMENT

Marshall was no egalitarian as an advocate; he was not an egalitarian as a jurist. His objective as NAACP advocate was to make sure his clients received equality of opportunity and were not treated as second-class citizens. Social injustice in America, he maintained, called for effective counsel to aid the poor, the weak, the unemployed, the aged, and criminal defendants in America in their effort to be treated fairly. There was, Marshall felt, a desperate "need for 'legal power' on the side of the socially and economically depressed." The goal of the legal community, he insisted, was the achievement of "justice through law." Nothing less would do.[1]

### EQUAL-PROTECTION LITIGATION

Three types of equal-protection issues came to the Court during Marshall's tenure. As the outsider, he tried to present his view of the general contours of the equality concept while addressing discrete events in cases that were beyond the understanding of some of the members of the Court.

One set of such cases focused on equality of educational opportunity for all young persons, regardless of race, color, economic status, or national origin. When Marshall joined the Court, public school "desegregation with all deliberate speed" was a failed strategy. Within the year, he and the brethren were to substantively reopen the question of equality in educational opportunity in an effort to determine what more, if anything, could be done by the federal courts to achieve it. Marshall and his colleagues were to wrestle with this issue for another two decades.

A second set of equal-protection cases that came to the Court while Marshall sat were the racial discrimination "state action" cases. ("State action" is action taken by a legislature, the executive branch, or judicial "instrumentalities" of the state or its local subdivisions [counties, towns, and cities], and is constrained by the language of the Fourteenth Amendment.) This litigation involved allegations by African Americans that states or local communities and—critically important—private persons who had some legal or commercial connection to the state engaged in racial discrimination, thereby violating the Fourteenth Amendment.

Before Marshall arrived in 1967, the Court had already discussed the scope of "state action" as it applied to SNCC sit-ins and the arrests that followed those peaceful demonstrations. The 1964 Civil Rights Act had made such demonstrations unnecessary because the new law prohibited racial and other kinds of discrimination in all places of public accommodation. Given the imagination and ingenuity of the bitter-enders in the South, however, racial discrimination continued in noneducational arenas. The third set of equal-protection cases heard by the Court during Marshall's time involved *nonracial discrimination* by states and local communities—that is, discrimination against the poor or the indigent, or against illegitimate children, or against the children of illegal aliens. In responding to these equality issues, the justices created and applied standards that tried to define the meaning of the Fourteenth Amendment and how it was to be applied.

Ratified in 1868 largely to protect the rights of the recently freed slaves, the amendment prohibits certain kinds of actions by official agents of the state or its local subdivisions. Section 1 states, in part, that "No state shall make or enforce any law which shall abridge the privileges or immunities of citizens of the United States; nor shall any state deprive any person of life, liberty, or property without due process of law; nor [shall any state] deny to any person within its jurisdiction the equal protection of the laws."

Marshall said of the Fourteenth Amendment that "it set forth the basic ideals of 1868 in positive form. It is self-executing on its face and declaratory in language. Various phrases were used to describe, in their different and overlapping aspects, the fundamental rights which were to be guaranteed to all men."[2] In it is the notion of legal equality before the law, but the U.S. Supreme Court had done little to effect the full application of the Fourteenth Amendment's equal-protection language until well into the twentieth century.

In a 1938 opinion, however, tucked away in a footnote to *United States v. Carolene Products Company*, were three paragraphs that had dramatic impact on subsequent equal-protection litigation. It was a case that upheld the Congress's authority to ban the shipment of adulterated skim milk in interstate commerce. Chief Justice Harlan F. Stone's majority opinion announced that the Court would no longer carefully scrutinize economic and social legislation passed by

Congress. Henceforth, the majority stated, it would assume that such legislation rested on "some rational basis," and unless it could be shown by the party bringing suit that the legislative action was irrational, the Court would defer to the legislature's judgment.

At that point in the opinion, Stone inserted the now-famous "footnote 4," stating that the justices would carefully scrutinize legislation that affected *fundamental rights*" of persons or that "discriminated against particular minorities based on race or color" and other "discrete and insular minorities." Such legislation, he thought, must be "subjected to more exacting judicial scrutiny under the general prohibitions of the Fourteenth Amendment than are other types of legislation." Unlike economic or social legislation, in which the presumption by the justices was statutory "rationality," where legislation discriminated on the basis of religion, race or color, national origin, or curtailed fundamental rights, the Court would apply "strict scrutiny" and demand a "compelling" justification from the government for its challenged action.

Ironically, the Court first applied the "strict scrutiny" standard in a case that upheld the incarceration of Japanese Americans during World War II. In *Korematsu v. United States* (1944) Justice Black wrote for the majority that "all legal restrictions which curtail the civil rights of a single racial group are immediately suspect. That is not to say that all such restrictions are unconstitutional. It is to say that courts must subject them to the most rigid scrutiny."

Was the two-tier standard (the "rationality" and "strict scrutiny" standards) too rigid, too confining? Were there unjust state laws validated because a classification—such as gender, indigency, or age—did not fall under the "suspect" standard, and therefore the Court had to judge only whether it was a reasonable law? Marshall thought so, and fought during his time on the Court to add to these standards. He "criticized the rigidity of the Court's formalistic analysis. Under the majority's approach, a judge asked whether a statute affected a suspect classification or a fundamental right; if it did, it was subjected to 'strict scrutiny,' which almost always meant that it would be found unconstitutional. If, however, a statute fell outside that narrow categorization, it would be upheld if it was rational—and virtually everything was found rational." He proposed what he believed was a more realistic and more flexible "sliding scale" standard for use in equal-protection litigation. "The more important the interests and the more insular and unpopular the affected group, the closer the scrutiny and the more justification the Court should demand," he argued.[3] The active task of judges, he asserted, in adjudicating equal-protection litigation was to "take into account the *importance* of the interest affected and the *nature of the classification involved* in deciding whether a statute violated the equal protection clause."[4]

Marshall's views on the criteria that should be applied were clearly enunciated in two dissents: *Dandridge v. Williams* (1970), and *San Antonio Independent School District v. Rodriguez* (1973). *Dandridge* involved Maryland's unique administration of the federal Aid to Families with Dependent Children (AFDC) program. The state imposed a "maximum limitation" on the amount any family could receive, based on the number of children in the family, even though the AFDC congressional legislation was supposed to provide assistance to *all* needy dependent children. Viewing the state legislation as economic, the Court used the "rational basis" standard and concluded that the state did not violate equal protection even though the classifications it made were imperfect. "It is enough," wrote Justice Potter Stewart for the majority, "that the state's action be rationally based and free from invidious discrimination."

Marshall dissented and was joined by Brennan. He criticized the majority for refusing to inquire about the reality of the discrimination. Stewart's opinion "avoids the task by focusing upon the abstract dichotomy between two different approaches to equal protection problems which have been utilized by this Court." The case was not an economic one, Marshall insisted. "This case, involving the literally vital interests of a powerless minority—poor families without breadwinners—is far removed from the area of business regulation." However, he concluded, it did not involve a suspect classification, which would trigger the "strict scrutiny" standard.

Marshall then suggested the employment of his intermediate, flexible standard, which contained three segments: "(1) the character of the classification in question, (2) the relative importance to [the individuals discriminated against]... of the governmental benefits which they do not receive, and (3) the asserted state interests in support of the classification." Use of such an intermediate calculus by the majority, he believed, would force them to acknowledge the reality they ignored when they used the "rational basis" standard: the missing government benefits would have provided "the stuff which sustains these children's lives: food, clothing, shelter."

The *San Antonio* dissent was, in his eyes and in the eyes of some of his law clerks, Marshall's "greatest opinion."[5] Demetrio Rodriguez and other Mexican American parents sued their school district, the Texas State Board of Education, the state's attorney general, and other public officials on the grounds that the Texas system of financing public education—because it discriminated on the basis of wealth—violated the equal-protection clause of the Fourteenth Amendment. Texas provided about 80 percent of the funding for all school districts, supplemented by funds apportioned by the state to local districts "under a [state] formula designed to reflect each district's relative taxpaying ability." Because property values varied, the richer school districts generated more local school funds than did the poorer districts. The federal three-judge district court ruled that Texas's school funding plan did violate the Fourteenth Amendment, and the state appealed to the Supreme Court.

The Court split five to four. The majority, in an opinion written by Lewis Powell, held that wealth was not a "suspect" classification and that no existing fundamental rights were impinged. (Powell rejected creating any new fundamental rights, saying that "it is not the province of this Court to create substantive constitutional rights [education] in the name of guaranteeing equal protection of the laws.") The majority concluded that "Texas' system of public school finance is an inappropriate candidate for strict judicial scrutiny." Therefore, employing the lower-tier "rational basis" standard, the majority concluded that the Texas public education funding program was rational and constitutional.

Justices Brennan, White, Douglas, and Marshall dissented. Marshall's dissent, joined in by only Douglas, addressed the bankruptcy of the two-tier standard: "The Court apparently seeks to establish today that equal protection cases fall into one of two neat categories which dictate the appropriate standard of review—strict scrutiny or mere rationality." Marshall insisted that, in equal-protection litigation, the justices must apply "a spectrum of standards in reviewing discrimination allegedly violative of the Equal Protection Clause."

Education's fundamental importance, wrote Marshall in his *San Antonio* dissent, had been accepted by the Court since *Brown*, because of its unique status "in our society, and by the close relationship between education and some of our most basic constitutional values." Marshall concluded that the Texas policy created invidious discrimination, in violation of the Fourteenth Amendment. "In my judgment, any *substantial degree of scrutiny* of the operation of the Texas financing scheme reveals that the State has selected means wholly inappropriate to secure its purported interest in assuring its school districts local fiscal control." (My emphasis.)

The Burger Court majority did create and, through the mid-1980s, did occasionally employ a third, intermediate standard to use when examining equal-protection litigation that did not clearly involve the "suspect" categories or state restrictions of fundamental constitutional rights that would trigger "strict scrutiny." It was a much more modest test than Marshall's. Employing what it called the "exacting scrutiny" or "strict rationality" standard,[6] the Burger Court looked for a *substantial* relationship, rather than a *rational* relationship, between the means and ends of legislation.

By the mid-1970s, then, and for another decade, there were two and one-half tiers that constituted the Court's tests for examining litigation that drew upon the constraints of the equal-protection clause of the Fourteenth Amendment. The upper tier was applied when neutral "suspect" classifications (race, religion, national origin) and/or fundamental rights (travel, voting) were involved in the litigation. If these appeared, then the standard employed was the "strict scrutiny" test, with the burden on the state to justify its discriminatory legislation or regulation by showing a "compelling state interest."

The intermediate tier was used by the brethren when a "quasi-suspect" category was present in the litigation (gender, age, indigency, legal and illegal aliens). The application of this standard meant that the state had to show in the briefs and in oral argument that there was a "substantial relationship in fact between the means and ends of legislation." (The lower tier was employed by the Court when the equal-protection litigation was ostensibly economic or regulatory in nature and did not involve suspect or quasi-suspect categories or fundamental civil rights.) Marshall could not get a Court majority to understand and then act on the reality of life for many millions of "desperate Americans."[7] As one of his former law clerks wrote about Marshall's conviction, "He moved very close to a belief in a constitutional right to freedom from desperate conditions."[8] His strong, unwavering position on this is seen in the many dozens of equal-protection cases and controversies that involved Marshall and the others, with Marshall, in most of them, raising his voice in dissent.

## EQUALITY OF EDUCATIONAL OPPORTUNITY AFTER *BROWN*

Marshall joined the Court at the very moment the judges had given up on the bitter-enders in the Deep South doing anything "in good faith" to end the dual school system. A decade after *Brown II,* there was virtually no desegregation in the region. In 1968 the Court finally gave up on the "with all deliberate speed" wording, and unanimously moved to an "integrate now" standard as expressed in *Green v. County School Board, New Kent County, Virginia.* In this freedom-of-choice school education clash, the Court said that the time for all deliberate speed had ended and that segregated school districts had to integrate at once. Brennan said, in conference, that Virginia "can't maintain a segregated school system. This one does and therefore since there are workable alternatives, this [freedom-of-choice plan] can't be sustained."[9]

The Court's "integrate now" order was reaffirmed in *Alexander v. Holmes County, Mississippi,* wherein a modest desegregation plan initiated in 1968 by the Johnson administration and approved by a federal appellate court for implementation in 1969 was stalled by Nixon's secretary of health, education and welfare, Robert Finch, who asserted that the time period allotted for desegregation was too short. The Fifth Circuit appeals court accordingly suspended its order. When the still-segregated Mississippi schools opened for the fall term, parents of the black children sought relief from the Supreme Court, which expedited consideration and issued an order on October 29 to proceed with desegregation.

The new Chief Justice, Warren Burger, another Nixon appointee, wanted to buck the case right back to the federal district court, but Marshall and Black, as well as Douglas, felt that the time for more talk and additional delay was over. Marshall wanted integration to take place within two months, but Burger drafted an order that effectively put it off until the following academic year. Black and Marshall revolted, and Black's draft dissent, when circulated, was a clear signal that the hard-won unanimity of the Court in this area might be openly and, for Warren Burger, embarrassingly blown apart. The new Chief was very much in the shadow of his predecessor, who had achieved unanimity of the Court in the seminal *Brown* decision through brilliant leadership. Burger wanted to be seen as the conservative version of "the Super Chief." Confronted with Black's draft dissent that pointed out how Burger's draft order could revitalize the repudiated "all deliberate speed" formula, the Chief backed down and Brennan, using language from Black's draft dissent, wrote the order for the district court to issue a decree, "effective immediately," to create unitary school systems in Mississippi.

The bitter-enders in the state continued to fight the desegregation orders and, in the 1970 term, their intransigence led to the case of *Carter v. West Feliciana, Mississippi, Parish School Board.* Once again the federal appeals court had granted a delay to the local school board in implementation of the HEW plan scheduled for February 1970. And once again the Supreme Court vacated the lower court's stay. But unanimity among the justices was wearing thin by this point. The struggle to achieve integration in Mississippi would continue through repeated NAACP efforts in the courts. Stubborn resistance would also continue; only by 1982 was there an end to *de jure* school segregation in that state.

### 1970: BUSING TO END SEGREGATED SCHOOLS (Swann)

*James E. Swann v. Charlotte-Mecklenburg, North Carolina, Board of Education,* a school desegregation case first filed in January 1965 and heard during the Court's 1970 term, was the first case that raised the question of whether busing to achieve desegregation was constitutionally permissible. It forced the Court to examine carefully what specific remedies could be used to end dual school systems. By the time the case came down, a year later, the Court had spent a great deal of time discussing the need to set guidelines for the lower courts, something the Court had avoided since *Brown II.*

The case also tested Burger's leadership ability and intellectual acumen. He failed on both counts; *Swann* in a way established, at least within the Court, Burger's reputation—and it was not a good one. As one justice said afterwards,

Burger "crossed the bridge with this [case]. He tried to take over the Court. He didn't succeed and never tried this blatantly again. The Chief Justice was determined to carry the day, and we were equally determined he wouldn't—and we had the votes."[10]

*Swann* followed on the heels of *Green.* After the Supreme Court announced *Green,* the North Carolina federal district court judge, James B. McMillan, finding *de jure* segregation in Charlotte, ordered the school board to submit a desegregation plan by May 15, 1969, for the 1969–70 school year. Sixty percent of the African American schoolchildren (14,000 of 24,000) attended schools that were 99 percent African American (with most of those students not having any white teachers), although 77 percent of all students in the system were white. Four plans were submitted, each of which was found inadequate by the federal judge, who then invited an educational consultant (Dr. James Finger) to develop a school desegregation plan for the city. Busing to achieve racial balance was an integral part of the plan finally accepted by the district court judge.

Implementation of the plan in the large urban area, with more than 84,000 children attending elementary and secondary schools, necessitated additional busing. The school board said it did not have the money to do it and couldn't get funding from the state because it had passed a law that prohibited the use of state funds for busing designed to achieve desegregation.

After the district court issued the order, the city appealed and also asked for a stay of the order pending the outcome of the appeal. The Fourth Circuit U.S. Court of Appeals issued a partial stay because of the alleged lack of funds for the busing. The African American petitioners asked the Supreme Court to review the case, vacate the stay, and reinstate the federal district court judge's original order requiring pairing and additional busing. In June 1970, the Court granted certiorari in *Swann,* and directed reinstatement of the district court's order pending further proceeding in that court.

By the end of the summer, the Court decided to expedite the case after all, even though Douglas's preference was to "leave [*Swann*] to the Court of Appeals." After hearing the arguments in court, the justices spent a number of weeks in conferences discussing the important case. During those meetings, they struggled to define what values and objectives were supported by busing. They also discussed the persistent dilemma of race that the case encapsulated. Burger, whose daughter was bused three hours a day in order to attend a private school in Virginia, spoke very briefly, arguing that the district court judge used too much discretion in his order to the school board. He maintained that there really was no *de jure* segregation, that the schools reflected the racial demographics of the city. As was becoming his custom, Burger delayed casting his vote "until all discussion is held." Black, the senior associate justice, spoke next and was one of the only two colleagues to support Burger (the other was Harry Blackmun).

The Alabaman's comments reflected his bitterness and pessimism. The problem of racism, he said, "will not be settled in our lifetimes or the lifetimes of our children.... We can't change attitudes—we can enforce 'equal protection,' but we can't write new laws." Like Burger, Black was protective of the neighborhood school and of the "idea of geographical integrity of schools." Black claimed that "the Constitution does not say there must be a certain ratio of blacks and whites in schools." Finally, he said that "I never thought it was for the courts to change the habits of the people in choosing where to live."

Douglas said that "it is not invidious to bus on account of race in order to disestablish a dual school," although he did believe that "there could be disestablishment without [mathematically correct] racial balance." Harlan, Black's close friend, disagreed with the southerner. Harlan agreed with the district court judge's view that "the neighborhood school is not a constitutional requirement if departure from it is necessary to disestablish a segregated system." He argued persuasively that if busing students to achieve desegregation was unconstitutional, then *Brown I* announced a self-defeating principle." He believed that disestablishment of the segregated system "means a constitutional duty to move students according to race," and that "busing is not an impermissible tool."

Brennan spoke next, flatly asserting that *Brown II* was wrong, that courts had to act aggressively to end the dual school system, and that court-ordered busing was a proper means for achieving desegregation. "Where busing is the only way to achieve the required amount of integration, the district judge has the power and duty to order it."

Potter Stewart reminded the brethren that the remedy problem "is our problem." White agreed with Stewart's assessment, as well as the others, that the court "can use prophylactic measures to avoid all racial schools." However, he worried about resegregation taking place, because no court can "take into consideration what individuals do for racial reasons."

It was Marshall's turn to talk about the case. "No white student wants to go to an inferior school and Negro schools are inferior." He said, sharply, that you can't disestablish the dual school system "and have a Negro school.... Every school must be disestablished and this is the time to 'bite the bullet.'" The "only place where Negro students know they have fully equal education is in a white school." To reach that goal, total mixing was necessary to overcome the segregated past, Marshall argued. He then reminded his colleagues of the reality black Americans faced in North Carolina and other Southern states: "The transfer of Negro students [to the white schools] is difficult because of the heavy [pressure by the segregationists put] on the Negro not to transfer." Quashing the notion of "freedom of choice" as a way to establish a unitary system, Marshall said, bluntly, "There is no such thing as freedom of choice for the Negro child in the South."

"Total mixing is not needed," Burger asserted, opening the discussion of
*Swann* at the next conference session; the age of the children and the length of
the busing ride "must be factors" in the determination of the issue. The majority
disagreed, and concluded that the district court judge's order had to be affirmed
and used by the Court as the *de minimus* guidelines for other school districts
preparing their desegregation plans. Marshall's words to Black, Blackmun, and
Burger were not comforting. He "angrily" said that there must be "affirmative
action" by the courts "to disestablish" segregated schools.[11] After these tense conferences in October, even though he was in a minority of three, Burger, to the
"surprise" of the others, gave himself the task of writing the opinion for a very
divided Court. This was seen as an exercise of raw power, an action that went
against one of the major unwritten rules of the Court: The Chief assigns opinions only when he is in the majority.

This opinion assignment decision led to an interminable delay in announcing
the decision in *Swann,* for the majority kept rejecting Burger's draft opinions,
which severely limited the remedial powers a federal judge could use to end segregation. It took no less than seven drafts before Burger's "majority" opinion
became acceptable to the others. They had been, in Douglas's words, "astounded"
when they read the initial draft opinion. It became agreeable only because
Burger was forced into accepting six other justices' language and views, including the fundamental acknowledgment that a federal district judge had broad
remediable powers. As Douglas recalled in a memo to his file, dated April 20,
1971, the day the opinion came down: "Changes were made haltingly and with
great resistance. We circulated new opinions, setting forth our views. At long
last—piece by piece—the suggestions were adopted. Black capitulated very, very
reluctantly."

While the painstaking drafting process went on, Marshall wrote a sixteen-
page memo and, on January 12, 1971, circulated it to the other eight justices. It
traced the sordid (yet all-too-common) history of the segregation mess in the
North Carolina school district, one that affected every one of the 106 schools in
the district. "When school boards fail to meet their obligations [to desegregate],
it is up to the courts to find remedies that effectively secure the rights of the
Negro children," he said, concluding that the busing requirement was fair, with
travel limited to no more than thirty minutes (whereas, prior to the order, children were bused over an hour each way to maintain segregated schools). While
the plan called for operating 138 more buses than planned, 105 buses were
already available and the balance "could easily be obtained," so the plan was an
equitable, reasonable one. Let's quickly close the matter and support the district
court judge's rulings, urged Marshall.[12]

Months later, however, the Court was still wrestling with its stubborn Chief.

His very restrictive, Nixonian view of court-ordered school desegregation orders was quite dramatically rejected by the majority when Stewart wrote a draft opinion representing the views of the seven angry men. The Chief capitulated in April 1971 and accepted all the ideas in the Stewart draft, as well as the ideas and suggestions passed on to him from Brennan and Marshall. "I believe I have demonstrated," he wrote in his cover memo, "a flexible attitude, even down to using words of others when I saw no real difference and preferred by own." In so doing, he disavowed the opinions he had expressed in his seven previous drafts. Blackmun joined the majority. Black finally, with great reluctance, and after circulating a draft dissent, joined in the opinion, in order that the Court might adopt a unanimous public stance.

Burger's "opinion" for a unanimous Court gave the federal district court judges broad powers to fashion remedies to ensure that a school system was "completely integrated." "If school authorities fail in their affirmative obligations...judicial authority may be invoked," he wrote. "Once a right and a violation have been shown, the scope of a district court's equitable powers is broad, for breadth and flexibility are inherent in equitable remedies." Federal district court judges could ensure racial balance; one-race schools were highly suspect and would be dismantled if a school board didn't meet the heavy burden of showing a valid reason for its retention; remedial altering by the federal judge of school attendance zones to achieve integration was authorized; transportation of students, including busing, could be ordered by a federal judge in order to achieve integration of the schools.

## 1973: THE QUESTION OF DE FACTO SCHOOL SEGREGATION (KEYES)

*Swann* involved a classic case of *de jure* school segregation, in which the segregation was the result of laws passed by the state legislators. *Keyes,* decided in the spring of 1973, was a case that involved the issue of *de facto* school segregation, that is, segregation without any *prima facie* demonstration that it was caused by state action of some kind.

The case of *Wilfred Keyes v. School District Number One, Denver, Colorado* had a long history in the Court. It came to the Court first in August 1969, and came back in the spring of 1971. From Marshall's success in *Brown* in 1954 through *Swann,* all school desegregation cases had their legal beginnings in the South or in border states touching the Mason-Dixon line. The first case from outside the South, *Keyes* involved allegations of segregation brought by African American and Hispanic parents against the Denver school system. (The racial breakdown in the Denver school population at the time was 66 percent white, 14 percent African American, and 20 percent Hispanic.) The federal district court concluded that the Denver school board, through a variety of mechanisms, "had engaged over almost a decade after 1960 in an unconstitutional policy of deliberate racial segregation with respect to the [primarily African American–populated core city] Park Hill schools."

Even though the core city schools were segregated, the federal court judge declined to order desegregation because there was no finding of *de jure* segregation on the part of the school board. The court of appeals upheld the decision of the district court and the minority plaintiffs appealed to the Supreme Court.

In conference, held on October 17, 1972, Burger argued for affirmance of the court of appeals decision. The Chief Justice did not think much of the plaintiffs' argument. Discrimination had not been shown. Unlike *Brown,* and all the other Southern *de jure* school segregation cases, he wrote, "no one was denied admission to school on racial grounds." The plaintiffs had not met the burden of showing intentional discrimination in the form of some kind of state action that suggested racial or ethnic discrimination against African American or Hispanic public school students.

Justices Douglas, Brennan, Stewart, and Marshall, and Powell all voiced the view that the court of appeals should be reversed—as did Blackmun, who joined the quartet to give them a narrow five-person majority opinion. (Burger concurred without writing an opinion.) Brennan wrote the opinion for the Court majority. If, as in *Keyes,* he said, the plaintiffs "prove that the school authorities have carried out a systematic program of segregation affecting a substantial portion of the students, schools, teachers, and facilities, [then] it is only common sense to conclude that there exists a predicate for a finding of the existence of a dual school system."

Brennan's opinion then pointed to the feature that differentiated *de jure* from *de facto* school segregation: In *de jure* discrimination, there is a proven *"purpose* or *intent* to segregate." The district court's finding of segregative practices in a segment of the Denver school system, for the majority, was a *"prima facie* case of unlawful segregative design on the part of school authorities." The Chief concurred as did Douglas, who maintained in his opinion "that there is no difference between *de facto* and *de jure* segregation."

Powell wrote a separate opinion, concurring and dissenting, to emphasize the fact that there was *no* difference between *de facto* and *de jure* segregation. He argued that there should be only one uniform national rule on segregation. If segregated schools exist, he argued in conference, then the federal courts could act to order their desegregation. If the school authorities were genuinely striving to integrate a school system, they must not be held to the unattainable integration goal "that *every* school must in fact be an integrated unit."

Rehnquist dissented in *Keyes.* Calling the Brennan opinion "judicial fiat," he maintained that "to require that school boards affirmatively undertake to achieve racial mixing in schools where such mixing is not achieved in sufficient degree by neutrally drawn boundary lines is quite obviously" not required by the Constitution's equal-protection clause but by result-oriented judges. Almost instantly, he and Marshall became bitter enemies on equal protection and most other civil liberties and civil rights issues. They would remain so during Marshall's tenure.

## 1974: COURT UNANIMITY DISINTEGRATES OVER THE QUESTION OF INTERDISTRICT BUSING (MILLIKEN)

"Keyes was, in retrospect, the high-water mark of the Supreme Court's commitment to busing."[13] During the following term of the Court, the brethren heard arguments in another non-Southern school segregation case. *Milliken v. Bradley* came to the brethren from Detroit, Michigan, and, like *Swann,* involved the question of whether busing to achieve school desegregation could be used—this time busing schoolchildren across school district boundary lines. It came to the Court after the justices, with Justice Powell not participating, in 1973, split four-to-four in a Richmond, Virginia, case, *Bradley v. State Board of Education of Virginia.* For the Court, the question in both cases, *Bradley* and *Milliken,* was the same: Did a federal district court judge, after finding discrimination in the public schools, have the authority "to require remedial plans that included more than one (and usually several) school districts."[14]

In *Milliken,* black parents brought suit against the state "because of [their] concern over the quality of the educational offerings to which their children were subjected."[15] Ronald Bradley, an African American student in Detroit's inner city, with the help of the NAACP, filed a lawsuit against the state's governor, William Milliken, claiming that school district lines were drawn in ways that discriminated on the basis of race, thereby depriving the children of equal educational opportunities. A federal district court agreed with them, and ordered the Detroit school board to draw up a desegregation plan that incorporated students from the surrounding eighty-five suburban school districts, located in local towns and cities adjacent to Detroit. The final plan adopted by the federal district court called for the busing of public school children to and from Detroit and its fifty-three surrounding suburban school districts. The federal court of appeals affirmed the plan, and the governor then appealed to the Supreme Court.

*Milliken* was the first case since *Brown* in which the Supreme Court ruled against a federal court–ordered school desegregation plan. Federal district court judge Stephen Roth heard the case brought by a number of African American parents. They claimed that the Detroit school board, aided and abetted by the State Board of Education and the Michigan legislature, had deliberately created and then sustained a segregationist public school policy that deprived minorities and the poor in the city of Detroit with equal educational opportunities. Detroit's school system was the fifth largest in the United States, covering over 140 square miles. It had a public-school student population of 290,000, with 65 percent of this number black students. In the city, 130,000 students attended 133 schools whose population was almost 100 percent African American. Detroit was poor; the majority of its population was black. It was surrounded by virtually all-white suburban school districts.

Judge Roth found numerous examples of deliberate Detroit school board activities that perpetuated school segregation, ranging from the creation of segregated housing patterns, neighborhood attendance policies, attendance boundaries changes, and grade structure, to building-site selection and construction policies, including one instance in which a school was built solely as a means to concentrate black students in it (rather than have them bused to a less-crowded, predominantly white public school in another section of the city).

He also found state actions that led to the segregated school pattern in the city, including differential bond rates that adversely affected Detroit. The state legislators had also rejected a Detroit desegregation plan in 1970, and the Michigan legislature refused to provide funds for busing. Given these facts, Roth concluded that there was *de jure* segregation, and ruled that Detroit schools could be desegregated and integration could take place only if the Detroit students and the white suburban students were reassigned and bused across city and county lines to end segregated schools both in Detroit and in the suburbs of the city. The federal judge therefore approved an integration plan that essentially ignored school district lines. It was a controversial decision, but the Sixth Circuit federal court of appeals, reviewing the data, concluded that Roth's plan was the only way segregation in Detroit could end. Roth was using the equitable discretionary powers of the federal court to end segregation in public schools the only way he felt segregation could realistically be ended. The federal court of appeals opinion noted that *not* to affirm Roth's plan would "nullify" *Brown* and turn the education clock back to the separate-but-equal doctrine of *Plessy*.

The case came to the Court in 1974. In conference after oral arguments, Burger argued that the "district court judge went way beyond what he could do and the court of appeals erred in affirming." He voted to reverse the appellate court decision. The other Nixon appointees also voted to reverse the court of appeals, with Powell in conference calling the Roth plan "a monstrosity on its face." They were joined by Potter Stewart, who had, until *Milliken*, voted with the Warren Court liberals on this issue. Justices Douglas, Brennan, White, and Marshall all spoke and voted in conference to affirm the court of appeals judgment. Chief Justice Burger, for the majority, concluded that court-ordered *inter-*

*district* public school busing was an inappropriate means for redressing *intra-district* segregation problems. While Burger acknowledged the unfair conditions that African American schoolchildren faced in the city, he argued that there was a showing of *de jure* segregation only in Detroit, and that the federal judge could not use his equity powers to cobble together an *effective* integration plan that impacted surrounding suburban counties in which there had been no showing of state-enforced segregation. Stewart's was the critical swing vote. He said that he would have sided with the African American plaintiffs "if they had shown that state officials had used housing or zoning laws in a purposefully racially discriminatory fashion." [16]

Yet the record presented clear evidence that that was precisely what the Michigan officials did. And these realities were pointed out by the four justices who dissented. Three wrote dissenting opinions, including Marshall. His opinion reflected all that he had experienced in the decades he'd spent trying to put an end to unequal school systems. The majority, he believed, was regressing to the separateness of *Plessy*.

Michigan's actions created a significant core of African American schools; they "inevitably acted as a magnet to attract Negroes to the areas served by such schools and helped drive whites to other areas of the city or to the suburbs." Marshall argued that having "created a system where whites and Negroes were intentionally kept apart so that they could not become accustomed to learning together, the State is responsible for the fact that many whites will react to the dismantling of that segregated system by attempting to flee to the suburbs."

When the opinion was announced in open court, Marshall added words to his written dissent to express his disdain and his sadness about the weakness of the majority opinion: "We deal here with the right of all our children, whatever their race, to an equal start in life and an equal opportunity to reach their full potential as citizens.... Our nation, I fear, will be ill-served by the Court's refusal to remedy separate and unequal education, for unless our children begin to learn together, there is little hope that our people will ever learn to live together and understand each other."

The Court remanded the case back to the federal district court, for the judge to act consistent with the majority opinion. That meant that the federal district court judge had to devise an integration plan that was limited to the Detroit city school district, with its overwhelmingly African American population.

Judge Roth had died in the interim, and the new judge assigned to the case, Robert DeMascio, had to develop such a plan. With the help of educational experts, a plan was developed that relied upon state financial support to pay for "educational components" to be created in the district. Those components included special reading programs, tutorial assistance, revised testing and counseling programs for the inner-city students, and a training program for the teachers. Michigan balked at paying for portions of the plan and appealed to the Sixth Circuit, which upheld the district court plan. Governor Milliken went, once more, to the U.S. Supreme Court. The Court, during its 1977 term, affirmed the lower federal courts. *Milliken I* was now precedent. During Marshall's remaining years on the Court, he could not persuade Court majorities to go beyond the narrowness of that case.

## AFTER MILLIKEN: *A COURT DIVIDED ON HOW TO ACHIEVE SCHOOL DESEGREGATION*

After *Milliken*, Marshall found himself dissenting regularly from the judgments of the Nixon quartet, joined by one or two other justices. In 1976, in the *Pasadena City Board of Education v. Spangler* litigation, Rehnquist, for the six-person Court majority, wrote an opinion that narrowed the supervisory powers of a federal judge. In 1970, a federal judge ordered a desegregation plan put into effect in Pasadena, California, to address racial imbalance in the public schools. (Pasadena was Jackie Robinson's home after his family left the South in the early 1930s. He found the Jim Crowism of that California city as bad as that in the place he had left.)[17] By 1974, five of the thirty-two schools in the district had more than 50 percent black pupils. The federal judge then ordered annual adjustments by the school board of attendance zones so that there would not be a majority of any minority in the schools. The white city leaders appealed the judgment, and the Court majority invalidated the order.

Although resegregation had occurred, Rehnquist admitted, it was a result of changing residential patterns, not of racially discriminatory state action. "These [population] shifts were not attributed to any segregative actions on the part of the defendants. Having once implemented a racially neutral attendance pattern in order to remedy the perceived constitutional violations..., the District Court had fully performed its function of providing the appropriate remedy for previous racially discriminatory attendance patterns."

Marshall and Brennan were the only dissenters. (Justice John Paul Stevens, recently appointed by President Gerald Ford to replace the retired William O. Douglas, did not participate in the discussion and vote.) Marshall argued that a "unitary system" had not been established in the school district in the few years since the initial district court order in 1970, and that the original finding of unconstitutional state racial discrimination had not diminished sufficiently "to justify a change in the level of judicial supervision."[18] He strongly believed that federal district court supervision was still appropriate, and that the equity powers of the judge should not have been diminished.

Marshall dissented alone in another California case, *Crawford v. Los Angeles Board of Education* (1982). After the California courts ordered busing to remedy *de facto* school segregation, California voters adopted Proposition 1, an amendment to the state's constitution, which said that "state courts shall not order mandatory pupil assignment or transportation unless a federal court would do so to remedy a violation of the Equal Protection clause." Black plaintiffs appealed to the California Supreme Court, which ruled that the voters "were not motivated by a discriminatory purpose."

Undaunted, the plaintiffs took their appeal to the U.S. Supreme Court. In an opinion by Justice Lewis Powell, for five other justices, the Court found no violation of equal protection owing to repeal of the state court action. Repeal of the antidiscrimination court order did not violate the Fourteenth Amendment. "Proposition 1 does not embody a racial classification," Powell wrote. "It neither says nor implies that persons are to be treated differently on account of their race.... Voters may have been motivated by...the educational benefits of neighborhood schooling."

Justice Blackmun, joined by Brennan, wrote a concurring opinion. State courts, he argued, "do not create the rights they enforce.... When one of those rights is repealed, and therefore is rendered unenforceable in the courts," it is not unconstitutional. "The people of California—the same 'entity' that put in place the state constitution, and created the enforceable obligation to desegregate— have made the [state] desegregation obligation judicially unenforceable [by the state's courts]." The Fourteenth Amendment did not bar such electoral behavior.

Marshall dissented. The proposition, he argued futilely, "was a fundamental reallocation of state power." It removed a judicial avenue for "obtaining compliance with the state constitution's guarantee that racial isolation will be alleviated by all reasonable means." The judiciary, Marshall pointed out, was "the only branch of government that has been willing to address this issue meaningfully." The only avenue left for minority parents lay in trying to "sear the conscience" of state legislators.

Marshall's very last school segregation case, during the Court's 1990 term, again saw him in dissent from a majority opinion authored by Rehnquist. *Board of Education of Oklahoma City, Oklahoma, v. Dowell* involved the question of when or whether a federal district court order could be terminated when its purposes had been achieved and a school system had been determined to have achieved a "unitary" status (rather than still having a "dual" school system). A federal judge had ordered the implementation of a desegregation plan to end the segregated dual-school system. After the system had complied with the plan for five years, the federal judge ceased its "active supervision" of the case, but did not dissolve the desegregation order.

The board of education, after this five-year period of judicial oversight ended, created and implemented a new pupil assignment policy, one that, because it focused on returning to the "neighborhood school" pattern, immediately led to racial imbalance. By the time the litigation came to the Court, a majority of the Oklahoma City elementary schools had student enrollments either 90 percent white or 90 percent black. Accompanying the chilling new demographics was the fact—no surprise to Marshall, who had seen this occur over the past sixty years—that funding to these schools was disproportionate in that fewer resources were provided to the mostly black schools.[19] There was a demand for reinstatement of supervisory authority by the federal judge, and the board of education appealed to the Court, arguing that the federal judge had already discontinued the supervision of the school board.

Rehnquist for the Court concluded that the federal decree should remain dissolved. Time and geography could work to end federal supervision of local school boards, he reasoned. The majority maintained that "it can be lifted when local authorities have obeyed it for a reasonable period of time." The case was remanded to the federal district court with instructions for the federal judge to review the school board's performance in all aspects of school management and operations.

Marshall's dissent, joined by Justices Blackmun and Stevens, ascertained that the dissolution was premature and that the Court should have *really* determined the degree of effective desegregation in these schools by asking some tough questions. (He found, for example, that racially restrictive housing patterns in Oklahoma City, based on local and state laws, created a segregated demographic pattern and that the school board maintained virtually all–African American schools in these highly segregated sectors of the city.) The Oklahoma City school board had, in Marshall's words, shown "unpardonable recalcitrance," complying with the order to decrease racial isolation in the city schools. He also found the board giving voice to the public's racist views when it argued that "public opinion was opposed to any further desegregation."

Clearly, in the school education cases after *Keyes,* Marshall "was increasingly alienated from the Supreme Court majority on integration issues."[20] He frequently pointed out the fact that school busing does not end segregated living in a city or a town, and if busing ends, segregated and unequal schools return. But his observations were ignored by a majority of the justices. Deep in his heart, Marshall knew that his colleagues were unwilling to decide these school segregation cases in a way that would truly "remake society."[21]

## RACIALLY DISCRIMINATORY STATE ACTION

The Civil War Amendments had abolished slavery and provided African Americans with the privileges and immunities of citizenship, due process, equal protection, and equal voting rights, as well as enabling the Congress—if it wished to act—to pass legislation to enforce these rights. Yet, a century later, black Americans were still trying to eradicate the "badges of slavery" that made them second-class citizens. These badges, in part, took the form of state laws and local customs that discriminated against black Americans and other minorities unfairly, denying them the equality of opportunity that was extended to white Americans.

The Reconstruction Congress, in 1866, passed a very powerful civil rights act. In part, it guaranteed that African Americans were entitled,

> in every State and Territory, to make and enforce contracts, to sue, be parties, and give evidence, to inherit, purchase, lease, sell, hold, and convey real and personal property, and to full and equal benefit of all laws and proceedings for the security of person and property, as is enjoyed by white citizens, and shall be subject to like punishments, pains, and penalties, taxes, licenses, and exactions of every kind, and to no other.

But it had been largely ignored after the Supreme Court eviscerated important segments of the legislation. In the *Slaughterhouse Cases* (1873), the Court dramatically narrowed the scope of the privileges and immunities clause of the Fourteenth Amendment. A decade later, in the 1883 *Civil Rights Cases* litigation, the Court greatly reduced the ability of the Congress to pass legislation that enforced the civil rights amendments, limiting the national legislature to enacting bills that prohibited race discrimination *only* when state action was involved. And finally, in 1896, there was *Plessy's* "separate but equal" doctrine. And so, for almost a century, African Americans were—constitutionally—racial outcasts in their land, denied basic equal rights and liberties.

As general counsel for the NAACP's Inc Fund after the Court's 1938 *Carolene Products* footnote 4, Marshall had been instrumental in getting a Court majority to play a significant role in ending racial discrimination. As an advocate and a jurist, Marshall knew the limits of Fourteenth Amendment protections for black Americans and others who suffered from discrimination. The amendment did not constrain purely private action, which "is any act or action engaged in or perpetrated by any individual in his private capacity and association."[22] However, if legal advocates could show a connection between the ostensibly private action and an instrumentality of the state, or a discriminatory custom or tradition of the state or community, a federal court judge could prohibit the discrimination because it was violative of the Fourteenth Amendment.

The Warren Court continued to address and try to cope with a variety of racially discriminatory state actions and local "customs," as seen in the *Adickes v. Kress* litigation. *Adickes*, which came to the Court from Mississippi in 1968, involved a refusal by the local Kress department store in Hattiesburg, Mississippi, to serve food at the lunch counter to a white female civil rights worker in the company of six young African American protesters seeking to desegregate the facility. (She was a SNCC "Freedom Summer" worker teaching in a "Freedom School" in the city, and the six young people were her students.)

She was told by the waitress that "we have to serve the colored, but we are not going to serve the whites that come in with them."[23] After leaving the Kress store, she was immediately arrested by police for vagrancy. The criminal conviction was reversed, and she then brought suit in federal court under an old civil rights act, charging that in refusing to serve her, Kress was acting "under color of" a discriminatory local "custom," a form of "state action" prohibited by the Fourteenth Amendment.

Although the lower federal courts summarily denied her the relief she sought, the Supreme Court heard the case and, in an opinion by Justice Harlan, the Court reversed the judgment and remanded the case to the federal district for a substantive hearing on the merits. (Marshall did not participate in the case because of his recent association with the Inc Fund.)

By 1969, however, the Court's personnel began to change, and with these personnel changes came a narrowing of the concept of state action. Marshall clashed with all of the Nixon appointees, especially Powell and Rehnquist. An example of this conflict is afforded by the 1982 case of *Memphis, Tennessee, v. Greene.* City officials had closed a street, West Drive, that ran through an affluent white section of the city, Hein Park. The public street was used primarily by African Americans to get to their subdivision on the other side of the white residential area. Residents challenged the action, asserting that the closing created a "badge of slavery" for them.

The Court majority, in an opinion by Justice Stevens, rejected their argument. The city's action was taken because of its interest "in protecting the safety and tranquility of a residential neighborhood." While African Americans were "slightly inconvenienced," the majority concluded, the record "discloses no racially discriminatory motive on the part of the city council" and it "could not be fairly characterized as a badge or incident of slavery."

Marshall was enraged at the actions of the Memphis officials and at the continuing insensitivity of his conservative colleagues on the Court. He dissented, joined by Brennan and Blackmun. The city's conduct was "egregious" because it was done to "prevent predominantly Negro traffic from entering a historically all-white neighborhood." Such an action—the erection of a barrier at the end of West Drive—was clearly a "badge of slavery."

## PRIVATE ACTS OF RACIAL DISCRIMINATION AND "STATE ACTION"

In his years with the Inc Fund, Marshall had sought ways to legally attack private acts of racial discrimination that went unpunished. Private discrimination, until passage of the 1968 Open Housing Act, was for the most part an invisible problem for Congress. At the very moment the Congress passed and President Johnson signed the 1968 Open Housing Act, the Warren Court, in *Jones v. Alfred E. Mayer Company,* actually minimized the need for the justices to creatively expand the state-action concept. The Court's conference session to discuss *Jones* took place amid the terrible rioting that engulfed Washington, D.C., and other urban areas of the nation in response to Martin Luther King's assassination in Memphis, Tennessee, on April 4, 1968.

The Court used *Jones* as an opportunity to limit further expansion of the "state action" concept to cover private discrimination when it ruled that the 1866 legislation *did* constitutionally cover such discrimination. The Court concluded, with Marshall joining the majority, that the Thirteenth Amendment prohibited all "badges and incidents of slavery" and that Congress could take action, such as it did with the 1866 legislation, to enforce the amendment.

In an opinion written by Justice Potter Stewart, who cast the deciding vote, the Court made a broad interpretation of this law to enable African Americans and others who were discriminated against on the basis of race in the sale, lease, purchase, transmittal, or rental of real and personal property to sue for damages in federal court.

Joseph Lee Jones was the African American plaintiff who went into federal court for relief after he was unable to purchase a home in a private subdivision, which contained many of the attributes of a small town, solely because of his color and race. The federal district court dismissed Jones's complaint, and its decision was affirmed by the Eighth Circuit federal court of appeals. He appealed to the Supreme Court, which heard the case during its 1967 term. For the Court, the question was the validity and the scope of Section 1982 of the 1866 legislation used by Jones to seek injunctive and monetary relief. In its April 5, 1968, conference, most of the brethren agreed that Jones had been discriminated against. The obvious question was, What legal foundation would be employed to justify a ruling in his favor?

The majority, including Warren, Harlan, White, Fortas, Brennan, and Marshall, initially argued that *Marsh v. Alabama* should be used to decide the case in Jones's favor. (*Marsh* was a First Amendment case decided in 1945, in an opinion written by Black, in which the Court ruled that a "private" company town that had all the conveniences and services of a public municipality had to be seen in that light, and its actions were subject to the constraints of the Constitution and its amendments.) In *Jones,* the six men argued that the racial discrimination Jones experienced was similar to the discrimination prohibited in *Marsh.*

Justices Douglas, Stewart, and Black, the author of *Marsh,* rejected the use of the *Marsh* precedent. They agreed with Stewart's view that the Court, if it was going to rule in Jones's favor, had to use much broader reasoning than that found in *Marsh*. Stewart argued that the Court should reinvigorate the 1866 statute that had been unused for a century. It had been written and passed before the Fourteenth Amendment and its state-action prohibitions; it clearly prohibited "private refusal to sell land because the man is a Negro any more than one can refuse to sell, lease or rent under Section 1982."

Marshall spoke again on the remedy. He would be "willing to go on Section 1982," he said, although he hoped it could be decided on narrow grounds *"or not decided at all if a new* [civil rights] *law passes."* He remained doubtful about basing the decision on the 1866 statute "as he fears Congress could repeal it."[24]

Justice Harlan "was not at rest," he said to his colleagues. He wrote a dissent that maintained that the Court should have dismissed the writ as improvidently granted because of the fact that the 1968 Open Housing Act had been signed into law by the President.

*Jones* became precedent, and in 1976, in another case involving the viability of the 1866 civil rights statute, *Runyon v. McCrary*, the Burger Court concluded that the congressional statute extended to private schools that refused to admit qualified African Americans. In a seven-to-two opinion, Justice Stewart wrote, "It is now well established [that the 1866 legislation] prohibits racial discrimination in the making and enforcement of private contracts....Private, commercially operated nonsectarian schools [may not] deny admission to prospective students because they are Negroes."

Marshall joined the Stewart opinion. Justices Stevens and Powell concurred. Justice White, joined only by Rehnquist, dissented, arguing that the 1866 statute "means what it says and no more, i.e., that it outlaws any legal rule [preventing] any person from making or enforcing a contract, but does not prohibit racially motivated refusals to contract....The statute by its terms does not *require* any *private* individual or institution to enter into a contract...under any circumstances."

In 1987 there was an even more solidly conservative "Rehnquist" Court. Marshall's foe had been elevated to the center seat by President Ronald Reagan in 1986, when Burger retired as Chief Justice. He had been joined by Associate Justices Sandra Day O'Connor (1981), the first woman appointed to the Court (and a classmate of Rehnquist's at Stanford Law School), Antonin Scalia (1986), the Court's first Italian American, and Anthony Kennedy. (Kennedy joined the Court in the spring of 1987, after Reagan's first choice, controversial jurist Robert Bork, was not confirmed by the Senate.) It was abundantly clear to Court watchers and to the justices themselves that Rehnquist was extremely conservative. Furthermore, he believed that *Jones* was terrible law and had to be overturned by the Court. Rehnquist felt that this was the right moment, given his new, conservative colleagues sitting with him on the high bench. In the case of

*Patterson v. McLean Credit Union,* the new Rehnquist coalition boldly attempted to revisit and to overturn *Runyon.*

*Patterson* was a case brought by an African American woman, Brenda Patterson, who charged that her employers had constantly harassed her over a ten-year period, in violation of the 1866 statute that, she claimed, prohibited racial and sexual harassment in the workplace. Rehnquist asked all parties to address the larger question: "whether or not the interpretation of the [1866 civil rights act] adopted by this Court in *Runyon*...should be reconsidered."

Rehnquist felt that *Jones* as well as *Runyon* should be overturned. Marshall, Brennan, Blackmun, and Stevens angrily dissented. Stevens wrote for the quartet that the Rehnquist majority's "spontaneous decision [suggested it was seeking] to cast itself adrift from the constraints imposed by the adversary process and to fashion its own agenda." Such action, the dissenters noted, damages both "the public's perception of the Court as an impartial adjudicator" as well as "the faith of victims of racial discrimination in a stable construction of the civil rights laws."

Marshall, given his dedication to playing by the rules, was furious. What especially galled him was the audacity of the new majority, led by his foe Rehnquist, to overturn precedents with power and ideology, not reason, as their guide for action.

The front-page headline in *The New York Times* announced the Rehnquist Court's order: "Court, 5–4, Votes to Restudy Rights in Minority Suits." Stuart Taylor's lengthy story began as follows: "In an extraordinary action, the Supreme Court decided today to reconsider the rights of minorities to sue private parties for racial discrimination under a post–Civil War statute. Over bitter dissents by the other four, the Court's five more conservative members agreed to consider overruling an important 1976 decision that had expanded such rights." [25]

A firestorm of national protest immediately greeted the announcement of the reconsideration question. Over one hundred groups, including the NAACP's Inc Fund, the American Civil Liberties Union, legislators (national and state), and forty-seven state attorneys general, prepared many briefs *amicus curiae* in opposing the overturn of *Runyon.* This message also got through to the justices. When the decision came down, written by Kennedy, it flatly stated that *"Runyon*...is not inconsistent with the prevailing sense of justice in this country. To the contrary, *Runyon* is entirely consistent with our society's deep commitment to the eradication of discrimination based on a person's race or color of his or her skin."

But the majority did not extend the 1866 legislation to hold employers liable for racial and sexual harassment on the job. The 1866 law covers "only conduct at the initial formation of the contract and conduct which impairs the right to enforce contract obligations through the legal process." Brennan dissented, joined by Marshall, Blackmun, and Stevens. He criticized the majority for "adopting a formalistic method of interpretation antithetical to Congress's vision of a society in which contractual opportunities are equal."

## ENDING NONRACIAL CLASS AND CASTE DISCRIMINATION IN AMERICA

What about a state or federal statute that discriminates against a group of persons because of gender, wealth, age, or sexual preference? Does the equal-protection clause's prohibition against such state action come into play in the federal courts? In the U.S. Supreme Court? Does such a nonracial caste designation fall into the "suspect category" class? Or is it a category that falls into the intermediate zone where the Court employs the "strict rationality" standard, a rule the Burger Court majority developed? Or does the Court employ the traditional "rational basis" test to determine whether the legislation is valid or not?

Those were the new kind of equal-protection questions that Marshall heard within a few years of his joining the Court in 1967. Marshall always believed in giving the Fourteenth Amendment the broadest possible scope in order to protect all persons, regardless of gender, class, caste, age, or race. As was to be the case in other areas of constitutional interpretation, Marshall was to find himself in the minority in this one.

### GENDER-BASED DISCRIMINATIONS

Through the early 1970s, the Court had traditionally treated women very differently than men, whether in suits upholding a state's right to bar women from service as lawyers, or in suits where the Court majority upheld legislation that "protected" the physiologically weaker women from certain hazards of employment, thereby underscoring the notion of women as the weaker sex, as family nurturers whose major tasks were child rearing and caring for their husbands. For these very traditional, sexist reasons, a state could bar women from being automatically placed on jury rolls and serving on juries unless they personally went down to the courthouse and requested that the registrar place their name on a list. And a state could bar a woman from serving as a barmaid unless the liquor establishment was owned by her husband or father.

After the civil rights legislation of the 1960s and a major movement for ratification of an equal rights amendment to the Constitution, gender discrimination litigation, slowly at first and then, by the mid-1970s, in a torrent, came into the federal courts and ultimately to the U.S. Supreme Court. *Reed v. Reed* (1971) and *Frontiero v. Richardson* (1973) pushed the Court into confronting gender discrimination.

*Reed,* decided unanimously by the Court, was a case challenging an Idaho statute that gave preference to the father over the mother in the administration of the estate of a deceased son. Burger, writing for the Court majority and using the "rational basis" standard, concluded that the statute failed to pass muster. There was no discussion of whether gender was a "suspect" classification until the *Frontiero* case two years later.

Sharon Frontiero was an air force officer whose husband, a full-time student and listed as her dependent, was denied spousal benefits available for female spouses of male military personnel. She went to federal court seeking an injunction against the enforcement of what she claimed was a discriminatory federal statute. Except for Rehnquist, who was the sole dissenter, the Court agreed with her contention. The split among the eight was over what standard to employ in reaching their justification.

In *Frontiero,* Brennan persuaded Marshall, White, and Douglas to agree that gender was a "suspect" category and that the standard that should be applied was "strict scrutiny." Brennan believed that the case "would provide an appropriate vehicle for us to recognize sex as a 'suspect criterion.'...Perhaps there is a Court [i.e., five justices to agree to] such an approach."[26] Immediately Douglas responded, saying, "I'd prefer that approach." Powell, however, told Brennan, "I see no reason to consider whether sex is a 'suspect' classification in this case. Perhaps we can avoid confronting that issue until we know the outcome of the Equal Rights Amendment."

Brennan responded to Powell's reference to the Equal Rights Amendment by writing him and stating, prophetically: "we cannot count on the Equal Rights Amendment to make the Equal Protection issue go away. Eleven states have now (March 8, 1973) voted against ratification....Since rejection in 13 states is sufficient to kill the Amendment it looks like a lost cause."

Marshall once more pointed out the need for a spectrum of standards, and White supported Marshall. White wrote Brennan: "I agree with Marshall that we actually have a spectrum of standards....Marshall is right about this." However, in the end, Marshall and White, with Douglas, joined Brennan's opinion.

By the beginning of March 1973, Brennan had written the *Frontiero* opinion and realized that he did not have five votes for declaring gender a "suspect category" and thus subject to "strict scrutiny." Very quickly, the others told Brennan they could not join him if he remained committed to that position. Blackmun told him that he could not join. So did the Chief, as did Stewart, who wrote Brennan to disagree with him on standards. "I see no need to decide in this case whether sex is a 'suspect' criterion." Powell also immediately wrote to Brennan, saying, "you have now gone all the way in holding that sex is a 'suspect classification'"; he was withdrawing his support for Brennan's opinion because he did not agree with the use of the strict-scrutiny standard in gender-based discrimination cases.

Douglas, reading these memoranda, wrote Brennan, telling him that he hoped Brennan would find a way "to sail between Scylla and Charybdis." He was very doubtful that Brennan would find the five votes needed to establish the precedent. He was also very correct in his count of the votes in *Frontiero*.

The gentle Virginian, Lewis Powell, wrote a concurring opinion, joined by Burger and Blackmun. He agreed with Brennan about the disposition of the case but disagreed with him regarding the reasoning. He cautiously rejected the proposed addition of gender to the list of "suspect" classifications, arguing, "it is unnecessary for the Court in this case to characterize sex as a suspect classification with all the far-reaching implications of such a holding."

Brennan's argument was that sex, like race, alienage, and national origin, was "an immutable characteristic determined solely by the accident of birth." It was, he argued, a neutral, "inherently suspect" characteristic, and the standard required in litigation involving gender-based discriminations had to be the "strict scrutiny" one. His view did not prevail, so there was no tough judicial standard to be applied in gender discrimination cases. A constitutional remedy was foreclosed when the proposed Equal Rights Amendment was defeated because it did not receive the approval of three-quarters of the states. Marshall, never comfortable with the country gentleman sitting on the Court, seethed with anger at Powell's conservatism on the constitutional status of gender.

Out of these two cases, and the battles within the Court about the standards to be employed in gender discrimination litigation, came the creation of the intermediate, or "heightened scrutiny," test. The new standard emerged when the Court heard *Craig v. Boren* during its 1976 term. It was an equal-protection case from Oklahoma involving the age differential at which women were allowed to drink beer (from age eighteen) and men (from age twenty-one). Brennan, who wrote the opinion for the majority, modified the standards language of *Reed* and *Frontiero*, concluding that "the gender based difference [was not] substantially related to the achievement of the statutory objective" and therefore was not an invidious discrimination, having no "substantial" relationship to an "important" governmental interest (i.e., highway safety). Rehnquist dissented on the grounds that the new standard or test was inappropriate and that the statute was constitutional under the "rational basis," or first-tier, standard.

However, *Michael M. v. Superior Court of Sonoma County* (1981) is an example of the Burger majority validating a gender-based legislative discrimination. Marshall, White, and Brennan dissented, with Brennan writing for the trio. Stevens wrote a separate dissent.

The case involved a young man seventeen years of age who was convicted of statutory rape in a California court. The crime was defined in the California criminal code as unlawful "sexual intercourse accomplished with a female not the wife of the perpetrator, where the female is under the age of 18 years." He appealed his conviction on the ground that the California law violated the Fourteenth Amendment's equal-protection clause because only males were held criminally liable in statutory rape cases. The Court, in a five-to-four vote, upheld the California law and the conviction of Michael M.

Rehnquist wrote the opinion, joined by Burger, Stewart, Blackmun, and Powell. He rejected the alternative type of legislation, one that was gender-neutral, punishing both the male and the female who engaged in such underage but consensual sex. The objective of the state was to try to "limit...illegitimate teenage pregnancy by prohibiting the male from having sexual intercourse with a minor female. We hold that such a statute is sufficiently related to the State's objectives to pass constitutional muster." He then argued that the risk of pregnancy is a "substantial deterrence to young females. No similar natural sanctions deter males. A criminal sanction imposed solely on males thus serves to roughly 'equalize' the deterrents on the sexes."

Brennan's dissent focused on the state's inability to show that the purpose of the law was better met by gender discrimination than by a gender-neutral statute. He noted that, at that time, thirty-seven states had such gender-neutral legislation that the legislators hoped would deter teenage pregnancy. The dissenters believed that the California statute violated the Fourteenth Amendment's equal-protection clause.

## WEALTH, POVERTY, ILLEGITIMACY

Marshall came to the Court at the wrong time. During the Warren Court's heyday, it had noted that "lines drawn on the basis of wealth or property...render a classification highly suspect."[27] That value was soon replaced by a much narrower, more conservative view of legislative classifications based on wealth—or the lack thereof. In cases involving legislative discriminations against the poor, the weak and indigent, the aged and the mentally incompetent, the Burger and Rehnquist Court majorities consistently used the lowest of the standards, the "rational basis" test, to determine whether the wealth-based discrimination was constitutional. And, most of the time, the Court found for the state and against the poor people who were adversely affected by the legislation.

Marshall first addressed the question of the (wealth versus) poverty classification in the 1969 case of *Shapiro v. Thompson,* which involved the question of residency requirements for poor persons in need of federal aid for themselves and their children.

Vivian Thompson, who was nineteen, the mother of a child and pregnant with another, applied for assistance under the federal AFDC program two months after moving from Massachusetts to Connecticut. The AFDC program was administered by the states, under guidelines the states themselves established. She was denied assistance because Connecticut had a one-year residency requirement. She sued Bernard Shapiro, Connecticut's commissioner of welfare, in a three-judge federal district court. That court ruled that the residency requirement violated the Fourteenth Amendment's equal-protection clause and also had a "chilling effect on the right to travel." Shapiro appealed to the Supreme Court, which upheld the judgment of the federal court.

Brennan, again, with Marshall's support, wrote the opinion for the Court. Rejecting the use of the "rational relation" standard in the case, Brennan's opinion emphasized the fundamental constitutional right of citizens to travel between states. For a state to curtail that right, there had to be a showing of a "compelling" government interest. Connecticut had not met the heavy burden of showing that the residency requirement was serving a compelling state need. There was a "clear violation" of the equal-protection clause, concluded Brennan.

Warren dissented, joined by Justice Black. Harlan wrote a separate dissent. Warren believed that Congress could "impose minimal nationwide residence requirements or authorize the states to do so. Since I believe that Congress does have this power and has constitutionally authorized it, I dissent." He disagreed with Brennan's reading of the congressional debates and argued that Congress had the right and did authorize the states to establish such residency requirements.

In 1971, a different Court majority retreated from *Shapiro*. In *James v. Valtierra*, Black, writing for the majority, upheld as valid an amendment to the California state constitution, even though it stated that no low-cost housing could be developed unless approved in a referendum held in the local community. "This procedure [the referendum] for democratic decision making does not violate the constitutional command that no State shall deny to any person 'the equal protection of the laws.'"

Marshall forcefully dissented, and was joined by Justices Brennan and Blackmun. He argued that there was a fundamentally unconstitutional discrimination "against persons of low income" in the amendment, one that was prohibited by the Fourteenth Amendment:

> Publicly assisted housing developments designed to accommodate the aged, veterans, state employees, persons of moderate income, or any class of citizens other than the poor, need not be approved by prior referenda. Article 34 is an explicit classification on the basis of poverty—a suspect classification which demands exacting scrutiny....It is far too late in the day to contend that the

Fourteenth Amendment prohibits only racial discrimination; and to me, singling out the poor to bear a burden not placed on any other class of citizens tramples the values that the Fourteenth Amendment was designed to protect. I dissent.

In a 1974 case involving the question of whether a one-year residency in Arizona was necessary before indigents could receive nonemergency hospital care, Marshall was able to write for a Court majority. In *Memorial Hospital v. Maricopa County*, Marshall concluded that such a residency requirement violated the Fourteenth Amendment's equal-protection clause.

This case was an example of clear invidious discrimination against the poor, not justified by the state. The law, he wrote, was a state classification that "operates to *penalize* indigents for exercising their right to migrate to and settle in [Arizona]." As such, it "must be justified by a compelling state interest." Medical care is a "basic necessity of life," and Arizona did not meet the "heavy burden of justification." Rehnquist, predictably, dissented.

While Marshall was on the Court, the jurists gave careful, though not strict, scrutiny to cases that discriminated against illegitimate children. In *Levy v. Louisiana* (1968), the majority held that a state could not create a right of action for children in the wrongful death of a parent and then exclude illegitimate children of the dead parent from benefiting from such a right. But in the 1971 case of *Labine v. Vincent*, also from Louisiana, Marshall dissented from a Court decision that upheld a Louisiana statute that denied an inheritance to an illegitimate child even though the father acknowledged his parentage while still alive. He argued, from the time of the conference session in January 1971, that the state had no right to draw the distinction.[28] (However, in the 1977 case of *Trimble v. Gordon*, from Illinois, the Court greatly narrowed the precedential impact of *Labine*.)

## RESIDENT AND ILLEGAL ALIENS

The Constitution's rights and liberties, for the most part, extend to all persons, including aliens. However, as Marshall was to note, legal aliens do not have the same freedom that citizens have when entering the country and trying to reside in America once here. They can also be deported and their property seized. Could laws that discriminate against aliens be validated by a federal court without "strict scrutiny"?

In the 1971 case of *Graham v. Richardson*, the Court majority, based on *Carolene*'s guidelines, said that the standard for reviewing cases involving aliens was the "strict scrutiny" standard. Aliens as a class, the Court stated, "are a prime example of a 'discrete and insular' minority." All legislation based on such a classification was "inherently suspect" and would be "subject to close judicial scrutiny." In 1973, in an opinion written by Blackmun, *Sugarman v. Dougall*, in which Marshall joined, the Court held that New York's Civil Service Law (requiring citizenship as a condition for employment) unconstitutionally discriminated against aliens. The statute, he wrote, "does not withstand the necessary close scrutiny." Once again Rehnquist dissented, rejecting the majority's disposition to protect minorities: "I cannot find, and the Court does not cite, any constitutional authority for such a 'ward of the Court' approach to equal protection."

In the late 1970s, however, the Court's treatment of cases discriminating against aliens changed significantly. In 1978, in *Foley v. Connelie*, the Court validated a New York law that excluded aliens from the New York City police force. (In 1982 the ban was extended to probation officers employed in New York City.) In 1979, in *Ambach v. Norwick*, the Court majority, in an opinion written by Powell, used the "rational relationship" standard to uphold a New York statute barring aliens "who have demonstrated their unwillingness to obtain United States citizenship" from becoming public school teachers. Blackmun dissented, joined by Marshall, Brennan, and Stevens. He maintained that the statute was irrational and in violation of the Fourteenth Amendment. "Is it better," he asked, for New York "to employ a poor [less capable] citizen-teacher than an excellent resident alien teacher?"

In 1982 the Court heard a controversial case from Texas involving free educational benefits for children of *illegal* aliens. (To that point, the cases heard by Marshall's Court had involved discrimination against legal aliens residing in the country.) Displaying a seesaw response to the issue, the Court majority's views were expressed in an opinion written by Brennan. *Plyler v. Doe* held that Texas could not deny the offspring of illegal aliens a public school education. The children did not engage in unlawful conduct. And, said Brennan, "legislation directing the onus of a parent's misconduct against his children does not comport with fundamental conceptions of justice." In this instance, he maintained, the state "imposes its discriminatory burden on the basis of a legal characteristic over which children can have little control." It did so in the absence of any articulated national policy "that supports the State in denying these children an elementary education."

In conference, he had argued that "strict scrutiny" could be applied in the case because the statute's discriminatory classification was national origin. (Later, Brennan changed his mind because there was an obvious difference between legitimate residential aliens and the undocumented, illegal aliens whose children were the focus of the litigation.) Marshall spoke plainly to his brethren in this conference: "The kids are not involved in anything illegal—they were victims of being born. It's the kids we must focus on, and I can't treat them as 'illegals.'"[29] He joined Brennan's opinion but added a short concurrence noting "that the facts of these cases demonstrate the wisdom of rejecting a rigidified approach to equal protection analysis, and of employing" his flexible standard.

What standard should be applied in the case? Brennan wrote to the justices who had joined him—Marshall, Powell, Blackmun, and Stevens—telling them that he could find no clear consensus among the group for the standard to be used. He suggested again that strict scrutiny be used. Powell, however, threatened to pull away from Brennan if he followed through with the use of the "strict scrutiny" standard. But Powell informed Brennan, "I would agree that a 'heightened' level of scrutiny is required." Brennan, ever the "wizard of five," took Powell's message, substantively changed the opinion to reflect Powell's views, and preserved his Court majority.

Burger wrote the opinion for the dissenters—himself, Rehnquist, White, and O'Connor. There was no arbitrariness in the Texas legislation, he asserted. The Fourteenth Amendment's equal-protection clause "is not an all-encompassing 'equalizer' designed to eradicate every distinction for which persons are not 'responsible.'" Texas did have a legitimate purpose in passing the exclusionary statute. Since illegal aliens are not a suspect class, and education is not a fundamental constitutional right, the "rational relationship" standard must be employed to determine whether the law in question serves a legitimate state purpose. Although Burger confessed that he would not have supported the Texas legislation if he were a legislator, the choice Texas legislators made, he felt, was not an unconstitutional one.

## AGE AND MENTAL RETARDATION DISCRIMINATION

In *Massachusetts Board of Retirement v. Murgia* (1976), the Court concluded that "age" was not a "suspect category." In a short, unsigned order, the Court employed the "rational basis" standard to uphold a state law that required state police officers to retire when they reached the age of fifty. Marshall dissented because of the Court's reliance on the rigid two-tier formula employed to validate the law.

The Court, he wrote, was "quite right in suggesting that distinctions exist between the elderly and traditional suspect classes.... The advantage of a flexible equal protection standard is that it can readily accommodate variables. The elderly are undoubtedly discriminated against, and when legislation denied them an important benefit—employment—I conclude that to sustain the legislation the Commonwealth must show a reasonably substantial interest and a scheme reasonably closely tailored to achieving that interest."

Can a state, consistent with the Fourteenth Amendment, discriminate against the mentally retarded? In *Cleburne, Texas, v. Cleburne Living Center* (1985), the Court heard a case involving a Texas city's denial, under its zoning ordinances, of a special permit for a group to run a professionally supervised home, the Featherston Home, for thirteen mentally retarded persons.

Justice White, for the majority, ruled that mental retardation was a classification that could be examined using the "rational relationship" or "rational basis" standard. The lower federal court was wrong when it applied the intermediate, "quasi-suspect" classification to adjudicate the case. Applying the lowest-tier standard, White concluded that the law was unconstitutional in that there was no requirement for a special-use permit for any other groups. "In our view, the record does not reveal any rational basis for believing that the Featherston home would pose any special threat to the city's legitimate interests....Mere negative attitudes, or fear, unsubstantiated by factors which are properly cognizable in a zoning proceeding, are not permissible bases for treating a home for the mentally retarded any differently than apartment houses, multiple dwellings, and the like."

Marshall concurred in part and dissented in part, and was joined by Justice Blackmun. He believed that the federal court of appeals was correct in using a standard that "subjected this zoning ordinance to the searching review—the heightened scrutiny—that actually leads to its invalidation." The majority's "refusal to acknowledge that something more than minimal rationality review is at work here is, in my view, unfortunate....For the retarded, just as for Negroes and women, much has changed in recent years, but much remains the same; outdated statutes are still on the books, and irrational fears or ignorance, traceable to the prolonged social and cultural isolation of the retarded, continue to stymie recognition of the dignity and individuality of retarded people."

The proper standard to be employed in *Cleburne* was that of "heightened scrutiny." The "mentally retarded" category, like that of gender, illegitimacy, or alienage, is a characteristic that is "relevant under some circumstances but not others" for legitimate state discrimination. Marshall argued that, employing the "heightened scrutiny" standard, the ordinance should have been struck down entirely, rather than the majority invalidating it "as applied to the respondents."

## MARSHALL'S CONCEPT OF GENUINE EQUALITY

Marshall wrote hundreds of dissenting opinions during his time on the Court; in fact, the majority of his writings while he served on the Court were dissents.[30] As the cases discussed above indicate, Marshall's invariable antagonist was Rehnquist. He was a man Marshall did not like and who was, in Marshall's mind, a racist. The two men argued continually over the meaning and the extent of the "equality" concept in the Constitution. As one observer has written, Marshall's "most enduring legacy as Justice" was in opinions in the equal-protection litigation before the Court.[31]

Marshall's understanding of equality was that of a traditional liberal. Equality's "defining feature" was the liberal democratic notion of equality of opportunity. All people had the right "to an equal start in life," he wrote in *San Antonio*. Differences matter, Marshall acknowledged, but they must be differences based on the content of a person's character and ability and not on the color of his skin, or her physical disability, or his sexual preference, or her age, or his wealth—or lack of wealth. Marshall "thought that the core meaning of the Equal Protection Clause was that the government could not translate morally irrelevant differences into a form of second-class citizenship."[32] As he said, in dissent, in *Flagg Brothers v. Shirley H. Brooks* (1978), "I cannot remain silent as the Court demonstrates, not for the first time, an attitude of callous indifference to the realities of life for the poor."

Rehnquist had written the opinion for the majority turning aside an appeal from a poor woman who was facing the imminent forced sale of all her possessions. Brooks and her family had been evicted from their New York City apartment. Their furnishings had been stored, consistent with a New York statute, at Flagg Brothers, a storage facility. After due notice for nonpayment of the storage bills, the company was about to sell the merchandise. She went into federal court arguing that, because the warehouse was an agent of the state, such threatened action was a form of "state action" that would violate her due process and equal-protection rights in the Fourteenth Amendment. The federal trial court dismissed her suit, but the Second Circuit federal court of appeals reversed, finding state action. The company appealed to the Supreme Court and, in the opinion for the majority, Rehnquist concluded that there was no state action and that the federal district court judge had acted properly in dismissing the complaint: acquiescence of the state to the proposed private action by the warehouse company in selling Brooks's property did not convert such action into that of the state.

Marshall dissented and wrote a blistering opinion. Basically, his concern about the case went to his notion of fairness and equality for people, especially those who were not as fortunate or as wealthy as federal judges. Brooks was, simply stated, not treated fairly by the Court. Rehnquist had "closed [his] eyes to the realities that led to this litigation." If the Court had carefully examined the history of lien executions in New York State, it would have realized that the warehouseman in New York played the role of sheriff in executing liens on property. As such, there was the requisite state action that warranted a review on the merits of whether there had been discrimination against Ms. Brooks. He "ignored this history" and dealt with the issue in an abstract way. Rehnquist "did not come down to earth and decide the issue here with careful attention to the State's traditional role."[33] Marshall, in equal-protection litigation, felt that a majority of his colleagues had closed their eyes to the realities that made relief by the Court essential. Until his failing health forced him to retire, he did all he could to bring the brethren "down to earth."

# 11

## *BAKKE* AND THE
## AFFIRMATIVE ACTION BATTLES:
## "THEY JUST DON'T GET IT!"

In 1978, during the Court's often heated internal battles regarding the constitutionality of a university affirmative action program in the Court's first major case in this area, *Regents v. Bakke*, William Brennan "resolved to get Marshall's reaction to the problem over lunch one day that week," Brennan recalled. "I asked whether if [his son] were a candidate for admission to medical school, he thought it would be proper for school administrators to accord his application special consideration because of his race. Thurgood's asseveration was: 'Damn right, they owe us!'"[1] A few years later, Marshall explained Brennan's astonishment at his answer. He told Carl Rowan, "I think [my colleagues on the Supreme Court] honestly believe that Negroes are so much better off than they were before."

Marshall knew that segregation was still deeply entrenched in American society, and his position on affirmative action reflected his view of the situation of black Americans: "It is impossible for the United States to assure equality for Blacks unless it is willing to factor into any remediation stratagem the reality of the continuing adverse effects of societal discrimination."[2] The consequences of such discrimination were outlined by Deval Patrick, President Clinton's assistant attorney general for civil rights in the Department of Justice. In March 1995, he testified before the Subcommittee on Employer-Employee Relations of the House of Representative's Committee on Economic and Educational Opportunities. Defending affirmative action, Patrick said:

> while meaningful progress has been made in eliminating discriminatory barriers to employment, education, and other economic opportunities, some barriers, and the effects of previous barriers, remain. African Americans and Hispanics

continue to lag far behind whites in rate of employment, income and educational level. The unemployment rate for African Americans was more than twice that of whites in 1993, while the median income of African Americans was barely more than one-half that of whites.... Tragically, in 1992, over 50% of African American children under 6 and 44% of Hispanic children lived under the poverty level, while only 14.4% of white children did so. The overall poverty rates were 33.3% for African Americans, 29.3% for Hispanics, as compared to 11.6% for whites.[3]

Almost two decades before Deval's comments, Justice Marshall had spoken in very similar terms:

A Negro child has a life expectancy which is shorter by more than five years than that of a white child. The Negro child's mother is over three times more likely to die of complications in childbirth, and the infant mortality rate for Negroes is nearly twice that for whites. The median income of the Negro family is only 60% that of the median of a white family, and the percentage of Negroes who live in families with incomes below the poverty line is nearly four times greater than that of whites.... For Negro adults, the unemployment rate is twice that of whites, and the unemployment rate for Negro teenagers is nearly three times that of white teenagers.... Although Negroes represent 11.5% of the population, they are only 1.2% of the lawyers and judges, 2% of the physicians, 2.3% of the dentists, 1.1% of the engineers, and 2.6% of the college and university professors.[4]

Affirmative action programs were an attempt to remedy past and present discrimination by leveling the playing field. "It is clear," Patrick told the legislators, "that many individuals, because of race, ethnicity and gender and associated stereotyping, have been denied the tools and the opportunity to share in and contribute to the wealth of our nation."[5]

## 1964: AFFIRMATIVE ACTION'S BEGINNINGS

When Marshall went to the Court in 1967, affirmative action was the emergent strategy of the executive branch to redress the harm done by racial segregation and discrimination. Its intent was to enable African Americans and other minorities to get equal education and employment opportunities through specific remedial efforts by government and the private sector, taking into account race, color, and gender. Affirmative action programs, initiated by Lyndon Johnson's executive order in 1965, ranged from "aggressive recruiting and remedial training programs, to setting goals and timetables, and to set-asides and quotas specifying an exact number or percentage of admissions or jobs for blacks, women, and other minorities."[6]

By the 1970s, during the Nixon administration, federal executive departments, primarily the Department of Labor (particularly its Equal Employment Opportunity Commission) and the Department of Education, formulated policies that required affirmative actions in employment and in education. And it naturally became a controversial political issue at the national and local levels, one that inevitably came before the U.S. Supreme Court.

Supporters of affirmative action—and Marshall was one of the major spokespersons for its need and its constitutionality—maintained that these programs were needed to overcome the devastating consequences of two centuries of slavery and a third century of second-class citizenship for African Americans.

Critics of affirmative action argued that the Constitution was "color-blind" and that the Fourteenth Amendment's equal-protection clause did not allow a "good," "benign" racial discrimination, even if it was to make up for centuries of cruel and unfair race discrimination. Such preferences in education and in employment, they asserted, disadvantaged whites who had nothing to do with past racial discrimination against African Americans. They labeled affirmative action programs as a form of "reverse racial discrimination" barred by the Fourteenth Amendment.

They also argued that Titles VI and VII of the 1964 Civil Rights Act, which prohibited discrimination in organizations that received federal funds and in employment on the basis of race, color, religion, national origin, and gender, invalidated all affirmative action programs. Title VI of the 1964 Civil Rights Act said that "no person in the United States shall, on the ground of race, color, or national origin, be excluded from participation in, be denied the benefits of, or be subjected to discrimination under any program or activity receiving federal financial assistance." Title VII of the Civil Rights Act focused on prohibiting employment discrimination in the private sector based on race, color, gender, or national origin. It also stated that no employer, employment agency, or labor union could "grant preferential treatment to any individual or to any group because of the race, color, religion, sex, national origin, of such individual or group on account of an imbalance which may exist with respect to the total number or percentage of persons of any race, color, religion, sex, or national origin employed by any employer."

Marshall's basic response to the critics of affirmative action, especially those on the Court, was to say, emphatically, that they just didn't get it! They didn't understand the societal context that made such programs necessary. Despite Brown's overturn of Plessy's "separate-and-unequal doctrine," racial discrimination was still present. Disparities of all kinds, in health, education, employment, housing, and morbidity and mortality (infant and adult alike), still existed for *all* African Americans as well as fundamental inequality of opportunity. *"Damn right, they owe us!"* as Marshall exclaimed to Brennan. The debt, even after *Brown* and civil rights legislation, was still a very large one. This remained Marshall's position from the very first case the Court heard on the merits, in 1978, until he retired in 1991. In all the major affirmative action cases that came before the Court, Marshall forcefully argued—in his opinions and in his memos to the conference—that remediation programs were vitally necessary and not prohibited by statute or by the Fourteenth Amendment.

The nation, he maintained, was nowhere near the ideal of equality, so affirmative action programs, whether voluntary or ordered by federal courts, were appropriate transitional remedies to the dilemma of inequality and lack of opportunity for African Americans, and other minorities as well. This was his conviction as *Bakke*, the first major case involving educational opportunity, came to the Supreme Court from California in 1978.

## THE *BAKKE* CASE: DEFINING AFFIRMATIVE ACTION

*Bakke* was not the first affirmative action litigation to be heard before the Supreme Court. A few years earlier the Court had granted certiorari in a case from Washington State involving a preferential admissions program implemented by the University of Washington's law school. In 1971, Marco DeFunis, a white Jewish student, applied for admission. He did not get into the law school, even though his scores were higher than those of many others who were admitted under the school's affirmative action program for minorities (specifically defined as African American, Chicano, American Indian, and Filipino; Asian Americans were excluded because the school felt that they were not an underrepresented category). The law school had argued that taking race and ethnicity into account was justified because the school was "in pursuit of a state policy to mitigate gross underrepresentation of certain minorities in the law school and in membership of the bar."

Under the University of Washington admissions protocol, the faculty-student admissions committee took into account an applicant's "racial or ethnic background." DeFunis's weighted average score was 76.23, which was high in the middle category. That year, 275 students were admitted; 74 of them had lower averages than DeFunis, including 36 minority students. DeFunis sued the university, asking for injunctive relief because the separate admissions program violated the Fourteenth Amendment's equal-protection clause. The state trial court judge ruled that the program was unconstitutional and granted the injunction; DeFunis was admitted to the law school in September 1971. The university appealed to the state supreme court, which reversed the lower court and lifted the injunction. By then, DeFunis was in his second year of law school.

DeFunis's attorneys petitioned the U.S. Supreme Court for a writ of certiorari. It was granted but, before oral arguments, the Court asked both sides to address, in a supplemental filing of briefs, the question of whether the issue was moot because DeFunis was in his third year of law school. Both parties did file and both argued that it was not a moot point and that the Court should decide the case on the merits. The Court majority, however, did not decide the constitutional issue. Rather, they concluded that, because of DeFunis's imminent graduation from law school, the case was indeed moot.

But Marshall, Brennan, Douglas, and White, dissenting, felt that the case should be considered on its merits. Brennan criticized the majority for "straining to rid itself of this dispute." Douglas felt that the racial classification used in the law school's admissions program should be subjected to the Court's "strict scrutiny" test for equal-protection cases. He believed that the Fourteenth Amendment's equal-protection clause required that race "not militate against an applicant or on his behalf." Ultimately the court avoided what Powell called "the sticky wicket" and, in a *per curiam* opinion, dismissed the case.

The Court, however, was able to avoid confronting the substantive issue for only three years. In 1978 the Court again faced the question in the case of *Regents of the University of California v. Bakke*. In 1973 and again in 1974, blond, blue-eyed military veteran Allan Bakke applied for admission to the brand-new medical school at the University of California at Davis.

Both times he was rejected for admission to the medical school while other students with poorer scores were admitted. The school had instituted a separate admission track for "disadvantaged" students—those who were African American, Hispanic, or Native American, and who desired to have their applications reviewed in the special affirmative action admissions program. It differed in two ways from the general admissions program: there was no summary dismissal for applicants who had a cumulative undergraduate grade point average of 2.5 (out of 4.0) or less; and the applicants competed with each other for the sixteen seats (out of one hundred seats available for the entire first-year class of medical students) that were set aside for "disadvantaged" applicants in both 1973 and 1974.

After failing to gain entrance the second time, Bakke filed suit in California, asking the court to order his admission on the grounds of racial discrimination in violation of the equal-protection clause of the Fourteenth Amendment, because the school's set-aside program "resulted in the admission of minority applicants less qualified than plaintiff and other non-minority applicants who were therefore rejected." The state court ruled in his favor, concluding that the special admissions program ran afoul of the Fourteenth Amendment, the California Constitution, and Title VI of the 1964 Civil Rights Act. However, while the court enjoined the university from considering the race of candidates in its admission process, it did not order Bakke to be admitted to the medical school.

Both parties, Bakke and the university, appealed the order to the California Supreme Court. That court, applying the strict scrutiny standard, agreed that the reasons for the special minority admission program were "compelling" ones, but thought that the school could have come up with less intrusive means for achieving its goals. It held that the admissions program was unconstitutional, on federal grounds, under the Fourteenth Amendment, and ordered Bakke admitted to the medical school. The university appealed the decision to the U.S. Supreme Court, which granted the request for a writ of certiorari on February 18, 1977, "to consider the important constitutional issue."

By this time there had been a significant personnel change on the Court since *DeFunis*. Justice Douglas had retired in 1975, replaced by John Paul Stevens, a federal appellate judge appointed by President Gerald Ford. And the Nixon quartet of Burger, Blackmun, Rehnquist, and Powell had grown closer on a number of constitutional issues, especially those involving the scope of equal protection under the Fourteenth Amendment.

Many months after certiorari was granted, in early September 1977, Ellen Silberman, one of Marshall's law clerks, wrote a bench memo to the judge arguing that *Bakke* "was an unfortunate case for the court to use to announce its views on affirmative action." The record in the case was undeveloped. Even though the California Supreme Court had argued that there were less intrusive ways for the university to accomplish its goals, as Silberman noted, "there is absolutely nothing in the record on that issue." She also raised the question of mootness because the California constitution had been amended, after the California Supreme Court ruling, to prohibit all racial preferences in admissions programs. The amended constitution stated that "no person shall be debarred admission to any department of the University on account of race, religion, ethnic heritage, or sex."

Another issue she raised in the memo was one that plagued the justices on this and other cases to come: "what level of scrutiny must be applied" by the Court in deciding the constitutional question of whether an affirmative action plan conflicted with equal protection. The question in *Bakke* "is whether this unconventional racial classification which discriminates against whites, requires [strict scrutiny]." In the end, she concluded, "what it all really comes down to is are we going to put an end to all attempts to bring minorities and particularly Negroes out of the lowest level occupations and into the mainstreams of American life. If this program is struck down by the Court, so much else will go with it." Marshall agreed—but could he persuade his colleagues to "get it"?[7]

Oral arguments were scheduled for October 12, 1977. Two "diametrically opposed" positions divided the court. On one side were the brethren who accepted the notion, first expressed in 1896 by the sole dissenter in *Plessy*, John Harlan, that the Constitution was color-blind and that therefore no racial discrimination, however benign or worthy, could pass constitutional muster. Marshall's position, after oral argument, was a reaffirmation of the need for "race-conscious remedies to correct a race-conscious past."[8]

Another major controversial issue that split the Court was whether Title VI of the Civil Rights Act was applicable. In the briefs filed in the Court and at oral argument, neither side had discussed the matter, and so the Court asked for supplemental briefs addressing the Title VI issue. As White said, in a memo to the conference written the day after oral argument, "we are at least *entitled* to consider the statutory ground....I think we *should* deal with the Title VI argument."

In all controversial cases heard by the Court, after oral arguments end, the fur begins to fly a few days later in the Court's conference session, where the case is discussed and viewpoints are aired, however briefly or tentatively. Memos are written, sometimes heated ones, tempers flare, voices are raised, and passionate debate—in the conference, in the memos to the conference, and in the draft opinions—takes place. *Bakke* was no exception. Almost all of the brethren were convinced that at some point they would have to answer the constitutional question—as well as the statutory one. As Powell wrote to his colleagues, if they decided *Bakke* on statutory grounds without dealing with the constitutional question,

> again we will have resolved finally nothing. Relevant prudential considerations weigh heavily in favor of our resolving the constitutional issue which is before us, which was the issue that prompted us to take the case....Any action by us that may be perceived as *ducking this issue for the second time in three years* would be viewed by many as a "self-inflicted wound" on the Court. (My emphasis.)[9]

Brennan and Marshall agreed with Powell's contention, although not with the standard he proposed that the Court use to decide the matter (i.e., strict scrutiny). Brennan believed that standard should be used in cases where race was used to stigmatize and demean. In the UC Davis case, where race was used for remedial purposes, the standard should not be strict scrutiny but "nonetheless... requires scrutiny more exacting than minimal rationality."[10] Marshall insisted on using his more flexible standard, one that he had discussed and used on a number of occasions before *Bakke*. It took into account the importance of the governmental purpose as well as the severity of the discrimination. He also argued, as he did in all "equality" cases, that the Court could not deal with the issue of affirmative action in the purely rational legalistic fashion appropriate for an ideal world. Furthermore, for Marshall, the "legality of affirmative action simply could not be resolved without consideration of the historical, legal, and sociological context of past racial policies and practices."[11]

William Rehnquist also believed that the Court had to deal with the *Bakke* case on the merits. Rehnquist wrote to his colleagues, "I take it as a postulate that difference in treatment of individuals based on their race or ethnic origin is at the bulls-eye of the target at which the Fourteenth Amendment's Equal Protection Clause was aimed." He rejected Marshall's law clerk's contention that the Fourteenth Amendment and Title VI "protects only minorities." For Rehnquist, "the *thing prohibited* [in the Constitution and in the statute] is discrimination on the basis of race, *any race*," and the standard the Court had to use was the strict-scrutiny standard, one that accepted the notion that the Constitution was color-blind.

Chief Justice Burger and the recently appointed Justice Stevens were the only ones who urged avoidance of the constitutional issue from the beginning of the *Bakke* discussions. They did not want the Court to decide the case by interpreting the Fourteenth Amendment's equal-protection clause. Ultimately, Stevens's insistence on this point led Rehnquist as well as Burger to resist confronting the issue. Burger hoped that the brethren would not imprudently move toward the constitutional issue simply because the "mildly hysterical media" urged them to do so.[12] Burger urged a prompt resolution, using the strict-scrutiny standard when the Court was prepared to address it. And even if it took years "to work out a rational solution of the current problem, so be it. That is what we are paid for," he wrote his colleagues.

By January 1978, the Court knew that it was badly split over *Bakke*. Although the Chief had decided that there would not be a decisive vote in conference on the case until later in 1978, the flood of memos circulated by all the brethren except Blackmun (who was at the Mayo Clinic recovering from prostate surgery) had given the justices a lot to digest as well as a clear sense of how eight of them lined up. (In one such extended multi-page memo, written in January 1978, Powell wrote, "[My] first impulse is to 'cringe' when I see another [memo].")[13]

Burger, joined by Rehnquist, Stewart, and Stevens, believed that the constitutional issue should not be addressed and that the Court should affirm the California Supreme Court decision on Title VI grounds alone. Three other jurists, Marshall, Brennan, and White, believed that the decision had to be overturned on both Title VI and constitutional grounds: The special admissions plan was permissible under Title VI because race was used in a benign manner in an affirmative action program. As a matter of constitutional law, the UC Davis special admissions plan was not violative of the Fourteenth Amendment's equal-protection clause.

Two men had not yet taken formal positions in *Bakke:* Powell and Blackmun. Powell, by late November 1977, however, had circulated a memo in which he said that the Davis plan did violate the Fourteenth Amendment. But Powell also noted that if the Court *merely* affirmed the state court judgment without giving further guidance about when and under what circumstances race might be used in affirmative action programs, it would be shirking its responsibility. Powell believed that it was erroneous to hold, as the state court did, "that race may never be considered to any extent in admitting students to a university." He would remain firmly in the middle. Unlike Burger's quartet, Powell believed that race could be a factor—one of many—taken into account by a college or graduate school's admissions committee. However, unlike Marshall's trio, he rejected the view that the UC Davis program—as it stood, with race as the *only* factor—was constitutional. For the Virginian, the UC Davis scheme was too extreme a remedy for past racial discrimination.

And so, by the beginning of February 1978, the votes were split four (Burger et al.), one (Powell) to three (Marshall et al.). All were clearly awaiting Harry Blackmun's input after he recovered from surgery. But they all knew that even when Blackmun was extremely healthy, his speed at getting the Court's work done was truly "deliberate." Although there were four justices (Powell, Marshall, Brennan, and White) who agreed that admissions decisions using race as a factor were not unconstitutional per se, they were fiercely divided on what standard should be used to determine the validity of various affirmative action programs. All of the brethren, even the four who wanted to rule on statutory grounds only, had something to say about what standard should be used in reaching a constitutional judgment.

Burger and Rehnquist argued for strict scrutiny. (As did Powell when pushed to opt for a standard, which caused Marshall to become enraged at him.) Marshall argued for a much more flexible standard in these equal-protection cases where race was used in an affirmative fashion to end caste/race discrimination in education. Brennan was in the middle, arguing for an intermediate standard of review. Justice White applied the strict-scrutiny test to the UC Davis program and came up with a different conclusion than Burger's. He found that the medical school preferential admission program passed the strict-scrutiny test. A compelling state interest was served by the admissions program, and there were no alternatives that would have served the important state goals.

Tempers grew frayed in April, as the justices waited for Blackmun and were increasingly angered by one another's hardening positions in *Bakke*. There were few personal interactions; most of the debate took place through memos and the circulation of draft opinions. During these tension-filled days, Brennan saw Marshall as an increasingly bitter and angry man. He commented that his colleague "had been extremely sensitive the entire Term regarding the Court's approach to the *Bakke* issue. He was livid over Powell's [draft] opinion which he regarded as racist."[14]

They were just not getting it, Marshall observed privately and then openly in a memo to his colleagues—a strong statement (an even tougher one was not sent) from the Court's outsider to the other justices. "I repeat, for the next to the last time," he began, "the decision in this case depends on whether you consider the action of the Regents as *admitting* certain students or as *excluding* certain other students." If his colleagues saw *Bakke* as admitting selected students, "then this is affirmative action to remove the vestiges of slavery and state imposed segregation by 'root and branch.' If you view the program as excluding students, it is a program of 'quotas' which violates the principle that 'the Constitution is color-blind.'" When the Court, in *Plessy*, explicitly rejected the principle of color-blindness, cases like *Bakke* were inevitable. Between 1896 and 1954, "ours was a nation where, by law, individuals could be given 'special' treatment based on race." He continued,

> For us now to say that the principle of color-blindness prevents the University from giving "special" consideration to race when this Court, in 1896 licensed the states to continue to consider race, is to make a mockery of the principle of "equal justice under law."…We are not yet all equals, in large part because of the refusal of the *Plessy* Court to adopt the principle of color-blindness. It would be the cruelest irony for this Court to adopt the dissent in *Plessy* now and hold that the University must use color-blind admissions.

Marshall then addressed the question of whether African Americans had "arrived." (In an earlier conference, Rehnquist had noted that great progress had been made by black Americans since 1954.)

> Just a few examples illustrate that Negroes most certainly have not. In our own Court, we have had only three Negro law clerks, and not so far have we had a Negro Officer of the Court. On a broader scale…the economic disparity between the races is increasing.…The gulf was brought about by centuries of slavery and then by another century in which, with the approval of this Court, states were permitted to treat Negroes "specially."…The dream of America as

the melting pot has not been realized by Negroes—either the Negro did not get into the pot, or he did not get melted down.

His deep anger at the obliviousness of his colleagues about the true condition of African Americans was expressed in the unsent portion of the draft of this memo: "Despite the fact that most if not all of the medical schools of this country have not enforced racial exclusion in recent years, the [Regents] found it had a new state medical school *with no Negro students!* They sought to remedy that situation effectively. So, we have this case with a lousy record and poorly reasoned court opinions. We must decide it." [15] To say that there was a muted response would be an overstatement. No one responded to Marshall's "cry from the heart" memo, not even Brennan. A few weeks later, another memo was received by the brethren, this one from the heretofore silent jurist, Harry Blackmun. Blackmun announced his views—and thanked Marshall for his tart, biting opinion.

Although he had returned to the Court in January 1978, Harry Blackmun had remained silent about the issues raised in *Bakke*—and about his decision in the case. Blackmun finally spoke on May 1, 1978. As someone noted afterwards, correctly, "it appears to have been Marshall's opinion that most affected Blackmun." [16] Brennan had said that "in April, the only wish shared by all the brethren regarding *Bakke* was that Harry cast his vote." [17] Brennan and Marshall got their wish granted as Harry Blackmun came down four-square on their side of the affirmative action issue. And it was a position he maintained throughout the years the three men sat on the Court. After reading the tons of paper on *Bakke* written by his brethren, especially Marshall's tough draft opinion, "and having given the matter earnest and, as some of my clerical friends would say, 'prayerful' consideration," Blackmun joined Brennan, Marshall, and White. What he said pleased Marshall more than anything any of his colleagues, including Brennan, said in the *Bakke* discussions.

Blackmun wrote that Title VI did not prohibit UC Davis's type of race-conscious special admissions program. He wrote that affirmative actions were necessary and not inconsistent with the Fourteenth Amendment. Addressing Rehnquist's abstract, rigid world, Blackmun stated, simply, "this is not an ideal world....We live in a real world." Blackmun understood what Marshall was trying to get the brethren to comprehend. For him, "Title VI, as with the Fourteenth Amendment, was concerned with the unconstitutional use of race criteria, not with the use of race as an appropriate remedial feature." Addressing the abstract notions of equality that Rehnquist relied on, Blackmun wrote:

> The original aims [of the Fourteenth Amendment] persist. And that, in a distinct sense, is what affirmative action, in the light of proper facts, is all about.

To be sure, it conflicts with idealistic equality in the sense that Bill Rehnquist proposes, but if there is tension here it is original Fourteenth Amendment tension and a part of the Amendment's very nature until equality is achieved....It is the unconstitutional use of race that is prohibited, not the constitutional use.

As he read the lengthy memo, Marshall was pleased that at least one of his colleagues had gotten the message he had sent three weeks earlier. It was in the final paragraph of his letter explaining his position that Blackmun credited Marshall with helping him reach it. "There is much to be said for Marshall's 'cruelest irony' approach as set forth in his memorandum of April 13," he concluded.

With Blackmun's thoughts now on the table, the Court was clearly split four-one-four. "It was immediately apparent that Blackmun's vote, if it could be counted upon, meant at least a partial victory for the view I had championed," Brennan decided after reading the Blackmun memo. The Court was now ready to have the opinion assigned and written.

Given the fractionated voting, Burger, as Chief Justice, would make the assignment. Brennan, the senior associate justice, knowing of Burger's "use [of the] assignment power in an unorthodox manner in other important cases," went to the Chief and suggested that Powell write the opinion. Powell was suggested because he was the only one of the nine justices "not in partial dissent." It was an unbelievably difficult task; he had to "find a common ground on which five could join with respect to both parts of the judgment." [18]

On May 2, 1978, the day after the brethren received and read Powell's letter, they received a memo from the Chief. Burger wrote:

> Given the posture of this case, Bill Brennan and I conferred with a view to considering what may fairly be called a "joint" assignment. There being four definitive decisions tending one way, four another, Lewis's position can be joined in part by some or all of each "four group." Accordingly, the case is assigned to Lewis who assures a first circulation within one week from today. [19]

Clearly, at this point and thereafter, the key justice in *Bakke* was Lewis Powell. He was to say, at the time of his retirement in 1986, that *Bakke* "was his most important opinion." [20] According to his biographer, Powell had resolved the affirmative action questions very early on in the *Bakke* discussions. He believed that it would be disastrous for the nation if the Court invalidated affirmative action programs. "On the other hand," Powell said, "it would be equally disastrous to give carte blanche for racial preferences [such as the UC Davis plan]." [21]

His support for some type of affirmative action came as a surprise to his colleagues. As a former school board administrator involved with desegregation of

the public schools, Powell "did no more than was required to hasten desegregation. On the great question of busing, he resolutely opposed minority aspirations....For this unresisting heir to the traditions of white supremacy to have
endorsed *reverse* discrimination would have been...inconceivable. Yet on the
Court he did just that." As a "pragmatic conservative," Powell accepted affirmative action, as he had accepted *Brown* in 1954, because it was necessary to do so.[22]
Within the week, by May 10, 1978, Powell had circulated a draft opinion.
Immediately, Brennan and Marshall told Powell they could not accept any of it
because he had used the strict-scrutiny standard to strike down the UC Davis
program (while agreeing with them that race could be considered as one of a
number of factors in university admissions programs).

Powell's use of the strict-scrutiny standard in *Bakke,* even though the university's discrimination was the central element in a remedial effort to improve professional opportunities for minorities, was at the very least insensitive, thought
Marshall. Furthermore, the expression of his views seemed patently racist to
Marshall. Powell had written (and was to leave the sentences in the final version), for example, that "it is far too late to argue that the guarantee of equal protection to *all* persons permits the recognition of special wards entitled to a degree
of protection greater than that accorded others. The Fourteenth Amendment is
not directed solely against discrimination due to a 'two-class theory'—that is,
based upon differences between white and Negro."

Marshall had fought legal battles for decades against gentrified education
board lawyers like Powell in Virginia, Mississippi, Alabama, and Georgia, precisely because of "racial discrimination due to a 'two-class theory.'" Powell, in
Marshall's view, retained "remnants of old [Southern ways and] attitudes." He
earned Marshall's disdain because he

> still had a gentleman's sense of responsibility for the less fortunate and a south-
> erner's instinct for paternalism toward blacks. No southerner could readily deny
> that blacks needed help, as the excesses of the past and the region were too
> familiar to ignore. The upper-class sense of *noblesse oblige* and the southerner's
> assumption of white control and responsibility conspired to the same conclu-
> sion: Racial justice required racial preference.[23]

These Southern traits of Powell's enraged Marshall, even though he understood what the Powell position on affirmative action meant for black Americans
and other minorities. Marshall wrote to him: "I will dissent 'in toto.' I doubt that
I can join any part of your opinion." The terrible irony in this horribly strained
relationship was that Marshall *knew* that without Powell's vote in *Bakke* (and in
affirmative action litigation that followed), all affirmative action programs would

have been killed then and there. Powell's was "the key vote." What galled Marshall was that "he owed his victory to the Court's lone southerner, a former segregationist and consistent foe of forced busing, the Justice whose background seemed least likely to produce the decisive vote for affirmative action."[24]

Without Powell's opinion on the value of racial preferences, strongly held from beginning to end, *"Bakke* would probably have been the death-knell of all voluntary affirmative action programs....It would have dealt as serious a blow to integration as *Plessy v. Ferguson."*[25]

Brennan, the Court's wizard of compromise and negotiation, knew that if Powell's opinion could not be fixed and if he could not lead a unified "gang of four" on behalf of UC Davis's plan, the affirmative action remedy, practiced across the nation in education and in employment, would be in jeopardy. And so he got to work on two fronts. He tried to persuade Powell (though ultimately he was largely unsuccessful) to modify his opinion, especially Powell's use of the strict-scrutiny standard with its racist implications. He also redrafted his proposed joint opinion to better reflect the views of the other three justices. Brennan wrote to White, one of the "gang of four": "I repeat I am determined to do what I possibly can to have Harry, you and I and, if possible at all, to have Marshall agree on a joint opinion."[26]

As a result of Brennan's herculean negotiating efforts, by the beginning of June, Marshall did finally join Brennan's opinion and he did accept, although not without considerable resistance, a portion of Powell's opinion. Of Marshall's joining the gang at the end, Brennan had only this to say: "Why he changed his initial adamant view that he would not join is still a puzzle to me."[27] However, Marshall, as well as Blackmun and White, wrote separate opinions in *Bakke.* In the end, there was no opinion of the Court because there were no five justices who joined any opinion in its entirety. Instead, there was a "bifurcated" judgment of the Court announced by Powell, with each of the groups of four joining in only a portion of his judgment.

From October to June, the justices debated the issue of affirmative action. They and their clerks had plowed through the fifty-eight *amicus curiae* briefs that had been filed with the Court, including one on behalf of Bakke by a young lawyer practicing in Seattle, Marco DeFunis, the plaintiff in *DeFunis v. Odegaard,* who was representing Young Americans for Freedom, a conservative pressure group. There was also the large amount of paper the justices generated themselves.

Finally, *Bakke* was ready to come down. There were six separate opinions written, totaling 154 pages in the *U.S. Supreme Court Reports,* and announced in Court on June 28, 1978. Powell presented the judgment of the Court, concluding that the UC Davis special admissions program unconstitutionally denied

Bakke equal protection and that therefore the California Supreme Court order admitting Bakke to the medical school was a valid one. These sections of his judgment were joined by Burger, Stewart, Rehnquist, and Stevens. But Powell also wrote that universities and colleges *could* develop an admissions formula that took the race of an applicant into account, and, in an appendix, he offered Harvard's admission program as an example. Powell was joined in these segments of his opinion by the other gang of four: Brennan, Marshall, White, and Blackmun.

Stevens wrote for Burger, Rehnquist, and Stewart, concluding that Bakke was excluded from UC Davis in violation of Title VI and there was no need to reach the constitutional question. Brennan wrote for his group of four, concluding that the UC Davis plan was valid in every respect, whether from the Title VI perspective or from the Fourteenth Amendment's equal-protection guideline. Justices Blackmun and White wrote brief separate opinions. Marshall wrote a much longer opinion in partial dissent.

Brennan's opinion from the bench reflected his group's views on the matter of affirmative action: "The *central meaning* of today's opinions is this: Government may take race into account when it acts not to demean or insult any racial group, but to remedy disadvantages cast on minorities by past racial prejudice, at least when appropriate findings have been made by judicial, legislative, or administrative bodies with competence to act in this area."

Brennan's introductory paragraph was technically correct, for his faction plus Powell added up to five, a Court majority on the issue of treating the race of a candidate affirmatively. (Since Brennan's group disagreed with Powell's view that the UC Davis admissions plan was unconstitutional, there was no "majority" opinion.) However, the placement and the language used by Brennan angered the other faction. Justice Stevens, in his opinion, noted that "it is hardly necessary to state that only a majority can speak for the Court or determine what is the 'central meaning' of any judgment of the Court." But Blackmun's brief concurring and dissenting opinion in the case gratified Marshall immensely. In a moving statement, he wrote: "in order to get beyond racism, we must take account of race. There is no other way."

Marshall's separate opinion in *Bakke* publicly revealed the thoughts he had shared privately with the brethren in his April 13 draft opinion. It was a lengthy one that recapitulated the shameful history of three centuries of "denial of human rights" to African Americans. He described the "enforced segregation of the races" from post–Civil War times "well into the middle of the twentieth century." Recent history, Marshall wrote, demonstrated that "the position of the Negro today in America is the tragic but inevitable consequence of centuries of unequal treatment. Measured by any benchmark of comfort or achievement, meaningful equality remains a distant dream for the Negro." Finally it was time to criticize the Court for their actions in *Bakke*. "The racism of our society has been so pervasive that *none*, regardless of wealth or position, has managed to escape its impact." In the end, he summed up what he had tried, unsuccessfully, to demonstrate to others on the Court: "If we are ever to become a fully integrated society, one in which the color of a person's skin will not determine the opportunities available to him or her, we must be willing to take steps to open these doors. I do not believe that anyone can truly look into America's past and still find that a remedy for the effects of that past is impermissible."

Following the Court's *Bakke* announcement came the press headlines. Conservative newspapers trumpeted the fact that the UC Davis affirmative action plan was invalidated by the Court. "WHITE STUDENT WINS REVERSE BIAS CASE; Justices OK Some Racial Preferences," shouted the *Chicago Sun-Times* headline. And *The Wall Street Journal* stated, in its fashion, correctly, that *Bakke* was "The Decision Everyone Won."

Liberal newspapers focused on the other side of the *Bakke* opinion. "High Court Backs Some Affirmative Action by Colleges, But Orders Bakke Admitted," headlined *The New York Times*, while the *Washington Post* stated in bold letters: "AFFIRMATIVE ACTION UPHELD: Court Orders School to Admit Bakke, Curbs Racial Quotas." And *Time* magazine put it simply and accurately: "Quotas, No; Race, Yes." Marshall would continue to defend the use of affirmative action programs. He believed it was vital to continue supporting these remedial programs for as long as it took to overcome centuries of racial discrimination and racial preferences for whites. Almost a dozen other affirmative action plans would be examined by the Court after *Bakke*.

## THE CONSTITUTIONALITY OF COURT-ORDERED AFFIRMATIVE ACTION PROGRAMS

As a consequence of an African American firefighter successfully suing the Memphis, Tennessee, fire department because of its racially discriminatory hiring and promotion practices, a federal court order issued in 1980 required that 50 percent of all new firefighters hired be African American until they made up 40 percent of the force. A budget cut in 1981 forced the city, with concurrence from the union, to reduce personnel on a "last-hired, first-fired" seniority basis, effectively targeting the new black firefighters. A suit was brought in federal court to enjoin the city from so proceeding. The federal court ordered the city to handle the reductions in accord with the original affirmative action decree. Three whites were fired, firemen more senior than the African Americans who remained. The city, with the union, appealed to the Supreme Court.

In *Firefighters Local Union 1784 v. Stotts* (1984), a six-to-three opinion written by Justice White, with Marshall, Brennan, and Blackmun in dissent, held that Title VII of the 1964 Civil Rights Act "protects bona fide seniority systems" unless evidence showed that the seniority plan was intentionally discriminatory or caused actual discrimination against individual African Americans. Absent such evidence, setting aside a seniority system for remedial purposes violated Title VII of the Civil Rights Act. Blackmun wrote the dissent on procedural grounds—the layoffs had been rescinded, no one had been injured, and therefore the issue was moot.

Many critics of affirmative action called this Court decision the "death knell" of affirmative action programs in America. U.S. Solicitor General Rex Lee, for one, appointed by President Reagan, "called *Stotts* a 'slam dunk' decision against affirmative action."[28] However, two years later the Court moved in another direction.

*Local 28, Sheet Metal Workers, v. EEOC* and *Local 93, International Association of Firefighters, v. City of Cleveland* involved lower federal court orders directing specific affirmative action hiring in New York City and in Cleveland. The New York case was a six-to-three decision, with Brennan writing the decision and with Burger, Rehnquist, and White in dissent. The Cleveland case was a five-to-four decision with Brennan, again, writing for the majority and recently appointed justice Sandra Day O'Connor joining Burger, Rehnquist, and White in dissent.

In the New York case, a federal judge issued an order that required a local sheet-metal union to meet a specific minority hiring target of 29 percent (which was the percentage of minority workers in the local workforce). Brennan's opinion upheld the order, on the grounds that there was nothing in Title VII that prohibited federal district courts from establishing a remedy such as "hiring goals and timetables [even if they] might incidentally benefit individuals who are not the actual victims of [past] discrimination." The relief ordered by the federal judge after the union refused to comply was "narrowly tailored to further the Government's compelling interest in remedying past discrimination," Powell concurred, supporting the federal judge's action because of the union's "particularly egregious conduct." All four dissenters, however, found the decision "simply incredible," with Rehnquist's dissent claiming that Brennan's opinion blatantly validated a minority hiring quota forbidden by Title VII of the 1964 Civil Rights Act.

In the Cleveland case, an agreement between city officials and African American and Hispanic firemen, ratified by a federal judge's consent decree, led to the establishment of racial goals and quotas for the hiring and promotion of firemen, including promotion of an African American when a white firefighter was promoted. The dissenters argued that the Civil Rights Act legitimized only federal court orders that remedied complaints of individuals who alleged specific, individualized racial discrimination in hiring or promotion.

For the majority, Brennan validated the court-approved plan, arguing in his opinion that the 1964 Civil Rights Act was not violated by the voluntary consent agreement that benefited a class of persons: in this case minority firefighters. Brennan wrote that Congress had not limited relief only to actual victims of discrimination but intentionally vested "district courts with broad discretion to award 'appropriate' equitable relief to remedy unlawful discrimination." These two 1986 cases caused significant divisions among the justices, divisions reflected in ten opinions and over 150 pages in the *Supreme Court Reports*.

In 1987 the Court heard *United States v. Paradise*, in which a deeply divided Court ruled, for the very first time, that federal district court judges could order strict racial quotas for promotion purposes, in order to "overcome long-term, open and pervasive discrimination." A federal district court judge in Alabama, in 1983 and 1984, had ordered the state police to carry out an affirmative action plan as the result of a suit brought by African American state troopers who claimed racial discrimination in promotion policy and practice within the department. The judge, noting that not one of the 232 Alabama state troopers with the rank of corporal or higher was black, ordered the promotion of one black trooper, if otherwise qualified, for each white trooper promoted by the state police, until the department developed a promotion plan that was approved by the federal court.

Brennan, joined by Marshall and Blackmun, wrote the opinion giving the Court's "judgment" (fewer than five brethren agreed on the reasons for so ruling). He found that the racial quota plan supported a "compelling governmental interest in remedying past and present racial discrimination." It was a flexible plan, whose requirements could be waived if there were no available black candidates and if it was applied only when the department needed to make promotions.

Powell and Stevens gave Brennan the votes necessary to make a majority, although they wrote separate concurring opinions. Powell departed from his view of quotas in *Bakke*, but justified his position in *Paradise* by noting that the state police "had engaged in persistent violation of constitutional rights and repeatedly failed to carry out court orders." Furthermore, the federal judge's quota order was "short in duration [and] the effect on innocent white workers [was] likely to be relatively diffuse."

There were four dissenters who joined in two dissenting opinions. One was written by White, who maintained that the federal judge had exceeded his constitutional and statutory authority by ordering the implementation by the state police of a strict quota. O'Connor wrote the other dissent, joined by Chief

Justice Burger and Justices Rehnquist and Scalia. She argued that while the federal district court judge had the discretion to fashion a remedy, it had to be one that was "narrowly tailored." In this case, however, there was an "extreme quota" that was unconstitutionally broad and beyond the judge's constitutional discretionary equity powers.

As in *Bakke,* Powell cast the critical vote in these court-ordered affirmative action programs and was in the majority in every one, as well as in other affirmative action litigation. Except for *Stotts,* which was a murky case, Marshall, voting with Brennan and Blackmun in all these cases, saw most of the court-ordered affirmative action plans validated by the Court.

## ARE "VOLUNTARY" AFFIRMATIVE ACTION PLANS CONSTITUTIONAL?

*United Steelworkers v. Weber,* a 1979 case before the Court, concerned a voluntary affirmative action plan implemented at the Kaiser Aluminum and Chemical Corporation plant in Gramercy, Louisiana. A year after *Bakke,* the Court majority validated the voluntary effort by the company to redress its racially discriminatory hiring and promotion practices. The plan, as approved by the company and the union, set aside half of the spaces in a small on-the-job training program.

Brian Weber, a white employee at the plant, was not able to enter the program and brought suit in federal district court arguing that the affirmative action plan was an unconstitutional racial quota prohibited by Title VII of the 1964 Civil Rights Act. The district court and the federal appellate court ruled in Weber's favor, finding that Title VII did specifically prohibit preferential treatment in employment.

The Supreme Court, however, in a five-to-two decision called by one observer "astonishing,"[29] overturned the lower court judgments and validated the affirmative action program. (Justices Powell and Stevens did not participate in the discussions and vote.) Brennan again wrote for the majority, which included Marshall, Stewart, White, and Blackmun, concluding that while the lower federal courts had followed the letter of the law in their rulings, they had not followed the *spirit* of the 1964 Civil Rights Act.

Chief Justice Burger and Rehnquist vehemently dissented. Burger accused the majority of judicial legislation, of fundamentally changing the content of Title VII in order to validate the preferential job training program. "Congress expressly *prohibited* the discrimination against Brian Weber," he wrote. He concluded by accusing the majority of "totally rewriting a crucial part" of the civil rights legislation to achieve "a good result." Rehnquist labeled Brennan's legal gyrations comparable to those of Harry Houdini. In his dissent, he wrote that

Brennan's opinion "introduced a tolerance for the very evil that the law was intended to eradicate.... The Court has sown the wind. Later courts will face the impossible task of reaping the whirlwind."

A few years later, in a 1986 case from Michigan, *Wygant v. Jackson, Michigan, Board of Education,* the Court divided five-to-four in another layoff plan keyed to race. At the conference session after oral argument, the Court seemed evenly divided. Four jurists (Burger, Powell, White, and Rehnquist) voted to reverse the lower court judgment in favor of the plan, and another four voted to affirm (Brennan, Blackmun, Stevens, and Marshall), with O'Connor voting to vacate. In late November 1985, Brennan saw that Burger had assigned *Wygant* to Powell. "I must assume," he wrote to Marshall, Blackmun, and Stevens, "that since the conference Sandra has joined the Chief.... I take it there will have to be a dissent to whatever Lewis circulates. May I ask, Thurgood, if you will take the dissent?" Marshall responded with alacrity: "I will be happy to do the dissent in this one."[30]

The Court majority struck down the Michigan school board's voluntary plan for laying off teachers that gave preference to minority faculty over more-senior white faculty. Such a plan was in violation of the Fourteenth Amendment's equal-protection clause, Powell argued. The school board had not presented compelling reasons for the plan, nor had they "narrowly tailored" its use of the racial criterion to remedy past discriminatory hiring practices. In comments off the point of law, Powell did write, however, that "in order to remedy the effects of prior discrimination it may be necessary to take race into account, [even though] innocent persons may be called upon to bear some of the burdens of the remedy."

Like *Bakke,* the *Wygant* case produced deep division among the jurists, and six opinions. Justice O'Connor wrote the critical concurring opinion. In opposition to other justices, who viewed Title VII relief in narrow terms, she noted that affirmative action programs could be devised "that need not be limited to the remedying of specific instances of identified discrimination." Justice White, also concurring, thought that none of the Court's affirmative action precedents supported "the discharge of white teachers to make room for blacks, none of whom has been shown to be a victim of racial discrimination."

Marshall's dissent in *Wygant,* joined by Brennan and Blackmun, employed his flexible standard to reach the conclusion that the school board plan's layoffs were "substantially related to important governmental objectives." The "goal of easing racial tension was an acceptable governmental objective whether or not the elimination of societal discrimination was a permissible governmental interest."[31] The fourth dissenter, John Paul Stevens, argued that the plan was constitutional because it advanced educational goals by having African American schoolteachers as role models for minority students in the school system. In this case,

Stevens had accepted Marshall's rationale for the necessity of affirmative action programs and was to remain allied with Marshall and the pro-preference group of justices until Marshall left the Court.

A year after *Wygant,* the Court, in a 1987 case from Santa Clara County, California, *Johnson v. Transportation Agency,* validated another voluntarily developed and implemented affirmative action program. Paul Johnson, a white male who had been employed by the county agency for fourteen years, was passed over for a promotion to road dispatcher and the job was given, for the very first time, to a woman, Diane Joyce, even though he had scored higher on a civil service test than Joyce. Under its guidelines, the Transportation Agency could factor into the promotion decision the gender of a person. However, there was no specific goal or quota that the agency had to follow. Could a public employer, in light of Title VII of the Civil Rights Act, voluntarily adopt an affirmative action program, one that allowed factors such as race and sex to be considered in hiring and promotion decisions?

Brennan, again writing for the majority of six, and following the suggestions in *Bakke,* concluded that an agency, in an effort to end past discrimination in hiring and promotions, could voluntarily take race *and* gender into consideration. Brennan wrote that the plan was "consistent with Title VII's purpose of eliminating the effects of employment discrimination." He concluded, "Given the obvious imbalance in the skilled craft division and given the agency's commitment to eliminating such imbalances, it was appropriate to consider as one fact the sex of Ms. Joyce in making the decision." Marshall joined in Brennan's opinion, as did Blackmun and, interestingly, Powell. Justices O'Connor and Stevens concurred, writing separate opinions. Justice O'Connor was uncomfortable with Brennan's ruling, but concurred "in light of our precedents." For her, the weight of precedent was central to her jurisprudence and it prevailed in *Johnson,* even though she believed that Brennan's view was "an expansive and ill-defined approach to voluntary affirmative action."

There were three dissenters: Chief Justice Rehnquist and Associate Justices White and Scalia. White, who had joined Brennan's opinion in *Weber,* now thought that Brennan had gone too far. Scalia's dissent was typically biting and withering. He claimed that *Johnson* "effectively requires employers, public as well as private, to engage in intentional discrimination on the basis of race or sex." Given Johnson's message, it would be "economic folly" for employers *not* to engage in reverse discrimination. Title VII was no longer viable: "the only losers in the process are the Johnsons of the country, for whom Title VII has not been merely repealed, but actually inverted. The irony is that these individuals—predominantly unknown, unaffluent, unorganized—suffer this injustice at the hands of a court fond of thinking itself the champion of the politically impotent."

In these voluntary affirmative action programs that were challenged in the courts, the justices concluded that they were not violative of either the civil rights statutes or the Fourteenth Amendment's prohibitions, unless the plan was seen as overly broad. The Court majority's message, to school boards, government agencies, and private firms alike, was that race- and gender-preferential hiring and promotion plans were constitutional so long as they were seen as "narrowly tailored" to address the effects of past racial and gender discrimination.

## GOVERNMENT CONTRACTING AND LICENSING AND AFFIRMATIVE ACTION GOALS

The Court, in the socially divisive affirmative action decade after *Bakke,* also had to tackle the question of whether federal and state affirmative action programs that *set aside* public funds for contracts to be given to minority firms doing business with government were constitutional. The first case to reach the Court was one in 1980 involving a 1977 federal law, the Public Works Employment Act, that set aside 10 percent of a $4 billion public works program for MCBs, "minority-controlled businesses." The legislation defined an MCB as one in which African Americans, Hispanic Americans, Oriental Americans, Native Americans, Eskimos, or Aleuts controlled at least a 50 percent interest in the company.

In a 1980 litigation, *Fullilove v. Klutznick,* Chief Justice Burger, surprisingly, wrote the plurality opinion that upheld the validity of the set-aside funding for MCBs. Using a form of strict scrutiny to determine whether the legislation was valid, he argued that Congress had the power to pass such legislation and that the statute did not run afoul of the equal-protection component of the Fifth Amendment's due-process clause. The legislation, wrote the Chief, was constitutional. "The limited use of racial and ethnic criteria, in the context of the case presented, is a constitutionally permissible *means* for achieving the congressional objectives." When acting in a remedial manner, Congress was not bound to act "in a wholly 'color-blind' fashion."

It was another divided, multi-opinion "judgment" of the Court. However, there were six justices who agreed on the result from the beginning of the discussions and remained committed to that result. The Court did vote six-to-three, but there was only a judgment of the Court, written by Burger and joined by White and Powell, because the six could not agree on the rationale and the standard to use in adjudicating the affirmative action issue. Powell, who also concurred separately, applied his strict-scrutiny standard and concluded that the congressional set-aside program was "justified as a remedy that serves the compelling interest in eradicating the continuing effects of past discrimination identified by Congress."

One of Marshall's law clerks, Philip Frickey, in a bench memo about *Fullilove*, wrote that the case was "more important than *Bakke*, since it involved an affirmative action plan developed by Congress."[32] Marshall concurred in the Court's judgment and was joined by Brennan and Blackmun. Using his more flexible standard, Marshall said: "the racial classifications employed in the set-aside provision are *substantially related* to the achievement of the important and congressionally articulated goal of remedying the present effects of past racial discrimination."

The dissenters were Justices Stewart, Rehnquist, and Stevens. Stewart's dissent, joined by Rehnquist, bluntly labeled the majority's decision "racist." Condemning his colleagues, Stewart said that the decision was "wrong for the same reason *Plessy v. Ferguson* was wrong." He called the controversial legislation an "invidious discrimination by government," and concluded by insisting that "our Constitution is color-blind, and neither knows nor tolerates classes among citizens." Justice Stevens also wrote a dissent. His scathing comments called the legislation and the majority's support for it a "perverse form of reparation.... Our statute books," he said bitterly, "will once again have to contain laws that reflect the odious practice of delineating the qualities that make one person a Negro and make another a white."

Eight years later, however, Stevens would concur in another set-aside case coming to the Court from Richmond, Virginia, Lewis Powell's hometown. (By then Powell was no longer on the Court, having been replaced in 1988 by Justice Anthony Kennedy.) In *City of Richmond, Virginia, v. Croson* (1989), the majority struck down as unconstitutional a 1983 minority set-aside affirmative action ordinance that dedicated 30 percent of its local construction funds for Minority Business Enterprises (MBEs). Half the city's population was African American, but only 1 percent of the over $25 million awarded in city contracts went to minority businesses. The set-aside plan was patterned after the federal law validated in *Fullilove*. Richmond, the capital of the Confederacy during the Civil War, was making a good-faith attempt to remedy past and present racial discrimination in this area of the local business economy.

However, the six-to-three Court that had validated the federal statute in 1980 was now rather different in its composition. In 1989, when *Croson* was heard, the three recently appointed Reagan justices—O'Connor, Scalia, and Kennedy—made a dramatic difference.

And so in *Croson* the vote was also six to three, but this time the six-person majority, including the three justices appointed after *Fullilove*, *invalidated* a set-aside program. The six separate opinions written in *Croson* reflected the continued disagreements among the justices over the constitutionality of affirmative action. Justice O'Connor wrote the opinion for the Court, joined by only

Rehnquist, White, and Kennedy. Justices Stevens, Kennedy, and Scalia wrote separate concurring opinions. Marshall wrote a dissent, joined by Brennan and Blackmun. Justice Blackmun wrote a separate dissent, joined by Brennan.

O'Connor's opinion striking down the Richmond set-aside effort focused in part on the differences between the sources of federal authority and state authority. The city of Richmond could not do what Congress did in 1977 because the state was bound by the "constraints" of the Fourteenth Amendment while Congress had "a specific constitutional mandate to enforce the dictates of the Fourteenth Amendment. The power to 'enforce' may at times also include the power to define situations which *Congress* determines threaten principles of equality and to adopt prophylactic rules to deal with those situations." Furthermore, Richmond's effort to remedy past racial discrimination was rigid and overinclusive at the same time, leading to "stigmatic harm," and for those reasons was unconstitutional. Past history, "standing alone, cannot justify a rigid quota in the awarding of public contracts in Richmond, Virginia." In concluding, O'Connor noted, "we think it obvious that such a program is not narrowly tailored to remedy the effects of prior discrimination." Because Richmond "failed to identify the need for remedial action in the awarding of its public construction contracts, its treatment of its citizens on a racial basis violates the dictates of the Equal Protection Clause."

Kennedy's concurrence, like Scalia's, addressed the "moral imperative of racial neutrality" as "the driving force of the Equal Protection Clause." The Fourteenth Amendment's "color-blindness" center was transformed, through their interpretation, into a core concept of "race neutrality." However, neither concept, for Kennedy and Scalia, allowed a state or a city "to act affirmatively to ameliorate the effects of past discrimination"—unless there was an identifiable victim of state racial discrimination.

Harry Blackmun's dissent was short and unusually acerbic. "I never thought that I would live to see the day when the city of Richmond, Virginia, the cradle of the Old Confederacy, sought on its own, within a narrow confine, to lessen the stark impact of persistent discrimination. But Richmond, to its great credit, acted. Yet this Court, the supposed bastion of equality, strikes down Richmond's efforts as though discrimination had never existed or was not demonstrated in this particular litigation."

Marshall dissented from the majority's "shallowness," and again he was joined by Brennan and Blackmun. *Croson* was "a deliberate and giant step backward in this Court's affirmative action jurisprudence." Race-conscious remedies that "serve important governmental objectives" and that are "substantively related to the achievement of these objectives" are constitutional, he maintained. He condemned the "majority's perfunctory dismissal" of the testimony of Richmond's appointed and elected leaders. This "armchair cynicism" of his colleagues in the majority was "deeply disturbing" to Marshall. Their failure to comprehend what was really going on in Richmond led them to minimize, to trivialize, the effects of past segregation and racial discrimination.

This case, wrote one of Marshall's clerks, "scarred" Marshall's heart. As he said in his dissent, the majority "sounds a full-scale retreat from the Court's long-standing solicitude for race conscious remedial efforts." It was the "civil rights massacre of 1989."[33] The majority still continued to maintain, Marshall wrote, that "racial discrimination [was] largely a phenomenon of the past, and that government bodies need no longer to preoccupy themselves with rectifying racial injustice."

However, only one year later, in what would be Bill Brennan's "last hurrah" in affirmative action litigation (he retired because of ill health at the end of the Court's 1989–90 term), the Court zigzagged once again on the question of governmental set-asides for minorities and women. *Metro Broadcasting v. FCC* involved a controversial Federal Communications Commission (FCC) policy promulgated in 1978 that gave minorities an opportunity to purchase licenses for radio and television stations. The FCC assigned a new UHF television channel to the Orlando, Florida, area. Of the three companies filing competing applications for the license, Rainbow Broadcasting was a minority-owned firm and, under the FCC guidelines, it was awarded the channel. The other two non-minority firms brought suit in federal court, charging that the FCC policy violated the equal-protection component of the Fifth Amendment's due-process clause.

Justice Brennan, for a five-person majority, upheld the constitutionality of the FCC policies. As usual, Marshall joined him, as did Harry Blackmun. The aged crafter of majority consensus wrote that "benign race conscious measures mandated by Congress—even if those measures are not 'remedial' in the sense of being designed to compensate victims of past governmental or societal discrimination—are constitutionally permissible to the extent that they serve important governmental objectives within the power of Congress and are substantively related to achievement of these objectives." There was an "empirical nexus" between minority ownership and broadcasting diversity. Further, "the FCC has determined that increased minority participation in broadcasting promotes programming diversity." Brennan then concluded by stating that the policies the agency created were substantively related to the governmental objective and offered an appropriate remedy because "long experience demonstrated [to the FCC] that race-neutral means could not produce adequate broadcasting diversity."

What was unusual was that White also concurred, as did Stevens. White concurred without saying a single word. Stevens wrote a concurring opinion that tried to distinguish *Metro* from his dissent in *Fullilove*. In the FCC case, Stevens admitted that it was an "extremely rare situation in which racial and ethnic characteristics" were applicable.

There were four dissenters in *Metro:* Chief Justice Rehnquist and Justices Scalia, Kennedy, and O'Connor. Two, O'Connor and Kennedy, wrote dissenting opinions. O'Connor's, joined by Rehnquist, Scalia, and Kennedy, noted that the Brennan majority opinion was a "departure [from *Croson* and] marks a renewed toleration of racial classifications and a repudiation of our recent affirmation that the Constitution's equal protection guarantees extend equally to all citizens. The Court's application of a lessened equal protection standard to congressional actions finds no support in our cases or in the Constitution. I respectfully dissent."

Kennedy's was a harsher dissent. It was hardly a respectful objection to Brennan's majority views. He hit Brennan, and especially Marshall, hard by comparing the majority opinion in *Metro* with the majority opinion in *Plessy.* The 1896 *Plessy* majority concluded that the equal but separate Louisiana legislation was a reasonable action of the lawmakers, and their "fundamental errors... distorted the law for six decades before the Court announced its apparent demise in *Brown.*" For Kennedy, there were "disturbing parallels [between *Plessy* and] today's majority opinion that should warn us that something is amiss here." He concluded the dissent in somber tones that deeply upset Marshall and the rest of the Brennan group: "History suggests much peril in...Government disfavoring some citizens and favoring others based on the color of their skin...and so the Constitution forbids us to undertake it. I regret that after a century of judicial opinions, we interpret the Constitution to do no more than move us from 'separate but equal' to 'unequal but benign.'"

## THE AFFIRMATIVE ACTION BATTLES

The affirmative action cases were extremely problematic for a number of the justices because, analytically, they were so different from earlier equal-protection cases heard by the Court. The strict-scrutiny standard was the one the Court applied in cases involving "suspect categories" such as race, alienage, and religion. In *Frontiero,* for example, Brennan and Marshall worked hard (but failed) to get the Court to agree that gender was a suspect classification, because such cases would then be subject to strict scrutiny by the Court. For the most part, a more lenient standard for adjudicating the affirmative action cases was developed and applied. During Marshall's remaining years after *Bakke,* ten major affirmative action cases were decided by the Court, involving a variety of race-conscious programmatic strategies. In seven of them, the race-conscious affirmative action plan was validated by five- and six-justice majorities.

Certainly the facts and the approaches to affirmative action in these cases were themselves always different. Some cases involved court-ordered race-conscious remedies, while others were voluntary private or public affirmative action plans. Some cases involved governmental contracting and licensing plans that were race-conscious, while others were plans for dealing with layoffs and firings. But the bottom line was that Marshall's position on affirmative action was the one often reflected in the Court's majority opinions. Even so, during the 1980s, the Burger Court and then the Rehnquist Court were "sharply divided" over the constitutionality of these different kinds of affirmative action programs. After all, some of the minority said (Rehnquist, Scalia, Kennedy), these contested race-conscious programs were actions that *did* discriminate on the basis of race, and the Fourteenth Amendment was race neutral or color-blind. Their view was that all such programs were unconstitutional.

On the other side were Brennan, Marshall, Blackmun, Stevens, and, to a much lesser extent, White, Stewart, and O'Connor, all of whom believed that there were either all or some narrowly tailored occasions on which race-conscious remedial programs were constitutional. And, ironically, there was the Virginian, Lewis Powell, whose votes were the decisive ones. "In nearly sixteen years on the Supreme Court, Powell never dissented in an affirmative action case. In every instance, his views prevailed—the only Justice of whom that can be said."[34] Powell participated in the deliberations and decisions of affirmative action cases from 1978 *(Bakke)* through 1987 *(Paradise)*. In four of those cases, affirmative action plans were validated by the Court; in two others, the plans were overturned by the Court—and there was *Bakke*.

Heated discussions among the justices about which standard should be used in these equal-protection affirmative action cases resulted from conflicting perceptions of race and racial discrimination in America. The strict-scrutiny jurists on the Court—Rehnquist, Burger, O'Connor, Scalia, and Kennedy—spoke also of the color-blindness and the race-neutrality norms at the center of the Fourteenth Amendment's equal-protection clause. Marshall could never convince them that the realities of race and racial discrimination in America made their views of the Fourteenth Amendment's intent quite mistaken and without a basis in historical fact. Marshall believed that "most racial discrimination was objectionable because of its particular purposes and its particular effects—that is, because it served to create and maintain a system of caste. When the use of race has quite different purposes and effects, it should be evaluated more leniently."[35] He believed that his colleagues' "constitutional assault on affirmative action 'perverted' the intent of the Framers by substituting abstract equality for the genuine equality the Amendment was intended to achieve."[36] Most of the battles over affirmative action, however, ended up with Marshall, Brennan, and the others in the "gang" victorious. It wasn't until Marshall retired in 1991 that the Court's affirmative action decisions moved in a very conservative direction.[37]

Marshall continually pleaded with his colleagues, especially Rehnquist, who regarded the Constitution as fundamentally color-blind, to recognize the "pervasive and ingrained effects of [three centuries of] racial discrimination in our society" that justified and necessitated affirmative action. Such remedial programs were necessary to "dismantle" the caste system in America that had robbed African Americans of their dignity as humans for centuries.[38] The effect of overturning these efforts in the name of an abstract ideal of genuine equality was to maintain institutional racism in education and in employment. He could not and did not forgive this application of an abstract notion of equality. His colleagues' insensitivity, he felt, bordered on racism, and it angered him until the day he died.

# 1 2

## PROCEDURAL FAIRNESS AND
## SUBSTANTIVE JUSTICE: REALITIES AND MYTHS

When Marshall joined the Court in 1967, he had already concluded that for black Americans, the poor, the illiterate, and the weak, the criminal justice system was a sham, a mockery of the Constitution and the Rule of Law. He had seen, close up, "first hand evidence of a frightening attitude by those who made and administered the laws—that there are people in the United States that just don't matter."[1] He spent years defending black Americans accused and convicted of crimes and treated in ways that violated all constitutionally and ethically derived notions of fairness and due process.

Marshall brought to the Supreme Court only those "legal defense cases... where there is injustice because of race or color, mob domination of the trials, [where] confessions were extorted by force and violence, [or where] the right of a defendant to a fair trial by a jury of his peers has long been established yet [as occurred in the South] Negroes have been systematically excluded from juries."[2] There were so many such legal travesties that he wrote an educational pamphlet on "legal defense" for the NAACP to distribute to its affiliates. What he wrote was shocking and explains Marshall's perennial concerns. There was no "absolute equality for Negroes in the courts of the land," he observed.

> As soon as it is discovered that a crime has been committed the local police seize a large number of Negroes without warrants and herd them to jail. They are held incommunicado and without formal charges or bail being fixed. They are all persistently questioned and tortured in an effort to make one or more of them "confess." Eventually some of the Negroes held are released...and the officers concentrate on the one left. [He] is placed in a dungeon without air, light, water or conveniences. His parents are arrested without warrants and held incommunicado. After being held in a dungeon for a week, the Negro is...

carried to police headquarters where he is beaten by the officers and strung up to the rafters in the ceiling until he "breaks." The Negro is then returned to the jail where a group of officials, not present at the beating, witness the fact that the confession is "free and voluntarily made." Then the Negro is formally charged for the first time. He is speedily tried and this "confession" is used to convict him.

This description of unfair and unconstitutional police and prosecutorial action, leading up to a "speedy" trial for a poor, often illiterate African American defendant was not hypothetical, Marshall told Wilkins when he sent him the report. "The facts in this typical case," he wrote, "are not from an imaginary case but are the facts in the record of the case of Dave Canty whose conviction [in a Montgomery, Alabama, courtroom] was reversed by the U.S. Supreme Court on March 11, 1940."[3]

In Marshall's experiences as the NAACP's trial advocate traveling across the South in the thirties and forties, the major procedural fairness amendments that were honored in the breach by racist sheriffs, judges, prosecutors, lawyers, and jurors were "arrest[ing] Negroes without warrants" (Fourth Amendment violation); "hold[ing] them incommunicado without formal charges or bail" (Fifth and Sixth Amendment violations); "beat[ing] 'confessions' out of them" (Fifth Amendment violation); "refus[ing] to make effective appointment of counsel to defend indigent Negroes" (Sixth Amendment violation); "refus[ing] to give counsel sufficient time to prepare the case" (Sixth Amendment violation); "exclud[ing] qualified Negroes from service on the jury" (Sixth Amendment violation); and "intimidat[ing] witnesses and attorneys" (Fifth and Sixth Amendment violations). Finally, he said, "often the trial is held in an atmosphere of mob violence" (Sixth Amendment violation).[4]

By the mid-1940s, Marshall and the NAACP Inc Fund had defended many poor African Americans who had "confessed" to crimes because police used the "special blackjack [an iron rod] called 'the nigger beater,' the rubber hose, and the electric prod to the genitals, in order to coerce a confession"[5] out of them. *Lyons v. Oklahoma*, heard in the Supreme Court during its 1944 term, was a coerced-confession case that Marshall never forgot, a case he lost. Both the loss of the appeal and the absolute unfairness faced by Lyons "nagged at him most" during his lifetime.[6]

## THE HUGO, OKLAHOMA, CRIMINAL JUSTICE HORROR: *LYONS*

W. D. Lyons, an African American handyman, was accused of the gruesome triple murder of a white farmer, his wife, and their four-year-old son in Hugo,

Oklahoma. (The murderer shot them to death, hacked their bodies into pieces, and then attempted to burn down their house with the body parts scattered about the premises.)

After eleven days of nonstop police interrogations, including constant use of a "nigger beater," deprivation of food and sleep, and denial of access to counsel, Lyons confessed to the murders. (He confessed immediately after the police dumped some of the alleged bones of the dead family members onto his lap.) Within the day, he signed a second confession in the state prison where he had been taken. The trial was delayed for over a year, owing to the weakness of the prosecution's case and the shadowy circumstances surrounding his arrest, including rumors that bootlegging was the reason for the murders.

The African American community believed that Lyons did not commit the murder, and asked the NAACP for help. In 1941, Marshall took the case himself and went to Oklahoma to defend Lyons at the criminal trial. "So intense was the racial animosity stirred up by the case that many Negroes smuggled weapons into the town from Oklahoma City and Tulsa. Elaborate precautions were taken for Marshall's safety, to the extent that he was to sleep at a different well-guarded home every night."[7] Marshall soon found out that an inmate at a nearby prison farm had admitted to the murders. The man, convicted for murdering his wife, was a trustee at the institution who was allowed to leave the prison unattended. According to Marshall, the local police arrested Lyons, an easy mark, rather than the trustee because they "didn't want it known that the inmates it [the prison] was letting out as trustees were committing murders."[8] There was nothing that Marshall could do except try to defend Lyons.

The local trial judge threw out the first confession but allowed the prosecution to refer to it during the trial. The only evidence available for the prosecution to use at the trial was Lyons's second confession. Marshall argued that the second confession was inadmissible, obtained only because Lyons feared a repetition of the beatings he had received prior to his first confession. Lyons, however, was found guilty and sentenced to life imprisonment.

A few years later, Marshall argued the case before the U.S. Supreme Court, when it came on appeal from the Supreme Court of Oklahoma (which had affirmed the conviction). He argued that Lyons's confession was coerced and therefore was an involuntary admission. Because it had been introduced as evidence against him in the trial, Lyons had been denied the due process of law guaranteed in the Fourteenth Amendment. The Court, however, by a six-to-three vote, declined to rule that there was a violation of due process. Justice Stanley Reed, for the majority, said that "the Fourteenth Amendment does not protect one who admitted his guilt because of forbidden inducements against the use at trial of his subsequent confessions." The second confession, given twelve hours after the first one, was "voluntary" and therefore admissible. That confession was not "brought about by the earlier mistreatments." Justice Frank Murphy, joined by Hugo Black, dissented, as did Wiley Rutledge. Murphy argued that "this flagrant abuse by the state of the rights of an American citizen accused of murder ought not be approved. The admission of such a tainted confession does not accord with the Fourteenth Amendment's command that a state shall not convict a defendant on evidence that he was compelled to give against himself."

*Lyons* convinced Marshall that criminal justice was parceled out on the basis of class and caste. African Americans and other minorities, the poor, and the ignorant were simply not treated fairly or equally in America's criminal justice system. Most Americans were unconcerned about the fates of these invisible victims. "Hell," said Marshall much later, "Lyons wouldn't have had a single sumbitch in the world to try to save him if the NAACP had not waded in."[9] To the end of his life, Marshall insisted that the family was killed because they were cheating others in a statewide bootlegging operation. "I am convinced that the governor's office was involved [in the murder too]. It was a bootleg thing. People who were killed were bootleggers. And it was obvious they were killed incident to their business of bootlegging.... Everybody was bootlegging around there."[10]

Marshall sent small gifts of money to Lyons at Christmastime and other holidays, telling him to "use this to buy some candy, or cigarettes, or whatever you need most." Lyons spent over two decades in prison. Marshall made two attempts in the 1940s to persuade Oklahoma's governor to grant clemency. On May 24, 1965, twenty-five years after his trial and conviction, Lyons was finally pardoned by Oklahoma's governor. Marshall told a reporter in the 1980s, "I *still* think Lyons was innocent."[11] These criminal trials left Marshall with an overriding concern about the "power of *undisciplined* state authority" and of "individual rights made vulnerable without the effective assistance of counsel."[12] While he was on the Court, especially after Warren and Black retired, Marshall was continually shocked at the refusal of the Burger and Rehnquist majorities to hold police and those involved in the criminal justice system responsible for acting according to the language and the spirit of fundamental procedural guarantees. As in equal protection and affirmative action, Marshall's chief ally was William Brennan. And, not surprisingly, Marshall's major antagonist in these cases during his tenure on the Court was William Rehnquist.

## MARSHALL VERSUS REHNQUIST: THE UNEVEN BATTLES

The influence and power of the staunchly conservative William Rehnquist increased as the Court changed over the years. When he became Chief Justice in 1986, Rehnquist quickly seized the reins of power. A small cohort invariably joined Rehnquist's opinions—Justices Scalia, O'Connor, White, and, on occasion, Stevens and Blackmun. With this majority, he began to move to restore a criminal justice system that had been weakened, Rehnquist believed, by the liberal judgments of the Warren Court majority. Jeffries wrote: "With Powell's retirement [in 1987, when he was replaced by another conservative jurist, Anthony Kennedy], there was little doubt which way the Court would jump."[13]

Marshall's great fear, after Powell's retirement, was that the new Chief Justice would take the Court in a radical, not a conservative, direction. Marshall knew that Rehnquist had a sharp mind, one that categorically, often haughtily, rejected Marshall's firsthand experience of persistent racism in American criminal justice. A younger Rehnquist, clerking for Justice Jackson in 1952, exhibited this radicalism when he wrote his boss: "I take a dim view of this pathological search for [racial] discrimination.... It is about time the Court faced the fact that the white people of the South don't like the colored people;...the Constitution...most assuredly did not appoint the Court as a sociological watchdog to rear up every time...discrimination raises its admittedly ugly head."[14]

Marshall believed that Rehnquist could not overcome his "mental block" when he considered cases involving African Americans and others in America who were disadvantaged in some manner. Marshall had encountered whites with such views all his life, and he feared the power they had to act on their ill-informed beliefs. Rehnquist had the ability to cobble together majorities that significantly narrowed and overturned some of the important criminal justice precedents created by both the Warren and the Burger Courts. By the time Rehnquist became Chief, Marshall could only protest through his dissents.

In the criminal justice cases that follow, one can see the true liberal and the true radical. The latter, Rehnquist, had the votes; Marshall had as his one constant ally the only other traditional liberal on the Court, William Brennan.

## PROTECTION AGAINST "UNREASONABLE" SEARCHES AND SEIZURES

The Fourth Amendment forbids "unreasonable searches and seizures" by officials of the government. In its entirety, the Amendment states:

> The right of the people to be secure in their persons, houses, papers and effects, against unreasonable searches and seizures, shall not be violated, and no warrants shall issue, but upon probable cause, supported by oath or affirmation, and particularly describing the place to be searched, and the persons or things to be seized.

In his Fourth Amendment decisions, mostly in dissent, Marshall emphasized "a strict interpretation of the warrant requirement and [was] extremely critical of the Court's decisions which expanded or created exceptions to this clause."[15] The amendment clearly had a warrant requirement. With a valid warrant, there was a reasonable search and seizure. Absent the warrant, there was unreasonableness in a search and seizure conducted by law enforcement officers. During his tenure on the Court, however, Marshall witnessed a continuing trend by the majority toward expansion of police search and seizure powers—*without a warrant*—at the expense of privacy rights. This was accomplished through the Court's creation of "exceptions" to the Fourth Amendment requirement for a valid search warrant. Without such a warrant, there was an "unreasonable" search and seizure—unless it was (1) a "plain view" search incident to an arrest or it was (2) a warrantless search done with the "consent" of the person whose room or house was the object of a police search.

These are only two of a number of exceptions that have been created by the Supreme Court in the past fifty years. These include the "open fields" exception (where police can seize illegal materials that are in open, public view), the "hot pursuit" exception (where evidence is seized by police after pursuing a suspect to prevent its probable destruction), and the "stop and frisk" exception (where, for his or her own protection, a police officer can search for possible weapons on a person stopped for questioning), created by the Warren Court, in *Terry v. Ohio*, during Marshall's first year.

Marshall believed that the Court should not back away from careful examination of all facts in situations where there was a claimed exception. The general search warrant requirement, he told his colleagues, "is *not lightly to be dispensed with.*" (My emphasis.) Simply "because an exception is invoked to justify a search without a warrant does not preclude further judicial inquiry into the reasonableness of that search," he argued in dissent in the 1973 case of *United States v. Robinson*. "It is the role of the judiciary, not of police officers," maintained Marshall, "to delimit the scope of exceptions to the warrant requirement."

*Terry v. Ohio* (1968), *United States v. Sokolow* (1989), *Schneckloth v. Bustamone* (1973), and *United States v. Ross* (1982) were four unsettled cases that came to the Court during Marshall's tenure. The first two involved the "stop and frisk" exception, while *Schneckloth* raised questions about the constitutionality of a consent search without a warrant, and *Ross* examined the issue of a search of an automobile incident to an arrest.

*Terry* was the result of a "stop and frisk" by a police officer of two persons he thought were acting suspiciously. After watching them case a store for about fifteen minutes, he walked over to them, briefly spoke, and then grabbed Terry and patted him down. He found one revolver inside Terry's coat and another inside the coat of Terry's accomplice, Richard Chilton. Terry was arrested and then convicted of carrying a concealed weapon and sentenced to one to three years in the state prison. The motion to suppress the evidence was denied in the state courts. The prosecutors successfully argued that the weapons were seized following a search incident to a lawful arrest. The trial judge denied the motion to suppress, finding that the policeman, "purely for his own protection, had the right to pat down the outer clothing of the men, who he had reasonable cause to believe might be armed." The conviction was upheld and Terry appealed to the Court.

In an opinion written by Chief Justice Warren, joined in by Marshall, the Court upheld Terry's conviction. For the Court, the "question [was] whether in all the circumstances of this on-the-street encounter, the individual's right to personal security was violated by an unreasonable search and seizure." Was there a traditional search and seizure that was governed by the Fourth Amendment's search-warrant requirement? Warren and the majority said that McFadden's contact with Terry and Chilton did not constitute such a formal Fourth Amendment search and seizure. Was there "justification" for McFadden's "invasion of Terry's personal security by searching him for weapons in the course of [his] investigation"?

The Court decided that there was. "We cannot blind ourselves," wrote Warren, "to the need for law enforcement officers to protect themselves...in situations where they may lack probable cause for an arrest." This type of limited "search," concluded the majority, when a police officer does so "purely for his own protection," is a reasonable one under the Fourth Amendment, "and any weapon seized may properly be introduced in evidence against the person from whom [it was] taken." Marshall and Brennan, though somewhat troubled by the "reasonable suspicion" decision, joined Warren's opinion. Brennan sent Warren a memo written in March 1968. Expressing his deep concern about "the terrible risk that police will conjure up 'suspicious circumstances' and courts will credit their versions," Brennan noted: "It will not take much of this to aggravate the already white heat resentment of ghetto Negroes against the police—and the Court will become the scapegoat."

The alternative was to reverse the conviction of Terry, but Brennan and Marshall felt that was inappropriate, given the facts. "I think the tone of our opinion," Brennan concluded, "may even be more important than what we say. I hope you will forgive me—[we are] truly worried."[16] Such fears were shown to be justified just a few years after the *Terry* decision. By 1972 the Court, with the appointment of the four Nixon justices (Burger, Blackmun, Powell, and Rehnquist), proved to be a willing accomplice in successful police efforts to expand the reach of *Terry*. Regardless of Warren's modification of the "tone" of the *Terry* opinion, Rehnquist and his allies moved quickly to expand the exceptions to the Fourth Amendment's "probable cause" search warrant requirements.

The 1989 *Sokolow* case is one example. Andrew Sokolow and a female accompanying him were stopped by U.S. Drug Enforcement Agency agents after he exited Honolulu's International Airport. Without a warrant, the agents stopped him on the airport walkway, brought him and his companion back into the airport, and then searched his possessions because he fit a DEA-created narcotic smuggler's profile.

The government-created profile targeted, as possible drug courier suspects, persons who (1) paid cash for airline tickets; (2) traveled under a different name; (3) traveled to a destination city (Sokolow traveled twenty hours, going from Honolulu to Miami and then returning to Honolulu) considered a source city for illicit drugs; (4) stayed at that city for a very short time (Sokolow stayed in Miami for two days); (5) appeared nervous; and (6) checked no baggage. According to the DEA reports, Sokolow fit all six profile characteristics. Over a kilogram of cocaine was found in Sokolow's carry-on luggage and he was arrested and convicted of violating a federal statute. The district court judge allowed the cocaine to be introduced at trial, rejecting his lawyer's motion to suppress the evidence. The judge found that "the DEA agents had a reasonable suspicion that he was involved in drug trafficking when they stopped him at the airport."

The Ninth Circuit federal appellate court reversed the conviction, "holding that the DEA agents did not have a reasonable suspicion to justify the stop, as required by the Fourth Amendment." On appeal to the Rehnquist Court, the federal appeals court ruling was overturned and the conviction upheld. Chief Justice Rehnquist wrote the opinion for the seven-person majority. His decision for the Court turned on "whether the agents had a reasonable suspicion that respondent was engaged in wrongdoing when they encountered him on the sidewalk." Noting that there was such "reasonable suspicion," he went on: "In evaluating the validity of a stop such as this, we must consider the 'totality of the circumstances—the whole picture.' We hold that the agents had a reasonable basis to suspect that respondent was transporting illegal drugs."

Once again, Marshall's ideal of due process and his sense of fairness was outraged by the judgment of the Rehnquist majority. He wrote, in dissent, that the majority opinion "diminishes the rights of *all* citizens to 'be secure in their persons,' as they traverse the Nation's airports." The Fourth Amendment, Marshall maintained, usually requires probable cause for *all* searches and seizures. *Terry* created the reasonable-suspicion "derivation" in order for police to question suspicious persons by taking certain protective precautions. "Law enforcement officers must reasonably suspect that he has engaged in, or [is] poised to commit, a criminal act *at that moment....* The facts about Sokolow known to the DEA agents at the time they stopped him fall short of reasonably indicating that he was engaged at the time in criminal activity."

The *Schneckloth* case, heard by the Burger Court in 1973, raised an issue about which Marshall was quite sensitive: whether a person ignorant of constitutional protections can give a constitutionally valid consent to a warrantless search if he does not know that he can refuse the police request to search the premises. During an automobile search, stolen checks were found, attributed to the actual owner of the car (who was not driving the car when the police stopped it). The owner's appeal of his conviction argued that the prosecution had failed to prove that the consent had been given with the understanding it could be freely withheld. The majority ruled that the state did not have to prove that the driver was aware that he had the right to refuse the search. Marshall, Brennan, and Douglas wrote separate dissents, with Marshall arguing that the Court was allowing the police "to capitalize on the ignorance of citizens so as to accomplish by subterfuge what they could not achieve by relying only on the knowing relinquishment of constitutional rights.... The holding today confines the protection of the Fourth Amendment against searches conducted without probable cause to the sophisticated, the knowledgeable and, I might add, the few."

In *United States v. Ross,* a case decided by the Court in 1982, the issue was the constitutionality of a "probing" warrantless search of an automobile by law enforcement officers who claimed they had probable cause to believe that the car contained illegal drugs. The Court majority "considered the *permissible scope*" of a police search of an automobile's concealed compartments and containers within the vehicle whose contents were not in plain view of the police. (From *Carroll v. United States,* decided in 1925, to *Ross,* the Court had said that an automobile search incident to an arrest—of materials *in plain view* of the officer—was not unreasonable under the Fourth Amendment.) But what about the glove compartment, the trunk, and other areas of the car not in plain view?

In late 1978, an informant told police that a District of Columbia drug dealer named "Bandit" was selling drugs from the trunk of his car. The informant gave the police a description of the dealer and the car he was driving. The police arrived on the scene and found the car parked exactly where the informant told them to look. But Bandit, legally known as Albert Ross, was nowhere near the car and the police left. A few minutes later, they saw Ross driving the car and pulled him over. Out of the car, one searched Ross, while the other police officer, searching the car, found a bullet on the driver's-side floor of the car. A pistol was found in the glove compartment, which was out of plain view of the officer. Ross was then arrested and handcuffed. The trunk was opened, and in it the police found a closed brown paper bag. Upon opening the bag, the officers found glassine envelopes containing a white powder (later determined to be heroin). They drove the car to police headquarters and thoroughly searched it, turning up $3, 200 in a red pouch found in the rear of the trunk.

Ross was charged with possession of heroin with intent to distribute, a violation of federal law. His lawyer moved to suppress the use of the seized evidence at trial (the money and the heroin), but the federal district court judge denied the motion. Convicted, he appealed to the federal appeals court, which held that the police should not have opened either container (the heroin and money containers) without first obtaining a warrant. The case was appealed to the Supreme Court, and the Court overturned the lower appellate court, upholding Ross's conviction. John Paul Stevens wrote the majority opinion, stating that "in this class of cases, a search is not unreasonable if based on facts that would justify the issuance of a warrant, *even though a warrant has not been issued.*" (My emphasis.) The police officers, reasoned Stevens, "had probable cause to search respondent's entire vehicle." He concluded that, on "grounds of practicability," police were allowed a warrantless search of all areas of an automobile if there was probable cause. Because there was probable cause to believe that the drugs would be found in the trunk, the evidence seized could be introduced at trial. The conviction was sustained.

Marshall was extremely agitated over this decision of the Court. "The majority today," he began his dissent, "not only repeals all realistic limits on warrantless automobile searches, *it repeals the Fourth Amendment warrant requirement itself.*" (My emphasis.) His and Brennan's warnings to Warren during the 1968 *Terry* discussions had clearly come to pass. The *Ross* opinion made a police officer's judgment the equivalent of a neutral, detached magistrate's finding of probable cause for issuing a warrant!

Almost twenty years after *Schneckloth*, in Marshall's last year on the Court, he once again dissented in a case involving a police search of an automobile's trunk without a search warrant. In *Florida v. Jimeno* (1991), the Court majority, in an opinion written by Rehnquist, determined that if a driver of an auto stopped by police gives the officers permission to search the car, they do not need a search warrant to open up any containers they find in the car. "Was it reasonable," asked the Chief, "for an officer to consider the suspect's general consent to a search of his car to include consent to examine a paper bag lying on the floor of the car[?] We think that it is."

Marshall dissented, noting that "an individual's consent to a search of the interior of his car should not be understood to authorize a search of closed containers inside the car." Marshall again accused Rehnquist and his group of deferring to police shortcuts, actions that deprived persons of their constitutional rights. He closed his dissent by quoting a segment of his dissent in *Schneckloth* decrying "the continued ability of the police to capitalize on the *ignorance of citizens*." The Fourth Amendment provides persons with an expectation of privacy, one that could not be invaded unless there was a valid search or arrest warrant, issued by a magistrate after he or she had been presented with specific information by law enforcement officers. Marshall had an absolutist view of this constitutional protection and fought to prevent its "erosion" by Court majorities through additional "exceptions" to the Fourth Amendment's prohibition. In one dissent after another, Marshall pleaded with his colleagues not to shrink the power of the Fourth Amendment for police convenience at the expense of private rights guaranteed by the Constitution.[17] He also continued to argue for the strict maintenance of the *Mapp* "exclusionary" rule in search-and-seizure activities.

In the 1961 case of *Mapp v. Ohio*, the Warren Court concluded that any and all evidence seized as a consequence of an unreasonable search and seizure could not be used against a person in a criminal prosecution. It was excluded because it was produced by a search and seizure that violated the Fourth Amendment. Police came to Ms. Mapp's home with what they said was a search warrant seeking an alleged bomber. They then forcibly entered the premises over her objections. They searched the apartment and the basement storage area completely, but the person they sought was nowhere to be found. They did, however, find some literature in the basement that they considered obscene under Ohio's obscenity statute that allowed conviction for knowing possession of lewd materials. Mapp claimed the stuff belonged to a previous boarder. She was nevertheless convicted of knowing possession of obscene materials and sentenced to one to seven years in prison. She appealed her conviction to the Supreme Court, arguing that the evidence seized could not be used against her because there was no valid search warrant. Justice Clark wrote for the Court, which concluded that there was a Fourth Amendment violation in this case and that it presented "what is tantamount to coerced testimony by way of unconstitutional seizure of goods, papers, effects, documents, etc."

Shortly after Marshall arrived on the Court, the *Mapp* "exclusionary" rule came under attack by the new brethren on the Court and remained under attack throughout Marshall's tenure. Burger and Rehnquist majorities, led by Rehnquist in both eras, crafted exceptions to the *Mapp* exclusionary rule. They argued that the exceptions were based on the reasonableness of the search and seizure, ignoring what Marshall took to be the essence of the law enforcement dilemma: lack of a valid search warrant. Marshall always demanded that there be strict application of the exclusionary rule if the police seized evidence without a valid warrant. In 1984, for example, in the case of *United States v. Leon*, an angry Marshall joined Brennan's dissent from a decision that created a "good faith" exception to the exclusionary rule. Alberto Leon was a drug seller known to police in Burbank, California. Based on informants' information and police observations of his behavior, law enforcement officials secured a warrant to search his residence for items related to drug trafficking. The search produced a large quantity of drugs, and Leon and his two colleagues were indicted and charged with conspiracy to possess and distribute cocaine and other drugs.

Leon's motion to suppress the evidence seized was granted in part by the federal district court judge, who believed that the police did not show probable cause in their warrant request. The trial judge also rejected the government's contention that the exclusionary rule should be waived because the police officers acted in good faith. The Ninth Circuit federal court of appeals affirmed the district court judgment about the evidence, and the Reagan administration took the case to the U.S. Supreme Court, asking the justices to "modify the Fourth Amendment's exclusionary rule so as not to bar the admission of evidence seized in reasonable, good-faith reliance on a search warrant that is subsequently held to be defective."

In a six-to-three decision, the Court majority overturned the rulings of the lower courts and remanded the case with instructions to have the seized evidence introduced at Leon's trial. Justice White wrote for the majority. His opinion allowed a "good-faith" exception to the exclusionary rule. The exclusionary rule, extended to the states in *Mapp*, was a "judicially created remedy to safeguard Fourth Amendment rights generally through its deterrent effect, rather than a personal constitutional right of the party aggrieved," White asserted. But, the majority concluded, there had been "substantial social costs exacted" by the Court's stipulation in *Mapp* that evidence seized illegally not be used in a criminal proceeding. For the majority, it was especially galling to see "some guilty defendants...go free [because of *Mapp*], when law enforcement officers have acted in objective good faith or their transgressions have been minor. The magnitude of the benefit conferred on such guilty defendants offends basic concepts of the criminal justice system."

The exclusionary rule was still valid in cases "where the Fourth Amendment violation has been substantial and deliberate." However, there has to be a "cost-benefit" balancing of interests in these cases—one that would in effect modify the exclusionary rule to favor the police forces.

Brennan's dissent, joined by Marshall, condemned the Burger Court's "gradual but determined strangulation of the [exclusionary] rule." Brennan wrote: "it now appears that the Court's victory over the Fourth Amendment is complete....*Lyon* represents the *pièce de résistance* of the Court's past efforts." The "crabbed reading" of the Fourth Amendment by the majority led them to distinguish between errors by the police and errors by the neutral, detached magistrate. The dissenters pointed out, however, that the Fourth Amendment drew no such line and that if a warrant was improperly issued, the evidence seized, however much "good faith" was exhibited by police, could not be used in the prosecution's case.

Further, until the narrowing of it, the exclusionary rule was a categorical one for Court majorities. It was "part and parcel of the Fourth Amendment's limitation upon governmental encroachment of individual privacy." As such, it cannot be subject to any form of balancing, especially of the absolutely artificial "benefit-cost" standard. Using such an approach to the rule, Brennan wrote, "has robbed the rule of legitimacy.... The extent of this Court's fidelity to Fourth Amendment requirements...should not turn on such statistical uncertainties."

Time and again Marshall, regularly joined by Brennan, dissented from Burger and Rehnquist majorities that reduced a person's notion of his or her legitimate expectation of privacy through increasingly aggressive narrowing of the exclusionary rule. "Your home is your castle" was the concept protected by the Fourth Amendment. It was also a belief of Marshall's, ever since he was a young boy listening to his father proclaim the primacy of that fundamental right. Outside that "castle," there was no need for a search warrant. However, did a person have an expectation of privacy when his or her garbage was put out? Could police search the garbage without a warrant? What about financial records located in the bank downtown? What about a motel room occupied by a person suspected of a crime? Could the police search that hotel room without a valid warrant?

In these Fourth Amendment cases, the basic conflict was between private rights guaranteed by the Fourth Amendment and effective law enforcement practices that made "end runs" around the constitutional constraints. In *National Treasury Employees Union v. Von Raab*, decided in 1989, Marshall dissented from a Court judgment that allowed the U.S. Customs Service to require a urinalysis test, without any showing of probable cause, from employees who sought a transfer or a promotion to a U.S. Customs Service position that involved any one of three things: involvement with drug enforcement; necessity of carrying a firearm; handling classified material. The customs workers' union successfully petitioned the federal district court for an injunction, alleging that the drug-screening program violated the Fourth Amendment. The Fifth Circuit U.S. Court of Appeals vacated the judgment, and the union appealed to the Supreme Court.

The Court majority, in an opinion written by Justice Kennedy, held that there was no government violation of the Fourth Amendment when they established the mandatory drug-screening program for all persons seeking a particular set of jobs in the Customs Service. In affirming the federal appellate court, Kennedy said that "requiring a warrant in this context would serve only to divert valuable agency resources from the Service's primary mission." Because the government agency has a compelling interest in seeking suitable individuals for certain dangerous jobs in the Customs Service, there is "a valid public interest" in such a testing program. The "operational realities of the workplace may render entirely reasonable certain work-related intrusions by supervisors...that might be viewed as unreasonable in other contexts." For the majority, the test for constitutionality was whether the practice was a reasonable one. The majority held that "suspicionless testing of employees who apply for promotion to positions involving the interdiction of illegal drugs, or to positions which require the incumbent to carry a firearm, is reasonable."

Marshall dissented, joined by Brennan. He again rejected the majority's balancing approach to the Fourth Amendment controversy and attacked the Court's continued deference to governmental authority. He believed that "the Court's abandonment of the Fourth Amendment's express requirement that searches of the person rest on probable cause is unprincipled and unjustifiable."

As he said in his dissent in *Skinner v. Railway Labor Executives' Association* (1989) (involving mandatory blood and urine tests of all employees involved in train accidents), "the Court today takes its longest step yet toward reading the probable cause requirement out of the Fourth Amendment [when it] holds that a 'special need, beyond the normal need for law enforcement,' makes the 'requirement' of probable cause 'impracticable.'"

Within the year, Marshall retired from the Court, leaving behind him a majority that he felt continued to ignore the commands of the Fourth Amendment in its attempt to support the forces of law and order against individuals in the society. "History teaches," he warned in *Skinner*, "that grave threats to liberty often come in times of urgency, when constitutional rights seem too extravagant to endure."

## THE FIFTH AMENDMENT AND THE SPECTER OF COERCED CONFESSIONS

The Fifth Amendment contains the important guarantee against self-incrimination as well as a protection against double jeopardy. In part, it states:

> No person shall be held to answer for a capital, or otherwise infamous crime, unless on a presentment or indictment of a Grand Jury;...nor shall any person be subject for the same offense to be twice put in jeopardy of life or limb; *nor shall be compelled in any criminal case to be a witness against himself,* nor be deprived of life, liberty, or property, without due process of law....

When he joined the Court, Marshall also had a definitive view of the value of the Fifth Amendment protection against official abuses of power against poor, ignorant, or minority persons. The Court had already expressed itself on the matter of self-incrimination and had done so in a way that greatly pleased Marshall. In the 1964 case of *Murphy v. Waterfront Commission,* the Warren Court's beliefs and values were clearly defined:

> [The right to remain silent] reflects many of our fundamental values and most noble aspirations: our unwillingness to subject those suspected of crime to the cruel dilemma of self-accusation, perjury, or contempt; our preference for an *accusatorial* rather than an *inquisitorial* system of criminal justice; our fear that self-incrimination would be elicited by inhumane treatment and abuses; our sense of fair play which dictates a "fair state-individual balance by requiring the government…in its contest with the individual to shoulder the entire load,"… our respect for the inviolability of the human personality and of the right of each individual "to a private enclave where he may lead a private life,"…our distrust of self-deprecatory statements; and our realization that the privilege, while "a shelter to the guilty," has often been "a protection to the innocent." (My emphasis.)

By the mid-1970s, these views were being gradually discarded by Burger and Rehnquist majorities, which, to Marshall's sadness, did not hold these values as highly as did he and Brennan. In Fifth Amendment cases involving the validity of a confession, Marshall "attempted to persuade a majority of the Court that the Constitution contemplates an accusatorial rather than an inquisitorial system of justice. He…argued assiduously for strict enforcement and expansion of the doctrine enunciated by the Court in *Miranda v. Arizona* [1965], that persons questioned while in custody be informed that their right to speak to counsel and to remain silent is constitutionally inviolate."[18]

The *Miranda* principle, written by Chief Justice Warren, emerged from a group of cases involving custodial interrogations in which the suspects did not have assistance of counsel, were not informed of their constitutional rights, and thereafter confessed to criminal activity. Warren's opinion changed the old, unsavory police practices that inevitably led to coerced confessions used to convict defendants in violation of due process. Marshall had seen the consequences during his decades of work with the NAACP Inc Fund.

In the end, in *Miranda,* the Court held that once a person is taken into custody and becomes the focus of the investigation, whether or not formal charges have been lodged, the police must inform the suspect that he or she has the right to remain silent, that anything said may be used against the suspect, and that the suspect has a right to have an attorney present before questioning and to have an attorney appointed if he or she cannot afford one. Further, if the suspect, "at any stage of the process...wishes to consult with an attorney before speaking there can be no questioning."

In an accusatorial system, the assumption is that the burden of proof lies with government, that prosecutors must acquire evidence that convinces a trial jury of "guilt beyond a reasonable doubt." Critically important, *silence* on the part of the accused is a constitutionally protected given, unless the person voluntarily and knowingly waives that constitutional right.

Marshall had defended men who had been beaten, detained without counsel for days and nights on end, and coerced into confessing to a crime they probably did not commit. As a jurist, Marshall tried to maintain the accusatory criminal justice system, largely in dissents. The Court majority, under Rehnquist's leadership, continued to accept confessions given under conditions Marshall found coercive.[19] Three such cases were *Fare v. Michael C.* (1979), *Rhode Island v. Innis* (1980), and *Duckworth v. Eagan* (1989).

*Fare v. Michael C.* was so labeled because it involved a juvenile held in police custody as a suspect in a crime. While being questioned, he asked to speak to his probation officer rather than to an attorney. His request was denied by the police, who continued questioning the young man until he confessed. The Rehnquist majority, using the "totality of circumstances" standard, concluded that the confession could be admitted at trial. The suspect's request was, under the circumstances, not the equivalent of a *Miranda* request. Marshall emphatically dissented from the majority's continued deference to police judgments involving procedural due process.

The *Innis* litigation involved a murder investigation in Providence, Rhode Island. Innis had been identified by a cabdriver as the person who robbed him at gunpoint. Innis, that same day, was arrested and advised of his *Miranda* rights by the arresting officer. Innis immediately asked to speak with a lawyer and was put in the rear section of a caged police van with two policemen sitting up front. The police then let him overhear their speculation that the unrecovered gun might bring harm to an innocent person, so Innis helped them recover the gun, which in turn was used to convict him of robbery with a deadly weapon. On appeal, the Rhode Island appellate court ruled that Innis had been subjected to "subtle coercion" that was the equivalent of "interrogation" within the meaning of the *Miranda* opinion. The Court granted certiorari to address the meaning of "interrogation" within *Miranda*. In a decision written by Justice Potter Stewart, the six-to-three majority overturned the decision of the state appellate court and upheld Innis's conviction. Marshall wrote a dissenting opinion, again joined by Brennan.

Stewart's opinion noted that custodial interrogation meant the "express questioning" of suspects by police after taking them into custody. This, however, differed from *voluntary statements* given by a suspect after being given his *Miranda* warnings. "We conclude that the *Miranda* safeguards come into play whenever a person in custody is subjected to either express questioning or its functional equivalent.... We conclude that [Innis] was not 'interrogated' within the meaning of *Miranda.*" Marshall was "utterly at a loss, however, to understand how this objective standard [the majority's definition of 'interrogation'] as applied to the facts before us can rationally lead to the conclusion that there was no interrogation." He rejected Stewart's totally unrealistic contention, upon which the Court's decision rested, that the policeman's statements "were 'no more than a few offhand remarks' which could not reasonably have been expected to elicit a response."

In *Duckworth v. Eagan,* a *Miranda* case decided a year before Marshall retired from the Court, he grimly spoke, again in dissent, of the Rehnquist Court's "disemboweling" of *Miranda.* Gary Eagan was a suspect questioned by the police as part of an investigation into the stabbing of a woman. He gave a non-incriminating statement to them after signing a waiver that said he would be provided with an attorney "if and when you go to court," because he spoke to them without an attorney present. The following day, Eagan confessed to the stabbing and took police to the scene, where they recovered physical evidence of the crime.

At trial, his two statements were introduced, although the defense attorney objected. Convicted, he appealed to the Indiana Supreme Court, which upheld the conviction. He then went into federal court, seeking to have the conviction overturned because the police did not give him a *Miranda* warning. The federal trial judge denied the motion, but the Seventh Circuit U.S. Court of Appeals reversed the conviction on the grounds that the first warning that Eagan would get a lawyer "if and when you go to court" was constitutionally defective. The state appealed to the Supreme Court and it granted certiorari to hear the case. The Court, in a five-to-four decision, overturned the federal appellate court. Rehnquist wrote the opinion for the majority and made light of the fact that Eagan had not been given the proper warnings: "We have never insisted that *Miranda* warnings be given in the exact form described in that decision.... Reviewing courts therefore need not examine *Miranda* warnings as if construing a will or defining the terms of an easement. The inquiry is simply whether the warnings reasonably 'convey to a suspect his rights as required by *Miranda.*'" Rehnquist concluded that Eagan's warnings "touched all of the bases required by *Miranda.*"

Marshall was outraged at the cavalier manner in which Rehnquist set aside the fundamental errors of the police when they gave Eagan his warnings. His dissent clearly expressed his rage at the majority's validation of a violation of a

Rule of Law. Through "mischaracterization" and the "continuing debasement of this historic precedent [*Miranda*]," the Court, he said, had ignored both the reality of police practices and the actual language in *Miranda*.

The Warren opinion clearly stated that a person taken into custody must be "clearly informed…that if he cannot afford an attorney one will be appointed for him *prior to any questioning* if he so desires." The Indiana police did not tell this to Eagan. In concluding, as Rehnquist did, that the warnings satisfied *Miranda*, "the majority makes a mockery of that decision," an outraged Marshall wrote for the dissenters. "What goes wholly overlooked in the CHIEF JUSTICE's analysis is that the recipients of police warnings are often frightened suspects unlettered in the law, not lawyers or judges or others schooled in interpreting legal or semantic nuance."

When Marshall left the Court in June 1991, the Rehnquist Court had significantly narrowed *Miranda* and other protections defined during the Warren Court era. Rehnquist's successful "continued retrenchment" of that important case's precedential value angered Marshall and left him profoundly disturbed by the shrinking definition of rights under the Fifth Amendment.

## THE RIGHT TO COUNSEL AND OTHER SIXTH AMENDMENT PROTECTIONS

The Sixth Amendment guarantees an accused the right to the assistance of counsel in a public trial before an impartial jury of his peers. It states:

> In all criminal prosecutions, the accused shall enjoy the right to a speedy and public trial, by an impartial jury of the State and district wherein the crime shall have been committed,…and to be informed of the nature and cause of the accusation; to be confronted with the witnesses against him; to have compulsory process for obtaining witnesses in his favor, and to have the Assistance of Counsel for his defense.

Equally important as his efforts to abolish the use of the coerced confession was Marshall's commitment to ensuring that all persons, especially those who could not afford to hire a competent attorney to defend them, had a competent lawyer assigned to them. On too many occasions, Marshall had interviewed clients after they had been miserably treated by attorneys appointed to defend them in the local courtroom. Marshall regarded effective representation by defense counsel as critically important to and for the accusatorial system under the Sixth Amendment, especially as it affected poor black American defendants.

Warren Court majorities had extended this right; if a suspect faced a "critical stage" of the state's criminal process, then he had the right to the assistance of counsel. Through the early 1970s, Warren and Burger Court majorities (with Chief Justice Burger and his "Minnesota Twin" colleague, Harry Blackmun dissenting) defined the "critical stages" in the criminal justice process where the assistance of counsel was constitutionally required. This was done on a case-by-case basis, as follows:

- quasi-arrest (*Orozco v. Texas*, 1969)
- arrest (*Miranda*, 1966)
- pre-indictment preliminary hearing (*Coleman v. Alabama*, 1970)
- pre-indictment confession (*Escobedo v. Illinois*, 1964)
- post-indictment (*Massiah v. United States*, 1964)
- arraignment (*Hamilton v. Alabama*, 1961)
- lineups (*United States v. Wade; Gilbert v. California*, 1967)
- trials (*Gideon v. Wainright*, 1963)
- appeals (*Douglas v. California*, 1963)
- probation hearings (*Mempa v. Rhea*, 1967)
- revocation of probation or parole (*Gagnon v. Scarpelli*, 1973)

These Court decisions were not easy ones to arrive at, even in a Court led by Warren, whose frequent question to lawyers and to his colleagues was, "But is it fair?" However, by the time Nixon appointees Powell and Rehnquist joined the Court in 1972, most of these "critical stage" issues had been identified, which led to a much-broadened interpetation of the Sixth Amendment's guarantee of the right to the assistance of counsel.

Given this constitutional reality, Marshall turned to an equally compelling matter involving the Sixth Amendment: Was a person entitled to the *effective* assistance of counsel? There were too many bargained guilty pleas, hurriedly worked up by defense counsel who didn't bother to consult their poor, minority clients. Marshall saw these guilty pleas, or "copping" arrangements, as fundamental violations of the Sixth Amendment's right to the assistance of *competent* counsel. Marshall argued repeatedly that to have some kind of equality in the clash between the accused defendant and the state, effective, competent counsel was necessary.

In a 1984 case, *United States v. Cronic*, the Court focused on this question. In an opinion written by Justice Stevens, the Court concluded that the "right to counsel" includes the idea that the Constitution implies *competent* counsel. Such effective assistance of counsel is a key to the basic fairness of the accusatory system of criminal justice in America; without competent counsel, the "reliability of the trial process" was placed in jeopardy. While Marshall did not disagree with *Cronic*, he was concerned about the fine print. Under what circumstances is competent counsel denied, therefore depriving the defendant of his Sixth Amendment rights, particularly in cases involving the death penalty, which Marshall regarded as unconstitutional per se.

In *Strickland v. Washington,* also in 1984, the opinion for the Court majority, written by Justice Sandra Day O'Connor, held that an attorney's performance was inadequate if it "fell below an objective standard of reasonableness." Two components had to be shown in such an appeal by a defendant who had been convicted in trial court: (1) that counsel was deficient and had committed substantive errors, and (2) that "the deficient performance prejudiced the defense." If these components were present, the conviction had to be reversed only if "there is a reasonable probability that, but for counsel's unprofessional errors, the result of the proceeding would have been different....More specific guidelines are not appropriate."

This majority opinion underscored its deference to the legal profession in cases in which the competency of defense counsel in criminal prosecutions was challenged. O'Connor maintained that "a Court must indulge a strong presumption that counsel's conduct falls within a wide range of reasonable professional assistance." But, Marshall protested, what about the rights of a poor, ignorant, often minority citizen who was "defended" by an ineffective, incompetent attorney? His objection fell on deaf ears; even Brennan concurred with O'Connor's majority opinion. Indeed, Brennan wrote to O'Connor to suggest ways she could counter some points in Marshall's outspoken dissent. He added that he would be "modifying my concurrence to account for some of the points made in Marshall's dissent." (She accepted his suggestions that same day.) Reviewing the trial record, Brennan felt that the lawyer in the case, which involved the death penalty, "took a very reasonable tack under the circumstances and [his errors]...could not have changed the sentencing judge's mind."

Marshall dissented vigorously in *Strickland.* What is the standard of reasonableness? he asked. Without clarification, which was not forthcoming in O'Connor's opinion, lower courts would continue to lack guidance. Requiring the defendant on appeal to show that there was a reasonable probability that the trial outcome would have been different with a competent lawyer was an impossible task. As Warren had done so often, Marshall asked: Where is the "fairness" in the review process for the poor defendant if there is a heavy presumption in favor of the attorney?

In my view, the [Sixth Amendment] guarantee also functions to ensure that convictions are obtained only through fundamentally fair procedures. The majority contends that the Sixth Amendment is not violated when a manifestly guilty defendant is convicted after a trial in which he was represented by a manifestly ineffective attorney. I cannot agree. Every defendant is entitled to a trial in which his interests are vigorously and conscientiously advocated by an able lawyer. A proceeding in which the defendant does not receive meaningful assistance in meeting the forces of the State does not, in my opinion, constitute due process.

The issue of fairly impaneled juries was another contentious criminal justice controversy during Marshall's tenure on the Court. As seen in *Batson v. Kentucky* (1987) and other cases, Marshall again and again clashed with Rehnquist on this Sixth Amendment issue. *Batson* was unusual because it was a case in which Marshall joined the majority opinion written by Justice Powell—and Chief Justice Burger and Justice Rehnquist each wrote dissenting opinions.

James Batson, a black American, was tried for second-degree burglary and receiving stolen goods. At the *voir dire* proceedings (to select the trial jury), the judge excused a number of potential jurors. The prosecutor then used his peremptory challenges to remove all four blacks remaining in the jury pool. Batson's lawyer then moved to dismiss the impaneled jury because his client's Sixth and Fourteenth Amendment rights had been violated by the actions that eliminated African Americans from the final pool of potential jurors. Such action violated Batson's guarantee of a jury drawn from a cross section of the community. The motion was denied, the trial took place, and Batson was convicted. The Kentucky Supreme Court affirmed the conviction, and Batson appealed to the U.S. Supreme Court.

In a majority opinion written by Powell, joined by Marshall, the Court reversed the judgments of the state courts. No state can provide a black defendant equal protection if he is tried before a jury "from which members of his race have been purposefully excluded." Furthermore, "the Equal Protection Clause... forbids the prosecutor to challenge potential jurors solely on account of their race or on the assumption that black jurors as a group will be unable impartially to consider the State's case against a black defendant."

Rehnquist's rare dissent from the majority condemned its "unprecedented use of the Equal Protection Clause to restrict the historic scope of the peremptory challenge....In my view, there is simply nothing 'unequal' about the State using its peremptory challenges to strike blacks from the jury in cases involving black defendants, so long as such challenges are used to exclude whites in cases involving white defendants, Hispanics in cases involving Hispanic defendants, Asians in cases involving Asian defendants, and so on."

## MARSHALL'S VIEWS ABOUT THE DEATH PENALTY

For Marshall, the death penalty was categorically immoral and unconstitutional, a form of cruel and unusual punishment. Furthermore, as he argued in the Court and in public, setting aside the moral question of the legitimacy of the death penalty, there was an *"extraordinary unfairness* that now surrounds the *administration* of the death penalty."[20] As a justice, he *always* voted against the death penalty. Marshall dissented, usually joined by Brennan, whenever the Court majority denied a petition for certiorari from a condemned petitioner. He wrote almost one hundred substantive dissents from the Court's denial of certiorari in capital punishment cases. And although he wrote for or voted with a Court majority nineteen times, the majority of his writings in plenary death penalty cases were either solitary dissents or ones in which he was joined by Brennan.

Shortly after Marshall joined the Court, in *Furman v. Georgia* (1972), the Court narrowly ruled, five to four, that the death penalty, as it was then implemented in the states, was unconstitutional. Again Marshall and Rehnquist were on opposite sides of the issue. But in 1972, by a single vote, Marshall was with the five-person majority (one that included Douglas, Brennan, Stewart, and White). Rehnquist dissented, along with the rest of the Nixon appointees (Burger, Blackmun, and Powell).

The Court, however, could not find any reasonable argument acceptable to a majority, so there was the issuance of the short *per curiam* opinion, followed by 231 pages containing *nine separate opinions.* Every justice expressed himself on the matter. Seven saw the death penalty as a legitimate punishment for crime (with Stewart, Douglas, and White stating that position—if the constitutional defects in its usage were rectified). Only Marshall and Brennan concluded that the death penalty was excessive and that it was cruel and unusual punishment prohibited by the Eighth Amendment. Marshall's opinion stated, bluntly, that "even if capital punishment is not excessive, it nonetheless violates the Eighth Amendment because it is morally unacceptable to the people of the United States at this time in their history."

> The burden of capital punishment falls upon the poor, the ignorant, and the underprivileged members of society. It is the poor, and members of minority groups who are least able to voice their complaints against capital punishment. Their impotence leaves them victims of a sanction that the wealthier, better-represented, just-as-guilty person can escape. So long as the capital sanction is used only against the forlorn, easily forgotten members of society, legislators are content to maintain the status quo....Assuming knowledge of all the facts...the average citizen would, in my opinion, find it shocking to his conscience and sense of justice. For this reason alone capital punishment cannot stand.

After the decision in *Furman* was announced, thirty-five states "enacted new legislation specifying the factors that juries must consider when issuing death sentences. [Twenty-five] states adopted laws requiring juries to consider specific aggravating factors (justifying the imposition of capital punishment) and mitigating factors (justifying the imposition of an alternative sentence to the death penalty)."[21]

Four years later, in *Gregg v. Georgia* (1976), another set of cases from Georgia, Texas, and Florida (consolidated by the justices), the seven-person Court majority found that the states had addressed the capricious and arbitrary ways the death sentence had been carried out, and validated the use of the penalty. The *Gregg* majority confirmed the legitimacy of the three states' new capital punishment statutes that had juries take into account aggravating and mitigating circumstances before passing sentence on defendants convicted of capital offenses. Only Brennan and Marshall dissented. In his dissent, Marshall called the death penalty a "vestigial savagery" that violated morality and the Eighth Amendment. Although he began to doubt whether the average citizen's conscience was shocked by the death penalty, Marshall nevertheless insisted that it was unconstitutional because it was excessive. "What disturbed him most was that several members of the Court's majority approved retribution as a legitimate reason for imposing the death penalty."[22] He concluded his dissent with the observation that "the taking of life 'because the wrongdoer deserves it' surely must fall, for such a punishment has as its very basis the total denial of the wrongdoer's dignity and worth...which is the goal of the Eighth Amendment to respect."

By this time, in addition to dissenting on principle in death penalty cases, both Marshall and Brennan began to file dissents from the Court's denial of certiorari in such cases. Marshall, seeing that his brethren (except for Brennan) were not willing to even consider that the death penalty per se violated the Constitution, shifted his attack on capital punishment. While still arguing that, on its face, the death penalty came into conflict with the Constitution, he hammered away at the fact that the new procedural safeguards introduced into state law after *Furman* were without value. There was still arbitrariness and capriciousness in the application of these newly revised statutes.[23] A disproportionate number of black American males were still put to death in the states.

In the 1980s, Marshall and Brennan, who continued to assert that the death penalty was per se unconstitutional, attempted to save condemned prisoners by arguing that *Gregg* was insufficient; defendants facing the death penalty needed new and greater procedural protections. Marshall was also deeply concerned about the poor quality—the essential incompetency—of counsel appointed to assist defendants facing the death sentence. "Capital defendants," he argued in 1986, "frequently suffer the consequences of having trial counsel who are ill-equipped to handle capital cases....[Many], though acting in good faith, inevitably make very serious mistakes....Trial counsel's lack of expertise takes a heavy toll.

"Whatever your views about the death penalty," Marshall told the assembled judges and lawyers attending the 1986 annual meeting of the Second Judicial Circuit, "we simply cannot accept this state of affairs. We must do something to improve the quality of representation at the trial stage."[24] Marshall called on the legal profession to address problems associated with capital punishment. He and Brennan attempted to persuade the other justices to improve the procedural protections for defendants facing the death penalty. They were not very successful. By 1991, however, Rehnquist had assembled majorities that overturned Brennan's and Marshall's modest successes in such cases as *Ford v. Wainright* (1986), *McCleskey v. Kemp I* (1987, as well as *II*, in 1991, and *III*, also in 1991), *Booth v. Maryland* (1987), and *Payne v. Tennessee* (1991).

In *Ford v. Wainright*, the Court, in a six-to-three decision written by Marshall, concluded that a defendant sentenced to death who has gone insane while on death row cannot be executed without violating the Eighth Amendment's prohibition against cruel and unusual punishment. It was a highly unusual case, one illustrating both Marshall's strength and the fluidity of choice in Supreme Court decision making. The Court majority initially refused to grant certiorari when the appeal was discussed in conference session. Marshall immediately wrote and circulated a substantive dissent from the denial of certiorari which, surprisingly, evolved into a Marshall opinion for the Court majority! He gathered the votes of Brennan, Blackmun, Powell (who concurred separately), and Stevens. Justices O'Connor and White agreed, in part, with the result. Rehnquist, once again, was on the other side of the issue and wrote a dissent that Chief Justice Burger joined.

*McCleskey*, however, was a very different and, for Marshall, a tragic death penalty case involving clear racial discrimination. In a closely divided opinion, with Marshall dissenting, the Court majority of five concluded that racial bias is not proven by the mere statistical fact that when African Americans murder whites, they are given the death sentence more frequently than are whites when they murder blacks. The Court had been presented with evidence, in briefs and in oral argument, "showing that despite the statutory procedural safeguards, racial discrimination still permeated Georgia's capital sentencing system."[25] It showed that defendants charged with killing white persons received the death penalty in 11 percent of the cases, while defendants charged and convicted of killing African Americans received the death sentence in only 1 percent of the cases. Defendants, basically nonwhites, charged with killing a white person were 4.3 times "as likely to receive a death sentence as defendants charged with killing blacks."

Justice Powell, for the majority, rejected McCleskey's argument that the "Georgia capital sentencing process is administered in a racially discriminatory manner in violation of the Eighth and Fourteenth Amendments." There was no "purposeful [racial] discriminaton shown in the litigation." McCleskey failed to show "that the decision makers in *his* case acted with discriminatory purpose," Powell concluded. Maintaining that the Georgia law had been properly applied, his opinion skirted the essential dilemma the evidence presented. By way of confessing an unwillingness to grapple with the dilemma, he wrote that ruling in McCleskey's favor would "throw into serious question the principles that underlie our entire criminal justice system." As one observer noted:

> rather than risk toppling the entire system of criminal sentencing, the Court chose to leave intact a racially discriminatory capital sentencing system that places a higher value on the lives of whites than blacks. Moreover, in upholding a black man's death sentence because he could not prove that anyone intended to discriminate against him personally, the Court ignored the fact that racism in America often operates on a systemic and unconscious level.[26]

Justice Brennan wrote an "impassioned" dissenting opinion, joined by Marshall, Harry Blackmun, and John Stevens. Had rational thinking been employed by the Court majority in this case, argued Brennan, then they would have clearly been led to the conclusion that

> the jury more likely than not would have spared McCleskey's life had his victim been black....Blacks who kill whites are sentenced to death at nearly twenty-two times the rate of blacks who kill blacks, and more than seven times the rate of whites who kill blacks. [Especially so in Georgia, where] "subtle, less consciously held racial attitudes" continue to be of concern, and the Georgia [criminal justice] system gives such attitudes considerable room to operate. The conclusions drawn from McCleskey's statistical evidence are therefore consistent with the lessons of social experience.

In *McCleskey,* the majority "for the first time required a capital defendant to prove that *his* particular sentence was based on impermissible factors."[27] Powell's majority opinion, much to Marshall's disgust, completely rejected the reality of an "unconscious racism" functioning across America, a racism that pervaded the capital sentencing process. "In fact, racial discrimination afflicting the capital sentencing system exists on a subtler, less overt, but more pervasive level than [Powell's opinion] was willing to acknowledge."[28]

Marshall was still sitting when *McCleskey* came back to the Court a second time in 1991. It was Marshall's last year on the Court. Following the 1987 decision, McCleskey's attorney filed a second petition arguing that his client's Sixth

Amendment right had been violated when the state placed an informant in the cell next to his client and the police spy prepared a twenty-one-page report that was never turned over to McCleskey's lawyers. Indeed, the prosecution had withheld it from the defense attorney during McCleskey's 1978 trial and for eight years afterwards.

The federal district court judge granted the petition, excusing defense counsel's failure to raise the Sixth Amendment issue the first time because it had no knowledge of the document. He also ruled that McCleskey's constitutional rights were violated. However, the federal appeals court reversed, and McCleskey came back to the Court.

Once again, the Court majority rejected his appeal, this time because, Kennedy argued for the majority, McCleskey had abused the writ of habeas corpus. The six-person majority concluded that second habeas corpus petitions had to be dismissed unless there were "exceptional circumstances" that warranted the granting of the petition.

Marshall wrote another scathing dissent, joined only by Blackmun and Stevens. His first draft labeled Kennedy's opinion "lawless," but a memo from Stevens led Marshall to take out that term. "I am with you even if you do not make the change, but I think in the long run it might be prudent to do so," wrote Stevens. After all, the Kennedy majority opinion in *McCleskey* was in fact the law of the land! That same day, Marshall wrote Stevens, "I took out the word 'lawless' within a minute after I received your note."[29]

*McCleskey* came back to the Court for a third time. On September 24, 1991, in *McCleskey v. Bowers,* the Court rejected the defendant's last-minute appeal for Court review. In a bitter memo to the conference, Marshall blasted his colleagues for their callousness:

> For the third time, this Court disregards Warren McCleskey's constitutional claims. In 1986, [he] presented uncontroverted evidence that Georgia murder defendants with white victims were more than four times as likely to receive the death sentence as were defendants with Afro-American victims....Last Term, the Court not only discounted [his] constitutional claim but sharply limited the opportunity of criminal defendants, even those on death row, to obtain federal habeas corpus....Now, in the final hours of his life, [he] alleges that he was denied an impartial clemency hearing....In refusing to grant a stay to review fully McCleskey's claims, the Court values expediency over human life. Repeatedly denying Warren McCleskey his constitutional rights is unacceptable. Executing him is inexcusable.

Early the next day, September 25, Warren McCleskey, the poor, ignorant black American petitioner, three times rejected by the Supreme Court, despite

Marshall's three dissents, was finally executed by the state of Georgia. In an ironic turn of events, just before McCleskey was executed, the now-retired Lewis Powell, the key vote and the majority opinion's author in the first *McCleskey* opinion, was asked if he would change his vote in any case he had heard. His immediate answer: "Yes, *McCleskey v. Kemp.*" Not because he now accepted the statistics-driven argument but because, as he put it, "I would vote the other way in *any* capital case....I have come to think that capital punishment should be abolished." After all, he said, capital punishment "serves no useful purpose."[30] Marshall was almost off the bench when Powell uttered these words. Marshall was not pleased by Powell's change of heart; he was angry and bitter because, even on the Court, there was an "unconscious racism" that made itself known in these anguishing criminal justice cases.

*Booth v. Maryland,* heard during the same term as *McCleskey I,* was a case that raised the question of whether a sentencing jury in a capital case could hear from the victim's relatives in victim-impact statements (VIS) presented to them. Maryland law required that "the pre-sentence report in all felony cases must also include a VIS, describing the effect of the crime on the victim and his family." A closely divided Court (five to four) ruled that use of VIS by the prosecutor in the sentencing phase of a capital murder trial violated the Eighth Amendment. Justice Powell wrote the opinion for the narrow majority, one that Marshall joined. The majority concluded that the VIS "information is irrelevant to a capital sentencing decision, and that its admission creates a constitutionally unacceptable risk that the jury may impose the death penalty in an arbitrary and capricious manner." Rehnquist, in 1987 the new Chief Justice, dissented, along with Justices Scalia, O'Connor, and White. White and Scalia wrote the dissenting opinions, with Scalia's the more scathing of the two. He wrote that "to require, as we have, that all mitigating factors which render capital punishment a harsh penalty in the particular case be placed before the sentencing authority, while simultaneously requiring, as we do today, that evidence of much of the human suffering that defendant has inflicted be suppressed, is in effect to prescribe a debate on the appropriateness of the capital penalty with one side muted."

*Booth,* however, did not last very long as precedent. There were two major personnel changes that led to the overturn: Powell's retirement, and his replacement by Anthony Kennedy, another Reagan administration conservative appointment; and Brennan's retirement in 1990, and his replacement by Justice David Souter (appointed by President George Bush). These two new critical votes provided the opportunity for Rehnquist, working with the other Reagan appointees and Byron White, to overturn the 1987 precedent.

That took place in 1991, in the case of *Payne v. Tennessee.* It was not a surprise to Court observers. When the Court granted certiorari in *Payne,* it directed the parties to argue "the question of whether the Court's prior rulings barring the use of VIS's ought to be overturned, despite the fact that that issue was not raised in the petition for certiorari." Twenty-two states, along with the Bush administration, all joined in one *amicus curiae* brief with the Court that urged the justices to overturn *Booth.*

*Payne* was announced four years after *Booth,* on Marshall's last day on the Court. It was a six-to-three majority decision, with an opinion written by Rehnquist, that overturned Marshall's majority decision for the Court in the *Booth* case, decided only four years earlier.

Pervis Payne, a borderline retarded defendant, was convicted of killing a mother and her two-year-old daughter. In closing arguments before the jury that convicted him, the prosecutor said that while there was nothing they could do for the dead females, "there is something you can do for Nicholas [the surviving three-year-old son]....He is going to want to know what type of justice was done."

Payne was sentenced to death, and his attorney immediately appealed on the grounds that the prosecutor had presented a VIS to the jury, which was in conflict with the Eighth Amendment—according to *Booth.* Rehnquist stated, in opposition to the earlier precedent, that the "individualized consideration" afforded the capital defendant should not occur "wholly apart from the crime" the defendant committed and its impact on the victims of the crime. The majority in *Payne* said that VIS evidence was "not only constitutional, but also beneficial in determining the culpability of capital defendants."[31] He concluded by reminding the nation that "the States remain free, in capital cases, as well as others, to devise new procedures and new remedies to meet felt needs. Victim-impact evidence is simply another form or method of informing the sentencing authority about the specific harm caused by the crime in question."

Equally important and scary to many was Rehnquist's views on the value and permanence of judicially created precedents. Judicial precedent, he concluded, "is not an inexorable command; rather, it 'is a principle of policy and not a mechanical formula of adherence to the latest decision.'...*Booth*...was wrongly decided and should be, and now [is], overturned." Furthermore, Rehnquist brazenly defended the overturn of *Booth* by noting that it was "decided by the narrowest of margins, over spirited dissents,...[and has] defied consistent application in the lower courts."

Rehnquist's decision thoroughly frightened Marshall and others who disagreed with the substantive views of the Constitution held by Rehnquist and his "gang." The Chief was announcing a new, flexible standard of *stare decisis,* or precedent. For observers of the judiciary, the Rehnquist group "signaled its willingness to reverse a host of decisions" not favored by the ideologically conservative Court majority.[32]

On this, his last day, Marshall dissented angrily. (His colleagues had not been informed of his decision to retire.) He spoke plainly to them and to the public beyond the marble palace.

> *Power, not reason, is the new currency of this Court's decision-making....*Neither the law nor the facts supporting *Booth*...underwent any change in the last four years. Only the personnel of this Court did. In dispatching *Booth* to its grave...the majority declares itself free to discard any principle of constitutional liberty which was recognized or affirmed over the dissenting votes of four Justices and with which five or more Justices now disagree. (My emphasis.)

Responding to his adversary's view of the value of precedent, Marshall wrote that "this Court has repeatedly stressed that fidelity to precedent is fundamental to 'a society governed by the Rule of Law.'" He concluded by stating that there were no reasons for the overturn except the power/ideological one. "If the majority's radical reconstruction of the rules for overturning this Court's decisions is to be taken at face value—and the majority offers us no reason why it should not—then the overruling of *Booth*...is but a preview of an even broader and more far-reaching assault upon this Court's precedents."

On January 25, 1993, the day after Marshall died and the flags on the U.S. Supreme Court building flew at half-mast, the Rehnquist Court announced its decision in the death-penalty case of *Graham v. Collins.* In a five-to-four decision, the Court ruled, in an opinion by Justice Byron White, that a challenge by a death-row inmate "could not be brought through a petition for a writ of habeas corpus in federal courts." Because of the Court's unwillingness to hear the complaint on substantive grounds, the petitioner was executed. (The petitioner's lawyers had challenged the conviction because the jury did not know that they could properly consider the fact "that the defendant committed murder before the age of eighteen.")[33] It was indicative of the Court majority's indifference to "people who just don't matter."

## MARSHALL'S CRIMINAL JUSTICE JURISPRUDENCE

Marshall was ever the liberal realist on the Court, but he had the misfortune to serve on it at a time when, for most of his tenure, his jurisprudential views were shared with a very small group of justices. He had the additional misfortune to serve on the Court at a time when a radical conservative (who was, at the same time, bright, articulate, and personable) by the name of William Rehnquist sat first as a justice and then, after 1986, as Chief Justice of the United States. By the end of his tenure, Marshall could say, openly in *The New York Times,* that the Rehnquist majority's "ill-considered reversals should be considered as no more than temporary interruptions."[34] Marshall was particularly angered by Rehnquist's categorical rejection of all he knew about the real world of criminal justice in America and its distortion by pervasive racism. Rehnquist was more concerned about the values of federalism and property rights than he was with the rights of individuals.[35]

If Rehnquist had his way, and Marshall feared that he would (given the new personnel on the Court), he would overturn *all* the Warren Court opinions that had brought into the Fourteenth Amendment's due-process clause most of the protections found in the Fourth through Eighth Amendments.[36] To Marshall, the Chief Justice's thoughts and his opinions in the area of criminal justice were "incontrovertible evidence of Rehnquist's insensitivity to the problems encountered by members of disadvantaged groups in American society."[37] And, deep in his heart as well as in his head, Thurgood Marshall always *knew* that the man from Arizona was a racist.

Statistically, the two men were unequivocal polar opposites. From the time Rehnquist became Chief, in 1986, through Marshall's retirement, in a total of 111 criminal due-process votes, Rehnquist voted against the defendant's due process claims 87 percent of the time, while Marshall voted against the defendant's claims 3 percent of the time. Rehnquist's was the highest percentage among the justices, and Marshall's was the lowest.[38] What offended Marshall most about the Rehnquist majority's criminal justice opinions was the continued deference shown to local police and local and state prosecutors by the Court majorities—and the use of a cost-effective balancing process that was always weighted to favor the government's arguments. As he said in *New York v. Quarles* (1984), where another exception to *Miranda* was created by the Rehnquist majority (police officers were permitted to question persons without giving the *Miranda* warnings when the public safety required such quick action): "The majority should not be permitted to elude the [Fifth] Amendment's absolute prohibition simply by calculating costs that arise when the public's safety is at issue. Indeed, were constitutional adjudication always conducted in such an *ad hoc* manner, the Bill of Rights would be a most unreliable protector of individual liberties."

# 13

## MARSHALL AND FIRST AMENDMENT FREEDOMS

*Congress shall make no law respecting an establishment of religion,*
*or prohibiting the free exercise thereof; or abridging the freedom of*
*speech, or of the press; or the right of the people peacefully to assemble,*
*and to petition the Government for a redress of grievances.*

Under the American federal system, every citizen has "dual citizenship." One is, simultaneously, an American citizen and a citizen of a particular state, and is subject to the laws of *both* the national and state governments, as well as local governments. Because America is a democratic republic, *all* governmental power is limited by the language of the U.S. Constitution and state constitutions. The Bill of Rights, the first ten amendments to the U.S. Constitution, were ratified in order to place very specific constraints on the central government's ability to restrict the freedoms and liberties of its citizens. The First Amendment, ratified in 1791, limited Congress from passing legislation that restricted an American citizen's free speech, religion, press, and assembly rights.

State constitutions generally had similar *but not identical* protections of individual rights and liberties for their residents. Moreover, while some state constitutions contained tougher restrictions on governmental power than did the U.S. Constitution, even as amended in 1791, there were some state constitutions that did not have all the protections found in the Bill of Rights. In the 1833 case of *Barron v. Baltimore,* the Supreme Court said that the Bill of Rights constrained only the *national* government; *state* constitutions were the source of curbs on state legislation that deprived a citizen of a civil or political right. If a particular state constitution did not contain such a protection, the Bill of Rights could not be used to invalidate the state action. The Fourteenth Amendment, ratified in 1868, was a limit on state power. As written and initially interpreted by the

Court, it enumerated civil rights, such as due process of law and equal protection of the laws, that could not be abridged by the state.

Beginning in 1925, however, Court majorities concluded that the First
Amendment contained "fundamental" rights for *all* persons in the nation.
If there was deprivation of these basic rights, then "liberty" was in jeopardy.
Therefore, in incremental fashion, the First Amendment's protections were
*incorporated* into the "due process" language of the Fourteenth Amendment. They were *nationalized;* a state law, for example, that restricted freedom of speech violated a person's right to "due process" that was protected by
the Fourteenth Amendment. Through interpretation of the various segments of the First Amendment (as well as other Bill of Rights guarantees—the Fourth through Eighth Amendments—by Supreme Court
majorities from 1925 through the late 1960s, state and local governments
found themselves constrained by the prohibitory language of the Bill of
Rights.[1]

## THE FIRST AMENDMENT:
## AN ABSOLUTE SET OF FREEDOMS?

Does this amendment absolutely prohibit a legislature from passing laws that
abridge the freedoms it protects? Or can the government abridge those freedoms
if it can show a compelling reason for so acting? From the very first occasion
when such questions came before the Supreme Court, they provoked fierce
internal debates among the Justices.

Only two justices have held that the First Amendment absolutely restricts the
powers of government: Hugo Black and William O. Douglas. For them, the language of the amendment admitted no exceptions. "Congress (and the States)
shall make no law…" meant exactly what the words said, Black maintained for
over three decades, on and off the high bench.[2] During their long tenures on the
Court, both men saw the amendment as a categorical constraint on all policy
makers.

For Black, "without deviation, without exception, without any ifs, buts, or
whereases, freedom of speech means that government shall not do anything to
people or, in the words of the Magna Carta, move against people, either for the
views they have or the views they express or the words they speak or write."[3]
William O. Douglas also believed deeply that an absolutely unfettered freedom
of speech, press, and religion was necessary for the maintenance of a functioning
political democracy. Freedom of speech in the Bill of Rights, he wrote, was "the
right of advocacy for the purpose of incitement, as well as for education.…Free
speech had traditionally included both.…The First Amendment…marks the

end of all censorship, it allows the ability of the mind to roam at will over the entire spectrum of ideas."[4]

Marshall believed in the primacy of the First Amendment,[5] but declined to let everything take shelter under First Amendment protections. Only in very rare circumstances was there justification for government's taking certain actions in the name of public order and morals. Marshall believed that if there was a "clear and present danger" to the community, then freedom of speech and expression had to be curtailed by government. His acceptance of the standard created by Justices Oliver Wendell Holmes and Louis Brandeis, in *Schenck v. United States* (1918) and *Debs v. United States* (1919), during the xenophobia of World War I, placed Marshall in conflict with Black and Douglas on occasion.

Marshall also shared the majority's view that some speech and expression was not protected by the First Amendment. This included such esoteric and rarely applicable categories as "fighting words" and "offensive" speech. Still other types of unprotected speech, press, and expression are much more problematic. Over the years, especially since 1957, the Supreme Court has validated a number of convictions involving the distribution of material thought to be obscene or pornographic. Furthermore, libel and slander (which the law defines as "defamation of character by print or visual [libel] or oral [slander] presentation"), if proven, are not a form of speech and expression protected by the First and Fourteenth Amendments.

Most of the brethren, except for Black and Douglas, also distinguished between commercial speech and other kinds of speech. The former has been given less protection than free expression of political, or social, or economic views. And *all* of the justices, including Black and Douglas, distinguished between pure speech and expression as opposed to speech "plus" some kind of conduct (such as marching, or picketing, or sitting in to protest discrimination, etc.).

The obvious problem, for Marshall and the others who did not believe in an "absolute" First Amendment, one that allowed *all* kinds of speech and expression, was in defining the difference between, for example, erotic but protected speech and pornography, which is unprotected "speech." Notwithstanding Potter Stewart's classic definition of pornography, "I know it when I see it," the justices believed that a somewhat less subjective standard was needed.

Except for Black and Douglas, the justices (and quite a few of their clerks) occasionally found themselves in a screening room viewing an allegedly pornographic film to determine whether it was indeed pornographic, or whether it had certain redeeming values that gave the film the protection of the First Amendment. Marshall always attended and greatly enjoyed these private screenings; he had great fun during the showings (regularly sitting next to an almost blind Justice John M. Harlan II, describing in vivid detail what was happening on the small screen). He enjoyed even more turning to Justice Blackmun at the end of the movies and saying, "Did you learn anything new from that one, Harry? I didn't."[6]

Marshall, while not in agreement with Black and Douglas that the First Amendment was an absolute bar to governmental actions, did believe that it was the primary set of values in the always-evolving Constitution. He believed that only very compelling reasons would justify the restriction, by government at any level, of First Amendment freedoms, and he invariably voted against such restrictions.

## FREEDOM OF SPEECH AND EXPRESSION

Although political speech and expression was important and should be protected, the First Amendment meant more than that for Marshall. *All persons,* criminals as well as playwrights, rich as well as poor, want to explore a wide range of experiences. He believed that those less fortunate, affluent, or powerful also had minds, ideas, and dreams, and that the First Amendment gave them the right to extend their world—however small and cramped it might be. As he said in 1974, "It is the role of the First Amendment and this Court to protect those precious personal rights by which we satisfy the basic yearnings of the human spirit."

His conception of a "just and humane society" was built on the First Amendment's protections against interference with one's personal liberties. In *Procunier v. Martinez,* a 1974 case involving First Amendment rights for persons in youth correctional facilities, Marshall stated that "when the prison gates slam behind an individual, he does not lose his human quality; his mind does not become closed to ideas; his intellect does not cease to feed on a free and open interchange of opinions; his yearning for self-respect does not end; nor is his quest for self-realization concluded."

Marshall usually ruled that "the First Amendment takes precedence over other individual rights that he cared deeply about, including privacy, fair trials for persons accused of crime, and racial integration."[7] He also tried, however, to discover ways to resolve conflicts *between* liberties. "Persons," he believed, "should not be put to a Hobson's choice—i.e., they should not be forced to renounce one right to enjoy another."[8] He and his colleagues were regularly involved in the resolution of clashes between the First Amendment freedom of the press and the Sixth Amendment right to a fair and open trial,[9] between the right of privacy versus the freedom of the press.[10] As the liberal in opposition to the Court radical, Rehnquist, Marshall prevailed over his nemesis in First Amendment cases more frequently than he did on other constitutional issues.

## PROTECTED SPEECH

In the Georgia pornography case *Stanley v. Georgia,* films found in Stanley's home during a warranted search for gambling evidence resulted in his conviction for possessing pornography. Stanley appealed to the U.S. Supreme Court, and the justices granted certiorari, heard the case, and overturned the conviction. Writing for a unanimous Court, Marshall maintained that Stanley's fundamental rights were violated by the Georgia statute. "If the First Amendment means anything, it means that a State has no business telling a man, sitting alone in his own house, what books he may read or films he may watch."

Obscenity standards were not affected by Marshall's decision in *Stanley.* His opinion stated that while "states retain broad power to regulate obscenity, that power simply does not extend to mere possession by the individual in the *privacy* of his own home." Therefore, "we hold," Marshall wrote, "that the First and Fourteenth Amendments prohibit making mere private possession of obscene material a crime." His writing echoed his father's long-held view that "every man's home was his castle," and nothing in the Constitution allowed this sanctuary of privacy to be violated unless a valid warrant was served.[11]

*Pickering v. Board of Education* (1968) was, in both his and his law clerks' judgment, one of Marshall's finest majority opinions. Marvin Pickering was a teacher in Township High School District, in Illinois, who had sent a letter to a local newspaper regarding a recently proposed tax increase. In it, he was critical of the way in which the school board and the superintendent of schools had used past funding. Determining that Pickering's letter was "detrimental to the efficient operation and administration of the schools of the district," the school board fired him. Pickering appealed in the Illinois courts, claiming that his letter was protected by the First Amendment. Rebuffed, he filed an appeal with the Supreme Court. The Court noted probable jurisdiction and heard the case. In an opinion written by Marshall, the Court overturned the Illinois Supreme Court. Using the "balancing" test (where the rights of the individual were weighed by the justices against the demands for public order by the state) that Black and Douglas rejected (they concurred in *Pickering*), Marshall concluded that the teacher had the right to comment as a citizen "upon matters of public concern." On the matter of school budgets, "Teachers are, as a class, the members of a community most likely to have informed and definite opinions as to how funds allotted to the operation of the schools should be spent. Accordingly, it is essential that they be able to speak out freely on such questions without fear of retaliatory dismissal."

Another landmark First Amendment case decided in 1976 still provokes debate today. The case was *James Buckley et al. v. Valeo et al.,* and it involved the legitimacy of congressional efforts to enact federal campaign finance reform legislation in the wake of the Watergate scandal. Argued in November 1975 and announced, in an unsigned opinion in early January 1976, there were eight opinions written. *Buckley* was, clearly, a case that fractured the Court along a number of First Amendment lines.

Congress had passed the Federal Election Campaign Act in 1971 in an effort to curb corrupt election practices. As amended in 1974, the act limited political *contributions* by individuals and political action committees (PACs). *Spending* by an individual, a group, or the candidate was limited as well. The Federal Election Commission (FEC) was created to oversee and implement the law, and IRS regulations were modified to provide for public financing of primary and general presidential elections.

The law was immediately challenged by Republican senator James Buckley of New York and others, who claimed that the act's limitations on a candidate's election campaign expenditures constituted *"a restriction on communication violative of the First Amendment,* since virtually all meaningful political communications in the modern setting involve the expenditure of money." Further, they argued that *the reporting and disclosure provisions of the Act unconstitutionally impinged on their right to freedom of association.* (My emphasis.) The federal appeals court (D.C. Circuit) rejected most of the claims, so Buckley and others appealed to the U.S. Supreme Court. The Court accepted the case, heard arguments, and handed down a hastily written decision in late January 1976—in time for the act to affect the 1976 presidential primaries and general election. Five justices, including Marshall, dissented in part in the case; there were different majorities among the eight participating justices in each of its major segments. "Teams" of justices, but not including Marshall (which angered him), were assigned to write different parts of the opinion.

On January 29, 1976, the *per curiam* opinion essentially upheld the *contribution* limits "as appropriate legislative measures to deal with the reality and appearance of improper influence stemming from the dependence of candidates on large campaign contributions." However, all the *expenditure* limits were declared unconstitutional because "these provisions place substantial and direct restrictions on the ability of candidates, citizens, and associations to engage in political expression protected by the First Amendment." Marshall dissented from the part of the opinion that invalidated the expenditure limitation because he felt that part of the law tried to level the political elections playing field for less affluent, minority candidates.

*Rankin v. McPherson* was a free-speech case heard by the Court in 1987. It involved the question of whether a government employee could be dismissed from work because of comments made on the job about the President of the United States. Ardith McPherson, who was a nineteen-year-old African American employee in a local constable's office, was fired for saying, after she heard that President Reagan had been shot and wounded, "He's [Reagan] cutting back Medicaid and food stamps, welfare and CETA....If they go for him again, I hope they get him." Rankin, her supervisor, fired her for that remark.

McPherson brought suit in federal court, contending that Rankin had violated her constitutional rights, and asking the federal court to reinstate her and to award her back pay, costs, and fees. The federal district court judge concluded that her speech was not protected by the First Amendment, but the federal court of appeals overturned the judgment because "however ill-considered [her] opinion was, it did not make her unfit" for her job in the constable's office. The government appealed and the Court, in a five-to-four opinion written by Marshall, affirmed the lower court's judgment. Justice Scalia wrote a dissent, joined by Chief Justice Rehnquist, and by Justices O'Connor and White.

Marshall, like most of his brethren, used the "balancing" test in this and other First Amendment cases. For him, the question was whether McPherson's angry comments about the President "constitut[ed] speech on a matter of public concern." That is determined, he wrote, by the Court reviewing "the content, form, and context of a given statement, as revealed by the whole record." For Marshall and the majority, McPherson's comments "plainly dealt with a matter of public concern" and thus outweighed the state's interest in "promoting the efficiency of the public services it performs through its employees." The Court concluded, finally, that the burden of proof ("justifying the discharge on legitimate grounds") in such First Amendment cases is on the government, and in this case it was not met by the constable's office. "While [McPherson's] statement was made at the workplace, there is no evidence that it interfered with the efficient functioning of the office."

While drafting and circulating the opinion, Marshall received a note from Justice Stevens that asked him to change some lines in the "excellent opinion" so as not to have the readers think "that we agree with what McPherson had to say [about Reagan]." Marshall quickly changed the offending sentence by incorporating Stevens's suggested modification. He was not going to risk losing the majority in this case—even though he had little regard for the President.[12]

## UNPROTECTED SPEECH

During the 1971 term, the Court received more than sixty certiorari petitions challenging obscenity convictions. Eight were selected for review and decision in the 1972 term. The new conservative justices could now prevail over the remaining liberals of the Warren Court. This meant that there could be significant modification of existing standards that defined what was obscene and pornographic (thus outside the protection of the First Amendment) and what challenged material was protected.

Justice Brennan had written the opinion defining the obscenity standards that was precedent in 1972, when the Burger Court majority overturned it. In 1957, in the combined opinion of *Roth v. United States* and *Alberts v. California,* he wrote for the Court majority that "implicit in the history of the First Amendment is the rejection of obscenity as utterly without redeeming social importance.... [The test for obscenity is] whether to the average person, the dominant theme of the material taken as a whole appeals to the prurient interest." The two absolutists dissented. Black and Douglas argued that "the First Amendment, its prohibition in terms absolute, was designed to preclude courts as well as legislatures from weighing the values of speech against silence."

Definitions determine constitutionality, and definitions are influenced by the climate and opinion and shaped by the character and beliefs of the justices sitting on the Court at any particular time. In 1972, in *Miller v. California,* Justice Byron White, a surprisingly conservative Kennedy appointee, joined all four of the Nixon appointees, Chief Justice Burger and Associate Justices Blackmun, Powell, and Rehnquist, to change the *Roth* standard for determining whether a book, film, or picture is or is not obscene and pornographic. Burger's opinion for the narrow five-person majority established a new, more restrictive standard. The "basic guidelines for the trier of fact must [now] be: (a) whether 'the average person, applying contemporary community standards' would find that the work, taken as a whole, appeals to the prurient interest; (b) whether the work depicts or describes, in a patently offensive way, sexual conduct specifically defined by the applicable state law; and (c) whether the work, taken as a whole, lacks serious literary, artistic, political, or scientific value."

Brennan, joined by Marshall and Potter Stewart, dissented; he felt it was impossible to legislate or adjudicate in this area. As he wrote to his colleagues after the conference session, "It has proved impossible to separate expression concerning sex, called obscenity, from other expression concerning sex, whether the material takes the form of words, photographs, or film."[13] Douglas wrote a separate dissenting opinion, saying: "I do not think that we, the judges, were ever given the constitutional power to make definitions of obscenity.... The idea that the First Amendment permits government to ban publications that are 'offensive' to some people puts an ominous gloss on freedom of the press. That test would make it possible to ban any paper or any journal or magazine in some benighted place." The majority ruled; the *Miller* precedent would be used throughout Marshall's remaining years on the Court.

In *Federal Communications Commission (FCC) v. Pacifica Foundation* (1978), the Court divided five to four, with Marshall joining the dissenting opinions of Justices Brennan and Stewart. Justice Stevens wrote for the majority. The question of law was whether the federal regulatory agency, the FCC, had the power to regulate a radio broadcast that contained indecent but not obscene material. The majority's answer was yes.

On a Tuesday afternoon in October 1973, a New York City FM station broadcast comedian George Carlin's "Seven Dirty Words" comedy monologue. It was done in violation of the FCC's regulations regarding indecent language. A listener complained to the FCC, and in February 1975, the agency issued a declaratory order declaring the monologue "patently offensive" but not obscene, granted the complaint, and held that Pacifica "could have been the subject of administrative sanctions." The federal court of appeals reversed the FCC order, and the government agency appealed. The Supreme Court majority overturned the lower federal appellate court.

Although offensive speech, Stevens wrote, ordinarily lacks "literary, political, or scientific value, [it is] not entirely outside the protection of the First Amendment. Some uses of even the most offensive words are unquestionably protected." Because broadcasts enter the privacy of a person's home, and are "uniquely accessible to children,…the individual's right to be left alone plainly outweighs the First Amendment rights of an intruder," so the FCC could lawfully issue regulations that ban offensive speech at certain times of the day. The Carlin comedy routine was a nuisance, said Stevens. It was speech; however, it was a "right thing in a wrong place," and the government could regulate it. "We simply hold that when the Commission finds that a pig has entered the parlor, the exercise of its regulatory power does not depend on proof that the pig is obscene."

Brennan's dissent, which Marshall joined, maintained that while "the privacy interests of an individual in his home are substantial and deserving of significant protection," the First Amendment takes priority over the right of privacy. First of all, Brennan observed, "the radio can be turned off." Whatever the "minimal discomfort" associated with this act of pushing a button or turning a knob, "it is surely worth the candle to preserve the broadcaster's right to send, and the right of those interested to receive, a message entitled to full First Amendment protection."

In *Renton, Washington, v. Playtime Theaters, Inc.,* a 1986 case, the issue was whether a municipality could use its zoning ordinances to restrict adult movie theaters "from locating within 1,000 feet of any residential zone, single- or multiple-family dwelling, church, park, or school." In a decision for the majority, Justice Rehnquist concluded that such local ordinances were constitutional. Reversing the judgment of the lower federal appellate court, Rehnquist concluded that it was passed to "protect and preserve the quality of the city's neighborhoods, commercial districts, and the quality of urban life, not to suppress the expression of unpopular views." Marshall and Brennan were the only dissenters, contending that the Renton ordinance was a content-based one, not content-neutral. "The ordinance discriminates on its face against certain forms of speech based on content.…[It] strongly suggests that Renton was interested not in controlling the 'secondary effects' associated with adult businesses, but in discriminating against adult theaters based on the content of the films they exhibit."

Libel and slander are other categories of speech that are unprotected and outside the coverage of the First and Fourteenth Amendments. Printed, verbal, visual defamation of character assaults can be subjected to civil suits by individuals allegedly libeled. If libel was proved at the trial, the person libeled can receive compensatory (actual loss of money due to loss of a job or damaged reputation) and punitive (mental suffering) monetary damages. By the time Marshall joined the brethren in 1967, Warren Court majorities had cobbled together a set of standards with which to adjudicate cases involving this issue.

By 1967 the Court had distinguished between public *officials* and public *figures* bringing libel suits against a magazine or a newspaper, and private *persons* who claim that they have been libeled or slandered by a magazine or newspaper. For a public official or a public figure (such as a major-league ball player or a movie star) to win a libel judgment, there had to be a showing at trial of (1) actual malice, that is, "with knowledge [by the reporter, for example] that it was false or (2) with reckless disregard of whether it was false or not."[14]

In 1974, after Marshall had been on the high bench for a number of years, the Court announced the standard for libel judgments when a private individual brings a civil suit to a court. In *Gertz v. Welch, Inc.* (1974), the Burger Court determined that private persons had to show only that a publisher was "negligent" in his failure to exercise due care in reporting a story that libeled a private person. Elmer Gertz was an attorney practicing in Chicago who was hired by a family to sue a police officer who had shot and killed their son. He was called a communist fronter by the right-wing journal *American Opinion*, owned by the Welch family of John Birch Society fame. Gertz sued for libel in federal district court. Using the "actual malice" standard, the court ruled in favor of the publication.

The federal appellate court upheld the ruling, and Gertz appealed to the Supreme Court. In a five-to-four opinion, featuring six different opinions (including four separate dissenting opinions), Justice Powell crafted the negligence standard for use in libel cases involving private, not public, individuals. Marshall joined Powell and his nemesis, Rehnquist, in this case, while his friend Brennan, with Douglas, White, and the Chief Justice, Burger, dissented. The majority opinion allowed the states to "impose liability on the publisher or broadcaster of defamatory falsehood [against a private person]" based on the "negligence" standard, but to restrict the award to nonexcessive actual injury only.

## PEACEFUL ASSEMBLY AND ASSOCIATION RIGHTS

Although freedom of association was not explicitly protected by the First Amendment, the Court, prior to Marshall's appointment, had "recognized that the freedom of association is implicit in the very structure of the First Amendment's guarantee of freedom of expression" (*NAACP v. Alabama,* 1958; Marshall had argued the case on behalf of the Inc Fund). A question closely related to peaceful assembly and freedom of association was the *places,* public and private, where such assembly could take place. Could protesters march on the streets, in front of police stations, in front of the state capitol, in front of or close to courtrooms? Some of these questions were answered by the Court when it examined the black American sit-in cases in the early 1960s.

What about private places such as large shopping centers? Did protesting demonstrators have the First Amendment right to speak and demonstrate on private property? This issue came to the Court shortly after Marshall joined it, and in 1968 he wrote the controversial opinion in *Amalgamated Food Employees Union Local 500 v. Logan Valley Plaza.*

Was the modern shopping center, Marshall asked, the equivalent of a public or a private town? Given the comprehensiveness of such complexes, and the large number of them across America—used by millions of shoppers—he argued that the shopping center was the mid-twentieth century's version of the downtown area of small-town America. In his opinion for the Court, Marshall used a 1946 case involving a private town as the central precedent for the 1968 opinion. However, his friend Hugo Black, the author of the 1946 opinion, *Marsh v. Alabama,* was still sitting on the Court in 1968 and vigorously objected to Marshall's use of that precedent.

Justice Black believed that if a private town was the absolute equivalent of a public town, then First Amendment activity could be carried out in that private place. In *Marsh v. Alabama,* for the Court majority, Black wrote that a person's First Amendment rights in the company-owned town of Chickasaw, Alabama, could not be denied by the owner of the private property. The town manager had denied Grace Marsh the right to preach on the sidewalks of the town's business block. Arrested by the company sheriff for violating Alabama's trespass statute, Marsh was subsequently convicted for entering and remaining on the premises of another after having been told to leave.

She appealed her conviction to the Supreme Court. The question for the Court was whether a state could impose criminal penalties on persons who distributed literature on the streets of a company-owned town, in the face of the owner's objections, and not violate the First Amendment. Black wrote the opinion for the Court. Certainly, he said, a public municipality could not completely prevent freedom of expression. Was the private town different? He concluded that if the private town had assumed "*all* the characteristics of any other American town," and "if it did not function differently from any other town," then it was the "functional equivalent" of a public municipality and subject to the commands of the First Amendment.

Was the huge shopping center in *Amalgamated* the functional equivalent of a company town, and therefore, did all persons entering the private mall retain their rights of free expression? Weis Supermarket in the Plaza employed non-union workers. The owner prohibited union organizers from "speaking" to his employees through picketing in front of his store in the private mall. After almost two weeks of picketing, Weis and the owners of the mall enjoined the protesters from picketing on the private property. The union appealed to the Pennsylvania Supreme Court, which upheld the injunction, and the union then appealed to the Supreme Court.

Marshall wrote the majority opinion for a divided Court. His argument was that peaceful picketing in a private facility open to the public, assuming no alternative picketing areas were available, was protected by the First Amendment. "The shopping center here is clearly the 'functional equivalent' of the business district in *Marsh*." Black fumed at what he regarded as Marshall's categorical misreading of his opinion in *Marsh*. Dissenting, he pointed to the gross misapplication of the precedent by Marshall and the Court majority. Chickasaw, Alabama, and Logan Valley Plaza, Pennsylvania, were not analogous. The union protesters, Black concluded, did not have a constitutional right to have Weis furnish them a place for them to protest against Weis's personnel policies.

After *Amalgamated* was handed down, Marshall received a letter from an L. B. Dent of Baltimore. It was an ugly letter:

> It is quite apparent that property rights mean nothing to a colored man at the top or at the bottom. During the recent riots we saw cheap niggers destroy property, steal and loot. We see a cheap nigger put on the Supreme Court to destroy property rights in another manner. Since you acted like a cheap nigger—I will treat you like one.[15]

Marshall did not bother to reply.

But, in a 1972 opinion, *Lloyd Corporation v. Tanner,* the new Nixon Court majority, in an opinion written by Lewis Powell, in effect overturned Marshall's shopping-center opinion. *Lloyd* involved a Portland, Oregon, shopping center, the Lloyd Center, and anti–Vietnam War protesters, the Resistance to the Vietnam War Committee, who were handing out flyers in the mall's central interior hall. There was a strictly enforced no-handbill ordinance in force at the time, and the protesters were forced to leave the premises. They sought a decree in federal district court enjoining the center from blocking their rights. The injunction was issued, in accordance with the *Amalgamated* precedent, and the Lloyd Corporation appealed to the Supreme Court.

There was a very close vote in conference. Douglas, on April 21, 1972, assigned to Marshall what he thought was the majority opinion affirming the lower federal court action. But Harry Blackmun was on the fence, and said so in a note to Marshall. That same day, Chief Justice Burger wrote Douglas and Marshall telling them that Douglas's five-to-four count to affirm was incorrect, "as I had reserved and not voted at all."[16] The assignment controversy escalated when Douglas wrote Burger, with copies to the conference, accusing him of manipulating writing assignments and breaking with Court traditions. "You apparently misunderstand. *Lloyd* is already assigned to Marshall and he's at work on an opinion....It is not for [one] in the minority to try to outwit [the senior associate justice in the majority] by saying 'I reserve my vote' and then recast it to control the assignment. This only leads to a frayed and bitter Court full of needless strains and quarrels. *Lloyd* stays assigned to Marshall."[17]

But not for long. A week after Douglas wrote his letter, the Chief was in the majority. On May 8, Harry Blackmun informed the Chief and the rest of the brethren: "I have spent a good bit of the weekend wrestling with this case. I have now concluded that my vote will be to reverse and not extend *Logan Valley* to the present situation."[18] Chief Justice Burger then announced his vote to reverse, and he had his narrow majority of five.

By early June 1972, Marshall's writing in *Lloyd* was in dissent. The Nixon quartet, joined by the ever-peripatetic Justice White, reversed the federal district court action. The fatal error in Marshall's 1968 opinion was his statement that whenever a private business serves the general public, "its sidewalks and streets become the functional equivalent of similar public facilities." Marshall's dissent repeated his view that the right of property owners to limit expressive freedoms diminishes as the private property expands its contacts with the public. At some point, the private restrictive practices of the owners become subject to the constraints of the First and Fourteenth Amendments.[19] This was the first of a number of decisions overturning Warren Court precedents during Marshall's remaining years on the Court. It would not be the last time he would write in dissent about the overturn of earlier precedents by the Burger and Rehnquist Courts.

Another question about the scope of the First Amendment protections arose in the 1960s: Could protesters picket and march and shout and sing in front of a public school? Could they use expressive conduct in a national park? In *Police Department, City of Chicago v. Mosely,* and in *Greyned v. City of Rockford, Illinois,* both decided the same day in June 1972, the justices addressed the former question. Marshall wrote the majority decisions in both cases. And in *Clark, Secretary of the Interior v. Community for Creative Non-Violence, et al.,* a case heard in 1984, the Court addressed the latter question.

In *Mosely,* a city of Chicago ordinance had prohibited all picketing in front of or next to a school, except for peaceful picketing by labor protesters. Marshall's opinion invalidated the statute on equal-protection grounds, although First Amendment rights were "closely intertwined" in the litigation. Marshall wrote that, "above all else, the First Amendment means that government has no power to restrict expression because of its messages, its ideas, its subject matter, or its content." The Chicago ordinance favored one group over other groups and was therefore in violation of the Fourteenth Amendment's equal-protection clause as well as in conflict with freedom of speech and expression.

*Greyned v. City of Rockford, Illinois* also involved protesters in front of a school. Marshall wrote the opinion for the Court majority of seven, including Rehnquist. The litigation involved more than two hundred high school students, mostly African Americans, who were protesting alleged racial discrimination at West Senior High School in Rockford, Illinois. Having gathered next to the school grounds in April 1969, the protesters then proceeded to march around on the sidewalk about one hundred feet from the school building.

The city relied on two ordinances to break up the demonstration and arrest some forty student demonstrators. One was an ordinance that prohibited picketing less than 150 feet from a public school (but did not "prohibit the peaceful picketing of any school involved in a labor dispute"), and the other was an anti-noise law that prohibited the willful "making of any noise or diversion which disturbs or tends to disturb the peace or good order of such school session or class thereof." For Marshall, the anti-picketing ordinance was clearly unconstitutional because, like *Mosely*, the statute was, in effect, one based on content. While labor groups could picket in front of a school, all other groups were restrained from doing so. The anti-noise ordinance, however, was constitutional. The ordinance, applied equally to all protesters, was neither unconstitutionally vague nor unconstitutionally overbroad because its "reach [did not] prohibit constitutionally protected conduct."

Despite his appreciation of the necessity for African Americans and others to protest racially based educational inequality, in *Greyned* he wrote that there are "special characteristics of the school environment" that adversely affect the First Amendment rights of potential demonstrators who wish to march and sing and yell in front of a school. "Expressive activity," he concluded, "may be prohibited if it 'materially disrupts classwork or involves substantial disorder or invasion of the rights of others.'" The judgment of the Illinois Supreme Court was affirmed in part (the anti-noise ordinance) and reversed in part (the anti-picketing ordinance) by the Supreme Court.

In *Clark*, the justices addressed the question of whether the National Park Service (NPS) could prohibit a group from using part of a national park for overnight expressive conduct purposes. (The demonstrators from the Community for Creative Non-Violence (CCNV) had camped overnight in Washington's Lafayette Park and the Mall, contrary to regulations forbidding this.) The Court majority, in an opinion written by Justice Byron White, ruled that the NPS regulation did not violate the First Amendment. It was a valid governmental regulation of expressive conduct, applicable to all groups, which served a governmental purpose (maintaining "attractive and intact" parks). White was joined in the opinion by Chief Justice Burger and Justices Blackmun, Powell, Rehnquist, Stevens, and O'Connor.

Marshall wrote a blistering dissent, joined by Brennan, arguing that the CCNV's symbolic speech was constitutionally protected. "Missing from the majority's description [of the two parks the CCNV wished to use to demonstrate against homelessness] is any inkling that Lafayette Park and the Mall have served as the sites for some of the most rousing political demonstrations in the nation's history." The CCNV, by "camping" in a version of a tent city, was protesting against something he had witnessed for decades: the hopelessness and misery of homelessness. The group's "primary purpose for making sleep an integral part of the demonstration was to reenact the central reality of homelessness and to impress upon public consciousness, in as dramatic a way as possible, that homelessness is a widespread problem, often ignored, that confronts its victims with life-threatening deprivations."

For Marshall, it was "political dynamics [that] led [NPS] officials to a disproportionate sensitivity to regulatory as opposed to First Amendment interests." He had seen and had battled against such disproportionate power of the white segregationists against his poor, uneducated African American clients. In *Clark,* he recognized the same triumph of power over fairness and justice. In this case it was the poor, the homeless, the powerless, represented by one marginal group, the CCNV, against the overwhelming power of the government. Movingly, drawing upon his bitter memories, Marshall wrote in his dissent that while "we all go to sleep as part of our daily regimen" in our comfortable bedrooms, many hundreds of thousands of impoverished persons in America sleep without homes. "By using sleep as an integral part of their mode of protest, [the CCNV] can express with their bodies the poignancy of their plight. They can physically demonstrate the neglect from which they suffer with an articulateness even Dickens could not match." Comparing this protest with earlier civil rights demonstrations, Marshall noted that while it was "commonplace activity" for many to sit or stand in a library in Louisiana in 1965, it was powerfully expressive for black people to do so. Such demonstrations were "'monuments of protest' against segregation." Unfortunately, for Marshall and Brennan, it was the Nixon-Reagan appointees who constituted the Court majority in 1984. (In a poignant footnote to the case, after the decision was announced, Mitch Snyder, the leader of the CCNV, sent Marshall and Brennan a short letter: "On behalf of the homeless, I thank you.")[20]

The notion of a public forum where people can use their First Amendment freedoms to protest has been broadly defined over the years. In 1939, in the case of *Hague v. CIO,* the Court said that "wherever the title of streets and parks may rest, they have immemorially been held in trust for the use of the public and, time out of mind, have been used for purposes of assembly, communicating thoughts between citizens, and discussing public questions." Except for secure public locations such as police stations and military bases, the Court has allowed protesters to use almost all public streets and buildings as a forum for expressing their ideas. Since the Court has insisted that any regulation of these groups must be done without regard to the content of the message, the only modest limitation on free expression has been the time, place, and manner restrictions—for public safety and convenience. This has come to mean that protesters must get a permit from the local law enforcement officials, but that the granting of the permit to march or protest must not be based on the content of the group's ideology.

### THE PREDICAMENT OF THE "SPEECH PLUS CONDUCT" CASES

The Supreme Court has always differentiated between pure speech and the communication of ideas through the conduct of protesters. As Justice Arthur Goldberg said, in a 1962 civil rights protest case, *Cox v. Louisiana:* "We emphatically reject the notion that the First and Fourteenth Amendments afford the same kind of freedom to those who would communicate ideas by conduct such as patrolling, marching, and picketing on streets and highways, as these amendments afford to those who communicate ideas by pure speech."

Henry Abraham, a noted constitutional scholar, has written about the First Amendment in a way that highlights the complex questions associated with speech plus conduct that the Court had to resolve. "There is no doubt that picketing, for example, is a vital prerogative of the freedom of expression," writes Abraham. "However, mass picketing, picketing that applies physical force to those who might wish to exercise their equal rights of freedom of expression by disregarding the picket line; or certain kinds of picketing violative of a picketee's property rights or picketing utterly unrelated to a picketee's 'operations'; or picketing in derogation of secondary boycott statutes, is *not.*"[21]

Picketing and other types of conduct, including the SNCC-inspired sit-in demonstrations by black Americans protesting racial discrimination, are particular forms of free expression. Ideas are communicated by the spoken and the printed word. However, ideas are also spread by the actions of persons and through symbols that often speak louder than printed and spoken words. And ideas are transmitted, by word, print, and conduct, on the public streets and on private property. Are all these varieties of expression of ideas protected by the First Amendment? If not, where does a judge draw the line?

Does a justice distinguish between pure speech and conduct associated with, or in place of, speech? If the speech is a part of unlawful conduct, then it cannot immunize the illegal conduct. There were many times when Marshall and his colleagues had to grapple with the meaning of freedom of speech in this more complex situation involving speech and some kind of conduct, whether it be a street demonstration, picketing by union workers, or the burning of a draft card or an American flag.

In the 1940 case of *Thornhill v. Alabama*, the Court determined that peaceful picketing in the context of a valid labor dispute was constitutionally protected free speech. A person picketing, for Black, was "not only communicating ideas…but pursuing a course of conduct in addition to constitutionally protected speech and press. [However, such a person] has no constitutional right to appropriate someone else's property to do so [use his free-speech rights]." Marshall agreed with these remarks, distinguishing the sit-in protesters because they peacefully and silently claimed the right to use accommodations that, according to the common law, should be open to the general public.

Dick Gregory, a nationally known African American comedian, led a group of about eighty-five black protesters on an evening march through the streets of Chicago from City Hall to Mayor Richard Daley's house to demand desegregation of the *de facto* segregated public schools in Chicago. White racist onlookers, over 1,200 by one police count, heavily outnumbered the African American marchers. The whites were unruly, shouting threats and screaming obscenities at the marchers and throwing rocks, bottles, and eggs. The local police did nothing to stop the onlookers. Instead, after asking Gregory five times to stop the march and disperse, they arrested Gregory and the others and charged them with disturbing the peace under a local ordinance that prohibited "making any improper noise, riot, disturbance, breach of the peace, or diversion tending to a breach of the peace." Convicted of the charge, Gregory appealed to the Illinois Supreme Court. After that court upheld the convictions, Gregory took his appeal to the U.S. Supreme Court.

*Gregory v. Chicago* was argued before the justices on December 10, 1968. Three days later, in the conference session, they discussed and voted on the case. The decision of the Court was to overturn the convictions because the defendants had not been disorderly and had not been charged with refusal to obey a police officer. Warren, in the conference, announced that he would reverse the convictions. "The police did a poor job at the event and the petitioners acted with restraint,…there was no parade statute that was violated, they were still very peaceful, there was no evidence of any damaging conduct," he concluded.

All the other justices voted to reverse the conviction, with Marshall, the freshman justice, speaking and voting last. There was little for him to add to the conversation, except to agree with his colleagues. Initially, Black was asked to write the opinion and Warren wrote a concurring opinion. After the initial circulations, most of the brethren quickly joined Warren's very short opinion and it became the majority opinion of the Court.

If picketing, a form of speech plus conduct, can be regulated by the state with regard to public safety concerns, what about the freedom to express oneself through a form of symbolic speech? Marshall sat on the Court when symbolic speech cases came to the Court in the late 1960s, including a number of the cases involving the actions of anti–Vietnam War protesters.

The justices heard a number of Vietnam War and civil rights symbolic-speech cases during Marshall's first years on the Court. Three of them, *United States v. O'Brien* (1968), *Tinker v. Des Moines Independent Community School District* (1969), and *Spence v. Washington* (1974), are particularly pertinent to an understanding of Marshall's position on symbolic speech. In all three, there was a "balancing" process employed by the justices: the symbolic speech activities of the protesters weighed against the government's responsibility to maintain order and prevent harm.

The Vietnam War ripped American society apart, as did the perceived excesses of the black power movement in the late 1960s. Intense criticism of the war swept the nation. By the time of the 1968 national party conventions, it had become a major fault line in politics and, ultimately, in law. Antiwar protesters generated a number of cases by venting their anger in mass demonstrations (picketing in private shopping centers) and in acts of symbolic speech (such as publicly burning their draft cards). They challenged the very constitutionality of the Vietnam War itself in state and federal courts.

*United States v. O'Brien* involved the burning of draft cards by O'Brien and three other protesters. (Marshall, the U.S. solicitor general who brought the case to the Supreme Court to justify the arrest of the protesters, obviously could not participate in *O'Brien*.) A federal statute made it a crime for a person to "forge, alter, knowingly destroy, knowingly mutilate, or in any manner change" a draft card. The Court, in an opinion written by Warren, upheld the conviction, rejecting O'Brien's argument that his symbolic-speech right was protected by the First Amendment. In cases where speech and non-speech action are present and combined, the government can punish the non-speech element if the regulation is (1) "within the powers of the government; (2) if it furthers an important or substantial governmental interest; (3) if the government interest is unrelated to the suppression of free expression; and (4) if the incidental restriction on alleged First Amendment freedoms is no greater than is essential to the furtherance of that interest." The congressional statute was not in violation of the First Amendment. Its major goal was to "insure the continued availability of issued certificates [and therefore the law] serves a legitimate and substantial purpose in the [selective service] system's administration." Justice Douglas dissented alone. His dissent asserted that "it is time that we made a ruling [as to the constitutionality of the Vietnam War]." To his continuing disappointment—and continuing anger at Marshall for not joining him in granting certiorari in those cases challenging the war's constitutionality—that never happened.

*Tinker v. Des Moines* (1969) involved junior and senior high school students, Christopher Eckhardt and siblings John and Mary Beth Tinker, who wore black armbands in their classes to protest the war in Vietnam, in violation of a school policy that outlawed such conduct. When they were suspended, an action was brought in federal district court to enjoin the school officials. After the case was dismissed in the lower federal courts, the Supreme Court granted certiorari and, in a seven-to-two vote, reversed the suspension orders.

Justice Fortas wrote for the majority and shifted the constitutional grounds away from *O'Brien.* "In order for the state to justify prohibition of a particular expression of opinion, it must be able to show that its action was caused by something more than a mere desire to avoid the discomfort and unpleasantness that always accompany an unpopular view." He concluded that the school students who wore black armbands and engaged in a "silent, passive expression of opinion, unaccompanied by any disorder or disturbance on the part of petitioners," and who were suspended for their actions, were practicing a constitutionally protected symbolic freedom of expression. Wearing of the black armband, concluded the Court majority, "was entirely divorced from actually or potentially disruptive conduct by those participating in it. It was closely akin to 'pure speech' which, we have repeatedly held, is entitled to comprehensive protection under the First Amendment." So long as the symbolic speech did not lead to disruption, the Court concluded that it was akin to pure speech and therefore protected from infringement, even by school authorities.

Black, joined by Harlan, dissented. School authorities had the legitimate authority to control the behavior of their students. The students' action was conduct, not expression, and it could be regulated by school authorities. Black wrote: "I have never believed that any person has the right to give speeches in demonstrations where he pleases and when he pleases." The Court majority, Black announced in open court, with bitterness in his voice, "wholly without constitutional reasons, subjects all the public schools in the country to the whims and caprices of their loudest-mouthed, but maybe not their brightest, students." It was one of the few occasions on which the coldly self-controlled justice showed his displeasure so openly.

In *Spence v. Washington,* a 1974 case before the Court, the brethren had to determine whether John Spence's protest against the Vietnam War was protected by the First Amendment's freedom of expression guarantees. On May 10, 1970, he had hung an American flag, upside down, with two peace symbols taped on it, from his apartment window. It was done to protest the recent killings of four college students on the Kent State University campus and the invasion of Cambodia by U.S. troops in Vietnam. He was arrested and convicted of violating a Washington State statute that made it illegal to "improperly use" the flag. He was convicted, and it was sustained by the state appellate courts. He appealed to the Supreme Court and the Court overturned his conviction. Although there was a six-to-three vote, with Marshall voting to overturn the conviction, there was not agreement on the justification for the overturn, so a *per curiam* order was issued. The short order noted that flag-burning was expressive conduct, which was defined in the opinion as the "intent to convey a particularized message and where in the surrounding circumstances, the likelihood is great that the message will be understood by those who view it."

Ironically, in both the Warren and Burger Courts, the moderate and liberal justices had not been able to cobble together a majority to directly uphold a person's right to desecrate the American flag as an expression of opposition to a public policy. It was in the more conservative Rehnquist Court era that the Court did address the issue squarely—twice in two years, 1989 and again in 1990. In both cases, Brennan wrote the opinion for the five-person majority he had assembled, one that included Marshall, Harry Blackmun, and, surprisingly, Justices Kennedy and Scalia. Chief Justice Rehnquist dissented, joined by Justices O'Connor, White, and Stevens. The cases were *Texas v. Johnson* (1989) and *United States v. Eichman* (1990).

In the Texas case, Gregory Lee Johnson, the putative leader of the Revolutionary Communist Youth Brigade, soaked a flag in kerosene and lit it in front of the Dallas city hall during the 1984 Republican presidential convention held in that city. He was arrested and convicted under a Texas statute that made it a crime to desecrate a state or national flag. The Texas Court of Criminal Appeals reversed the conviction, and the State appealed to the Supreme Court. Certiorari was granted in October 1988, with many liberals fearing that the Rehnquist Court majority would uphold the Texas statute and Johnson's conviction.

Court-watchers knew that Brennan, Marshall, and Blackmun would vote to affirm the Texas appellate court decision, but were shocked when Scalia and Kennedy did as well. The oral arguments revealed Scalia's views. Counsel for the state had said that if the flag "over a period of time is ignored or abused, it can lose its symbolic effect." Scalia immediately responded, "I think not at all. I think that when somebody does that to the flag, the flag becomes even more a symbol of the country. It seems to me that you just don't make that argument because then you're getting into a sort of content preference."

In June 1989, Brennan read the opinion for the Court, which addressed two related questions: Did Johnson's burning of the flag constitute expressive conduct, "permitting him to invoke the First Amendment in challenging his conviction"? Even Texas accepted the premise that Johnson's action was expressive conduct, Brennan pointed out. Texas was attempting to punish him for his expressive conduct, but the First Amendment forbids such state actions. "The State's interest in preventing breaches of the peace does not support his conviction because Johnson's conduct did not threaten to disturb the peace. Nor does the State's interest in preserving the flag as a symbol of nationhood and national unity justify his criminal conviction for engaging in political expression."

In his concurring opinion, Kennedy wrote that the case "exacts its personal toll":

> The hard fact is that sometimes we must make decisions we do not like. We make them because they are right, right in the sense that the law and the Constitution, as we see them, compel the result....His acts were speech, in both the technical and the fundamental meaning of the Constitution.

Rehnquist's dissent was a cry from the heart. "Millions and millions of Americans regard [the flag] with an almost mystical reverence regardless of what sort of social, political, or philosophical beliefs they may have." The American flag is simply not "just another symbol," he noted, sadly.

The following year, 1990, in *United States v. Eichman*, the Court invalidated a statute passed by Congress after *Johnson* was handed down. The legislation, reflecting the great irritation of the Congress and President George Bush, barred the desecration of the American flag. However, in his very last publicly read opinion for the same five-person Court majority, Justice Brennan ruled that it was an unconstitutional action because "the government's asserted interest is related to the suppression of free speech and concerned with the content of such expression."

## FREEDOM OF THE PRESS AND CLASHES WITH FAIR TRIAL GUARANTEES

Before Marshall's arrival on the Court, the justices, in *Garrison v. Louisiana* (1964), said that "speech concerning public affairs is the essence of self-government." A free press plays a major role in America's commitment to democratic government. As the press—the "fourth branch" of government, as some refer to it—is chiefly responsible for informing the public about the affairs of government, there must be no prior restraints placed on it. If a government attempts to restrain the press, as Marshall observed in his opinion in *New York Times v. United States* (1974), it bears the heavy burden of showing compelling necessity to deny the press its First Amendment freedom to publish. Furthermore, in Court decisions from the 1930s until Marshall joined the Court, the Justices had broadly defined free press to include almost all methods for transmitting information to the public, including signs, leaflets, booklets, books, magazines, motion pictures, radio, and television broadcasts.

In *Branzburg v. Hayes, In Re Pappas,* and *United States v. Carroll,* a consolidated 1972 case, the Court had to grapple with the question of whether the First Amendment allowed reporters to protect their sources when asked questions by prosecutors and grand juries. Paul Branzburg, Paul Pappas, and Earl Caldwell were reporters who were independently covering stories involving different militant African American organizations. Each of them refused to reveal the sources for his story to a grand jury, and each was found in contempt of court for failing to answer the questions. The Court granted certiorari to resolve the constitutional question.

Justice Byron White, joined by the Nixon quartet, wrote the majority opinion for a divided five-to-four Court. Marshall joined Stewart's dissent (as did Brennan). Douglas dissented separately. For White, the constitutional issue was whether "requiring newsmen to appear and testify before state or federal grand juries abridges the freedom of speech and press guaranteed by the First Amendment. We hold that it does not." The heart of the reporters' constitutional claim, he wrote, "is that the burden on news gathering resulting from compelling reporters to disclose confidential information *outweighs* any public interest in obtaining the information." (My emphasis.) For the slim majority, the reporters' argument did not make the case for not giving information to the grand jury. The press do not have a testimonial privilege not to talk to a grand jury "that other citizens do not enjoy": "Citizens generally are not constitutionally immune from grand jury subpoenas;...It is clear that the First Amendment does not invalidate every incidental burdening of the press that may result from enforcement of civil or criminal statutes of general applicability."

Balancing the need for the grand jury to acquire information in law enforcement matters against the reporters' claim of testimonial privilege was rather easy for the Nixon justices and White:

> We perceive no basis for holding that the public interest in law enforcement and in ensuring effective grand jury proceedings is insufficient to override the consequential, but uncertain, burden on news gathering that is said to result from

insisting that reporters, like other citizens, respond to relevant questions put to them in the course of a valid grand jury investigation or criminal trial.

Stewart wrote for the three dissenters criticizing the Court's "'crabbed view of the First Amendment,'" a majority belief that "reflects a disturbing insensitivity to the critical role of an independent press in our society." The news reporter, they argued, does have a First Amendment right to protect his news sources. This right "stems from the broad societal interest in a full and free flow of information to the public. It is this basic concern that underlies the Constitution's guarantee of a free press.... The right to gather news implies, in turn, a right to a confidential relationship between a reporter and his source."

They did not accept Black's and Douglas's categorical First Amendment free press protection. Instead, emphasizing the primacy of the First Amendment, the three men said that the press's right to protect sources cannot be abridged *unless* the government demonstrates a "compelling and overriding interest in the information.... Government officials must, therefore, demonstrate that the information is *clearly* relevant to a *precisely* defined subject of governmental inquiry. They must demonstrate that it is reasonable to think the witness in question has that information. And they must show that there is not any means of obtaining the information less destructive of First Amendment liberties."

For the staunch First Amendment absolutist Douglas, there was "no way of making mandatory the disclosure of a reporter's confidential source of the information on which he bases his news story." More in sadness than anger, he concluded, "Now that the fences of the law and the tradition that has protected the press are broken down, the people are the victims. The First Amendment, as I read it, was designed precisely to prevent this tragedy."

A watershed First Amendment case came to the Court a few years later, in the late spring of 1971. It involved the Nixon administration's efforts to use the federal judges to prevent two major newspapers from publishing a purloined secret analysis of the Vietnam War. Marshall was not at all happy with the administration's strategy. Nixon's attempt at government by injunction provoked the landmark case, *New York Times v. United States*. On June 15, 1971, two days after *The New York Times* ran the first two installments of a series of confidential Defense Department studies of America's involvement in Vietnam—the "Pentagon Papers"—Attorney General John Mitchell obtained a restraining order from a U.S. District Court judge in New York, enjoining the *Times* from publishing additional segments.

Later that week, the *Washington Post* began to publish segments of the Pentagon Papers, but Mitchell secured a restraining order against that paper as well. The Nixon administration's argument was that publication of the Pentagon

Papers while America was still at war in Vietnam posed a severe threat to the nation's security. By June 24, the cases were before the U.S. Supreme Court. In twenty-four hours the Court had to prepare the certiorari conference. For a majority of the justices, a bad precedent had already been established, in that both papers did not run further installments of the Vietnam study because of the restraining orders issued by federal judges.

Black knew that four judges would act quickly to restore the First Amendment's freedom of the press to the newspapers. These brethren were himself, Brennan, Douglas, and Marshall. (Interestingly, as disclosed when Marshall's papers were released to the public after his death, Marshall initially had grave doubts about lifting the restraining orders.)

Black also concluded that Chief Justice Burger, along with Justices Blackmun and Harlan, would support Nixon's efforts to gag the press through the use of the injunction strategy. That meant that Black, the senior justice favoring the lifting of the restraints, had to get and keep either Potter Stewart or Byron White in his potential majority in order for the Court to set aside the restraining orders.

On Friday, June 25, 1971, the Court, without Douglas participating because he had already left for his summer retreat in Goose Prairie, Washington, met to discuss the cases and decide whether it should hear arguments in an expedited manner. Without hesitation, Black stated that there was no need to listen to oral argument or read briefs; the Court must lift the restraining orders without further delay. Douglas called on the phone and agreed with Black, and Brennan and Marshall also supported this view. Because it was an expedited "Rule 20" appeal to the brethren, there had to be five votes to grant certiorari.

Harlan, White, Blackmun, and Chief Justice Burger, however, wanted to hear arguments during the October 1971 term of the Court, and to restrain the newspapers until then. Stewart's was the key vote. He concluded that he could not tolerate a restraining order lasting through the October term, and voted to grant certiorari and to take the case from the district court. Harlan joined in the vote to grant expedited review, and oral arguments were set for the following day. An order was issued scheduling oral arguments for Saturday, June 26, 1971. The temporary restraints placed on the papers would continue until the Court resolved the matter. Burger's order had a footnote: "Mr. Justice Black, Mr. Justice Douglas, Mr. Justice Brennan, and Mr. Justice Marshall would not continue the restraint."

Before a full courtroom, at 11:00 A.M., with Douglas sitting (having flown in from Goose Prairie the evening before), oral argument commenced for one hour. The government argued that the publication of the Papers would adversely affect national security and that the restraining orders should stand. Alexander Bickel, once a Frankfurter law clerk and, in 1971, a Yale Law School professor, argued on behalf of the *Times* that the Pentagon Papers did not pose a grave danger to the nation's security and that therefore the restraints should be removed. After oral arguments ended, Black expressed his displeasure at the presentation made by Bickel. He told his clerks, "Too bad *The New York Times* couldn't find someone who believes in the First Amendment."

When the justices met later that afternoon, Douglas's notes show how charged the atmosphere was. Black "insisted that no notes be taken in this conference as they would be bound to leak out somewhere," but Douglas, obviously, ignored his colleague's request and took copious notes. Black could count on only himself, Douglas, and Brennan to argue that the press had an absolute right to publish. Burger, Harlan, and Blackmun would argue for further argumentation in the lower courts, with the restraining orders in force. Marshall and White did not accept the "absolute freedom" argument but would vacate the order if there was no national security threat. Stewart wanted to review the record to determine whether there was a national security danger. Whichever side received two of these three votes would carry the day.

The Chief, as is customary, began the discussion with the argument that the case should be sent back to the lower courts in order to develop the appellate record. He argued that the cases were being heard on a "panic basis" and that, because there was no time to reflect on the constitutional issue, he was "unable to vote on the merits." He concluded by stating that "we have been rushed in this case and if the *Times* and the *Post* win I will write at once and more fully during the Summer."

Black disagreed, and urged immediate publication of the Pentagon Papers. He argued that "we should not destroy the First Amendment" by approving the use of the courts to restrict the press. Such an action, he said, "would be the worst blow to the First Amendment." Douglas simply noted that Black's comments echoed "my view."

Harlan voted for the government's position, arguing that the "judicial process has been made a travesty—[the judges, including his friend Black] have been panicky and hurried." Maintaining that there were "many imponderables in national security and only the judgment of men in the field can be relied upon," he sided with the government. From a review of Harlan's files, one can see Harlan insisted that he "wanted to read the documents—he needs the help of the law clerks," and "to write out his views will take time and he'll file [his dissent] later."

Brennan sided with Black and Douglas, but used the balancing-test argument in his observations. He insisted that it was a prior-restraint case, with the "heavy burden on the U.S." to justify the suppression of the publication. The Nixon administration had not met that burden, and therefore Brennan would lift the restraints immediately. Then it was Stewart's turn; he argued that the government had not made the case for suppression of the information. Douglas commented in his notes on the conference discussion that, while Stewart was not an absolutist on freedom of the press, he was tending in Black's direction. Stewart, however, said that if the publications would "result in immediate grave and irreparable harm to the U.S. or the sentencing to death of 100 young men, this court as a court of equity would have the power to enjoin publication." For him, the question was, "Is there here any such threat?" Since the Pentagon Papers "ended in 1968," he didn't think there was any future threat to national security that would lead to the deaths of young servicemen. Justice Byron White argued for lifting the injunction, although he rejected Black's absolutist perspective. He insisted that the Executive had broad powers in the national security area, and that included the right to confidentiality but that, in this case, Nixon went too far.

It was Marshall's turn to talk about the matter. Clearly, Nixon as Chief Executive, had "broad powers," including the "power to classify [documents]." However, for Marshall, "the First Amendment, when it says 'no law,' applies to all three branches of government. The Executive can't do what Congress can't do. There is no 'inherent' [presidential] power to stop the *Times* from printing. There is no Act of Congress [and] the [Executive's] 'inherent' power is limited by the First Amendment. [I] am close to Hugo and Bill Douglas on that point." Harry Blackmun, the junior justice, spoke last and joined Burger and Harlan on the side of the government. Blackmun believed that the Papers contained "dangerous material that will harm this nation. The publication is reprehensible—[I] have nothing but contempt for the *Times*. We should write on the criminal aspect of the problem."

The final tally of the brethren that morning, according to Douglas's conference notes, stood at six to three in favor of immediately setting aside the restraining orders. Given the imperative need for a quick order to stop the prior restraint of the press, the justices agreed to a short, unsigned *per curiam* order, written by Brennan, that lifted the restraining orders, followed by opinions written by each of the nine men. Black had the feeling that this was to be the last opinion he would write. Angrily telling his clerks that the Johnson and Nixon administrations "deceived us all this time," Black set about writing his last major opinion—appropriately, one that defended the First Amendment. It was a stern yet moving statement that reaffirmed his view that the First Amendment was framed in absolute terms and was "the very foundation of constitutional government." No governmental agency, least of all a federal court of law, had the legitimate authority to suppress free speech or press. "The First Amendment was offered to *curtail* and *restrict* the general powers granted to the Executive, Legislative, and Judicial branches." However, he said, "for the first time in the 182 years since the founding of the Republic, the federal courts are asked to hold that the First Amendment does not mean what it says, but rather means that the Government can halt the publication of current news of vital importance to the people of this country. I can imagine no greater perversion of history." Shortly after the announcement of the Court's decision, the judge found himself, for the final time, in the Naval Hospital at Bethesda, Maryland. In mid-September 1971, he retired from the Court. Less than two weeks later he was dead.

Marshall's first draft had an ominous tone, for he wrote about the conspiracy between the staffs of the two national newspapers involved in the case. The President had an "effective remedy" under traditional criminal law: arrest everybody involved in the publication of the Pentagon Papers!

A "good faith prosecution" against the newspapers would, he said, deal with the problem quickly, without resorting to Executive requests to the federal courts to enjoin publication of the newspapers. Under the existing espionage laws, it was a crime for "a person to receive, disclose, communicate, withhold and publish certain documents, photographs, instruments, appliances and information."

> If the Executive Branch believes a crime has been committed or that there is a conspiracy by the staff, editors, and publishers of either paper to commit future crimes, it can arrest the people who are responsible.... If people are in jail and the documents have been seized, future publications would clearly be stopped.... The publication of any of these documents could be stopped by the arrest of staff, editors, for *willfully retaining and failing to deliver to the appropriate officials* [the copies of the Pentagon Papers they had received].... *It would appear that there is probable cause to believe that there is a conspiracy within the staffs of both the* Washington Post *and* New York Times. (My emphasis.)[22]

Marshall had been outraged by the publication of the Pentagon Papers—but his anger was directed at the reporters and executives of the two newspapers. Rules is Rules; both the *Times* and the *Post* intentionally, "willfully," conspired to evade the statutes enacted by Congress. But he eventually calmed down. After conversations with Brennan and his clerks, Marshall's final opinion in the case did not call for the arrest of the reporters, editors, and publishers of the *Times* and the *Post*.

## FREEDOM OF THE PRESS VERSUS THE RIGHT TO A FAIR TRIAL

Another set of free-press problems confronted the Supreme Court during the Warren Court era and well into Marshall's tenure. Could a criminal defendant receive a speedy, public, and, essentially, fair trial, a Sixth Amendment right, if the press, including radio and television, given its First Amendment rights, had blanketed the area with daily stories about the crime and about the alleged criminal? Was there anything that could be done to minimize or neutralize the clash between competing constitutional rights? Can a trial judge ban the press from covering a preliminary hearing, or forbid the publication of the names of rape victims who are mentioned in a public court document?

By the time Marshall joined the Court, it had ruled (*Estes v. Texas*, 1965) that cameras in a courtroom were disruptive and that their presence denied a defendant due process of law, and (*Sheppard v. Maxwell*, 1966) that televising a coroner's inquest or allowing reporters to overhear and then publish conversations between a defendant and his attorney also violated due process. (In *Chandler v. Florida*, 1981, however, the Burger Court, in an opinion written by the Chief Justice, modified the earlier precedents, saying that "an absolute ban on broadcast coverage of trials cannot be justified simply because there is a danger that, in some cases, prejudicial broadcast accounts of pretrial and trial events may impair the ability of jurors to decide the issue of guilt or innocence uninfluenced by extraneous matter.")

Soon after 1966, trial judges began to issue orders preventing reporters from covering sensational preliminary hearings and some trials. This led to a major Supreme Court decision regarding this power of judges. The case was *Nebraska Press Association v. Stuart* (1976), in which the Court for the first time addressed the question.

In October 1973, Erwin Simants was arrested and charged in Sutherland, Nebraska, with the murders of six members of the Kellie family. His attorney and the local prosecuting attorney asked the judge to issue a restraining order against the press not to talk about, in print, on radio, and on television, five subjects associated with the crime. It was issued and the Nebraska Press Association immediately asked the judge to stay the order. It also took its appeal to the state supreme court. That court upheld the restraining order but limited the restraints to only three subjects. The press association then appealed to the U.S. Supreme Court, which granted certiorari.

There was a unanimous judgment to declare the restraining order invalid; but there were five different opinions. Chief Justice Burger wrote the judgment for the Court, joined only by Blackmun and Rehnquist. Brennan, joined by Marshall and Potter Stewart, wrote a separate concurring opinion, as did Justices White, Powell, and Stevens. Burger's opinion was a modest one, noting the "tensions between the need to protect the accused as fully as possible and the need to restrict publication as little as possible." Reviewing the facts in the case, Burger concluded that "it is far from clear that prior restraint on publication would have protected Simants' rights."

The four other opinions were more emphatic in their rejection of the gag order and in defense of the First Amendment. Brennan's concurrence reflected Marshall's views on the issue of conflict between the First and the Sixth Amendments. The opinion "reject[ed] the notion that a choice is necessary, that there is an inherent conflict that cannot be resolved without essentially abrogating one right or the other." Trial judges can use methods ("requiring greater sensitivity and effort") other than the gag order to maintain both a free press and a fair trial, he concluded.

Could a judge bar the press and the public from pretrial hearings? was another question addressed by the Court. In 1982, in the case of *Globe Newspaper Co. v. Superior Court for the County of Norfolk, Massachusetts,* the justices, by a six-to-three vote, answered the question in the negative. Justice Brennan wrote the opinion, joined by his colleague Marshall. Chief Justice Burger, joined by Justice Rehnquist, dissented. Justice Stevens also dissented separately.

A section of the Massachusetts General Laws, as it was interpreted by the state supreme court, required state judges to exclude the press and the public from hearing testimony involving sexual offenses given by a victim who had not reached eighteen years of age. For Brennan, writing for the Court, the question was whether "the statute... violates the First Amendment as applied to the states through the Fourteenth Amendment." Broadly defining the First Amendment, rather than giving it a "narrow, literal interpretation," the Court found the section to violate the First Amendment. Brennan said that the "right of access to *criminal trials* in particular...while not absolute...is properly afforded protection by the First Amendment."

In a 1989 case before the Court involving the constitutionality of a Florida statute that prohibited the publication of the name of a victim of a sexual assault, *Florida Star v. B.J.F.,* Marshall wrote the opinion for the Court majority. The *Florida Star* argued that the law infringed on the First Amendment rights of the press to print truthful information for the public to read, and that the First Amendment had priority over the victim's right to privacy. B.J.F., who had been robbed and sexually assaulted, had been awarded monetary damages (both compensatory and punitive) in a civil suit against the paper. The *Star,* in its "Police Reports" section, had published her name in violation of the state law and its own internal policy. (The local police department investigating the crime had prepared a report, using her full name, and then posted it in its press room.)

Marshall's opinion tried to moderate the "clashes" between these two constitutionally derived rights and crafted a judgment he hoped would "sweep no more broadly than the appropriate context in the instant case." His opinion reversed the damage award because the victim's name had already been released by the local police in a public report that the *Star* reporter used to write the story. Furthermore, the story as published, a one-paragraph item, was truthful. In addition, the state had selectively enforced its statute against small weeklies such as the *Star* (with a circulation of eighteen thousand) while turning a blind eye when major media outlets published or announced names of persons who had been sexually assaulted. For those reasons, the damage judgment against the *Star* violated the First Amendment's freedom of the press.

In *Cable News Network (CNN) v. Noriega* (1990), the issue for the Court to grapple with was whether the media could be forced to disclose information obtained from tape recordings of conversations between an attorney and his client (the recently apprehended dictator of Panama, Manuel Noriega). Noriega was in a federal prison facing drug-trafficking charges when illicit tapes were made of conversations between the dictator and his attorney. These tapes found their way to CNN.

CNN notified Noriega's attorney that the network planned to broadcast segments of the tape. The attorney immediately sought to suppress the playing of the tapes by going to the federal district court judge. The judge requested that CNN provide him with the tapes so that he could make a determination whether playing them would jeopardize Noriega's receiving a fair trial. The network refused, and the federal judge issued a temporary restraining order barring CNN from broadcasting and telecasting the tapes. CNN appealed to the federal appellate court, arguing that the First Amendment enabled the network to broadcast the material. At the same time, CNN did broadcast a segment of the tapes. The Eleventh Circuit Court of Appeals upheld the district court judge and ordered CNN to turn over the tapes to the federal trial judge. CNN then appealed the decision to the Supreme Court.

The Court denied certiorari; the lower federal appellate court order stood unchanged. Marshall dissented angrily from the denial of certiorari, joined by Justice O'Connor. He felt that the case should have been heard on the merits, arguing that "the prior restraint imposed in this case cannot be reconciled" with earlier Court precedents such as *Nebraska Press Association* and the Pentagon Papers cases.

## THE "NO ESTABLISHMENT OF RELIGION" AND "FREE EXERCISE" CLAUSES

In addition to protecting freedom of speech, expression, assembly, and association, the First Amendment guarantees religious freedom. It protects religious beliefs and organized religions in two ways: Congress (and, through incorporation, the states) is prohibited from acting in any way that *aids, endorses, or establishes* a "state" religion; and all governments, federal, state, and local, are also prohibited from proscribing the free exercise of religion. In but one sentence,

"Congress shall make no law respecting an establishment of religion, or prohibiting the free exercise thereof," the men of the First Congress defined and
protected a right; the practical application of that definition and protection has
occasioned disagreement among the men and women who have sat on the
Supreme Court, as well as among politicians and the lower courts, for many
decades. For Thomas Jefferson, and for modern Supreme Court justices such as
Hugo Black, William O. Douglas, William J. Brennan Jr., and Thurgood
Marshall, the "no establishment of religion" clause created an impenetrable and
very high "wall of separation between Church and State." Government, according to this understanding of the Constitution, cannot aid religion in any way.

Marshall believed in this absolute separation of church and state. He thoroughly rejected Rehnquist's more accommodating (to the government) view of
the religion clauses in the Constitution. When he became Chief Justice, he
began the tradition of having a Court Christmas party hosted by the justices in
the building's Great Hall. "You and your spouse are invited," he wrote to all the
Supreme Court employees. "Please come to the party with your best singing
voice!"

Marshall's response was always short and to the point. In 1988, for example,
he wrote to Rehnquist and to the other justices, "I have your memorandum concerning the annual Christmas Party. As usual, I will not participate. I still prefer
to keep church and state apart." In 1990, he wrote, "As usual, I will *not* attend
the Christmas Party, but I will pay my share of the bill. I still believe in the separation of church and state." [23]

Other justices occasionally declined to participate in these Christmas festivi-
ties, but none of their refusals was as pointed as Marshall's. For example, Justice
Stevens wrote Rehnquist to say that, "like Marshall, I will not be able to attend,
…but my excuse is perhaps less principled and more secular than his." And, in
1990, his first term on the Court, Justice David Souter excused himself, explaining that it was "not because of any particular reservation, but because I'd best not
take time to get up to speed on anything not required just now." [24]

Unlike Marshall's clear definition of the separation of church and state, other
recent views, held by men such as former U.S. attorney general Edwin Meese III
(appointed during the Reagan administration) and Chief Justices Burger and
Rehnquist, represent the *accommodationist* perspective. In this interpretation, the
"no establishment" clause prohibits the government from creating a state religion
but does allow it to accommodate, without any preferences, the needs of *all* religions. This conflict of views regarding the correct way to interpret the
Constitution led to what Marshall referred to as the "scourge of the contemporary Supreme Court: multiple opinions." [25]

There was also disagreement on the scope of a person's freedoms under the "free exercise of religion" clause. For all the justices, from Marshall to Rehnquist, that clause allowed persons to believe in and assert the truths of their religion without governmental interference. It also protected the rights of unbelievers, atheist or agnostic. Actions based on religious beliefs, however, were subject to governmental restrictions.

As with the interpretation of other protections in the First Amendment by members of the Court, with the exception of Justices Black and Douglas, the justices have said that religious freedom protections in the First Amendment are not absolute. Under certain conditions, the government can support religious groups and can prohibit certain exercises (actions) of religious belief. And that view still provokes controversy—on the Court and in the country. What is permissible conduct by a person acting out of religious beliefs? Cases raising these questions have led to the writing of many opinions, concurring as well as dissenting, by various justices, with varying views, over the years.

In the 1940 case of *Cantwell v. Connecticut,* where the Court incorporated the First Amendment's "free exercise of religion" protection into the Fourteenth Amendment, the justices said religious freedom "embraces two concepts—freedom to *believe* and freedom to *act.* The first is absolute but, in the nature of things, the second cannot be. *Conduct remains subject to regulation of society."* (My emphasis.) In 1947 the Supreme Court "incorporated" the "no establishment of religion" clause into the Fourteenth Amendment. Justice Black, writing for a majority of five in *Everson v. Board of Education of Ewing Township, New Jersey,* included the clause in the Fourteenth Amendment, quoting Jefferson's admonition that there was a high (but, in *Everson,* a *penetrable*) wall of separation between Church and State.

Since 1947, the Supreme Court has been caught up in a variety of religion cases that sought clarification about the meaning and scope of the First Amendment's religious freedom language. When Marshall arrived on the Court, he quickly became embroiled in the controversies surrounding the meaning and scope of the two religion clauses in the First Amendment.

## THE "NO ESTABLISHMENT OF RELIGION" CLAUSE
Are there any circumstances under which government can constitutionally provide aid to religion (basically state aid, either financial or the sharing of human and other resources, to sectarian—primarily Catholic—schools), given the "no establishment of religion" clause? By 1971, with Marshall joining in the majority opinion of the Court (written by Chief Justice Burger), the answer was in the affirmative—provided the state assistance did not violate one of the three tests announced in the opinion *Lemon v. Kurtzman.*

State aid to religion was permissible, said the Court majority in *Lemon,* provided that (1) the challenged legislation had a "*secular* legislative purpose," (2) the "*principle and primary effect*" of the challenged statute was *neutral* in that it neither advanced nor inhibited religion, and (3) the challenged statute did not "foster an *excessive government entanglement* with religion."

Marshall did not participate in the discussion and vote in the *Lemon* case because, as he reported in the conference session of March 5, 1971, the NAACP was a party in the litigation.[26]

Implementing *Lemon* case by case led to heightened tension among the justices and, as Justice Scalia was to say later, in 1987, to the creation of a bewildering establishment-clause "maze." By 1980, Marshall, joined by Brennan and Stevens, had given up on *Lemon's* accommodationist interpretation of the "no establishment of religion" clause and, in the case of *Committee for Public Education and Religious Liberty v. Regan,* the trio dissented in an opinion written by Stevens. They believed that "the entire enterprise of trying to justify various types of subsidies to nonpublic schools should be abandoned. [We] would resurrect the 'high and impregnable' wall between church and state constructed by the Framers of the First Amendment. See *Everson v. Board of Education.*"

By 1984, in *Lynch v. Donnelly,* a narrow five-to-four Court majority upheld the city of Pawtucket, Rhode Island's Christmas display of a creche. Burger transmogrified the Christian symbol of the holy day into a secular symbol and found no excessive governmental entanglement with religion. Because the creche was part of a display that included Christmas trees and other "secular" symbols of the season, there was no sectarianism associated with the display. In a dissent joined by Marshall, Brennan wrote, the placement of the creche in the city's display was evidence of "the government's imprimatur of approval on the particular religious beliefs exemplified by the creche. The effect on minority religious groups, as well as on those who may reject all religion, is to convey the message that their views are not similarly worthy of public recognition nor entitled to public support."

The following year, Justice Stevens assembled a six-person majority to overturn, in *Wallace v. Jaffree,* an Alabama statute that required all students and teachers to observe a moment of silent prayer or meditation each school morning. Burger and Rehnquist, the accommodationists on the Court at the time, along with Justice White, vehemently dissented from Stevens's opinion.

In the December 7, 1984, conference session, three days after the oral arguments, Marshall maintained that students in these schools "were not absolutely free to think of what you will—[They] must do what the school tells you to do and here the clear purpose was to get prayer back into the schools."[27] However, for the dissenters, the law was, in Burger's words, "completely neutral." White said that he "agreed with the Chief—the addition of a moment of prayer language posed no problem" for him. Rehnquist agreed with Burger, adding that there was no attack on constitutional principles by the state legislators. William Brennan stated that "on the record in this case, there can be no doubt that the legislative purpose in passing the statute was to endorse religious practice in the public schools....This statute was intended to bring back school prayer."

For the majority, the law conflicted with the First Amendment. However, because only three of the justices (Marshall, Brennan, and Stevens) thought the three-pronged *Lemon* test should be set aside for the "high wall" standard discussed by Black in his *Everson* decision, *Lemon* was used by Stevens to rule the Alabama statute unconstitutional (in order for Stevens to "hold the Court"). For the majority, the question was "whether government's actual purpose is to endorse or disapprove of religion." Stevens then noted that the "answer to that question is dispositive....The enactment of the Alabama statute was not motivated by any clearly secular purpose—indeed, the statute had *no* secular purpose."

Rehnquist's dissent emphasized his reading of "the true meaning" of the original intent of the men who wrote the First Amendment.

> [The framers] intended the Establishment Clause to prohibit the designation of any church as a "national" one. The Clause was also designed to stop the Federal Government from asserting a preference for one religious denomination or sect over others....As its history abundantly shows, however, nothing in the Establishment Clause requires government to be strictly neutral between religion and irreligion, nor does the Clause prohibit Congress or the States from pursuing legitimate secular ends through nondiscriminatory sectarian means.

Again, in 1987, Brennan was able to command a seven-person Court to overturn a Louisiana statute requiring the teaching of the religious theory of "creationism" in the public schools. Justices White, O'Connor, and Blackmun joined in the opinion while writing two separate concurring opinions. Chief Justice Rehnquist and Justice Scalia angrily dissented in this case, *Edwards v. Aguillard.* Using the *Lemon* test, Brennan concluded that the Louisiana "Balanced Treatment for Creation-Science and Evolution-Science in Public School Instruction" law was "facially invalid" because it violated the First Amendment's "no establishment of religion" clause. Louisiana's legislation would require any science instructor teaching the theory of evolution to also teach the sectarian theory of "creationism" as well.

For the majority, the essential purpose of the legislation was sectarian and therefore, on its face, the law violated the First Amendment:

> The purpose of the Creationism Act was to restructure the science curriculum to conform with a particular religious viewpoint. Out of many possible science

subjects taught in the public schools, the legislature chose to affect the teaching of the one scientific theory that historically has been opposed by certain religious sects.... The legislature passed the Act to give preference to those religious groups which have as one of their tenets the creation of humankind by a divine creator.

And in *County of Allegheny, Pennsylvania, v. American Civil Liberties Union* (1989), a bitterly divided Court voted five to four on the constitutionality of the public display of a creche and a menorah. In Pittsburgh, Pennsylvania, a creche was constructed by a local Roman Catholic church, and then prominently displayed in the center of the county courthouse in downtown Pittsburgh. A block away, in front of the City-County building, public officials put up a huge Christmas tree, a smaller (Jewish) Hanukkah menorah, and a large banner that celebrated liberty. The local ACLU chapter challenged the first two displays, arguing that they were an establishment of religion by the city in violation of the First Amendment.

In the conference session, Brennan argued vigorously that both displays violated the Constitution's "no establishment of religion" clause in the First Amendment. Marshall supported his friend's position in the conference. The *Lemon* test was the relevant standard for the Court to use in the case, maintained Brennan. It was to no avail, for they, along with Stevens and Blackmun, were in the minority—again. And so, a few days later, Stevens sent the other three a note: "We four are in dissent in *Lynch [v. Donnelly].* I shall attempt a dissent, although I can well understand that each of you may also want to write separately."[28]

In *Lynch,* there were five separate opinions. Blackmun's opinion for the fragile majority concluded that the creche placement violated the First Amendment, but that the second challenged display, the eighteen-foot-high menorah, placed next to a forty-five-foot gaily decorated Christmas tree, was not a violation of the First Amendment. The creche's placement and significance underlined the unconstitutionality of the display. It was clearly sectarian in its message, not secular, even though it was erected in a "secular" setting. Wrote Blackmun: "Here nothing in the context of the display detracts from the creche's religious meaning." Regarding the other challenged display, Blackmun, who was joined by O'Connor and Stevens, wrote that "the display of the Chanukah menorah in front of the City-County building may well present a closer constitutional question."

Was the city celebrating the two holidays as religious ones or as secular ones? If the former, then the second display violated the First Amendment. If, however, the second display celebrated Christmas and Hanukkah as secular holidays, then the display was constitutional. Blackmun's opinion held that the intent was to mark secular holidays and validated the display of a Hanukkah menorah and a Christmas tree.

In the shadow of the tree, the menorah is readily understood as simply a recognition that Christmas is not the only traditional way of observing the winter holiday season....The combination of the tree and the menorah communicates, not a simultaneous endorsement of both Christian and Jewish faith, but instead, a secular celebration of Christmas coupled with an acknowledgment of Chanukah as a contemporaneous alternative tradition.

Brennan, joined by Marshall and Stevens, wrote an opinion that concurred with parts of Blackmun's decision, and dissented from other elements of it. For Brennan, both displays violated the "no establishment of religion" clause of the First Amendment. Criticizing the grounds on which the display was validated, Brennan disagreed with Blackmun's three points, that (1) the Christmas tree is a secular symbol, that (2) Chanukah is a secular holiday and the menorah is largely a secular symbol, and that (3) "the government may promote pluralism by sponsoring or condoning displays having strong religious associations on its property."

Marshall and Brennan also joined in Stevens's opinion, which was also one that concurred in part and dissented in part. His opinion clashed with the Kennedy opinion, and Stevens attacked Kennedy's reasoning and his jurisprudence. "I find wholly unpersuasive Justice Kennedy's attempts to belittle the importance of the obvious differences between the display of the creche in this case and that in *Lynch v. Donnelly.*" Stevens could not accept the Blackmun reasoning in the menorah display issue because "juxtaposition of this tree with an eighteen-foot menorah does not make the latter secular, as Justice Blackmun contends. Rather, the presence of the Chanukah menorah, unquestionably a religious symbol, gives religious significance to the Christmas tree. The overall display thus manifests governmental approval of the Jewish and Christian religions."

Justice Kennedy wrote a strongly worded dissent, joined by Chief Justice Rehnquist and Justices Scalia and White. For them, both displays were constitutional actions by the local government. Supporting a much more accommodationist view of what government can do in the area of passive religious actions, Kennedy said:

this Court is ill-equipped to sit as a national theology board, and I question both the wisdom and the constitutionality of its doing so....The principles of the Establishment Clause and our Nation's historic traditions of diversity and pluralism allow communities to make reasonable judgments respecting the accommodation or acknowledgment of holidays with both cultural and religious aspects. No constitutional violation occurs when they do so by displaying a symbol of the holiday's religious origins.

It was a rancorous Court that decided the *Allegheny* case. The Kennedy dissent accused Blackmun and his group of an "Orwellian rewriting of history," a "latent hostility" or "callous indifference" toward religion. Blackmun responded by labeling his colleague Kennedy's charges as "offensive" and "absurd." Said the angry Minnesotan, "perhaps it is Justice Kennedy himself who has slipped into a form of Orwellian newspeak when he equates the constitutional command of secular government with a proscribed orthodoxy."

The Court was to remain fundamentally divided until Marshall's retirement in 1991 and in the years that followed. Indeed, in Marshall's last year, the Court majority granted certiorari (over Marshall's vote to deny certiorari) in a case, *Lee v. Weisman,* that gave the Rehnquist Court the opportunity to overturn the three-prong standard in *Lemon v. Kurtzman.*

After Marshall retired, the *Lee* case came from Rhode Island and raised the question of whether invocations and benedictions that mentioned God and other religious figures (Jesus, etc.) during public-school graduation ceremonies violated the First and Fourteenth Amendments. The Bush administration's brief, prepared by the solicitor general, had asked the Court to dismantle the *Lemon* standard and not use it in *Lee* and other cases where there was very little or no coercion. When the case came down the following year, with Justice Clarence Thomas sitting in Marshall's seat, the Court barely declined to reconsider *Lemon.* Thomas voted with the conservative trio of Scalia, Rehnquist, and White to junk the *Lemon* standard, but they did not have the votes. The key vote in *Lee* was Kennedy's; his was the fifth vote that joined with a moderate conservative quartet of Souter, O'Connor, Blackmun, and Stevens to rule that the graduation prayers were, for some students, coercive and therefore violative of the First and Fourteenth Amendments. Marshall must have been delighted.

## THE "FREE EXERCISE OF RELIGION" CLAUSE

Freedom of religion is a hallowed right of all persons in America. It is one of the small set of neutral factors that, if legislation is enacted to somehow limit religious practice, the Court will employ its "strict scrutiny" standard to determine whether the legislation is constitutional—with the burden of showing constitutionality placed on the shoulders of the government attorneys. By the time Marshall joined the Court, it had ruled many times that government, whether national, state, or local, could not discriminate on the basis of religion.

By 1967, however, the Court had also permitted governments to *restrict* in some basic ways many religious practices. A congressional ban on polygamy was validated by the Court in 1879 *(Reynolds v. United States).* In 1934, a unanimous Court allowed the University of California to require all male students to enroll in military training courses, even though religious students objected to the invasion of their religious beliefs by the state. In a number of Jehovah's Witnesses cases in the early 1940s, the Court upheld a compulsory flag-salute statute (*Minersville v. Gobitis,* 1941) and a Massachusetts statute that prohibited minors from selling religious tracts on street corners (*Prince v. Massachusetts,* 1944). Just a few years before Marshall joined the brethren, in the Sunday Closing Law cases of 1961, Warren Court majorities validated ordinances requiring the closing of stores on Sundays, over the objections of Orthodox Jews, whose holy day is Saturday (*McGowan v. Maryland* and *Braunfield v. Brown,* 1961).

Court majorities had also upheld many "free exercise of religion" claims raised by religious groups who were adversely affected by local laws and ordinances. In 1940, there was the *Cantwell* case, in which the Court invalidated a Connecticut statute that required Jehovah's Witnesses to obtain permits for solicitation of funds on the public streets. In 1943, in *Martin v. Struthers,* another Jehovah's Witnesses case, the Court invalidated a local ordinance that had been used to prohibit Jehovah's Witnesses from going door-to-door to solicit funds for their religion. And in 1943 the Court majority overturned *Gobitis,* in *West Virginia Board of Education v. Barnette,* and ruled that a government cannot punish persons (Jehovah's Witnesses) for refusing, on religious belief grounds, to salute the American flag.

In 1946, in the already mentioned case of *Marsh v. Alabama,* the Court, in an opinion written by Hugo Black, ruled that a private town was not immune from the coverage of the First Amendment and that its prohibition of the distribution of religious literature on its streets was an unconstitutional infringement of a person's freedom of religion. The use of public parks, the Court said in 1951, in *Niemotko v. Maryland,* had to made available to Jehovah's Witnesses and other religious groups, while in 1961 the Court invalidated a state requirement that all public officials had to declare their belief in God in order to hold public office *(Torasco v. Watkins).*

In *Sherbert v. Verner,* an important case decided in 1963, the Court, by a seven-to-two vote (with Justices White and Harlan dissenting) overturned a South Carolina agency ruling denying a Seventh-Day Adventist unemployment benefits because she had refused to work on her Sabbath (Saturday) and had been fired as a result. *Sherbert*'s precedent, written by Justice Brennan, was to last until 1991, when the Rehnquist majority, finding the *Sherbert* test to be an expensive and dangerous "luxury," struck it down. Brennan's majority opinion stated that a state law that burdened a person's free exercise of religion could only be validated if the government showed a sufficiently compelling reason for restricting a First Amendment freedom. The government must also show that the legislation was "the least drastic means" for achieving the state's goals. And, in the midst of the Vietnam War, the Court majority, in *United States v. Seeger* (1965), held that conscientious objectors had to be exempted from military service if they held a belief, religious or otherwise, that prevented them from serving in the military.

Marshall joined the Court during the period in which it continued to define what free exercise means, and whether or not the government meets the burden, in strict-scrutiny litigation, of justifying constraints on a group's religious beliefs. As in the other areas of First Amendment controversy, Marshall would clash with Burger, Rehnquist, Scalia, and Kennedy. And in most of those battles he was joined by, or he joined with, Brennan and Stevens.

In *Wisconsin v. Yoder*, a 1972 case involving the religious freedom of the Amish, the Court majority ruled in favor of the small religious sect. Jonas Yoder, Adin Yutzy, and Wallace Miller, members of an Amish Mennonite church in Wisconsin, were convicted in state court for violating the state compulsory school attendance law and fined five dollars each. (In Wisconsin, state law compelled children to attend school, public or private, until they reached sixteen years of age.) The three men refused to send their children to public school beyond the eighth grade, even though the students had not reached the age of sixteen. (Through the eighth grade, the children receive basic education in the three R's; after that grade they are exposed to secular moral, ethical, and societal values, which are antithetical to Amish religious beliefs.) They appealed their convictions, arguing that the Wisconsin law violated their First and Fourteenth Amendment freedom of religion. The Wisconsin Supreme Court agreed with them and reversed their convictions. The state appealed to the U.S. Supreme Court, and the Court affirmed the state court's decision in the conference session held on December 10, 1971, a few days after the oral arguments. The brethren were unanimous in their judgment. A point made repeatedly, especially by Burger and Marshall, was that the Amish were not a fly-by-night religious cult but a religious group hundreds of years old. Burger noted that the Amish follow "an ancient religion, not a new cult." Furthermore, "being raised on an Amish farm is equal [to] or better than vocational school training." Though it was a difficult situation, he voted to affirm the state court.[29]

Marshall had no difficulty with the case, and also voted to affirm the judgment. White affirmed and raised a question that Douglas picked up and led to his writing a partial dissent. White said that "there was little talk of the interest of the children—the rights of the children have an independent standing and they are not competent to make the decision [whether to stay in public school or leave after the eighth grade]."[30]

Chief Justice Burger wrote the majority opinion, which Marshall joined. Justices Stewart and Brennan concurred, while Justice Douglas dissented in part. The two new Nixon appointees, Powell and Rehnquist, did not participate. After reviewing the religious and community values of the Amish, including the conviction that "formal high school education beyond the eighth grade is contrary to Amish beliefs," Burger concluded that the sect's religious beliefs were indeed unconstitutionally abridged by the state. They affirmed the judgment of the Wisconsin court, and concluded "that the First and Fourteenth Amendments prevent the State from compelling respondents to cause their children to attend formal high school to age 16." Douglas dissented in part because only one of the children expressed an opinion about religion and secular education. "I think the children should be entitled to be heard.... The education of the child is a matter on which the child will often have decided views."

*Employment Division, Department of Human Resources of Oregon v. Smith,* decided in 1990, involved the firing of two Native Americans, Alfred Smith and Galen Black, who were employed in a private drug rehab program, because they took peyote. It was the case that overturned the *Sherbert* precedent penned by Brennan in 1963 for a seven-person Court majority. The two men, members of the Native American Church, ingested hallucinogenic peyote mushrooms as part of their religious ceremonies. Though they were never charged by law enforcement with criminal violation of the state's antidrug statutes, they were denied Oregon unemployment benefits because their firings were due to "misconduct" on the job.

An Oregon court overturned the decision, on First Amendment freedom of religious expression grounds, balancing that right against the state's effort to prohibit the use of the drug, even for religious purposes. On appeal, the Oregon Supreme Court affirmed the lower court's judgment, but on different grounds. The Court concluded that Smith should collect unemployment payments because Oregon's "interest in [preserving the integrity of] its compensation fund [from payouts to persons who used prohibited drugs] did not outweigh the burden imposed on Smith's religious beliefs and practices."

The state appealed the judgment to the U.S. Supreme Court. The Court returned the case to the state court in 1987, in order to have the Oregon Supreme Court determine "whether the use of peyote was protected by the Federal Constitution." That Court, using the U.S. Supreme Court's balancing test and the *Sherbert* "compelling interest" precedent, interpreted the First Amendment as protecting Smith's religious use of the drug and, again, concluded that Smith was entitled to unemployment insurance. (In *Sherbert*, the Seventh-Day Adventist case decided in 1963, the Court held that "a State could not condition the availability of unemployment insurance on an individual's willingness to forgo conduct required by his religion.")

The state once again appealed to the Supreme Court, which granted certiorari and overturned the Oregon Supreme Court decision. Justice Scalia wrote the decision in *Smith* for the conservative majority. They reversed the state court decision and, in so doing, addressed the question of balancing. There were three dissenters: Marshall, Brennan, and Blackmun. Blackmun wrote the dissent, joined by the other two men.

For Scalia, Rehnquist, and the others in the majority, the bottom line was that "Oregon does prohibit the religious use of peyote." For the majority, such a prohibition was constitutional. While the First Amendment "excludes all governmental regulation of religious *beliefs* as such," religious *conduct* based on belief can be regulated by government. "We have never held that an individual's religious beliefs excuse him from compliance with an otherwise valid law prohibiting conduct that the State is free to regulate." They set aside the "compelling interest" balancing test created in the 1963 *Sherbert* decision because, Scalia argued, "many laws will not meet that test. Any society adopting such a system would be courting anarchy, but that danger increases in direct proportion to the society's diversity of religious beliefs, and its determination to coerce or suppress none of them."

Blackmun wrote a blistering dissent, joined by Brennan and Marshall, in which he defended the strict-scrutiny standard "painstakingly developed" by the Court in the freedom of religion cases decided by the Court—until *Smith*. Until *Smith* was announced, statutes that burdened the free exercise of religion stood "only if the law in general, and the State's refusal to allow a religious exemption in particular, are justified by a compelling interest that cannot be served by less restrictive means." After *Smith*, strict scrutiny of such statutes had become an unaffordable "luxury," according to Scalia and his group. The dissenters thought that "[*Sherbert*] was a settled and inviolate principle of this Court's First Amendment jurisprudence, unlike the majority, who perfunctorily dismisse[d] it as a 'constitutional anomaly.'" By so deciding, the majority "effectuates a wholesale overturning of settled law concerning the Religion Clauses of our Constitution."

There was no sufficiently compelling state interest in enforcing its drug laws as balanced against the Native Americans' "right to the free exercise of their religion." Blackmun, Marshall, and Brennan would have affirmed the judgment of the Oregon Supreme Court. It was a dreadful day for them, for in this one case the Rehnquist majority had invalidated a principle of constitutional law that had been implemented continually since 1963. For Marshall and the others, however, it was not surprising to see the Rehnquist majority move in these new directions.

## MARSHALL AND THE FIRST AMENDMENT FREEDOMS

Marshall's friend Carl Rowan wrote that Marshall

was as passionate in his defense of First Amendment rights as he was in his support of affirmative action. He clearly extended the parameters of freedom of speech in this society....He tried to sell to the Court and the nation the idea that a parking lot in a shopping center, a prison hall, an army base, was a public forum, and that the government always had to show compelling reasons for limiting free speech there or anywhere else.[31]

For Marshall, in First Amendment litigation as in the other areas of constitutional conflict he dealt with while on the Court, the freedoms were as important to poor, ignorant minorities as they were to other, more affluent groups. We all have the human need to communicate, with ourselves, our God, our family, our community, and the First Amendment freedoms guarantee almost complete freedom to so communicate.

There is also a privacy element attached to these freedoms, especially when a person is in his or her home. One's residence cannot be invaded unless the government has probable cause and shows such cause to an impartial magistrate. Marshall didn't accept Hugo Black's absolutist views of the First Amendment. As was the case in other areas of constitutional jurisprudence, Marshall's views were closer to Brennan's "compelling reason" view of limits on First Amendment freedoms than to any other judicial theory of First Amendment adjudication.

During the few years he worked with the Warren Court, and in the early years of the Burger Court, Marshall, joined by Brennan, Douglas, Black, and Stewart, among others, was able to emerge victorious in many First Amendment clashes within the Court. By the middle of the 1970s, however, after Douglas retired from the Court, things changed, personnel changed. Marshall fought off the inroads made by an ascendant conservative Court majority, led by Rehnquist.

So, for his last fifteen years on the Court, Marshall found himself increasingly in the minority on First Amendment issues as well as in other areas. But, until the last year, a year without his good friend Bill Brennan sitting on the Court with him, Marshall rose time and again to the challenge of writing dissents for future courts to consider. As he said, "I love a dissent. You have to get real mad to write a good dissent. I loved a war. When young lawyers apply to clerk for my office, the first thing I ask is, 'Do you like writing dissents? If you don't, baby, this is not the office for *you.*' Yep, get my juices jiggling and I'll write a helluva dissent. I admit, though, that I sometimes wonder what a difference it might make for the country if I were writing for the majority."[32]

Marshall came to write many dissents in his last years on the high bench. He would never know what kind of difference he would have made if he were writing for the Court majority.

# 14

## THE CONSTITUTION AS EVOLVING GUARANTOR OF NEW RIGHTS

W
e the People," the opening words of America's Constitution, excluded women from voting, and treated African Americans as property, "although they were counted for representational purposes—at three-fifths each," Marshall reminded lawyers at a meeting in May of 1987 during the celebration of the two hundredth anniversary of the adoption of the Constitution by the states. "These omissions were intentional....The more fitting commemoration would acknowledge that the Constitution was then and now an *evolving* document of justice and fairness."[1] Unfortunately, he sat on the Court at a time when a majority of his colleagues, especially William Rehnquist and Antonin Scalia, argued for an interpretation of the Constitution's language that reflected the "original intent" of the Framers. These conservative "originalists" argued that modern judicial interpreters of the Constitution had to faithfully reflect the original values of the men who wrote the document in 1787. Former U.S. attorney general Edwin Meese expressed this view when he said, in a major address in the summer of 1985 to the American Bar Association, that the task of the Supreme Court is to "resurrect the original meaning of constitutional provisions...as the only reliable guide to judgment. [It] must adopt a jurisprudence seriously aimed at the explication of original intention which would produce defensible principles of government that would not be tainted with ideological predilection."[2]

This prescription was intolerable to Marshall and William Brennan because it did not acknowledge that 1787 marked only the turbulent and defective *birth* of a living document, one that has been given new meaning by men and women who have interpreted it over a span of two centuries, in the Congress, in the Executive, and in the federal courts, but definitively in the Supreme Court. The 1787 document had too many defects to be relied upon by twentieth-century jurists to answer legal questions regarding the relationship between governmental powers and individual rights.

Brennan spoke for himself and Marshall when, a few months after Meese's address, he spoke at Georgetown Law School in October 1985. Both men had bristled at Meese's undisguised attack on the Warren Court majority's actions in the area of constitutional rights and liberties, and Brennan elected to blast Meese in public. Some interpreters of the Constitution, both on and off the Court, Brennan said, "find legitimacy in fidelity to what they call the 'intentions of the Framers.'" Their attitude, he said, "in truth, is little more than arrogance cloaked in humility. It is arrogant to pretend that from our vantage point we can gauge accurately the intent of the Framers on applications of principle to specific, contemporary questions."[3] Such a jurisprudential position would "turn a blind eye to social progress and eschews adaptation of overarching principles to changes of social circumstances." These fundamental differences were abundantly clear whenever the justices addressed the question of new rights, especially the right to privacy and personal autonomy.

## THE RIGHT TO PRIVACY

Marshall believed, as he demonstrated in his opinion for the Court majority in the 1969 case of *Stanley v. Georgia,* that the evolving Constitution guaranteed the fundamental right of privacy for all citizens. Even though the term itself was not specifically enumerated in the document, he and others argued that it could be discovered in the basic principles inherent in the various clauses in the Bill of Rights. By 1965 the right of privacy had been firmly established by a landmark Court decision, *Griswold v. Connecticut,* which arose from the conviction of Estelle Griswold, the executive director of the Planned Parenthood League of Connecticut, for giving married people advice about avoiding unwanted pregnancy. She had violated a state statute dating from 1879 that prohibited anyone from using a drug or device to prevent conception.

Justice Douglas, who had been married four times and thus could be considered something of an expert on the subject, wrote the majority opinion: "We deal with a right of privacy older than the Bill of Rights—older than our political parties, older than our school system—marriage." In *Griswold,* the Court had determined that where rights are concerned, the Bill of Rights guarantees are but expressions or examples of those rights, and do not preclude applications or extensions of those rights to situations unanticipated by the Framers.

Marshall was on the Court when other cases gave him an opportunity to elaborate on what he believed the Constitution said regarding "the right to be left alone—the most comprehensive of rights and the right most valued by civilized man."[4] As seen in a previous chapter, Marshall believed that there was a *privacy of place,* where there existed a reasonable expectation of personal, intimate, privacy. For Marshall, privacy of place included the home and its functional equivalent (hotel room, etc.), and such places could not be invaded by government unless probable cause was shown to an impartial magistrate.

He also believed that there was a privacy guarantee inherent in a person's personal *decision* to marry, to have—or not to have—a family, and in other decisions involving personal autonomy. Clearly, he would have extended the right of privacy to "unconventional personal relationships."[5] Because of the appointment of the four conservative Nixon justices, however, by the mid-1970s Marshall was increasingly in dissent, as seen, for example, in *Kelly v. Johnson* (1976) when the Court, in a six-to-two opinion written by Rehnquist, upheld a Suffolk County, New York, statute that limited the length of a policeman's hair. Showing their usual deference to authority, the majority found that there was a rational relationship between the state's regulation of hair length and "the promotion of safety for persons and property."

In response to and in dissent from the majority's rejection of Johnson's claim to a "liberty" interest covered by the Fourteenth Amendment, both Brennan and Marshall held that there was such protection. "An individual's personal appearance may reflect, sustain, and nourish his personality and may well be used as a means of expressing his attitude and lifestyle. In taking control over a *person's personal appearance,* the government forces him to sacrifice substantial elements of his integrity and personality as well." Unless there were significant reasons for government to intrude into this area of personal autonomy, the Constitution prohibits such interference. The "right to be let alone," Brandeis's observation in his 1928 *Olmstead* dissent, was for Marshall a fundamental right every person has and that right extended to "one's personal appearance."

*Village of Belle Terre v. Bruce Boraas, et al.* was another case from Suffolk County, New York, that came to the Court and raised the right-of-privacy claim. It involved the specific issue of privacy of a place and, again, Marshall disagreed with the Court majority (in this case with Douglas, the author of the majority opinion). A small upper-middle-class village adjacent to the campus of the State University of New York at Stony Brook, in an effort to restrict occupancy of homes to prevent groups of university students from moving into the area, passed a zoning ordinance that restricted land use to "one-family dwellings," expressly excluding boardinghouses, fraternity houses, or multiple dwellings.

Bruce Boraas was a co-owner of a building in the village who rented it to six unrelated university students. The owners were cited for violating the ordinance, and Boraas brought an action in federal court, maintaining that the local ordinance was in violation of the First and Fourteenth Amendments' rights of association and privacy. The federal district court held the ordinance to be constitutional, but the federal appellate court overturned the ruling, asserting that there was a constitutional violation. The village then appealed to the Supreme Court.

For Douglas and the majority, including Brennan, the ordinance was a piece of economic and social legislation and was upheld because there was shown to be a *reasonable*, "not an arbitrary," relationship between the ordinance and a "state objective." (Belle Terre officials claimed the law was passed to keep "transients" out of their community, and the Court majority concluded that that was a reasonable goal of the local government.)

Marshall dissented. For him, because the "disputed classification burdens the students' fundamental rights of association and privacy guaranteed by the First and Fourteenth Amendments,...the application of *strict scrutiny* is therefore required." While some "deference should be given to governmental judgments concerning proper land-use allocation,...*deference does not mean abdication....* The village had "infringed upon fundamental constitutional rights." (My emphasis.) There is, he concluded, "the freedom to choose one's associates... [and] the freedom of association is often inextricably intertwined with the constitutionally guaranteed right of privacy."

During the 1975 term of the Court, an action of the now-emergent conservative Burger Court majority deeply upset Marshall. The case, *Doe v. Virginia Commonwealth's Attorney*, came to the brethren on direct appeal from a three-judge federal district court. Virginia's anti-sodomy law had been challenged, and the federal judges had validated the statute (which prohibited homosexual acts, including those performed in the privacy of one's home, as well as heterosexual oral sex). The Court summarily affirmed the lower court's decision. "Marshall was outraged" and dissented from the order.[6]

A decade later, in another controversial right-of-personal-privacy decision, *Bowers v. Hardwick*, a 1986 Georgia sodomy case, Marshall was, once again, in the minority. Five opinions were written in the case. Justice Byron White eventually wrote the opinion for the very narrow majority, with Chief Justice Burger and the pivotal swing vote, Lewis Powell, writing their own separate concurrences. Marshall joined both dissenting opinions written by Justices Blackmun and Stevens. The case involved the constitutionality of a nineteenth-century Georgia sodomy statute that made it a criminal offense, punishable by up to twenty years in prison, for a person to commit heterosexual or homosexual sodomy, that is, "when [a person] performs or submits to any sexual act involving the sex organs of one person and the mouth or anus of another."

Michael Hardwick was charged with committing that act with another adult male in his own bedroom. Police went to his apartment to serve him with an arrest warrant because Hardwick did not appear in a local court to answer a charge that he was drinking in public. Another male in Hardwick's apartment told the police that Hardwick was not home, but that they could look into his home. The police then discovered Hardwick in bed with another man and arrested him. However, after a preliminary hearing, the local district attorney decided not to bring the charge of sodomy against Hardwick to the grand jury.

Hardwick then sought a declaratory judgment in federal district court, charging that the Georgia statute was unconstitutional in that it punished consensual sodomy. (Since he had not been charged, tried, and convicted of violating the sodomy statute, he was not "injured" and could not challenge the statute. He could, and did, request that the district court judge issue a declaratory judgment in which, if granted, the judge would declare Hardwick's legal right to engage in consensual sodomy and invalidate the Georgia statute.) The federal judge did not issue the declaratory judgment, but the federal appellate court reversed, holding that the Georgia statute violated Hardwick's "fundamental rights because his homosexual activity is a private and intimate association that is beyond the reach of State regulation by reason of the Ninth Amendment and the Due Process Clause."

In an evidently intense battle between the justices, one that swung one way and then the other, the Court majority *initially* reversed the lower federal appellate court. On the merits, the Court divided five to four. On one side of the issue, holding that the Georgia statute violated Hardwick's right of privacy, were Marshall, Brennan, Blackmun, Stevens, and Lewis Powell. On the other side stood Chief Justice Burger, and Associate Justices White, Rehnquist, and O'Connor.

Weeks later, however, after long and considerable thought and then reading Blackmun's draft majority opinion—whose primary focus was on the broad scope of the right of privacy—Powell concluded that he could not join the majority. He notified the conference that he had changed his mind, and White, who had written a dissent, was given a new assignment by the Chief: author a majority opinion for the Court. For them, the constitutional question was placed in sharp focus: Does the Constitution "confer a fundamental right [of privacy] upon homosexuals to engage in sodomy and hence invalidates the laws of the many States that still make such conduct illegal"? No, they answered. "None of the rights announced in [*Griswold* and *Roe*] bears any resemblance to the claimed constitutional right of homosexuals to engage in acts of sodomy." Unwilling to invalidate the sodomy laws of "some 25 States," the majority reversed the decision of the federal appellate court. Burger wrote a separate concurring opinion to point out that to make such sexual conduct a protected fundamental right "would be to cast aside millennia of moral teaching." Nothing in the Constitution, from Burger's reading of it, "deprives a State of power to enact the statute challenged here." Powell's concurring opinion was the critical fifth vote that made the new majority. He explained his switch by noting, "I cannot say that conduct condemned for hundreds of years has now become a fundamental right."

Harry Blackmun, who started off drafting the majority opinion, now found himself writing a four-person dissent. For Blackmun and the others, the case was "about the right to be let alone....If that right means anything, it means that, before Georgia can prosecute its citizens for making choices about the most intimate aspects of their lives, it must do more than assert that the choice they have made is an 'abominable' crime not fit to be named among Christians." They argued that the right to privacy extends to decisions a person makes, as well as "to certain *places* without regard for the particular activities in which the individuals who occupy them are engaged." Hardwick's activities were protected because they took place in a space, the bedroom, that was protected by the right of privacy.

In a somewhat tragic footnote to the case, Powell, *after* he retired from the Court, announced that he had voted the wrong way in *Bowers* and, had he to do it over again, he would have stayed with Blackmun's opinion. As with his recantation in *McKleskey*, the death-penalty decision, Powell was, of course, too late to have any effect other than to admit the dictates of conscience. This ineffectual *post hoc* gesture angered Marshall a great deal.

Toward the very end of his tenure on the Court, during the 1989 term, Marshall and his colleagues faced a question that had never been argued before the Court: Does personal autonomy and the right to privacy encompass a person's right to die by shutting off the life-support system that maintains said person's life? The case, *Cruzan by Cruzan v. Director, Missouri Department of Health,* came to the Court from Missouri.

Twenty-five-year-old Nancy Cruzan had been in a terrible auto accident in which her brain had been deprived of oxygen for many minutes. She never regained consciousness and soon become brain-dead. She would remain unconscious in a vegetative state for decades unless the feeding tube was removed and she was allowed to die a natural death. The accident occurred in 1983. In early 1987 her parents requested that the tube be removed and that their daughter be allowed to die a natural death. They based their request on the constitutional right to privacy, which, in their situation, involved the very personal decision to allow their child to die.

In 1988 a state court granted permission for the parents to have the feeding tube removed, but, on appeal by the state, the Missouri Supreme Court reversed the judge's order, maintaining that the state was committed to the "sanctity of human life" as expressed in the state's "living will" law, which stated that "clear and convincing evidence" had to be presented showing that an incompetent patient such as Nancy Cruzan, when she had previously been competent, had clearly indicated that life-support systems should not be used on her in the event she became medically incompetent. The Cruzans then appealed to the U.S. Supreme Court, which granted certiorari and heard the case during its 1989–90 term. In a narrow five-to-four vote, the Court, with Chief Justice Rehnquist writing the majority opinion, upheld the judgment of the state supreme court.

The case focused national media attention on the Court's struggle to resolve the question of who was empowered to make life-and-death decisions in such a situation—the family, the doctor, or the state. The Court received *amicus curiae* briefs from medical groups such as the American Medical Association and a great many religious organizations, most of them supporting the family's right to make the choice for an incompetent, comatose patient.

As with so many other controversial right-of-privacy cases, *Cruzan* had five separate opinions; there were the majority and two concurring opinions (written by Justices Scalia and O'Connor), while the other two were dissents written by William Brennan and John P. Stevens. Marshall, along with Harry Blackmun, joined both dissents.

At the very end of the term, June 25, 1990, the Court announced its decision upholding the state court's decision. The dissent in *Cruzan* was one of Brennan's last; he announced his retirement less than one month later. The majority wrestled with the possibility of expanding the right of privacy to difficult decisions involving the death and dying of persons who are incapable of making their own choices. Naturally, Rehnquist's opinion rejected such an expansion to include the "right to die." All the justices in this case accepted the premise that a competent person can elect not to receive life-sustaining medical technology. But what about a patient such as Nancy Cruzan, comatose when brought into the hospital? She was clearly incompetent, so the question for the justices was whether a state could establish guidelines by which doctors could "pull the plug" or not, on such comatose, brain-dead, incompetent patients—without facing criminal charges for murder. For the Rehnquist majority, "the question is simply and starkly whether the U.S. Constitution prohibits Missouri from choosing the rule of decision [the 'clear and convincing evidence' rule] which it did."

The majority concluded that the state's rule was not in violation of the Constitution's prohibitions. They refused to extend the right of privacy to an unconditional right to die. The state, they concluded, and not the family, was better able to serve as the surrogate for an incompetent patient like Nancy Cruzan. (Justice Scalia's concurring opinion maintained, "federal courts have no business in this field....The Constitution has nothing to say about the right to die.")

Justice Brennan dissented, joined by Marshall and Harry Blackmun. They believed that Nancy Cruzan had "a fundamental right to be free of unwanted artificial nutrition and hydration, which right is not outweighed by any interests of the State.... [She was] entitled to choose to die with dignity." They accepted as factual the family's and friends' assertion that Nancy Cruzan did not wish to continue to exist "metabolically alive." There was a choice made, and it should have been honored by the state. For Brennan, family members were more competent than the state to make these life-and-death decisions. For the three men, "the state is a stranger to the patient," and they concluded that the Missouri statute violated the Fourteenth Amendment's due-process clause and that Nancy Cruzan had the right to die.

The Court's narrow five-to-four holding in *Cruzan* was a setback for Marshall and his colleagues who believed in the broad right of privacy. As Rehnquist argued successfully in other constitutional cases before his Court, the balance between individual rights and the powers of the states had to tip in favor of the states, thereby narrowing the judicially constructed right to privacy. Nancy Cruzan, despite the majority's ruling in her case, did not "remain a passive prisoner of medical technology." In a follow-up hearing before the state probate judge, Cruzan's parents presented additional witnesses in an effort to meet Rehnquist's requirement that "clear and convincing evidence" be presented to show Nancy's views on death. The probate judge granted, again, the family's petition and the state supreme court affirmed that decision. On December 26, 1990, Nancy Cruzan died.[7]

Clearly, in right-of-privacy litigation, the Court found itself dealing with controversial questions that literally involved life and death. Birth and abortion, in the early 1970s, were thrown into the legal equation as the brethren heard cases that raised the possibility of extending the right of privacy, announced in 1965, to a woman's choice to have an abortion.

## ABORTION AS A WOMAN'S PERSONAL—AND PRIVATE—CHOICE

Court opinions and files "indicate that no justice ever supported a woman's right to [choose to have an abortion] as uncompromisingly as Marshall did."[8] He, of all the justices who sat on the Court and heard and decided abortion decisions, knew about "the circumstances of life of pregnant women in our pockets of rural poverty, or in the worst of our urban ghettos." He was the only justice, of the 108 men and women who have sat on the Court, "who had defended and worked with so many poor women that he actually knew how they suffered financially, were pained emotionally, [and] often became psychological wrecks over knowledge that another baby was on the way."[9] When the Court heard the abortion cases, Marshall argued vigorously on behalf of these forgotten women who desperately needed the freedom to choose—and to have Medicaid and other public funding used to provide them with counseling and coverage of their medical expenses.

The abortion controversy has fiercely engaged millions of persons since the late 1960s. The Supreme Court soon found itself in the middle of the political thicket of abortion rights. The justices themselves, especially Brennan (a Roman Catholic), Blackmun (the author of *Roe*), and Marshall, received thousands of abusive letters and threats on their lives.

## ROE'S *ANTECEDENTS*

In 1965, in *Griswold v. Connecticut,* the "right of privacy" was announced as a "fundamental" constitutional norm, one that could be found in the cracks and crevices of the various amendments in the Bill of Rights. Seven years after *Griswold,* the Court heard *Thomas Eisenstadt, Sheriff v. William R. Baird.* Massachusetts law prohibited the sale or distribution of contraceptives to unmarried persons. Bill Baird, a birth-control activist, gave a speech at Boston University in 1967, in which he exhibited a number of contraceptive devices and invited audience members to come up and take free samples. He personally handed an unmarried adult woman a package of vaginal foam. Sheriff Eisenstadt witnessed the transaction and arrested Baird. He was convicted of distributing contraceptives to unmarried persons.

Baird appealed the conviction on the ground that the statute violated the due-process clause of the Fourteenth Amendment. The federal court of appeals agreed with his contention and declared the statute unconstitutional. The state appealed the decision to the Supreme Court. Probable jurisdiction was noted by the Court in March 1971, and the Court heard the case the following term.

Oral argument took place in mid-November 1971, and the seven-person conference met on November 19 to discuss the case. (Justices Black and Harlan had retired in September 1971, and their replacements, Powell and Rehnquist, had not yet joined the Court.) Voting to affirm, but for different constitutional reasons, were Douglas (on First Amendment free-speech grounds), and a small cohort led by Brennan, and including Potter Stewart, Marshall (Brennan noting in conference that "this [case] is in the *penumbra* of *Griswold*"), and a hesitant Harry Blackmun. Voting to reverse the lower federal court was Justice White. Chief Justice Burger passed because, recorded Douglas in his notes, the Chief "can't discover what the issue is." A few days later, Burger wrote to Douglas and Brennan, "my vote is a questionable reverse with a note 'could affirm—depends on how written.'"[10]

Brennan, with Marshall joining him, wrote the majority opinion that overturned the Massachusetts statute. In *Eisenstadt,* Brennan said that "whatever the rights of the individual to access to contraceptives may be, the rights must be the same for the unmarried and the married alike." He concluded by stating that "if the right of privacy means anything, it is the right of the *individual,* married or single, to be free from unwarranted intrusion into matters so fundamentally affecting a person as the decision whether to bear or beget a child."

In *United States v. Vuitch,* a 1971 case heard the term before the *Roe* case was brought to the Supreme Court, the Court initially examined the validity of anti-abortion statutes. The case, which came to the justices from the District of Columbia, questioned the constitutionality of a statute that made it a crime to perform an abortion except where "necessary for the preservation of the mother's life or health." The trial judge focused on the vagueness of the meaning of the term "health" in the statute, and concluded that the phrase was "so vague in its interpretation and the practice under the act that there is no indication whether it includes varying degrees of mental as well as physical health."

The Court avoided the question of whether a state could regulate the abortion process at all, and set aside for vagueness the lower federal court ruling that the act was unconstitutional. It sent the case back on remand to the federal court. Black's opinion, handed down in April 1971, noted that the term "health" was clear enough to cover psychological as well as physical health of pregnant women.

Shortly after announcing *Vuitch,* the Court granted certiorari in the cases of *Roe v. Wade,* from Texas, and *Doe v. Bolton,* a Georgia case. By the time *Roe* and *Doe* came to the Court, it was a seven-man tribunal because Black and Harlan had both retired in September 1971. This fact was to become a significant one during the Court's deliberations in its 1971–72 term. (Both Doe and Roe were legal pseudonyms given to the women in these cases in order to protect their privacy.)

## ROE V. WADE

Abortion rights of women was one of a number of demands of the women's rights movement that emerged in the 1960s. It was an explosive public policy controversy at the time President Richard Nixon was appointing four new men to the Court. These were men the President hoped would reverse much of the Warren Court's revolution in civil rights and liberties, especially the recently crafted privacy right.

*Roe* and *Doe* were granted certiorari during the Court's 1970 term. As with all contemporary controversial cases that come to the Supreme Court, many briefs *amicus curiae* were filed. The pro-choice briefs, filed by groups of medical experts (such as the American College of Obstetricians and Gynecologists) as well as civil rights and civil liberties groups and groups such as Planned Parenthood and the American Public Health Association, were more numerous than the pro-life briefs.[11]

The medical briefs emphasized two points: the associational rights that existed between a patient and her doctor as well as the woman's right to privacy, to be left alone, with her doctor, to make a very difficult choice. Those were rights that were denied in the challenged Texas and Georgia anti-abortion statutes. The doctors from the Mayo Clinic, for example, argued in an *amicus curiae* brief that the state laws "unfairly discriminate against physicians and deny physicians equal protection of the laws."

The pro-life briefs, such as the one submitted from Americans United for Life, argued that the unborn had the constitutional right to life, a life guaranteed in the Fourteenth Amendment's due-process and equal-protection clauses: the unborn child is a person, it is human, it is living, and it has "being," the term used in a Supreme Court opinion, *Levy v. Louisiana*. That person's rights had to be balanced against those of the woman and, on balance, the child's life outweighed the right of a woman to choose to have an abortion.

*Roe* involved the constitutionality of a nineteenth-century Texas statute that prohibited all abortions except those for the specific purpose of saving the mother's life. In *Doe,* a more recent state anti-abortion statute was challenged. The Georgia statute allowed abortions if the woman's life was endangered, or if the fetus was likely to be born with a serious mental or physical defect, or if the pregnancy resulted from rape. The statute also mandated some minimal procedural safeguards that had to be met if there was to be a legal abortion: the procedure had to be done in an accredited hospital, with the doctor using an approved procedure, and after the need for the procedure had been validated by two other doctors.

The woman in the Texas case was not allowed to have the abortion because her life was not in danger; the woman in Georgia was not able to have a legal abortion because none of the three substantive conditions was met in her case. In *Roe,* a three-judge federal district court declared the Texas statute unconstitutional because it was vague and overbroad and infringed on the woman's Ninth and Fourteenth Amendment rights. It did not enjoin the state from enforcement of the law, and Roe appealed to the U.S. Supreme Court. In *Doe,* another three-judge federal district court granted declaratory relief to Doe; however, while the three substantive bases for having an abortion were invalidated, the three procedural requirements were deemed constitutional by the federal judges. Doe appealed the ruling to the U.S. Supreme Court.

After oral arguments, they met in conference to discuss and vote on the cases. Burger started off the discussion by noting that while the Texas statute was obsolete, it was constitutional, as was the Georgia statute.[12] All but White, including Burger's close friend Harry Blackmun, emphatically disagreed with the Chief, arguing that there was a constitutional right of privacy that extended to the woman's right to have an abortion. Burger's switch to the majority angered Douglas a great deal. As the senior associate justice, he would have made the assignment if Burger had not changed his vote and would have given it to himself or to Brennan and it would have been written with the "privacy" argument as the rationale. Instead, Burger's tactics resulted in the assignment being given to Blackmun, who based his judgment that the statutes were unconstitutional on other, less precedentially impactful grounds.

Burger counted on Harry Blackmun's inordinate slowness in the drafting and circulating of the majority opinion. If he ran true to form, Blackmun's circulation would come toward the end of the term, and its lateness would give the Chief the opportunity to have it reargued so that the two new Nixon appointees, Powell and Rehnquist, could participate. This could result in enough voters to support Burger's original view that the statutes were constitutional.

For Brennan, and for Marshall, the strategy in these two abortion cases was to build a bridge from *Griswold* and *Eisenstadt* to *Roe* and *Doe.* There was a right to privacy that protected a woman's right to choose to have a baby or have an abortion. The cases were assigned to Blackmun in mid-November, but as Burger and the rest suspected, he did not circulate a draft until May 18, 1972, six months later and little more than one month away from the informal close of the term of the Court. Furthermore, Blackmun's draft opinion distressed Douglas, Brennan, and Marshall because it was based on his observation that the law was unconstitutionally vague and overbroad, thus denying a medical doctor his Fourteenth Amendment equal-protection right to carry out his professional obligations and duties.

Brennan wrote Blackmun a letter, with copies to the conference, saying: "a majority of us feel the Constitution required the invalidation of abortion statutes save to the extent they required that an abortion be performed by a licensed physician within some time limit after conception. Your circulation invalidates the Texas statute only on the vagueness ground." Despite this admonishment, Blackmun's second circulation, in early June, produced no change in the reasoning for the overturn of the statutes. The three liberal justices concluded that this was the best they could hope to get from the Court on the issue of abortion.

Burger then asked Blackmun to consider carrying the cases over to the following term, when a full Court would participate in the discussion and the vote. Blackmun agreed, much to the chagrin and anger of Brennan, Douglas, and Marshall. Blackmun wrote a letter to the brethren, saying that he was "not yet certain about the details. I have now concluded, somewhat reluctantly, that reargument in both cases at an early date would perhaps be advisable....I believe..., the country deserves the conclusion of a nine-man, not a seven-man, court, whatever the ultimate decision may be."

Just before the critical conference session on the issue of carrying over the abortion cases, Potter Stewart vented his feelings about the Chief Justice's machinations to Brennan, who then sent a confidential memo to Marshall: "I will be God-damned! At lunch today, Potter expressed his outrage at the high-handed way things are going, particularly the assumption that a single Justice, if CJ, can order things his own way, and that he can hold up for nine anything he chooses."

Douglas was also boiling with anger at Burger, and on June 1, 1972, just before the decision was made to carry the two cases over, Douglas wrote a short letter to the brethren. "If the vote of the conference is to reargue, then I will file a statement telling what is happening to us and the tragedy it entails." After the vote to reargue carried, he drafted and circulated, after again having Brennan review the draft, a dissent from the order of the Court scheduling reargument in *Roe* and *Doe* in the fall 1972 term of the Court.

> When the minority seeks to control the assignment there is a destructive force at work in the Court. When a Chief Justice tries to bend the Court to his will by manipulating assignments, the integrity of the institution is imperiled. The abortion cases are symptomatic. This is an election year. Both parties have made abortion an issue....To prolong these abortion cases into the next election is a political gesture unworthy of this Court....I dissent with the deepest regret that we are allowing the institution to be manipulated for political objectives.[13]

During the summer, Harry Blackmun retreated to Minnesota, and to the Mayo Clinic, where he continued to reflect on the abortion issue. He brought with him the many memos that had been circulated, including the critically important Brennan letters that argued that the Court had to rest its decision in *Roe* and *Doe* on the core constitutional issue of the right to privacy.

After oral argument ended on October 11, 1972, the colleagues met in conference and discussed the cases.[14] By this time, Potter Stewart had joined with Brennan, Marshall, and Douglas in asserting the primacy of the woman's right of privacy. But, to the surprise and dismay of Burger's faction, so too did the new justice, Lewis Powell! William Rehnquist, however, viewed the statutes as constitutional and joined White in making that argument. With Powell in the Brennan camp, that meant that there were now six justices who saw the Texas and Georgia statutes as unconstitutional, Harry Blackmun (on First Amendment "vagueness" grounds) and the rest (Brennan, Stewart, Douglas, Powell, and

Marshall) on privacy grounds. Burger, who had passed, now joined the majority and immediately assigned the opinions, again, to Harry Blackmun—even though he was clearly expressing the minority rationale for the statutes' overturn. Douglas was, again, affronted by Burger's maneuvers.

Blackmun, however, surprised the brethren on two counts. First, he had his opinions drafted in short order, and second, after the summer's period of reflection and additional notes from Brennan and Marshall, his rationale for overturn was no longer vagueness. Instead, Blackmun switched to the privacy argument. In December 1972, Blackmun received important input from Marshall. Blackmun had raised a question and sought help from his colleagues in answering it: Was it better to provide a woman with free choice to the end of the first trimester of pregnancy (twelve weeks) "as the point beyond which a state may appropriately regulate abortion practices," or might not the point of "viability" (which is when the fetus can live outside the womb, at approximately 20–28 weeks into the pregnancy) be "a better choice."

The following day, Marshall responded with a "Dear Harry" letter. There was always the element of "balancing" in these very difficult and controversial cases before the Court: "At some point the State's interest in preserving the potential life of the unborn child overrides any individual interests of the women. I would be disturbed if that point were set before viability." Marshall, who was all too aware of the ignorance and fears that constrained poor, pregnant women, was "inclined to agree that drawing the line at viability accommodates the interests at stake better than drawing it at the end of the first trimester." Marshall, however, did accept the fact that the state had a legitimate interest "in insuring that abortions be done under safe conditions." He then suggested to Blackmun that "if the opinion stated explicitly that, between the end of the first trimester and viability, state regulations directed at health and safety alone were permissible, I believe that those concerns would be adequately met." [15]

Blackmun did indeed incorporate Marshall's suggestions, and Marshall, only a few days later, joined in the Blackmun majority opinion. By January 1973, only some two months after the brethren met to discuss and vote on the two cases, Blackmun's opinions were ready for announcement. In the end, the Court voted seven to two to invalidate the state laws (with White and Rehnquist the only dissenters). Blackmun's decision for the Court majority established the right of privacy in this area and, relying on Brennan's and Marshall's comments and thoughts, concluded that until the fetus is viable, the woman has a great deal of freedom to choose, without restrictions by the state. Blackmun had incorporated *in toto* Marshall's suggestions made in December 1972. Only in the third trimester does the state's interest in preserving the life of the unborn child become a "compelling" one and the government can pass legislation that severely limits or prohibits abortions at this point in the pregnancy.

After *Roe* came down, there were significant changes in abortion statutes in most of the states. Some of the changes liberalized the states' abortion policy. However, most of the changes "sought to limit the impact of *Roe*.... In addition, ten states passed laws or resolutions pledging to ban or severely restrict abortions, and fifteen others left their pre-*Roe* laws on the books, in anticipation of *Roe*'s being eventually overturned."[16] Moreover, a short time after *Roe*, with Douglas no longer on the Court, replaced by John P. Stevens, there was movement within the Court toward restricting the *Roe* opinion.

## ROE'S PROGENY: THE WOES OF ROE

In *Maher v. Roe*, one of three 1977 decisions of the Court involving the question whether a state can limit the use of Medicaid funds to cover the medical costs of an abortion, the justices, in a six-to-three vote, upheld such state restrictions on a woman's right to get an abortion. (The two other cases were *Beal v. Roe* [from Pennsylvania] and *Poelker v. Doe* [from Missouri].) It was a devastating decision for Marshall, who dissented in all three cases (as did Brennan and Harry Blackmun), for he saw poor, impoverished women as the unfortunate target of the legislation as well as the majority decision of the Court.

Connecticut passed a state regulation that prohibited the funding (through the Medicaid monies received from the national government) of abortions that were not medically or psychologically necessary for the health of the mother. Two indigent women (one an unmarried mother of three, and the other a sixteen-year-old high school student) challenged its constitutionality. The federal district court ruled in favor of the women, and the Second Circuit U.S. Court of Appeals remanded the case back to the district court, stating that the federal law allowed but did not require Medicaid funding for abortions. After the federal judge ruled, again, against the state, Edward Maher, Connecticut's commissioner of social services, appealed to the U.S. Supreme Court.

Justice Lewis Powell wrote the opinion for the six-person majority in the three cases. Concluding that the Constitution "imposes no obligation on the States to pay the pregnancy-related expenses of indigent women, or indeed to pay any of the medical expenses of indigents," Powell said that the equal-protection clause of the Fourteenth Amendment was not violated if Connecticut decided to use federal funds to pay for childbirth but not for nontherapeutic abortions.

As he had said a few years earlier in the San Antonio school education case (in which he and Marshall clashed over the issue of poverty as a "suspect class"), in *Maher*, Powell said that "this case involves no discrimination against a suspect class.... This Court has never held that financial need alone identifies a suspect class for purposes of equal protection analysis." And, under the rational-relationship test, Powell concluded that the Connecticut "funding scheme satisfies this standard [for the state has a 'strong interest in protecting the potential life of the fetus']....While indigency may make it difficult—and in some cases, perhaps, impossible—for some women to have abortions," Powell concluded, the Connecticut statute "neither created nor in any way affected" the decision not to have an abortion. In effect, then, Powell's opinion maintained that both the rich and the poor have an equal right to get a privately funded abortion!

Marshall, as was the case in the *San Antonio* clash with Powell, was outraged at the insensitivity of Powell and the majority. These statutes, he argued, involved the "most vicious attacks yet devised" by the "ethically bankrupt" opponents of *Roe* to "circumvent the commands of the Constitution and impose their moral choices upon the rest of society." The impact of those state regulations fell "upon those among us least able to help or defend themselves." As Powell "well knows, these regulations inevitably will have the practical impact of preventing nearly all poor women from obtaining safe and legal abortions." Marshall pointed out that the practical consequence of Powell's decision was the birth of unwanted children by desperately poor women. "An unwanted child may be disruptive and destructive of the life of any woman, but the impact is felt most by those too poor to ameliorate those effects."

These powerful angry words were not said lightly. Marshall knew the pain and mental anguish that would be visited "with great disparity upon women of minority races." Almost half of all minority women—"more than five times the proportion of whites"—depended on Medicaid for their health care. For Marshall, with the 1973 *Roe* decision, the Court "properly embarked on a course of constitutional adjudication no less controversial than that begun by *Brown*." Yet the Court flinched in *Maher* as it had in *Milliken*, and as a result, Marshall wrote, the opinion "will be an invitation to public officials, already under extraordinary pressure from well-financed and carefully orchestrated lobbying campaigns, to approve more such restrictions. The effect will be to relegate millions of people to lives of poverty and despair, only to serve the moral vanity of those who presume to dictate where righteousness lies."[17]

Marshall's dissent in these cases, along with the dissents of Brennan and Blackmun, did not stem the tide of criticism against the *Roe* precedent. Abortion became an issue, a very controversial one, in the presidential campaigns of 1980, 1984, and 1988. All three elections were won by conservative Republican candidates (Ronald Reagan in 1980 and 1984, and George Bush in 1988) who argued on behalf of the rights of the unborn and against the right of a woman to choose freely to have an abortion.

By the time *Webster v. Reproductive Health Services* was heard by the Court during its 1989 term, there had been significant changes in the Court's personnel. Only three justices remained from the seven-person 1973 *Roe* majority:

Marshall, Blackmun, and Brennan. The two dissenters in *Roe,* Rehnquist and White, had been joined by the conservative Reagan appointees. Stewart had been replaced by Sandra Day O'Connor (1981); federal appeals judge Antonin Scalia had taken Rehnquist's associate seat when Rehnquist was made Chief Justice (replacing Burger in 1986); and Lewis Powell had been replaced in 1987 by another Republican conservative appointee, federal appeals court judge Anthony Kennedy.

The Court's first female justice, Sandra Day O'Connor, a legislator and state judge from Arizona, was instantly critical of the *Roe* precedent. In the 1983 case of *Akron v. Akron Center for Reproductive Health,* in which the Court majority invalidated portions of an Ohio city ordinance that restricted a woman's right to an abortion, she was one of three dissenting justices (along with Rehnquist and White). She wrote that Blackmun's trimester approach was unworkable and that the framework created in *Roe* was "clearly on a collision course with itself." For her, the important question for the Court to raise in any abortion rights litigation was whether the state regulation placed an "undue burden" on a woman's right to an abortion.

When *Webster* was heard in 1989, given the Court's lineup, everyone thought that the case, from Missouri, would be the vehicle the Court majority would use to overturn *Roe.* The Eighth Circuit U.S. Court of Appeals had invalidated a number of provisions in Missouri's very restrictive 1986 abortion statute, and William Webster, the state's attorney general, appealed to the U.S. Supreme Court. The provisions invalidated by the federal appeals court were that (1) life begins with the act of conception itself, and "unborn children have a protectable interest in life, health, and well-being"; (2) medical doctors, before performing an abortion on a woman more than twenty weeks pregnant, were required to test the fetus's "gestational age, weight, and lung maturity"; (3) no public employee or public medical facility could be involved in a nontherapeutic abortion; and (4) no public funds could be used to "encourage or counsel" women about the value of an abortion.

The case became a *cause célèbre* when the Court announced that it would hear oral arguments and decide the issue on the merits. An unprecedented number of organized groups, seventy-eight in all, filed briefs *amicus curiae* with the Court in *Webster.* Forty-six sided with the appellant, the state of Missouri (including the U.S. solicitor general's brief), while another thirty-two *amicus* briefs were filed on behalf of the appellee, Reproductive Health Services.

The Court narrowly—five to four—overturned the lower federal court decision and restored the four contested provisions in Missouri's abortion law. *Webster,* much like other controversial cases brought into a fragmented Court, led to the writing of five separate opinions. A great deal of fur flew in the discussions, and the printed opinions revealed the depth of the Court's differences. While the Rehnquist majority just barely overturned the judgment of the lower federal appellate court, Rehnquist did not have the votes to overturn *Roe*. Only four justices voted to overturn: Rehnquist, White, Scalia, and Kennedy. Though weakened seriously, *Roe* was not overturned in *Webster*, but Harry Blackmun, *Roe's* author, was less than sanguine about its future: "For today, at least, the women of this Nation still retain the liberty to control their destinies. But the signs [of overturn] are evident and very ominous, and a chill wind blows."

For Rehnquist, the conclusion that *Roe* had to be dramatically modified, if not overturned outright, followed. According to him, *Roe* was "unsound in principle and unworkable in practice." The state regulation was one that "*reasonably furthers* the state interest in protecting potential human life." In so stating the preference for reasonable state abortion regulations, the Rehnquist opinion narrowed the impact of *Roe* by allowing the state to specify medical procedures, effective in the second trimester, in order to protect the unborn fetus. However, because he lacked O'Connor's vote, Rehnquist could not overturn *Roe*. And so he wrote, "to the extent indicated in our opinion, we would modify and narrow *Roe* and succeeding cases." Justice Scalia's concurrence was scathing, calling O'Connor cowardly for not directly overturning *Roe* in *Webster*. It should have been done "more explicitly," he argued. Given the lack of a majority, however, "it thus appears that…*Roe* must be disassembled door-jamb by door-jamb, and never entirely brought down, no matter how wrong it may be."

In a ringing defense of the *Roe* trimester framework, Blackmun's dissent argued that the 1973 framework "simply defines and limits the right of privacy in the abortion context to accommodate, not destroy, a state's legitimate interest in protecting the health of pregnant women and in preserving potential human life." Blackmun's dissent, joined by Marshall and Brennan, was a fierce, emotive defense of *Roe* by its bitterly attacked author. For them, Missouri's "viability testing" requirement was "patently irrational." It was "an arbitrary imposition of risk, and expense, furthering no discernible interest except to make the procurement of an abortion as arduous and as difficult as possible."

The result in *Webster* was the rejection of the abortion choice as a "fundamental" right of privacy possessed by all women—certainly up to the point of fetal viability. Rehnquist and his group argued instead that there was a less essential "liberty" interest women had, a part of the due-process clause, that gave them certain freedom to act, subject to reasonable governmental regulations.[18] Marshall, Brennan, and Blackmun, joined separately by Stevens, dissented from the affirming of the constitutionality of the Missouri regulations as well as from the view that *Roe* was no longer viable precedent.

*Webster* left the country anxiously awaiting the next round in *Roe's* deconstruction by a very conservative Supreme Court. Many felt it would formally and directly strike down *Roe* as soon as the next case came along. In effect, the decision encouraged states to pass restrictive antiabortion laws, noting that there was at least a five-person majority that either saw a weak personal "liberty" interest outweighed by the authority of the state or, in O'Connor's case, regarded the state laws as imposing no "undue burden" on a woman's right to have an abortion. Some states, including Utah and Pennsylvania, passed very restrictive abortion laws.

In 1991, Marshall's last year on the high bench, the Court heard the case of *Rust v. Sullivan*, which involved the constitutionality, in light of the Court's abortion decisions, of a number of Reagan administration amendments to Title X of the Public Health Service Act. Written in 1970, Title X authorized the government to provide financial grants to clinical organizations that engaged in family planning projects. The 1988 amendments, in a major change from the funding guidelines in place since 1970, prohibited funds from going to any project in which the organization counseled pregnant women about abortions; the prohibition included distributing materials about the abortion procedure, and forbade the organization to be physically associated with or attached to a facility that did the abortion procedure. Such organizations were forbidden to lobby for state or federal laws that would liberalize the availability of abortions.

Dr. Irving Rust, a medical doctor who was the recipient of Title X funds, immediately challenged the constitutionality of the federal amendments. His argument was that the new legislation deprived individuals and groups of their First and Fourteenth Amendment freedoms of speech and association if they supported a woman's right to reproductive choice. The lower federal courts upheld the amendments, and Rust appealed to the Supreme Court.

A sharply divided Court ruled, five to four, that the amendments did not violate the Constitution and that the Reagan administration officials in the Department of Health and Human Services (HHS) did not unconstitutionally abuse administrative discretion. Nor was the woman's liberty interest, found in the due-process clause, "impermissibly burdened" by the administrative restrictions on free speech and association. Marshall's polar opposite, Rehnquist, once again wrote the majority opinion for the Court.

Marshall joined a dissenting opinion written by Justice Blackmun. For Blackmun, joined by Marshall, with Stevens and O'Connor joining parts, the Court, by validating the 1988 amendments, for the first time had "upheld viewpoint-based suppression of free speech simply because that suppression was a condition upon the acceptance of public funds." And he saw in the majority decision another attack on the *Roe* precedent: *"Roe* and its progeny are not so much about a medical procedure as they are about a woman's fundamental right to self-determination. [They] serve to vindicate the idea that 'liberty,' if it means anything, must entail freedom from governmental domination in making the most intimate and personal of decisions."

In *Rust*, Justice O'Connor once again parted company with Rehnquist. She dissented in part from his decision affirming the lower federal courts' decisions upholding the 1988 changes in the law, joining Blackmun's opinion regarding the amendments' denying women and their doctors freedom of speech. Because of Justice O'Connor's change and a similar change in Kennedy since 1990, *Roe* was not overturned—but its full impact has been greatly blunted by the conservative Court majority ever since *Webster*. Only an overturn of the 1989 abortion decision would restore *Roe* to its full potency as constitutional precedent in the area of abortion.

One year after Marshall retired from the Court, in the 1992 case of *Planned Parenthood of Southeastern Pennsylvania v. Casey*, O'Connor and Kennedy, joined by Justice David Souter, the Bush administration's "stealth" candidate who took Brennan's seat in 1990, took part in writing a unique joint opinion that, with the two votes of Blackmun and Stevens, upheld the *Roe* precedent, although in writing the opinion the trio adopted O'Connor's "no undue burden on women" standard for evaluating the constitutionality of state and federal abortion legislation. As one observer commented, "the story of *Casey*—and Rehnquist's failure to find five votes to overturn *Roe*—is one of the most extraordinary in the annals of the modern Supreme Court."[19]

In 1988 and 1989, Pennsylvania had passed a number of prohibitive amendments to its abortion law. They called for (1) a doctor to inform a woman contemplating an abortion about "fetal development," (2) a woman to give her formal consent or, if she was a minor, to get the consent of her parents, (3) a waiting period of one full day before the abortion procedure could take place, (4) notification of the woman's spouse, (5) antiabortion counseling, and (6) the establishment of certain reporting procedures that all doctors had to follow when performing abortion procedures.

The Court was divided three ways over *Casey*. One view was held by Blackmun and Stevens, who continued to argue for the viability of the *Roe* trimester framework. Blackmun voted to strike down all the challenged Pennsylvania amendments as violative of *Roe*, while Stevens would have validated some and struck down others in light of the *Roe* judging framework. The conservative Rehnquist quartet—consisting of the Chief and Justices White, Scalia, and the recently appointed and controversial Clarence Thomas—who voted to validate all the Pennsylvania abortion law amendments and insisted that *Roe* be directly overturned. (Again, they came up one vote shy of a majority.) And then there was the newly emergent, moderately conservative trio of Justices O'Connor, Kennedy, and Souter, who argued, in their jointly written opinion, that all the Pennsylvania amendments were constitutional because no "undue burden" was placed upon the woman by the state. Evidently, Souter had proposed that the three jurists meet secretly "to explore the possibility of an opinion that would preserve the core of *Roe*."[20] They met and, with the help of only a few of their law clerks, drafted and then announced their joint decision to their surprised colleagues.

While Rehnquist took the news without any apparent rancor, Scalia was so angry with Kennedy that he "walked over to Kennedy's nearby house in McLean, Virginia, to upbraid him."[21] "The essential holding of *Roe*," Souter, Kennedy, and O'Connor asserted, "should be retained and once again reaffirmed," and they concluded that the Pennsylvania statute did not "unduly burden" women seeking an abortion in the state.

Harry Blackmun, in *Casey*, applauded the trio's opinion, which he called "an act of personal courage and constitutional principle": "In brief, five members of the Court today recognize that 'the Constitution protects a woman's right to terminate her pregnancy in its early stages.'" For Blackmun, O'Connor's "undue burden" standard required the Court to apply the standard of strict scrutiny when judging the validity of abortion regulations. That was fine with him, even though it clearly moved away from *Roe*'s trimester framework—which was at the heart of the *Roe* precedent.

Blackmun was still extremely pensive and certainly not sanguine about the future of *Roe*. He wrote, "I remain steadfast in my belief that the right to reproductive choice is entitled to the full protection afforded by this Court before *Webster*. I fear for the darkness as four Justices anxiously await the single vote necessary to extinguish the light." Blackmun knew that only he and Stevens stood by the fundamental constitutional principle espoused in *Roe*, and also knew that the other seven members had totally "abandoned *Roe*'s assertion of a 'fundamental right' of women to choose abortion [and] a bare majority stood against expressly overturning *Roe* and allowing states to ban abortions prior to fetal viability."[22]

The year 1992, however, saw the conservative Republican incumbent President, George Bush, defeated in the presidential election by the moderate Democratic presidential candidate, Arkansas governor Bill Clinton, a vocal supporter of a woman's right of freedom of reproductive choice. Furthermore, with his appointment of two abortion-rights supporters, Ruth Bader Ginsburg in 1993 (replacing retired Byron White, who was a perennial opponent of *Roe*) and Stephen Breyer in 1994 (replacing retired Justice Harry Blackmun), the threat of a direct overturn of *Roe* subsided. Clinton's reelection in 1996 guaranteed continued support of the reproductive rights of women—at least from the Executive.

Marshall always believed *Roe* would not be overturned. Asked in 1987 if *Roe* would fall, Marshall answered: "Nope....Because I believe in the Court....The only sure way [conservative Republican President Ronald Reagan could get his appointee to overturn *Roe*] would be to get on the Court himself."[23] He derived great comfort from his conviction that freedom, liberty, and the right of privacy would prevail over those who argued for the primacy of traditional values and the constitutionality of state and federal laws that expressed these norms in legislation that inhibited the freedom to choose. Perhaps Marshall's belief was correct, for *Roe*, though battered, was still precedent when he died in 1993.

# 15

## JUSTICE MARSHALL:
## ALWAYS THE OUTSIDER, ALWAYS DEFIANT

Cissy Marshall was sitting in the Supreme Court's small courtroom on June 29, 1990, the last day of the Court's 1989–90 term. She and her husband knew that it was Bill Brennan's last day on the Court, although the public announcement would not come for another month. Suffering from ill health, this deeply committed and resourceful liberal was retiring from the institution he loved after thirty-four years of service. He and Marshall, the remaining liberal holdovers from the Warren Court era, had tried to "hold the line" against Burger and especially Rehnquist Court inroads on the premier decisions of the Warren Court. They had been worn out by that increasingly difficult task, especially after Rehnquist became Chief in 1986.[1]

Brennan had suffered a series of strokes, and his doctors strongly urged him to step down. As he said, retirement "wasn't anything I wanted to do and, indeed, tried my best to avoid doing it, but the doctors persuaded me that unless I wanted to risk another stroke (I've had two), I should retire. I must say, it was a very difficult thing to do."[2] Appropriately, Brennan was able to achieve one last consensus, a five-person majority in an affirmative-action case (the *FCC* opinion) on his last day sitting on the Court.

With Brennan retired, Marshall was the last remaining liberal from the Warren Court days. Marshall missed Brennan greatly. As he said on the ABC News program *Primetime Live*, "There's nobody here that can persuade the way Brennan can persuade. Brennan can sit down and talk to you and show you where you are wrong. There's nobody with that power on the Court today. [He] cannot be replaced."

Without his ally Brennan beside him in the wars against the Rehnquist faction, now a potential majority of six, Marshall was isolated, cantankerous, and deeply frustrated. He was also in failing health. He had very poor eyesight, was short of breath, had suffered a heart attack, and had very poor circulation in his legs. Decades of heavy smoking and drinking, poor eating habits, and lack of exercise had taken their toll on the big man. Throughout his tenure, he had insisted that he was on the Court for the long haul. As he said, in 1987, to an audience at the annual Second Circuit U.S. Court of Appeals conference: "For all those people who wish very dearly for me to give up and quit and what-have-you, I hope you will pardon me for saying it, but, don't worry, I'm going to out-live those bastards."[3] Even though Marshall had always promised his friends and defiantly told his enemies that he was serving a "life term" on the Court and that he would have to be carried out or else get shot by a jealous husband when he was 120 years old, his wife and his doctor finally persuaded the nearly eighty-three-year-old justice that it was time to step down. And so, on June 27, 1991, on the last day of the 1990–91 term, Cissy Marshall paid another melancholy visit to the Court's courtroom.

Only a few people knew that this was her husband's last day on the Court. Bill Brennan was also present and aware of Marshall's decision. Cissy was accompanied by her sons, Thurgood junior and John. Brennan leaned against one of the pillars in the rear of the courtroom, watching events unfold and pos-sibly thinking about his own retirement the year before. Justice Anthony Kennedy vividly recalled that day, because Marshall "took the unusual step of leaving the bench and going to the well of the Court to move the admission of his son John to the Court's Bar." Kennedy later admitted, "All of us missed the clue [that it would be Marshall's last day on the Court]. I suppose we did not recognize that a man of such immense power could become tired."[4]

After the formalities, the justices got down to business and announced a number of controversial opinions. In keeping with his role on the Court over the years, Marshall's last day on the bench was marked by his reading of dissents he had written in response to Rehnquist-penned majority opinions in a number of death-penalty cases. He was leaving the Court partly because this "dance" between two bitter adversaries had become tiring. And Marshall almost always lost on the merits. Worst of all, it had become routine.

As if to underline some of the reasons behind his decision to retire, he ended his twenty-four years by reading portions of his fiery dissent in *Payne v. Tennessee.* Marshall began by observing acidly that "power, not reason, is the new currency of this Court's decision-making." It was, noted one writer, a "grim judi-cial farewell of a man who had spent more than fifty years in courtrooms as an attorney and judge defending the rights" of all persons to equality, fairness, and, in a word, justice.[5]

On the twenty-seventh of June, 1991, Marshall sent his retirement letter to President Bush, and announced his retirement to his colleagues at the end of the final, private, conference session of the 1990–91 term, held the following day. It was to take effect as soon as Marshall's replacement was confirmed by the U.S. Senate, "when my successor is qualified," he wrote Bush. In his letter to the President, he stated that "the strenuous demands of Court work and its related duties required or expected of a Justice appear at this time to be incompatible with my advancing age and medical condition."

A few days later, Marshall held a press conference in the Court's East Conference Room to announce his retirement publicly and answer questions from the crowd of reporters in attendance. Asked what was wrong with him that was causing him to retire, after promising so many times that he would never retire, Marshall responded, "What's *wrong* with me? I'm old. I'm getting old and coming apart!"

In retiring when he did, Marshall very reluctantly gave the opportunity to name his replacement to a man he truly scorned and had publicly ridiculed on a major television network news show, George Bush. On *Primetime Live,* he told his interviewer, Sam Donaldson, what he thought of the President: "Let me put it this way. It's said that if you can't say something good about a dead person, don't say it. Well, I consider [Bush] dead." When Donaldson, incredulously, said, "He's still alive, Mr. Justice," Marshall said: "You're damn right he is! I just don't understand it."

Marshall knew that Bush would replace him with yet another conservative Republican appointee. His apprehension was justified; within days of Marshall's announcement, Bush nominated Clarence Thomas. Thomas was a controversial, conservative African American, a man who had served as a political appointee in the Reagan and Bush administrations.

Alan Simpson, a conservative U.S. senator from Wyoming, had known Marshall for some time and wrote him a letter on July 2, 1991. He and others knew how difficult it was for Marshall to step down, especially with George Bush still in the White House.

"I know this was a damn tough decision for you," Simpson wrote. "It would be absurd to say that I have agreed with all of your actions in these past years. It would, however, surely be honest to say that ever since I met you at Milt Kronheim's liquor warehouse when I was a brand-spanking new United States Senator back in 1979, I have always very much enjoyed being in your presence."

Simpson closed on a "wishing you well" note: "Your place in history is assured. It must give you a great sense of well-being and satisfaction of a life well-lived."[6]

Marshall's life was indeed one "well lived," but at the end of his public service it was a lonely, often miserable life, in part because of his anger and frustration. Although he had said, decades earlier, "I intend to wear life like a very loose garment, and never worry about nothin'," in his last years on the Court he was, as

Justice Kennedy said, very tired. Very tired and also very worried about the future of personal liberties and freedom for the millions of "Joe Doakeses" he cared so much about, spoke for, and defended as an advocate and as a judge.

His last decade of service on the Court was terribly painful for Marshall. During those years, his frustration often moved him to "train his sarcasm on his colleagues" in open court, as Linda Greenhouse recalled in 1993.[7] Carl Rowan, who spoke regularly with Marshall, confirmed that the 1989 and 1990 terms of the Court were the "most frustrating, angry, disillusioning years of Marshall's entire legal life."[8] Rehnquist finally had his conservative majority. With the appointment of New Hampshire Republican David H. Souter as Brennan's replacement, it appeared that Rehnquist was in almost complete control of the Court's docket and of its substantive output.

With Bill Brennan gone, the typical vote on controversial constitutional cases was Rehnquist 5/6/7 against Marshall 4/3/2.[9] Furthermore, there was no one on Marshall's side who had the capacity to pull together majorities under the most difficult circumstances, as Brennan had been able to do for so long. Marshall was joined regularly by Harry Blackmun and, occasionally, by the rather unpredictable John P. Stevens. He "found himself increasingly isolated on a Court hostile to his liberal views of the broad constitutional protections" guaranteed to all persons. In case after case, on issues ranging from free speech and civil rights to criminal justice to the right of privacy, from affirmative action to cruel and unusual punishment, the Rehnquist majority "brushed Marshall's positions aside."[10] Marshall ended up angrily firing off dissent after dissent. In his last term, Marshall wrote seventeen dissents and joined in forty-one others written by his colleagues. He wrote only twelve majority opinions in 1990–91.[11]

Stuart Taylor, in reviewing that term, wrote that Marshall "did not conceal his dismay" with the Rehnquist Court's jurisprudence. "This Court has gone to pot, that's for sure," he said once. Another time, he asked, with reference to his upper-class colleagues, "How can you understand poor people if you've never known any except as servants?"[12]

In April 1991, Marshall wrote a memo to his colleagues chastising them for forgetting their "inviolable obligation to treat rich and poor alike, [which is] echoed in the oath taken by each Justice prior to assuming office: 'I do… solemnly swear that I will administer justice without respect to persons, and do equal right to the poor and to the rich." The memo was sent in response to a change in Rule 39 by the majority, one that applied to all litigants who asked the Court to review their case. "Under the amendment adopted today," Marshall noted, "an indigent defendant may be denied a disposition on the merits of a petition for certiorari, jurisdictional statement, or petition for an extraordinary writ following a determination that the filing is 'frivolous or malicious.'" There was no clause that permitted "dismissal of 'frivolous or malicious' filings by paying litigants." A primary value of the Court, that "'All men and women are entitled to their day in Court,'" had been erased by the Rehnquist majority. As Marshall said bitterly, "That guarantee has now been conditioned on monetary worth. It now will read: 'All men and women are entitled to their day in Court only if they have the *means* and the *money*.'"[13]

Karen Hastie Williams said that Marshall "clearly felt that the Constitution and the Bill of Rights were the keys to a more open, more supportive society." Implicit in this view was an understanding that equality of opportunity, freedom of expression, and personal autonomy formed the essential bedrock on which such an open, supportive community rested. "True justice," he said to a law school audience in 1969, "requires that the ideals expressed...in the Bill of Rights and the Civil War Amendments...[are] translated into economic and social progress for all of our people....There can be no justice until [these ideals] together with the broader ideals they embody, become more than mere abstract expressions." The law was intended to be the primary instrument to be employed to open the doors to the just society—not to keep them closed. For Marshall, "true justice can only be obtained through the actions of committed individuals, individuals acting both independently and through organized groups." Whether through calling for new, more empathetic legislation or instituting lawsuits in the courts that challenged the constitutionality of archaic and unfair legislation, there is much people can do, Marshall believed, both individually and in organized groups, to make the society a more just one. A monument to Marshall at the very least would have to state that he continually insisted that lawyers, working with organized public interest groups, "push the law to be more fair, more inclusive, more sensitive, and more responsive."[14]

Law is a series of rules made, modified, discarded, and remade by legislators, judges, and others, Marshall insisted throughout his life as an advocate and a jurist. If the law is too unfair, or too exclusive, or too insensitive and unresponsive to the needs of some persons living in the society, it can be challenged by them, with the help of lawyers. The "Rules is Rules" principle Marshall absorbed at Howard Law School was confirmed by his practical legal experiences with Charlie Houston in the 1930s. But Marshall, as the leader of a successful civil rights legal organization for three decades, understood that Rules can be changed and that the task of lawyers is to use the law to change the bad ones. Hard work and patience were essential to success.

Where could citizens employ the law as an instrument of social change? The courts, for Marshall, were "vehicles of social transformation." Civil rights groups had found that state and federal courts were the only governmental arena in which their claims could be voiced and heard. As Marshall said in 1968, "courtrooms are perhaps the most accurate barometers of the extent to which we have succeeded in building a just society." Lawyers functioning as social engineers, receptive federal judges, and an evolving U.S. Constitution, as interpreted by the U.S. Supreme Court, were critical components of his strategy for dealing with and overcoming racial and other unconstitutional discriminations. Marshall never lost his fundamental belief that "law cannot only respond to social change but can initiate it, and lawyers, through their everyday work in the courts may become social reformers."[15]

In his James Madison lecture in April 1969, Marshall reminded his audience "that organized groups are becoming increasingly necessary in the pursuit of... the rights and liberties encompassed by the term...justice." How did legal racial segregation, Jim Crow, end? he asked his audience. "What happened?" Change came about from the ordinary "Joe Doakes," he answered. The "citizen who believed that equal protection meant just that—the citizen who, with the assistance of those lawyers who still believed in the promise of justice and equality, never gave up the fight against the relics of slavery."

However, given the leviathan of modern government and its Byzantine bureaucracy, "individual effort is not enough to secure justice. Today, even more than in the past, only organized action can hope to insure that the concept of justice remains meaningful to *all* our people." Marshall always challenged bar associations to provide assistance to those who needed help the most: "the... poor,...minorities,...indigent criminal defendants....If the bar is to live up to its social responsibilities," he would tell his audiences, "it cannot let the narrow interests of a few practitioners stand in its way." He called for his audiences to support and work in legal aid services and other such groups that aided people who desperately needed such help in order to survive.[16] Marshall's ultimate goal was "making the law a reality for those to whom it is now largely meaningless." This meant that law schools and bar associations had to instill in men and women the "commitment" to the "ideals of justice" for all.

## MARSHALL FOR THE DEFENSE

Thurgood Marshall was a tireless advocate for the less fortunate—they were his "constant companions" and stood as invisible presences behind him when he sat on the Court, a Court he constantly sought to make aware of the grim realities of life for millions of Americans. During the 1977 term, the case of *Inez Moore v. East Cleveland, Ohio* clearly illustrated the dilemma Marshall constantly faced when dealing with the Court's conservative majority. *Moore* involved the question of how far a municipality could constitutionally intrude into the privacy rights of an "extended" family.

East Cleveland, Ohio, a suburb of Cleveland, had a zoning ordinance that limited residential occupancy to single families, with "single family" defined as husband and wife and their unmarried children, or a grandparent, *one* child as parent, and the children of *only* that one parent. Inez Moore, a resident of the town, had her two divorced sons, with *their* two sons, living with her in her house—in violation of the ordinance. In January 1973 she was cited for violating the single-family ordinance because the two youngsters were cousins, not brothers. Either she had to leave the house or one of her grandchildren had to leave; either way the citation threatened to disrupt the relationship of an extended family living under one roof, a family in which the grandmother was the person holding the family together. Inez Moore defended her family and challenged the constitutionality of the zoning ordinance in federal courts, arguing that her privacy and associational rights were violated by implementation of this law. She lost her case and appealed to the Supreme Court.

The Court heard the case in its 1976 term and, after first voting five to four to validate the zoning ordinance, finally voted five to four to invalidate it—because Justice John Paul Stevens changed his mind. Marshall tried and failed to get the majority to understand the importance of allowing people like Inez Moore to do what millions of poor people—mostly black Americans and other disadvantaged minorities—did to survive in an affluent America. "I cannot agree that the norms of middle-class suburban life set the standards of constitutional law for all people at all times," he asserted in his draft dissent. He was preparing a dissent because the Court, after oral argument, had tentatively concluded that the local ordinance was a rational one and hence constitutional. Marshall was furious with those justices in the apparent majority, led by Chief Justice Burger, and including Justices Rehnquist, Stewart, and White, as well as, until April 1977, John P. Stevens. In December 1976, Potter Stewart had been assigned the task of writing the majority opinion in *Moore* upholding the ordinance. Stewart's draft majority opinion initially reflected Burger's views. In a memo to the brethren dated November 22, 1976, the Chief Justice contended that "the basic unit of society [is] parents and their offspring.... This 'nuclear' family is the basic building block of our society and it is a rational place to draw a line."

The following day, Marshall wrote Burger disagreeing with his understanding of what a family was in American society:

> I have seen too many situations where a strong grandparent literally held the family together, and was responsible for the education and upbringing of decent, law-abiding youngsters, to agree as a matter of constitutional law that the "nuclear family" is "the basic building block of our society." That is a middle class norm that government has no business foisting on those to whom economic or psychological necessity dictates otherwise.[17]

Justice Stevens was the only one of the five in the majority who was truly perplexed by and uncomfortable with the case from the very beginning. In the conference session a few days after oral arguments, he told the brethren that "something smells about this case." But, at the time, he couldn't find any "Court handle [to overthrow the ordinance] except substantive due process—and I won't go for that." And so Stewart was asked to write for the majority.

After reading Marshall's draft dissenting opinion, however, and considering other memos from him, as well as the draft dissents of Blackmun, Brennan, and Powell, Stevens wrote the brethren a memo on April 12, 1977, informing them that he had changed his mind and was joining the quartet who viewed the ordinance as unconstitutional. Brennan immediately assigned the opinion to Lewis Powell. Marshall did not have to write a dissent after all. Instead, he concurred in a separate opinion written by Brennan, who had told Burger, in November 1976, that the Chief Justice's "nuclear family" concept "seems to me to be completely out of touch with the reality of a vast number of relationships in our society, including my own as a youngster growing up....In urban areas a grouping such as the Moores remains an economic necessity....I cannot believe that the Constitution embraces purely and simply an affluent suburban concept of what is a family." Marshall completely agreed with Brennan's observations.

On May 31, 1977, Powell read the judgment of the majority of the Court in *Moore*. Sadly, *Moore* was one of only a few times in his twenty-four years on the Court that Marshall had the pleasant experience of seeing one of his passionate dissents against the insensitivity of the Court majority transformed into a majority vote.

Inez Moore's plight was but one of literally over a thousand cases in which Marshall dissented from the views of his less empathetic colleagues—Burger, Rehnquist, Scalia, and others. His well-informed concern for society's less fortunate meant that Marshall had neither the time nor the inclination to associate with a privileged elite—even if they had deemed him worthy to enter their clubs and their homes. He was an unwelcome witness to the failure of his country to keep its promises. When Marshall became a judge and then an associate justice, his opinions were always, in the view of one of his law clerks, "characterized by his sensitivity to the effect of rules on people, a sensitivity which, in part, emanates from his experience as an advocate who was actively and personally involved in the struggles of the individuals that he represented."

Three years after Marshall's death, the Court heard a case from Mississippi, *M.L.B. v. S.L.J.*, involving the constitutionality of a statute that barred poor people from appealing the termination of parental rights if they could not pay for court costs. The state law permitted a person to appeal the adverse decision of a family court judge, but required the appellant to pay in advance for all court costs, including the costs of copying the transcript of the court proceedings. In *M.L.B.*, the appellant did not have two thousand dollars to pay for the transcript, and was not able to appeal the permanent loss of her two children to her former husband and his new wife. She appealed the judgment of the Mississippi Supreme Court to the U.S. Supreme Court.

In a six-to-three decision, written by Ruth Bader Ginsburg (who replaced Byron White in 1993), the Court ruled that the parent-child relationship was so fundamental that, in light of the Fourteenth Amendment's equal-protection and due-process clauses, no state could deny a poor parent the right to appeal an adverse judgment because she lacked the money to pay the court costs. "We place," Ginsburg wrote for the six-person majority, "decrees forever terminating parental rights in the category of cases in which the State may not bolt the door to equal justice [because of a person's poverty]."

The "usual suspects" dissented: Rehnquist, Scalia, and the man who took Marshall's seat, Clarence Thomas, who wrote the dissent. In it he said that "the Equal Protection Clause is not a panacea for perceived social or economic inequality.... Any adverse impact that the transcript requirement has on any person seeking to appeal arises not out of the state's action, but out of factors entirely unrelated to it." Thomas concluded his dissent with the observation that the Court majority continued to validate "an equalizing notion of the Equal Protection Clause that would, I think, have startled the Fourteenth Amendment's Framers."

Had Marshall been alive to read the Court's opinions, he would have been very pleased with Ginsburg's reliance on an expansive view of the Fourteenth Amendment, one also evidently held by his former colleagues, Justices Souter, O'Connor, and Kennedy. He would have been especially pleased by the size of the majority vote supporting this new, broader understanding of the Amendment. He would also have been gratified by the Court majority's understanding of the cruel realities of life as faced by those living at the margins of American society. And he would have been delighted with the Court majority's actions to remedy an unfairness brought about by state legislation that unconstitutionally discriminated against the poor.

Marshall, were he still sitting on the high bench, would have lashed out at Thomas's dissent because of the ease with which the African American jurist rejected, as *The New York Times* put it in an editorial, "the idea of granting the poor greater access to civil appeals." He would also have attacked Thomas's unrealistic, idealized perception of the world beyond the Marble Palace, just as Marshall continually fought against Rehnquist's apparently limited concern for and knowledge of the real world of the poor, the homeless, the victims of discrimination, the aged, and the infirm.

"There is another world out there," he said again and again to Rehnquist and the others. Don't forget about it when ruling on cases and controversies. Don't make "unfounded assumptions about how people live," and don't enact "'wishful thinking' into law."

While there were still three justices who insisted on exhuming the originalist argument in constitutional adjudication, Marshall would have been relieved to know that there were six others who decided the case with fundamental fairness in mind. By Thurgood Marshall's standards, Ginsburg's ruling was right and just; Thomas's dissent was wrong, cruel, and unfair. When he was nominated to the U.S. Supreme Court in 1967, Marshall spoke directly to the tension between government and the individual. "A lot of people talk in terms of balancing the public interest against the individual's rights. My position is that personal rights take precedence." He then stated emphatically, "I am not a conservative."

His commitment to the primacy of the individual's rights meant that the legal process had to be responsive to the needs of *all* individuals, regardless of class, color, or caste. For African Americans, and others discriminated against, Marshall was "held in extraordinary esteem, not only as having been one of the nation's most powerful blacks, but as one who used his life and power to win legal equality for all."[18]

Juan Williams, a newspaper reporter and biographer of Marshall, recalled how African Americans reacted to Marshall, then a justice of the U.S. Supreme Court and the legendary former NAACP advocate. One day when he was well into his seventies, Marshall made his way haltingly through a hotel lobby in Washington, D.C., on his way to give a speech. "Black bellhops and maids and doormen freeze in place pointing. Black waiters and waitresses begin streaming out of the kitchen for a glimpse of the man. Elderly black people, some with tears in their eyes, stand on tiptoes to see better and wave."[19]

Marshall's many vigorous dissents were intended to reach the audience of lawyers and judges and law school students beyond the Court—and to leave behind a strong message for future Supreme Court majorities. His role as a dissenter was inevitable, given the politics of his era. "What marked these dissents," commented Harvard law professor Kathleen Sullivan, "was a candor that cut through legal abstractions to the social reality and human suffering underneath." Marshall, as dissenter, became the "conscience of the Court—a constant reminder [to his brethren] of the human consequences of legal decisions."[20]

Marshall's life is the story of the persistence of racism in American life. From birth to death, from 1908 (when eighty-nine African Americans were lynched in the United States) to 1993, Marshall had no difficulty remembering who he was. He never had to hold his hand in front of his face to remind himself that he was African American. His racial identity, and the racial segregation that accompanied it, was established by the norms of a predominantly white—racist either consciously or unconsciously—society. He devoted his life to helping all citizens in his beloved country overcome the consequences of racism. As the NAACP's legal advocate for almost a quarter of a century, Marshall was "run out of towns. He was threatened with death. He had clients pursued by lynch mobs." He "was a man of action, simple and direct. His glory years came when he was putting his life on the line in racist towns throughout the South—traveling 50,000 miles a year to help criminal defendants and civil rights plaintiffs—as a trial lawyer fighting an entrenched system of oppression."[21]

## MARSHALL'S EPITAPH

At his retirement press conference in the Supreme Court's East Conference Room in late June 1991, he said, about the continuance of racism in America: "All I know is that years ago, when I was a youngster, a Pullman porter told me that he had been in every city in this country...and he had never been in any city in the United States where he had to put his hand up in front of his face to find out he was a Negro. I agree with him. [Even today? a reporter asked.] I agree with him."

However, while he acknowledged the persistence of racism, he still believed that it could be eradicated in America. Perhaps "defiantly hopeful" is the phrase that best describes Marshall. He drew the strength from his belief in the logic and the fairness of the Rule of Law. Marshall's actions required what Yale law school professor Paul Gewirtz called the "heroic imagination": "He grew up in a ruthlessly discriminatory world—a world in which the segregation of the races was pervasive and taken for granted, where lynching was common, where the black man's inherent inferiority was proclaimed widely and wantonly."

From his earliest days as a lawyer, Marshall "had the capacity to imagine a radically different world, the imaginative capacity to believe that such a world was possible, the strength to sustain that image in the mind's eye and the heart's longing, and the courage and ability to make that imagined world real." Marshall believed that, using the law as Charlie Houston had taught at Howard Law School, he and others could change the "ruthlessly discriminatory world" he lived in.

But he knew that the real work had barely begun. There was still a great deal to be done before America reached the stage of freedom and liberty where the Constitution's guarantees were truly color-blind. In his very last public statement, just before he died in January 1993, Marshall called upon young men and women to join in the struggle against racism, to dissent from the fear, hatred, and mistrust that existed in the land. "We must dissent," he said, "because America can do better, because America has no choice but to do better." Acknowledging the limits of even his beloved Rule of Law, he said that while "the legal system can force open doors,...it cannot build bridges [between people]....Take a chance, won't you? Knock down the fences that divide. Tear apart the walls that imprison. Reach out; freedom lies just on the other side."

Thurgood Marshall, from birth to death an outsider in America, deeply felt the slights and the insults from his brethren; he endured what he regarded as the racist attitudes of the justices of the nation's highest court, just as he uncomplainingly and bravely endured the hatred he had encountered in the South. Other than Bill Brennan, and a few brethren of the Warren Court era, he really did not have any colleagues on the Court who were also friends. While Justices O'Connor and Kennedy appreciated Marshall's insights, as well as his recollection of that part of America's history he had experienced as a civil rights advocate, and learned from his experiences, they, too, were not his friends. Isolated, often discouraged but never despairing, Marshall fought on, defiantly, until the ravages of age and poor health overwhelmed him. He told many that his epitaph should read: "He did the best he could with what he had." And he did a great deal with what he had. As Benjamin Hooks, the NAACP's executive director at the time of Marshall's death, said, "It's my belief that without Thurgood Marshall, we would still be riding in the back of the bus, going to separate schools and drinking 'colored' water."[22]

Marshall's death, on January 24, 1993, evoked an outpouring of love and affection from millions of African Americans who knew him as Mr. Civil Rights and who saw him as the Moses who brought the Constitution and its proclamations of justice and equality to them. "I owe him a lot," said Medell Ford, a sixty-eight-year-old retired African American postal worker who never met Marshall. "My future wasn't very bright then. But because of his tenacity in the civil rights area, I had a chance to support my family." After Marshall's death in 1993, a reporter remarked: "Not all great men are good men. Marshall was both."[23] *That* is the fitting epitaph for lawyer and jurist Thurgood Marshall.

# RESEARCH NOTES

*Abbreviations Used in Notes*

| | |
|---|---|
| ASP | Arthur Spingarn Papers, Library of Congress (LOC), Washington, D.C. |
| CHHP | Charles Hamilton Houston Papers, LOC, Washington, D.C. |
| CUOHP | Columbia University Oral History Project (Thurgood Marshall), New York |
| DDEPP | Dwight David Eisenhower Presidential Papers, Abilene, Kans. |
| EWP | Earl Warren Papers, LOC, Washington, D.C. |
| FFP | Felix Frankfurter Papers, LOC, Washington, D.C. |
| FVP | Fred M. Vinson Papers, University of Kentucky Library, Lexington, Ky. |
| HFSP | Harlan Fiske Stone Papers, LOC, Washington, D.C. |
| HHBP | Harold H. Burton Papers, LOC, Washington, D.C. |
| HLBP | Hugo L. Black Papers, LOC, Washington, D.C. |
| HSTPP | Harry S Truman Presidential Papers, Independence, Mo. |
| JFKOH | John F. Kennedy Library Oral History, Boston, Mass. |
| JFKPP | John F. Kennedy Presidential Papers, Boston, Mass. |
| JMHP | John M. Harlan II Papers, Mudd Library, Princeton University, Princeton, N.J. |
| KCP | Kenneth C. Clark Papers, LOC, Washington, D.C. |
| LBJOH | Lyndon Baines Johnson Oral History, Austin, Tex. |
| LBJPP | Lyndon Baines Johnson Presidential Papers, Austin, Tex. |
| NAACPP | National Association for the Advancement of Colored People Papers, LOC, Washington, D.C. |
| RCP | Ramsey Clark Papers, LBJ Presidential Library, Austin, Tex. |
| RHJP | Robert H. Jackson Papers, LOC, Washington, D.C. |
| SRP | Stanley Reed Papers, University of Kentucky Library, Lexington, Ky. |
| TCCP | Tom C. Clark Papers, University of Texas Law Library, Austin, Tex. |
| TMP | Thurgood Marshall Papers, LOC, Washington, D.C. |
| WHP | William Hastie Papers, LOC, Washington, D.C. |
| WJBP | William J. Brennan Papers, LOC, Washington, D.C. |
| WODP | William O. Douglas Papers, LOC, Washington, D.C. |
| WRP | Wiley Rutledge Papers, LOC, Washington, D.C. |

CHAPTER 1

1. Ayers, *Promise*, 27, passim.
2. Nieman, *Promises to Keep.*
3. *Dred Scott v. Sandford* (1857).
4. Baudouin, *Ku Klux Klan*, 10.
5. Nieman, *Promises*, 75. See also Woodward, *Strange Career.*
6. Williamson, *Crucible*, 43.
7. Ibid., 4, 6.
8. Lewis, *W. E. B. Du Bois*, 34.
9. Ayers, *Promise*, 17.
10. Wilkins, *Standing Fast*, 2.
11. Woodward, *Strange Career*, 7n.
12. Ayers, *Promise*, 264.
13. Egerton, *Speak Now*, 29; Wilkinson, *From Brown to Bakke*, 27.
14. Quoted in Ayers, *Promise*, 43.
15. Ibid., 44.
16. Woodward, *Strange Career*, 70.
17. Ayers, *Promise*, 88.
18. Woodward, *Strange Career*, 82.
19. Du Bois, *Souls of Black Folk*, 79, 88-89.
20. Egerton, *Speak Now*, 19; Williamson, *Crucible*, 28-32.
21. Egerton, *Speak Now*, 51.
22. Wilkinson, *From Brown to Bakke*, 35/ff.
23. Williamson, *Crucible*, passim.
24. Fisher, *A Matter of Black and White*, 8.
25. Whitfield, *Death in the Delta*, 6.
26. Cobb, *The Most Southern Place*, 113.
27. Whitfield, *Death in the Delta*, 8.
28. Du Bois, *Souls of Black Folk*, 275-76.
29. Lewis, *W. E. B. Du Bois*, 275.
30. Woodward, *Strange Career*, 85.
31. Ayers, *Promise*, 267.
32. White, *A Man Called White*, 266/ff.
33. CUOHP.
34. Ibid.
35. Quoted in Rowan, *Dream Makers.*
36. David, *Growing Up Black*, 3.
37. CUOHP.
38. Ibid.
39. Quoted in *Time*, "The Tension of Change," 19 September 1955, 24.
40. Tushnet, *Making Civil Rights Law*, 4.

CHAPTER 2

1. MacLean, *Behind the Mask*, 30.
2. Duberman, *Robeson*, 31.
3. Lewis, *W. E. B. Du Bois*, 389.
4. Goings, *NAACP Comes of Age*, 46.
5. CUOHP, 4-190.
6. ASP.
7. NAACPP.
8. ASP.
9. Ibid.
10. Alexander, *KKK in the Southwest*, 13; McNeil, *Groundwork*, 46/ff.
11. Ellsworth, *Death in a Promised Land.*
12. MacLean, *Behind the Mask*, 10-11, 90/ff.
13. Ibid., 12.

14. McRae, *Groundwork*, xvi; Duberman, *Robeson*, 15.
15. ASP.
16. W. E. B. Du Bois, "Defeat of Judge Parker," 26.
17. Goings, *NAACP Comes of Age*, 53.
18. NAACP, *First Line*, 1.
19. Greenberg, *Crusaders*, 5.
20. *Douglas*, quoted in McNeil, *Groundwork*, 3.
21. Ibid., 42.
22. Quoted in Gormley, "A Mentor's Legacy," 63.
23. Slocum, "'I Dissent,'" 889.
24. Ware, *William Hastie*, 29.
25. Quoted in McNeil, *Groundwork*, 71.
26. Greenberg, *Crusaders*, 5.
27. Ibid., 4; Ware, *William Hastie*, 30.
28. CUOHP, 3-4.
29. TMP.
30. CUOHP, 1-84-5.
31. CUOHP, 1-19.
32. Greenberg, *Crusaders*, 71.
33. CUOHP.
34. Quoted in Rowan, *Dream Makers*, 68.
35. Quoted in Hengstler, "Looking Back," 57.
36. ASP.
37. See Goodman, *Stories of Scottsboro*.
38. CUOHP, 2-96.
39. NAACP, I-C-198.
40. White, *A Man Called White*, 142.
41. Quoted in Egerton, *Speak Now*, 52.
42. Quoted in Wilkins, *Standing Fast*, 153.
43. Egerton, *Speak Now*, 151.

CHAPTER 3
 1. Quoted in Note, "The Power of One," 40.
 2. *Time*, 19 September 1955, 24.
 3. *Afro-American*, 12 May 1947.
 4. Rowan, *Dream Makers*, 4-5.
 5. Fisher, *A Matter of Black and White*, 50.
 6. Greenberg, *Crusaders*, 29.
 7. Wilkins, *Standing Fast*, 161-62.
 8. *Afro-American*, 12 May 1947, 2.
 9. White, *A Man Called White*, 154.
10. Poston, "On Appeal," 4.
11. *Afro-American*, 12 May 1947, 2.
12. Quoted in Tushnet, "Thurgood Marshall and the Rule of Law," 7; see also Oliver Hill, "Recollections," 51.
13. Quoted in Goldman and Gallen, *Thurgood Marshall: Justice for All*, 159.
14. Wilkins, *Standing Fast*, 163.
15. Quoted in Greenhouse, "Ex-Justice Marshall Dies."
16. *Afro-American*, 23 February 1952, 2.
17. Davis and Clark, *Thurgood Marshall*, 101.
18. Robinson, "Thurgood Marshall: The Lawyer," 234; see also Motley, 237.
19. CUOHP, 1-6-7, 24.
20. Quoted in McNeil, *Groundwork*, 123.
21. Quoted in Greenberg, *Crusaders*, 3.
22. CUOHP, 2-111.
23. White, *A Man Called White*, 157-58.

24. CUOHP, 3-10.
25. ASP.
26. NAACPP, I-C-198.
27. CUOHP, 1-32.
28. Davis and Clark, *Thurgood Marshall*, 103.
29. NAACPP, I-C-656.
30. Ibid., I-C-198.
31. Davis and Clark, *Thurgood Marshall*, 103.
32. Quoted in McNeil, *Groundwork*, 129.
33. Greenberg, *Crusaders*, 8.
34. CUOHP, 3-5.
35. Greenhouse, "Ex-Justice Marshall Dies."
36. Ware, *Hastie*, 190.
37. CUOHP, 1-48.
38. *Afro-American*, 12 May 1947.
39. CUOHP, 1-46.
40. Wilkins, *Standing Fast*, 93.

CHAPTER 4

1. TMP.
2. WHP.
3. Rowan, *Dream Makers*, 103.
4. CUOHP, 1-26.
5. NAACPP, II-A-325.
6. Wilkins, *Standing Fast*, 174.
7. Greenberg, *Crusaders*, xvi; Bland, *Private Pressure*, 22; Tushnet, *Making Civil Rights Law*, 20/ff.
8. Greenberg, *Crusaders*, 20.
9. LBJOH, 4-5.
10. CUOHP, 6-28.
11. Ibid., 6-29.
12. Greenberg, *Crusaders*, 25-27.
13. *Afro-American*, 12 May 1947.
14. NAACPP, I-C-69.
15. Quoted in *Time*, "The Tension of Change," 19 September 1955, 30.
16. *Afro-American*, 12 May 1947.
17. TMP.
18. Ibid.
19. Lewis, "Files Say."
20. Goldberg et al., "The Long Distance Runner," 70-76, 73.
21. Watson, "Thurgood Marshall's Red Menace."
22. TMP.
23. Ibid.
24. NAACPP, II-A-410.
25. Ibid.
26. Greenberg, *Crusaders*, 40.
27. Quoted in Kluger, *Simple Justice*.
28. TMP.
29. Ibid.
30. Ibid.
31. NAACPP, II-B-100.
32. HSTPP.
33. EWP.
34. Greenberg, *Crusaders*, 72
35. Tushnet, *Making Civil Rights Law*, 170.
36. Fisher, *Matter of Black and White*, 136.
37. NAACPP, II-A-15.

38. Baker, *Second Battle,* 125/ff.
39. Poston, "On Appeal," 3.
40. Greenberg, *Crusaders,* 65.
41. Fisher, *Matter of Black and White,* 146/ff.
42. NAACPP, II-B-147.
43. Ibid., II-B-140.
44. TCCP.
45. FMVP.
46. TCCP.
47. NAACPP, II-B-100.
48. CUOHP.
49. Ibid., 2-82.
50. Quoted in Baker, *Second Battle,* 74.
51. HSTPP, Bon-3.
52. Fisher, *Matter of Black and White,* 89.
53. Ibid., 90/ff.
54. Poston, "On Appeal," 3.
55. NAACPP, II-B-183.
56. Ibid., II-B-133.
57. Ibid.
58. FMVP.
59. Wilkins, *Standing Fast,* 195.
60. Ibid., 194.
61. ASP.
62. See Ball, *Hugo L. Black.*
63. Quoted in Rowan, *Dream Makers,* 131.
64. Quoted ibid., 132.
65. HSTPP, N-58.
66. Wilkins, *Standing Fast,* 183.
67. Ibid.
68. NAACPP, II-A-73.
69. CUOHP, 1-39.
70. HSTPP, N-27.
71. Wilkins, *Standing Fast,* 192.
72. McCullough, *Truman,* 53-54.
73. CUOHP, 2-84.
74. HSTPP, N-36.
75. NAACPP, II-B-192.
76. Tushnet, *Making Civil Rights Law,* 151/ff; Greenberg, *Crusaders,* 86/ff.
77. Greenberg, *Crusaders,* 87.
78. NAACPP, II-B-192.
79. Quoted in Davis and Clark, *Thurgood Marshall,* 120.

CHAPTER 5

Racism was at its most virulent and humiliating in the armed forces in all American wars until Vietnam. The NAACP papers contain file after file labeled "Soldier Troubles," beginning with NAACP II-B-12 through II-B-135. These files contain the tragedy of segregation in the military, and have such titles as "Soldier Killings," "Soldier Complaints," and "Soldier Troubles." There is also, under NAACP, Veterans' Affairs, many files, from II-G-1-9 (Investigations of racism at military camps), through II-G-15-17 (post-World War II segregation troubles that faced African American soldiers and sailors). These files contain the poignant letters from African American soldiers and their families, and the follow-up by the NAACP. They also include court-martial files of African Americans during the wars, clearly revealing the depth and the breadth of the policy of racism in the military and the basic inability of the NAACP to do very much to help individual African Americans in the military.

Until 1997, the Congressional Medal of Honor had been awarded to 433 white military personnel for their bravery in World War II. Although 1.2 million African Americans served in that war, not a single African American had received the nation's highest honor. In late January 1997, six African American men were awarded the medal posthumously. The seventh recipient, a tearful seventy-seven-year-old Vernon Baker, was presented the Medal of Honor by President Bill Clinton, who said that "history has been made whole today." Baker then said, "The only thing I can say to those who were not here with me today is, 'Thank you, fellows. Well done. I'll always remember you.'"

1. ASP.
2. NAACPP, II-A-325.
3. HSTPP, Nash-54
4. McNeil, *Groundwork*, 164-65.
5. Wilkins, *Standing Fast*, 175.
6. Gillem Report, 5, HSTPP.
7. Quoted in McNeil, *Groundwork*, 45.
8. Quoted in Goodwin, *No Ordinary Time*, 169-70.
9. NAACPP, I-C-64.
10. Goodwin, *No Ordinary Time*, 165/ff.
11. Gillem Report, 6.
12. CHHP.
13. Goodwin, *No Ordinary Time*, 171.
14. NAACPP, II-A-300.
15. Wilkins, *Standing Fast*, 181.
16. NAACPP, II-A-15.
17. Ambrose, *Citizen Soldiers*, 322.
18. White, *A Man Called White*, 207-8.
19. Quoted in Staples, "Citizen Sengstacke," 28.
20. See NAACPP II-B-12 through II-B-135.
21. Ibid., II-B-148.
22. Ibid., II-B-152.
23. Goodwin, *No Ordinary Time*, 524.
24. CUOHP, 5-31.
25. NAACPP, II-B-156.
26. CUOHP, 5-35.
27. Ibid., 5-7, passim.
28. Quoted in McCullough, *Truman*, 737/ff.
29. NAACPP, II-A-300.
30. Ware, *Hastie*, 103.
31. HSTPP, N-4.
32. White, *A Man Called White*, 325.
33. See ibid., 324/ff.
34. HSTPP, N-37.
35. Gillem Report, 18/ff.
36. HSTPP, N-34.
37. KCP.
38. Ibid.
39. HSTPP, Nash-28.
40. TMP.
41. CUOHP, 2-56.
42. Quoted in Hengstler, "Looking Back," 58.
43. TMP.
44. Ibid.
45. Ibid.
46. CUOHP, 2-59.
47. Quoted in Hengstler, "Looking Back," 58.

CHAPTER 6

1. Quoted in *Time*, 19 September 1955, 24.
2. Quoted in *Harvard Black Letter Journal* 6 (1989), 1.
3. Quoted in Wilkinson, *From Brown to Bakke*, 27.
4. Sunstein, "On Marshall's Conception of Equality," 1268.
5. NAACPP, II-B-215.
6. KCP.
7. Quoted in *New Leader*, 22 December 1952, 4.
8. Clark and Clark, "Development of Consciousness," 593.
9. Clark, "Racial Prejudices," 1.
10. CUOHP, 4-168-70.
11. Quoted in Aldred, *Thurgood Marshall*, 78.
12. NAACPP.
13. Kluger, *Simple Justice*, 298, 304; see also Yarbrough, *A Passion for Justice*.
14. TMP.
15. KCP.
16. Robertson, *Sly and Able*, 51, 34.
17. Ball, *Hugo L. Black*.
18. FMVP.
19. Elman, "Solicitor General's Office," 817, 822.
20. RHJP.

21. Ibid.
22. Elman, "Solicitor General's Office," 829.
23. Baker, *Second Battle*, 479.
24. Hugo L. Black Jr., *My Father*, 208.
25. Kluger, *Simple Justice*, 560.
26. Elman, "Solicitor General's Office," 832.
27. Quoted in Kluger, *Simple Justice*, 608-9.
28. TCCP.
29. Brownell, *Advising Ike*.
30. DDEPP, Box 20.
31. Brownell, *Advising Ike*, 192.
32. Ibid., 189-91, passim.
33. Ibid., 195.
34. Robertson, *Sly and Able*, 517-18.
35. NAACPP, II-B-138.
36. NAACPP, II-B-140.
37. WHP.
38. Quoted in Elman, "Solicitor General's Office," 840.
39. Ibid.
40. Quoted in Schwartz, *Super Chief*, 446.
41. TCCP.
42. SRP.
43. EWP.
44. Ibid.
45. Goldman and Gallen, *Thurgood Marshall*, 151/ff.
46. SRP-OH, 10-12.
47. Wilkins, *Standing Fast*, 213.
48. Lomax, 84.
49. Kluger, *Simple Justice*, 708.
50. EWP.
51. TCCP.
52. SRP.
53. TCCP.
54. TMP.
55. SRP.
56. Ibid.
57. EWP.
58. ASP.
59. Peltason, *Fifty-Eight Lonely Men*.
60. Goldberg, "Justice Marshall," 72.
61. TMP.
62. Wilkins, *Standing Fast*, 216.
63. TMP.
64. Quoted in NAACPP, II-B-141.
65. LBJOH.
66. TMP.
67. FBI Report to DOJ, DDEPP, 15.
68. Robertson, *Sly and Able*, 521.
69. KCP.
70. FBI Report to DOJ, DDEPP, 2, 20.
71. Ibid., 15-16.
72. Ibid., 17.
73. LBJOH, 5.
74. Payne, *Light of Freedom*, 41-42.
75. FBI Report to DOJ, DDEPP, 18.
76. Ibid.

77. Ibid., 15-16.
78. Vollers, *Ghosts of Mississippi*, 54/ff.
79. Payne, *Light of Freedom*, 53.
80. TMP.
81. Vollers, *Ghosts of Mississippi*, 53/ff.
82. FBI Report to DOJ, DDEPP, 18-19.
83. Quoted in Bland, *Private Pressure*, 100.

CHAPTER 7
 1. Taper, "A Reporter at Large," 106.
 2. TMP.
 3. KCP.
 4. Quoted in Hengstler, "Looking Back," 61.
 5. LBJOH, 13.
 6. CUOHP, 3-125.
 7. Wilkinson, *Brown*, 61-80, passim.
 8. See Whitfield, *A Death in the Delta*.
 9. Wilkins, *Standing Fast*, 224.
10. Moody, *Coming of Age*, 125-26.
11. Wilkins, *Standing Fast*, 225.
12. Ibid., 327/ff.
13. Vollers, *Ghosts*, 90.
14. LBJOH, 6.
15. Moody, *Coming of Age*, 129, 187.
16. Abernathy, *And the Walls*, 152.
17. TMP.
18. CUOHP, 10-113-4.
19. Ibid., 4-193.
20. Wilkins, *Standing Fast*, 269.
21. Carson, *In Struggle*, 25.
22. Quoted in Bell, "Epistolary Explanation," 55.
23. Quoted in Davis and Clark, *Thurgood Marshall*, 217.
24. King, *Freedom Song*, 35/ff.
25. Carson, *In Struggle*, 304.
26. Quoted in Davis and Clark, *Thurgood Marshall*, 217.
27. DDEPP, 15.
28. CUOHP, 3-124.
29. *Cooper v. Aaron*, at 9.
30. DDEPP, 16.
31. Bates, *Long Shadow*.
32. *Cooper v. Aaron*, at 10.
33. DDEPP, 8.
34. Brownell, *Advising Ike*, 207.
35. Wilkins, *Standing Fast*, 248.
36. DDEPP, 8.
37. Ibid.
38. Wilkins, *Standing Fast*, 253-54.
39. CUOHP, 2-90-1.
40. DDEPP, 8.
41. HHBP.
42. Quoted in Schwartz, *Super Chief*, 293.
43. WODP.
44. HLBP.
45. Quoted in Schwartz, *Super Chief*, 300.
46. U.S. Commission on Civil Rights Report, 4.
47. Reed, "Resegregation."
48. Sack, "In Little Rock."

49. Ambrose, *Eisenhower*, 125.
50. Rampersad, *Jackie Robinson*, 342.
51. Quoted in Robertson, *Sly and Able*, 512.
52. Wilkins, *Standing Fast*, 222.
53. Ambrose, *Eisenhower*, 191.
54. Quoted in Belknap, *Federal Law*, 34.
55. Quoted in Ambrose, *Eisenhower*, 190.
56. Quoted in Belknap, *Federal Law*, 36.
57. DDEPP, 31.
58. Ambrose, *Eisenhower*, 191.
59. Rampersad, *Jackie Robinson*, 342.
60. CUOHP, 3-126.
61. Ibid., 4-136.
62. Wermiel, "Brennan," 536.
63. Wilkins, *Standing Fast*, 234.
64. Ibid., 257.
65. DDEPP, 20.
66. Cohodas, *Strom Thurmond*, 290.
67. Ibid., 291.
68. Brownell, *Advising Ike*, 219.
69. Wilkins, *Standing Fast*, 244.
70. JFKPP, 758.
71. LBJOH, 3.
72. Ambrose, *Eisenhower*, 498.
73. DDEPP, 23.
74. Bell, "Epistolary," 60.
75. LBJOH, 8.
76. While with the NAACP, Marshall participated in the preparation and/or argument in forty-three cases argued before the U.S. Supreme Court, winning thirty-seven of them. **(D)** denotes cases in which the U.S. Supreme Court decision went against the NAACP position:

*I. Cases for which Thurgood Marshall wrote briefs but did not argue in the U.S. Supreme Court, 1936-61:*

1. *Missouri ex rel Gaines v. Canada*, 1938
2. *Chambers v. Florida*, 1940
3. *McLaurin v. Oklahoma State Regents*, 1950
4. *Grey v. University of Tennessee*, 1952 (D)
5. *Burns v. Wilson*, 1953 (D)
6. *Barrows v. Jackson*, 1953
7. *Reeves v. Alabama*, 1954
8. *NAACP v. Alabama ex rel Patterson*, 1958
9. *Anderson v. Alabama*, 1961
10. *Hamilton v. Alabama*, 1961
11. *Garner v. Louisiana*, 1961

*II. Cases for which Thurgood Marshall prepared briefs and argued before the U.S. Supreme Court, 1936-61:*

1. *Adams v. U.S.*, 1943
2. *Smith v. Allwright*, 1944
3. *Lyons v. Oklahoma*, 1944 (D)
4. *Morgan v. Virginia*, 1946
5. *Patton v. Mississippi*, 1947
6. *Sipuel v. Oklahoma*, 1948
7. *Fisher v. Hurst*, 1948 (D)
8. *Rice v. Elmore*, 1948
9. *Shelley v. Kraemer*, 1948
10. *Taylor v. Alabama*, 1948 (D)
11. *Watts v. Indiana*, 1949
12. *Sweatt v. Painter*, 1950
13. *Brown v. Board of Education*, 1954
14. *Florida ex rel Hawkins v. Board of Control*, 1954
15. *Brown v. Board of Education*, 1955
16. *Lucy v. Adams*, 1955
17. *Mayor and City of Baltimore v. Dawson*, 1955
18. *Holmes v. Atlanta*, 1955
19. *Florida ex rel Hawkins v. Board of Control*, 1956
20. *Frazier v. University of North Carolina*, 1956

21. *South Carolina Electric and Gas Co. v. Flemming*, 1956
22. *Gayle v. Browder*, 1956
23. *Bryan v. Austin*, 1957
24. *Florida ex rel Hawkins v. Board of Control*, 1957 (D)
25. *Cooper v. Aaron*, 1958
26. *State Athletic Commission v. Dorsey*, 1959
27. *Harrison v. NAACP, et al.*, 1959 (D)
28. *NAACP v. Alabama ex rel Patterson*, 1959
29. *Faubus v. Aaron*, 1959
30. *Boynton v. Virginia*, 1960
31. *U.S. v. Louisiana; Bush v. Orleans Parish School Board*, 1961
32. *Tinsley v. City of Richmond, Va.*, 1961

77. Quoted in *Miami Herald*, 14 June 1967.
78. CUOHP, 2-100.

CHAPTER 8
1. JFKOH, 1.
2. CUOHP, 3-138.
3. Quoted in Weisbrot, *Federal Law*, 45.
4. Quoted in Whalen and Whalen, *The Longest Debate*, xvii.
5. JFKPP, 1071; see also Wofford, *Of Kennedys and Kings*.
6. JFKPP, 1071.
7. Ibid.
8. Whalen and Whalen, *The Longest Debate*, xvii.
9. JFKOH, 9.
10. Wilkins, *Standing Fast*, 279.
11. JFKOH, 14.
12. Quoted in Weisbrot, *Federal Law*, 51.
13. JFKOH, 7.
14. LBJOH, 6.
15. Quoted in Davis and Clark, *Thurgood Marshall*, 236.
16. Weisbrot, *Federal Law*, 76.
17. JFKOH, 18.
18. CUOHP, 2-100-101; 3-140.
19. *Time*, 22 September 1961, 25.
20. *U.S. News and World Report*, 14 May 1962, 16.
21. Morris, *Federal Justice*, 165.
22. Ibid., 183.
23. Bland, *Private Pressure*, 120/ff.
24. Quoted in Rowan, *Dream Makers*, 285-86.
25. Pierce, "The Solicitor General," 74.
26. Sandler, "Thurgood Marshall," 16, 21.
27. LBJOH, 11.
28. Quoted in Ball et al., *Compromised Compliance*, 42-43.
29. Ibid., 43.
30. Ibid., 44 /ff.
31. *U.S. News and World Report*, 3 July 1967, 57-58.
32. President Johnson, said Roy Wilkins, echoing Marshall's views, "became the greatest civil rights President of our lifetime, and if he hadn't stumbled into Vietnam, he might have come out of the 1960s as a liberal hero." Wilkins, *Standing Fast*, 297.
33. Quoted in Rowan, *Dream Makers*, 287-88.
34. LBJOH, 10.
35. LBJPP.
36. Quoted in Rowan, *Dream Makers*, 295.
37. LBJOH, 28-29.
38. Claiborne, "The Noblest Roman," 19, 20.
39. Clymer, "New Supreme Court Justice," 25-26.
40. *Washington Post*, 14 June 1967.

41. Rowan, *Dream Makers*, 19.
42. "School Segregation Before High Court," 20-25, passim.
43. CUOHP, 2-110.
44. JFKOH, 17-18.
45. LBJOH, 1-30-31.
46. Ibid., 14.
47. Rowan, *Dream Makers*, 297.
48. RCP.
49. Clymer, "The New Supreme Court Justice," 25.
50. *New Republic*, 24 June 1967, 9.
51. *New York Times*, 14 June 1967.
52. LBJPP.
53. CUOHP, 1-41.
54. *Washington Post*, 31 August 1967.
55. See Hearings Before the Committee on the Judiciary, U.S. Senate, 90th Congress, First Session, *On Nomination of Thurgood Marshall, of New York, to Be an Associate Justice of the Supreme Court of the United States*, 1967.
56. Ibid., 158-78; *New York Times*, 14 July 1967.
57. LBJOH, 16.
58. *Time*, 28 July 1967, 16.
59. *Washington Post*, 31 August 1967.
60. Wilkins, "Justice as Narrative," 69.
61. Carter, in Guinier, *Tyranny of the Majority*, xvii.
62. LBJPP.
63. CUOHP, 3-160.
64. Goldman and Gallen, *Thurgood Marshall*, 169.
65. Karen Hastie Williams, interview with Laryn Ivy, Esq., 9 November 1993, Washington, D.C.
66. EWP.

CHAPTER 9

1. See, generally, Davis and Clark, *Thurgood Marshall*.
2. *Newsweek*, 26 June 1967, 34.
3. See Kalman, *Abe Fortas*.
4. Jeffries, *Justice Lewis F. Powell, Jr.*, 260.
5. White, "A Tribute," 1215, 1216.
6. Tushnet, "Thurgood Marshall and the Brethren," 2109.
7. Schwartz, *Super Chief*, 679.
8. TMP.
9. See Ellison, *Invisible Man*.
10. Williams, "Humanizing," 90-92.
11. Burt, *Two Jewish Justices*, 9.
12. Seidman, "A Modest Proposal," 33.
13. Lehman, "The Lawyer as Hero," 132.
14. Quoted in Rowan, *Dream Makers*, 415.
15. TMP.
16. Ibid.
17. Quoted in Taylor, "Glimpses."
18. Jeffries, *Powell*, 260.
19. TMP.
20. Tushnet, "Thurgood Marshall and the Brethren," 2124-25.
21. Sullivan, "Candor," 84.
22. Wilkins, "Justice as Narrative," 70.
23. Sullivan, "Candor," 86.
24. *Kras*, at 460.
25. O'Connor, "Thurgood Marshall," 1217-18.

26. Laryn Ivy interview with Karen Hastie Williams, 9 November 1993.
27. Kennedy, "Voice," 1221-22.
28. Jeffries, *Powell*, 261.
29. Seidman, "A Modest Proposal," 33.
30. Quoted in Jeffries, *Powell*, 261.
31. TMP.
32. Ibid.
33. Woodward and Armstrong, *The Brethren*, 209.
34. Schultz and Smith, *Jurisprudential Vision*, 100.
35. Garrow, "The Rehnquist Years," 68-69.
36. Douglas, *The Court Years*, 149.
37. Quoted in Jeffries, *Powell*, 262.
38. Bloch, "Remembering," 1.
39. Note, "Mr. Civil Rights."
40. Black and Black, *Mr. Justice and Mrs. Black*, 176.
41. Quoted in White, "A Tribute," 1216.
42. Tushnet, "Marshall and the Brethren," 2112, 2115.
43. Ibid., 2119.
44. LBJOH, 18-19.
45. Interview with the author, 22 May 1996, Washington, D.C.
46. Tushnet, "Marshall and the Brethren," 2124.
47. Tushnet, "Themes," 763, 766.
48. Bloch, "Remembering," 1.
49. Clark, *Brennan*, 277-78.
50. Quoted in Urofsky, *The Douglas Letters*, 137.
51. Jeffries, *Powell*, 255.
52. Quoted ibid.
53. WODP.
54. Woodward and Armstrong, *The Brethren*, 32, 98.
55. Douglas, *The Court Years*, 235-36.
56. Ibid., 236-37.
57. Jeffries, *Powell*, 261.
58. Powell, "Tribute," 1229-30.
59. Ivy interview with Williams.
60. Quoted in *New York Times*, 8 November 1981.
61. TMP.
62. Hentoff, "Marshall and the Chief."
63. See, generally, Cooper and Ball, *United States Supreme Court*.
64. Bloch, "Privilege," 25.
65. Ivy interview with Williams.
66. Alexander, "Thurgood Marshall," 1233.
67. Ivy interview with Williams.
68. Austin, "Write On, Brother," 82.
69. Bloch, "Foreword," 2003-6, passim.
70. TMP.
71. WODP.
72. TMP.
73. Ibid.
74. Sunstein, "Marshall's Conception of Equality," 1274.

CHAPTER 10
1. TMP.
2. Ibid.
3. Bloch, "Foreword," 2005.
4. Tushnet, "Themes," 770.
5. TMP.

6. Gerald Gunther, "Foreword," 2.
7. Sunstein, "On Marshall's Conception of Equality," 1274.
8. Ibid., 1272.
9. WJBP. The "freedom of choice" plan invalidated by the Court was one that allowed parents to choose the school their children would attend, which meant that African American parents did not send their children to the predominantly white schools because of fears for their safety.
10. Quoted in Schwartz, *Decision,* 135.
11. WODP.
12. JMHP.
13. Jeffries, *Powell,* 306.
14. *Cooper,* at 13.
15. Jones, "Milliken v. Bradley," 54.
16. Ibid., 53.
17. Rampersad, *Jackie Robinson,* 22.
18. Marcus, "Learning Together," 76.
19. Ibid., 79, n. 72.
20. Ibid., 85.
21. Shaw, "Missouri v. Jenkins," 60.
22. Abraham and Perry, *Freedom and the Court,* 383.
23. WODP.
24. Ibid.
25. Taylor, "Court, 5-4."
26. WJBP.
27. *Harper v. Virginia Board of Elections,* 1966.
28. WODP.
29. WJBP.
30. Thurgood Marshall wrote 322 majority opinions for the Court in his twenty-four years on the high bench. However, he wrote more dissents—363—and joined 1,021 other written dissenting opinions penned by others on the Court. He dissented 1,384 times, over 40 percent of all the cases he participated in (3,430) as an associate justice of the U.S. Supreme Court between 1967 and 1991. Source: November issues of *Harvard Law Review* 82-105 (1968-91).
31. Goldman and Gallen, *Thurgood Marshall,* 210.
32. Sunstein, "On Marshall's Conception of Equality," 1270.
33. TMP.

CHAPTER 11
1. WJBP.
2. Belton, "Sociology of Affirmative Action," 103.
3. Deval Patrick testimony, 4-5.
4. *Bakke.*
5. TMP.
6. O'Brien, *Constitutional Law,* 1343.
7. TMP.
8. Jeffries, *Powell,* 463, 464.
9. TMP.
10. WJBP.
11. Belton, "Sociology of Affirmative Action," 104.
12. WJBP.
13. Ibid.
14. Ibid.
15. TMP.
16. Tushnet, "Racial Discrimination, 1967-1991," 529.
17. WJBP.
18. Ibid.

19. Ibid.
20. Quoted in Jeffries, *Powell,* 456.
21. Ibid., 469.
22. Ibid., 469, 470.
23. Ibid., 470-71.
24. Ibid., 493.
25. Belton, "Sociology of Affirmative Action," 103, n. 11.
26. WJBP.
27. Ibid.
28. Quoted in *Washington Post,* 13 June 1984.
29. Abraham and Perry, *Freedom and the Court,* 425.
30. WJBP.
31. Belton, "Sociology of Affirmative Action," 105.
32. TMP.
33. Rowan, *Dream Makers,* 439.
34. Jeffries, *Powell,* 499.
35. Sunstein, "On Marshall's Conception of Equality," 1271.
36. Quoted ibid., 1271.
37. Note, for example, the Supreme Court's refusal to hear the case from Texas, *Cheryl Hopwood v. Texas,* in its 1995 term. In deciding not to hear the case, the Court let stand a federal appeals court ruling that rejected the use of race in admissions programs as outlined in Powell's *Bakke* opinion.
38. Belton, "Sociology of Affirmative Action," 110.

CHAPTER 12
 1. TMP.
 2. NAACPP, II-A-15.
 3. Ibid.
 4. Ibid.
 5. CUOHP.
 6. Quoted in Rowan, *Dream Makers,* 383.
 7. Goldman and Gallen, *Thurgood Marshall,* 47.
 8. TMP.
 9. Quoted in Rowan, *Dream Makers,* 96.
10. CUOHP, 6-33.
11. Quoted in Rowan, *Dream Makers,* 97.
12. Kennedy and Minnow, "Thurgood Marshall and Procedural Law," 95, 97.
13. Jeffries, *Powell,* 450.
14. Quoted in Savage, *Turning Right,* 37.
15. Ogletree, "Marshall's Criminal Justice Jurisprudence," 111, 112.
16. WJBP.
17. Ogletree, "Marshall's Criminal Justice Jurisprudence," 114-17, passim.
18. Ibid.
19. Ibid., 119-21, passim.
20. TMP.
21. O'Brien, *Constitutional Law and Politics,* 1075.
22. Goldman and Gallen, *Thurgood Marshall,* 232.
23. Ogletree, "Marshall's Criminal Justice Jurisprudence," 126.
24. TMP.
25. Ogletree, "Marshall's Criminal Justice Jurisprudence," 150.
26. Ibid.
27. "McCleskey," *Harvard Law Review* 101 (1987), 119, 155.
28. Ogletree, "Marshall's Criminal Justice Jurisprudence," 156.
29. TMP.
30. Quoted in Jeffries, *Powell,* 451-52.
31. "Criminal Law and Procedure," *Harvard Law Review* 105 (1991), 177, 181.

32. Ibid., 178.
33. TMP.
34. Quoted in Rowan, *Dream Makers*, 406.
35. Davis, *Justice Rehnquist*, 19/ff.
36. As one biographer noted: "If Rehnquist was to lead a majority, the Court would overrule a large body of precedent in order to 'unincorporate' the Bill of Rights. The states would then be released from the restrictions of the Bill of Rights and would be free to define due process regarding the rights of the accused....A majority guided by Rehnquist would take the law back to the days...when the states were marked by a particularly unpredictable lack of uniformity regarding the protections of the rights of the accused." Davis, *Justice Rehnquist*, 205-6
37. Ibid., 62.
38. Schultz and Smith, *Jurisprudential Vision*, 5.

CHAPTER 13

1. Following are the "incorporation" actions of the U.S. Supreme Court in the area of First Amendment freedoms prior to Marshall's joining the Court in 1967:

| Year "Incorporated" by Supreme Court | First Amendment Segment | Case |
|---|---|---|
| 1927 | Freedom of Speech | *Fiske v. Kansas* |
| 1931 | Freedom of the Press | *Near v. Minnesota* |
| 1934 | Freedom of Religion | *Hamilton v. Regents, Univ. of California* |
| 1937 | Freedom of Assembly | *DeJonge v. Oregon* |
| 1940 | Free Exercise of Religion | *Cantwell v. Connecticut* |
| 1947 | No Establishment of Religion | *Everson v. Board of Education* |
| 1958 | Freedom of Association | *NAACP v. Alabama* |

2. Black, *Constitutional Faith*.
3. Ibid., 45.
4. Douglas, *Court Years*.
5. He once said, "I'm a believer in freedom of speech,...as my father used to say: 'Everyone to their own liking, said the old lady as she kissed the cow.'" TMP.
6. Quoted in Rowan, *Dream Makers*, 341.
7. Goldman and Gallen, *Thurgood Marshall*, 264.
8. Fisher, 132.
9. *Nebraska*, 1979.
10. *Rosenbloom v. Metromedia*, 1971; *Florida Star v. B.J.F.*, 1989.
11. CUOHP, 1-24.
12. TMP.
13. WJBP.
14. *New York Times v. Sullivan*, 1964.
15. TMP.
16. Ibid.
17. WODP.
18. WJBP.
19. In the 1975 term, the Nixon Court majority, in the case of *Hudgens v. NLRB*, formally overturned Marshall's majority decision in *Amalgamated v. Logan Valley Plaza*. Marshall, of course, dissented again, saying that *"Logan* has been laid to rest without ever having been accorded a proper burial."
20. WJBP.
21. Abraham and Perry, *Freedom and the Court*, 166.
22. TMP. On April 23, 1971, on a related matter involving Vietnam War protesters in conflict with the Nixon administration's continuation of the Vietnam War, Marshall wrote a short memo to the brethren. He had just found out that the government lawyers had told a federal district court judge that "the Justice Department had changed its mind,"

about enjoining the protesters from demonstrating on the Mall. The federal judge, "scowling and shouting, told the...government lawyers that 'this Court feels that one equal and coordinate branch of the government, the judiciary, has been dangerously and improperly used by another, the executive.'" Marshall concluded his memo with the following observation: "While I will neither scowl or shout, I find myself in complete agreement with Judge Hart. I suppose this is another anomaly inherent in 'government by injunction.'" TMP.

23. WODP.
24. TMP.
25. Ibid.
26. WODP.
27. WJBP.
28. Ibid.
29. WODP.
30. Ibid.
31. Rowan, *Dream Makers*, 337.
32. Ibid., 347.

## CHAPTER 14

1. TMP.
2. Meese, "The Attorney General's View," 701, 702.
3. Quoted in *New York Times*, 13 October 1985.
4. Brandeis, J., dissenting, *Olmstead v. U.S.*, 1929.
5. As noted by his dissent in the 1986 *Bowers v. Hardwick* case. It involved the constitutionality of a Georgia law that punished voluntary homosexual sodomy, an issue that sharply divided the justices along both moral and legal lines.
6. Woodward and Armstrong, *The Brethren*, 505.
7. Savage, *Turning Right*, 342. During its 1996 term, in the case of *Compassion In Dying v. State of Washington*, the Court continued to confront privacy dilemmas when it agreed, as it did in this instance, to hear cases involving the question of whether a *competent* person could end life through physician-assisted suicide. The state statute, it was claimed by plaintiffs, violated the "liberty" interest of *competent* but terminally ill patients, found in the Fourteenth Amendment's due-process clause, who wished to bring about their own death through physician-assisted suicide. Such a liberty interest, they argued, was also found in the *Cruzan* precedent, which said, in effect, that a *competent* person had the right to choose death over life. The Clinton administration's brief *amicus curiae* filed with the justices argued that there was a difference between withdrawing life-support systems from a patient and allowing a patient to actively hasten his death, with the assistance of doctors, by committing suicide. Linda Greenhouse, "Clinton Admin Asks Supreme Court to Rule Against Assisted Suicide," *New York Times*, 13 November 1997. In its decision, the Court deferred, for the time being, to state actions in this area of physician-assisted suicide. See *Washington v. Gluckstern*, 1997.
8. Rowan, *Dream Makers*, 323.
9. Ibid., 325.
10. WODP.
11. Craig and O'Brien, *Abortion and American Politics*, 97-98.
12. All comments from the *Roe* conference session taken from Brennan's notes, WJBP.
13. WODP. Although Douglas's dissent was never formally published, because he was persuaded not to air the Court's internal conflicts publicly, his draft was leaked to the press and caused some embarrassment for the Chief. And Burger expressed his anger at the leak to Douglas during the summer break between terms.
14. All comments from Douglas's notes, WODP.
15. TMP.
16. O'Brien, *Constitutional Law and Politics*, 1153.
17. TMP.
18. Jeffrey Toobin, "The Agonizer," *The New Yorker*, 11 November 1996, 82, 86.

19. Simon, *The Center Holds*, 156.
20. Toobin, "The Agonizer," 87.
21. Ibid.
22. O'Brien, *Constitutional Law and Politics*, 1992.
23. Quoted in Rowan, *Dream Makers*, 331.

CHAPTER 15

1. See Heck, "Holding the Line," 1, 13. Heck notes that there were thirty-seven five-to-four votes in Rehnquist's first term as Chief and that his conservative coalition was victorious in twenty-five of the thirty-seven while Brennan and Marshall succeeded in putting together five-person majorities in only twelve. That was the duo's high point. In succeeding terms, they wrote more dissents. Ibid., 2.
2. Letter, Brennan to author, 3 August 1990.
3. TMP.
4. Kennedy, "The Voice of Thurgood Marshall," 1221.
5. Simon, *The Center Holds*, 211.
6. TMP.
7. Greenhouse, "Ex-Justice Marshall Dies at 84."
8. Rowan, *Dream Makers*, 322.
9. See Heck, "Holding the Line," 9-13, passim.
10. Simon, *The Center Holds*, 209.
11. The following table summarizes Marshall's votes while a member of the Supreme Court of the United States, showing that he dissented in over 40 percent of all the Court's decisions handed down while he was on the Court, and showing also that he wrote more dissenting opinions than majority opinions for the Supreme Court. The data was collected from reviewing the November issues of the *Harvard Law Review* from November 1968 (vol. 82) through November 1991 (vol. 105).

### Thurgood Marshall Opinions, 1967-1990 Terms of the Supreme Court

| Term | Opinion of Court* | Concurrences | Dissents† Opinions written/Votes |
|------|-------------------|--------------|----------------------------------|
| 1967 | 10/127 | 1/75 | 1/1 |
| 1968 | 13/122 | 0/67 | 3/7 |
| 1969 | 9/94 | 1/52 | 2/4 |
| 1970 | 9/122 | 4/82 | 10/30 |
| 1971 | 15/151 | 3/69 | 20/34 |
| 1972 | 12/164 | 8/67 | 21/48 |
| 1973 | 13/157 | 4/57 | 19/53 |
| 1974 | 11/137 | 4/51 | 8/31 |
| 1975 | 17/156 | 7/86 | 16/50 |
| 1976 | 12/142 | 6/91 | 21/48 |
| 1977 | 15/135 | 4/81 | 20/41 |
| 1978 | 13/138 | 4/78 | 15/48 |
| 1979 | 14/149 | 7/79 | 21/47 |
| 1980 | 13/138 | 1/91 | 12/48 |
| 1981 | 15/167 | 5/95 | 4/47 |
| 1982 | 17/162 | 3/70 | 27/59 |
| 1983 | 15/163 | 2/68 | 16/56 |
| 1984 | 13/151 | 6/62 | 13/48 |

*The Chief Justice tries to ensure that there is a fairly even division of the work of writing majority opinions for the Court. Marshall wrote his share of opinions; however, given that he was not very often in the majority in major constitutional decisions handed down by the Court during his tenure, his majority opinions generally touch on less controversial and lesser constitutional and statutory questions.

†This column reflects the number of dissents written by Marshall as well as the number of other dissenting opinions he joined but did not write.

### Thurgood Marshall Opinions, 1967-1990 Terms of the Supreme Court

| Term | Opinion of Court* | Concurrences | Dissents† Opinions written/Votes |
|---|---|---|---|
| 1985 | 15/159 | 6/89 | 31/62 |
| 1986 | 16/152 | 1/76 | 20/61 |
| 1987 | 15/142 | 1/64 | 13/37 |
| 1988 | 14/143 | 0/88 | 18/63 |
| 1989 | 14/139 | 4/85 | 15/57 |
| 1990 | 12/120 | 2/47 | 17/41 |
| *TOTALS* | 322 written opinions for Court majority | | 363 dissents |

12. Taylor, "Glimpses," 8.
13. TMP.
14. Ibid.
15. Ibid.
16. Ibid.
17. Ibid.
18. Savage, *Turning Right,* 75.
19. Quoted ibid.
20. Kathleen Sullivan, "Sea Change at the High Court," *Los Angeles Times,* 5 July 1991.
21. Taylor, "Glimpses," 8.
22. Quoted in *People,* 8 February 1993, 40.
23. Taylor, "Glimpses," 8.

*The Chief Justice tries to ensure that there is a fairly even division of the work of writing majority opinions for the Court. Marshall wrote his share of opinions; however, given that he was not very often in the majority in major constitutional decisions handed down by the Court during his tenure, his majority opinions generally touch on less controversial and lesser constitutional and statutory questions.

†This column reflects the number of dissents written by Marshall as well as the number of other dissenting opinions he joined but did not write.

# BIBLIOGRAPHY

Abernathy, Ralph D. *And the Walls Came Tumbling Down.* New York: Harper & Row, 1989.
Abraham, Henry J., and Barbara Perry. *Freedom and the Court: Civil Rights and Liberties in the United States.* New York: Oxford University Press, 1994.
*Afro-American.* "Thurgood Marshall." 12 May 1947.
*Afro-American.* "Marshall Hailed as Greatest Civil Liberties Lawyer." 23 February 1952.
Aldred, Lisa. *Thurgood Marshall: Supreme Court Justice.* New York: Chelsea House, 1990.
Alexander, Charles C. *The Ku Klux Klan in the Southwest.* Norman, Okla.: University of Oklahoma Press, 1995.
Alexander, Janet Cooper. "TM." *Stanford Law Review* 44 (Summer 1992), 1231-35.
Ambrose, Stephen E. *Citizen Soldiers.* New York: Simon and Schuster, 1997.
———. *Eisenhower.* Vol. 2, *The President.* New York: Simon and Schuster, 1984.
Austin, Regina. "'Write On, Brother' and the Revolution Next Time: Justice Marshall's Challenge to Black Scholars." *Harvard Blackletter Journal* 6 (Spring 1989), 79-82.
Ayers, Edward L. *The Promise of the New South: Life After Reconstruction.* New York: Oxford University Press, 1992.
Baine, Kevin T. "Wit, Wisdom, and Compassion of Justice Thurgood Marshall," 20 *Hastings Constitutional Law Quarterly* 20, no. 3 (Spring 1993), 497-502.
Baker, Liva. *The Second Battle of New Orleans: The Hundred-Year Struggle to Integrate the Schools.* New York: HarperCollins, 1996.
Ball, Howard. "Careless Justice: The U.S. Supreme Court's Shopping Center Opinions, 1946-1976." *Polity* 6, no. 2 (Winter 1978), 200-228.
———. *Judicial Craftsmanship or Fiat: Direct Overturn by the United States Supreme Court.* Westport: Greenwood Press, 1978.
———. "The Convergence of Constitutional Law and Politics in the Reagan Administration: The Exhumation of the 'Jurisprudence of Original Intention' Doctrine." *Cumberland Law Review* 17, no. 3 (1986-1987).
———. *Hugo L. Black: Cold Steel Warrior.* New York: Oxford University Press, 1996.
Ball, Howard, and Phillip J. Cooper. *Of Power and Right: Hugo Black, William O. Douglas, and America's Constitutional Revolution.* New York: Oxford University Press, 1992.
———. "Fighting Justices: Hugo L. Black and William O. Douglas and Supreme Court Conflict." *American Journal of Legal History* 38, no. 1 (January 1994), 1-37.
Ball, Howard, Dale Krane, and Thomas P. Lauth Jr. *Compromised Compliance: Implementation of Section Five of the 1965 Voting Rights Act.* Westport: Greenwood Press, 1982.
Barker, Lucius J. "Thurgood Marshall, the Law and the System: Tenets of an Enduring Legacy." *Stanford Law Review* 44 (Summer 1992), 1237-47.
Barringer, Felicity. "Thousands Bid Farewell to Marshall." *The New York Times,* 28 January 1993.
Bates, Daisy. *The Long Shadow of Little Rock.* New York: McKay, 1962.
Battle, Thomas C. "Thurgood Marshall: The Power of His Legacy." *Howard Law Journal* 37 (Fall 1993), 117.
Baudouin, Richard, ed. *Ku Klux Klan: A History of Racism and Violence.* 5th edition. Montgomery, Ala.: Southern Poverty Law Center, 1977, 1996.
Belknap, Michael R. *Federal Law and Southern Order: Racial Violence and Constitutional Conflict in the Post-Brown South.* Athens, Ga.: University of Georgia Press, 1987.
Bell, Derrick. "An Epistolary Exploration for a Thurgood Marshall Biography." *Harvard Blackletter Journal* 6 (Spring 1989), 51-67.
Belton, Robert. "Justice Thurgood Marshall and the Sociology of Affirmative Action." *Harvard Blackletter Journal* 6 (Spring 1989), 102-10.

Berry, Mary Frances. *Black Resistance, White Law: A History of Constitutional Racism in America.* New York: Allan Lane, Penguin Books, 1994.

Black, Elizabeth. "Hugo Black: A Memorial Portrait." *Supreme Court Journal* (1980), 77-84.

Black, Hugo L. *A Constitutional Faith.* New York: Knopf, 1968.

Black, Hugo L., and Elizabeth Black. *Mr. Justice and Mrs. Hugo L. Black.* New York: Random House, 1986.

Black, Hugo L., Jr. *My Father: A Remembrance.* New York: Random House, 1975.

Bland, Randall W. *Private Pressure on Public Law: The Legal Career of Justice Thurgood Marshall, 1934-1991.* Lanham, Md.: University Press of America, 1971, 1993.

Bloch, Susan Low. "The Privilege of Clerking for Thurgood Marshall." *Supreme Court Journal* (1992), 23-25.

———. "Foreword: Thurgood Marshall: Courageous Advocate, Compassionate Judge." *The Georgetown Law Review* 80 (1993), 2003-9.

———. "Remembering Justice Thurgood Marshall: Thoughts from His Clerks." Eulogy presented at Georgetown Law School, 27 January 1993, and reprinted in *Georgetown Journal on Fighting Poverty* 1 (1993).

Branch, Taylor. *Parting the Waters: America in the King Years, 1954-1963.* New York: Simon and Schuster, 1988.

Brennan, William J., Jr., "Justice Thurgood Marshall: Advocate for Human Need in American Jurisprudence." *Maryland Law Review* 40 (1981), 390-97.

———. "Response to Attorney General Meese's Speech Concerning a Jurisprudence of Original Intent." Speech at Georgetown Law School, 12 October 1985, reprinted in *New York Times,* 13 October 1985.

———. "A Tribute to Thurgood Marshall." *Supreme Court Journal* 1992, 1-13.

Brownell, Herbert, with John P. Burke. *Advising Ike: The Memoirs of Attorney General Herbert Brownell.* Lawrence, Kans.: University Press of Kansas, 1993.

Burt, Robert A. *Two Jewish Justices: Outcasts in the Promised Land.* Berkeley, Calif.: University of California Press, 1988.

Caplan, Lincoln. *The Tenth Justice: The Solicitor General and the Rule of Law.* New York: Vintage, 1988.

Carson, Clayborne, ed. *The Eyes on the Prize Civil Rights Reader.* New York: Penguin, 1991.

———. *In Struggle: SNCC and the Black Awakening of the 1960s.* Cambridge, Mass.: Harvard University Press, 1995.

Carter, Robert L. "Reflections on Justice Marshall." *Supreme Court Journal* 1992, 15-18.

Carter, Stephen L. Foreword to Lani Guinier, *The Tyranny of the Majority.* New York: Knopf, 1994.

Chesnut, J. L., Jr., and Julia Cass. *Black in Selma.* New York: Farrar, Straus, and Giroux, 1990.

Claiborne, Lewis. "The Noblest Roman of Them All: A Tribute to Thurgood Marshall." *Journal of Supreme Court History* 1992.

Clark, E. Culpepper. *The Schoolhouse Door: Segregation's Last Stand at the University of Alabama.* New York: Oxford University Press, 1993.

Clark, Hunter. *Justice Brennan: The Great Conciliator.* New York: Birch Lane Press, 1995.

Clark, Kenneth B. "Racial Prejudices Among American Minorities." *International Social Science Bulletin,* Winter 1950.

Clark, Kenneth B., and Mary P. Clark. "The Development of Consciousness of Self and the Emergence of Racial Identification in Negro Pre-School Children." *Journal of Social Psychology* 10 (1939), 591-99.

Clark, Ramsey. "This Gentle Giant." *Hastings Constitutional Law Quarterly* 20, no. 3 (Spring 1993), 493-96.

Clymer, Adam. "The New U.S. Supreme Court Justice: Thurgood Marshall." *American Trial Lawyer,* June/July 1967, 25-26.

Cobb, James C. *The Most Southern Place on Earth: The Mississippi Delta and the Roots of Regional Identity.* New York: Oxford University Press, 1992.

Cohen, Lawrence M. *"PruneYard Shopping Center v. Robins:* Past, Present, Future." *Chicago-Kent Law Review* 57 (1981), 373-95.

Cohodas, Nadine. *Strom Thurmond and the Politics of Southern Change.* New York: Simon and Schuster, 1993.

"Content Regulation and the Dimensions of Free Expression." *Harvard Law Review* 96 (1983), 1854-73.

Cooper, Phillip J. *Battles on the Bench.* Lawrence, Kans.: University Press of Kansas, 1995.

Cooper, Phillip, and Howard Ball. *The U.S. Supreme Court: From the Inside Out.* New York: Prentice-Hall, 1995.

Craig, Barbara H., and David O'Brien. *Abortion and American Politics.* Chatham, N.J.: Chatham House, 1993.

"Criminal Law-Constitutional Law-Due Process-Admissibility of Confessions." *George Washington Law Review* 13 (1944-45), 109-11.

Daniels, Roger, Sandra C. Taylor, and Harry Kitano, eds. *Japanese Americans: From Relocation to Redress.* Salt Lake City: University of Utah Press, 1986.

David, Jay, ed. *Growing Up Black.* New York: Avon, 1992.

Davis, Michael D., and Hunter Clark. *Thurgood Marshall: Warrior at the Bar, Rebel on the Bench.* New York: Birch Lane Press, 1992.

Davis, Sue. *Justice Rehnquist and the Constitution.* Princeton, N.J.: Princeton University Press, 1989.

"Death Penalty-Racial Discrimination." *Harvard Law Review* 101, no. 1 (November 1987), 149-68.

"Death Penalty-Victim Impact Evidence." *Harvard Law Review* 105, no. 1 (November 1991), 177-81.

Douglas, William O. *The Court Years, 1939-1975.* New York: Random House, 1980.

Du Bois, W. E. B. "The Defeat of Judge Parker." *The Crisis,* July 1930, 225-28.

———. *The Souls of Black Folk.* New York: Signet Classics, 1995.

Duberman, Martin B. *Paul Robeson: A Biography.* New York: Ballantine, 1989.

Dunne, Gerald T. *Hugo Black and the Judicial Revolution.* New York: Simon and Schuster, 1977.

Egerton, John. *Speak Now Against the Day.* New York: Knopf, 1994.

Ellison, Ralph. *Invisible Man.* New York: Vintage, 1980.

Ellsworth, Scott. *Death in a Promised Land: The Tulsa Race Riot of 1921.* Baton Rouge, La.: LSU Press, 1982.

Elman, Phillip. "The Solicitor General's Office, Justice Felix Frankfurter, and Civil Rights Litigation, 1946-1980: An Oral History." *Harvard Law Review* 100 (1987), 817-86.

Farmer, James. *Lay Bare the Heart: An Autobiography of the Civil Rights Movement.* New York: Plume, 1985.

*The First Line of Defense: A Summary of Twenty Years of Civil Rights Struggle for American Negroes.* New York: NAACP, 1930.

Fisher, Ada Lois Sipuel. *A Matter of Black and White.* Norman, Okla.: University of Oklahoma Press, 1996.

Fisher, William, III. "The Jurisprudence of Thurgood Marshall." *Harvard Blackletter Journal* 6 (Spring 1989), 131-40.

Fiss, Owen M. "A Vision of the Constitution." *Harvard Civil Rights-Civil Liberties Law Review* 13 (1978).

Franklin, John Hope, and Genna Rae McNeil, eds. *African Americans and the Living Constitution.* Washington, D.C.: Smithsonian Institution Press, 1995.

Garrow, David. "The Rehnquist Years." *The New York Times Magazine,* 6 October 1996, 65-69.

Goings, Kenneth. *The NAACP Comes of Age: The Defeat of Judge John J. Parker.* Bloomington, Ind.: Indiana University Press, 1990.

Goldberg, Stephanie, ed. "Justice Thurgood Marshall: The Long Distance Runner." *American Bar Association Journal* 78 (June 1992), 70-76.

Goldman, Roger, and David Gallen. *Thurgood Marshall: Justice for All.* New York: Carroll and Graf, 1992.

Goodman, James. *Stories of Scottsboro.* New York: Vintage, 1994.

Goodwin, Doris Kearns. *No Ordinary Time: Franklin and Eleanor Roosevelt: The Home Front in World War II.* New York: Simon and Schuster, 1994.

Gormley, Ken. "A Mentor's Legacy." *American Bar Association Journal* 78 (June 1992), 62-69.

Greenberg, Jack. *Crusaders in the Courts.* New York: Basic Books, 1994.

Greene, Linda S. "The Confirmation of Thurgood Marshall to the U.S. Supreme Court." *Harvard Blackletter Journal* 6 (Spring 1989), 27-50.

Greenhouse, Linda. "Ex-Justice Marshall Dies at 84." *The New York Times,* 25 January 1993.

———. "Clinton Administration Asks Supreme Court to Rule Against Assisted Suicide." *The New York Times,* 13 November 1996.

Grey, Fred. *Bus Ride to Justice.* Montgomery, Ala.: Black Belt Press, 1995.

Gunther, Gerald. "Foreword." *Harvard Law Review* 86, no. 1 (November 1972).

———. *Learned Hand: The Man and the Judge.* New York: Alfred A. Knopf, 1994.

Hall, B. C., and C. T. Wood. *The South.* New York: Scribner's, 1995.

Hall, Kermit L., ed. *Oxford Companion to the Supreme Court of the United States.* New York: Oxford University Press, 1992.

Heck, Edward V. "Holding the Line: Justices Brennan and Marshall in the 5:4 Decisions of the Rehnquist Court." Paper presented at Western Political Science Association Meeting, San Francisco, March 1988.

Hengstler, Gary. "Looking Back." *American Bar Association Journal* 78 (June 1992), 56-61.

Hentoff, Nat. "Thurgood Marshall and the Chief." *The Village Voice,* 9 March 1993.

Hill, Oliver W. "A Classmate's Recollections of Thurgood Marshall in the Earlier Years." *Howard Law Journal* 35, no. 1 (Fall 1991), 49-52.

*Houston Advocate.* "Thurgood Marshall: Counsel in a Showdown Fight." 12 May 1947.

James, C. L. R. *Fighting Racism in World War II.* New York: Pathfinder, 1980.

James, Daniel. "Supreme Court Tries School Segregation." *The New Leader,* 22 December 1952.

Jeffries, John C., Jr. *Justice Lewis F. Powell, Jr.* New York: Scribner's, 1994.

Jones, Nathaniel R. *"Milliken v. Bradley:* Brown's Troubled Journey North." *Fordham Law Review* 61 (1992), 49-55.

Kalman, Laura. *Abe Fortas.* New Haven: Yale University Press, 1991.

Kennedy, Anthony M. "The Voice of Thurgood Marshall." *Stanford Law Review* 44 (Summer 1992), 1221-25.

Kennedy, Randall, and Martha Minow. "Thurgood Marshall and Procedural Law: Lawyer's Lawyer, Judge's Judge." *Harvard Blackletter Journal* 6 (Spring 1989), 95-101.

King, Mary. *Freedom Song: A Personal Story of the 1960s Civil Rights Movement.* New York: Morrow, 1987.

Kluger, Richard. *Simple Justice.* New York: Vintage, 1977.

Lehman, Nicholas. "The Lawyer as Hero." *New Republic,* 13 September 1993, 132-35.

Lewis, Anthony. "Mr. Justice Marshall: A Symbol of Possibility." *The New York Times,* 28 June 1991.

Lewis, David L. *W. E. B. Du Bois: Biography of a Race.* New York: Henry Holt, 1993.

Lewis, Neil A. "Files Say Justice Marshall Aided FBI in 50's." *The New York Times,* 4 December 1996.

Lofgren, Charles A. *The Plessy Case: A Legal-Historical Interpretation.* New York: Oxford University Press, 1987.

Luney, Percy R., Jr. "Thurgood Marshall as Solicitor General: An Opportunity to Fulfill a Dream." *Harvard Blackletter Journal* 6 (Spring 1989), 18-26.

MacLean, Nancy. *Behind the Mask of Chivalry: The Making of the Second Ku Klux Klan.* New York: Oxford University Press, 1994.

Marcus, Maria L. "Learning Together: Justice Marshall's Desegregation Opinions." *Fordham Law Review* 61 (1992), 69-104.

Marshall, Thurgood. "The Gestapo in Detroit." *The Crisis,* August 1943.

———. "An Evaluation of Recent Efforts to Achieve Racial Integration in Education Through Resort to the Courts." Speech, 16 April 1952, Howard University, Washington, D.C.

———. "An Evaluation of Recent Efforts to Achieve Racial Integration in Education Through Resort to the Courts." *Journal of Negro Education* 21, no. 3 (Summer 1952), 316-22.

————. "The Fifty-Year Fight for Civil Rights." Speech, Freedom Fund Dinner, New York City, 16 July 1959.

————. Commencement Address, Kalamazoo College, 4 June 1961.

————. "Of Law and Lawyers." *The Advocate,* December 1962, 7-10.

————. "Law and the Quest for Equality." *Washington University Law Quarterly* (1967), 1-8.

————. "The Continuing Challenge of the Fourteenth Amendment." *Georgia Law Review* 3, no. 1 (Fall 1968), 1-10.

————. "Financing Public Interest Law Practice: The Role of the Organized Bar." *American Bar Association Journal* 61 (December 1975), 1487-91.

————. "Group Action in the Pursuit of Justice." In *Essays on the Evolving Constitution,* edited by Norman Dorsen. New York: New York University Press, 1986, 97-106.

————. "Remarks on the Death Penalty Made at the Judicial Conference of the Second Circuit." *Columbia Law Review* 86, no. 1 (January 1986), 1-8.

————. "Reflections on the Bicentennial of the United States Constitution." *Harvard Law Review* 101, no. 1 (November 1987), 1-5.

————. "A Tribute to Justice William J. Brennan, Jr." *Harvard Law Review,* November 1990.

"Marshall's Son Recalls His Dad Was 'Disappointed' When He Left College to Be Cop." *Jet,* June 1991, 16-17.

McCullough, David. *Truman.* New York: Simon and Schuster, 1992.

McNeil, Genna Rae. *Groundwork: Charles Hamilton Houston and the Struggle for Civil Rights.* Philadelphia: University of Pennsylvania Press, 1983.

Meese, Edwin, III. "The Attorney General's View of the Supreme Court: Toward a Jurisprudence of Original Intent." *Public Administration Review* 45 (1985), 701-4.

Mello, Michael. *Against the Death Penalty: The Relentless Dissents of Justices Brennan and Marshall.* Boston: Northeastern University Press, 1996.

*Miami Herald.* "Johnson Names First Negro to Top Court," 14 June 1967.

Miller, Keith D. *Voice of Deliverance.* New York: Free Press, 1992.

Mills, Kay. *This Little Light of Mine: The Life of Fannie Lou Hamer.* New York: Plume, 1994.

Moody, Anne. *Coming of Age in Mississippi.* New York: Dell, 1968.

Morris, Jeffrey B. *Federal Justice in the Second Circuit.* New York: Second Circuit Historical Committee, 1987.

Motley, Constance B. "Thurgood Marshall." *Harvard Civil Rights-Civil Liberties Law Review* 13 (1978).

"Mr. Civil Rights." *Howard University Magazine,* no. 2 (January 1963), 4-8.

Nieman, Donald G. *Promises to Keep.* New York: Oxford University Press, 1989.

O'Brien, David M. *Constitutional Law and Politics.* Vol. 2, *Civil Rights and Liberties.* New York: Morrow, 1991.

O'Connor, Sandra D. "Thurgood Marshall: The Influence of a Raconteur." *Stanford Law Review* 44 (Summer 1992), 1217-20.

Ogletree, Charles J. "Justice Marshall's Criminal Justice Jurisprudence: 'The Right Thing to Do, the Right Time to Do It, the Right Man, and the Right Place.'" *Harvard Blackletter Journal* 6 (Spring 1989), 111-30.

Ovington, Mary White. "The Year of Jubilee: 25 Years of the NAACP." *The Crisis,* June 1934.

Patrick, Deval L. *Testimony of Assistant Attorney General, Civil Rights Division, U.S. Department of Justice, Before the Subcommittee on Employer-Employee Relations, Committee on Economic and Educational Opportunities. U.S. House of Representatives.* Washington, D.C.: U.S. Government Printing Office, 24 March 1995.

Payne, Charles. *I've Got the Light of Freedom: The Organizing Tradition and the Mississippi Freedom Struggle.* Berkeley, Calif.: University of California Press, 1995.

Peltason, Jack. *Fifty-Eight Lonely Men.* Urbana, Ill.: University of Illinois Press, 1962.

Pierce, Ponchita. "The Solicitor General." *Ebony* 21 (1965).

Pollak, Louis H. "The Limitless Horizons of *Brown v. Board of Education.*" *Fordham Law Review* 61 (1992), 19-22.

Poston, Ted. "On Appeal to the Supreme Court." *The Survey,* January 1949.

Powell, Lewis F., Jr. "Tribute to Justice Thurgood Marshall." *Stanford Law Review* 44 (Summer 1992), 1229-30.

"Power of One, The," *People,* 8 February 1993, 40.

Rampersad, Arnold. *Jackie Robinson: A Biography.* New York: Knopf, 1997.

Reed, Roy. "Resegregation: Segregation Problems in the Urban South." *The New York Times,* 28 September 1970.

Rehnquist, William H. *The Supreme Court: How It Was, How It Is.* New York: Morrow, 1987.

———. "Tribute to Justice Thurgood Marshall." *Stanford Law Review* 44 (Summer 1992), 1213.

Robertson, David. *Sly and Able: A Political Biography of James F. Byrnes.* New York: W. W. Norton, 1994.

Robinson, Spottswood, III. "Thurgood Marshall: The Lawyer." *Harvard Civil Rights-Civil Liberties Law Review* 13 (1978).

Rosen, Jeffrey. "Annals of Law: The Agonizer." *The New Yorker,* 11 November 1996, 82-90.

Rowan, Carl T. *Dream Makers, Dream Breakers: The World of Justice Thurgood Marshall.* Boston: Little, Brown, 1993.

Sack, Kevin. "In Little Rock, Clinton Warns of Racial Split." *The New York Times,* 26 September 1997.

Sandler, Paul. "Thurgood Marshall: Advocate on the Bench." *Res Ipsa Loquitur,* Fall 1967. 16-21.

Savage, David G. *Turning Right: The Making of the Rehnquist Supreme Court.* New York: John Wiley and Sons, 1992.

"School Segregation Before the High Court." *NEA News* 6, no. 19 (19 December 1952).

Schultz, David A., and Christopher E. Smith. *The Jurisprudential Vision of Justice Antonin Scalia.* Lanham, Md.: Rowman and Littlefield, 1996.

Schwartz, Bernard. *Super Chief: Earl Warren and His Supreme Court.* New York: New York University Press, 1980.

———. *Swann's Way: The School Busing Case and the Supreme Court.* New York: Oxford University Press, 1986.

———. *Decision: How the Supreme Court Decides Cases.* New York: Oxford University Press, 1996.

———. *The Unpublished Opinions of the Rehnquist Court.* New York: Oxford University Press, 1996.

Seidman, Louis M. "A Modest Proposal for Solving the Marshall Mystery." *Legal Times,* 7 June 1993.

Shaw, Theodore M. *"Missouri v. Jenkins:* Are We Really a Desegregated Society." *Fordham Law Review* 61 (1992), 57-61.

Simon, James F. *The Center Holds: The Power Struggle inside the Rehnquist Court.* New York: Simon and Schuster, 1995.

Slocum, Alfred A. "'I Dissent': A Tribute to Justice Thurgood Marshall." *Rutgers Law Review* 45 (Summer 1993), 889.

Smead, Howard. *Blood Justice: The Lynching of Mack Charles Parker.* New York: Oxford University Press, 1986.

Smith, J. Clay, Jr. "Thurgood Marshall: An Heir of Charles Hamilton Houston." *Hastings Constitutional Law Quarterly* 20, no. 3 (Spring 1993), 503-20.

Smith, Tim. "Justice O'Connor and the Pragmatic Approach to Stare Decisis." Unpublished essay, 1996.

Spingarn, Arthur. *The First Line of Defense: A Summary of Twenty Years of Civil Rights Struggle for American Negroes.* New York: NAACP, 1930.

Staples, Brent. "Citizen Sengstacke." *The New York Times Magazine,* 4 January 1998.

Steinberg, Jacques. "Marshall Is Remembered as More Than a Justice." *The New York Times,* 28 January 1993.

Sullivan, Kathleen M. "The Candor of Justice Marshall." *Harvard Blackletter Journal* 6 (Spring 1989), 83-89.

———. "Marshall's Prophetic Dissents Will Be Rediscovered Some Day." *Los Angeles Daily Journal,* 5 July 1991.

Sunstein, Cass. "On Marshall's Conception of Equality." *Stanford Law Review* 44 (Summer 1992), 1267-75.

Taper, Bernard. "A Reporter at Large: Meeting in Atlanta." *The New Yorker,* 17 March 1956, 106.

Taylor, Stuart, Jr. "Court, 5:4, Votes to Restudy Rights in Minority Suits." *The New York Times,* 26 April 1987.

———. "Glimpses of the Least Pretentious of Men." *Legal Times,* 8 February 1993.

Tushnet, Mark. *The NAACP's Legal Strategy Against Segregated Education, 1925-1950.* Chapel Hill, N.C.: University of North Carolina Press, 1985.

———. "Thurgood Marshall and the Rule of Law." *Howard Law Review* 35 (Fall 1991), 7-22.

———. "Thurgood Marshall and the Brethren." *The Georgetown Law Journal* 80 (1992), 2109-32.

———. "Public Law Litigation and the Ambiguities of *Brown.*" *Fordham Law Review* 61 (1992), 23-28.

———. "Rule of Law, or Rule of Five?" *The Nation,* 1 November 1993, 497-99.

———. *Making Civil Rights Law: Thurgood Marshall and the Supreme Court, 1936-1961.* New York: Oxford University Press, 1994.

———. "The Supreme Court and Race Discrimination, 1967-1991: The View from the Marshall Papers." *William and Mary Law Review* 36 (1995), 473-545.

———. "Themes in Warren Court Biographies." *New York University Law Review* 70, no. 3 (June 1995), 748-70.

Urofsky, Melvin I., ed. *The Douglas Letters.* Bethesda, Md.: Adler and Adler, 1987.

U.S. Commission on Civil Rights, Staff Report. *School Desegregation in Little Rock, Arkansas.* Washington, D.C.: U.S. Government Printing Office, June 1977.

"Verbatim: Marshall and the FBI: Uneasy Allies." *Legal Times,* 9 December 1996, 7-9.

Vollers, Maryanne. *Ghosts of Mississippi.* Boston: Little, Brown, 1995.

Ware, Gilbert. *William Hastie: Grace Under Pressure.* New York: Oxford University Press, 1984.

Watson, Denton L. "Thurgood Marshall's Red Menace." *The New York Times,* 10 December 1996.

Weisbrot, Robert. *Freedom Bound: A History of America's Civil Rights Movement.* New York: Plume, 1991.

Wermiel, Stephen J. "The Nomination of Justice Brennan: Eisenhower's Mistake? A Look at the Historical Record." *Constitutional Commentary,* 11, no. 3 (Winter 1994-95), 515-537.

Whalen, Charles, and Barbara Whalen. *The Longest Debate: A Legislative History of the 1964 Civil Rights Act.* New York: New American Library, 1985.

White, Byron R. "A Tribute to Justice Thurgood Marshall." *Stanford Law Review* 44 (Summer 1992), 1215-16.

White, Walter. *A Man Called White.* New York: Viking, 1948.

Whitfield, Stephen J. *A Death in the Delta: The Story of Emmett Till.* New York: Free Press, 1988.

Wilkins, David B. "Justice as Narrative: Some Personal Reflections on a Master Story Teller." *Harvard Blackletter Journal* 6 (Summer 1989), 68-78.

Wilkins, Roy. *Standing Fast: The Autobiography of Roy Wilkins.* New York: Viking, 1982.

Wilkinson, Harvey, III. *From Brown to Bakke: The Supreme Court and School Integration, 1954-1978.* New York: Oxford University Press, 1979.

Williams, Juan. "The Triumph of Thurgood Marshall." *The Washington Post Magazine,* 7 January 1990, 12-29.

Williams, Karen Hastie. "Humanizing the Legal Process: The Legacy of Thurgood Marshall." *Harvard Blackletter Journal* 6 (Spring 1989), 90-94.

Williamson, Joel. *The Crucible of Race: Black-White Relations in American Society Since Emancipation.* New York: Oxford University Press, 1984.

Wofford, Harris. *Of Kennedys and Kings: Making Sense of the 1960s*. Pittsburgh: University of Pittsburgh Press, 1980.

Woodward, C. Vann. *The Strange Career of Jim Crow*. New York: Oxford University Press, 1955, 1974.

Woodward, Robert, and Scott Armstrong. *The Brethren: Inside the Supreme Court*. New York: Simon and Schuster, 1979.

Yarbrough, Tinsley E. *A Passion for Justice: J. Waties Waring and Civil Rights*. New York: Oxford University Press, 1987.

———. *John Marshall Harlan: Great Dissenter of the Warren Court*. New York: Oxford University Press, 1992.

# CASE INDEX

# GENERAL INDEX